# Civil Procedure

ASPEN PUBLISHERS

EXAMPLES & EXPLANATIONS

# Civil Procedure

*Sixth Edition*

**Joseph W. Glannon**
Professor of Law
Suffolk University Law School

 Wolters Kluwer
**Law & Business**

AUSTIN   BOSTON   CHICAGO   NEW YORK   THE NETHERLANDS

Aspen Publishers
Attn: Permissions Department
76 Ninth Avenue, 7th Floor
New York, NY 10011-5201

To contact Customer Care, e-mail customer.care@aspenpublishers.com, call 1-800-234-1660, fax 1-800-901-9075, or mail correspondence to:

Aspen Publishers
Attn: Order Department
PO Box 990
Frederick, MD 21705

Printed in the United States of America.

2 3 4 5 6 7 8 9 0

ISBN 978-0-7355-7033-7

**Library of Congress Cataloging-in-Publication Data**

Glannon, Joseph W.
Civil procedure: examples and explanations/Joseph W. Glannon. — 6th ed.
    p. cm.
Includes index.
ISBN 978-0-7355-7033-7
    1. Civil procedure — United States — Cases.    2. Civil procedure — United States — Problems, exercises, etc.    I. Title.
    KF8839.G58 2008
    347.73′5 — dc22

                                                                    2008009076

# About Wolters Kluwer Law & Business

Wolters Kluwer Law & Business is a leading provider of research information and workflow solutions in key specialty areas. The strengths of the individual brands of Aspen Publishers, CCH, Kluwer Law International and Loislaw are aligned within Wolters Kluwer Law & Business to provide comprehensive, in-depth solutions and expert-authored content for the legal, professional and education markets.

**CCH** was founded in 1913 and has served more than four generations of business professionals and their clients. The CCH products in the Wolters Kluwer Law & Business group are highly regarded electronic and print resources for legal, securities, antitrust and trade regulation, government contracting, banking, pension, payroll, employment and labor, and healthcare reimbursement and compliance professionals.

**Aspen Publishers** is a leading information provider for attorneys, business professionals and law students. Written by preeminent authorities, Aspen products offer analytical and practical information in a range of specialty practice areas from securities law and intellectual property to mergers and acquisitions and pension/benefits. Aspen's trusted legal education resources provide professors and students with high-quality, up-to-date and effective resources for successful instruction and study in all areas of the law.

**Kluwer Law International** supplies the global business community with comprehensive English-language international legal information. Legal practitioners, corporate counsel and business executives around the world rely on the Kluwer Law International journals, loose-leafs, books and electronic products for authoritative information in many areas of international legal practice.

**Loislaw** is a premier provider of digitized legal content to small law firm practitioners of various specializations. Loislaw provides attorneys with the ability to quickly and efficiently find the necessary legal information they need, when and where they need it, by facilitating access to primary law as well as state-specific law, records, forms and treatises.

Wolters Kluwer Law & Business, a unit of Wolters Kluwer, is headquartered in New York and Riverwoods, Illinois. Wolters Kluwer is a leading multinational publisher and information services company.

*I dedicate this book to my parents,*
*Edward and Helen Glannon.*

# Contents

## PART I. CHOOSING A PROPER COURT

## PART II. STATE LAW IN FEDERAL COURTS

**ix**

# PART III. THE SCOPE OF THE ACTION

# PART IV. STEPS IN THE LITIGATION PROCESS

# PART V. THE EFFECT OF THE JUDGMENT

## Contents

---

# PART VI. THINKING PROCEDURALLY: THE RULES IN ACTION

# Preface to Students

Everyone comes to law school with some idea of what a contract is or the meaning of assault and battery, but who ever heard of supplemental jurisdiction, impleader, or res judicata? Abstract concepts such as these make civil procedure the most unfamiliar and intimidating of the basic law school courses.

However, civil procedure can also be fascinating if you can get by the initial strangeness. Many of the topics covered in the course appear baffling upon first acquaintance but begin to make sense when you see how they apply in particular cases and how they relate to other topics in the course. The goal of this book is to demystify civil procedure by providing concrete examples of procedural doctrines and rules in operation, together with full explanations of how these abstract concepts apply to each example.

Most casebooks contain major or representative cases but provide little discussion of what the cases mean or "what the law is" on a particular topic. I hope that you will find, as my students have, that the discussion in this book helps to tie the cases together into a coherent picture of the law. In addition, the opportunity to try your hand at the examples and then to compare your answers with mine will provide an incentive to analyze the examples and make that process more rewarding — perhaps even enjoyable.

Each chapter (except for the pleading chapters in Part VI) includes an introduction that gives a basic explanation of the relevant procedural concept followed by a series of examples. The "Explanations" section of each chapter presents my analysis of the examples in that chapter. The most effective way to use the book is to read each chapter when that topic is covered in your civil procedure course and to try to answer the questions yourself, based on my introductions and your reading for class. To keep yourself honest, write out your own analysis of each example, if only in a few sentences, before comparing it to mine. You may also want to review the chapter again after class coverage or discuss with your civil procedure professor any issues that you don't fully understand.

One of my principal frustrations as a first-year law student was that the questions posed in the casebooks were too hard. (Many are still beyond me, even after teaching procedure for twenty-five years.) I think you will find that the examples in this book are geared to cover the basics as well as more sophisticated variations; you really will be able to answer many of them, and the explanations will help to deepen your understanding of the issues.

You certainly will want to use *Civil Procedure: Examples and Explanations* for reviewing your civil procedure course at the end of the year. My students have found that these chapters are an excellent way to test their understanding of each topic and to fill in any gaps in class discussion or case reading. The examples provide an efficient means of learning the material because they help you to actively apply the concepts. You will learn a lot more by doing that than by passively rereading cases. In addition, the process will give you a sense of mastery of the material. As the year progresses, you will find that your ability to analyze the examples improves markedly, and that this positive feedback will help you feel more confident about your analytical skills. Surely every first-year law student will be thankful for that.

If you would like to listen to *Civil Procedure* as well as read it, consider buying Aspen's *Audio Guide to Civil Procedure*, which will be published in August 2008. In this series of lectures (broken down into individual lectures and tracks for easy I-Pod listening), I review all the major topics in the course. Each lecture includes a set of questions to test your understanding of the material, followed by an analysis of the correct response to each question.

If you have any comments, suggestions, or corrections for future editions, please e-mail me at jglannon@suffolk.edu.

*Joseph W. Glannon*

March 2008

# Acknowledgments

In addition to those who offered advice in the original creation of this book, and in earlier editions, I would like to express my appreciation to Professor Karen Blum, of the Suffolk University Law School faculty, for reviewing parts of the manuscript.

As always, I appreciate the excellent support and advice provided by the editors at Aspen Publishers, including Carol McGeehan and Melody Davies. Thanks, too, to Peter Skagestad, Kathy Yoon, Gretchen Otto, Rebecca Logan, and Frances Andersen for their patient and professional assistance in guiding the manuscript through the book production process.

# Special Notice

For several frequently cited treatises I have used shortened versions after the initial citation to the work. These are as follows: Friedenthal, Kane, and Miller, Civil Procedure (4th ed. 2005), cited as Friedenthal, Kane, and Miller; James, Hazard, and Leubsdorf, Civil Procedure (5th ed. 2001), cited as James, Hazard, and Leubsdorf; Moore's Federal Practice, cited as Moore's; Wright, Federal Courts (5th ed. 1994), cited as Wright; and Wright and Miller, Federal Practice and Procedure, cited as Wright and Miller. (My apologies to supplementary co-authors of the Moore's and Wright and Miller treatises.)

# PART I

# Choosing a Proper Court

# Personal Jurisdiction

## The Enigma of Minimum Contacts

# INTRODUCTION

There is no place to start like the beginning, and the usual beginning for the defendant is the receipt of a summons from the court with an order to appear and defend a lawsuit. It is never a prospect that evokes much enthusiasm, but the reception is likely to be even chillier if the suit has been filed in a distant state. The defendant will want to know why on earth the plaintiff has chosen to sue in a court a thousand miles away and, perhaps more to the point, whether she *can* sue there. The answer to the second question lies shrouded in one of the foggiest realms of civil procedure, the doctrine of personal jurisdiction.

Ever since the landmark case of *Pennoyer v. Neff*, 95 U.S. 714 (1877), the Supreme Court has consistently held that plaintiffs are not free to bring suit wherever they choose. The Fourteenth Amendment to the United States Constitution forbids the states from "depriv[ing] any person of life, liberty or property, without due process of law." A state would violate this guarantee if its courts entered judgments against defendants without following a fair judicial procedure, and fair procedure includes not only such traditional elements as the right to counsel or to cross-examine witnesses, but also appropriate limits on the places where a defendant can be required to defend a lawsuit.

The Supreme Court has repeatedly attempted to define the appropriate limits on the power of state courts to "exercise personal jurisdiction over" defendants, that is, to require them to come into the state to defend lawsuits there. A number of bases for personal jurisdiction have evolved, including domicile, consent, physical presence, and the enigmatic "minimum contacts" standard. In many cases in which the defendant is not from the forum state (the state where suit is brought), the only basis for exercising personal jurisdiction over her will be the minimum contacts test developed in *International Shoe v. Washington*, 326 U.S. 310 (1945). This chapter focuses on the meaning of that test.

## THE MINIMUM CONTACTS TEST

In *International Shoe*, the Supreme Court held that the courts of a state may exercise personal jurisdiction over a defendant if she has such minimum contacts with the state that it would be fair to require her to return and defend a lawsuit in that state. The Court did not elucidate this somewhat circular proposition by providing a list of what minimum contacts are sufficient, nor did it base the test on the number of contacts with the state. Instead, the Court suggested that whether jurisdiction is permissible depends on the "quality and nature" of the contacts with the state. 326 U.S. at 319. In some cases, the Court indicated, even a single contact will do, but not contacts that are "casual" or "isolated."

This language is too vague to provide much guidance in applying the minimum contacts test, but the rationale of *International Shoe* is more helpful. The *Shoe* Court suggested that a corporation that chooses to conduct activities within a state accepts (implicitly, of course) a reciprocal duty to answer for its in-state activities in the local courts. A defendant should understand that her activities within the state will have an impact there, that those activities may lead to controversies and lawsuits there, and that the state has a right to enforce the orderly conduct of affairs within its borders by adjudicating disputes that arise from such in-state activities. The defendant who deliberately chooses to take advantage of the "benefits and protections of the laws" (326 U.S. at 319) of a state will not be heard to cry "foul" when that state holds her to account in its courts for her in-state acts.

This rationale suggests an important limitation on minimum contacts jurisdiction. Because the court's power to exercise jurisdiction derives from the defendant's voluntary relation to the state, the power should be limited to cases arising out of that relation. *International Shoe* implies such a limitation, and subsequent cases have confirmed that minimum contacts jurisdiction is limited to claims arising from (or, perhaps, related to) the defendant's contacts with the forum state. In *Shoe*, for example, the corporation was held subject to personal jurisdiction in Washington for claims arising out of its shoe sales in that state, but the corporation could not have been required to defend a claim in Washington arising from shoe sales in Texas under a minimum contacts analysis. Sales in Texas are unrelated to Washington; the corporation would certainly not expect to be sued in Washington by a Texas shoe buyer, nor does the corporation take advantage of the benefits and protections of the laws of Washington by its activities in Texas. The analysis must always consider the relationship between the contacts that gave rise to the suit and the state where the suit is brought. Miscellaneous contacts are not minimum contacts. It is the contacts that spawned the lawsuit that are crucial to the minimum contacts analysis.

# SPECIFIC AND GENERAL JURISDICTION: THE "*SHOE* SPECTRUM"

Although *International Shoe* is primarily viewed as a minimum contacts case, the opinion analyzes a broad spectrum of possible contacts with a state and their jurisdictional consequences. Figure 1-1 illustrates this spectrum of increasing contacts.

At one end of the "*Shoe* spectrum" are cases in which a defendant has no contact with the forum state. In such cases, *Shoe* indicates that the state has no authority to exercise personal jurisdiction over the defendant, unless she consents to it. "Casual" or "isolated" contacts (whatever they may be) are also insufficient to support jurisdiction. But other single acts, because of their "quality and nature," will support "specific in personam jurisdiction," that is, jurisdiction over claims arising out of that single act. See, e.g., *McGee v. International Ins. Co.*, 355 U.S. 220 (1957) (upholding jurisdiction over claim arising out of a single contract solicited in the state). Continuous but limited activity in the forum state, such as the ongoing business relationship in *Burger King Corp. v. Rudzewicz*, 471 U.S. 462 (1985), will also support "specific" jurisdiction, that is, jurisdiction over claims arising out of that continuous activity. In each of these categories of cases, the in-state activity is limited. In each, the defendant is only subject to jurisdiction for claims arising out of those "minimum contacts."

The *Shoe* opinion also suggests that if the defendant's forum contacts fall at the far right end of the spectrum, where the in-state contacts are very substantial, the defendant is subject to "general in personam jurisdiction." This means that the defendant may be sued in the state for any claim, even one completely unrelated to its in-state activities. Several cases since *International Shoe* affirm that general in personam jurisdiction is sometimes permissible (see *Helicopteros Nacionales de Colombia, S.A. v. Hall*, 466 U.S. 408 (1984); *Perkins v. Benguet Consolidated Mining Co.*, 342 U.S. 437 (1952)), but the Supreme Court has not clearly indicated where the line (marked "G" on Figure 1-1) lies between contacts that support general in personam

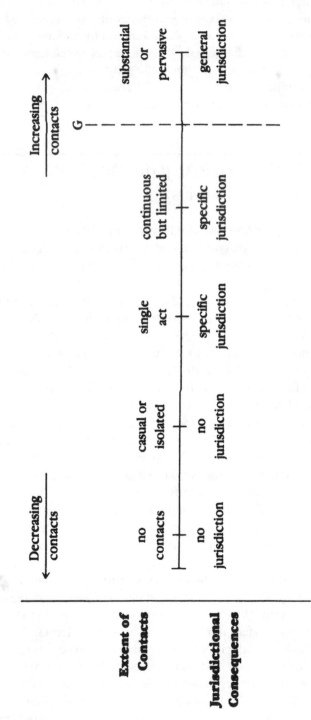

**Figure 1-1.** The *Shoe* spectrum.

jurisdiction and those that support only specific, minimum contacts jurisdiction.

General jurisdiction is apparently appropriate when the defendant's activities in the state are so substantial and continuous that she would expect to be subject to suit there on any claim and would suffer no inconvenience from defending there. See generally Friedenthal, Kane, and Miller, Civil Procedure §3.10 (4th ed. 2005, pp. 129-130) (hereinafter cited as Friedenthal, Kane, and Miller).

Under general in personam jurisdiction analysis, for example, a major American oil company would be subject to personal jurisdiction in many, if not all states, regardless of whether the claim arose in the state where suit was brought. Companies that have such extensive activities, personnel, and facilities in a state may fairly be considered "at home" there and, therefore, subject to the burden of submitting generally to jurisdiction there.[1] This approach is analogous to general jurisdiction over individual defendants based on domicile in the state, which was approved in *Milliken v. Meyer*, 311 U.S. 457 (1940).[2]

# SOME GUIDELINES IN APPLYING MINIMUM CONTACTS

Several important aspects of the minimum contacts test have been settled by cases since *International Shoe*. First, the minimum contacts test applies to individual as well as corporate defendants. See, e.g., *Kulko v. Superior Court*, 436 U.S. 84 (1978). This makes good sense, since individuals benefit from their voluntary in-state contacts just as corporations do and should likewise understand that those benefits may carry with them the burden of related litigation. *Second*, the limitations on personal jurisdiction found in long-arm

---

1. Be careful not to confuse general in personam jurisdiction over a corporation with the corporation's state citizenship for diversity purposes under 28 U.S.C. §1332(c)(i). A corporation will almost certainly be subject to general in personam jurisdiction in the states where it is incorporated and has its principal place of business, but it may also be subject to general in personam jurisdiction in many additional states, as in the oil company example described above. General in personam jurisdiction is explored more fully in Chapter 9.
2. One Supreme Court opinion suggests in dicta that general in personam jurisdiction based on extensive in-state contact may only apply to corporations. *Burnham v. Superior Court of California*, 495 U.S. 604, 610, n.1 (1990). Whether or not this is true, the overwhelming majority of general in personam cases involve corporate defendants. Individuals' contacts with states other than their domicile are seldom so extensive as to support an argument for general in personam jurisdiction.

statutes are distinct from the constitutional limit imposed by the minimum contacts test. See Chapter 2, which compares these two related concepts.

Third, it is clear that a defendant may have sufficient contacts with a state to support minimum contacts jurisdiction there even though she did not act within the state. If a defendant commits an act outside the state that she knows will cause harmful effects within the state, she will be subject to minimum contacts jurisdiction there for claims arising out of that act. In *Calder v. Jones*, 465 U.S. 783 (1984), for example, the defendant was held subject to personal jurisdiction in California for an allegedly defamatory article written in Florida, since the article was to be circulated in California, the plaintiff lived there, and the plaintiff's career was centered there. Similarly, if Healy, a Minnesota lawyer, calls a Missouri client on a regular basis to give her legal advice and bills the client for that advice, Healy derives benefits from conducting activities in Missouri. Even if she has never visited Missouri, she will have to answer there for a legal malpractice claim that arises from her deliberate business activity there.

Fourth, minimum contacts analysis focuses on the time when the defendant acted, not the time of the lawsuit. Even if Healy stopped representing her Missouri client a year before being sued and now has no contacts with Missouri, Healy is subject to jurisdiction in Missouri for claims arising from these prior contacts. Minimum contacts jurisdiction is based on the premise that parties who conduct activities in a state accept the risk that those activities will give rise to suits and understand that they may have to return to the state where the activity was conducted to defend such suits. This rationale applies whether or not the defendant is still acting in the state at the time the suit is actually filed. Compare jurisdiction based on service of process on the defendant within the state, which was reaffirmed in *Burnham v. Superior Court of California*, 495 U.S. 604 (1990). Jurisdiction based on in-state service only requires that the defendant be present in the state at the time that the summons and complaint are served upon her. In such cases, the defendant need not have had *any* contact with the state at the time of the events giving rise to the suit.

# PURPOSEFUL AVAILMENT

The toughest problem in applying the minimum contacts test has been defining the "quality and nature" that makes a contact sufficient to support jurisdiction. Many cases have relied on the statement in *Hanson v. Denckla* that the defendant must have "purposely avail[ed] itself of the privilege of conducting activities within the forum State, thus invoking the benefits and protections of its laws." 357 U.S. 235, 253 (1958). This language emphasizes that the defendant must have made a deliberate choice to relate to the state in some meaningful way before she can be made to bear the burden of defending there. Unilateral contacts of the plaintiff or others will not do.

Although scholars have criticized this emphasis on the defendant's purposeful in-state contacts,[3] the Court has consistently required it. In *World-Wide Volkswagen v. Woodson*, 444 U.S. 286 (1980), for example, the Court concluded that a New York Audi dealer, Seaway, had not purposely availed itself of the opportunity to conduct activities in Oklahoma, although it could foresee that its buyers might take its cars there. The dealer had not sold cars there, advertised there, cultivated Oklahoma customers, or deliberately focused on Oklahoma as a market. Thus, it had not sought any direct benefit from Oklahoma activities sufficient to require it to submit to jurisdiction there. In *Keeton v. Hustler Magazine, Inc.*, 465 U.S. 770, 780 (1984), by contrast, the defendant had purposely availed itself of the opportunity to engage in in-state activities, by distributing its magazines within the state. Those contacts supported jurisdiction even though the defendant's acts had greater impact in other states, and the plaintiff had few contacts with the forum state.

Much debate has swirled around application of this purposeful availment requirement in cases where the defendant's goods reach the forum state through the so-called "stream of commerce." This often happens in one of two ways. First, an out-of-state component manufacturer sells components to a manufacturer of a finished product outside the state. That manufacturer then incorporates the component into a finished product and distributes the finished product into the forum state. *Asahi Metal Industry Co. v. Superior Court*, 480 U.S. 102 (1987), is an example of this situation. Second, a manufacturer sells finished products to a wholesaler outside the state, the wholesaler then resells to a retailer in the forum state, and the retailer resells to the consumer. In these situations, the party at the beginning of the stream of commerce (the component maker in the first situation, and the manufacturer in the second) did not import the product into the forum state itself; it sold to others who did. The manufacturer or component maker may know that such resales take place in the state, may think it highly likely, or may not know or care about the ultimate destination of its product.

In *Asahi*, the Court split on the question of whether the mere act of selling goods outside the forum state that will likely be imported into the forum state for resale suffices to support jurisdiction. Justice O'Connor's opinion, joined by three other Justices, rejected the premise that "mere awareness" that the stream of commerce may sweep goods into the state

---

3. See, e.g., M. Weber, Purposeful Availment, 39 S.C.L. Rev. 815, 865-871 (1988).

after they leave the defendant's hands suffices to satisfy "purposeful avail-ment." O'Connor would require clearer evidence that the defendant seeks to serve the market in the particular state, such as designing the product for the market in that state or advertising there. 480 U.S. at 112-113. However, the concurring Justices in *Asahi* would find that sending goods into the stream of commerce, at least in substantial quantities, constitutes "pur-poseful availment," whether or not the original maker knows that the goods will be sold in a particular state or cultivates customers there. The rationale for this view is that the maker both foresees and benefits from such sales in other states, whether it distributes them there directly or indirectly profits from the fact that another entity conveniently does so in its place.

Since the *Asahi* Court split sharply on this issue, and since the mem-bership of the Court has changed significantly since *Asahi* was decided, it is difficult to say what "the law" is on stream-of-commerce cases today. Some courts continue to apply a fairly broad stream-of-commerce approach based on *World-Wide*, and take jurisdiction in cases that the O'Connor approach would not reach. See, e.g., *Ruston Gas Turbines, Inc. v. Donaldson Co., Inc.*, 9 F.3d 415 (5th Cir. 1993); *Barone v. Rich Bros. Interstate Display Fireworks*, 25 F.3d 610 (8th Cir. 1994). Others appear to adopt the O'Connor view. See, e.g., *Lesnick v. Hollingsworth & Vose Co.*, 35 F.3d 939 (4th Cir. 1994). Many avoid lining up on either side by finding that jurisdiction would be proper (or lacking) under either approach. See, e.g., *Kernan v. Forbes Products Corp.*, 175 F.3d 236 (2d Cir. 1999). This ambiguity is not very satisfying to an attorney who has to advise a client, or to a first year law student, but it is, as of this writing, the state of the law.[4] It is clear, however, that if the defendant's contacts satisfy Justice O'Connor's test they will support jurisdiction, since the other *Asahi* opinions would require a lesser showing.

# OTHER FACTORS IN THE JURISDICTIONAL CALCULUS

There is also a great deal of talk in the cases about factors other than the defendant's in-state contacts, such as the interest of the forum state in providing redress to its citizens, the interest of the plaintiff in obtaining relief in a convenient forum, the interest of the states in enforcing their substantive law or policy, and the extent of the inconvenience to the defendant if she is forced to defend away from home. The cases have repeatedly cited such factors in determining whether it would be fair to assert personal jurisdic-tion over the defendant. See *Keeton*, 465 U.S. at 775-780; *Burger King*, 471 U.S.

---

4. For the author's prediction on this point, see infra example 11 and n.5.

at 476-477. However, *Burger King* suggests that, where the defendant has purposely directed activities to the forum state, jurisdiction is presumptively reasonable, and she will have to make a "compelling case" that other considerations make the exercise of jurisdiction unreasonable. *Burger King* at 477. In *Asahi*, on the other hand, the Court found such a case to be made: There, a clear majority of the justices concluded that, even if minimum contacts were established, it would be unreasonable to exercise jurisdiction on the unusual facts of that case.

While the plaintiff's interest, the forum state's interest, and other fairness issues enter the balance once minimum contacts are found, they are not sufficient to support jurisdiction if those contacts are lacking. The defendant must first have purposely availed herself of the opportunity to conduct activities in the state. It is only when such deliberate contacts exist between the defendant and the forum state (and in specific jurisdiction cases, when those contacts give rise to the claim) that other factors will be weighed in determining whether the exercise of jurisdiction would comport with "fair play and substantial justice."

Thus, although some principles are established in the minimum contacts area, the test still remains difficult to state and even more difficult to apply in close cases. Over the course of your lawyering life it will take on clearer meaning as you handle personal jurisdiction issues and begin to see how courts give flesh to the bare-bones test. The following examples will provide a start in that direction. In answering them, focus on the constitutional issue of minimum contacts only; do not worry about statutory problems under long-arm statutes. Also, assume that the contacts mentioned are the only contacts the defendant has with the forum state.

## Examples

### Opening Rounds

1. Austin is a traveling salesman who lives in North Dakota and sells Fuller brushes in parts of North Dakota, South Dakota, and Minnesota. While en route to deliver brushes to a Minnesota customer, he is involved in an auto accident in Minnesota with Healy, a Minnesota citizen. He brings suit against Healy in North Dakota for his injuries in the accident. Does the court have personal jurisdiction over Healy?

2. As a result of the same accident, Healy brings suit against Austin for her injuries. She sues in South Dakota. Does the court have jurisdiction over Austin based on minimum contacts?

3. To be on the safe side, Healy also files suit against Austin in Minnesota. Does that court have personal jurisdiction over Austin based on minimum contacts?

## A Parade of Perplexities

4. *The Volkswagen.* Many of the most difficult personal jurisdiction cases involve commercial contacts, that is, contacts that arise out of business done in the state, either directly or indirectly, by a corporation acting outside the state. *World-Wide Volkswagen v. Woodson*, 444 U.S. 286 (1980) sets out the basic framework for analyzing these cases. The motorcade of hypotheticals that follows may help you to assess the importance of various contacts with the forum state.

   Hudson, an Ohio citizen, buys a Volkswagen from Smoky Mountain VW, located on the east side of the Smoky Mountains in North Carolina, while she is on vacation in North Carolina. Shortly after she returns home, all four wheels fall off while she is driving, and Hudson is injured. Understandably upset, Hudson sues Smoky Mountain in an Ohio court for negligence. Does the Court have personal jurisdiction over the dealer?

5. *The Chevy.* After Hudson leaves, Ford pulls into Smoky Mountain's lot with his engine belching smoke. His car is clearly a total loss, and he tells De Soto, the salesman, that he must have a car to get back home to Florida. De Soto sells him a (very) used Chevy. After crossing into Florida, Ford pushes the windshield wiper button, and the engine automatically ejects into the Everglades. Ford sues De Soto and Smoky Mountain in Florida. Is personal jurisdiction proper there?

6. *The Maserati.* De Soto has an eye for fast cars. At the moment, he has a nice Maserati on the lot, with all the extras (engine, wheels, brakes). A customer tells him that a trucker buddy of his, Packard, from Pennsylvania, might be interested in buying the Maserati. De Soto calls Packard in Pennsylvania, extols the Maserati's virtues and encourages her to come in and test drive the car on her next delivery in North Carolina. Packard does stop to see the car, likes it, and buys it. She makes the mistake of towing it home, only to discover upon arrival that the engine, lights, carburetor, and exhaust system are missing. She sues De Soto in Pennsylvania. De Soto has no other contacts with Pennsylvania. Will the Pennsylvania court have personal jurisdiction over De Soto?

7. *The Audi.* After lunch, Rambler comes in. Rambler lives across the border in Tennessee, where he read in a Tennessee paper Smoky Mountain's ad for a one-year-old Audi for $1,100. Because the Smoky Mountain dealership is located ten miles from the Tennessee border, it advertises frequently in Tennessee, as well as in North Carolina. Rambler visits the dealership, talks De Soto down to $1,025 and buys the car. He barely gets across the Tennessee line when the steering wheel comes off in his

hand, and the body comes entirely loose from the frame of the car. Rambler sues Smoky Mountain in Tennessee. Does the court have personal jurisidiction over Smoky Mountain?

8. Assume, on the facts of example 7, that Smoky Mountain only advertises occasionally in Tennessee and derives only 5 percent of its business ($40,000 of its annual gross sales of $800,000) from sales to Tennessee customers. The rest of its sales are in North Carolina. Rambler sees the ad and buys the Audi at Smoky Mountain's dealership; it breaks down in Tennessee on the way home. Can Rambler sue Smoky Mountain in Tennessee?

## Sports Cars

9. *The Ferrari.* You can't work all the time. When De Soto relaxes, he likes to go to the Georgia coast for some deep sea fishing. While drinking at a bar in the fishing lodge there, he gets to talking with Lenoir, another guest at the lodge. Lenoir asks De Soto about his work. The two get into a car lovers' debate over the relative merits of various sports cars. Before leaving the bar, Lenoir asks De Soto for his card.

Two months later, Lenoir visits Smoky Mountain and buys a jazzy looking Ferrari from De Soto. Imagine for yourself what happens to the Ferrari when Lenoir gets it back to Georgia. Lenoir sues De Soto in Georgia. Will the court have personal jurisdiction over De Soto?

## Changing Cars in Midstream

10. *The Off-Road Vehicle.* Nippon Auto Unlimited is a Japanese corporation that manufactures off-road vehicles in Japan for sale worldwide. It sells substantial numbers of these vehicles in Japan to A-1 Wholesalers, Inc., a California dealer in off-road vehicles, which resells them in various Western states, including Nevada. Nippon sells an off-road vehicle to A-1, which then sells it to Fred's Recreational Emporium in Reno, Nevada. Fred's sells the off-road vehicle to Lincoln, who is injured (in Nevada) when the vehicle collapses while driving over a crack in the sidewalk. Lincoln sues Nippon in a state court in Nevada.
    a. Does the Nevada court have jurisdiction over Nippon?
    b. Would it have jurisdiction over A-1 if Lincoln sued it in Nevada?

11. Assume that A-1 bought the off-road vehicle from Atlanta Importers, Inc., a large importer of off-road vehicles in Atlanta, Georgia. A-1 has the off-road vehicles shipped to California and resells some to Fred's in Nevada, where Lincoln bought hers. Could Lincoln sue Atlanta Importers in Nevada?

12. *The Edsel.* Andretti is an Indiana race car driver whose hobby is collecting antique cars. He notices an ad in *Antique Auto,* a national magazine, for a mint condition Edsel for sale by a Michigan collector, Studebaker. He calls Studebaker, gets further information on the car, and decides to go up to look at it. While he is in Michigan, he and Studebaker discuss price but do not settle the deal. After Andretti returns to Indiana, he calls Studebaker back, agrees to his price, and arranges to pick up the car the following month. After buying the car and returning with it to Indiana, he discovers that it is a cleverly disguised Dodge Dart. He sues Studebaker in Indiana. Will the court dismiss for lack of personal jurisdiction?

13. Reconsider the case just described, involving Andretti's purchase of a car from Studebaker. However, assume that, instead of reading about the car in *Antique Auto,* Andretti dialed up Studebaker's "Hot Cars" website and learned of the Edsel through the Internet. He then called Studebaker, and the transaction unfolded as above in example 12. Could Andretti sue Studebaker in Indiana on his fraud claim arising out of the sale?

## The Rental Car

14. Patrikas, an elderly widow with minimal income, lives in Georgia. Her daughter is getting married in California. Patrikas scrimps and saves for two years (it was one of those long engagements) to set aside funds to fly out for the wedding. She rents a car to drive to the wedding, but on the way back to the airport she runs into an Acme International Conglomerated Enterprises truck. She flies back to Georgia, broke.

    Acme International Conglomerated Enterprises is an international company worth billions. It sues Patrikas for damage to the truck in California. Does the court have personal jurisdiction over Patrikas?

## Fundamental (Un)truths

15. Every year, the following statements sprout like dandelions in civil procedure bluebooks. What is wrong with them?
    a. "Even if the defendant lacks minimum contacts with the state, the plaintiff may be able to get jurisdiction over him if he has taken advantage of the benefits and protections of the laws of the state."
    b. "The defendant may be sued in the state because she has engaged in deliberate acts there and thus has minimum contacts sufficient to support personal jurisdiction."

## Explanations

### Opening Rounds

1. In this case Austin has sued Healy in a state in which Austin has contacts, but Healy has none. As far as the example tells us, Healy has never been there, has not formed any deliberate relationship to or performed acts within the state, and has done nothing to derive benefits from North Dakota. Consequently, she has no reason to expect to be sued there and has not impliedly swallowed that bitter pill in exchange for the benefits of in-state activity. She lacks minimum contacts with North Dakota and may not be sued there on this claim.

   As this conclusion suggests, the personal jurisdiction rules are defendant-oriented: The plaintiff's contacts with the forum state will not do; the court must find some basis for forcing the defendant, the unwilling litigant, to appear before it. Conversely, if the defendant has minimum contacts with the forum state, it is irrelevant (at least, for personal jurisdiction purposes) that the plaintiff has none.

   One might well ask why Austin should have to go to Healy instead of Healy coming to Austin. If someone will have to be inconvenienced by the suit, shouldn't it be the defendant rather than the injured plaintiff? On the other hand, the defendant may be completely blameless; plaintiffs lose law suits as well as win them. If so, it seems unfair to add the insult of distant litigation to the injury of being sued in the first place. Perhaps more importantly, the defendant (unlike the plaintiff, who started the suit) has not chosen the forum and ought to have some veto power over unreasonable choices by the plaintiff.

2. The South Dakota court will not have personal jurisdiction over Austin under the minimum contacts test. It is true that Austin has some contacts with South Dakota because he travels there to sell brushes. However, *International Shoe* does not hold that a defendant may be sued in a state simply because she has some contacts with that state. *Shoe* holds that a defendant may, by committing limited acts within a state, submit herself to jurisdiction for claims arising out of the in-state acts themselves. Here, Healy's claim is unrelated to Austin's brush sales in South Dakota. Austin had no reason to believe that he was submitting himself to the jurisdiction of the South Dakota courts for auto accidents in Minnesota by selling brushes in South Dakota. The situation would be different if the claim were for faulty brushes sold to a South Dakota customer. In that case, the claim would arise directly from Austin's voluntary contacts with the state, and jurisdiction would be proper.

   However, Healy may still be able to sue Austin in South Dakota for the auto claim. Ever since *Pennoyer v. Neff*, 95 U.S. 714 (1877), it has been permissible to obtain personal jurisdiction over an individual defendant (that is, a person) by serving her with the summons in the state where suit is brought. In *Burnham v. Superior Court*, 495 U.S. 604 (1990), the Supreme Court concluded that such "transient jurisdiction" is still a valid means of obtaining jurisdiction over an individual defendant, even if the defendant is in the state briefly or for reasons unrelated to the litigation. Thus, if Healy is determined to sue in South Dakota, she may bring suit there and have the process server await Austin's next sales trip into the state.

3. Healy has gotten it right by suing Austin in Minnesota. Austin's act of driving in Minnesota provides a minimum contacts basis for a suit against him there for injuries suffered in the accident. Motorists who use the roads of a state should realize that this purposeful activity in the forum subjects other drivers to serious risks, that people may be injured and may sue. It would be unfair to allow drivers to take advantage of Minnesota's highways but not to call them to account there for accidents they are involved in on those highways.

   Even if causing the accident in Minnesota were Austin's only contact with the state, it would support specific in personam jurisdiction in this case. The "quality and nature" of this single, purposeful act, and the consequences that may predictably ensue from it, are so serious as to make it reasonable to force the driver to return to defend a suit that arises from the accident. This is true whether Austin causes an accident while in Minnesota on business or in Florida on vacation.

## A Parade of Perplexities

4. As the heading suggests, this case bears some resemblance to *World-Wide Volkswagen v. Woodson*. Here, as in *World-Wide*, the plaintiff purchased the car in one state and took it to another where she suffered injury from alleged defects in the car. As in *World-Wide*, the plaintiff sues where the injury is suffered, although the defendant acted in another state and is still in that state. And, as in *World-Wide*, the court will dismiss this case for lack of personal jurisdiction. Smoky Mountain (like Seaway in the *World-Wide* case) has committed no deliberate act that affiliates it with Ohio. It does not sell cars there, has not availed itself of the protection of Ohio's laws, and has no reason to expect that it will be sued there. Although it is foreseeable that the car will be driven through or end up in Ohio, it is equally foreseeable that it will go to many other states. A rule that such foreseeability establishes jurisdiction would essentially subject the seller of any portable product to nationwide jurisdiction, making "the chattel [product] his agent for service of process" (*World-Wide Volkswagen* at 296) wherever the buyer takes it.

5. This case is somewhat stronger than Hudson's, since De Soto at least knew he was dealing with a Florida citizen who would use the Chevy in

Florida. However, it is very doubtful that this knowledge is enough to support jurisdiction over De Soto or Smoky Mountain in Florida. Personal jurisdiction is the price defendants pay for deliberate efforts to derive benefits from or conduct activities in a state. These defendants did not solicit any business in Florida; they did not even solicit business from a Floridian. Ford rolled into the dealership under his own steam and initiated the transaction in North Carolina. It was only by chance that Ford told De Soto why he needed the car; it is reasonable to infer that it was irrelevant to De Soto that Ford planned to drive it to Florida. (A sale is a sale, right?) De Soto and his employer derived benefits from dealing with a Floridian in North Carolina, not from conducting business activities in Florida. Ford's Florida domicile is a unilateral contact of the plaintiff, not the defendant, with the forum state. See *Hanson v. Denckla*, 357 U.S. 235, 253 (1958); compare *Burger King*, 471 U.S. at 478-482, in which jurisdiction was upheld because the defendants had an on-going contractual relationship with a large Florida franchise, agreed that Florida law would govern the relationship, and regularly related to the Florida headquarters of the franchise regarding important aspects of their business.

It is true that the Supreme Court cases emphasize that the plaintiff's interest in a remedy and the forum state's interest in providing one are part of the personal jurisdiction calculus. See, e.g., *Asahi*, 480 U.S. at 113-115; *Keeton v. Hustler Magazine*, 465 U.S. at 775. However, before those factors can be weighed in favor of jurisdiction, the defendant must be shown to have appropriate purposeful contacts with the state asserting jurisdiction. *Burger King Corp. v. Rudzewicz*, 471 U.S. at 474-478. De Soto's relation to Florida on these facts appears too attenuated to support such a finding.

Nor is it sufficient that the defendants could anticipate that the car would be used in Florida. If that were sufficient to support jurisdiction, then the local store that sells a defective mountain climbing rope could be sued in any mountainous state, or a farmer who sells rancid tomatoes to railroad dining cars could be sued in any state the railroad serves. The Court has chosen a narrower view of personal jurisdiction, focusing on the scope of the activity of the seller, rather than the predictable area of use of the product by the buyer.

6. Here, as in example 5, De Soto has consciously dealt with an out-of-stater, but here, unlike the earlier situation, he has voluntarily affiliated himself with the plaintiff's state. He not only anticipates that his acts will have consequences in the other state, but he has also deliberately set those events in motion by his own in-state act. De Soto voluntarily reached into Pennsylvania to conduct business with a Pennsylvanian. He made representations to Packard in Pennsylvania that encouraged her to

come to North Carolina to buy the car. He can reasonably anticipate that Packard will use the car extensively in Pennsylvania and likely suffer harm there from any defects in the car. De Soto should realize that his deliberate relationship with a Pennsylvanian, which he initiated by calling into that state, may lead to a lawsuit and that if a claim arises out of the sale, Packard will likely bring the suit in Pennsylvania. Thus, De Soto will be subject to personal jurisdiction in this action. His single contact with Pennsylvania is sufficient to support specific in personam jurisdiction (that is, jurisdiction for claims arising out of the contact itself), although it would not support jurisdiction for claims that did not arise out of the sale.

7. In this case the dealership has reached into Tennessee to solicit business. It has attempted to draw customers from there into North Carolina, and in Rambler's case it succeeded. Although the actual sale took place in North Carolina, the claim arises directly out of deliberate efforts to serve the Tennessee market. Smoky Mountain can hardly plead unfairness or surprise when suits that arise from those efforts are brought in Tennessee. Even Justice O'Connor should have no problem upholding jurisdiction in this case, since the defendant has intentionally attempted to derive profits from dealing with Tennessee customers.

    It is important that the dealership is the defendant here, instead of De Soto, because it is the dealership that solicited the business in Tennessee, not the salesman. It is unlikely that the dealership's contacts with Tennessee will be imputed to its employees. (Compare example 6, in which De Soto personally initiated contacts with the forum state.) Thus, if Rambler wanted to sue De Soto and Smoky Mountain together, he would probably have to bring suit in North Carolina.

8. This hypo makes an important point. Personal jurisdiction is not based on the most contacts or the best contacts but on minimum contacts. Here, Smoky Mountain has a great deal more contact with North Carolina than it has with Tennessee, but the dealership has solicited business in Tennessee, and the claim arises out of its efforts to obtain that business. That is enough to support jurisdiction in Tennessee. Smoky Mountain will not be able to defeat jurisdiction there by arguing that it has more contacts with North Carolina.

    A corollary of this point is that a defendant may be subject to minimum contacts jurisdiction in more than one state for a claim that arises from a transaction involving contacts with a number of states.

## Sports Cars

9. In my estimation, this is the kind of "casual" or "isolated" contact (*International Shoe*, 326 U.S. at 317) that is insufficient to subject the

defendant to personal jurisdiction. Although De Soto did act in the state, he was not soliciting business and did not initiate the conversation for business purposes. He gave Lenoir his card at Lenoir's request. He did not encourage Lenoir to go to North Carolina to buy a car. In the "but-for" sense, this contact did give rise to the claim Lenoir asserts, but it was not a purposeful act intended to take advantage of the benefits and protections of conducting activity in Georgia. De Soto would be justifiably upset if this offhand interaction led to a suit in Georgia. He would hardly expect that to be the consequence of responding to a request for a business card, and jurisdictional doctrine is largely based on a common sense appraisal of what people should expect.

There is room for debate on this case, but it is doubtful that this constitutes deliberate in-state activity intended to exploit the local market or affect local citizens. In this regard, it is clearly distinguishable from the Maserati case, in which De Soto deliberately initiated a business contact with the in-state plaintiff, or *McGee v. International Ins. Co.*, 355 U.S. 220 (1957), in which the insurer reached into California by sending an offer there to reinsure a Californian.

## Changing Cars in Midstream

10. a. This is a relatively typical stream of commerce example, in which an out-of-state (in this case, out-of-country) manufacturer sells its product to a wholesaler in one state, which then resells the product into the forum state for final sale to consumers. As in most cases, the original seller, Nippon, does not control the subsequent flow of the "stream." Nippon may or may not know that A-1 resells in Nevada, though it certainly could predict that it will. Doubtless, it hopes that A-1 will sell as widely as possible and profits from those sales regardless of what it knows about A-1's market area.

   In the first edition of this book, written before *Asahi* was decided, I offered the following analysis of a similar example:

   > *World-Wide Volkswagen* clearly supports jurisdiction over such out-of-state (or out-of-country) suppliers who deliver "products into the stream of commerce with the expectation that they will be purchased by consumers in the forum State." 444 U.S. at 298.
   > Here, Nippon has purposely taken advantage of the benefits and protections of the laws of Nevada by importing cars to that state and deriving a profit from those sales. It cannot insulate itself from the jurisdictional consequences of that activity by using wholesalers to channel the goods into the state.

   Since *Asahi*, however, it is not so clear that putting goods into the stream of commerce constitutes sufficient "purposeful availment" to support jurisdiction over Nippon in Nevada. Nippon has not done any of the things Justice O'Connor would require to cultivate the Nevada market. It neither markets directly there, nor advertises there, nor designs its goods for Nevada buyers. It just sells its product in Japan to a foreign wholesaler.

Arguably, this example is distinguishable from *Asahi*. The defendant there was a component maker, not a manufacturer of a final product. Also, it was a third-party defendant, not a direct defendant as here. More importantly, Nippon sold to an American buyer, while *Asahi* sold to a Taiwanese corporation. But it does not appear that these distinctions would make a difference to Justice O'Connor. Her position requires an active effort to serve the forum state market to support stream-of-commerce jurisdiction; Nippon merely sells its off-road vehicles to a wholesaler in Japan. If O'Connor's view is "the law," or becomes the law, Nippon would apparently not be subject to jurisdiction in Nevada.

The concurring opinions in *Asahi* suggest that jurisdiction should be proper in this case, assuming that a reasonable quantity of Nippon's products are resold in Nevada, since Nippon predictably derives benefits from the ultimate sale of its goods in Nevada. Those benefits are the same, whether Nippon directs A-1 to sell in Nevada, knows that it does, suspects that it does, or deliberately avoids finding out. Arguably, that economic reality should support jurisdiction over Nippon, even though it does not control the means by which its product enters the forum state.

b. There is no question about jurisdiction over A-1 in Nevada on this claim. It imported the vehicle into the state, a purposeful contact, which directly gives rise to the claim.

11. The main difference here is that the defendant is an out-of-state corporation, not a corporation from another country. This might influence the second prong of the jurisdictional inquiry, the reasonableness of taking jurisdiction. Almost all the Justices considered it relevant to the fairness analysis that Asahi would be dragged into a foreign court halfway around the world. Here, unlike *Asahi*, the defendant, Atlanta Importers, has imported the product into the United States. Clearly, it is trying to serve the United States market.

It is not clear, however, that these distinctions would lead Justice O'Connor to a different conclusion on the issue of purposeful availment. Atlanta Importers has still sold a product to a buyer in Georgia, with no special knowledge or effort to serve the Nevada market where its buyer resold the product. If the O'Connor view would reject jurisdiction in cases like this, and if it becomes the position of the Court, this would be a very substantial change in the limits of jurisdiction in stream of commerce cases. Compare *World-Wide*, 444 U.S. at 297-298 (reasonable to subject manufacturer to suit if it "serves, directly or indirectly, the market for its product" in the state). Indeed, this reasoning could lead to a rejection of jurisdiction, even if Atlanta *manufactured* the off-road vehicles in Georgia but sold to wholesalers there for marketing in other states. Cf. *Rodriguez v. Fullerton Tires Corp.*, 115 F.3d 81, 84-86 (1st Cir. 1997) (company that sold tire rims to manufacturer in California not subject to personal jurisdiction in Puerto Rico, where manufacturer redistributed tires equipped with those rims).[5]

Because *Asahi* is such an important and complex case, my students tend to analyze all personal jurisdiction issues on my exams under the *Asahi* case. Remember that *Asahi*, like the other post–*International Shoe* cases, elaborates the meaning of minimum contacts in a particular context: cases involving an on-going flow of the defendant's goods into the forum state through a distributor or final manufacturer. In analyzing personal jurisdiction issues that do not involve commercial distribution of a product, other cases, such as *Burger-King*, *McGee*, or *World-Wide Volkswagen*, frequently provide closer analogies for making effective arguments.

12. This is a close case indeed, perhaps too close to call. Studebaker does have a contact with Indiana: He advertised in a magazine circulated there with the express purpose of selling his Edsel. On the other hand, the magazine is a specialty publication circulated nationally. Studebaker was not specifically soliciting an Indiana buyer but was willing to sell to anyone, in or out of the state. Once Andretti learned of the car's availability, he took the initiative: He went to Michigan to see the car; he called back to make an offer; and he picked up the car in Michigan. Studebaker remained in Michigan and passively responded. It was irrelevant to him that Andretti was from Indiana. He may not even have known where Andretti was from.

I think this is a case in which the defendant does have a deliberate contact with the forum state, but the totality of the circumstances weighs against jurisdiction in Indiana. At least eight of the *Asahi* Justices agreed that, once a jurisdictionally significant contact with the forum state is found, the Court must consider whether it would be fair

---

5. If you want this author's view on how this will be resolved, it is that it won't be. The Court is likely to proceed on a case by case basis, and each will turn, as personal jurisdiction cases inevitably do, on its facts. If the Court ultimately requires more than placing goods into the stream, it is likely to require *very little more*. On the facts of this example the Court would likely recognize the economic reality that the very purpose of the importer is to serve the United States market, not just the Georgia market. Thus, the resale of its off-road vehicles in Nevada is consistent with Atlanta Importers goals and expectations, and the company should be subject to jurisdiction there, even if it does not have the various in-state contacts referred to in the O'Connor plurality.

and reasonable under all the circumstances to take jurisdiction. 480 U.S. at 113-116. Given the lack of deliberate acts by Studebaker in Indiana, that all the negotiations took place at Andretti's initiative, and that Studebaker never left Michigan, it appears unreasonable to expect Studebaker to defend this claim in Indiana. Once again, compare example 6, in which the seller solicited the sale in the forum state.

13. Doubtless the Internet has changed a great many things, but it hasn't really changed the basic principles of personal jurisdiction. In this case, as in example 12, Studebaker has advertised the car but has not really reached into Indiana specifically. The initiative came from Andretti and the transaction unfolded in Michigan. The court would likely conclude that the act of posting the car on a website accessible in Indiana (or anywhere else, for that matter) is like the advertisement in example 12, and insufficient to constitute purposeful availment by Studebaker. See, e.g., *Mink v. AAAA Development, LLC.*, 190 F.3d 333 (5th Cir. 1999) (website which constituted "passive advertisement" not sufficient to support jurisdiction).

   However, where the defendant engages more actively in in-state commerce over the Internet, jurisdiction will be found. If, for example, substantial negotiations take place between the defendant and the plaintiff in the forum state over the Internet, or products are sold into the forum state over the Internet, purposeful availment is likely to be found, just as it would be if the same contacts arose in person or by phone or fax. See, e.g., *Euromarket Designs Inc. v. Crate & Barrel Ltd.*, 96 F. Supp. 2d 824 (N.D. Ill. 2000) (jurisdiction upheld over defendant who conducted catalogue sales in Illinois over the Internet); see also *Hy Cite Corp. v. Badbusinessbureau.com LLC.*, 297 F. Supp. 2d 1155, 1160 (W.D. Wis. 2004) (jurisdiction based on Internet contacts requires inquiry as to whether defendant "is expressly targeting residents of the forum state and not just making itself accessible to everyone regardless of location"). Basically, analysis in Internet jurisdiction cases requires the same examination of the defendant's contacts with the forum and the relation of those contacts to the plaintiff's claim, that is necessary in any other type of personal jurisdiction case.

## The Rental Car

14. The first part of the minimum contacts test is satisfied here: the claim arises out of a deliberate contact of Patrikas in California, driving a car there, which imposes the predictable risk of causing an accident. But might the court hold that it isn't "fair and reasonable," under the second part of the test, to drag the widow back to California on these facts? Shouldn't that deep pocket corporation go to her instead?

Probably not. The Supreme Court suggested in *Burger King Corp. v. Rudzewicz* that a defendant who has directed activities to the forum must present "a compelling case" (471 U.S. at 477) before jurisdiction will be found unreasonable. Patrikas probably cannot make that case. Acme's claim arises out of her deliberate choice to engage in conduct in California. California has an interest in regulating that conduct and compensating injuries that result from it. And Acme has an interest in bringing suit where the accident happened, since witnesses and evidence may be located there. Despite some language in *Burger King* that might support the argument,[6] it is hard to find cases that reject jurisdiction under circumstances like this, involving an imbalance in the economic resources of the parties. Patrikas will probably have to defend this action in California, even though it would be a huge inconvenience to her to do so, and it would be much easier for Acme to litigate in Georgia than for her to do so in California.

## Fundamental (Un)truths

15. a. This statement implies that taking advantage of the benefits and protections of the laws of the state is an alternative basis for personal jurisdiction, independent of the minimum contacts test. On the contrary, the purpose for asking whether the defendant has taken advantage of the benefits and protections of the state's laws is to *evaluate* the defendant's contacts with the state, to ascertain whether they are of the "quality and nature" to support jurisdiction. If the defendant's in-state acts demonstrate a deliberate effort to take advantage of the benefits and protections of the forum state's laws, it is a fair inference that these acts satisfy the minimum contacts test, since minimum contacts jurisdiction is based on the defendant's deliberate decision to act in the forum state for her own purposes.

    b. The problem with this statement is that it suggests that a defendant is subject to jurisdiction in a state for any claim if she has *some* contacts with the state. Not so. Conducting some activity in a state does not support such wide jurisdiction. Unless the contacts are so substantial as to pass that ambiguous "G" line in Figure 1-1, the defendant is only subject to jurisdiction for claims *related to the in-state contacts.*

    Precision and clarity are the stock-in-trade of the law student as well as the lawyer. A few students who make statements like this on

---

6. "Jurisdictional rules may not be employed in such a way as to make litigation 'so gravely difficult and inconvenient' that a party unfairly is at a 'severe disadvantage' in comparison to his opponent." 471 U.S. at 478.

the exam have not really grasped the distinction between specific and general in personam jurisdiction. But most really mean to say, "The defendant may be sued in the state on this claim under the minimum contacts test because it has purposely conducted activities there, and the claim arises out of this purposeful contact." This second statement is not only a great deal more precise than the first, but it is accurate, while the other, as it stands, is not. It is differences like this that separate the daffodils from the dandelions in the Merry Month of May.

# Statutory Limits on Personal Jurisdiction

## The Reach and Grasp of the Long-Arm

# INTRODUCTION

As Chapter 1 explains, the due process clause of the Fourteenth Amendment to the Constitution imposes fundamental limitations on the power of state courts to exercise personal jurisdiction over defendants in civil suits. Under that clause states may only assert jurisdiction over defendants who have established a significant relationship to the forum state, such as domicile, in-state presence, continuous and substantial business within the state, consent to suit in that state, or minimum contacts with the state that gave rise to the claim in suit. If the defendant is not subject to personal jurisdiction within the forum state on one of these limited bases, the court will be unable to adjudicate the plaintiff's claim.

However, even if it is constitutionally permissible for a court to exercise personal jurisdiction in a case, that court may still lack the power to call the defendant before it. The due process clause does not actually confer any jurisdiction on state courts; it only defines the outer bounds of permissible jurisdictional power. That is, it says to the state legislatures: "When you authorize your courts to exercise jurisdiction, you may not go any further than this." It is up to the legislature of each state to actually grant the power to its courts to exercise personal jurisdiction, through jurisdictional statutes. Thus, every personal jurisdiction issue involves a two-step analysis. First, the court must ask whether there is a state statute that authorizes it to exercise personal jurisdiction under the circumstances

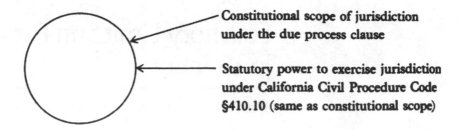

Figure 2-1.

of the case. *Second*, if there is, the court must ask whether it would be constitutional under the due process clause to do so.

State legislatures are free to grant their courts the power to exercise personal jurisdiction to the limits of the due process clause or to confer only part of the constitutionally permissible jurisdiction. In some states the legislature has granted the courts the full scope of personal jurisdiction permissible under the due process clause. California's statute, for example, authorizes its courts to exercise jurisdiction "on any basis not inconsistent with the Constitution of this state or of the United States." Cal. Civ. Proc. Code §410.10. In states with statutes like California's, the two inquiries are collapsed into one: If the court has the constitutional power to assert jurisdiction, it automatically has the statutory power to do so as well. Visually the relationship may be (somewhat simplistically) portrayed in Figure 2-1. One advantage of such expansive provisions is that they are "self-adjusting"; that is, if the courts reinterpret the due process clause to allow the exercise of personal jurisdiction in additional circumstances, these statutes automatically authorize the courts of the state to exercise jurisdiction in such cases. See K. Beyler, The Illinois Long-Arm Statute: Background, Meaning and Needed Repairs, 12 S. Ill. L.J. 293, 319, 320 (1988).

## "ENUMERATED ACT" LONG-ARM STATUTES

Other states, however, have not given their courts blanket authority to exercise personal jurisdiction to the limits of due process. Instead, these states have passed "long-arm" statutes, which authorize their courts to exercise jurisdiction over defendants based on specific types of contact with the forum state. Historically, these "enumerated act" long-arm statutes were passed in reaction to *International Shoe* and its progeny. Once

*International Shoe* and succeeding cases established that certain types of contacts were constitutionally sufficient bases for exercising personal jurisdiction over nonresidents, the states adopted long-arm statutes to authorize their courts to hear cases arising out of such contacts. Such enumerated act long-arm statutes frequently authorize state courts to exercise jurisdiction over cases arising out of contacts such as committing a tortious act within the state, transacting business in the state, or owning property in the state. A fairly typical provision is the Uniform Interstate and International Procedure Act, 13 U.L.A. 355 (West 1986), which has served as the model for the long-arm statutes of some 20 states. It is reproduced on p. 32 for use in the examples in this chapter.

Visually the relation of such statutes to the due process clause is represented by Figure 2-2. Such provisions convey a good deal of the jurisdiction authorized by the due process clause, but not necessarily all of it. Some areas remain (represented by the shaded area in the diagram) in which jurisdiction could be exercised, but the statute does not authorize it.

Students often ask why a state would enact an enumerated act long-arm when the California model is simpler and broader. One reason is historical: The first modern long-arm statute, the Illinois statute, used the enumerated act approach, and many states later used it as a model. Even if California's mellow approach is preferable in the abstract, many states are reluctant to tinker with statutes that have worked satisfactorily for years and have been construed repeatedly by their courts. In addition, the list of jurisdictionally sufficient acts in enumerated act long-arm statutes provides some guidance to nonresidents about the jurisdictional consequences of their choice to conduct particular activities in the state. Finally, some legislatures may not want to authorize jurisdiction in every case that barely passes constitutional muster. The enumerated act statutes give courts some

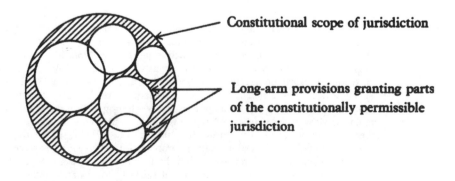

Constitutional scope of jurisdiction

Long-arm provisions granting parts of the constitutionally permissible jurisdiction

**Figure 2-2.**

leeway to reject jurisdiction in cases having little connection to the state, without making constitutional pronouncements.[1]

Long-arm statutes take their colorful name from their primary purpose, which is to reach out of the state to call nonresident defendants back into the state to defend lawsuits.[2] Even though a defendant has left the forum state before he is sued (or in some cases has never been in the state at all), he may be required to defend a suit there under the *International Shoe* analysis if the suit arises out of his prior contacts with the forum. Legislatures tend to grant such long-arm jurisdiction liberally since it is usually invoked by plaintiffs who live in the state and prefer to sue at home.

Be careful, however, not to conclude that every assertion of jurisdiction under a long-arm statute is automatically constitutional simply because the statute purports to authorize it. In the area of personal jurisdiction, it is not always easy to tell what is and is not constitutional. Consequently, the reach of a state's long-arm statute may sometimes exceed its constitutional grasp. Suppose, for example, that an Iowa long-arm statute authorized its courts to take jurisdiction in all cases brought by resident plaintiffs. It would certainly be unconstitutional to apply such a statute to a case in which the Iowa plaintiff purchased goods from a Colorado defendant in Colorado. Assuming that the defendant has no other contacts with Iowa, there would be no constitutional authority to assert personal jurisdiction over the defendant, since the claim does not arise out of any minimum contacts with Iowa. This case falls within the "bulge" area in Figure 2-3, in which the statute authorizes jurisdiction (because the plaintiff is a resident), but it would exceed the limits of due process to exercise that jurisdiction.

However, the statute could be applied in other cases without violating due process. For example, if the case arose from a sale by the defendant to the plaintiff that took place in Iowa, the exercise of jurisdiction would be constitutionally permissible because the defendant's voluntary contacts

---

1. A few states have taken the curious approach of adding a California-type, anything-constitutional-goes provision to their enumerated act statute. This seems calculated to confuse: Why specify enumerated acts which support jurisdiction, if everything else within due process limits does too? For a defense of this strategy, see K. Beyler, The Illinois Long-Arm Statute: Background, Meaning and Needed Repairs, 12 S. Ill. L.J. 293, 412-414 (1988).
2. Long-arm statutes generally authorize jurisdiction over out-of-state actors who have minimum contacts with the forum state, such as selling goods in the state, contracting to provide services in the state, or driving in the state. Where courts exercise jurisdiction on other constitutionally adequate bases, there still must be a statute authorizing the court to do so. For example, it is constitutionally permissible for a state court to exercise jurisdiction over a defendant who is domiciled within the forum state. *Milliken v. Meyer*, 311 U.S. 457 (1940). However, the court may only do so if a jurisdictional statute authorizes it: It is the state legislature, not the Constitution, that actually grants jurisdiction to the courts of a state. For a statute that authorizes jurisdiction based on in-state domicile, see N.C. Gen. St. Ann. S. 1-75.4.

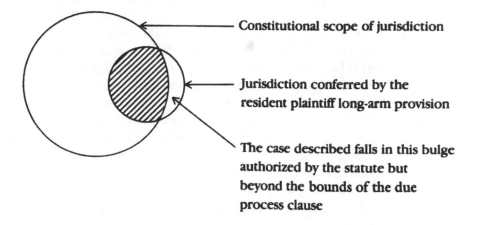

Constitutional scope of jurisdiction

Jurisdiction conferred by the
resident plaintiff long-arm provision

The case described falls in this bulge
authorized by the statute but
beyond the bounds of the due
process clause

Figure 2-3.

with Iowa gave rise to the claim. This case would fall in the shaded area on
the diagram. In such cases, where the statute may be constitutional as
applied to some cases but not all, the courts do not invalidate the statute
entirely; they simply refuse to apply it to cases that fall outside the bounds
of due process. Consequently, the statute remains in force and may be
applied in other cases that are within due process limits.

All long-arm statutes that base personal jurisdiction on specific
enumerated acts require that the claim sued upon arise out of the act itself.
See, e.g., Uniform Interstate and International Procedure Act §1.03(b),
infra p. 32. This limitation is rooted in the *International Shoe* analysis, which
holds that limited in-state contacts only support jurisdiction over claims
that arise from those contacts. See the "*Shoe* spectrum" at p. 6. By echoing
that limitation in the long-arm statute itself, the legislature insures that the
statute will not be used to reach cases beyond the constitutional bounds of
due process.

# JURISDICTION BASED ON ACTS COMMITTED OUTSIDE THE STATE

In many cases, a party commits acts that have an impact in a state, even
though he doesn't actually enter the state. A party may contract to deliver
goods in the state, or develop a computer program for an in-state company
and deliver it over the Internet. A party might call into the state and defame
a local citizen. A manufacturer might make its goods in Oregon and sell
them to a wholesaler in Arizona, which resells them to consumers in Texas.

In each of these cases, the out-of-state party has engaged in conduct that ultimately has effects in the state, without physically entering it.

In some circumstances, such contacts suffice, under the due process clause, to support the exercise of personal jurisdiction over the out-of-state actor. For example, in *International Ins. Co. v. McGee*, 355 U.S. 220 (1957), an insurer sent an offer to re-insure to a policy holder in California. The Supreme Court held that this was a deliberate reaching in that supported jurisdiction over the insurer. In *Calder v. Jones*, 465 U.S. 783 (1984), the defendant published an allegedly defamatory article about a California actress and distributed it in California. That too was held a deliberate reaching in that supported personal jurisdiction. And in *Burger King Co. v. Rudzewicz*, 471 U.S. 462 (1985), one of the defendants was held subject to jurisdiction in Florida when it established a twenty-year franchise relationship to a Florida franchisor, even though he never actually went to Florida.

A number of provisions in enumerated act long-arm statutes authorize jurisdiction in such cases, in which the defendant acts outside the state but causes an effect within it. Many such cases, for example, would satisfy subsection 103(a)(1) of the Uniform Act, which authorizes jurisdiction for claims that arise out of "transacting business" in the forum state. In others, subsection 103(a)(2), dealing with contracting to supply services or things in the state, will apply. In others, subsection 103(a)(4), which premises jurisdiction on an out-of-state tortious act that causes tortious injury in the state, will authorize jurisdiction.

Perhaps the most extravagant example of a long-arm statute that authorizes jurisdiction for out-of-state acts is found in the Illinois Supreme Court's opinion in *Gray v. American Radiator and Standard Sanitary Corp.*, 176 N.E.2d 761 (1961). The *Gray* case interpreted Ill. Rev. Stat. Chap. 110, s. 17(1)(b),[3] which allowed jurisdiction if the defendant "commits a tortious act" in Illinois. In *Gray*, the plaintiff sued a defendant in Illinois that had negligently manufactured a water heater valve in Ohio, which was incorporated in a water heater in Pennsylvania by a different manufacturer. The assembled water heater was later sold in Illinois and exploded there. The *Gray* court concluded that the Ohio valve maker — which had done nothing in Illinois — had "committed a tortious act" in the state, since the explosion that injured the plaintiff took place in Illinois. This expansive interpretation of the Illinois long-arm statute (much criticized, but never overruled) authorizes jurisdiction in many cases in which the defendant did not act in Illinois, did not send goods there, and did not know or anticipate that its product would end up in Illinois. As the examples that follow will illustrate, in many cases, application of this provision

---

3. See now 735 I.L.C.S. 5/2-209.

would fall in the "bulge area" in Figure 2-3, in which the statute authorizes jurisdiction, but exercising that jurisdiction would exceed constitutional limits.

# GOING TO THE LIMITS OF DUE PROCESS

You will frequently read in the cases that an enumerated act long-arm statute is "intended to reach to the limits of due process." This is one of the most frequently misunderstood phrases in the civil procedure lexicon. Although innumerable cases broadly hold that the long-arm statute in question is intended to extend jurisdiction to the constitutional limits, this is not generally intended to mean that a statute like the Uniform Act occupies the entire constitutional field, as the California statute does. It would make little sense for the legislature to pass a statute enumerating specific contacts that support jurisdiction if it actually intended all minimum contacts to do so. Instead, this phrase is better interpreted to mean that the *specific categories* of jurisdiction conveyed by the long-arm statute are to be interpreted as liberally as the due process clause will allow.

For example, the phrase "transacting business" in a long-arm statute might be interpreted quite narrowly, to apply only in cases where the defendant has ongoing commercial activities and permanent employees within the state. Alternately it might be interpreted more broadly, to apply whenever the defendant enters into a single business transaction with an in-state party. If the statute is intended to go to the limits of due process, the court will interpret this language to reach all cases that are within the statutory language and can be reached under the due process clause. See Casad and Richman at §4-1[1][b]; Moore's Federal Practice §108.60[3][a]. Since a single business transaction (depending on the facts) may be sufficient under due process analysis to give rise to personal jurisdiction over claims arising out of it, the statute should be broadly interpreted to reach such a case. In other words, the going-to-the-limits-of-due-process language commands liberal interpretation of the specific provisions of the long-arm statute; it does not fill in any interstices those provisions fail to cover.

Unfortunately, courts have not always grasped this distinction between broad interpretation of the enumerated acts and absorbing the whole constitutional sphere. Many decisions holding that the relevant long-arm is intended to "go to the limits of due process" really do mean, rightly or wrongly, that it fills all the shaded interstices in Figure 2-2.[4] Thus, if you

---

4. For an example of the confusion such loose language has generated under one long-arm provision, see Comment, Georgia's Not-So-Long Arm Statute: Exposing the Myth, 6 Ga. St. L. Rev. 487 (1990).

are researching a case and find such language, it should set off a little alarm in the personal jurisdiction corner of your brain, stimulating some very careful reading of the cases under your long-arm statute to determine what the court really means to say.

In analyzing the following examples, consider first whether the applicable long-arm statute authorizes the court to exercise jurisdiction. Then consider whether it would be constitutional under the minimum contacts test for the court to exercise jurisdiction on the facts given. The Uniform Act, which is used in the examples, is set forth below.

### UNIFORM INTERSTATE AND INTERNATIONAL PROCEDURE ACT

**§1.03. [Personal Jurisdiction Based upon Conduct]**

    (a) A court may exercise personal jurisdiction over a person, who acts directly or by an agent, as to a [cause of action] [claim for relief] arising from the person's

        (1) transacting any business in this state;

        (2) contracting to supply services or things in this state;

        (3) causing tortious injury by an act or omission in this state;

        (4) causing tortious injury in this state by an act or omission outside this state if he regularly does or solicits business, or engages in any other persistent course of conduct, or derives substantial revenue from goods used or consumed or services rendered, in this state; [or]

        (5) having an interest in, using, or possessing real property in this state; or

        (6) contracting to insure any person, property, or risk located within this state at the time of contracting,

    (b) When jurisdiction over a person is based solely upon this section, only a [cause of action] [claim for relief] arising from acts enumerated in this section may be asserted against him.

## Examples

### Torts and the Long-Arm: Basic Cases

1. Hardy throws a pie at Fields while the two are making a movie in New York. Fields fails to see the joke and sues Hardy for assault in Pennsylvania, where Fields lives. Hardy has no other contacts with Pennsylvania.
   a. Could the Pennsylvania court assert jurisdiction over Hardy if the Uniform Act applied in Pennsylvania?
   b. Would it be constitutional for the court to do so?

2. Assume that Hardy, a comedian, performs two or three times a year at clubs in Pennsylvania. Fields sues him in Pennsylvania for the New York assault.
   a. Is jurisdiction proper under the Uniform Act?
   b. Would it be constitutional for the court to take jurisdiction?

3. While traveling to Pittsburgh for a performance, Hardy collides with Fields on Interstate 83 near Harrisburg. After the performance, Hardy returns to New York. Fields, fast losing his sense of humor, sues Hardy in Pennsylvania.
   a. May Fields do so under the Uniform Act?
   b. Would it be constitutional for the Pennsylvania court to take personal jurisdiction over Hardy?

4. West, in California, learns that Paramount Pictures plans to offer Fields a lucrative contract to make a movie in New York. She calls the producer in New York and tries to talk him out of it. During the conversation, she offers several vivid and distinctly uncomplimentary opinions concerning Field's sense of humor. Fields is not amused; he sues West in New York for defamation.
   a. Does the Uniform Act authorize jurisdiction on these facts?
   b. Would it be constitutional for the New York court to exercise jurisdiction over West on this claim?

## Torts and the Long-Arm: *Gray* Areas of Products Liability

5. Chaplin manufactures stunt cars in Michigan for use in movie and television chase scenes. Paramount Pictures of Hollywood, California, a regular customer of Chaplin's, orders ten cars from Chaplin, which are shipped to California. Paramount takes one of the cars to Colorado, where it is used to film a cliff-hanging scene in Rocky Mountain Park. Brice, the star of the show, is injured when the brakes fail at 14,000 feet. Brice sues Chaplin in Colorado.
   a. Would jurisdiction be authorized by a long-arm statute that allowed jurisdiction for claims "arising out of a tortious act committed in this state"?
   b. Would long-arm jurisdiction be proper under the Uniform Act if it applied in Colorado?
   c. Would it be constitutional for the Colorado court to exercise jurisdiction over Chaplin in this action?

6. Assume the same facts as example 5, except that the accident took place on location in Hollywood.
   a. Would jurisdiction be proper under the Uniform Act if it applied in California (instead of California's anything-constitutional-goes version quoted at p. 26)?

    b. Would it be constitutional for the California court to exercise personal jurisdiction on these facts?

7. In this same case against Chaplin in California, Brice also sues Gleason Brake Corporation, the Michigan manufacturer of the brakes in the stunt car.
   a. Would the Uniform Act authorize jurisdiction if it were applicable in California?
   b. Would it be constitutional to require Gleason to defend this action in California?

8. Assume that Oklahoma has a long-arm statute that authorizes jurisdiction over a defendant who "commits a tortious act in Oklahoma." Assume also that it interprets that statute the way Illinois interpreted the same language in *Gray v. American Radiator and Standard Sanitary Corp.*, that is, that the statute is satisfied if the plaintiff suffers the injury in Oklahoma. The Robinsons buy an Audi from Seaway Volkswagen in New York and drive through Oklahoma on their way to their new home in Arizona. While passing through Oklahoma, they have an accident, and the gas tank explodes, allegedly due to a defect in the car sold to them by Seaway.
   a. Is Seaway subject to personal jurisdiction in Oklahoma under the assumed provision of the long-arm statute?
   b. Would it be constitutional for the Oklahoma court to exercise personal jurisdiction over Seaway?

## Famous Foibles

9. The following dandelion sprouts all too frequently in student answers to personal jurisdiction questions:

   > If the defendant does not have minimum contacts with the state, he may still be required to defend a suit there if a provision of the state long-arm statute authorizes jurisdiction.

   What is wrong with this weedy analysis?

## Transacting and Contracting

10. Chaplin sells ten stunt cars to Paramount in California. Paramount sues Chaplin for breach of contract and breach of warranty after one of the cars repeatedly breaks down during filming in Hollywood. Assume that suit is brought in California and that the Uniform Act applies. (Assume for purposes of examples 10 and 11 that breach of warranty is not a tort action.)
    a. Does the Uniform Act authorize jurisdiction over the suit?
    b. Does the court have power to hear the suit under the due process clause?

11. Chaplin manufactures stunt cars and sells them to a distributor, Indestructible Auto, Inc. in Salt Lake City, Utah. Indestructible in turn sells the cars to movie studios. Indestructible sells ten of Chaplin's specials to Paramount in California. Paramount sues Chaplin in California for breach of warranty after three of the cars break down repeatedly during filming.
    a. Is jurisdiction proper under the Uniform Act?
    b. Is jurisdiction permissible under due process analysis?

## Statutory Restraint, and . . .

12. An agent for International Insurance Company calls Skelton in North Carolina and offers him a deal on some life insurance. Skelton agrees, fills out the policy application, and sends in his premium. He then moves to California and dies three weeks later. His mother sues in California to collect the proceeds of the policy. International Insurance has no other business in California.
    a. Would there be jurisdiction over this case under the Uniform Act?
    b. Would it be constitutional to sue International Insurance Company in California on these facts?

## . . . Constitutional Constraints

13. Meadows, a mechanic, repairs a tire for Van Dyke, a tourist heading east, at a service station in Indiana. As Van Dyke later drives through Pennsylvania, the tire falls off the rim, causing an accident. Van Dyke, convinced that Meadows failed to secure the tire properly, wants to sue her in Pennsylvania. His lawyer looks up the Pennsylvania long-arm statute and finds 42 Pa. C.S.A. s. 5322(a)(4), which authorizes jurisdiction over a defendant for "causing harm or tortious injury in this Commonwealth by an act or omission outside this Commonwealth."
    a. Does s. 5322(a)(4) authorize suit against Meadows in this case?
    b. Would it be constitutional for the court to exercise jurisdiction over Meadows?

# Explanations

## Torts and the Long-Arm: Basic Cases

1. Long-arm jurisdiction:   No      Constitutional power:   No
    a. The Uniform Act does not provide statutory authority for Fields to sue Hardy in Pennsylvania. Although §§1.03(a)(3) and 1.03(a)(4) of the Uniform Act authorize jurisdiction in tort cases, neither applies in the circumstances of this case. Subsection 1.03(a)(3)

authorizes jurisdiction over claims arising out of tortious injuries caused by an act or omission in the state (meaning the state where the suit is brought). This subsection does not apply because Hardy's act took place in New York. Subsection 1.03(a)(4) allows the plaintiff to sue in Pennsylvania if he suffered tortious injury in Pennsylvania from an out-of-state act and if the defendant does business in the state or derives revenues from goods used or consumed in the state. This doesn't help Fields either. First, any injury he suffered took place in New York, where the assault occurred. Second, the example states that Hardy does not do business in Pennsylvania or have any other contacts with the state. No matter how liberally interpreted, the long-arm is too short to reach this case.

b. Had the statute purported to confer jurisdiction over this case, its reach would have exceeded its constitutional grasp, Although Fields has minimum contacts with Pennsylvania, Hardy does not. Nor do the facts suggest any other basis for personal jurisdiction, such as consent or domicile. Field's domicile in Pennsylvania is irrelevant; it is the defendant who is being forced into the state to defend. The plaintiff's unilateral contacts with the forum do not create a constitutional basis for requiring the defendant to defend there. *Hanson v. Denckla*, 357 U.S. 235 (1958).

2. Long-arm jurisdiction:   No      Constitutional power:   No
   a. Hardy's occasional forays into Pennsylvania do not lead to a different result from example 1. Subsection (a)(3) of the Uniform Act still doesn't apply because the tortious act took place in New York. Nor does subsection (a)(4) reach this case because the injury also occurred in New York. Even if the injury could be construed to take place in Pennsylvania, it is doubtful that the proviso in (a)(4) could be met. Such sporadic performances in Pennsylvania probably do not amount to "regularly do[ing] business" in the state or "deriving substantial revenue from . . . services rendered" in the state.

   Fields might argue that Hardy has "transacted business" (Uniform Act §l.03(a)(1)) in Pennsylvania by his performances there. Indeed he has, but this is insufficient to subject him to personal jurisdiction for Fields's New York tort claim. The Uniform Act and all long-arm provisions limit jurisdiction based on specific contacts to claims *arising out of* the contacts. Indeed, this point is so fundamental that the Act says it twice, in the first sentence of §l.03(a) and in §1.03(b) as well. Hardy could be sued in Pennsylvania under §1.03(a)(1) for a breach of contract claim resulting from his performances there, but not for an unrelated claim arising in New York.

   b. In this case, Hardy has contacts with Pennsylvania but the claim doesn't arise from them. As the *"Shoe* Spectrum" on p. 6 illustrates, when the defendant's contacts with the state are limited, he is only subject to "specific in personam jurisdiction," that is, jurisdiction for claims that arise out of those in-state contacts. It is because of this constitutional limitation that long-arm statutes also restrict jurisdiction to claims arising from the listed contacts. Otherwise, their reach would frequently exceed their constitutional grasp in cases like this one.

3. Long-arm jurisdiction: Yes    Constitutional power: Yes
   a. In this case, Fields gets the last laugh. The case is clearly covered by subsection (a)(3) of the Uniform Act because Fields's suit arises from Hardy's tortious act (the negligent driving) in Pennsylvania. An argument might also be made, since Hardy was driving to a performance, that the claim arose out of Hardy's transacting business in Pennsylvania (subsection (a)(1)). (It is certainly possible for a defendant's acts to satisfy more than one provision of a long-arm statute, as illustrated by the intersecting circles in Figure 2-2.) The argument is dubious here, however, since the claim is for a tort to a person not involved in Hardy's in-state business. In any event, it is unnecessary, since subsection (a)(3) squarely applies.
   b. Courts have consistently held that committing a tortious act within the state is a minimum contact of the "quality and nature" that gives rise to personal jurisdiction. Because the claim arises out of this in-state act, jurisdiction is proper under the minimum contacts test. The fact that Hardy left the state before suit was brought does not preclude jurisdiction. *International Shoe* premises jurisdiction on the in-state contacts that gave rise to the claim, not presence at the time of suit.

4. Long-arm jurisdiction: Maybe    Constitutional power: Yes
   a. Assuming that West has no other contacts with New York, the only likely basis for jurisdiction is subsection (a)(3) of the Uniform Act. The problem, of course, is that that section requires that the tortious injury result from an "act or omission in this state," yet West has not entered New York. In *Gray v. American Radiator and Standard Sanitary Corp.*, 176 N.E.2d 761 (Ill. 1961), the Illinois Supreme Court concluded that a "tortious act" took place where a negligently constructed product caused an injury. The Uniform Act precludes this extravagant interpretation by specifying that the act or omission that causes the injury, not the injury itself, must take place in the state. See §1.03(a)(3). Indeed, provisions like §1.03(a)(3) and (a)(4), which distinguish between in-state tortious acts and out-of-state tortious acts causing in-state injuries, were drafted to clarify the statutory ambiguity discussed in *Gray*.

   However, a strong argument can be made that West *did* commit the tortious act in New York. West has deliberately projected her voice into the state via the telephone wires for the purpose of making the defamatory statement to a person in that state. (Compare *Gray*, in which the tortious act was done entirely in Ohio, but the harm was suffered after the water heater was shipped into Illinois.) Some courts have concluded in such cases that the act takes place where the statements are heard, rather than where they are uttered. Other courts have concluded that the act takes place where the actor acts, not where the statement is heard. These latter courts view such cases as out-of-state act/in-state injury cases and refuse to take jurisdiction unless the defendant has engaged in business or other persistent activity in the state under subsection (a)(4).

This is a good example of a case in which interpreting the long-arm statute to "go to the limits of due process" makes a difference. If this is the governing rule of interpretation, the court should interpret the "act or omission within this state" language as broadly as due process allows and conclude that the act took place in New York.

It appears that New York does not interpret its "commits a tortious act in the state" provision to reach cases like West's. In *Bensusan Restaurant Corp. v. King*, 126 F.3d 25 (2d Cir. 1997), for example, the New York federal court reiterated that this provision of New York's statute is satisfied only if the defendant acted while physically in New York. 126 F.3d at 27-29. See also Practice Commentary to C.P.L.R. s. 302(a)(2) ("if a New Jersey domiciliary were to lob a bazooka shell across the Hudson River at Grant's tomb, [New York's approach] would appear to bar the New York courts from asserting personal jurisdiction over the New Jersey domiciliary in an action by an injured New York plaintiff"). Id. at 28. In this bazooka hypothetical, it would clearly be constitutional to exert jurisdiction over the New Jersey assailant, as it probably would be in West's case as well. New York has simply chosen a more restrained interpretation of its statute, which does not "go to the limits of due process."

b. West's act is deliberately aimed at causing harm to Fields in New York. Such an act, undertaken with the intent to injure the plaintiff in New York and involving direct contact with the producer there, constitutes a voluntary affiliation with the forum of the "quality and nature" to support jurisdiction under the due process clause. West can hardly claim surprise when the harm she intended eventuates where she intended it, and Fields sues her there. See *Calder v. Jones*, 465 U.S. 783, 788 (1984); compare *Wilson v. Belin*, 20 F.3d 644 (5th Cir. 1994), *cert. denied*, 513 U.S. 930 (1994) (no jurisdiction over defendants who *were called by* reporter from the forum state and made allegedly defamatory statements about the plaintiff that were then published in the state).

## Torts and the Long-Arm: *Gray* Areas of Products Liability

5. Long-arm jurisdiction:   (a) Possibly   (b) Uniform Act: No   (c) Constitutional power:   No

   a. The long-arm statute quoted here is similar to the Illinois statute interpreted in *Gray v. American Radiator and Standard Sanitary Corp.*, 176 N.E.2d 761 (Ill. 1961). In *Gray* the court interpreted this language to apply if the *plaintiff's injury* occurred in the state, even though the defendant's negligence occurred elsewhere. 176 N.E.2d at 763. However, other courts have refused to accept this strained interpretation. See *Feathers v. McLucas*, 209 N.E.2d 68, 79 (N.Y. 1965), in which the court concluded that the *Gray* interpretation "disregards [the statute's] plain language and exceeds the bounds of sound statutory interpretation" and that the phrase only applies to cases in which the defendant's tortious conduct took place in the state. Thus, whether Chaplin is subject to jurisdiction under this long-arm provision depends on the court's willingness to stretch the language as the court did in *Gray*.

   b. The Uniform Act does not reach this case. Subsection (3) does not apply; it focuses specifically on the place where the defendant's negligent act (here the negligent manufacture) took place, which was Michigan in this case. Subsection (4) does not apply either. Although Chaplin may have caused tortious injury in Colorado by his out-of-state act, there is no indication that the additional requirement of regular in-state conduct or profits is met.

   c. The only contact Chaplin has with Colorado in this case is that the motion picture company took one of his stunt cars from California to Colorado to make a movie, and the brakes failed there. Like the Volkswagen in *World-Wide Volkswagen v. Woodson*, the car reached Colorado by the unilateral act of a third party, not as the result of any deliberate contact by Chaplin with Colorado. Although it may be foreseeable that Paramount will use the car to make chase scenes in the Rockies, this foreseeability is not a sufficient basis for exercising jurisdiction over Chaplin there. *World-Wide Volkswagen v. Woodson*, 444 U.S. 286, 295-296 (1980). It would exceed the limits of due process for the Colorado court to exercise jurisdiction over Chaplin wherever Paramount chooses to film movies. Thus, this is another example in the "bulge" area of Figure 2-3, in which the long-arm statute might be interpreted to authorize jurisdiction (under the *Gray* approach), but it would exceed the bounds of due process to exercise that jurisdiction.

6. Long-arm jurisdiction:   Yes   Constitutional power:   Yes

   a. If Brice's accident takes place in California, subsection (4) will authorize jurisdiction. Chaplin has caused Brice's injuries in

**39**

California by an out-of-state act. In addition, he apparently does business with Paramount in California on a regular basis. Note that subsection (4) includes two requirements: an in-state injury from an out-of-state act and an ongoing relationship to the state. The second requirement may be satisfied by one of several alternative showings: regular solicitation of business, regularly doing business, any other persistent course of conduct in the state, or deriving substantial revenue from goods or services used or consumed in the state.

It may also be possible to argue that Brice's claim in this case arises from Chaplin's "transacting business" in California, under §1.03(a)(1) of the Uniform Act. Although Brice's claim does not arise directly out of the transaction itself (as a claim by Paramount for defects in the cars would, for example), it does "arise out of" the sale of the cars in California in a more general sense. Many courts would uphold jurisdiction in these circumstances under §1.03(a)(1). See Casad and Richman at §4-2[1][b].

b. There is a constitutionally significant difference between this case and the last. Here, the brake failure and resulting injury is not the sole contact Chaplin has with the forum state. The presence of the car in California arose through deliberate efforts by Chaplin to serve the market for his product in California. This is a voluntary affiliation with the state that changes the "quality and nature" of Chaplin's in-state act of causing injury in California. The Supreme Court's stream-of-commerce analysis in *World-Wide Volkswagen* and *Asahi* supports jurisdiction over out-of-state defendants in these circumstances on the theory that a defendant who persistently takes advantage of the opportunity to market his product in the state may fairly be called to account in the state if a product he sold into the state causes tortious injury there.

Even under Justice O'Connor's view in *Asahi*, jurisdiction would be proper in this case. Unlike the valve maker in *Asahi*, Chaplin in this example has deliberately shipped his cars — including the one that caused the injury — to California. Thus, there is no question of being subjected to jurisdiction due to the unilateral acts of a subsequent distributor. Chaplin has chosen to sell cars directly to California, and this purposeful conduct gives rise to the claim in suit.

7. Long-arm jurisdiction: Maybe    Constitutional power: Maybe
   a. The issue here is whether the component part manufacturer, who has dealt with the final manufacturer but has not directly done business or sold goods in California, can be required to defend there in a products liability case arising out of injury in California allegedly resulting from a defect in its product. Gleason is analogous to Titan Value company in *Gray*. Gleason caused tortious injury in California by an out-of-state

act. It also derives substantial revenue from goods used or consumed in California, assuming that Chaplin, and perhaps others as well, sell a substantial number of cars in California made with Gleason brakes. Jurisdiction would likely be upheld over component part manufacturers in such circumstances, under §1.03(a)(4) of the Uniform Act, and perhaps §1.03(a)(1) as well.

It will not always follow that the component part manufacturer will fit subsection (4) just because the final manufacturer does. For example, if Chaplin sold only 50 cars in California, this may be enough to constitute doing or soliciting business there or deriving substantial revenue from goods sold there. The company that makes the windshield wipers, however, at $6 a pair does not derive substantial revenue from goods used or consumed in California if the only wipers that go there are on Chaplin's 50 stunt cars. If the wipers failed and caused the accident, Chaplin would be subject to jurisdiction under this language but the wiper manufacturer probably would not.

b. Prior to *Asahi*, a number of courts held it within the bounds of due process to exercise jurisdiction over an out-of-state component manufacturer in this type of case. These courts reasoned that a component maker who derives revenue from substantial sales of its product in a state should not be able to accept that benefit without submitting to jurisdiction when the product causes injury there. Some courts reached this conclusion even if the component maker was unaware that the finished product for which it provided parts was being resold in the forum state. See, e.g., *Bean Dredging Corp. v. Dredge Technology Corp.*, 744 F.2d 1081 (5th Cir. 1984).

However, as Chapter 1 indicates, *Asahi* has thrown some doubt on the question of whether component makers who do not direct their goods into a state or cultivate the market there are subject to personal jurisdiction if their product reaches the forum state through resale of the finished product and causes injury there. The O'Connor approach would require more to establish "purposeful availment." Four other Justices (all no longer on the Court) apparently would not. A distinction might be premised on the fact that the component maker is in Michigan rather than Japan, but this seems to go more to the second prong of the analysis (reasonableness once minimum contacts are shown) than to the issue of minimum contacts themselves.

8. Long-arm jurisdiction:   Yes      Constitutional power:   No
   a. If Oklahoma had this provision in its long-arm statute, and if it adopted the Illinois interpretation, the provision would authorize jurisdiction over Seaway. All that provision requires, under the *Gray* interpretation, is that the injury to the plaintiff take place in the state, not the conduct of the defendant. Since the car exploded in

Oklahoma, the statute would authorize jurisdiction over Seaway, since its negligent act in New York caused injury in Oklahoma when the Audi blew up there.

b. Clearly, it would exceed constitutional limits for Oklahoma to exercise jurisdiction over Seaway on these facts . . . the Supreme Court told us that in *World-Wide Volkswagen*. Seaway has not purposely availed itself of the benefits of conducting activities in Oklahoma or focused on Oklahoma. It acted only in New York; it was the unilateral act of the Robinsons that brought the car to Oklahoma. Thus, this example illustrates a situation in which the "tortious act" long-arm, interpreted as the Illinois court did in *Gray*, would authorize jurisdiction that would be impermissible under the Fourteenth Amendment Due Process Clause. This case falls in the bulge area in Figure 2-3.

## Famous Foibles

9. The fallacy in this foible is the student's conclusion that satisfying a provision of a long-arm statute is *an alternative* to satisfying constitutional due process analysis. Not so! In every case, a state statute must authorize the court to exercise personal jurisdiction over the defendant. But — also in every case — it must be constitutional for the court to do so. It's not an "either/or" proposition; the court must always have both statutory authority to exercise jurisdiction, and it must be constitutionally proper for the court to exercise that authority as well. One, without the other, will not do.

## Transacting and Contracting

10. Long-arm jurisdiction:   Yes      Constitutional power:   Yes
    a. This claim squarely fits subsection (2) of the Uniform Act because it arises directly out of Chaplin's agreement to sell the allegedly defective car to Paramount in California. It would likely satisfy subsection (1) as well. Even if Chaplin does not have a business office in California, most courts would hold that he transacts business there by selling his product to a California buyer, at least where the sale is as substantial as this one.
    b. The decision to sell goods to buyers in another state is a deliberate, profit-oriented contact with that state. When the sale is substantial (as here) or part of a series of such sales, the seller enjoys the benefits and protections of doing business in the state and may have a significant effect on the commerce of the state. In such cases, the seller should expect to defend suits there arising out of those business transactions with forum-state customers. See *Burger King*, 471 U.S. at 475-476.

11. Long-arm jurisdiction: Probably    Constitutional power:    Unclear

    a. Paramount might argue that several provisions of the Uniform Act apply but will probably have to fall back on §1.03(a)(1), the "transacting business" provision. Subsection 1.03(a)(2) was probably meant to apply to cases in which the defendant directly contracted to supply goods in the state, not stream of commerce cases like this one where a distributor resells the defendant's goods in the state. Section 1.03(a)(4), the tortious-act-outside/injury-inside-the-state provision probably can't be stretched to reach the case either: The claim is for failure of the goods to perform properly, not for personal injury or property damage.

       However, many courts would conclude that Chaplin did "transact business" in California, albeit indirectly. Chaplin has delivered his goods into the stream of commerce. He may well know that they are destined for California or hope that they are. Where he profits from these resales in the state, it appears likely that the long arm's "transacting business" language was intended to reach his conduct even though he used a distributor rather than sending the goods directly to California. See, e.g., *Stabilisierungsfonds Fur Wein v. Kaiser Stuhl Wine Distributors Pty. Ltd.*, 647 F.2d 200, 204-206 (D.C. Cir. 1981); Casad & Richman, §4-2[1][a][4].

    b. This is another stream of commerce case. It differs from *Asabi* and example 7 in that Chaplin is a final manufacturer rather than a component maker. But it is still indirect, as Chaplin sold his cars to Utah, and they were then resold into California. The reasoning of Justice O'Connor's opinion would seem to bar jurisdiction in both types of cases. Because of the split in the Court and the change in its composition, it is hard to say whether jurisdiction is proper in such cases, in which a predictable stream of commerce sweeps the defendant's goods into the state.

       Note that, should the O'Connor view prevail, interpreting "transacting business" provisions to apply to defendants who indirectly sell their goods in the state would often exceed the bounds of due process. This example, then, would fall in the bulge area of Figure 2-3, in which the statute authorizes jurisdiction but it would exceed due process limits to assert that jurisdiction.

## Statutory Restraint, and . . .

12. Long-arm jurisdiction: No    Constitutional power: Probably not

    a. Subsection (a)(6) of the Uniform Act specifically addresses claims arising out of insurance contracts. That subsection limits jurisdiction to claims arising from contracts to insure risks present in the state at the time the insurance contract was made. Skelton was not present in California when the insurance contract was made, so this subsection doesn't apply.

One might argue — though it's a stretch — that the claim arises from International's "transacting business" in California. But the court is very unlikely to apply this general provision where subsection (a)(6) specifically addresses insurance cases and limits the claims that can be brought to those involving risks in the state at the time of contracting. That would allow cases through the back door that the legislature pretty clearly barred explicitly in s. (a)(6).

b. The drafters of the Uniform Act probably included the in-state-risk limit in s. (a)(6) because they thought the limit was necessary to avoid constitutional problems. On the facts of the example (an obvious twist on *McGee v. International Ins. Co.*, 355 U.S. 220 (1957)) the insurer really has no deliberate contacts with California: it simply entered into an insurance contract with a North Carolinian in North Carolina. Perhaps one could argue that Skelton's listing of a California beneficiary provides some contact with California, but it is a very tenuous one at best. Thus, allowing suit wherever the insured dies, or a beneficiary lives, would often allow jurisdiction in states where it would exceed constitutional bounds. Drafting the long-arm statute to apply only if the risk was in the forum state at the time of contracting limits jurisdiction to cases which will virtually always involve a sufficient, related contact to constitutionally support jurisdiction there. Thus, the restraint exercised by the drafters will avoid constitutional problems in applying the statute.

## . . . Constitutional Constraints

13. Long-arm jurisdiction:   Yes      Constitutional power:   No
    a. Subsection 5322(a)(4) clearly authorizes jurisdiction over Meadows in Van Dyke's case. It only requires that the defendant have acted outside the state and caused an injury within it. Meadows did just that when she repaired the tire in Indiana, leading to Van Dyke's injury in Pennsylvania.

    Note that s. 5322(a)(4) does not require additional, on-going contacts with the state, such as deriving profits from goods sold in the state, or ongoing solicitation of sales. Compare s. 1.03(a)(4) of the Uniform Act, which allows jurisdiction based on out-of-state acts that cause in-state injuries, but only if such additional contacts exist.

    b. This provision of the Pennsylvania long-arm statute is living proof that legislatures do enact long-arm statutes whose reach, in many cases, exceeds their constitutional grasp. In this case, Meadows has no contacts with Pennsylvania that would support personal jurisdiction over her, but the statute allows jurisdiction solely on the ground that the *plaintiff's injury* occurred in Pennsylvania. *Worldwide Volkswagen* clearly rejects resulting in-state injury — even foreseeable resulting injury — as a basis for minimum contacts jurisdiction. "Foreseeability of harm within the forum state must be accompanied by conduct directed at the forum state in order for the defendant to reasonably anticipate being haled into the state's courts. There is a critical difference between an act which has an effect in the forum and one directed at the forum itself." *Surgical Laser Technologies, Inc. v. C.R. Bard, Inc.*, 921 F. Supp. 281, 285 (E.D. Pa. 1996) (footnote omitted).

One consequence of such broad jurisdictional statutes is increased litigation over personal jurisdiction. Subsection 5322(a)(4) is a clear invitation to lawyers to file cases like Van Dyke's: after all, the statute says that you can! So plaintiffs do, and the courts end up dismissing these cases, after substantial litigation, on the ground that the exercise of jurisdiction, though authorized by s. 5322(a)(4), would be unconstitutional. See, e.g., *Santana Products, Inc. v. Bobrick Washroom Equipment*, 14 F. Supp. 2d 710, 715-716 (M.D. Pa. 1998) (discussing cases rejecting, on constitutional grounds, jurisdiction based on s. 5322(a)(4)).

CHAPTER 3

# Seeking the Home Field Advantage

## Challenges to Personal Jurisdiction

# INTRODUCTION

Surely one of the most fundamental principles of civil procedure is that the courts of a state may not exercise judicial power over a defendant unless that defendant has, in one way or another, submitted to the jurisdiction of the courts of that state. A century of case law has given some specificity to this requirement. As Chapter 1 indicates, defendants may be subject to jurisdiction under the due process analysis on the basis of domicile in a state, in-state service of process, consent to jurisdiction, continuous or substantial in-state contacts, or as a result of "minimum contacts" with the forum state that give rise to a particular cause of action.

It is not always clear when a plaintiff sues a defendant in a particular state whether one of these bases for personal jurisdiction is met. Suppose, for example, that Wolfe, a North Carolina novelist, gives a newspaper interview in North Carolina in which he disparages Hemingway's writing abilities. Hemingway sues Wolfe in Oregon for libel. When Wolfe is served with the complaint, he may be unsure whether the Oregon court has the right to exercise jurisdiction over him. For example, he may not know whether the newspaper that interviewed him is circulated in Oregon or whether Hemingway has suffered any injury in Oregon as a result of the alleged libel. If Wolfe has no other connections with Oregon, he may well conclude that the courts of Oregon have no right to order him to appear and defend the suit in Oregon.

This chapter explores the options available to a defendant like Wolfe to present his objection to the exercise of personal jurisdiction over him by the courts of another state. Generally, these options involve a challenge either in the court in which the original action is brought (the rendering state) or in another state where enforcement of the original judgment is sought (the enforcing state).

## CHALLENGING JURISDICTION IN THE RENDERING STATE ("DIRECT ATTACK")

The defendant's first option is to appear in the original action at the beginning of the suit and object to the court's exercise of jurisdiction over her. For example, Wolfe may decide to appear in the Oregon court and ask the court to dismiss the action for lack of personal jurisdiction. The procedure for doing this varies from state to state. In some states, the defendant who objects to jurisdiction files a "special appearance." Under a special appearance, the defendant is allowed to appear before the court at the beginning of the action for the sole purpose of challenging its power to exercise personal jurisdiction over her. If the defendant is careful to appear "specially," she may litigate the jurisdictional question without submitting to jurisdiction by the very act of appearing before the court.

However, the defendant who files a special appearance must exercise extreme care not to raise any other issue: If she raises any objection or argument that the court can construe as a defense on the merits, the court may conclude that she has waived her jurisdictional objection. For example, in *Koplin v. Saul Lerner Co.*, 201 N.E.2d 763 (Ill. App. 1964), the defendant entered a special appearance to object to the court's jurisdiction and also moved to strike the complaint for vagueness. The court held that this hapless defendant, by raising the vagueness issue, had addressed an issue going to the merits, and thereby had submitted to the court's jurisdiction. The pitfalls of making a successful special appearance are discussed in Casad and Richman ¶3-1[5][a][i].

A growing number of states have abandoned the common law special appearance device in favor of the more liberal approach to challenging personal jurisdiction used in federal courts. Under the Federal Rules, as under the special appearance, a defendant may appear before answering to the merits of the complaint and object to personal jurisdiction. Fed. R. Civ. P. 12(b)(2). However, under the Federal Rules approach, the defendant may also raise other objections at the same time, without waiving the objection to personal jurisdiction. For example, under Fed. R. Civ. P. 12(b), a defendant may move to dismiss for lack of personal jurisdiction and, at the same time, for failure to state a claim upon which relief can be granted (see Rule 12(b)(6)). This second objection clearly goes to the merits of the suit; if a defendant did this in a state that adheres to the older special appearance rule, the court would hold that she had waived her objection to personal jurisdiction by bringing up matters going to the merits of the case.[1]

Thus, in the federal courts under Rule 12(b), and in the numerous state courts with similar rules, the defendant has a little more flexibility in raising the objection and is less likely to be tripped up by the procedural technicalities of doing so. But under either approach, the objection to jurisdiction must be raised immediately or it is lost. A defendant who answers on the merits and later concludes that personal jurisdiction is lacking will have waived the objection by failing to raise it at the outset. See generally Chapter 19.

If Wolfe properly raises his objection in the rendering court, under either the special appearance approach or the Federal Rules approach (whichever applies in that state), the court will hold a hearing on the issue. If the court concludes that there is no basis to exercise jurisdiction over Wolfe, it will dismiss the suit. However, if the court concludes that it does have the power to exercise jurisdiction over him for the claim asserted by Hemingway, it will proceed with the case.

In most states a defendant who challenges jurisdiction at the beginning of the suit and loses may defend the merits of the suit without waiving her objection to the court's jurisdictional ruling. If she loses the suit on the merits, she may appeal to an appellate court in the rendering state, claiming that the trial court's conclusion that it had personal jurisdiction was wrong. Friedenthal, Kane and Miller, 196-197 (4th ed. 2005). This scenario is hardly palatable to Wolfe, of course, since it requires him to do exactly what he believes he should not have to do, defend the action in a state that (allegedly) lacks personal jurisdiction over him. However, it at least leaves him an avenue to correct the trial judge's mistake and to avoid being bound by a decision rendered by a court that lacks jurisdiction to render it.

In some state court systems, a defendant whose challenge to the rendering court's jurisdiction is rejected may take an immediate appeal to the appropriate appellate court in that state. This has a great advantage for the defendant. If the appellate court concludes that she is not subject to jurisdiction in the action, it will order it dismissed, and the defendant will avoid litigating the case in that court. In *World-Wide Volkswagen v. Woodson*,

---

1. Under Fed. R. Civ. P. 12(b), the defendant may also raise the jurisdictional objection in her answer to the complaint, if she did not file a pre-answer motion. The crucial thing is to raise it immediately, either in the answer or a pre-answer motion. See Chapter 19. For an example in which the objection was raised in the answer, see the defendant's answer in the *Schulansky* case, infra p. 665 (Third Defense).

444 U.S. 286 (1980), for example, several defendants sought a "writ of prohibition" from the Oklahoma Supreme Court, before trial, to bar the trial judge from subjecting them to jurisdiction in Okalahoma. A few states even *require* a defendant to take interlocutory review, presumably on the rationale that dismissal of the case, if jurisdiction is lacking, will save everyone the useless exercise of a trial destined to be nullified on appeal. See, e.g., *Mosier v. Kinley*, 702 A.2d 803 (N.H. 1997).

Other states, however, do not allow interlocutory appeals on personal jurisdiction. And the federal courts generally do not allow them either. Although the argument for allowing such appeals seems strong (especially to the defendant), there is also a strong counter argument: If the appellate court affirms the trial court's conclusion that the defendant is subject to jurisdiction, the case will go back to the trial court for further proceedings, after a lengthy delay to process the appeal.

## CHALLENGING JURISDICTION IN THE ENFORCING COURT ("COLLATERAL ATTACK")

The second option for the defendant who objects to personal jurisdiction is to ignore the original suit entirely. If Wolfe is truly convinced that Oregon lacks personal jurisdiction over him, he may view the suit as mere harassment, an ineffective proceeding that can give rise to no binding judgment and that can therefore be ignored with impunity. If the Oregon court lacks personal jurisdiction over Wolfe, any judgment it enters in Hemingway's suit will be unenforceable anyway. If that's true, why bother to respond at all?

Procedurally, it is true that Wolfe has a right *not* to appear in Oregon if the Oregon court lacks jurisdiction over him for the claim asserted in the suit. However, this course poses a serious risk: If Wolfe fails to appear at all in Oregon, either to object to personal jurisdiction or to defend on the merits of the libel claim, the court will probably enter a default judgment for Hemingway — that is, a judgment that Wolfe is liable to Hemingway on the claims asserted in the complaint. If that judgment is enforceable, Wolfe will have lost his suit without ever having had a chance to defend it on the merits.

The usual method of enforcing money judgments against out-of-state defendants is for the plaintiff to take her judgment against the defendant to a state where the defendant lives or has property and seek a court order from the courts of that state authorizing the sheriff to sell the defendant's assets to satisfy the judgment. Hemingway, for example, may take his Oregon judgment to North Carolina, where Wolfe lives, and ask the court to authorize a judicial sale of Wolfe's house to pay off the judgment.

However, the North Carolina court will not directly enforce the Oregon judgment. Hemingway must first obtain recognition of the Oregon judgment (called "domesticating the judgment," like finding a home for a wild animal) in one of two ways. The traditional procedure is to file a new action on the judgment in the enforcing state — North Carolina in this case — seeking a "judgment on the judgment." A good many states now provide an alternative statutory procedure for domesticating foreign[2] judgments. The judgment creditor (Hemingway in our example) simply files a certified copy of the Oregon judgment in the North Carolina court, eliminating the need to file a new suit there.[3] In states that have such a procedure, the judgment creditor may either file a traditional action on the judgment or use the statutory filing procedure.

The Full Faith and Credit Clause of the United States Constitution (Article IV, §1) requires the courts of each state to honor the judgments of other states by entering judgments upon them and allowing out-of-state creditors like Hemingway to use court process to collect them. Once Hemingway obtains a judgment on the judgment (or under a registration statute, registers the judgment in the enforcing state), he may invoke North Carolina procedures for collecting it, including placing liens on Wolfe's assets in the state, forcing sale of those assets, or initiating court hearings to determine Wolfe's ability to pay.

There is, however, an important exception to a state's duty to give full faith and credit to a judgment of another state: The enforcing court may always inquire as to whether the rendering state had jurisdiction in the original action and refuse enforcement if it did not. See *Pennoyer v. Neff*, 95 U.S. 714, 732 (1877). For example, if the North Carolina court concludes after a hearing on the jurisdiction issue that the Oregon court had jurisdiction over Wolfe, the North Carolina court must enforce the Oregon default judgment by entering a North Carolina judgment on the original judgment and making its procedures for execution[4] of judgments available to Hemingway. However, if the North Carolina court concludes that the Oregon court did not have jurisdiction over Wolfe, it will refuse to honor the Oregon judgment, and Hemingway will not be able to levy on Wolfe's property in North Carolina.

Thus, if Wolfe ignores the Oregon proceeding, he will still have an opportunity to protect his property from being sold on execution in North

---

2. The word "foreign" in this context refers to a judgment of another state, not that of another country.

3. Most such statutes are based on a model act, the Uniform Enforcement of Foreign Judgments Act (1964 Revised Act), 13 U.L.A. 155 (2002). There is also a federal statute authorizing registration of federal judgments in other federal districts. 28 U.S.C. §1963.

4. This grim sounding term refers to the various court procedures available for obtaining satisfaction of a judgment by seizure and sale of the defendant's assets. See generally Friedenthal, Kane and Miller, §15.7.

Carolina. Even if a default judgment is rendered in the original Oregon law suit, Wolfe may oppose enforcement of that judgment by asserting in the North Carolina enforcement action that the Oregon court lacked personal jurisdiction over him.[5] This is referred to as a "collateral attack" on the judgment because the defendant challenges the original court's jurisdiction in the enforcement action rather than directly in the original suit. Collateral attack is clearly more convenient for Wolfe because he does not have to go to Oregon, something that from his point of view he shouldn't have to do. It also allows him to litigate the jurisdictional issue in his home state. While the issue of whether the Oregon court had jurisdiction over Wolfe will theoretically be the same in either state, it is at least possible that a North Carolina court will be more sympathetic to Wolfe's objection than the Oregon court would be.

However, this strategy poses a great risk for Wolfe. The Full Faith and Credit Clause allows Wolfe to question the rendering court's jurisdiction but not to reopen the merits of the underlying libel action. If the North Carolina court concludes that the Oregon court had jurisdiction over Wolfe, it will automatically enforce the Oregon default judgment. If Wolfe's original conclusion that the Oregon court lacks jurisdiction is wrong (and many conclusions in this area are only educated guesses), the default judgment will be valid and enforceable, in Oregon or any other state. The idea is that a defendant has the right to stay away if a court lacks jurisdiction but not if it has jurisdiction. In the latter situation, the defendant is deemed to have waived her defense on the merits by failing to appear. That is a very considerable price to pay to avoid contesting the jurisdictional issue in the plaintiff's chosen forum.

All this is complex enough, but one further wrinkle is also important. It is true that the Full Faith and Credit Clause allows defendants such as Wolfe to resist enforcement of another state's judgment on the ground that the rendering state never obtained personal jurisdiction over them. But there is an exception to this rule as well. A defendant may not challenge personal jurisdiction in the enforcement action if she has already done so in the original action. Suppose, for example, that Wolfe had appeared in the Oregon action and moved to dismiss for lack of personal jurisdiction. If the motion was denied, and Wolfe then defaulted on the merits, he could not renew his challenge to jurisdiction in an enforcement action in North Carolina, because he had already litigated and lost on that issue. Once is enough; the rules of collateral estoppel provide that a party who has fully

---

5. If Hemingway brings a suit to obtain a judgment on the original judgment, Wolfe can raise this objection as a defense to the enforcement suit. If Hemingway files the judgment under a registration statute, Wolfe can raise the objection by a motion asking the court not to enforce the judgment. See Uniform Enforcement of Foreign Judgments Act §2, 13 U.L.A. at 163.

litigated an issue in one action may not relitigate it in another. See Chapter 28. Thus, Wolfe gets his choice to raise the objection in one court or the other but not to resurrect it after it has been fully litigated and decided.

While the explanation of these principles is lengthy, their application is fairly straightforward. The following examples should help. See also Figure 3-1, which illustrates the various possibilities. Please assume that all

| Defendant's Response to the Original Suit | Action in the Rendering Court | Action in the Enforcing Court |
| --- | --- | --- |
| D appears, defends on merits, and loses | Enters judgment for P | Must enforce the rendering court's judgment, even if D challenges the rendering court's jurisdiction; D has waived his objection |
| D makes special appearance or 12(b)(2) motion; court agrees that it lacks jurisdiction | In most cases, dismisses action for lack of jurisdiction; in some, may order proper service to cure jurisdictional defect | If original suit dismissed, there will be no judgment to enforce. However, P may file a new suit in a court that has jurisdiction over the defendant |
| D makes special appearance or 12(b)(2) motion; court upholds jurisdiction; D defaults | Enters judgment for P | Must enforce judgment because D already litigated the rendering court's jurisdiction and lost |
| D loses on objection to jurisdiction; defends action on the merits; loses; appeals | In most states, appellate court may review decision that jurisdiction was proper; a few may treat defense on merits as a waiver of the jurisdictional objection | If jurisdiction upheld on appeal, or objection waived by defense on merits, must enforce the rendering court's judgment |
| D defaults, contests jurisdiction in enforcing court | Enters default judgment for P, unless lack of jurisdiction is clear from the complaint | Enforcing court may decide whether rendering court had jurisdiction; if it finds it did not, it refuses enforcement. If it finds that it did, it must enforce the judgment |
| D defaults, denies liability on merits in the enforcing court | Enters default judgment for P, unless lack of jurisdiction is clear from the complaint | Enforces the judgment; full faith and credit clause precludes reexamination of merits, which are settled by default |

**Figure 3-1.** Challenges to personal jurisdiction: some common scenarios.

cases are brought in state court unless the example specifies otherwise. Also assume that the special appearance rule applies in Mississippi.[6]

## Examples

### Novel Developments

1. Lewis publishes books in Ohio. He agrees to sell a thousand copies of *Brandywine, Ohio*, a popular novel, to Faulkner, a book wholesaler with offices in Mississippi. At Faulkner's request Lewis ships the books to Faulkner's Louisiana warehouse. Faulkner subsequently discovers that the books are damaged and sues Lewis in Mississippi to recover the price of the books. Lewis claims that the books were damaged later, while stored in Faulkner's warehouse. He also doubts that the Mississippi court has jurisdiction over him because all the negotiations took place in Ohio and the parties contemplated from the beginning that the books would be shipped to Louisiana.

   Lewis makes a special appearance in Mississippi to contest the Mississippi court's jurisdiction over him. The court concludes after holding a hearing that it lacks jurisdiction. What will the court do?

2. When first served with the complaint in *Faulkner v. Lewis*, Lewis is confident that he can win on the merits and therefore answers the complaint and defends the damage claim on the merits. Just before trial, however, he gets nervous about the outcome and decides to move to dismiss for lack of personal jurisdiction. How will the court respond to the motion?

3. Assume that Lewis decides to appear in the Mississippi action, despite his doubts that the court has jurisdiction over him. He files an answer, defends that action on the merits, and loses. Judgment is entered for Faulkner. Faulkner brings a suit on the judgment in Ohio, and Lewis opposes enforcement of the judgment on the ground that the Mississippi court lacked personal jurisdiction over him. What will the court do?

### The Silent Treatment

4. Lewis is convinced from the outset that the Mississippi court lacks jurisdiction over him. Consequently, he does not respond to the complaint, and a default judgment is entered for Faulkner, who then brings an action on the judgment in Ohio.

---

6. Until 1982 Mississippi practice required defendants to raise objections to personal jurisdiction by special appearance. Mississippi now follows the Federal Rules model, which allows defendants to raise the objection by a pre-answer motion to dismiss or in their answer to the complaint. Miss. R. Civ. P. 12(b)(2). Assume in analyzing the examples that the special appearance rule still applies.

    a. Lewis defends the Ohio enforcement action on the ground that he is not liable for the damage because the books were damaged after delivery. Assuming that Lewis can prove this, what will the court do?

    b. Lewis defends the enforcement action on the ground that the Mississippi court never obtained personal jurisdiction over him. Assuming this is true, what will the court do?

    c. Lewis defends the enforcement action on the ground that the Mississippi court lacked jurisdiction over him. The Ohio court, however, concludes that the Mississippi court *did* have jurisdiction. What will the court do?

5. Lewis appears specially in the original suit in Mississippi to challenge personal jurisdiction. The court holds a hearing on the objection, and concludes that it has personal jurisdiction. Lewis, convinced that the court is wrong, defaults. Faulkner gets a default judgment and seeks enforcement in Ohio. Lewis defends on the ground that the Mississippi court lacked jurisdiction over him. What result?

6. Assume that Faulkner's suit is brought in a state that follows the Federal Rules model. Lewis appears and moves to dismiss for failure to join an indispensable party. The motion is denied. He then moves to dismiss for lack of personal jurisdiction. How will the court rule?

## The Plot Thickens

7. Assume that Faulkner brings suit in Louisiana, the state where Lewis has agreed to deliver the books, and the Louisiana long-arm statute authorizes personal jurisdiction over a nonresident defendant as to all claims arising out of "contracting to supply goods in the state." The Ohio long-arm statute, however, has no such provision, nor any other that would apply on the facts of the case. Lewis defaults in the Louisiana action. When Faulkner seeks to enforce his default judgment in Ohio, Lewis defends on the ground that the court lacked personal jurisdiction under the Ohio long-arm statute. Will his defense be upheld?

8. Assume that Lewis is sued in Mississippi and makes a special appearance to object to the court's exercise of personal jurisdiction over him. The court concludes that it has jurisdiction and therefore refuses to dismiss the case. Lewis, fearful lest he lose his right to defend on the merits, decides to defend the case on the merits in Mississippi and loses. May he appeal the trial court's initial decision that it had personal jurisdiction over him?

9. Lewis makes a special appearance in Mississippi to challenge personal jurisdiction and loses. He is frustrated; he knows that decision is wrong. He foresees the following scenario: litigating the merits, losing, appealing on jurisdiction, winning the appeal, the case being dismissed

for lack of jurisdiction, and Faulkner starting over in Ohio (where he ought to have started anyway). Is there any way Lewis can short-circuit this procedural nightmare?

## Double Trouble

10. Lewis defaults in Mississippi and challenges enforcement of the resulting default judgment in Ohio. The Ohio court refuses to enforce the Mississippi judgment, on the ground that the Mississippi court lacked personal jurisdiction over Lewis. Faulkner, convinced that the Ohio decision is wrong, brings another action on the judgment in Illinois, where Lewis owns other property subject to execution. What do you think the Illinois court will do?

## Hostage Taking

11. Faulkner learns that Lewis has a summer cottage in Wisconsin and brings suit against Lewis on his book damage claim in a Wisconsin court.
    a. What will the court do if Lewis fails to appear and defend the action?
    b. If Faulkner gets a default judgment in his Wisconsin action on the book damage claim, what is he likely to do next?
    c. What is Lewis virtually forced to do to assert his objection to jurisdiction in this case?

## Explanations

### Novel Developments

1. In most cases, the court will dismiss the case because it lacks the power to render a binding decision if it lacks personal jurisdiction over the defendant. Thus, by entering a special appearance (or a motion to dismiss in a state that follows the Federal Rules model), Lewis will avoid litigating the merits in Mississippi without risking a default judgment that might be enforced in Ohio or some other state where Lewis has property.

   In a few cases the court may agree with Lewis that it has not acquired jurisdiction over Lewis and yet still refuse to dismiss. For example, if the defendant is subject to jurisdiction in the forum state but has not been properly served with process, the court may simply order process to be served in an appropriate manner and then proceed. See Chapter 18 on the proper methods for service of process. In most cases, however, the defendant's objection will not be to the method of service but the power of the court to exercise jurisdiction. This objection, if valid, will usually require dismissal.

2. In this case Lewis has waived his objection to personal jurisdiction by appearing and defending on the merits without raising his jurisdictional challenge. In states that follow the special appearance rule, the defendant waives her jurisdictional objection unless she raises it immediately, before pleading to the merits. The states that follow the federal approach similarly provide that objections to personal jurisdiction are waived unless raised by motion before answering or in the initial answer to the complaint. See Fed. R. Civ. P. 12(g)(2), (h)(1). Thus, under either approach, objections to personal jurisdiction must be raised immediately, or they are waived. Lewis may not hold back on this defense and spring it on the plaintiff later if things go badly on the merits. The motion will be denied.

3. The answer to this example follows from the last. Lewis has waived his jurisdictional objection by defending on the merits without objecting to jurisdiction and is barred from raising it later, either by direct attack in the Mississippi court or by collateral attack in the Ohio enforcement action. It is true that it is ordinarily open to the defendant to resist enforcement in the enforcing state on the ground that the original, rendering court lacked personal jurisdiction over her. Here, however, Lewis waived the objection by appearing on the merits in the initial action. The raise-it-or-lose-it rule forces Lewis to assert his objection to jurisdiction (or to default) *before* the court invests time in litigating the merits of the case in the Mississippi action. He may not sandbag the court and the plaintiff by holding back his jurisdictional objection, trying to win on the merits in the Mississippi court and then asserting the jurisdictional objection later in Ohio.

## The Silent Treatment

4. a. Lewis defaulted on the merits in Mississippi. That precludes him from litigating any of the underlying substantive issues that Faulkner had to prove to recover, such as whether the books were damaged and whether the damage resulted from Lewis's negligence. Even if Lewis can conclusively prove that the damage was not his fault, the Ohio court will not listen. The Full Faith and Credit Clause prevents it from reexamining issues that have been settled — even by default — in another state's courts.

   If this seems like a victory of form (or procedure) over substance, consider what would happen if the opposite were true. If defendants could litigate the merits in the enforcement action, they could simply ignore the plaintiff's original suit and have the substantive issues heard in the forum of the defendant's choice instead. The plaintiff's traditional right to choose the forum (subject, of course, to venue and jurisdictional restrictions) would be replaced by the defendant's right always to litigate at home.

b. In this hypo, Lewis decided to ignore the Mississippi action, because he is convinced that the rendering court had no power to order him to appear there. He may raise the defense of lack of personal jurisdiction in the Ohio enforcement action since the enforcing court need not give full faith and credit to the Mississippi judgment if the Mississippi court lacked jurisdiction over Lewis. If it is true that the Mississippi court lacked jurisdiction, the Ohio court will refuse to enter a judgment on the Mississippi judgment, Faulkner will be unable to collect on his default judgment, and Lewis will suffer no harm from it — except, of course, the anxiety over whether the Ohio court will agree with him on the jurisdictional question. If I were Lewis, I would prefer to litigate the jurisdictional issue in the Mississippi court, by filing a special appearance there, rather than risk losing the chance to litigate the merits entirely by staking all on the chance that the Ohio court will agree that the Mississippi court lacked jurisdiction to hear the case.

c. As in example 4b, it is open to Lewis to challenge the personal jurisdiction of the original court in this enforcement action. However, if the Ohio court concludes that the Mississippi court had jurisdiction, the Ohio court is bound under the Full Faith and Credit Clause to enter judgment on the original judgment and order execution of it on Lewis's assets. Thus, by postponing his jurisdictional challenge, Lewis has abdicated his chance to defend the substance of the claim in either Mississippi or Ohio. This is an extreme price to pay for the convenience of litigating the jurisdictional issue in your home state. This price was paid, for example, in *McGee v. International Life Ins. Co.*, 355 U.S. 220 (1957), in which the insurer ignored the original California suit, and the California judgment was subsequently held enforceable in Texas.

5. Once again, Lewis has run afoul of the rules. He has already raised his challenge to jurisdiction in the initial action. One bite at the apple is all that he gets; he may not challenge jurisdiction in Mississippi, lose, and try again in the enforcing court in hopes of getting a more favorable reading from an Ohio judge. See *Baldwin v. Iowa State Traveling Men's Association*, 283 U.S. 522 (1931). The plaintiff should not have to prove twice that the first court had jurisdiction, nor should the defendant be allowed to keep raising the issue until she finds some court that agrees with her. If Lewis insists on challenging jurisdiction in Ohio, he must default in Mississippi to preserve his right to do so.

6. Alas, poor Lewis. All these arbitrary rules and traps for the unwary. Here, he has fallen into another by misconstruing Rule 12. That rule, as well as state rules modeled on it, allows the defendant to raise the jurisdictional

objection along with other objections but not to raise other objections first and then challenge the court's personal jurisdiction in a subsequent motion. Responding with other objections and defenses (such as failure to join an indispensable party, failure to state a claim, or denials on the merits) without raising the personal jurisdiction objection operates as a waiver of that objection. See Fed. R. Civ. P. 12(g)(2), (h)(1). The jurisdictional challenge must always be raised in the defendant's first response to the complaint. Lewis's motion will be denied.

## The Plot Thickens

7. This example raises two important points. First, the rendering court must have jurisdiction not only under the minimum contacts standard of *International Shoe* but also under the applicable long-arm statute. Thus, even if Lewis's contacts with Louisiana are sufficient to support jurisdiction under the constitutional standard, Lewis could still argue (in the original suit or the enforcement action) that the rendering court lacked jurisdiction under the applicable long-arm statute.

    The second point is, what is the applicable long-arm statute? Ohio's, where enforcement is sought? Or Louisiana's, where the initial suit was brought? The relevant issue is whether the Louisiana court had the right to exercise jurisdiction over Lewis. Therefore, the Ohio court must ask whether the Louisiana long-arm statute authorized jurisdiction in Louisiana, not whether the Ohio statute would have allowed it if Faulkner had sued there. Lewis's defense fails again.

8. As the introduction indicates, most states allow the defendant, after raising the jurisdictional objection and losing, to take the safer course of defending on the merits and then appealing the decision on jurisdiction.[7] This way, Lewis may still obtain appellate review of the decision on personal jurisdiction without abandoning his opportunity to defend the case on its merits. If he wins on the merits, he will be content and obviously will not appeal the decision on jurisdiction. If he loses on the merits, he may appeal the trial court's decision that he was subject to personal jurisdiction in Mississippi. If the Mississippi appellate court concludes that he was subject to jurisdiction, it will affirm the judgment. If, however, it concludes that he was not subject to jurisdiction in Mississippi, it will order the case dismissed, even though there has been a full trial on the merits.

    A few states used to follow the more formalistic rule that the defendant waives the jurisdictional objection by defending the case on the merits. The theory behind this approach is that it is inconsistent for the

---

7. Mississippi follows the majority rule. See *E. B. Kaiser Co. v. Ludlow*, 243 So. 2d 62, 66 (Miss. 1971).

defendant to appear and litigate in that court and at the same time claim that the court lacks jurisdiction over her. If you object to jurisdiction, these courts held, you should stick to your guns by refusing to litigate the merits and appeal solely on the jurisdictional issue. See, e.g., *Kotlisky v. Kotlisky*, 552 N.E.2d 1206 (Ill. App. 1990). See generally 62 A.L.R.2d 937 (1958). However, it isn't clear that any state still adheres to this approach.

9. Clearly the most efficient course for Lewis would be to file an immediate appeal in the Mississippi appellate court, challenging the trial court's decision that it had jurisdiction. That way he could avoid going through a trial on the merits in Mississippi, assuming that the trial judge was wrong.

   This strategy would not be open to Lewis in the federal courts. Ordinarily, parties in federal cases can only take appeals after the case goes to a final judgment in the district court. 28 U.S.C. §1291. The Supreme Court has held that decisions upholding personal jurisdiction are "interlocutory" orders because they do not finally resolve the suit and are therefore not appealable until the end of the suit. See *Van Cauwenberghe v. Biard*, 486 U.S. 517, 526-527 (1988).

   However, state practice varies considerably on this issue. Some states allow interlocutory appeals of orders upholding personal jurisdiction or appellate relief through some extraordinary method of review. A good example is *World-Wide Volkswagen v. Woodson*, 444 U.S. 286 (1980), in which the defendants sought a "writ of prohibition" from the Oklahoma Supreme Court to prohibit the trial judge from acting in excess of his jurisdiction.

## Double Trouble

10. This is an interesting strategy on Faulkner's part. Because Court Number Two has held that Court Number One lacked jurisdiction, Faulkner tries Court Number Three, in hopes that it will disagree with Two and enforce One's judgment. It is reminiscent of Lewis's attempt in example 5 to have the enforcing court reexamine the jurisdictional issue already litigated and decided in the rendering court.

    For the same reasons, it won't work. The issue of whether the original court had personal jurisdiction over Lewis was litigated and decided in Ohio. Under the principle of collateral estoppel Faulkner will be barred from relitigating the jurisdiction issue in Illinois or any other state. Note that the Illinois court, by refusing to reopen the jurisdiction issue, is not choosing between the two courts and deciding to honor the judgment of one over the other. Only the Ohio court decided the issue of jurisdiction over Lewis in the original action; the Mississippi court never did because Lewis defaulted. Thus, the Illinois court is honoring the holding of the one court that reached the jurisdictional issue. See Restatement (Second) of Judgments, §81, comm. b.

## Hostage Taking

11. a. Lewis may not be subject to personal jurisdiction in Wisconsin for this claim simply because he has a summer place in the state. See *Shaffer v. Heitner*, 433 US. 186, 208-209 (1977) (questioning jurisdiction based on presence of property unrelated to claim in suit). However, if Lewis defaults, the Wisconsin court may not ever consider the point. It may assume that Faulkner has no defense to the action, enter a default judgment for Faulkner on the claim, and assess damages for the books.

    b. Since Faulkner chose to sue in Wisconsin, presumably Wisconsin is a convenient forum for him to enforce his judgment as well. Very likely, he will do what Mitchell did in *Pennoyer v. Neff*: take out a writ of execution on the Wisconsin judgment and commence proceedings to have Lewis's summer house sold to satisfy the damage judgment.

    c. Can you see that in this predictable scenario, Lewis's only realistic option is to appear and object to personal jurisdiction in Wisconsin when the suit is originally brought? If he does not, and Faulkner obtains a default judgment and executes the judgment against Lewis's property in Wisconsin, Lewis will naturally have to resist the sale of his cottage by appearing in Wisconsin to object. On what ground? The same ground, of course, that Neff asserted in *Pennoyer v. Neff*: that the Wisconsin court had no jurisdiction to render the judgment which Faulkner now seeks to execute.

       So, he will have to go to Wisconsin one way or the other, either to object to personal jurisdiction at the outset or to contest the sale of his house on execution. However, if he waits and objects to the sale, he is out of luck if the court holds that it had jurisdiction to render the default judgment. There goes the house, and Lewis will never have had the chance to defend the book claim on the merits. By contrast, by appearing at the outset, he preserves his right to defend on the merits if the Wisconsin court concludes that it has jurisdiction over him.

       Thus, the presence of the defendant's property in the state may force him to make a direct attack on the court's jurisdiction in the rendering state. A defendant in Lewis's situation can't wait and make a collateral attack when Faulkner brings the judgment to his home state, because Faulkner never will bring it to Lewis's state; he can collect on it in Wisconsin.

# Federal Questions and Federal Cases

Jurisdiction over Cases "Arising under" Federal Law

# INTRODUCTION

Our first three chapters dealt with personal jurisdiction — the power of a court to require a defendant from outside the state to defend a lawsuit in that state. Now we turn to *subject matter jurisdiction*, a separate, additional requirement for a court to hear a case. Suppose, for example, that Engle wishes to sue her employer, Consolidated Packing Corporation, after she is fired from her job for reporting acts of fraud committed by Consolidated officers to federal authorities. She needs to choose a court which has personal jurisdiction over Consolidated for her claim, but she must also choose one which can hear the type of lawsuit she plans to file against Consolidated.

To understand the principles governing subject matter jurisdiction in American courts, we have to start with those courts themselves. The United States Constitution created a system of divided sovereignty, in which the states and the national or "federal" government share power. Not only is legislative power split between the two levels of government, but the judicial power is as well. Thus, in every state there is a state court system and a branch of the federal court system. Some cases must be brought in the state courts. Others (though not many) must be brought in federal court. And still others may be filed in either court system. The trick is to know which ones go where, and that depends on which court has "subject matter jurisdiction" over the case, that is, the power to hear the particular type of case the plaintiff plans to file.

## 4. Federal Questions and Federal Cases

Let's start with the reach of subject matter jurisdiction in the state courts. Every state defines the types of cases its courts may hear in its constitution or by statute (or both), and all states have conferred very broad subject matter jurisdiction on their courts. That isn't particularly surprising: Plaintiffs generally prefer to sue at home, so broad jurisdiction accommodates local citizens, who, after all, elect the legislators who write jurisdictional statutes. So it's a fair working principle that the state courts in every state have very broad jurisdiction to hear most types of cases. For example, the state courts will be able to hear garden variety tort and contract claims, property claims, divorce claims, cases involving wills and trusts, and claims under state statutes. Indeed, it is hard to think of a case arising under state law that could not be filed in some court within the state, and most cases do arise under state law.

While the state courts will be able to hear most claims, statutes vary as to which court within the state hears those claims. All states have a trial court of general subject matter jurisdiction that can hear common types of suits. This court may be called the superior court, the circuit court, the district court, or something else, depending on the state.[1] In addition, states usually establish specialized courts to hear some types of cases requiring particular expertise, such as probate courts, municipal courts, land courts, or housing courts. Some of our thirstier western states even have water courts.

The state courts handle by far the greatest part of the judicial business. In 2002 an astounding 96,000,000 cases were filed in the courts of the fifty states,[2] while some 1,900,000 were filed in the federal courts.[3] The respective numbers of judges also convey a sense of the extent to which state courts carry the laboring judicial oar. As an example, the California state trial courts had about 1500 judges in 2004, while there were only about 180 federal judges (including magistrate judges) sitting in the federal district courts in California.[4]

---

1. For a list of the courts of general jurisdiction in each state, see D. Meador, American Courts 90-91 (West 2000).

2. B. Ostrom, N. Kauder, and R. LaFountain, eds., Examining the Work of State Courts, 2003: A National Perspective from the Court Statistics Project, National Center for State Courts 2002, p.10 (includes all types of filings).

3. The Year-End Report of the Federal Judiciary, 35 The Third Branch, No. 1, p.4 (Jan. 2003) (including bankruptcy cases).

4. Want's Federal-State Court Directory (Washington D.C.: Want Pub. Co. 2005), pp. 29-36, 157.

# THE SOURCE AND LIMITS OF FEDERAL SUBJECT MATTER JURISDICTION

Unlike the state courts, which exercise very broad subject matter jurisdiction, the type of cases that federal courts can hear is extremely limited. The subject matter jurisdiction of federal courts is defined in Article III, s. 2 of the Constitution, which lists the categories of cases federal courts may hear. Generally speaking, any case not on the Article III, s. 2 list must be brought in state court: the basic premise of the Constitution is that the federal government has the authority to exercise powers expressly or impliedly granted in the Constitution, but that all others—those not granted to the feds—are reserved to the states. U.S. Constitution, Amendment X.

Under Article III, s. 2 the federal courts are authorized to hear cases between states, between citizens of different states, between citizens and aliens, cases involving foreign ministers and consuls, admiralty and maritime cases, cases arising under the federal Constitution and federal law, and a few other narrow categories of suits. In each of these types of cases, the Framers perceived an important national interest. In cases between states, between citizens of different states, and cases between citizens and aliens, for example, they foresaw a risk of prejudice against the outsider—generally, the defendant—in state court. Admiralty and maritime cases and those involving ministers and consuls involve international relations, as to which the nation should speak with one voice. Similarly, it makes sense that federal courts should be able to hear cases that involve the application and interpretation of federal law, both to protect it from unsympathetic construction by state courts and to allow definitive interpretation of federal law.

With this background, let's return to Engle's case. Several of the categories in Article III, s. 2, might give a federal court constitutional authority to hear this case. Federal subject matter jurisdiction may be proper if Engle is "diverse" from (that is, a citizen of a different state than) Consolidated. Article III, s. 2 also provides federal courts the constitutional authority to hear Engle's case if it arises under a federal statute or under the federal Constitution. If her case doesn't fit into one of these two cubbyholes in Article III, s. 2, it appears that Engle will have to sue in state court: remember the general premise that if a power is not granted to the federal government under the Constitution, it remains with the states.

These two categories of federal subject matter jurisdiction—cases that arise under federal law and cases "between citizens of different states" (diversity cases)—are by far the most common types of civil cases filed in federal court. This chapter will focus on the first category, which I shall refer to as "arising-under jurisdiction." The next chapter will tackle diversity.

# JURISDICTION OVER CASES ARISING UNDER FEDERAL LAW: THE PROBLEM

Article III, s. 2 authorizes federal courts to hear cases "arising under this Constitution, the Laws of the United States, and Treaties made, or which shall be made, under their Authority." This provision obviously authorizes federal courts to hear at least some claims which involve federal constitutional issues or federal statutes, but the trick is to determine which claims that grand phrase, "arising under" federal law, includes. Does it authorize federal jurisdiction over a case which involves federal law in any way, or some more limited set of cases? Here are some examples that illustrate the problem:

- Engle sues Consolidated under a federal "whistle-blower" statute, which authorizes an employee who is discharged or disciplined for reporting violation of federal regulations to obtain reinstatement and damages from her employer.
- Engle sues Consolidated for breach of contract, for firing her in the first year of a three-year contract. Consolidated answers the complaint, raising the defense that it was required to discharge Engle under a federal statute barring employment of illegal aliens.
- Engle sues Consolidated for bad faith discharge, a state tort claim which allows damages if the defendant discharges an employee for reasons which violate certain public policies. She claims that Consolidated fired her because she refused to engage in accounting practices which violate federal statutory accounting requirements for government contractors.
- Engle sues Consolidated for breach of contract, claiming that her contract was for three years, but Consolidated fired her after one. She claims that Consolidated hired her to administer a research program partially funded by grants from the federal government, but fired her for taking time off to stay home with a sick child.

Federal law lurks in each of these cases in one way or another. In the first case, Engle has actually brought suit under a federal statute. In the second, she sues on the state contract claim, but Consolidated has asserted a defense involving federal law. In the third example, plaintiff sues on a state law bad faith dismissal claim, but tries to establish the defendant's bad faith by showing that it required her to violate federal law. In the last, federal law is only vaguely relevant, if at all. Examples like these illustrate that the courts need to develop some working standards to determine when a case which somehow *involves* federal law will "arise under" federal law.

# JURISDICTION OVER CASES ARISING UNDER FEDERAL LAW: THE CONSTITUTIONAL SCOPE

The Supreme Court has long taken an expansive view of the "arising under" language in Article III, s. 2. In *Osborn v. Bank of the United States*, 22 U.S. 738 (1824), Chief Justice Marshall, who advocated a strong national government, held that a case arises under federal law — as that phrase is used in Article III, s. 2 — if

> the title or right set up by the party, may be defeated by one construction of the constitution or law of the United States, and sustained by the opposite construction. We think, then, that when a question to which the judicial power of the Union is extended by the constitution, forms an ingredient of the original cause, it is in the power of Congress to give [the lower federal courts] jurisdiction of that cause, although other questions of fact or law may be involved in it.

22 U.S. at 822-823.

Under the broad holding in *Osborn*, the federal court could clearly hear the first case above, since the federal statute is the source of the substantive right Engle claims. Jurisdiction under this "federal ingredient" approach would also extend to the second example case, in which Engle sues under state contract law, but Consolidated claims as a defense that it was required to discharge her under a federal statute. The validity of this defense will clearly be an "ingredient" of the case, although that ingredient is injected by the defendant, not the plaintiff.[5] The third case would arguably also come within this broad "ingredient" approach to arising-under jurisdiction. Although Engle has sued under state tort law, in order to prove her bad faith dismissal claim she will have to show that she was fired because of her refusal to violate federal regulations. Thus, proving her state law contract claim will require her to show that the accounting practices she refused to adopt would violate federal law.

The last case described above would not "arise under" federal law even under the broad test of *Osborn*. Presumably, for federal law to be an "ingredient" of a case, one of the parties in the case would have to rely on federal law to establish either a claim or a defense in the lawsuit, or at least raise a federal issue in proving her case. While there is some peripheral relationship to a federal program in the fourth example, neither Engle nor

---

5. Chief Justice Marshall's reference in *Osborn* to "the original cause" means to the case itself, not, as under *Mottley*, only to the claims asserted by the plaintiff in that case. A federal issue raised by the defendant would suffice under this reading. See Wright, Federal Courts 5th ed. 1994, p. 102.

Consolidated would need to refer to federal law to litigate the case. If Engle sued under a federal parental leave act, the result would be different, but on the facts given neither her claim nor the company's defense would require evidence about any proposition of federal law.

So, the bottom line is that the phrase "arising under" in Article III, s. 2 is very broadly construed. It is probably satisfied in any case in which a party seeks to rely on or establish a proposition of federal law in order to prove either a claim or a defense in the case. In *Osborn*, Chief Justice Marshall even opined that *any case* brought by the Bank of the United States would "arise under" federal law, since the Bank was incorporated under a federal statute. Thus, the Bank's very existence, and its right to sue or be sued, are an issue in any such case. This is a very broad — perhaps extravagantly broad — conception of the reach of the Framers' "arising under" language in Article III. The Court has never been called upon to accept or reject the outer reaches of Marshall's view, but it has reaffirmed that the "arising under" language in Article III is broad enough to apply if substantial issues of federal law are raised by either party to the case.

# JURISDICTION OVER CASES ARISING UNDER FEDERAL LAW: THE NEED FOR BOTH CONSTITUTIONAL POWER AND STATUTORY AUTHORITY

Now comes the problem. The Court's decision in *Osborn* indicates that the constitutional reach of arising-under jurisdiction in Article III, s. 2 is broad. However, Article III *does not confer subject matter jurisdiction on the lower federal courts.* In fact, Article III does not even create lower federal courts; it authorizes Congress to do so. See Article III, s. 1 (judicial power "shall be vested in one Supreme Court, and in such inferior Courts as the Congress may from time to time ordain and establish" ). Since Congress has the authority to create lower federal courts — or not to — it has long been held that it also has the authority to define their jurisdiction, within the outer bounds of possible cases described in Article III, s. 2. *Kline v. Burke Construction Co.*, 260 U.S. 226, 233-234 (1922). In other words, if Congress chooses to establish federal trial courts — like the federal district courts as they exist today — it may give them the authority to hear all the cases listed in Article III, s. 2. But it may also — as it has — authorize them to hear some, but not all, of the cases described in Article III, s. 2. It could authorize them to hear diversity cases but not cases arising under federal law, or cases between states but not cases between citizens of different states, or cases between citizens of different states only if an amount-in-controversy requirement is met.

[F]ederal courts may assume only that portion of the Article III judicial power which Congress, by statute, entrusts to them. Simply stated, Congress may impart as much or as little of the judicial power as it deems appropriate and the Judiciary may not thereafter on its own motion recur to the Article III storehouse for additional jurisdiction. When it comes to jurisdiction of the federal courts, truly, to paraphrase the scripture, the Congress giveth, and the Congress taketh away.

*Senate Select Committee v. Nixon*, 366 F. Supp. 51, 55 (D.D.C. 1973).

It follows from this basic fact that a lawyer seeking to file a lawsuit in federal court must ask two questions in determining whether a suit may be filed there. *First*, is this case one which constitutionally may be granted to the federal courts, because the power for them to hear it is granted in Article III, s. 2 of the Constitution? And *second*, if the case does fall into one of the categories in Article III, s. 2, has Congress actually conveyed jurisdiction over this type of case in a federal statute?

There are many illustrations of cases within the federal judicial power under Article III that Congress has *not* authorized federal courts to hear. For example, for many years there was no broad grant of arising-under jurisdiction to the lower federal courts. Prior to 1875, there were narrow statutes authorizing jurisdiction over cases arising under *particular* federal laws, such as the federal revenue statutes or federal patent statutes, but there was no broad grant of arising-under jurisdiction.[6] It was only after the Civil War, when Congress doubted the willingness of the state courts in the southern states to enforce the new federal civil rights statutes, that it granted broad jurisdiction over cases arising under federal law to the lower federal courts.

Today 28 U.S.C. s. 1331, the statute by which Congress bestows arising-under jurisdiction on the federal district courts, authorizes jurisdiction over "cases arising under the Constitution, laws, or treaties of the United States." Because the statute conveys the arising-under jurisdiction in the same language used in Article III, s. 2, one might reasonably conclude that Congress intended to grant the full reach of such jurisdiction to the federal district courts — to the broad extent of the Court's interpretation of the "arising-under" language in *Osborn*. However, such a reasonable conclusion would, perplexingly, be wrong.

---

6. Another example is a case between a citizen of Minnesota and a citizen of Illinois demanding $35,000 in damages. This is a case "between citizens of different states," so it is within the diversity jurisdiction authorized in Article III, s. 2. However, Congress has not seen fit to allow this diversity case into federal court: 28 U.S.C. s. 1332(a), the statute that confers diversity jurisdiction on the federal district courts, limits that jurisdiction to cases in which more than $75,000 is in controversy.

# CONSTRUING THE STATUTORY ARISING UNDER GRANT: THE ENIGMATIC MOTTLEY RULE

Even though 28 U.S.C. s. 1331 grants jurisdiction in the same language as Article III, s. 2, the federal courts have interpreted the reach of the statute much more narrowly than the constitutional scope of arising-under jurisdiction. The cases consistently hold that s. 1331 only applies if the plaintiff's claim requires proof of federal law. The statute does not confer jurisdiction on the federal district courts over cases that involve federal law unless the federal issue is necessary to the proof of the plaintiff's claim.

*Louisville & Nashville R.R. v. Mottley*, 211 U.S. 149 (1908), illustrates the puzzling distinction between the meaning of "arising under" in Article III, s. 2 and the meaning of the same phrase in s. 1331. In *Mottley*, the plaintiffs were given lifetime passes for free travel on the railroad, in settlement of a claim for injuries the Mottleys had suffered in an accident. After honoring the passes for thirty-some years, the railroad refused to renew them, because Congress had passed a statute barring railroads from giving free transportation. The Mottleys sued to obtain their passes, and the railroad defended on the ground that the federal statute barred renewal. The Mottleys had two responses to this argument. First, they argued that the statute was prospective only: surely Congress must not have meant the statute to apply to passes granted by the railroad before its enactment. *Second*, argued the Mottleys, if the statute were interpreted to bar their passes, it would be unconstitutional under the Fifth Amendment to the United States Constitution, since it would deprive them of vested property rights without due process of law.

These were two substantial, hotly contested questions of federal law. A person of common sense would be justified in concluding that a case which raised them — which, indeed, turned on them — would "arise under" federal law. Indeed, the parties and the trial court thought so, for no one questioned the federal court's jurisdiction in the trial court. No party questioned it on appeal to the United States Supreme Court, either. Yet the Court raised the subject matter jurisdiction issue itself and concluded that the lower federal court had lacked jurisdiction to hear the Mottleys' case.

How can this be? The Court explained that, for a plaintiff to sue in federal court under the statutory test for arising-under jurisdiction, she must assert a claim that arises under federal law. The Mottleys' case did not: they had sued for breach of contract, a state law cause of action that did not require them to prove any proposition of federal law. They could establish their right to relief simply by proving that the railroad had agreed to renew the passes and then refused to do so. True, the railroad had given the federal statute as its reason for failing to renew the passes, and it was clear that they would rely on the statute as a defense in responding to the Mottleys' suit. However, the statute would naturally arise as a defense, not as an element of the Mottleys' case in chief. It was up to the Mottleys to state their claim in their complaint and to leave it to the railroad to raise whatever defenses it chose. And it was clear that the Mottleys' claim arose under state contract law, not federal law.

Note several things about this counterintuitive holding. First, it is clear that the case would come out differently if the Court interpreted the statute (now, 28 U.S.C. s. 1331) as broadly as it has interpreted Article III, s. 2 under *Osborn*. The federal statute was clearly an "ingredient" of the case; indeed, the irony of *Mottley* is that the only disputed issues in the case were issues of federal law. *Second*, under *Mottley*, it is not enough that the plaintiff refers to federal law in her complaint: the Mottleys *did* refer to both federal issues in their pleadings. The problem was that they didn't have to; they could have stated a perfectly adequate claim for relief by alleging only contract breach, and a demand for specific performance. Under *Mottley's* "well pleaded complaint" rule, the court, in deciding whether the case "arises under federal law" for purposes of s. 1331, asks whether the plaintiff would have to raise the federal issue in a complaint which includes the elements she needs to prove to establish her claim, and *only those elements*. Jurisdiction under 28. U.S.C. s. 1331 "must be determined from what necessarily appears in the plaintiff's statement of his own claim in the bill or declaration" (*Taylor v. Anderson*, 234 U.S. 74, 75-76 (1914)), not from any anticipated defenses the complaint alleges that the defendant will assert.

The *Mottley* case illustrates and applies the well-pleaded complaint rule, but provides the beleaguered student with precious little to explain its rationale. Why shouldn't a case that involves a genuine issue of federal law qualify for federal court jurisdiction, regardless of who raises the federal issue? Perhaps it should, yet the *Mottley* rule remains the law today, primarily because it furthers sensible judicial administration. Courts need to determine their jurisdiction from the outset; the *Mottley* rule allows the court to do so based solely on the plaintiff's case, before the defendant answers. If *Mottley* had been decided the other way, plaintiffs might invoke federal jurisdiction simply by referring in their complaints to defenses they expected the defendant to raise — or by speculating about ones the defendant could raise — simply to create federal subject matter jurisdiction. Under the well-pleaded complaint rule, the court is able to determine at the outset whether it has jurisdiction, based on the claims the plaintiff has asserted, without waiting for the defendant's answer.

## An Early Question

1. Suppose that federal courts did not use the *Mottley* rule; instead, they upheld jurisdiction under 28 U.S.C. s. 1331 if either the plaintiff's

complaint or the defendant's answer raised an issue of federal law. The Mottleys bring suit in federal court, demanding specific performance of their contract. You represent the railroad, which is considering raising several defenses to the Mottleys' claim, some based in federal law and some in state law. If you wanted to avoid federal court, what would you advise the railroad to do in answering the complaint?

## APPLYING THE *MOTTLEY* RULE: THE HOLMES "CREATION TEST"

Justice Oliver Wendell Holmes suggested a test for determining when *Mottley*'s well-pleaded complaint rule is met: he suggested that a suit arises "under the law that creates the cause of action." *American Well Works v. Layne*, 241 U.S. 257, 260 (1916). The Holmes test would find jurisdiction under s. 1331 if the source of the plaintiff's enforceable legal right against the defendant is federal law. In *Mottley*, the source of the plaintiffs' right to demand relief from the court was state contract law. The Mottleys could sue the railroad because the state common law of contracts allows courts to order specific performance where a party makes a contract and fails to perform its obligations. Since the "law that creates the cause of action" was state law, the claim did not "arise under" federal law within the meaning of 28 U.S.C. s. 1331.

By contrast, in our first example case, if Engle sues under the federal whistle-blower statute, the Holmes test is met. The reason that Engle can demand damages from Consolidated is that the federal statute bars employers from discharging or disciplining their employees for reporting violation of federal regulations, and authorizes such employees to sue for reinstatement or damages if the employer does so. Thus, the federal law is the direct source of Engle's right to sue. If it did not exist, she would not be able to sue (at least, not under federal law); because Congress created that right, she can.

Compare the third example case, in which Engle sues for bad faith discharge, a state law cause of action. This case fails the Holmes test, since Engle sues on a state law claim. Here, her right to relief is created by state tort law, the common law cause of action for bad faith discharge. However, to *recover* on her state law claim, Engle will have to *prove* a proposition of federal law: that the accounting practices she refused to engage in violated the federal statute, so that she was justified in refusing to engage in them. Arguably, this should be sufficient to support arising-under jurisdiction (since the plaintiff will have to establish a proposition of federal law in order to prevail). However, the Holmes test would leave this one out.

One fair rule of thumb in this area (in which, unfortunately, most "rules" turn out to have exceptions) is that, if a case meets the Holmes test, it does "arise under" federal law for purposes of section 1331. "Mr. Justice Holmes' formula is more useful for inclusion than for the exclusion for which it was intended." *T. B. Harms v. Eliscu,* 339 F.2d 823, 827 (2d Cir. 1964). The vast majority of cases brought under the arising-under jurisdiction fit neatly within the Holmes test, and consequently there is no question that the federal court has jurisdiction under 28 U.S.C. s. 1331. Here are two easy examples:

- The federal copyright statute, 17 U.S.C. s. 106, provides that authors have the exclusive right to perform or reproduce their original works. The statute also authorizes injunctive relief against any person who uses copyrighted works without permission. 17 U.S.C. s. 502. Shakespeare writes a play about a prince. The Elizabethan Publishing Company gets hold of a copy and announces publication of the same play. Shakespeare sues for an injunction under 17 U.S.C. s. 502.

  > Here, the federal copyright statute both creates a federal substantive right — the right to exclusive use of original works — and authorizes him to sue for violation of that right. Thus, his suit clearly satisfies the Holmes test.

- The Eighth Amendment to the United States Constitution, which bars "cruel and unusual punishment," has been interpreted to require jailers to provide medical care for prisoners in their charge. Willson, a prisoner in a state prison, is taken violently ill, but the guards ignore his pleas for medical help, leading to serious complications. He sues under 42 U.S.C. s. 1983, which authorizes any person deprived of rights under the United States Constitution by state actors to sue for damages.

  > Here, the United States Constitution creates a substantive right — the right of a prisoner to be free of deliberate indifference to his serious medical needs — and a federal statute authorizes him to sue for damages for deprivation of that right. Again, there is no question that federal law is the source of Willson's claim and that jurisdiction would be proper under s. 1331.

# BEYOND THE CREATION TEST: STATE LAW CLAIMS TURNING ON A SUBSTANTIAL FEDERAL ISSUE

Despite Justice Holmes' suggested test, federal courts have occasionally upheld arising-under jurisdiction where federal law does not create the right to sue, but the plaintiff, in order to establish her state law claim, must prove a proposition of federal law. An oft-cited example is *Smith v. Kansas City Title and Trust Company*, 255 U.S. 180 (1920). In *Smith*, the plaintiffs sued to enjoin Kansas City Title & Trust from investing in certain bonds issued by federal banks under the authority of a federal statute. The plaintiffs claimed that investing in the bonds would exceed the company's corporate powers, since it was only authorized to invest in valid securities, and the bonds at issue in the case were invalid because the federal statute authorizing them was unconstitutional.

The claim in *Smith* does not satisfy the Holmes test: the plaintiffs sued to enjoin the corporation from exceeding its powers under state corporation law, a state law claim (just as the Mottleys sued to enforce a contract in *Mottley*). However, the plaintiffs in *Smith* could not prove this state law claim without establishing a proposition of federal law: that the federal statute under which the bonds were issued was unconstitutional under the United States Constitution. The federal issue was embedded in the state law claim and essential to its resolution. The Supreme Court held that this claim satisfied arising-under jurisdiction, since "the controversy concerns the constitutional validity of an act of Congress which is directly drawn in question. The decision depends upon the determination of this issue." 255 U.S. at 201. Justice Holmes dissented in *Smith*, arguing that "the [federal] law must create at least a part of the cause of action by its own force, for it is the suit, not a question in the suit, that must arise under the law of the United States." 255 U.S. at 215.

Later Supreme Court cases suggest that the *Smith* exception is still a viable basis for finding jurisdiction under s. 1331. In *Franchise Tax Board v. Laborers' Vacation Trust*, 463 U.S. 1, 9 (1983), for example, the Court stated:

> It is well settled that Justice Holmes' test is more useful for describing the vast majority of cases that come within the district courts' original jurisdiction than it is for describing which cases are beyond district court jurisdiction. We have often held that a case "arose under" federal law where the vindication of a right under state law necessarily turned on some construction of federal law. *See, e.g.*, *Smith v. Kansas City Title & Trust Co.*

However, the Court's decision in *Merrell Dow Pharmaceuticals Inc. v. Thompson*, 478 U.S. 804 (1986), appeared to reject jurisdiction based on such embedded federal issues. In *Merrell Dow*, the plaintiffs sued for damages allegedly caused by Bendectin, a drug manufactured by Merrell Dow. They asserted claims based on negligence, breach of warranty, and strict liability, all state law tort theories. One of their negligence theories was that Merrell Dow gave inadequate warnings of the risks of Bendectin, because the warnings did not meet the labeling requirements of the Federal Food, Drug, and Cosmetic Act (FDCA).

Thus, the complaint in *Merrell Dow* alleged a state cause of action (negligence) but asserted that the plaintiffs could *prove* this state cause of action by showing a violation of the standard governing warnings in the federal statute. In this sense, the case resembled *Smith v. Kansas* City Title & Trust, in which the plaintiffs brought a state law claim to enjoin the corporation from investing in bonds, but had to establish that those bonds were issued under an unconstitutional federal statute.

In *Merrell Dow*, however, there was a twist that led the Court to distinguish *Smith*: All parties agreed that Congress did not intend to authorize parties who claimed injury from the failure to comply with the FDCA to sue for damages. To allow the *Merrell Dow* plaintiffs to turn their negligence claim into one "arising under" federal law, simply by alleging that the defendant was negligent for failure to provide the warnings required by the statute, would fly in the face of Congress's decision *not* to create a federal right to sue for damages for FDCA violations. It would effectively create a federal court remedy where Congress had decided not to do so. Consequently, the Court held that the reference to the FDCA in the state negligence claim was "insufficiently 'substantial' to confer federal-question jurisdiction" under s. 1331.

In *Merrell Dow*, the plaintiff had based the argument for federal jurisdiction on *Smith v. Kansas City Title & Trust*, so the Court's rejection of the argument raised considerable controversy about whether the Court was overruling *Smith's* federal-issue-embedded-in-a-state-claim exception to the Holmes test. The Supreme Court's decision in *Grable & Sons Metal Products Inc. v. Darue Engineering and Manufacturing*, 545 U.S. 308 (2005), has put that speculation to rest.

In *Grable & Sons*, the federal government had taken Grable & Sons' real property for non-payment of taxes, and conveyed it to Darue. Later, Grable & Sons brought an action to quiet title, claiming the conveyance to Darue was not valid, because it had not received proper notice of the sale under the federal statute authorizing sales for non-payment of taxes. Darue removed the case to federal court, arguing that the case arose under federal law because the nature of the notice required under the federal statute is a question of federal law. The case went up to the Supreme Court on the question of whether the federal district court had arising-under jurisdiction over the case.

The Supreme Court recognized that Grable & Sons' action arose under state law, a traditional property action to quiet title. It also recognized, however, that as in *Smith*, Grable & Sons could only establish its right to reclaim the property by proving a proposition of federal law:

> Whether Grable was given notice within the meaning of the federal statute is thus an essential element of its quiet title claim, and the meaning of the federal statute is actually in dispute.

545 U.S. at 315. The *Grable* Court held unequivocally that "a federal court ought to be able to hear claims recognized under state law that nonetheless turn on substantial questions of federal law. . . . " 545 U.S. at 312.

The Court's opinion makes clear that the need to resolve a federal question to decide a state law claim will not always support arising-under jurisdiction, however. The embedded federal issue must be substantial to support jurisdiction, and delicate judgments will have to be made about the importance of the federal issue and the danger of opening the federal courts to an excessive number of claims. So, nothing is simple in this area, but *Grable* certainly reaffirms that sometimes the need to resolve an issue of federal law to prove a state cause of action will support federal jurisdiction.

The *Grable* Court explained *Merrell Dow* as a case that actually undertook the type of individualized judgment about the substantiality of the embedded federal issue called for by *Smith*. It noted that recognizing federal arising-under jurisdiction based on an allegation that non-compliance with federal regulations constitutes negligence would have "attracted a horde of original filings and removed cases raising other state claims with embedded federal issues." 545 U.S. at 318. Further, the Court noted that Congress's refusal to create a federal cause of action for violations of the misbranding statute at issue in *Merrell Dow* suggested that such claims were not sufficiently "substantial" to support arising-under jurisdiction. Thus, *Grable* portrayed *Merrell Dow* as a sensitive application of a long-standing exception to the Holmes test, rather than a rejection of the *Smith* analysis.

Justice Thomas, concurring in *Grable*, suggested that the court should reconsider whether to confine arising-under jurisdiction to cases that satisfy the Holmes test. "Jurisdictional rules," he suggested, "should be clear. Whatever the virtues of the *Smith* standard, it is anything but clear." 545 U.S. at 321. Doubtless the *Grable* majority recognized that the Holmes test would provide more certainty as to which cases fall within the arising-under jurisdiction. However, they concluded that allowing certain state law claims into federal court, because of the importance of the federal issues involved, was more important than increased certainty in defining the reach of federal court jurisdiction.

Note that, while cases such as *Smith* and *Grable & Sons* go beyond Holmes' "creation test," they are faithful to *Mottley*'s well-pleaded complaint rule in a broader sense, since in determining jurisdiction, the court looks at what the *plaintiff* must establish as part of her case.

Under this "substantial federal issue" approach, Engle could argue that the federal court has subject matter jurisdiction over the third example case given on p. 66, in which Engle sues for bad faith discharge (a state law claim), but alleges that she was fired for refusing to violate federal accounting requirements. Although state tort law creates the right to sue, in order to prove her claim Engle would have to prove that she was fired for refusing to engage in conduct that violated federal law.

All of this seems confusing, but at least the fundamentals are fairly clear. If you feel at sea, perhaps the following examples will provide a few beacons of light to guide you toward an understanding of the fundamentals. Assume in considering the examples that there is no basis other than arising-under jurisdiction for suing in federal court.

## Examples

### Charting the Waters

2. Landry wishes to sue Deveaux for violation of the New Mexico Consumer Protection Act. Does her case arise under the "laws of the United States"?

3. Costa is injured in an accident with Prior on Interstate 95. Prior is a trucker who is engaged in interstate commerce, transporting goods among the various states on the eastern seaboard. Costa claims that Prior was negligent, in that he fell asleep and swerved into her lane, causing the accident. Does the claim come within the arising-under jurisdiction authorized by 28 U.S.C. s. 1331?

4. Gould, who works at an auto assembly plant, sues Rambler Company, his employer, for failure to pay him overtime as required by the Federal Fair Labor Standards Act. He claims that he is an employee of Rambler, that he worked more than forty hours per week for twenty-one weeks, and that he is entitled to time-and-a-half for his overtime hours during those weeks. Rambler answers the complaint, denying the allegation in Gould's complaint that he is an "employee" entitled to extra pay for overtime work. Rambler's position is that Gould is a manager, who does not meet the definition of "employee" in the Act and is not entitled to overtime pay.

   a. Rambler, after filing its answer, moves to dismiss for lack of subject matter jurisdiction, arguing that the court lacks jurisdiction because the Fair Labor Standards Act does not apply to Gould. What should the court do?

   b. Rambler moves for summary judgment, submitting with its motion affidavits of various corporate officers and a copy of Gould's job description, to prove that Gould's duties were managerial. Gould submits evidence of his own on the point, but the court concludes based on the supporting materials that Gould is, as a matter of law, a manager and not entitled to overtime under the Act. Should it dismiss for lack of jurisdiction or on the merits?

5. Steinberg, the public relations manager for Pinnacle Engineering Company, is fired. He concludes that he was fired simply because the company wanted a younger person in his job and brings suit against

Pinnacle under the Age Discrimination in Employment Act (ADEA), a federal statute that bars discharge or other discrimination in employment based on age. The statute expressly creates a right for employees to sue for damages for acts of age discrimination.

Pinnacle admits that the ADEA governs its employees, and that Steinberg, who is 57, is protected under the statute. It defends on the ground that it fired him for incompetence, not based on his age. Is the case properly brought in federal court under 28 U.S.C. s. 1331?

6. Suppose that Steinberg is from Florida and sues both Pinnacle (a Florida corporation) and Swift, president of Pinnacle and a Florida citizen. His suit alleges that he was fired because of his age and demands damages under the ADEA. Can he bring the action in federal court?

## Concurrents

7. Steinberg's counsel brings suit against Pinnacle in state court on his ADEA claim. (The ADEA statute says nothing one way or another about where suit must be brought.) Pinnacle moves to dismiss the case, on the ground that the case must be brought in federal court, since it arises under federal law. What should the state court do?

8. Pinnacle sues Steinberg in state court for conversion (a state tort claim), for removing confidential company records when he cleared out his office after being fired. Steinberg counterclaims — that is, asserts a claim of his own against Pinnacle — demanding damages from it under the federal ADEA. Could the case be brought in (or removed to) federal court based on federal arising-under jurisdiction?

## Stemming the Flood

9. Senator Doe, fed up with the continual demands for more federal judges, concludes that the problem could be alleviated by adding an amount-in-controversy requirement to 28 U.S.C. s. 1331 (that is, a provision limiting federal court jurisdiction to arising-under cases in which a minimum amount of money is in dispute). He asks you, his legislative counsel, for advice on whether a bill adding such a requirement to s. 1331 would be constitutional. What would you advise him?

10. Senator Jones, upset that the Mottley rule keeps many cases which involve important federal issues out of federal court, proposes to amend 28 U.S.C. s. 1331 to authorize federal jurisdiction if the plaintiff's complaint or the defendant's answer raises a substantial issue of federal law. He asks you whether it would be constitutional to expand arising-under jurisdiction in this way. What would you advise him?

11. Einstein, holder of a patent on a new computer technology, licenses the idea to Gates, an entrepreneur, under a contract which requires Gates to pay Einstein a license fee for every computer sold with the new technology. Gates makes the computers, sells them, and pays royalties to Einstein. However, Einstein claims that Gates has understated the number of units sold and therefore underpaid. He sues Gates in federal court. Does the court have jurisdiction over the case under 28 U.S.C. s. 1331?[7]

12. Suppose that, on the facts of the last example, Einstein sued Gates for breach of the licensing contract *and* for an injunction to prevent him from continuing to manufacture the computers, on the theory that making them without paying the proper royalty is an infringement of his patent rights. Would asserting the claim for injunctive relief allow Einstein to sue in federal court?

## Another Port in the Storm

13. Caprano is arrested by Quan, a police officer. Quan allegedly used excessive force in making the arrest, causing serious injury to Caprano. Bryan, Caprano's lawyer, believes that Judge Kane, the only federal judge sitting in the federal district where the claim arose, takes a very defense-oriented view of cases under 42 U.S.C. s. 1983, the federal civil rights statute. Consequently, Bryan decides to sue in state court and to assert only a state law battery claim. Quan tries to remove the case to federal court. (A defendant can remove a case to federal court if it could have been brought there originally.) Quan is not diverse from Caprano, but she argues that the complaint arises under federal law, because use of excessive force in the course of arrest would constitute a violation of the Fourth Amendment, a claim arising under the United States Constitution. Is the case removable?

14. Suppose that you represent Engle in the third example case on p. 66, in which she sues for bad faith discharge and alleges that she was fired for refusing to violate federal accounting requirements. You want to sue Consolidated in federal court.
    a. Would the case fall within the Article III, s. 2 grant of jurisdiction over cases arising under federal law?
    b. Which of the cases discussed in the Introduction would provide the most support for an argument that Engle's cases satisfies the arising-under requirement in s. 1331?

---

7. Actually, there is a special statute conferring jurisdiction on federal courts for patent claims. 28 U.S.C. s. 1338. However, the issue of when a case "arises under" that statute is substantially similar to that under s. 1331.

## Second Time Around

15. When the Supreme Court held that the lower federal court had lacked subject matter jurisdiction over the Mottleys' case, it ordered the case dismissed from federal court. The Mottleys still wanted their passes, so they started over in a Kentucky state court, which clearly had subject matter jurisdiction over their breach of contract case. That court heard the case, accepted the Mottleys' rebuttal to the railroad's defense based on the federal statute, and ordered the railroad to renew the passes. The railroad appealed to the Kentucky Court of Appeals, which affirmed the judgment. The railroad then appealed to the United States Supreme Court. Although it had held in its first *Mottley* decision that it lacked jurisdiction to hear the case, this time the Court took jurisdiction and decided the appeal. See 219 U.S. 467 (1911). How can it be that it lacked jurisdiction the first time, when the case was appealed from the lower federal court, but had it the second time?

## Explanations

### An Early Question

1. Naturally, you would advise the railroad, in answering the complaint, to assert only their state law defenses and then move to dismiss for lack of subject matter jurisdiction. Since neither the complaint nor the answer would raise federal law issues, that motion would presumably be granted and the Mottleys would have to start over in state court. (Remember that state courts have very broad subject matter jurisdiction; there will be no problem with a state court hearing a state contract claim.)

   Suppose the railroad took your advice, the federal suit was dismissed, and the Mottleys sued in state court. If, in answering the state court complaint, the railroad confined itself to state law defenses, the case would obviously remain in state court. But suppose it now raised its federal defenses? Should the case then be removed to federal court? If so, the rule could lead to delay in determining which court will hear the case. Or should the railroad be barred from raising federal issues, to punish its manipulative effort to avoid federal court? This could lead to disputes about the defendant's reason for failing to assert the federal defense earlier. If the railroad only raises state law defenses in state court, should it be barred from later raising federal defenses which it discovers in preparing for trial? Or should it be entitled to raise them, but the case then removed to federal court?

   These are perhaps not insuperable problems, but they do illustrate that practical difficulties would arise if potential defenses were considered in determining jurisdiction.

## Charting the Waters

2. Perhaps this is belaboring the obvious, but let's just eliminate one source of confusion at the outset. The language "laws of the United States" refers to laws made by Congress, not to the laws of the various states. A New Mexico statute is a law of *one of the states of the United States*, not of the United States, that is, of the national government. Unless she is diverse from Deveaux, Landry will have to proceed in state court.

3. In this case, there is some vague presence of federal law lurking on the periphery, since the accident takes place on an interstate highway and involves a defendant engaged in interstate commerce. But the claim clearly does not arise under federal law as that phrase is construed in 28 U.S.C. s. 1331. Costa's suit will be for negligence, a claim based in state tort law. She is not suing for violation of any interstate commerce regulation, just for negligence. Her "well pleaded complaint" will be entirely sufficient if it alleges the basic elements of a negligence claim: that Prior owed her a duty of due care, that he breached that duty, and that the breach caused her damages. Nor will Costa have to prove anything about federal law in order to establish her state law claim.

4. a. The court should deny the motion. Gould has sued under a federal statute, claiming that he is entitled to benefits under that statute. There is no question that the Fair Labor Standards Act creates a federal right to overtime, and that Gould is claiming recovery under that federal right. Rambler's position is simply that Gould isn't actually entitled to overtime under the statute, because he doesn't qualify as an "employee." This is simply a denial on the merits of Gould's claim; it does not alter the fact that federal law creates the cause of action that Gould asserts.

   There is a crucial difference between challenging jurisdiction on the ground that the plaintiff has not asserted a federal claim, on the one hand, and claiming that he can't *prove* the federal right he has *asserted*, on the other. Think of it this way: if the defendant could defeat federal jurisdiction simply by denying that the plaintiff is entitled to win on her federal claim, the federal court would seldom have any arising-under jurisdiction!

   b. Here, the court has taken jurisdiction over the case, as it properly should, since Gould asserts a federal claim. However, after receiving evidence on the issue of whether Gould is an "employee" under the Fair Labor Standards Act, the court concludes as a matter of law that he is not and, therefore, cannot recover overtime under the statute. Thus, judgment should enter against him on the merits: Gould has asserted a claim under federal law and lost on it, but this does not change the fact that the court had jurisdiction to hear the case.

Gould's failure to prove his federal claim does not mean that he failed to *assert* one sufficient to give the federal court arising-under jurisdiction.

5. Applying the Holmes test to this case, there is no question that the case arises under federal law even within the narrow definition in 28 U.S.C. s. 1331. The ADEA creates Steinberg's right to be free of age discrimination and expressly provides that employees who suffer such discrimination may sue for damages. Steinberg can sue *because* the federal statute exists and says that he can. He relies on the statute as the source of his right to relief.

The irony of the example, of course, is that the parties will not be litigating any issues of federal law in this case. No one is challenging the applicability of the statute, or even whether it protects employees in Steinberg's position. The only dispute between the parties is whether he was fired because of his age or because he couldn't cut the mustard. While *Mottley* makes the well-pleaded complaint approach to arising-under jurisdiction appear too restrictive, examples like this suggest that the test is overinclusive: it brings into federal court large numbers of cases in which the parties are suing under federal law, but not *disputing about* federal law at all: they're only disagreeing about the facts.

On the other hand, a convincing case can be made that federal jurisdiction in such cases is entirely appropriate. Patient, sympathetic application of federal statutes to the facts of particular cases may be as important to effective implementation of national policy as the legal interpretation of those statutes by federal courts. Particularly where subtle, subjective issues like intent must be assessed in order to apply the statute, administration by federal judges may go a long way to ensure that congressional policy is implemented where it really counts — in individual cases.

6. This example is meant to dispel one potential source of confusion about federal court jurisdiction. Here, the defendants are from the same state as the plaintiff, so there is no diversity of citizenship. However, the federal court still has subject matter jurisdiction over the case: Steinberg brings his suit under a federal statute, so the case "arises under federal law." A plaintiff can sue in federal court if his case falls into any category of federal subject matter jurisdiction; he doesn't have to sue under federal law *and* be diverse from the defendant. Thus, it is irrelevant that Steinberg is from the same state as the defendants.

## Concurrents

7. The issue posed by this example is whether a case which *may* be brought in federal court (because it arises under federal law) *must* be brought

there. Nothing in Article III states that cases within the federal judicial power *must* be brought in federal court. Article III, s. 2 provides that the federal judicial power "shall extend to" the cases delineated in that section, but does not withdraw jurisdiction over such cases from the state courts. The general principle is that cases within the jurisdiction of the federal courts may also be brought in the state courts; the state and federal courts have "concurrent jurisdiction" over such cases. However, Congress may provide that particular types of cases within the federal subject matter jurisdiction must be brought in federal court. Wright, 5th ed. 287. For an example, see 28 U.S.C. s. 1338(a), which makes federal court jurisdiction exclusive in patent, plant variety, and copyright cases.

Since (the example indicates) the ADEA does not provide that ADEA suits must be brought in federal court, Steinberg's counsel may file the action in state court if she chooses. In fact, many cases arising under federal law are litigated in the state courts. In such cases, state judges routinely interpret and apply the provisions of federal statutes — just as they do in the myriad cases in which issues of federal law are raised as a defense to a state law claim.

8. In this case Pinnacle sues on a state law claim, and Steinberg counterclaims — that is, he asserts a claim for damages against Pinnacle — arising under federal law. Under *Mottley*, the court will look at the *plaintiff's claim*, that is, Pinnacle's, to determine whether the case arises under federal law. Pinnacle's claim clearly does not, so the case does not fit within the arising-under jurisdiction.

The irony here is that if Steinberg had sued first on his ADEA claim, he could have sued in federal court, since his claim is based on the federal statute. If Pinnacle, as the defendant, counterclaimed for conversion, this would not defeat federal jurisdiction: Under *Mottley*, the court assesses jurisdiction based solely on the claim asserted by the plaintiff. By losing the race to the courthouse, Steinberg loses the federal forum.[8]

## Stemming the Flood

9. You should advise Senator Doe that there is nothing in the Constitution that would prevent Congress from limiting the arising-under jurisdiction of the federal district courts by introducing an amount-in-controversy requirement into s. 1331. As the Introduction indicates, the Supreme Court has held that Congress is free to grant the federal district courts less than the full scope of Article III jurisdiction. Article

---

8. Steinberg would not be able to remove the case to federal court based on the counterclaim either. See Chapter 7, ex. 13.

III defines the *outer bounds* of what they may be given, but does not require that all cases which could be granted to the lower federal courts must be. If Congress wishes to grant a part, but not all, of the arising-under jurisdiction, it may do so.

Historically, Congress has often made this choice. For example, for many years there was no general grant of jurisdiction over cases arising under federal law. There were narrow statutes granting federal courts the authority to hear particular types of federal claims, but no broad arising-under statute like s. 1331. Indeed, if you had been a devotee of federal jurisdiction for long enough, you could advise Senator Doe that 28 U.S.C. s. 1331 actually *had included* an amount-in-controversy requirement until 1980.

10. This expansion of statutory arising-under jurisdiction would be constitutional. As the Introduction suggests, a case "arises under" federal law, as that phrase is used in Article III, s. 2, if federal law is an "ingredient" of the case. This is true whether the federal issue is raised by the plaintiff or the defendant. Thus, Senator Jones's amendment would authorize federal district courts to exercise more of the constitutionally permissible arising-under jurisdiction.

    The American Law Institute proposed an amendment along these lines in 1969. An ALI study recommended that s. 1331 be changed to allow removal to federal court if "a substantial defense arising under the Constitution, laws, or treaties of the United States is properly asserted that, if sustained, would be dispositive of the action or of all counterclaims therein." American Law Institute, Study of the Division of Jurisdiction between State and Federal Courts, p. 25 (1969). However, Congress has never adopted this expansion of arising-under jurisdiction.

11. Einstein's case involves a contract dispute about a patented device, but it does not involve a question of patent law, or a claim under the patent laws. The "law that creates the cause of action" is state contract law, just as it was in the Mottleys' suit. Federal patent law is certainly tangentially involved in the action — if Einstein didn't have a patent on the device, Gates would presumably not have agreed to pay licensing fees. But the claim is a claim for breach of contract, not a claim for patent infringement. Einstein has a right to the money because Gates agreed to pay it, not because the device was patented. He would have the same right to royalties if Gates had agreed to pay them on a device that wasn't patented. Nor will Einstein have to establish a proposition of patent law in order to recover, analogous to *Smith v. Kansas City Title & Trust Co.* Presumably, he could enforce the contract whether the patent was valid or not.

12. Bringing suit for an injunction probably would change the result. The contract claim still doesn't arise under federal law, but the claim for

injunctive relief to stop the infringement does. In order to obtain the injunction against Gates, Einstein will have to prove that he holds a patent on the technology. If he proves that he holds the patent, and that Gates is selling the technology without permission (or, at least, in excess of his permission since he isn't paying the proper fees), patent law expressly allows the court to enter an injunction to prevent Gates' use of the technology. See 35 U.S.C. ss. 281, 283. Here, Einstein relies directly on federal patent law as the source of the substantive right he seeks to enforce, and it is clear (unlike in *Merrell Dow*) that federal patent law expressly creates the right to seek an injunction if the federal right is violated.

If this seems to put the power to "create federal jurisdiction" in the hands of Einstein's counsel, in a sense it does. The plaintiff is free to bring whatever colorable claims he has against the defendant. Here, Einstein has a right to enjoin Gates from using his technology without paying the license fee, and that right to an injunction is based on his federal patent right to control the sale of the technology. If he chooses to assert the injunction claim, his claim arises under federal law, and the federal court will have jurisdiction over it under 28 U.S.C. ss. 1331 and 1338.[9]

## Another Port in the Storm

13. In this case, Caprano has brought a state law claim for battery. She could not have sued in federal court, since battery is a state tort claim, and there is no diversity of citizenship between her and Quan. Consequently, Quan cannot remove to federal court, unless she can claim that the case "arises under" federal law because Caprano *could have* asserted a claim under federal law.

Federal jurisdiction generally turns on the claims the plaintiff actually asserts, not on those she could have asserted but didn't. Even though Caprano could have asserted a claim arising under federal law, she is entitled to choose the claims she wishes to bring. If, for tactical reasons, she is sufficiently anxious to avoid federal court to forgo her federal claim in order to do so, she may.[10]

---

9. The related contract claim could then be heard in federal court along with the federal claim, under "supplemental" jurisdiction, discussed in Chapter 16.

10. There is an exception to this. If the true nature of the plaintiff's claim is federal, she may not "artfully plead" it as a state law claim to avoid federal court. For example, in *Bright v. Bechtel Petroleum, Inc.*, 780 F.2d 766 (9th Cir. 1986), the plaintiff sued Bechtel, claiming that it had breached its contract with him by paying him less than his agreed salary. However, it was clear that the basis of Bright's claim was that Bechtel had withheld sums from his wages for federal taxes, and that this was illegal under the Internal Revenue Code. The court held that Bechtel's claim actually arose under federal tax law and upheld removal to federal court based on arising-under jurisdiction.

14. a. This case is within the *constitutional* grant of arising-under jurisdiction, as broadly interpreted by Chief Justice Marshall in *Osborn v. Bank of the United States*. In *Osborn*, Chief Justice Marshall interpreted the constitutional scope of the arising-under jurisdiction to be met if federal law was an "ingredient" of the case. Here, the federal accounting statute is an integral part of Engle's claim, since she will have to establish that it barred the practices Consolidated fired her for refusing to employ. In Marshall's language, Engle's right will be "defeated by one construction of the . . . law of the United States, and sustained by the opposite construction."

   b. Engle would rely on *Smith* and *Grable* as the basis for arising-under jurisdiction over her claim. Federal law does not create Engle's right to sue here: it is a state law claim for bad faith dismissal. But Engle intends to establish this state law claim by reference to federal law — the federal accounting statute which she refused to ignore. To premise federal jurisdiction on this federal-proof-of-a-state-law-claim argument, Engle will have to convince the court that the federal accounting standards are central to her case and raise a sufficiently important federal issue to support federal jurisdiction.

   The Fifth Circuit Court of Appeals confronted a similar case in *Willy v. Coastal Corp.*, 855 F.2d 1160 (5th Cir. 1988). In *Willy*, the plaintiff, a lawyer, alleged that he was discharged for failing to engage in activities that would violate federal environmental laws. Like Engle's claim, Willy's was based on state tort law, but he sought to prove it by reference to federal law. The *Willy* court's analysis suggested that arising-under jurisdiction might still be premised on the reasoning in Smith but, for several reasons, including the centrality of state law to Willy's claim, held that it could not hear his claim.

## Second Time Around

15. The subsequent history of the *Mottley* case nicely illustrates the difference between the statutory and constitutional scope of the arising-under jurisdiction. Under Chief Justice Marshall's expansive interpretation of the constitutional scope in *Osborn*, a federal court — either the federal trial court or the Supreme Court — could take jurisdiction if federal law formed an "ingredient" of the case. Surely, the railroad's federal statutory defense would meet this constitutional test for jurisdiction. But

---

In a sense, this "artful pleading" exception to the principle that the plaintiff may avoid federal court by pleading only state claims is simply an application of *Smith v. Kansas City Title and Trust*. The plaintiff in *Bechtel* could not establish his breach of contract claim without establishing a proposition of federal law: that the IRS regulation requiring withholding was invalid under the federal tax laws.

because the Court interpreted the statute which conveyed jurisdiction to the federal trial court—the predecessor of s. 1331—to require the *plaintiff* to rely on federal law, it held that the *federal trial court* had lacked subject matter jurisdiction under the statute. Since the trial court lacked jurisdiction, its judgment was of no effect, and the Court could not review it.

The situation was different when the case came to the Supreme Court on appeal from the Kentucky state courts. Those courts certainly had jurisdiction over the case, a common law claim for breach of contract. And the statute which conveyed arising-under jurisdiction to the *Supreme Court* on appeal was worded more broadly than s. 1331. It read much like 28 U.S.C. s. 1257, which currently authorizes Supreme Court review of state court judgments

> where the validity of a treaty or statute of the United States is drawn in question . . . or where any title, right, privilege, or immunity is specially set up or claimed under the Constitution or the treaties or statutes of . . . the United States.

Clearly, the railroad in *Mottley* "claimed an immunity" under a statute of the United States; in addition, the Mottleys' claim that the statute was unconstitutional "drew into question" the validity of that statute. So the jurisdiction provision just quoted authorized Supreme Court review. And clearly, it makes sense for Congress to authorize Supreme Court review in cases involving federal defenses. If it did not, state court interpretations of federal law in cases like *Mottley*, where the issue arises as a defense, would never be subject to review or correction in the United States Supreme Court.

# Diversity Jurisdiction

## When Does Multiplicity Constitute Diversity?

# INTRODUCTION

A major premise underlying our Constitution is that the states function quite well in most respects and that federal interference should be confined to those areas where there is a special need for national policy. For example, in 1787, when the Constitution was drafted, every state already had its own system of courts. The framers of the Constitution saw no need to abolish those courts in favor of federal courts administered by the national government. Instead, they authorized the creation of a separate federal court system (see U.S. Const. Art. III, §1), but only authorized those courts to hear limited categories of cases that, for one reason or another, involved a particular national interest. U.S. Const. Art. III, §2. Jurisdiction of all other cases was left to the courts of the states.

One of the major categories of cases that the framers authorized federal courts to hear is the so-called diversity jurisdiction, described in Article III, §2, as cases "between citizens of different states." In diversity cases, as in some others enumerated in Article III, §2, the subject matter jurisdiction of the federal courts is defined by who the parties to the suit are, rather than the subject matter of the underlying dispute.[1] The plaintiff in a diversity case may seek recovery on a battery theory, a fraud claim, a right created by state statute, or any other state law cause of action. So long as he sues a

---

1. Other examples in Article III that authorize jurisdiction based on the nature of the parties include cases to which the United States is a party; cases involving ambassadors, ministers, and foreign citizens; and cases between states.

diverse defendant and the claim is for more than $75,000, the federal court will have subject matter jurisdiction on the basis of diversity.

The framers' apparent reason for singling out diversity cases for federal jurisdiction was a fear that out-of-state citizens would suffer prejudice if they were forced to litigate against local citizens in the local state courts. That rationale has long been disputed by the scholars,[2] and repeated efforts have been made to abolish diversity jurisdiction. For example, the 1990 report of the Federal Courts Study Committee recommended abolishing diversity jurisdiction in all but a few unusual types of cases. Report of the Federal Courts Study Committee (April 2, 1990) pp. 38-42. However, reports of its death, in the words of Sam Clemens, have been greatly exaggerated.

Although Article III authorizes jurisdiction over diversity cases, it does not directly confer the diversity jurisdiction, or any other category of jurisdiction, on the lower federal courts. Rather, it authorizes Congress to create lower federal courts and to confer jurisdiction upon them to hear the types of cases enumerated in Article III, §2. This important additional requirement is succinctly explained in Judge Sirica's Watergate opinion:

> [F]ederal courts may assume only that portion of the Article III judicial power which Congress, by statute, entrusts to them. Simply stated, Congress may impart as much or as little of the judicial power as it deems appropriate and the Judiciary may not thereafter on its own motion recur to the Article III storehouse for additional jurisdiction. When it comes to jurisdiction of the federal courts, truly, to paraphrase the scripture, the Congress giveth, and the Congress taketh away.[3]

Thus, a plaintiff invoking federal jurisdiction must always be prepared to show that his case is not only within the constitutional bounds of Article III, §2, but has also been granted to the federal district courts by Congress in a statute.

In the case of diversity jurisdiction, Congress has granted to the federal courts some, but not all, of the Article III diversity jurisdiction. The statutory grant in 28 U.S.C. §1332 is narrower than Article III, §2, in that it includes an amount-in-controversy requirement, while Article III authorizes jurisdiction over *all* diversity cases, regardless of the sum in dispute. In addition, Chief Justice Marshall held in *Strawbridge v. Curtiss*, 7 U.S. 267 (1806), that a case is not within the statutory grant of diversity jurisdiction unless there is "complete diversity" between the parties, that is, all plaintiffs in a suit are from different states than all defendants at the time suit is brought. It is now clear, however, that Article III, §2, allows diversity

---

2. For a review of the debate, see Wright & Miller, Federal Practice and Procedure §3601.
3. *Senate Select Committee v. Nixon*, 366 F. Supp. 51, 55 (D.D.C. 1973).

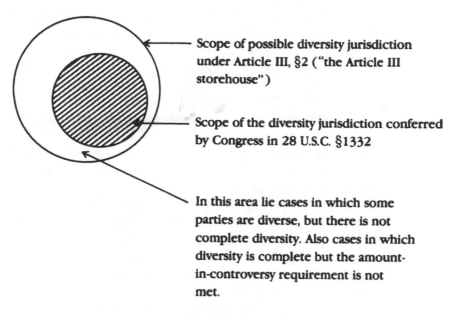

Scope of possible diversity jurisdiction under Article III, §2 ("the Article III storehouse")

Scope of the diversity jurisdiction conferred by Congress in 28 U.S.C. §1332

In this area lie cases in which some parties are diverse, but there is not complete diversity. Also cases in which diversity is complete but the amount-in-controversy requirement is not met.

**Figure 5-1.**

jurisdiction as long as *some* opposing parties to the action are diverse. *State Farm Fire & Casualty v. Tashire*, 386 U.S. 523 (1967). As with arising-under jurisdiction, the *statutory* grant of diversity jurisdiction has historically been narrower than the *constitutional* grant of jurisdiction. See Figure 5-1. Consequently, many diversity cases within the "Article III storehouse" may not be brought in federal court.

## THE MEANING OF STATE CITIZENSHIP

Constitutions establish grand principles but seldom explain exactly how to apply them. In the area of diversity jurisdiction, for example, it has been left to the courts to determine what it means to be "citizen" of a state. For natural persons (that is, human beings), the courts have equated state citizenship for diversity purposes with the common law concept of domicile. A person's domicile is usually defined as the state where he has taken up residence with the intent to reside indefinitely. Under this definition, residence is not equivalent to domicile; having a residence in the state is necessary but not sufficient to establish a domicile for diversity purposes. If Hawes owns houses in both Missouri and Wyoming and spends a good deal of time in both states, he will still have only one domicile. Which state it is depends on his subjective intent — sometimes almost impossible to ascertain — to make one particular state his "home."

The major problem in applying the domicile concept is determining what it means to "intend to stay indefinitely" in a state. It is not necessary to make an irrevocable commitment to stay in a place "permanently" to establish intent under the domicile test. That would be an unduly stringent requirement; few of us make such a firm decision about what we will do in the long term. Rather, "indefinitely" means that a person's presence in the state is open-ended; that is, he has no definite intent to leave to make a home elsewhere. This test can be met, even though a person expects that he probably will move on at some point, so long as he has no definite plans to do so at a particular time or upon the occurrence of a particular event. A person who is not committed to leaving is thought to be "at home" even though, like all of us, he may choose to leave at some time in the future.

For example, if Hawes quits his job and moves to Florida in hopes of finding a good job, he establishes a new domicile, even though he may leave if the job market proves unpromising. However, if Hawes goes to Florida for a few months as an undercover agent for the FBI, with the intent to return to his home in Missouri when the case is closed, he remains domiciled in Missouri, even if the exact length of time it will take to crack the case is unknown. Although the exact date of his departure from Florida is unknown, Hawes does not intend to stay "indefinitely" but rather to leave upon the occurrence of a particular event.

In addition, subjective intent to stay indefinitely is necessary but not sufficient: It must coincide with physical presence within the new domicile. Even if Hawes firmly intends to move to Florida after he retires next month, he does not acquire a domicile there until he physically arrives there to stay. Until then, he keeps his last domicile.

# CORPORATE CITIZENSHIP FOR DIVERSITY PURPOSES

Although it is hardly a foregone conclusion from the language of Article III and §1332, corporations have long been held to be state "citizens" authorized to invoke the diversity jurisdiction. Until 1958 they were held to be citizens of the state in which they were incorporated, regardless of where they actually conducted their daily business activity. In 1958 Congress enacted 28 U.S.C. §1332(c), which provides a statutory definition of the state citizenship of corporations for diversity purposes. Under §1332(c)(1) corporations are now citizens for diversity purposes of both the state where their principal place of business is located and the state in which they are incorporated. Consequently, if an opposing party is a citizen of either of those states, diversity does not exist.

The "principal place of business" provision in §1332(c)(1) has also created some interpretive problems. Most corporations carry on their business totally or predominantly in one state, so there is no problem in ascertaining their principal place of business for diversity purposes. In other cases, however, particularly cases involving very large corporations whose business involves commerce or transportation among numerous states, it is difficult to point definitively to one state as the corporation's principal place of business. If there is a definable center of the productive activities of the corporation, that is, the manufacturing or other profit-making activity that the corporation is engaged in, most courts tend to choose that state. The term "place of business," after all, connotes the place where you do what you exist to do, and the term "principal" suggests the place where you do the most of it. This is sometimes referred to as the "place of operations" or the "bulk of the corporate activity" test. The asserted rationale for diversity jurisdiction, to avoid prejudice against "outsiders," supports the use of this test. The corporation will most likely be perceived as "local" where it employs the most people, conducts the most activities, and has the most interaction with the public. See generally Wright & Miller §3625.[4]

However, the day-to-day activities of some corporations may be so dispersed as to make it artificial to characterize one state as the center of their productive activities. For example, it may be difficult to say that the productive activity of an insurance company that insures risks in many states or an airline that flies to destinations in many states is centered in any one of those states. In cases involving such widely dispersed corporate activities, courts have sometimes looked to the so-called "nerve center" of the corporation, the corporate headquarters or home office from which its activities are coordinated, to determine the principal place of business. See, e.g., *Egan v. American Airlines, Inc.*, 211 F. Supp. 292 (E.D.N.Y. 1962).[5]

A good many courts use a "total activity" test, which determines the corporation's principal place of business based on all aspects of the corporation's activity. See, e.g., *Teal Energy USA Inc. v. GT, Inc.*, 369 F.3d 873, 876 (5th Cir. 2004). This test, which considers both the nerve center and the production activities of the corporation, seems to make sense, but doesn't resolve the fairly common case in which the corporate headquarters are in one state and the daily conduct of business in another. Typically, these courts also look to the place of daily activities in these bipolar cases as well.

In analyzing the following examples assume that all actions are brought in federal court, that the amount-in-controversy requirement is

---

4. On the other hand, this logic suggests that corporations should *not* be deemed citizens of their state of incorporation, if, as is often true, they conduct no activities in that state. But, of course, under §1332(c)(1), they are.

5. Like so many procedural issues, however, this one is not entirely settled. The Seventh Circuit uses the nerve center test alone to establish a corporation's principal place of business. *Wisconsin Knife Works v. National Metal Crafters*, 781 F.2d 1280, 1282-1283 (7th Cir. 1986).

met in each case, and (unless otherwise specified) that each case is based on state law. The explanations begin on p. 100.

## Examples

### The Basic Diversity Requirements

1. Is there diversity between the parties in the following cases?
   a. Marlowe, from California, sues Archer, from California, in a federal district court in Illinois.
   b. Carella, from New York, sues Marlowe (California) and Archer (California).
   c. Carella (New York) sues Marlowe (California) and McGee, a Floridian, in a federal district court in California,
   d. Carella (New York), McGee (Florida), and Spenser (Massachusetts) sue Marlowe (California), Archer (California), and Meyer (New York).
   e. Marlowe (California) sues Carella (New York) and Marple, an Englishwoman.
   f. Same facts as (e), except that Marple, still an Englishwoman, lives in California.

2. Marlowe (California) sues Archer (California) in federal court in California for damages under a federal firearms control statute. May the court hear the case?

3. Marlowe (California) sues Carella (New York) for breach of contract in state court. Can he do this?

4. Marlowe (California) sues McGee (Florida) and Archer (California). Marlowe's claim against McGee is for defamation, a state law claim. His claim against Archer arises from the same incident but is based on federal law. Will the federal court have jurisdiction?

5. Marlowe (California) sues McGee (Florida) in federal court for libel. A month later he amends his complaint to add a libel claim against Archer, a California citizen who co-authored the offending article. Will the federal court have jurisdiction over the action?

### Homes Away from Home

6. Carella (New York) collides with McGee (Florida) during a car chase in New York City. Carella is disabled in the accident, retires to Florida, and sues McGee in a federal district court in Florida. Does the court have jurisdiction on the case based on diversity?

7. Meyer, a New Yorker, decides to move to Arizona. He buys an Audi from Isola Volkswagen, a New York dealership incorporated in New

York, and sets off with his family for Arizona, While driving through Oklahoma, he is involved in an accident and hospitalized.

   a. Two months later, while still in the hospital, Meyer files a negligence suit against Isola in an Oklahoma federal court. Does the court have diversity jurisdiction?

   b. While in the hospital, Meyer receives an offer to stay in Oklahoma and work as a detective for an oil company. He accepts and several months after beginning work sues Isola in federal court. Is the suit proper?

   c. Meyer is released from the hospital after six months. The company he planned to join in Arizona has rescinded its job offer since he was unable to start work when it needed him. He still has six months of rehabilitation ahead of him in Oklahoma. After that, he plans to begin looking for a job as a detective in the oil industry, wherever one turns up. Is he diverse from Isola?

## Corporate Diversity

8. Carella (New York) sues Underworld, Inc., incorporated in Delaware, doing business in every state, with its principal place of business in Florida. Suit is brought in the federal district court for the Northern District of Florida. Does the court have jurisdiction?

9. McGee (Florida) sues Underworld in a New York federal court. Is there diversity jurisdiction?

10. Marlowe (California) sues Gamblers International, Inc., a corporation incorporated in Nevada. Gamblers has two casinos: one very large casino in Reno, Nevada, which grosses $40 million per year, and another casino in California, which does $35 million in business each year. The corporate offices are in Reno. Is there diversity jurisdiction in Marlowe's suit?

11. Prior to the 1958 amendment that provided for dual citizenship of corporations for diversity purposes, corporations were considered citizens of their state of incorporation only. Did the amendment expand or contract corporate access to federal court?

# THE AMOUNT-IN-CONTROVERSY REQUIREMENT

As stated above, Article III, §2, broadly grants federal court jurisdiction over cases "between citizens of different states" without any requirement that a particular amount be in dispute between the parties. But Congress has always chosen to keep minor diversity cases out of the federal courts by providing that such cases can only be brought there if the amount in controversy exceeds a given figure. The figure started out at $500 in 1789, and has been periodically increased in pursuit of inflation, to the current $75,000 plus.

Courts face an awkward problem in applying the amount-in-controversy requirement, particularly in cases that involve intangible damages such as pain and suffering, emotional distress, loss of goodwill in a business, or punitive damages. There is no objective yardstick for lawyers to use in predicting the amount a jury will assess for such damages, or for juries to use in awarding them. Thus, it is difficult to determine at the outset of a case whether the recovery will meet the amount requirement.

Indeed, a plaintiff may legitimately seek more then $75,000 and recover nothing: The jury may conclude that the defendant was not negligent or that some defense to the claim is established. Thus it is impossible to know what value the jury will put on plaintiff's claim, or whether they will find for him at all, until the case is tried. How is the court to determine its power to hear the case without hearing the case?

This paradox is addressed by the very sensible rule in *St. Paul Mercury Indemnity Co. v. Red Cab Co.*, 303 U.S. 283 (1938), which holds that a plaintiff's good faith claim for more than the amount required controls, unless it "appear[s] to a legal certainty that the claim is really for less. . . ." 303 U.S. at 288-289. This means that the court must find the amount-in-controversy requirement met unless it is quite clear that there is no way the recovery will reach $75,000.01. The *St. Paul Mercury* rule is heavily weighted toward the plaintiff. Where the plaintiff might get more or might get less, the amount-in-controversy requirement is deemed satisfied. Where he will probably get less, but just might get more, it is deemed satisfied. It is only where the judge, looking at the pleaded facts, concludes "to a legal certainty" that the plaintiff could only be awarded less that the amount-in-controversy requirement is not met.

This rule makes sense because Congress has not provided that jurisdiction exists only where the plaintiff *recovers* more than $75,000. The requirement is that more than $75,000 be in *controversy*. Where there is legitimate debate as to whether the jury might return a verdict above that amount, the Congressional mandate is satisfied. However, while the *St. Paul Mercury* rule makes sense, it is ineffective at keeping many types of diversity cases involving intangible damages out of federal court. Because intangible damages (such as pain and suffering, emotional distress, or punitive damages) are hard to value, it will often not be possible in such cases to conclude that there is no way the plaintiff will recover more than the amount required.

# AGGREGATION OF CLAIMS TO MEET THE AMOUNT-IN-CONTROVERSY REQUIREMENT

There is another tough interpretive problem in applying the amount-in-controversy requirement. Suppose a plaintiff has two claims against a defendant, each less than the required amount, but that add up to more? Here's an example:

- Case #1. Holmes sues Watson for $50,000 for injuries in an auto accident caused by Watson, and for $60,000 for breach of a contract to promote Holmes's book. Is the amount requirement satisfied?

Or, suppose a plaintiff sues one defendant for $50,000, and, in the same case, sues another for $50,000:

- Case #2. Holmes sues Watson for $50,000 for injuries in an auto accident, and, in the same action, sues Meyer for $50,000, claiming that she was also negligent in causing the injury. Is the amount requirement satisfied?

Or, suppose that one plaintiff sues the defendant for $50,000, and another plaintiff joins in the same action against the defendant, seeking $40,000:

- Case #3. Holmes is injured in an auto accident, and sues Meyer for $50,000 for his personal injuries. His wife also suffered an injury in the same accident. She joins as a co-plaintiff, seeking $30,000 in damages. Is the amount requirement satisfied?

Or, suppose that the plaintiff sues one defendant for more than the required amount, and another defendant for less:

- Case #4. Holmes sues International Investigations Inc., his employer, for breach of contract, for firing him. He claims $200,000 in damages for loss of his job. In the same suit, he sues Watson, his supervisor, for libel, claiming that Watson libeled him in a memo to the president of the company. He claims $50,000 in damages for the libel.

Or, one last variation, suppose one plaintiff sues the defendant for more than the required amount, and a second plaintiff joins to sue the same defendant for less:

- Case #5. Holmes sues International Investigations Inc., his employer, for breach of contract, for firing him. He claims $200,000 in damages for loss of his job. Spenser, who was demoted based on the same incident, joins as a co-plaintiff, seeking $35,000 in damages.

The "rules" as to when claims can be added together to meet the amount requirement are more the result of historical accident than impeccable logic. They will be discussed more fully in Chapter 16, examples 10-14. For now, here are the basic answers to the configurations above:

Where a single plaintiff asserts two or more claims against a single defendant, the amounts may be added together to reach the required amount. Thus, in Case #1 the amount requirement is met.

A single plaintiff cannot aggregate amounts sought from different defendants. He must meet the amount requirement against each individually. Thus, in Case #2, Holmes cannot add his claims against Watson and Meyer together to meet the amount requirement. Similarly, if he sues one defendant for more than $75,000, and a second defendant for less, he cannot bootstrap the insufficient claim onto the other. Thus, in Case #4, he would meet the amount requirement against International Investigations, but not against Watson. Even if there was complete diversity, he could not make Watson a co-defendant in the action, since his claim against Watson does not independently satisfy the amount requirement. His claim against International Investigations could proceed in federal court, since this claim does meet the amount requirement.

Plaintiffs may not add their claims together to meet the amount requirement in cases like Case #3, in which neither party meets the amount requirement. This case would have to be dismissed, since neither plaintiff meets the amount-in-controversy requirement.

That leaves Case #5, in which one plaintiff satisfies the amount requirement, and another does not. The Supreme Court recently held that the federal court has "supplemental jurisdiction" over the $35,000 claim in cases like this, but only in a case against a *single defendant*. As long as one plaintiff asserts a claim that satisfies the amount requirement, others may join as co-plaintiffs even though they are seeking less. *Exxon Mobil Corporation v. Allapattah Services Inc.*, 545 U.S. 546 (2005). Note, however, that the converse isn't true: in Case #4, in which the plaintiff seeks more than $75,000 from one defendant and less from another, the amount requirement is not met against the second defendant. As already mentioned, history more than logic explains these variations. The reasoning for this last variation will be more apparent after you read Chapter 16, on supplemental jurisdiction.

The following examples will help you to apply the aggregation rules, if not to appreciate them. Assume in analyzing them that the traditional rules apply.

# Examples

## Aggravation of Damages

12. Is the amount-in-controversy requirement met in each of the following cases? (Assume that diversity is otherwise proper and that there is no common undivided interest involved in the suit.)

    a. Hammer sues Holmes for $70,000 for his personal injuries suffered in an auto accident and for $15,000 for damage to his car in the same accident.

    b. Hammer sues Holmes to recover $60,000 on a loan he made to Holmes and for $50,000 for an unrelated libel.

    c. Hammer sues Holmes for $60,000 for damages suffered in an accident. In the same action, Marlowe, who was a passenger in Hammer's car, sues Holmes for $25,000 for his injuries.

    d. Hammer sues Holmes for $80,000 for his injuries in the accident. In the same suit, Marlowe, the passenger in Hammer's car, sues for $25,000.

    e. Hammer sues Holmes for $80,000 for injuries suffered in an auto accident. He also sues Dr. Watson, claiming that Watson negligently treated his injuries, causing $20,000 in additional damages.

## Adding Insult to Injury

    f. McGee sues Spenser for causing $50,000 worth of damage to McGee's houseboat. His complaint contains two counts. Count One seeks $50,000 from Spenser for negligently ramming the boat while docking in Fort Lauderdale. Count Two seeks $50,000 from Spenser on the theory that he intentionally damaged the boat.

    g. McGee's $100,000 houseboat is destroyed in a collision with boats piloted by Spenser and Carella. He claims that either Spenser, Carella, or both, were negligent and sues them both to recover for the damage to the boat.

    h. McGee sues Spenser for $60,000 for intentionally damaging his boat and for $50,000 in punitive damages.

## Another Famous Foible

13. Here is another dandelion from the bluebook garden. What is wrong with it?

    The plaintiff's claim must be dismissed for failure to meet the amount-in-controversy requirement unless it appears to a legal certainty that he will recover more than seventy-five thousand dollars.

## Explanations

### The Basic Diversity Requirements

1. a. Marlowe and Archer are both from California. You can't get any less diverse than this, under any definition of diversity. The fact that Marlowe has sued in an Illinois federal court is irrelevant. No matter which district he chooses, the parties are from the same state. Don't be thrown off the track by the fact that the suit is brought in a third state. For diversity purposes (unlike personal jurisdiction purposes), the crucial question is where the opposing parties live, not where they sue.

   b. This is a proper diversity case even though both defendants are from California. The *Strawbridge* rule requires that all defendants must be from different states than all plaintiffs; parties on the same side of the "v" may be co-citizens. While this might not satisfy one's intuitive notion of "complete diversity," it is diverse enough to satisfy Chief Justice Marshall and §1332.

   c. This is the completest of all possible diversities because all parties are from different states. It is therefore a proper diversity case. Once again, the place of suit is irrelevant to the diversity analysis. Carella's choice to sue in a defendant's home state does not destroy diversity, just as the choice of forum could not create it in example 1a.

   d. There is no diversity jurisdiction here. While there are diverse citizens on both sides of the "v," there are also New Yorkers on both sides, which violates the *Strawbridge* rule. This is an ironic result: Why should a New York state court jury be any less prejudiced against Marlowe and Archer, simply because Meyer has been sued as well? Indeed, might not the jury shift the blame from the in-state defendant to the out-of-state defendants? It is easy to poke holes in the *Strawbridge* rule in cases like this; indeed, Chief Justice Marshall is said to have regretted the decision himself. C. Wright, the Law of Federal Courts, 156. On the other hand, this application of the rule is not entirely irrational. Carella could not sue Meyer in federal court alone, since they are both from New York. Why should he be able to do so simply by joining other defendants who are diverse?

   Note the various ways in which the plaintiffs could restructure this suit to use the federal courts. All three plaintiffs could sue Marlowe and Archer, or McGee and Spenser could sue all three defendants. In either case, diversity would exist, but some part of the controversy would have to be heard separately in state court.

   e. This is a suit between diverse citizens with an additional party who is an alien (a harsh-sounding term for a person who is a citizen or subject of another country). Article III, §2, does not specifically provide for this kind of case, but it does separately authorize jurisdiction over cases between citizens of different states and cases between citizens and aliens ("between a State, or the Citizens thereof, and foreign States, Citizens or Subjects"). It is a fair inference that a combination of the two is also proper. Congress has expressly authorized jurisdiction in such cases in 28 U.S.C. §1332(a)(3).

f. Marple is an alien whether she is currently living in California or England. She cannot become a state citizen without first becoming a United States citizen or a recognized "permanent resident."[6] Thus, even if she is domiciled in California, this is a proper diversity case. See, e.g., *Mas v. Perry*, 489 F.2d 1396 (5th Cir. 1974). For an interesting variation on this case, see *Twentieth Century-Fox Film Corp. v. Taylor*, 239 F. Supp. 913 (S.D.N.Y. 1965), in which Elizabeth Taylor was sued for various claims arising out of the filming of the movie "Cleopatra." Although Taylor was an American citizen at the time suit was filed, she was domiciled abroad. Consequently, she was not subject to suit in federal court under the diversity statute: she was not a citizen of any state because, while a U.S. citizen, she was not domiciled in any state. But she was not an alien either, since she had not relinquished her American citizenship. Id. at 914 n.2.

2. This example is meant to dispel one potential source of confusion. It is only necessary to have one basis of federal jurisdiction to sue in federal court. Here, Marlowe's suit is brought under a federal statute. It is a case "arising under federal law," a separate basis for federal subject matter jurisdiction authorized by Article III and 28 U.S.C. §1331. It is therefore irrelevant that the parties are from the same state, since diversity is not needed to support federal jurisdiction.

3. This example illustrates a point already raised in the last chapter: that a case within the federal court's jurisdiction may usually be filed in a state court instead. Marlowe's is a proper diversity case, so he could have filed it in federal court. But state courts have jurisdiction over contracts cases too. Under the principle of concurrent jurisdiction, Marlowe may file this case in state court if he wishes. (However, as we will see in Chapter 7, Carella may have a right to "remove" it to federal court if Marlowe does file in state court.)

4. This suit is proper even though Archer and Marlowe are both from California. Marlowe has a federal claim against Archer, a separate basis for suing him in federal court. Thus, he is not relying on diversity between himself and Archer as a basis for jurisdiction. In determining

---

6. §1332 treats an alien "admitted to the United States for permanent residence" as a citizen of the state where he is domiciled. See the last paragraph of 28 U.S.C. §1332(a).

diversity, you can disregard parties who are properly before the federal court on another basis and focus on the part of the case for which diversity is argued as the basis for jurisdiction. *Kauth v. Hartford Ins. Co. of Illinois*, 852 F.2d 951, 958-959 (7th Cir. 1988). Because Marlowe is diverse from McGee, his claim against him is proper, so there is a basis for jurisdiction over all claims in the case.

Put another way, it is clear on these facts that Marlowe could sue McGee and Archer in separate actions in federal court, one based on federal question jurisdiction and the other on diversity. It would hardly make sense to allow him to do that, but not to allow him to sue them in a combined action.

5. This looks like an obvious ploy to invoke federal jurisdiction for a case that fails the *Strawbridge* test. Marlowe sues a diverse defendant, gets into federal court, and then adds the non-diverse defendant by amending his complaint. The federal court will probably either refuse to allow the amendment or dismiss this action for lack of diversity jurisdiction, since Marlowe's amendment has "destroyed diversity" by adding a party from his home state. Even though the court had jurisdiction over the action as originally filed, it must dismiss once the non-diverse party is added. Otherwise, the plaintiff would be able to gain access to federal court by suing diverse parties in the initial action and adding home-state defendants later on. See *Owen Equipment & Erection Co. v. Kroger*, 437 U.S. 365 (1978).

## Homes Away from Home

6. The court does not have jurisdiction in this case. Although the parties were diverse at the time of the incident that gave rise to Carella's claim, they are not diverse at the time of the suit: Carella has apparently changed his domicile by retiring to Florida. Although it is unclear from the statute, courts have held that the magic date for determining diversity is the date of filing suit. *Hawes v. Club Ecuestre El Comandante*, 598 F.2d 698, 701 (1st Cir. 1979). Since the parties were not diverse on that date, there is no jurisdiction. If they are, it does not matter that they were from the same state when the claim arose. The fact that the accident took place in New York does not affect the analysis; the place of the underlying events in suit, like the place where the plaintiff brings the action, is irrelevant to the determination of diversity.

7. a. You may recognize this hypo as a slightly modified version of the facts in *World-Wide Volkswagen v. Woodson*, 444 U.S. 286 (1980). The case could not be properly brought as a diversity case, since Meyer is still a New Yorker. Even though he intends to settle in Arizona and has left New York, perhaps never to return, he has not yet established

a domicile in Arizona. To do so, he must physically arrive in the state with the intent to remain indefinitely.

Nor may Meyer argue that he is domiciled in Oklahoma based on his two-month stay there. He has arrived there and established a residence of sorts,[7] but as far as we know, he has not changed his intent to go on to live in Arizona. Residence in Oklahoma without the necessary intent is just as ineffective to create a new domicile as intent to live in Arizona without residence there. Until the two co-incide in a new state, Meyer remains a New York domiciliary.

Most federal courts apply the intent-to-remain-indefinitely test in determining domicile, but a few offer a looser test for establishing a domicile. In *Sadat v. Mertes*, 615 F.2d 1176 (7th Cir. 1980), for example, the court held that a person must "be physically present at the location and intend to make that place his home for the time at least" to establish a new domicile. This test would probably yield a different result in this example, since presumably Meyer intends to make Oklahoma his home "for the time at least" — until he gets out of the hospital. However, this test raises problems if taken literally. If Hawes goes to Florida for four months to conduct an investigation, he intends to remain in Florida "for the time at least," but even the *Sadat* court would probably not find him domiciled in Florida.

b. A frequent mistake in applying the domicile rule is to conclude that intent and residence must coincide when a person originally arrives in the state. That is not so; as long as the two coincide at some time while he is there, a new domicile is established. In this case, Meyer does not intend to stay in Oklahoma when he arrives but forms that intent later, while residing there. When he does form that intent, Oklahoma becomes his domicile. Restatement (Second) of Conflicts of Law §15, illustration 2 (1971). Consequently, this is a proper diversity case.

c. This is a difficult case. Meyer has not made any commitment to stay in Oklahoma after he finishes rehabilitation; nor does he have a reason any longer to go on to Arizona; nor is he likely to return to New York where they don't drill an awful lot of oil. Nor can you argue that he is in Oklahoma for a definite period of time, the six-month rehabilitation period. He will definitely be there for *at least* six months, but he is not definitely there for *only* six months. He may stay until Armageddon for all we know.

---

7. Establishing a residence for domicile purposes need not entail purchasing a house or leasing an apartment. Even an overnight stay in a hotel or a night spent in the family camper may suffice. See Restatement (Second) of Conflicts of Law §12, illustration 2; cf. T. P. *Laboratories v. Huge*, 197 F. Supp. 860, 863 (D. Md. 1961). Some authorities state the re-quirement as one of "physical presence" rather than residence. See, e.g., *Holmes v. Sopuch*, 639 F.2d 431, 433 (8th Cir. 1981).

Of course, the rule is that you don't lose your old domicile until you acquire a new one. But I would conclude that Meyer has acquired domicile in Oklahoma. He might stay in Oklahoma — where they clearly do have oil wells — or he might go elsewhere. While he's not irrevocably committed to staying, he's not committed to leaving either. Meyer's plans are "indefinite."

A generation of civil procedure students have done battle with me over examples like this, resisting the idea that a person can be domiciled in a state where they have so little commitment or expectation of remaining. Many argue that Meyer remains domiciled in New York, since he is not committed to staying in Oklahoma; but I say he is domiciled in the state where he currently resides unless he is committed to going somewhere else. Meyer was committed to leaving in example 7a, but that isn't true here.

## Corporate Diversity

8. Diversity jurisdiction is proper here, since Carella is not from either Underworld's state of incorporation or the state where it has its principal place of business. The fact that Underworld does business in New York, the plaintiff's home state, does not affect diversity as long as New York is not Underworld's principal place of business. Distinguish personal jurisdiction over the corporation, which may be established (in appropriate cases) in a state where the corporation does substantial business, even though it does a great deal more business in other states.

9. There is no diversity jurisdiction here because the plaintiff is a citizen of the state in which Underworld has its principal place of business. McGee may not claim diversity on the ground that he is from Florida and Underworld from Delaware: Underworld is *also* from Florida under §1332(c)(1). Neither the corporation nor the opposing party can pick and choose between these two states in order to establish diversity. The corporation is from both states, and therefore, complete diversity is lacking.

10. In this case, the defendant has very large facilities in two states, both of which might ordinarily be deemed "principal" places of business. While it may seem artificial to designate either as more "principal" than the other, §1332(c)(1) has been consistently interpreted to mean that a corporation can have only one principal place of business for diversity purposes. See 28 U.S.C. §1332(c)(1) ("the state where it has its principal place of business") (emphasis supplied). Thus, the court will have to choose California or Nevada. Because the corporate headquarters and the larger casino are both in Nevada, the court will

likely conclude that Gamblers' principal place of business is Nevada, especially if it applies the "total activity" test. Thus, it will be a citizen of Nevada on this basis as well as on the basis of its incorporation there and will be diverse from Marlowe. In many cases, as in this one, corporations will be citizens of only one state under §1332(c)(1) because they are incorporated in the state where their principal place of business is located.

11. The amendment restricted corporate access to the federal courts by increasing the number of cases in which corporations share the same state citizenship with opposing parties. For example, a mining corporation might incorporate in Delaware for tax or legal reasons, but do all its mining business in Colorado. Under the earlier interpretation, it was diverse from a Colorado citizen and could invoke federal jurisdiction even though, in day-to-day reality, it functioned as a local Colorado corporation. Under §1332(c)(1), however, that corporation is deemed a citizen of Colorado as well as a citizen of Delaware and confined to the state courts in suits against Colorado citizens.

## Aggravation of Damages

12. a. Hammer may aggregate any claims he has against Holmes, a single defendant, to reach the required jurisdictional amount. Because the two claims combined exceed $75,000, the amount-in-controversy requirement is met.

   b. Aggregation is proper because the plaintiff may aggregate his claims against a single defendant even if, as here, the two claims are totally unrelated.

   c. Both of these claims will be dismissed. Just as Hammer is barred from aggregating claims against separate defendants, he may not aggregate his claims with those of another plaintiff to reach the $75,000-plus threshold. When you look separately at each plaintiff's claim against Holmes, neither satisfies the amount-in-controversy requirement. Nor does 28 U.S.C. §1367, the supplemental jurisdiction statute, change the result. It only allows additional plaintiffs to bootstrap on where *one* plaintiff satisfies the amount requirement.

   d. In this case, one plaintiff meets the amount requirement and another joins as co-plaintiff, seeking less than the jurisdictional amount. In *Exxon Mobil*, the Supreme Court interpreted the supplemental jurisdiction statute to allow this. There is one claim that supplies a basis for original federal jurisdiction—Hammer's claim. And Marlowe's arises from the same events, so it qualifies for supplemental jurisdiction. Again, this will make more sense to you after you have studied 28 U.S.C. s. 1367, the supplemental jurisdiction statute. But the short answer is that Marlowe can tag along, as long as Hammer, or *some* plaintiff, asserts a claim that meets the amount requirement.

e. Hammer's claim against Holmes is fine, but his suit against Watson fails, since Hammer does not seek more than $75,000 from Watson. Under the traditional aggregation rules, he cannot add his claim against one defendant to his claim against a different defendant to meet the amount requirement. Each must independently meet the requirement. Neither 28 U.S.C. §1367 nor *Exxon Mobil* has changed the result in this case.

## Adding Insult to Injury

f. If you thought carefully about this case, you should have concluded as a matter of common sense that the amount-in-controversy requirement is not met. The rule that the plaintiff may aggregate his claims against a single defendant applies to claims for *separate losses*, such as those asserted in example 12b, not to demands for the same damages based on different theories. McGee has only suffered $50,000 in damages; that is what he is suing to recover. Granted, he has two possible theories of relief, but he will clearly not recover a separate $50,000 on each theory. Spenser could not have been negligent *and* intentionally caused the damage. If McGee wins at all, he will win on only one theory and will only recover the amount of his loss.

Indeed, even in cases where a plaintiff might recover on both theories, he will not be awarded more than his actual damages, absent a claim for punitive damages. For example, McGee might sue a truck dealer for breach of contract and breach of implied warranty to recover for a truck worth $50,000 less than he paid for it. Even if the court finds for McGee on both counts, he will still recover only the $50,000 he has lost; no court will give him double damages simply because he advances two theories for the same relief.

g. In this case McGee is claiming that one or both defendants' negligence contributed to cause the loss of his boat. If only Spenser was at fault, McGee would recover the entire $100,000 from him. If Carella caused the collision, McGee would recover the $100,000 loss from him. If they are both found negligent, the law in some states would allow McGee to collect the full $100,000 from either, assuming McGee was not negligent himself.[8] Thus, since either defendant might be liable for the entire $100,000, the

---

8. In other states, the damages would be apportioned according to fault.

amount-in-controversy requirement is satisfied against each. Of course, either might be absolved completely, but as long as each *might* by liable for more than the jurisdictional amount, the requirement is met.

h. Here, McGee's actual damages are $60,000, but he may recover more than his actual damages if the governing law allows recovery of punitive damages. If the state allows punitive damages in the kind of action McGee brings, the amount requirement is likely met. Under *St. Paul Mercury*, the plaintiff's demand controls, unless it appears to be a legal certainty that he could not recover the jurisdictional amount. It is extremely difficult to say for sure that McGee will not recover $15,000.01 in punitive damages, since punitive damages turn on a jury's subjective assessment of the extremity of the defendant's conduct and, at the time the defendant challenges the sufficiency of the amount sought, the court will have little familiarity with the underlying facts of the case.

However, if relevant state law bars punitive damages, the amount-in-controversy requirement will not be met, and the case will be dismissed, since the only allowable damages do not exceed $75,000.

## Another Famous Foible

13. This too-frequent misstatement of the *St. Paul Mercury* rule exactly reverses its meaning: It requires the plaintiff to prove that he *will* recover more than $75,000 to satisfy the amount-in-controversy requirement and stay in federal court. On the contrary, the rule gives the plaintiff every benefit of the doubt. If, looking at the pleaded facts, it appears that the plaintiff *might* recover more than $75,000, the requirement is met. It is only where it is clear to a legal certainty that the plaintiff *definitely will not* recover that much on the claim he has asserted that the court dismisses for failure to meet the monetary threshold.

# Personal and Subject Matter Jurisdiction Compared

## The First Two Rings

---

# INTRODUCTION

Much of the civil procedure course is devoted to the fundamental issue of choosing the proper court in which to bring a lawsuit. As we have already seen, there is quite a choice: Each of the 50 states has its own court system, not to mention the District of Columbia and other territories. In addition, there is a separate system of federal courts, established and administered by the federal government but geographically located throughout the United States. Thus, in any particular state there will be both the local state courts and one or more "branches" or districts of the federal court system.

The plaintiff is not free to choose indiscriminately among the various federal and state courts in the 50 states. There are three basic requirements that limit the proper courts for any lawsuit. First is the need to find a court that can exercise personal jurisdiction over the defendant. Second, not all courts can hear all types of cases: The plaintiff must choose a court that has "subject matter jurisdiction" over the kind of case she wishes to litigate. Third, the chosen forum must be a proper "venue" under the applicable venue statute. I call these the three rings of civil procedure and visualize them as in Figure 6-1.[1] As a rule, courts can only hear those cases that satisfy all three rings (the shaded area in the diagram). Frequently, a case will satisfy one or two of these prerequisites but fail the third. For example,

---

1. I am indebted to the late Professor Abram Chayes, of Harvard Law School, my own civil procedure teacher, for this helpful diagram.

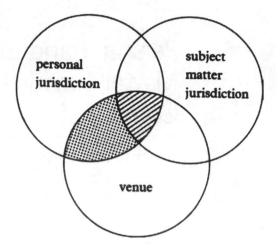

**Figure 6-1.**

the plaintiff may have chosen a court that has personal jurisdiction over the defendant and is a proper venue under the relevant venue statute (see the dotted area in the diagram), but the court will still have to dismiss the action if the third ring, subject matter jurisdiction, is not met.

This chapter compares the first two rings, personal and subject matter jurisdiction. The reasons for these two limitations on the right to bring an action are quite different, yet the concepts used to define them are sometimes confusingly similar. It is worth getting the distinctions clear in your mind before wading too deeply into the procedural morass.

## BASIC DISTINCTIONS

Personal jurisdiction, as Chapter 1 explains, is a geographical limitation on the places where a plaintiff may choose to sue a defendant for a particular claim. It is intended, as a matter of basic fairness, to prevent a plaintiff from suing a nonresident defendant in a state unless that defendant has established a relationship to that state that would reasonably lead her to anticipate being sued there.

Personal jurisdiction turns in each case on the relationship between the defendant and the state where suit is brought. Consequently, it may be proper to bring a particular action in one state but not in another. For example, if Gable sues Leigh, a Texan, for assault arising out of threats Leigh made at a Hollywood movie opening, it would be unreasonable to force Leigh to defend the action in Minnesota. She has (presumably) no minimum contacts with Minnesota, did not make the threats in Minnesota, and has no reason to expect this suit to be brought there. However, she could be sued in California for this claim, since she has relevant contacts with California: She made the threats there and can expect them to injure Gable there.

Similarly, the courts of a single state may have jurisdiction over one suit between particular litigants but not over another between the same parties, if the second suit is unrelated to that state. Although Gable's first assault action could not be brought in Minnesota, he would be able to sue Leigh there for another assault if Leigh repeats her threatening statements at a Minneapolis opening. Thus, the answer depends in every case on the defendant's contacts with the state where the suit has been brought.

Subject matter jurisdiction, by contrast, concerns the court's authority to hear generic types of cases. All state court systems have a set of trial courts with very broad subject matter jurisdiction. These courts (sometimes confusingly referred to as courts of "general jurisdiction") have subject matter jurisdiction over a wide range of suits, such as torts, contracts, property, and other common types of disputes. These state courts of broad subject matter jurisdiction have different names in different states. In California they are called the Superior Courts; in Pennsylvania, the Courts of Common Pleas; in New York, perversely, they are called the Supreme Courts. In addition, a state may create specialized courts to hear certain types of claims, such as landlord/tenant cases (housing courts) or family and inheritance matters (probate courts).

The subject matter jurisdiction of the *federal* courts, by contrast, is much more limited than that of the state courts. The federal courts were not created to displace the preexisting state systems, but only to provide a federal forum for specific categories of cases of national concern. The federal courts have jurisdiction over cases arising under federal law, cases between citizens of different states (the so-called diversity jurisdiction), and other more limited categories of cases. United States Constitution, Article III, §2. By contrast, they have no jurisdiction over most common types of suits, such as tort suits, contract actions, or actions seeking recovery under state statutes (unless the parties are diverse or some other narrow category of Article III jurisdiction applies).

Unlike personal jurisdiction, the subject matter jurisdiction of a court does not usually depend on the location of the particular court the plaintiff chooses. For example, if a case arises under federal law, any federal district court will have subject matter jurisdiction over it. Since Article III, §2, and 28 U.S.C. §1331 authorize "the [federal] district courts" to hear cases arising under the laws of the United States, they all have jurisdiction over such cases. If subject matter jurisdiction were the only limit on a plaintiff's right to sue, she could bring a case arising under federal law in any federal district court in the country.

# SOURCES OF CONFUSION

A number of factors conspire to make these differing concepts difficult to sort out. First, although Article III, §2, of the Constitution confers jurisdiction over various categories of cases on federal courts, it does not withdraw jurisdiction over those cases from the state courts. The state courts have "concurrent jurisdiction" over cases within the federal judicial power unless Congress has made federal court jurisdiction exclusive for a particular type of claim. Wright & Miller, §3527. Thus, a state court may hear many claims arising under federal law, such as federal civil rights cases, even though the plaintiff would have the option to bring the action in federal court as well. By contrast, the federal courts do not have concurrent jurisdiction over state law actions (unless the parties are diverse); they may only hear those cases specifically provided for in Article III of the Constitution and jurisdictional statutes passed by Congress.

The framers of the Constitution made the situation particularly confusing by creating the diversity jurisdiction, in Article III, §2, which authorizes the federal courts to hear cases between citizens of different states. In most situations, subject matter jurisdiction is defined by the nature of the controversy (such as housing cases, probate cases, or tax cases), but here the framers chose to confer upon federal courts the power to hear cases on the basis of where the parties are from. Despite this focus on the domicile of the parties, this is not personal jurisdiction; it does not focus on the geographical relationship of the events giving rise to the suit to the state where suit is brought but broadly grants subject matter jurisdiction to any federal court, no matter where located, so long as the case is between citizens of different states. For example, if Flynn, from Oregon, sues Peck, from Maryland, for a breach of contract arising in Montana, the case is a proper diversity case (assuming the amount in controversy exceeds $75,000). Any federal district court will have subject matter jurisdiction over it, though many will not have personal jurisdiction over Peck.

Another potential source of confusion arises from the fact that the concept of domicile is relevant to both personal and subject matter jurisdiction. A natural person (that is, a human being) is subject to personal jurisdiction in the state where she is domiciled, the last state where she has established a residence with the intent to reside indefinitely. See Restatement (Second) of Conflicts of Law §27 (1971). An individual's state citizenship for purposes of determining diversity jurisdiction is also determined by this same domicile concept. But in applying the concept to determine personal jurisdiction, the court will ask whether the defendant's domicile is in the state where suit is brought. When invoking this concept to determine subject matter jurisdiction based on diversity, the court will simply compare the plaintiff's domicile to the defendant's to make sure they differ.

Yet another piece of terminology that breeds confusion is the concept of "general jurisdiction," which is used in connection with both personal and subject matter jurisdiction. The basic trial courts of each state, for example, are said to exercise "general jurisdiction." This means that they have very broad *subject matter jurisdiction* over many types of suits, unless the type of dispute has been delegated to a specialized state court or is within those few categories of cases in which Congress has made federal subject matter jurisdiction exclusive. By contrast, when used in the *personal juris-diction* context, "general jurisdiction" refers to the authority of a state's courts to hear any claim against a particular defendant, whether or not it is related to the defendant's in-state contacts. Such general in personam jurisdiction may be based on domicile in the state or substantial and continuous in-state business activities. See Chapter 1, pp. 5-7.

# PERSONAL JURISDICTION IN THE FEDERAL COURTS

For the purposes of this chapter, it is necessary to touch briefly on a problem that puzzles lawyers as well as law students — the reach of personal jurisdiction in the federal courts. As a matter of *constitutional power* the federal courts' power to exercise personal jurisdiction is not limited by the Fourteenth Amendment due process clause: That amendment, by its terms, only applies to the *states*, not to the federal government. However, the Fifth Amendment imposes its own limits on the power of federal courts to exercise personal jurisdiction. L. Teply & R. Whitten, Civil Procedure (3rd ed. 2004) 318.

Under Fourteenth Amendment analysis, state courts may only exercise personal jurisdiction over parties who have formed a relationship to that state. By contrast, under the Fifth Amendment a defendant need only have an appropriate relationship to the United States — such as being found or domiciled in the United States or having minimum contacts here that give rise to the claim — in order to be subject to personal jurisdiction in a federal court. Thus, it is generally held that Congress has the power to authorize federal courts to exercise nationwide jurisdiction, that is, to require parties with contacts anywhere in the United States to respond to suits brought in any federal district court. See generally R. Casad, Personal Jurisdiction in Federal Question Cases, 70 Tex. L. Rev. 1589, 1599-1606 (1992).[2]

---

2. A frequent argument in support of this conclusion is that Congress did not have to create separate federal courts in each state. It might have created regional courts or a single court located at the seat of the federal government. Had Congress taken this course, it would obviously have been necessary to authorize such a court to exercise broad jurisdiction over defendants from all over the country. Since such nationwide jurisdiction might well have been necessary, it would be incongruous to hold that it is constitutionally impermissible.

In some types of actions Congress *has* authorized nationwide jurisdiction in the federal courts through special jurisdictional provisions governing particular types of actions. An example is 28 U.S.C. §2361, which authorizes nationwide service in interpleader actions. Unless such a special provision applies, however, the authority for federal courts to exercise personal jurisdiction over out-of-state defendants is restricted by the Federal Rules of Civil Procedure. Under Fed. R. Civ. P. 4(k)(1)(A), a federal court is authorized to exercise jurisdiction over a defendant "who is subject to the jurisdiction of a court of general jurisdiction in the state where the district court is located." In other words, the federal court may exercise personal jurisdiction only to the extent it could be exercised by the courts of the state in which the federal court sits. Thus, if Gable sues Leigh in federal court in California, and Congress has not authorized broader jurisdiction for the type of suit involved, the court will only exercise personal jurisdiction over Leigh if the California courts could do so under the California long-arm statute and the due process clause of the Fourteenth Amendment.

This is really a very sensible rule. By generally confining the reach of personal jurisdiction in the federal court to that of the state courts of the same state, the Rules eliminate a potential ground for "forum-shopping" based on purely procedural considerations. As indicated above, in many cases plaintiffs will have a choice of state or federal court because both systems have subject matter jurisdiction over the suit. If the reach of personal jurisdiction were generally broader in federal court, plaintiffs would frequently choose to bring suit there for this reason alone, even though state court would otherwise be a more appropriate forum.

The following examples should help you sort out these related concepts. Assume in all cases that the relevant state long-arm statute authorizes exercise of all constitutionally permissible jurisdiction. See the California statute, supra p. 26.

## Examples

### Distinctions and Differences

1. Stewart, a California citizen, wishes to sue Cagney, also a Californian, for battery, to recover for injuries he suffered in a fight between them on a Los Angeles street. Stewart prefers to sue Cagney in California.

---

See, e.g., *Briggs v. Goodwin*, 569 F.2d 1, 8-10 (1st Cir. 1977), rev'd on other grounds sub nom. *Stafford v. Briggs*, 444 U.S. 527 (1980).

There may be limits to this; some courts have held that the Fifth Amendment, like the Fourteenth, includes a basic fairness requirement which may restrict the places where defendants can be required to defend a federal action. See, e.g., *Peay v. BellSouth Medical Assistance Plan*, 205 F.3d 1206, 1211-1213 (10th Cir. 2000). Even if so, however, it will probably be the unusual case where a court would reject jurisdiction on this basis. Id. at 1212-1213.

    a. Would a California state court have personal jurisdiction over Cagney?

    b. Would a California federal court have personal jurisdiction over Cagney?

    c. Would a California state court have subject matter jurisdiction over the action?

    d. Would a California federal court have subject matter jurisdiction over the action?

2. Assume that Cagney is from New York and that he attacked Stewart while visiting California to make a movie. Stewart, a California citizen, prefers to sue Cagney in California.

    a. Would the California state court have personal jurisdiction over Cagney?

    b. Would the California federal court have personal jurisdiction over Cagney?

    c. Would a California state court have subject matter jurisdiction over the action?

    d. Would a California federal court have subject matter jurisdiction over the action?

3. On the facts of example 2, could Stewart have sued Cagney in either a state or federal court in New York?

4. On the facts of example 2, could Stewart have sued Cagney in either a state or federal court in Nevada?

## Variations

5. One more variation on the facts of example 2: Assume that after the Los Angeles battery but before Stewart brings suit, Cagney moves to California.

    a. May Stewart sue him in federal court in California?

    b. May Stewart sue him in a New York state court?

6. Colbert sues Hepburn in the federal district court for the Southern District of California for breach of a contract to star in a movie. Both parties are domiciled in New York, the contract was entered into there, and the movie was to be made there. However, Colbert prefers to sue in California, where she is currently working, and also prefers to sue in federal court. Hepburn, who is currently working in Arizona, does not object to the California court hearing the case. May it do so?

7. Colbert, a New Yorker, sues Kojak for a violation of her federal civil rights. Suit is brought under 42 U.S.C. §1983, the federal statute that authorizes suit for such violations. The claim arises out of an unlawful arrest that took place in New York. Kojak is also domiciled in New York.

    a. May Colbert bring the suit in a New York state court?

    b. May she bring the suit in a California federal court?

    c. Assume, on the same facts, that Colbert is from California. Could she bring the action in a California federal court?

8. May Colbert sue Hepburn in a New York state court for violation of a copyright she holds on a book about the golden age of the movies? See 28 U.S.C. §1338(a).

## Explanations

## Distinctions and Differences

1. a. The California state court will have personal jurisdiction over Cagney on several bases. First, the California court may exercise personal jurisdiction over Cagney on the basis of his California domicile. Domicile in the forum state has been held an adequate basis for asserting personal jurisdiction, even if the claim sued upon did not arise in the state. *Milliken v. Meyer*, 311 U.S. 457 (1940). A person who has chosen the state as his domicile may fairly be said to have submitted himself generally to the judicial power of that state's courts, as a quid pro quo for enjoying the benefits and protections of living within the state.

    In addition, Cagney has (allegedly) committed an in-state tortious act by assaulting Stewart in California. Virtually every state's long-arm statute authorizes personal jurisdiction over defendants for claims arising out of torts committed within the state, and this assertion of jurisdiction is clearly constitutional under *International Shoe*. Where Cagney has entered the state and consciously committed an act intended to harm Stewart in California, it is both fair and foreseeable to require him to respond to a California suit arising out of those in-state acts. See Chapter 2, example 3.

    b. As stated in the introduction, the federal district courts' reach of personal jurisdiction is restricted in most cases to that of the courts of the state. Under Fed. R. Civ. P. 4(k)(1)(A), the federal court first looks to the statutes or court rules governing personal jurisdiction in the state where the federal court sits. For example, the Idaho federal court will look to the Idaho long-arm statute. If the statute authorizes the assertion of jurisdiction and such an exercise of jurisdiction would not exceed the Fourteenth Amendment due process limits on *state* court jurisdiction, then the federal court will have personal jurisdiction. Similarly, the California federal court will look to the California jurisdiction statutes as well as the constitutional limits on state court jurisdiction. Since the California state court will have personal jurisdiction over Cagney, the federal court will too.

One interesting consequence of this rule is that the reach of personal jurisdiction may vary from one federal court to another because each exercises jurisdiction to the extent permitted in the state in which it sits, and the reach of long-arm statutes varies from state to state.

c. Every state court system has a set of courts that has broad subject matter jurisdiction over state law claims, including battery claims. These courts of "general jurisdiction" are the workhorses of the state court systems, the basic trial courts for most types of claims. In California they are called the superior courts, and their jurisdiction includes tort claims such as the battery alleged in *Stewart v. Cagney*. Note that the analysis here for subject matter jurisdiction focuses on the nature of the case Stewart is asserting, rather than the relationship of the underlying events to the state of California, as in the personal jurisdiction analysis.

d. The California federal district court will not have subject matter jurisdiction over this case. The federal courts are not courts of general jurisdiction, but are limited to the types of cases listed in Article III, §2, and the federal statutes, such as 28 U.S.C. §§1331 and 1332, which confer this subject matter jurisdiction on the federal courts. Because nothing in Article III grants federal courts jurisdiction over battery cases, Stewart's suit may not be properly brought in federal court.

It is true that cases involving state claims, such as battery, negligence, or breach of contract may be brought in federal court if there is diversity between the parties. The Framers, in their wisdom, saw fit to allow even cases based on state theories of recovery to be brought in federal court, if the parties are from different states. But here they are not, so there is no basis for federal subject matter jurisdiction. Only the California state court has both personal and subject matter jurisdiction over Stewart's suit; if venue is also proper, it may proceed to hear the case.

2. a. On these facts Cagney is not subject to personal jurisdiction in California on the basis of his domicile, but the minimum contacts analysis in example 1a remains unchanged. Cagney has still committed a tortious act in California, which is likely to injure Stewart there. He will be subject to specific in personam jurisdiction there for suits arising out of this in-state conduct. Even though it may be extremely inconvenient for Cagney to return to California to defend the action, under due process analysis the California court may require him to do so.

b. As suggested above, the federal court under Fed. R. Civ. P. 4(k)(1)(A) will exercise personal jurisdiction to the same extent as the state court. Since the California state court may require Cagney to return and defend, the federal court may as well.

c. The answer here is the same as example 1c: The California superior court is a court of general subject matter jurisdiction that may hear tort claims. Thus, as in example 1, the California state court satisfies both rings; if venue is proper, it may hear this case.

d. It is still true, as in example 1d, that the federal courts have no subject matter jurisdiction over battery cases because nothing in Article III bestows jurisdiction over common law tort claims on the federal courts. However, Article III, §2, does authorize federal courts to hear cases between citizens of different states, regardless of the nature of the underlying dispute between them, and Congress has conferred that jurisdiction on the federal district courts in 28 U.S.C. §1332, subject to the amount-in-controversy requirement. Because Cagney and Stewart are diverse in this example, the federal court has subject matter jurisdiction over the suit between them if Stewart seeks more than $75,000 in damages. So here, too, the two rings intersect: Stewart may choose a California state or federal court for this suit, assuming he can satisfy the third ring, venue, in both courts.

3. Stewart may sue Cagney in state or federal court in New York. Here, there is no minimum contacts basis for personal jurisdiction, but Cagney is subject to personal jurisdiction there because New York is his domicile. When jurisdiction is based on domicile it is irrelevant that the cause of action did not arise there. Thus, the state courts in New York may exercise personal jurisdiction over him, and a New York federal court may do so as well, under Fed. R. Civ. P. 4(k)(1)(A).

Subject matter jurisdiction is also proper in the state court in New York. The state trial courts of New York, the inaptly named supreme courts, have broad subject matter jurisdiction, including battery cases. That does not mean "battery cases arising in New York," but battery cases *as a class*. Thus, it does not matter for subject matter jurisdiction purposes that this battery took place in California.

The federal district court in New York also has subject matter jurisdiction based on diversity since Stewart and Cagney are still diverse. Note that Cagney's New York domicile is essential to establish a basis for personal jurisdiction over him in this case. For subject matter jurisdiction, however, he need only be domiciled in some state other than California. The fact that he happens to be domiciled in the state where suit is brought is not essential for establishing diversity. Forty-eight other states would do as well.

4. If Stewart sues in Nevada, the subject matter analysis is the same as example 3. Nevada's trial level courts (called district courts) have broad

subject matter jurisdiction, including tort claims. Further, the federal district court in Nevada will have diversity jurisdiction over this case; Stewart and Cagney are just as diverse there as they are anywhere else.

The personal jurisdiction analysis differs from example 3, however, because Cagney has no minimum contacts with Nevada that gave rise to this claim, and he is not domiciled there. Absent consent or service of process on Cagney in Nevada, neither the Nevada state court nor the federal court sitting in that state will have the power to require Cagney to come to Nevada to defend this particular suit. Here, Stewart will come up at least one ring short.

Note, in particular, that the existence of diversity here does not substitute for personal jurisdiction; diversity is a separate requirement for a separate purpose. To rephrase the old song, you *can* have one without the other.

## Variations

5. a. Personal jurisdiction would be proper in this case based on minimum contacts analysis and Rule 4(k)(1)(A), but subject matter jurisdiction is not. Cagney and Stewart were diverse at the time of the events giving rise to the suit. However, as a result of Cagney's move, they are no longer diverse when suit is brought. Because the relevant date for determining diversity is the date suit is filed (*Smith v. Sperling*, 354 U.S. 91, 93 n.1 (1957)), there is no diversity. Nor is there a federal claim or other basis for federal subject matter jurisdiction.

   b. The New York state court would have subject matter jurisdiction since it has broad jurisdiction over common law claims, but personal jurisdiction is not proper. The claim arises out of events that took place in California. Because the claim is unrelated to New York, the only possible basis for personal jurisdiction is Cagney's domicile. Cagney was domiciled in New York at the time of the assault but is not at the time of suit.

   The rationale for allowing a state to exercise personal jurisdiction on the basis of domicile is that a party living in the state is so integrally related to the state that it is fair to require him to appear in its courts. *Milliken v. Meyer*, 311 U.S. at 463. In addition, it is unlikely to be inconvenient to defend in the state of one's domicile. This rationale suggests that domicile jurisdiction should require domicile at the time of suit, not at the time of the events that led to the suit. See *Nicholas v. Inglimo*, 421 N.E.2d 1014, 1016-1017 (Ill. App. 1981) (taking this view). Assuming the New York court takes this approach, it will dismiss for lack of personal jurisdiction over Cagney.

   Minimum contacts (specific in personam) jurisdiction provides an interesting contrast. Cagney could be required to return to defend a California suit arising out of the assault there, even if he has had no contact with California since then. The rationale underlying minimum contacts jurisdiction is that performing certain acts in a state carries with it predictable consequences, including a duty to return to defend those acts in court. The defendant cannot avoid those consequences by subsequently avoiding the state. If he could, minimum contacts jurisdiction would be meaningless.

6. This example highlights an important distinction between personal and subject matter jurisdiction. The California court lacks any basis for personal jurisdiction over Hepburn on this claim, which arose in New York. However, personal jurisdiction is deemed a privilege of the defendant, which will be waived if she fails to assert it. *Rauch v. Day & Night Manufacturing Corp.*, 576 F.2d 697, 701 (6th Cir. 1978). Consequently, a court that lacks personal jurisdiction may still hear the case if the defendant does not object. Because Hepburn is willing to litigate the claim in California, she will presumably waive her objection by failing to raise it. See Fed. R. Civ. P. 12(b)(2), (g)(1), (h)(1).

However, the California federal court also lacks subject matter jurisdiction over this action. Nothing in Article III, §2, or the federal jurisdictional statutes gives the federal courts jurisdiction over state contract claims between nondiverse citizens. Hepburn's willingness to have the federal court hear the case is irrelevant: The parties cannot confer subject matter jurisdiction on the court. Subject matter jurisdiction allocates governmental power among different tribunals. That allocation is made by the Constitution and Congress, not by the parties. Consequently, even if neither party objects to the federal court hearing the case, it will refuse to do so. See Fed. R. Civ. P. 12(h)(3).

7. a. This suit is proper in state court in New York. Personal jurisdiction is satisfied because the claim arises out of alleged deprivation of rights taking place in New York. Under the minimum contacts test, Kojak could fairly be required to defend a suit arising out of these in-state acts in a New York court. In addition, he is subject to personal jurisdiction in New York on the basis of his domicile in the state.

Subject matter jurisdiction is also proper in the New York state court, even though this is a case arising under federal law. As a rule, the general trial courts of each state have subject matter jurisdiction over almost any kind of case, unless it has been exclusively delegated to a specialized state court or (for some cases within the federal subject matter jurisdiction) to the federal courts. Even though federal civil rights cases arise under federal law and are therefore properly brought in federal court under 28 U.S.C. §1331, Congress has not made federal jurisdiction over such cases exclusive. Consequently, the state courts also have jurisdiction to hear such claims.

b. Because the case arises under federal law, the California federal court will have subject matter jurisdiction. 28 U.S.C. §1331. However, the federal court will not exercise personal jurisdiction if the California state court could not do so. Fed. R. Civ. P. 4(k)(1)(A). Here, the claim does not arise out of any contacts with the state of California. The California courts therefore lack personal jurisdiction over Kojak (absent some other basis such as in-state service or consent), since there are no "minimum contacts" among the claim, Kojak, and the forum state.

c. Moving Colbert's domicile to California creates some distinctions from the prior case, but distinctions without any relevant difference. Colbert's California domicile would be an adequate basis for personal jurisdiction over her, were she the defendant, but it does not alter the due process requirement that the defendant, the party being unwillingly haled before the court, must have minimum contacts with the state that is doing so. Kojak lacks any such contacts, at least for this claim. Personal jurisdiction is therefore lacking.

The other difference here is that the parties in this case are diverse. This gives the court an alternative source of subject matter jurisdiction (which is unnecessary, since it is a federal-question case anyway), but it is irrelevant to personal jurisdiction. Innumerable first-year exam answers not withstanding, diversity is not a substitute for personal jurisdiction.

8. Although the general rule is that the federal and state courts have concurrent jurisdiction over cases arising under federal law, Congress may make federal court jurisdiction over cases within Article III exclusive. Wright & Miller §3527. It has done so for copyright cases, presumably because of the specialized nature of these suits and the national scope of the protection conferred by the copyright laws. See 28 U.S.C. §1338(a). Consequently, the state court lacks subject matter jurisdiction over this case.

# Second-Guessing the Plaintiff's Choice of Forum

## Removal

---

# INTRODUCTION

The traditional rule in American courts has been, and largely still is, that the plaintiff chooses the forum in which to bring a suit, subject to the limitations of personal jurisdiction, subject matter jurisdiction, and venue. He may choose the geographical place of suit by suing in the courts of the state he prefers. And, assuming proper subject matter jurisdiction, he may also choose the court system in which to litigate by starting the action in either a federal or state court.[1] In this respect, and in others, it is said that "the plaintiff is master of his claim."

Removal is an exception to this rule, however. The federal removal statutes allow the defendant, after the plaintiff has chosen a state court, to "second-guess" that choice by "removing" some types of cases from the state court to a federal court. Once properly removed the case becomes a federal case, and the state court loses jurisdiction over it. Both pretrial litigation and trial will take place in the federal court.

The rationale for removal is that defendants as well as plaintiffs should have the option to choose federal court for cases within the federal jurisdiction. That jurisdiction is intended to protect both parties, and therefore, both parties should have access to it. If a federal court is particularly qualified to decide cases arising under federal law, then a

---

1. As Chapter 6 explains, the state and federal courts will frequently both have subject matter jurisdiction over a case. See pp. 111-113.

defendant should be able to ask it to do so, just as a plaintiff may. Similarly, if an out-of-state defendant may suffer prejudice from litigating in a state court, he should have the same right as an out-of-state plaintiff to avoid that prejudice by invoking federal diversity jurisdiction.

A natural corollary of this rationale is that removal jurisdiction should be available to the defendant only in cases that the plaintiff could have commenced in federal court. Removal is not meant to expand federal jurisdiction but merely to make it available to defendants. Therefore, 28 U.S.C. §1441(a) only authorizes removal of state court actions "of which the district courts of the United States have original jurisdiction." If the plaintiff could not have chosen to bring the action in federal court initially, the defendant cannot remove it. For example, if Oakley sues Cody, a fellow Kansan, on a state law contract claim, she could not sue in federal court, since there is neither diversity nor a federal question. Consequently, if she sues Cody in state court, her action against Cody will not be removable. By contrast, if she sued Cody in state court under a federal age discrimination statute, or if they were citizens of different states, Cody could remove because Oakley could have chosen to sue him on that claim in federal court.

A caution is in order here, however. Some cases are not removable *even though* the plaintiff could have brought them in federal court originally. In particular, 28 U.S.C. §1441(b) provides that a diversity case is only removable if "none of the parties in interest properly joined and served as defendants is a citizen of the State in which such action is brought." In other words, if a defendant is sued in his home state, he may not remove on the basis of diversity. If Pike, from Nevada, sues Cody, from Kansas, on a state law claim in Kansas state court, Cody cannot remove. The rationale for this exception is that Cody has no need to be protected from local prejudice, since he has been sued in his own home state.

Interestingly, there is no explicit authority in the Constitution for snatching cases out of the hands of state courts by removal to federal court. Yet the First Congress provided for removal in the Judiciary Act of 1789, and it has been with us in one form or another ever since. The courts have consistently upheld the constitutionality of the removal procedure. See Wright & Miller, §3721. Because removal only applies to cases that could have been brought *originally* in federal court, there seems little constitutional distinction between allowing the plaintiff to choose the federal court in a case within the federal court's jurisdiction and allowing the defendant to do so by removing a state court action.[2]

Traditionally, removal jurisdiction depended not only on the scope of original federal jurisdiction, but also on the jurisdiction of the state court

---

2. However, §1441(c), the enigmatic provision for removal of "separate and independent" claims, may be an exception to this principle. See L. Teply and R. Whitten, Civil Procedure, 3rd ed. 2004, 165-166 (noting cases that question constitutionality of §1441(c)).

from which it was removed. The federal court's removal jurisdiction was said to be "derivative" (Moore's Federal Practice, §107.14[3][a][iv]) of the state court's. Thus, removal jurisdiction was only proper if the removed case was properly before the state court to begin with. For example, if Butterfield brought a patent infringement action in state court, it could not be removed because the federal courts have exclusive jurisdiction over patent cases. 28 U.S.C. §1338(a). Thus, because only the federal court had jurisdiction, it had to dismiss the case when it was removed to federal court! However, if Butterfield was not too bewildered to press on (and if the statute of limitations had not passed), he could bring an *original* action on the patent claim in federal court.

This long-standing but impractical rule was changed by statute in 1986. Congress added §1441(e) (subsequently renumbered as §1441(f)) to the removal statute, which provides that the federal court is not precluded from hearing the case simply because the state court lacked jurisdiction over it. Thus, a case like Butterfield's would now be removable, despite the fact that the state court had no power to hear his patent claim. Clearly, however, §1441(f) does not change the requirement that the case be within *federal* jurisdiction to be removable. Section 1441(a) still requires that.

Even if a state court case satisfies the jurisdictional requirements for removal, there are drastic limits as to which court it may be removed *to*. You can't remove to another state court or to a state court in a different state. You can't remove to a federal court in another state or even in another district in the same state. There is only one lonely court that can host a removed action: the federal district court "for the district and division embracing the place where such action is pending [in the state court]." 28 U.S.C. §1441(a). For example, Figure 7-1 shows the configuration of the four federal districts in Texas. Each federal district spans a number of counties. Cases filed in any county within that district will be removed to that district. If Pike sued Cody in the District Court for Lipscomb County (the Texas *state* court of general jurisdiction, even though it is confusingly called a "district" court), the action would be removed to the federal district court for the Northern District of Texas. If he sued in Dimmit County, it would be removed to the Western District of Texas, and so on.[3] Thus, removal only partially displaces the plaintiff's choice of forum: He still gets to choose the state where the action will be litigated, even if he ends up in federal court in that state due to removal by the defendant.

---

3. Of course, the federal court may well sit in a city some distance from the place where the state court action was filed. For example, the Texas District Court for Lipscomb County sits in Lipscomb, Texas. If Cody removes his case from that court to the federal district court for the Northern District of Texas, however, court hearings will take place in Amarillo, where the Amarillo Division of the federal court for the Northern District sits, some 130 miles from Lipscomb.

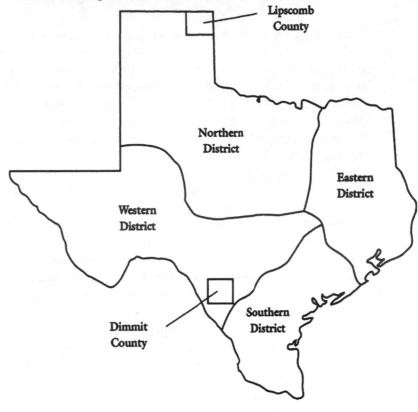

**Figure 7-1.** Federal districts — Texas.

The usual federal venue rules do not apply in removed actions. A case that is removable must be removed to the "district and division embracing the place where such action is pending" (§1441(a)), even if that federal district would not have been a proper venue under 28 U.S.C. §1391 if the case had been brought in federal court initially. In the *Schulansky* case (see Part VI), for example, Ronan may only remove to the District of Massachusetts because the Plymouth County Superior Court, where the suit was initiated, falls within that district. Even if the District of Massachusetts would not have been a proper venue if Schulansky started her suit in federal court, it is the proper district when Ronan removes it on these facts.

It may be helpful to compare removal under §1441 with transfer of venue under 28 U.S.C. §1404(a). Section 1404(a) provides for geographical transfer from one district court within the federal system to another in a different state or district. See Jones's motion to transfer venue from the District of Massachusetts to the District of New Hampshire in the

*Schulansky* case, infra Chapter 35. Removal, by contrast, authorizes transfer from the state court system to the federal court system within the same state. Transfer displaces the plaintiff's geographical choice for litigation, while removal displaces the plaintiff's choice of the state court system in favor of a federal court within the same geographical area. It may even be possible to use both devices in a single suit. For a case that was removed and then transferred (and then dismissed for forum non conveniens!), see *Piper Aircraft Co. v. Reyno,* 454 U.S. 235 (1981).

The general removal statute applies to cases, not claims: When the defendant properly removes a suit to federal court, the defendant's entire suit is removed, including not only the specific claim that gives rise to removal jurisdiction, but also any related claims that the federal court has the power to hear under supplemental jurisdiction. Suppose, for example, that Colter sues Bridger (a citizen of the same state) for violation of Colter's federal civil rights (a claim based on federal law, which state courts as well as federal courts may hear) and asserts a claim for relief on a state law battery theory as well. If Bridger removes, the federal court acquires jurisdiction of the entire action, including the civil rights claim that provides the basis for federal court jurisdiction and the supplemental state law claim. Neither the plaintiff nor the defendant can dissect a single case and send only parts of it to the federal forum.[4] In addition, remember that removal is a one-way street: A defendant who is properly sued in federal court cannot remove to state court.

After removal, a case proceeds in federal court under the Federal Rules. See Fed. R. Civ. P. 81(c). Essentially, that court picks up the ball in mid-air and continues to juggle it. The state court complaint and answer (if one has been filed before removal) will be filed with the notice of removal. 28 U.S.C. §1446(a). See the notice of removal in *Schulansky v. Ronan,* infra p. 653. The court may order the parties to file discovery material and other filings from the state court in the federal court for use in the action. 28 U.S.C. §1447(b). If the state court has entered any orders prior to removal, such as a preliminary injunction or a protective order concerning discovery, those orders remain in effect in the federal court, unless modified by the federal judge. 28 U.S.C. §1450. It's a little like the Red Sox being whisked out of Fenway Park to Dodger Stadium in the second inning and being told to just finish the game under the National League rules.

The following examples illustrate the substantive limits on removal jurisdiction. The second set of examples deals with removal procedure. For purposes of this chapter, I have stubbornly ignored the murky mysteries of §1441(c), dealing with removal of certain "separate and independent"

---

4. However, the federal court may, in its discretion, remand or dismiss supplemental state law claims in appropriate cases. See 28 U.S.C. §1367(c); *United Mine Workers v. Gibbs,* 383 U.S. 715, 726-727 (1966); *Carnegie-Mellon University v. Cohill,* 484 U.S. 343 (1988).

claims. You should do the same in analyzing the examples. Also, where it is relevant, assume that the amount-in-controversy requirement is met.

## Examples

### The Power to Remove

1. Earp, from Kansas, sues Dillon, also a Kansan, in a state court in Kansas. His claim is based on a violation of his federal civil rights. May Dillon remove?

2. Suppose Earp (still from Kansas) sues Carson, from Colorado, in the Colorado state court on a state law assault claim. May Carson remove?

3. Assume the same facts as example 2, but Earp sues a second defendant, Hickok, as well. Hickok is from Missouri. Can the defendants remove?

4. Consider the same facts again, with another twist: Earp, from Kansas, sues Carson (Colorado) and Hickok (Missouri) on the assault claims in a Kansas state court. Can the defendants remove?

5. Chester, from Iowa, sues Carson, a Coloradan, and James, a Kansan, in Kansas state court on a federal civil rights claim.
   a. May the defendants remove?
   b. If so, to which court or courts?

6. Recall that old chestnut case, *Louisville and Nashville R.R. v. Mottley*, 219 U.S. 467 (1911), in which the Supreme Court dismissed for lack of subject matter jurisdiction because the federal question in the case arose as a defense. Suppose that the plaintiffs in that case sued the (nondiverse) railroad in the state court for breach of contract. Ten days later the railroad answered, raising the defense that the federal statute precludes it from renewing the Mottleys' passes. Ten days after answering, the railroad removes the case to federal court. Is removal proper?

### Some Refinements

7. Suppose, on the facts of example 4, that Carson wants to remove, but Hickok likes the state court. Can Carson remove the case? See 28 U.S.C. §1441(a).

8. Earp sues James, a fellow Kansan, on a state law assault claim. Six months later Earp's lawyer decides, on the basis of his further knowledge of the case gleaned from discovery, that Earp also has a claim against James for a federal civil rights violation arising out of the same facts. Earp amends to assert the federal claim. May James now remove?

9. Earp, a Kansan, sues Bean, a Texan, on a state law abuse-of-process claim in an Iowa state court. Bean removes to federal court. Subsequently, Earp

amends to add James, a fellow Kansan, as a second defendant. Should the federal court remand the case to state court? See 28 U.S.C. §1447(e).

10. On the facts of example 9, suppose that Earp (Kansas) has claims against Bean (Texas) and James (Kansas) for abuse of process arising from the same incident. Earp deliberately decides to sue them jointly in a single action in state court in order to avoid removal to federal court. Is this permissible? Will it work?

11. Suppose that Earp, a Kansan, has a claim against Bean, from Texas, for abuse of process. For tactical reasons, Earp is anxious to avoid federal court. He recognizes that, if he sues a Kansan along with Bean, there will not be complete diversity, so the case will not be removable. Therefore, he sues James, from Kansas, as a co-defendant with Bean in the suit. James is a colleague of Bean's, but really had almost nothing to do with the misuse of legal procedure that underlies Earp's abuse of process claim. Earp realizes that he will not be able to establish a claim against James, but that's all right; his real agenda isn't to recover from James, but to avoid federal court. Will this ploy work?

12. Suppose, on the facts of example 9, that Earp sues Bean in state court. Anticipating removal, Earp seeks only $70,000 in damages, leaving out a demand for certain consequential damages worth $8,000. May Bean remove?

13. James sues Earp, his fellow Kansan, on an assault claim. Earp counterclaims for damages for violation of his federal civil rights, arising out of the same encounter. See Fed. R. Civ. P. 13(a). Does §1441 allow James to remove?

## Unlucky Number 14

14. Dillon (a Kansan) sues Greeley (a New Yorker) for $90,000 for breach of contract. Dillon claims that he had contracted with Greeley to allow Greeley to manufacture electrical circuits upon which Dillon held a patent. In return, Greeley agreed to pay Dillon royalties but has failed to do so. Dillon also claims that Greeley, by making the circuits covered by his patent, has committed patent infringement. Suit is brought in state court in Kansas. Greeley removes.
    a. If the suit had been brought prior to 1986, how would this case have been resolved?
    b. How would it be resolved under current removal law?

# THE PROCEDURE FOR REMOVAL

The procedure for removal, set forth in §1446, is relatively straightforward. The defendant (or defendants) must file a notice of removal in the appropriate federal district court, together with all pleadings, process, and other papers on file in the state action. 28 U.S.C. §1446 (a). The notice must be filed within 30 days of receiving the plaintiff's pleading in the state suit. 28 U.S.C. §1446(b). Once the notice is filed and the state court is notified, the state court loses control of the case automatically. It may not proceed with discovery, try the case, or issue orders to the parties. 28 U.S.C. §1446(d). The *Schulansky* case in Part VI provides a full example of the removal process. See Chapter 32.

Although the state court loses power over the case once it has been removed, the removal decision is not irrevocable. If the plaintiff contends that the case is not within the federal court's subject matter jurisdiction, or that the defendant has not properly followed the requirements of removal procedure, his recourse is to move in the federal court to remand the case back to state court. If the basis for the motion is failure to comply with the procedural requirements (such as failure of all defendants to join in the notice, or failure to remove within the thirty day period), the remand motion must be made within thirty days after removal, or the objection is waived. 28 U.S.C. §1447(c). A motion to remand on the basis of lack of subject matter jurisdiction, however, may be made at any time prior to final judgment in the case. Id.

This procedure, under which removal automatically moves the case to federal court, prevents any confusion as to which court has jurisdiction to proceed: Even if the federal court has no jurisdiction, the state court loses power to proceed. That way, the decision as to whether the federal court has jurisdiction over the case will be made, quite properly, by the federal court when the plaintiff challenges its jurisdiction by moving to remand. If that court lacks jurisdiction, it will remand the case to the state court, which will once more pick up the ball and run with it.

In many cases, the right to remove will not be clear from the face of the complaint. For example, most states do not require the plaintiff to allege the citizenship of the parties because state court jurisdiction does not depend upon it. Compare Fed. R. Civ P. 8(a)(1); see p. 641. Thus, a defendant who claims the right to remove on the ground of diversity may have to ascertain the citizenship of the plaintiff and allege in his notice of removal that diversity exists. Section 1446(a) explicitly allows the removing defendant to allege in the notice of removal any facts necessary to demonstrate the grounds for removing the suit.

## Examples

### Some Technicalities

15. Chester, an Iowa citizen, sues Holiday, of Kansas, for malpractice in a leg operation. Suit is brought in an Iowa state court. His complaint does not state a dollar demand for relief (some states don't require it; others don't even allow it). Holiday wants to remove. Can he?

16. Long Branch Saloons, a corporation, sues Holiday (a Kansan) in Nebraska to collect $90,000 in rent due on Holiday's offices above its saloon in Dodge City, Kansas. The state court complaint makes no allegation about Long Branch's principal place of business. Several months later Holiday discovers, much to his surprise, that the Long Branch saloon in Dodge City is the smallest of three such establishments run by Long Branch. Its principal place of business and state of incorporation is Colorado. Holiday removes on the basis of diversity. Can he do so?

17. Assume that James sues Earp, and Earp removes the suit within 30 days. However, James disputes the right to remove since he claims that his action is based on state law rather than federal law.
    a. James moves in the state court to have the case remanded for lack of removal jurisdiction. The court agrees that removal was improper. What should it do?
    b. James moves for remand in the federal court. That court agrees that removal was improper. What should it do?

18. Masterson (Nebraska) sues Hickok (Missouri), Earp (Kansas), and Bean (Texas) for assault, arising out of a fight at a corral. He serves the complaint and summons on Hickok on June 1 and Earp on June 15. As of June 25 Bean has not yet been served. If Earp wants to remove, what should he do?

19. Assume on the facts of example 18 that Earp and Hickok remove the case on June 27. On July 12 Bean is served. If he prefers state court, does he have any recourse? Should he?

### Hoist with His Own Petard

20. Masterson sues Hickok, Earp and Bean in state court. The defendants file a notice of removal in federal district court. Six weeks later, Masterson's counsel examines the docket and determines that the notice of removal was filed on the thirty-third day after service of the complaint. He moves to remand the case on the ground that the case was not removed within the thirty-day period for removal in 28 U.S.C. s. 1446(b). What should the court do?

## A Final, Fundamental Point

21. Chester (Iowa) sues Holiday (Kansas) in an Iowa state court. Holiday removes. Three days later Holiday moves to dismiss the case, on the ground that the court lacks personal jurisdiction over him. Is this motion permissible?

## Explanations

### The Power to Remove

1. Earp has asserted a right to relief under federal law. Had he chosen to do so, he could have commenced this case in federal court under 28 U.S.C. §1331. Thus, the case satisfies the requirement of §1441(a) that the federal courts have original jurisdiction over the action (or, more accurately, *would* have had original jurisdiction over it had it been brought in federal court).

    However, §1441(b) must also be considered since it places some further restrictions on removal jurisdiction. That section does not restrict removal of Earp's suit. It provides that cases "founded on a claim or right arising under the Constitution, treaties or laws of the United States shall be removable without regard to the citizenship or residence of the parties." Since Earp's claim is based on a federal question, it is irrelevant that the parties are not diverse and that there is an in-state defendant in the action. Removal is proper.

2. This is a straightforward diversity case. A federal district court would have original jurisdiction over the case, but this illustrates the situation in which the federal courts' removal jurisdiction is narrower than their original jurisdiction. Section 1441(b) provides that actions based on diversity ("[a]ny other such action") cannot be removed if any defendant is from the forum state. Under this provision Carson is barred from removing this case.

    The logic behind this limitation is that diversity jurisdiction was intended to protect out-of-state parties from local prejudice, so there is no need to extend it to cases where suit is brought in the defendant's home state. Of course, that rationale would support a similar restriction on *original* diversity jurisdiction in the plaintiff's home state, but there is no such restriction. Logic has its limits.

3. This example makes one narrow point: §1441(b) precludes removal of a diversity case if *any* defendant is from the state where the state court action is brought ("only if none of the parties . . ."). Carson is still in the case; ergo, no removal. Here again, Earp could have initiated the action in federal court as a diversity action in Colorado or elsewhere, but removal is narrower.

4. Moving the case back to Kansas changes the result. The case is still within the federal court's diversity jurisdiction, but now no defendant is from the forum state, so they may remove despite §1441(b). Note that this configuration, with the Kansas plaintiff using the Kansas state courts to recover from two non-Kansas defendants, presents the strongest risk of prejudice to the defendants and therefore is the best candidate for removal jurisdiction.

5. a. This case, like that in example 1, is a federal question case and is still removable as such. Here, however, there is also diversity of citizenship, a separate basis for federal jurisdiction. The interpretive problem raised is whether it is removable "without regard to the citizenship or residence of the parties" (§1441(b)) where there is both a claim under federal law and diversity. If not, removal would be barred due to the presence of an in-state defendant, James. The answer is "yes"; the case may be removed because it is just as squarely founded on a claim under federal law when there is diversity as when there is not.

   b. Carson would clearly prefer to remove to the Colorado district court, to get the benefit of the home forum. However, removal is not meant to give the defendant a geographical choice of forum, only a choice to use the federal court system. The action can only be removed to the federal district court for the District of Kansas. If there were more than one federal district in Kansas (as there is in Texas, for example), the defendants could only remove the case to the district in which the state court where Chester brought suit is located.

6. On the facts given here, there is no original federal jurisdiction because it is a state law claim between nondiverse parties. Of course, when the railroad answers the complaint in the state court, raising the federal statute as a defense, it becomes clear that a federal issue exists in the case. However, that does not make it a case that "arises under" the laws of the United States. Jurisdiction is determined by looking at the plaintiff's complaint, to determine if he seeks recovery under federal law. See Chapter 4, pp. 70-71. The Mottleys did not. The only difference between this hypo and *Mottley* is that in the hypo we know the railroad relies on a federal defense at the time when removal is sought. But it is a defense, nonetheless, and it does not convert the Mottleys' contract action into a federal question case. Because the federal issue does not arise on the face of the well-pleaded complaint, there is no original federal jurisdiction. Since there is no original jurisdiction, the case cannot be removed.

   A number of commentators have suggested that this rule makes little sense because the assertion of the federal defense clearly indicates that the case involves federal issues. See, e.g., American Law Institute,

Study of the Division of Jurisdiction Between State and Federal Courts §1312(a)(2) and accompanying commentary (1969) (suggesting legislation — never enacted — to authorize removal in such cases).

## Some Refinements

7. The answer to this example depends on the meaning of §1441(a), which provides that the "defendant or defendants" may remove. Although it is not a foregone conclusion from the language of the statute, the courts have held that the alternative reference to the "defendants" means that, in a multi-defendant case, all defendants must agree to remove. See *Chicago, Rock Island & Pacific Railway Co. v. Martin*, 178 U.S. 245 (1900); *Tri-Cities Newspapers, Inc. v. Tri-Cities Printing Pressmen and Assistants' Local 349*, 427 F.2d 325, 326-327 (5th Cir. 1970). Since Hickok will not agree, Carson will be stuck in state court, even though he may be subject to prejudice as an out-of-stater. While this is a reasonable interpretation of the statute, it prevents removal in cases in which the policy underlying diversity jurisdiction — avoiding prejudice against out-of-state defendants — would support it.

8. Again, removal jurisdiction turns on original jurisdiction. In this example, there was no original federal jurisdiction over the case when it was filed; the claim was based on state law and was between nondiverse parties. However, once Earp amends to assert a federal claim, the case looks different. Earp is now relying on federal law as a basis for relief. If the case had been brought in this amended form initially, it would have been removable as a federal question case with a supplemental state law claim.

   The removal statute specifically provides for removal in cases like this, when the case becomes removable after the filing of the original complaint. See 28 U.S.C. §1446(b), second paragraph, which gives the defendant 30 days from the amendment to file a notice of removal. This approach is clearly necessary; otherwise plaintiffs could avoid removal by suing in state court on a state law theory alone and later amending to assert their federal claims.

   Once Earp's case is removed, both the federal claim and the related state assault claim will be heard in the federal court. If the combined action had been brought originally in federal court, the court could have heard the state law claim under principles of supplemental jurisdiction. See Chapter 16, example 1. Consequently, the court may also do so in a removed action.

9. Whatever answer you come up with for this example is troubling. By adding a Kansas defendant after removal, Earp has "destroyed diversity." If he had started this case in federal court and later added James, the

court would have dismissed for lack of subject matter jurisdiction. *Owen Equipment & Erection Co. v. Kroger*, 437 U.S. 365, 373-374 (1978). On the other hand, if Earp can win a remand by this device after Bean removes, it allows Earp to defeat the right to removal by his subsequent choice of defendants, a choice he was not inclined to make until the defendant invoked the removal jurisdiction.

Because the addition of the nondiverse party destroys the basis for subject matter jurisdiction, the court will have to remand the case if it allows the amendment. In some cases, when the amendment was apparently offered for the sole purpose of defeating removal, courts have simply refused to allow the amendment, thus preserving diversity jurisdiction. See, e.g., *Boyd v. Diebold, Inc.*, 97 F.R.D. 720, 722-723 (E.D. Mich. 1983). In other cases, however, in which the nondiverse party was added in good faith for independent reasons (such as efficiency or belated discovery of a claim against the added party), courts have allowed the amendment and then remanded the case to state court under 28 U.S.C. §1447(c). See, e.g., *McIntyre v. Codman & Shurtleff, Inc.*, 103 F.R.D. 619, 621-623 (S.D.N.Y. 1984). In 1988 Congress codified these options by adopting 28 U.S.C. §1447(e), which authorizes the court to refuse the amendment or allow it and remand the case.

10. There is nothing improper in Earp's choice here. It will work, so long as he really has colorable claims against both defendants. The joinder rules in most states allow Earp to choose to sue the defendants together. The fact that he has exercised that option in part to secure his preferred state forum is a permissible form of "forum shopping."

11. Clearly, it should not work . . . indeed, Earp's ploy is itself an abuse of the litigation process. It would very likely violate the pleading rules of the state court in which he has filed suit, as it would the federal pleading rules had it been filed in federal court. Fed. R. Civ. P. 11(b)(2), (3). Such rules generally bar bringing an action against a party if there is no viable claim for relief against that party.[5]

Federal courts have consistently recognized that parties should be disregarded in determining removal jurisdiction if there is no viable claim against them. See, e.g., *Rodriguez v. Sabatino*, 120 F.3d 589, 591-592 (5th Cir. 1997), *cert. denied*, 523 U.S. 1072 (1998); see generally Wright & Miller, s. 3723, at n.80. Thus, Bean should remove the case, and argue that James was fraudulently joined solely to defeat removal. If the court agrees, it will accept removal jurisdiction based on diversity between Earp and Bean (and, presumably, dismiss James from the case).

---

5. Earp's counsel would likely be subject to disciplinary sanctions for such conduct as well. See A.B.A. Model Rules of Prof'l Conduct, R. 3.1 (a lawyer shall not assert an issue in a legal proceeding without a non-frivolous basis for doing so).

As a practical matter, however, it may not be immediately clear to Bean that Earp's claim against *the other defendant*, James, is frivolous. Since he only has thirty days to remove, Bean's counsel will have to be alert to the possibility of removal, investigate the possible claim against James immediately, and prepare a notice of removal that appropriately sets forth the basis for removing a case that appears non-removable on its face — all this within thirty days, while tending to the usual round of events in other cases as well.

12. Here again Earp has structured his lawsuit to prevent removal by seeking damages that do not satisfy the amount-in-controversy requirement of §1332. This is permissible, even if Earp could have sought higher damages. If Earp is willing to pay the price — foregoing his other $8,000 claim — to buy a state forum, he may do so. *St. Paul Indemnity Co. v. Red Cab Co.*, 303 U.S. 283, 294-295 (1938).

13. The issue here is whether a plaintiff can remove. James could not have started in federal court because he had no basis upon which to invoke federal jurisdiction. However, if Earp had started the litigation by suing on the civil rights claim first, James could have removed. Shouldn't James have the same right to remove, whether as the original defendant or as the "defendant" on the counterclaim?

    The Supreme Court says no, as a matter of statutory interpretation. Section 1441 (a) authorizes removal by the "defendant or defendants." In *Shamrock Oil and Gas Corp. v. Sheets*, 313 U.S. 100 (1941), the Court concluded that only the original defendant satisfies this language, so that a plaintiff may not remove under the statute.

## Unlucky Number 14

14. a. Even before 1986, this case would have been removable in part. Dillon's first claim is for breach of contract. True, it is a claim for breach of a contract involving a patent, but the source of the claim is still state contract law. See *Schwartzkopf Development Corp. v. Ti-Coating, Inc.*, 800 F.2d 240, 244 (Fed. Cir. 1986) (contracts for patent royalties have consistently been held to arise under state contract law). Since the parties are diverse and the amount in controversy requirement is met, this part of the case is removable.

    However, the related claim for patent infringement was barred (before 1986) by the "derivative" jurisdiction doctrine. Since Congress has made federal jurisdiction exclusive in patent cases (28 U.S.C. §1338(a)), the state court in which the claim was brought lacked jurisdiction, and the federal court could not acquire jurisdiction of the infringement claim on removal. The federal court would have to dismiss it. Then, presumably, Dillon would have moved to amend the contract action (now in federal court) to add a claim for patent infringement.

b. As the Introduction states, Congress has jettisoned the derivative jurisdiction rule by enacting 28 U.S.C. §1441(f), which provides that the federal court acquires jurisdiction on removal even if the state court where the case was brought lacked the power to hear it. Under §1441(f) the patent claim would be proper in the federal court, so both could proceed. Even if there were no diversity between the parties, there would be supplemental jurisdiction over the contract claim (see Chapter 16), so the federal court would have jurisdiction over the entire action.

## Some Technicalities

15. The problem for Holiday here is that removal turns on original federal jurisdiction, in this case, diversity jurisdiction. The federal court only has diversity jurisdiction if more than $75,000 is in dispute, but the court can't tell from the complaint whether this prerequisite is met, and Holiday must remove within 30 days or waive his right to do so. Section 1446(a) allows the defendant in situations like this to include in his notice of removal any further allegations that are necessary to demonstrate his right to remove. Thus, Holiday could allege in the notice that Chester's claim might support damages in excess of $75,000. Such allegations are subject to the same ethical standards as the allegations in pleadings. See §1446(a) (incorporating by reference the pleading standard in Fed. R. Civ. P. 11).

16. The smart aleck answer to this question is "yes": You can always remove, even if you have no valid ground, by filing a notice of removal, which automatically removes the action whether it is within federal jurisdiction or not. But of course it will be remanded on the plaintiff's motion if that jurisdiction is lacking.

    The problem here, of course, is that the notice of removal was filed after the thirty-day period in 28 U.S.C. §1446(b) had gone by. But . . . Holiday did not know the case was removable at that time. But . . . should he bear the burden to find out if the parties are diverse within the removal period? The cases take the view that the thirty days for removal only commence when the defendant receives a pleading or other paper (such as a response to discovery) from which she should realize that the case is removable. In *Lovern v. General Motors Corp.*, 121 F.3d 160, 161-163 (4th Cir. 1997), for example, the court held that the defendant, who had not initially removed the case, could remove within thirty days of receiving a police report that first put it on notice of the plaintiff's diverse citizenship. See also *Harris v. Bankers Life and Cas.Co.*, 425 F.3d 689 (9th Cir. 2005) (case removable within thirty days after basis for removal manifested in a pleading or other paper). Similarly, some courts have held that the period for removal did not commence until the defendant received actual notice that the required jurisdictional amount was in dispute. See, e.g., *Chapman v. Powermatic, Inc.*, 969 F.2d 160 (5th Cir. 1992). Naturally, if the defendant has grounds to believe the case is removable, the wisest course is to do so, rather than waiting to be sure it is removable

17. a. Although the state court is convinced that it alone has jurisdiction over the case, it can do nothing to help James. Once the case is removed, the state court loses all power over it, even if it was improperly removed. 28 U.S.C. §1446(d).

   b. Here, James has followed the proper procedure for objecting to removal: a motion in the federal court to remand the action to the state court. See 28 U.S.C. §1447(c). The federal court will hear the motion and resolve any factual issues necessary to determine its jurisdiction. If it concludes that jurisdiction is lacking, it will remand the case to state court. Note that it does not *dismiss* the case, but *remands* it. The plaintiff does not have to refile, pay a new fee, or worry about the statute of limitations, since the original suit continues its wobbly way in the state court.

18. The problem here is that §1441(a) has been interpreted to require all defendants to join in the notice of removal. See example 7. Bean has not even been informed of the suit yet. Do the other defendants have to find Bean, tell him the bad news, and convince him to join in removing the case?

   Although it is not entirely clear from the statute, the cases hold that only the defendants actually served need join in the removal. See 28 U.S.C. §1441(b) (referring to "parties in interest properly joined and served as defendants"); 14C Wright & Miller, §3731 at n.26.

19. If all defendants are served at the same time, each will have the power to prevent removal by refusing to join in the removal. In this case, however, Bean finds himself in federal court without having had the chance to forestall removal by refusing to agree to it. However, Bean may still prevent the case from being heard in federal court by moving to remand on the ground that he does not consent to removal. See 28 U.S.C. §1448; *Hutchins v. Priddy*, 103 F. Supp. 601, 607 (W.D. Mo. 1952) (subsequently served defendant may move to remand to state court).

## Hoist with His Own Petard

20. The court should deny the motion. Masterson has fallen afoul of the *separate* thirty-day period for the plaintiff to seek remand for non-jurisdictional defects in the removal. Under 28 U.S.C. s. 1447(c), a motion to remand "on the basis of any defect other than lack of subject matter jurisdiction" must be made within thirty days after the notice of removal is filed in the federal court. Because late filing of the notice of removal is not a defect in subject matter jurisdiction, Masterson's failure to move to remand within thirty days waives the objection. *Wisconsin Dep't. of Corrections v. Schacht*, 524 U.S. 381, 392 (1998).

## A Final, Fundamental Point

21. The motion is proper. Holiday does not waive his objection to personal jurisdiction just because he prefers to litigate in federal court. Indeed, he may have removed precisely because he believes that a federal judge will take a more objective view of the jurisdiction question. Removal does not affect Holiday's right to raise any objections or defenses he may have; it only changes the court in which they will be presented. On the other hand, had Holiday waived his personal jurisdiction objection by answering in state court before removal without raising the jurisdiction objection, removal would not revive it.

# CHAPTER 8

# Proper Venue in Federal Courts

## A Rough Measure of Convenience

---

## INTRODUCTION

Earlier chapters have considered personal and subject matter jurisdiction, two crucial restrictions on the forums in which a lawsuit may be brought. Frequently, these "first two rings" will dramatically limit the plaintiff's choice of forum. For example, if Jones comes to Alabama, Smith's home state, and is injured there in a collision with Smith, Jones will likely be able to obtain personal jurisdiction over Smith only in Alabama.

However, personal and subject matter jurisdiction will not always limit the plaintiff's choice of forum so significantly. Suppose, for example, that Smith travels a great deal in her work, so that she could be personally served with process in other states. Under *Burnham v. Superior Court of California*, 495 U.S. 604 (1990), such personal service in another state — say Illinois or Oregon — would probably suffice to support jurisdiction in that state. And, because Smith and Jones are diverse, the federal district courts in every state would have subject matter jurisdiction. Even if they were not diverse, the broad subject matter jurisdiction of the state courts in every state would support jurisdiction over this ordinary tort case. Thus, if only the first two "rings" limited Jones's choice of courts, she might well be able to sue Smith in any state in the United States, quite possibly in either federal or state court in each one.

Venue rules are meant to further restrict the places where the plaintiff may choose to bring suit, to assure that suits are tried in a place that bears some sensible relationship to the claims asserted or to the parties to the action. Such venue rules form a third "ring," apart from and in addition to personal and subject matter jurisdiction, which must be satisfied (or waived) if a court is to hear a particular case. Every court system, state or federal, has venue rules, generally established by statute. State court venue provisions often provide that cases must be brought in the county where one of the parties resides or does business, where the claim arose, or where property in dispute is located. Friedenthal, Kane and Miller 4th ed. §2.15.

---

# THE BASIC FEDERAL VENUE PROVISIONS

To provide an example of how venue provisions work, this chapter will focus on 28 U.S.C. §1391, the federal venue statute. Sections (a) and (b) of §1391 provide the basic options for venue in most federal cases. Section 1391(c) defines the "residence" of corporate defendants for purposes of applying sections (a) and (b) to cases involving corporations.

Section 1391(a), which governs venue in diversity cases, authorizes venue in

(1) a judicial district where any defendant resides, if all defendants reside in the same state,

(2) a judicial district in which a substantial part of the events or omissions giving rise to the claim occurred, or a substantial part of property that is the subject of the action is situated, or

(3) a judicial district in which any defendant is subject to personal jurisdiction at the time the action is commenced, if there is no district in which the action may otherwise be brought.

All other cases ("a civil action wherein jurisdiction is not founded solely on diversity of citizenship") are governed by §1391(b), which provides that such cases may be brought in

(1) a judicial district where any defendant resides, if all defendants reside in the same state,

(2) a judicial district in which a substantial part of the events or omissions giving rise to the claim occurred, or a substantial part of property that is the subject of the action is situated, or

(3) a judicial district in which any defendant may be found, if there is no district in which the action may otherwise be brought.

If you compare §1391(a) and (b), you will see that subsections (1) and (2) are the same in both sections. Subsection (b)(3) differs slightly from subsection (a)(3), but, as is explained below, both are very limited "fallback" provisions, which only apply in the rare case when no district is a proper venue under subsection (1) or (2).

Wouldn't it be nice if Congress would tidy up this statute, by collapsing sections (a) and (b) into a single provision, thus removing one small aggravation from the lives of bewildered first-year law students? Yes, it would be nice, but Congress hasn't, and probably won't, so let's analyze the two sections in tandem, starting with the identical provisions in subsections (a)(1) and (b)(1).

# VENUE BASED ON INDIVIDUAL "RESIDENCE"

Both §§1391(a)(1) and (b)(1) authorize venue in a judicial district where any defendant resides, *if they all reside in one state*. First, note that these provisions focus on judicial districts, not on states. Suppose, for example, that Sherman sues Stuart, from the Western District of Virginia, and Lee, from the Eastern District of Virginia, in a diversity case. Venue would be proper in either district, because both are from the state and §1391(a)(1) authorizes jurisdiction in such cases in any district in which a defendant resides. The same would be true if the case arose under federal law, since §1391(b)(1) parallels §1391(a)(1).

However, if Stuart was from the Southern District of California and Lee from the Central District of California, suit would not be proper in the Northern District of California under either §1391(a)(1) or (b)(1) since no defendant is from that district. This focus on districts contrasts with personal jurisdiction doctrine: A person who is subject to personal jurisdiction in a state is subject to jurisdiction *anywhere* in that state.

As in other areas of civil procedure, the venue provisions in §1391 include ambiguous terms that have required judicial interpretation. For example, the term "reside" spawned contradictory holdings under earlier versions of the venue statute. Some courts held that an individual defendant "resided" only in the state of her domicile. Others, however, concluded that a person could "reside" for venue purposes in several districts if she maintained residences in more than one, even though she could only have one domicile for diversity purposes. The weight of authority appears to equate an individual's "residence" for venue purposes with domicile, but the issue is not clearly resolved.[1] See Moore's Federal Practice §110.03[1].

---

1. Professor Wright's treatise suggests that the drafters used the term "reside" instead of "domicile" because the venue statute restricts suit to the *district* in which the party is domiciled; Congress used "reside" to avoid awkward references to parties as "citizens" or "domiciliaries" of a district. Wright, 5th ed. at 263.

Assuming that an individual defendant's "residence" under §1391 is her "domicile," she will be deemed to reside only in the district where she actually lives. If Greeley lives in Manhattan, she will "reside" only in the Southern District of New York for venue purposes, even though the state of New York has three other federal districts.

# VENUE BASED ON EVENTS OR OMISSIONS GIVING RISE TO THE CLAIM

Prior to 1990, §§1391(a) and (b) authorized venue in the judicial district "where the claim arose." This created interpretive problems in cases involving activities in a number of states. For example, an action for violation of the federal trademark laws might involve: 1) a decision made in one state to market the goods in violation of the trademark; 2) sales of the goods by the defendant in several states; and 3) harm to the plaintiff's business in other states where it manufactured goods or had its headquarters. The Supreme Court never established a single test for where a claim "arose" in such cases.

In 1990, Congress amended §1391 to substitute the current language in §§1391(a)(2) and (b)(2) for the "where-the-claim-arose" formula. Under these subsections, venue is proper in a judicial district in which "a substantial part of the events or omissions giving rise to the claim occurred, or a substantial part of property that is the subject of the action is situated." Although there will certainly be close questions as to what constitutes a "substantial part" of the relevant events, these provisions will often authorize venue for a particular suit in several districts. In the trademark example above, this language would presumably authorize venue in the district where the decision to market the infringing product was made and in districts where the product was sold. See, e.g., *Pilates, Inc. v. Pilates Institute, Inc.*, 891 F. Supp. 175, 182-183 (S.D.N.Y. 1995). In a products liability case, this language would likely authorize venue in both the district where the product was manufactured and the district where it caused injury. This is a perfectly sensible result. The purpose of this venue provision is to assure a relation between the underlying events that are litigated and the place where the case is tried. Such a relation will exist in each of the districts where significant events involved in the case took place.

# THE "FALLBACK" PROVISIONS IN SECTION 1391

Both §1391(a) and §1391(b) contain a third subsection, which authorizes an additional basis for venue in certain cases. Section 1391(a)(3) authorizes venue in "a judicial district in which any defendant is subject to personal jurisdiction at the time the action is commenced, if there is no district in which the action may otherwise be brought." Section 1391(b)(3) authorizes venue in "a judicial district in which any defendant may be found, if there is no district in which the action may otherwise be brought." These two subsections are similar, but not the same: (a)(3) allows venue in a district where any defendant is subject to personal jurisdiction, while (b)(3) authorizes venue in a district where any defendant may be "found."

It is unclear what it means for a defendant to be "found" in a district. An individual defendant is probably "found" in a district if she is served with process there, but something less, such as being subject to personal jurisdiction in the district, may also suffice. Nor is it clear how a corporate defendant may be "found" in a district, though it is probably "found" in any district where it would be subject to personal jurisdiction for the plaintiff's claim. The quirks and quidditics of these provisions are more readily explained as historical accidents than as logical distinctions.

One thing, however, is clear, and luckily it is the most important thing: Both of these subsections are "fallback" provisions that only apply if there is no district, *anywhere in the United States*, in which the case can be brought under the other subsections of the statute. Let's consider an example to illustrate the point: Suppose that Stuart, from California, brings a diversity action against Sheridan, from Colorado, and Hooker, from Ohio, for an accident that took place in Illinois. No district will be a proper venue under §1391(a)(1) because the defendants do not reside in a single state. However, there will be at least one proper venue under §1391(a)(2): the district within Illinois where the accident occurred, since a substantial part of the events giving rise to the suit took place in that district. Because there is a proper venue under one of the first two subsections, Stuart cannot invoke §1391(a)(3).

If Stuart's accident had taken place in Canada, he could try to lay venue under subsection (3), since on these facts there would be no proper venue under either §1391(a)(1) or (a)(2). However, to find a proper venue under subsection (3), he would have to find a district in which either Sheridan or Hooker was subject to personal jurisdiction.[2]

# THREE OTHER IMPORTANT POINTS

Three other aspects of venue analysis should be noted. First, venue, like personal jurisdiction, is considered a personal privilege of the defendant,

---

2. Presumably, this means a district in which a defendant is subject to personal jurisdiction for this claim. It hardly seems likely that Congress meant to authorize venue in a district simply because a defendant could be sued there for some unrelated claim.

which may be waived. See *Neirbo Co. v. Bethlehem Shipbuilding Corp.*, 308 U.S. 165, 168 (1939). Under the Federal Rules of Civil Procedure, the defendant waives her objection to venue by failing to raise it when she responds to the plaintiffs complaint. See Fed. R. Civ. P. 12(h)(1); Chapter 19, pp. 369-370. Parties may even agree in advance to a particular venue for suits that may arise between them. Many contracts contain such "forum selection clauses," and these have generally been held enforceable in the federal courts, even if they lay venue in a district that would not be proper under §1391. See *Carnival Cruise Lines, Inc. v. Shute*, 498 U.S. 807 (1991) (upholding forum selection clause in absence of showing of unfairness).

Second, §§1391(a) and (b) are general venue provisions that apply to diversity and other federal cases "except as otherwise provided by law." An important caveat is in order based on this exception: Specialized venue provisions govern many types of claims that appear to be covered by §§1391(a) and (b). For example, one would reasonably conclude from §1391(b) that patent infringement claims, which arise under federal law, may be brought wherever the defendant resides or wherever events giving rise to the claim occurred. Not so; lurking elsewhere in the United States Code is 28 U.S.C. §1400(b), which restricts venue in patent infringement actions to the district where the defendant resides or where she committed acts of infringement *and* has a regular and established place of business. Special venue provisions also govern copyright suits, interpleader actions, and actions against federal officials. See generally 15 Wright & Miller §§3810-3825.[3] There is no way to guard against such pitfalls other than a careful search of the statutes prior to bringing suit.[4]

Finally, you should be aware of another exception to the general venue statute for so-called "local actions." From the early days of the common law, courts have treated certain actions relating to interests in land as "local actions," which must be prosecuted in the county or district in which the land is located. See generally 17 Moore's Federal Practice §110.20. Although there is no explicit exception in §1391 for such cases, the federal courts continue to distinguish between "transitory actions" (the vast majority of suits that are not "local" and may be brought in any

---

3. Actually, things get even more confusing. Special venue statutes may be exclusive, or they may supplement the general venue statute. An exclusive venue provision is just what it says: It specifies the only proper venues for the action. If the special venue statute is interpreted to supplement §1391, it provides additional options, but the plaintiff may also file in any venue that is proper under §1391. Whether a special venue statute is exclusive or supplementary is a matter of statutory interpretation in each case, so you just have to check the case law . . . and hope that the cases have resolved the question one way or the other!
4. Similar traps for the unwary may await the state court plaintiff. In Massachusetts, for example, there is a general venue statute, Mass. Gen. L. ch. 223, §1, analogous to 28 U.S.C. §1391, but an ancient venue statute provides that an action in replevin "shall be brought in the county where the goods or beasts are detained." Mass. Gen. L. ch. 223, §4.

venue that is proper under the statute) and local actions, which still must be brought in the district where the land is located.

Although these federal venue provisions seem daunting at first, they basically require in most cases that the defendants must be sued in a district where they reside or where important events relevant to the suit took place. In at least a rough way, these provisions assure some reasonable connection between the court where suit may be brought and the suit itself. The first set of examples below considers venue in cases involving individual defendants. Then, after an introductory discussion of §1391(c), a second set deals with venue in cases brought against corporate defendants. In considering the examples, assume that all actions are brought in federal court, that the amount-in-controversy requirement is met where it is relevant, and that no special venue statute or local action rule applies.

## Examples

### The Basic Venue Provisions

1. Grant, who lives in the Northern District of Ohio, sues Lee, who lives in the Eastern District of Virginia and has his architectural office there, for breach of a contract to design a building. Grant claims that Lee agreed, after extensive negotiations in the Northern District of Ohio, to design a building to be built in Nashville, in the Middle District of Tennessee. Subsequently, however, Lee refused to follow through on the contract. In which of the following districts would venue be proper?
   a. The Eastern District of Virginia?
   b. The Western District of Virginia?
   c. The Middle District of Tennessee?
   d. The Northern District of Ohio?

2. Grant sues Lee and Stuart, Lee's partner who lives in the Western District of Virginia, for the same claim. What venues in Virginia are proper?

3. Assume that Grant sues Lee and Longstreet (from the District of South Carolina) for breach of contract. Longstreet, an engineer, had represented to Lee (in a conversation that took place at Longstreet's Charleston, South Carolina, office) that he would do the mechanical engineering on the building for a certain price but then backed out. Lee then recalculated the cost of doing the job with the higher engineering costs and decided to renege on his contract with Grant. In which of the following districts would venue be proper?
   a. The Eastern District of Virginia?
   b. The Western District of Virginia?
   c. The Middle District of Tennessee?
   d. The Northern District of Ohio?

4. On the facts of example 3, assume that Grant also asserts a federal question claim against Lee. How would this affect the available venues?

5. Assume that venue is improper in Grant's case against Lee, but Lee does not raise an objection. May the judge dismiss the case sua sponte (on her own initiative, without a request to do so by the parties)?

### Fallback Fallout

6. Reconsider the example in the Introduction, in which Stuart, from California, wants to bring a diversity action against Sheridan, from Colorado, and Hooker, from Ohio, for an accident that took place in Canada. Assume that Hooker lives in the Northern District of Ohio, and Stuart sues Hooker and Sheridan in that district. Is venue proper?

# VENUE IN CASES INVOLVING CORPORATIONS

Although the basic venue statutes can be seriously confusing, the real topper is 28 U.S.C. §1391(c), concerning venue in cases involving corporate defendants:

> For purposes of venue under this chapter, a defendant that is a corporation shall be deemed to reside in any judicial district in which it is subject to personal jurisdiction at the time the action is commenced. In a State which has more than one judicial district and in which a defendant that is a corporation is subject to personal jurisdiction at the time an action is commenced, such corporation shall be deemed to reside in any district in that State within which its contacts would be sufficient to subject it to personal jurisdiction if that district were a separate State, and if there is no such district the corporation shall be deemed to reside in the district within which it has the most significant contacts.

This is formidable language, but on closer examination it's not really as bad as it seems.

First, to clear away a little underbrush, note that §1391(c) applies only to corporate defendants. It says nothing about cases in which corporations bring suit as plaintiffs. Because §1391(c) does not apply, venue in such cases is governed by the basic venue provisions in §§1391(a) and (b).

Second, it is crucial to understand that §1391(c) is not a separate, exclusive provision governing venue in cases against corporations. All it does is define corporate "residence" for purposes of applying §§1391(a)(1) and (b)(1). Thus, it is proper to lay venue in a case against a corporation, for example, in a district where a substantial part of the events giving rise to the claim took place, under §1391(a)(2) or (b)(2). Section 1391(c) is irrelevant in applying these subsections because venue under those provisions does not depend on where the corporation "resides."

If, however, the plaintiff wants to lay venue in the district where a corporate defendant "resides," under either §1391(a)(1) or (b)(1), she must look to §1391(c) to determine where the corporation resides. Section 1391(c) defines corporate "residence" as any district in which the corporation is subject to personal jurisdiction. Suppose, for example, that Mead sues Jackson Corporation for breach of a contract that the parties made and performed in South Carolina (which only has one district, the District of South Carolina). If Mead bases venue on Jackson's residence under §1391(a)(1), he must refer to §1391(c) to determine where Jackson "resides." Under that section, it "resides" in the District of South Carolina because it would be subject to personal jurisdiction there based on the contacts of negotiating and performing the contract in South Carolina.

Jackson may also "reside" in other districts under §1391(c). For example, if it is incorporated in Delaware, the District of Delaware would be a proper venue, since corporations are subject to general in personam jurisdiction in the state where they are incorporated. Or, if Jackson has extensive production facilities in the District of Maryland, it will be subject to general in personam jurisdiction there (see Chapter 1, pp. 5-7), and thus "resides" there as well under §1391(c). Consequently, it may be sued in those districts in a diversity case under §1391(a)(1).

The more confusing part of the new §1391(c) is the second sentence, which applies this concept of corporate "residence" to states with more than one judicial district.

> In a state which has more than one judicial district and in which a defendant that is a corporation is subject to personal jurisdiction at the time an action is commenced, such corporation shall be deemed to reside in any district in that State within which its contacts would be sufficient to subject it to personal jurisdiction if that district were a separate state. . . .

Suppose, for example, that Jackson Corporation negotiated and breached the contract with Mead in Richmond, Virginia, but has no other contacts with Virginia. As Figure 8-1 shows, Virginia is divided into an Eastern District and a Western District, and Richmond is in the Eastern District of Virginia. Under §§1391(a)(1) and (c), venue would be proper in the Eastern District of Virginia. If the Eastern District were a separate state, Jackson's contacts in that district — negotiating and breaching the contract with Mead — would support personal jurisdiction there for this lawsuit under the minimum contacts test. Consequently, Jackson "resides" there under §§1391(a)(1) and (c). However, there would not be jurisdiction over Jackson in the Western District if it were a separate state, since the

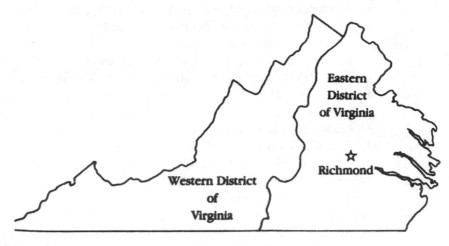

**Figure 8-1.**

corporation has no contacts in the Western District. Therefore, the Western District would not be a proper venue under §§1391(a)(1) and (c).

Now, suppose that Jackson has a permanent production facility in Atlanta, Georgia, but no other contacts with Georgia. As Figure 8-2 shows, Georgia has three districts. Jackson would be subject to personal jurisdiction in the Northern District of Georgia since, if that district were treated as a separate state, Jackson's Atlanta facility would support general in personam jurisdiction over it there. Thus, Jackson "resides" there under §1391(a)(1) and the Northern District is a proper venue. However, because Jackson has no contacts in the Middle or the Southern District of Georgia, venue would not be proper in either of those districts under §§1391(a)(1) and (c). Got that?!

## Examples

### Applying §1391(c)

7. Mead, who lives and works in the Northern District of Ohio, sues Dixie Corporation for a defamatory statement made about him by an officer of the corporation. Dixie is incorporated in Maryland and has large factories in Atlanta, Georgia (in the Northern District of Georgia), and Nashville, Tennessee (in the Middle District of Tennessee). The statement about Mead was made in Philadelphia, in the Eastern District of Pennsylvania. As a result of the statement, Mead was fired from his job.

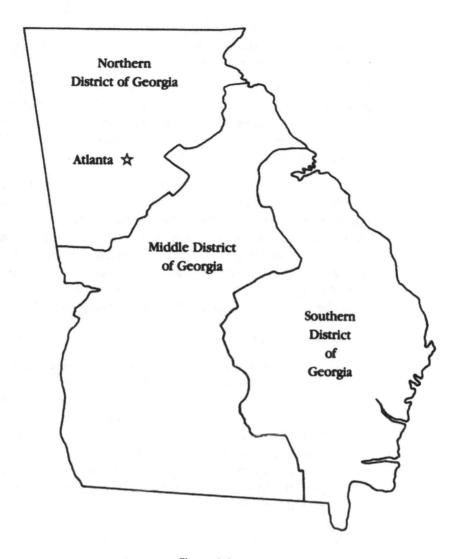

Figure 8-2.

If Mead sues Dixie, which of the following districts would be proper venues?

a. The District of Maryland?
b. The Middle District of Tennessee?
c. The Southern District of Georgia?
d. The Eastern District of Pennsylvania?

8. On the same facts, suppose Mead sues both Dixie and Calhoun, the officer who made the statement. Calhoun lives in Atlanta. Which of the following districts is a proper venue?

    a. The Northern District of Georgia?
    b. The Southern District of Georgia?
    c. The Eastern District of Pennsylvania?
    d. The Middle District of Tennessee?

9. Suppose that Dixie Corporation sues Mead for a violation of the federal trademark laws, arising from Mead's distribution throughout Ohio of products bearing the Dixie logo. What venues are proper? (Ohio has two districts, the Northern and Southern.)

10. Consider the facts of *World-Wide Volkswagen Corp. v. Woodson*, 444 U.S. 286 (1980), in which the Robinsons were injured when an Audi they bought from Seaway in New York exploded while driving across Oklahoma. Assuming that Seaway is a New York corporation doing business only in the Northern District of New York, and that the Robinsons (having established a new domicile in Oklahoma) sued Seaway based on diversity, can you think of a district in which venue would be proper but personal jurisdiction would not?

## Unlucky Number 11

11. Sumner, from Massachusetts, sues Davis, from Louisiana, in Massachusetts Superior Court, for an allegedly libelous statement Davis made in Louisiana. He bases venue on a statute authorizing venue in the county where the plaintiff resides. He gets jurisdiction over Davis by serving him with process in Massachusetts while he is there at a convention. Davis removes to the federal district court for the District of Massachusetts, and then files a motion to dismiss for improper venue, claiming that the District of Massachusetts is not a proper venue under §1391. Should the motion be granted?

## Unlucky Number 12

12. Mead sues Dixie Corporation for the defamatory statement made by an officer of Dixie. He brings the action in the Eastern District of Pennsylvania, where the statement was made, basing venue on 28 U.S.C. §1391(a)(2). Dixie moves to dismiss the action, on the ground that, when he was hired, Mead signed a contract that included a forum selection clause requiring all suits arising from his employment to be filed in the District of Maryland. Should the motion be granted?

## Explanations

### The Basic Venue Provisions

1. a. Because this is a diversity case, §1391(a) prescribes the proper venues. Under §1391(a)(1) the Eastern District of Virginia is proper, since "a defendant" resides there and all defendants (Lee only) are from the same state. The Eastern District of Virginia would presumably be a proper venue under §1391(a)(2) as well, on the ground that Lee's "omission" to design the building took place there.

   b. The Western District of Virginia is not a proper venue under §1391(a), since Lee doesn't "reside" there and none of the relevant events took place there. It is true that the concept of "residence" in the venue statute is generally equated with domicile and that Lee is domiciled in the *state* of Virginia. But for venue purposes, the term "reside" refers to the district within the state in which Lee actually has his domicile, that is, where he actually lives.

      The Western District of Virginia is not a proper venue under §1391(a)(3), even though Lee would be subject to personal jurisdiction there based on his domicile in the state. Section 1391(a)(3) does not apply to this case, since it is a fallback provision that only applies if there is "no district where the action may otherwise be brought." Here, there are several proper venues for Grant's suit under §§1391(a)(1) and (a)(2), so §1391(a)(3) is irrelevant.

   c. The only potential basis for venue in the Middle District of Tennessee is that the building was to be constructed there. Lee might be subject to venue in that district if he was to render services at the site during construction, since he "omitted" (see §1391(a)(2)) to render those services there. However, if he was solely to provide design services in Virginia, this provision would not support venue in the Middle District of Tennessee.

   d. The Northern District of Ohio may be a proper venue under §1391(a)(2) on the ground that "a substantial part of the events or omissions giving rise to the claim occurred" there. The courts will have to decide whether the negotiations that took place in the Northern District "gave rise to the claim." Arguably, the claim arose from the failure to follow through on the agreement rather than the contract formation. However, given the purpose of venue provisions — to site the litigation in a place with a substantial connection to the case — the court may well take the more flexible view of this phrase and conclude that venue is proper where the parties negotiated the contract.

2. On these facts either district in Virginia is a proper venue under §1391(a)(1), since all defendants reside in the same state and one of the defendants ("any defendant") resides in each district.

3. a. This is also a diversity case, so §1391(a) applies. Subsection (1) authorizes venue in a judicial district where any defendant resides, if they all reside in the same state. Here, they don't, so §1391(a)(1) is no help.

   But how about §1391(a)(2), which makes a district a proper venue if "a substantial part of the events or omissions giving rise to the claim" occurred there? If Lee did his recalculations and decided to back out of the deal at his office in the Eastern District, this language in §1391(a)(2) is apparently satisfied, even though Longstreet was not involved in that "event." Of course, there would still have to be personal jurisdiction over Longstreet in Virginia, under the three-ring analysis, before suit could be brought against him there.

   b. Venue is not proper in the Western District of Virginia. All defendants are not from the same state, so §1391(a)(1) does not apply. Nor does §1391(a)(2) apply, since none of the relevant events took place there. Finally, §1391(a)(3) does not apply, since there will be at least one proper venue under §1391(a)(2).

   c. Once again, venue would only be proper in the Middle District of Tennessee if Lee omitted to render substantial services there. If he did, venue is apparently proper there under §1391(a)(2), even though it was *Lee's* omission, not Longstreet's, that took place there: The standard in §1391(a)(2) apparently focuses on the events or omissions giving rise to the claim, not the acts or omissions of each individual defendant. But see *Kaplan v. Reed*, 28 F. Supp. 2d 1191 (D. Colo. 1998) (venue improper under s. 1391(b)(2) as to those defendants who did not engage in "events" in the forum district). Here again, however, Grant would have problems with personal jurisdiction over Longstreet.

   d. The Northern District of Ohio would probably be a proper venue under §1391(a)(2), based on the extensive negotiations between Grant and Lee there. Note again that, even though venue is proper there, Grant will probably not be able to satisfy the personal jurisdiction "ring" as to Longstreet in Ohio, since Longstreet dealt only with Lee, and did so in Virginia rather than Ohio.

4. Because Grant has asserted a federal claim against one of the defendants, the case is "not founded solely on diversity of citizenship." Consequently, §1391(b) applies rather than §1391(a). However, this doesn't provide any additional venue options in this case. Subsections (1) and (2) are the same in sections (a) and (b), and §1391(b)(3), which authorizes venue in a district where any defendant may be "found," does not apply because there are other districts that are proper venues under the first two subdivisions of §1391(b). This "catch-all" provision, like §1391(a)(3), is apparently included to assure that there will be *some* proper venue in federal question cases, even if the events giving

rise to the claim took place outside the United States. It does not apply unless no federal district is a proper venue under subsection (1) or subsection (2).

5. Several cases have held that it is improper for the court to dismiss an action sua sponte for improper venue, since venue is a privilege of the defendant, which she may waive. See, e.g., *Concession Consultants, Inc. v. Mirisch*, 355 F.2d 369, 371 (2d Cir. 1966); see also 15 Wright & Miller at §3826 (noting conflicting cases on the point). However, the court ought to have some control over inappropriate venue choices even if the parties are satisfied. The purpose of venue statutes is not only to prevent inconvenience to defendants, but also to allocate judicial business to courts with some connection to the case. See *Gulf Oil Corp. v. Gilbert*, 330 U.S. 501, 508-509 (1947) (listing various private interests and public interests that may make a court an inappropriate place to conduct the litigation.) The public interest may suggest that a particular venue is inappropriate even if the parties are willing to litigate there. However, this public interest may be protected by 28 U.S.C. §1404(a), which authorizes a court to transfer cases to other districts when justice so requires.

## Fallback Fallout

6. In this case, venue cannot be based on s. 1391(a)(1), since the defendants do not reside in the same state. Nor is s. 1391(a)(2) satisfied in any judicial district, since the events giving rise to the suit did not take place in any judicial district in the county. Thus, it is appropriate to look to the "fallback" provision, s. 1391(a)(3), which authorizes venue in a district where "any defendant is subject to personal jurisdiction at the time the action is commenced, if there is no district in which the action may otherwise be brought." This "fallback" venue provision is satisfied, since Hooker is subject to personal jurisdiction in Ohio.

This satisfies the venue requirement, but of course Stuart still faces the problem that Sheridan is not subject to personal jurisdiction in Ohio. Proper venue is a separate, additional requirement along with personal jurisdiction. If, however, Sheridan waived her objection to personal jurisdiction or was served with process while in Ohio, the suit could proceed.

## Applying §1391(c)

7. a. This is a diversity case, so venue is governed by §1391(a). Under that section, venue is proper in a district where the defendant resides (§1391(a)(1)) or in a district where events giving rise to the claim took place. Section 1391(a)(2). A corporation's "residence" is defined by §1391(c) to include any district in which it would be

subject to personal jurisdiction. Because corporations are subject to general in personam jurisdiction in the state where they are incorporated, Dixie would be subject to jurisdiction in the District of Maryland (which encompasses the entire state of Maryland). Thus, it is a proper venue.

Note that this analysis makes the District of Maryland a proper venue even though the case does not arise out of events that took place there. But venue provisions often lay venue where the defendant has important connections, such as a residence or a place of business, even if the claim arose somewhere else. Thus, it is not anomalous that the place of incorporation is a proper venue under §1391(c).

b. Once again, venue will be proper under §1391(a)(1) if Dixie "resides" in the Middle District of Tennessee. And again, §1391(c) provides that Dixie resides in any district in which its contacts would subject it to personal jurisdiction. Here, Dixie is probably subject to general in personam jurisdiction in the district based on its large factory there. Thus, the Middle District of Tennessee is a proper venue.

c. Dixie does not "reside" in the Southern District of Georgia under §1391(c). True, Dixie is probably subject to personal jurisdiction throughout Georgia because of its large factory in Atlanta. But, under §1391(c), Dixie is only deemed to "reside" in those districts within a state in which its contacts would support jurisdiction if the district were a state. Thus, since Georgia is a multi-district state, we must look at the contacts Dixie has with each district, not at its contacts with the state as a whole. Here, Dixie has no contacts with the Southern District of Georgia. If that district were a state, Dixie would not be subject to personal jurisdiction in it for this claim. Thus, it does not "reside" there under §1391(c), even though it has substantial and continuous contacts with another district within the state.

d. The Eastern District of Pennsylvania is a proper venue on several grounds. First, venue is proper there under §1391(a)(2), since a substantial part of the events giving rise to the claim took place there. Second, venue is proper under §1391(a)(1), since the corporation "resides" (so says §1391(c)) in any district where its contacts would support personal jurisdiction. Here, Dixie would be subject to minimum contacts jurisdiction in the Eastern District of Pennsylvania because its officer made the defamatory statement there.

8. a. Section 1391(a)(1) authorizes venue where any defendant resides, if they both reside in the same state. Calhoun resides in Georgia, as does Dixie, as "residence" is defined for corporations in §1391(c). Thus, any district in Georgia in which either defendant resides is a proper venue. Because they both "reside" in the Northern District of Georgia, that is a proper venue.

b. Although both defendants "reside" in Georgia, neither resides in the Southern District of Georgia. Consequently, it is not a proper venue under §1391(a)(1). And, since no events took place in that district, §1391(a)(2) does not apply either.

c. The Eastern District of Pennsylvania is a proper venue under §1391 (a)(2), since a substantial part of the events giving rise to the claim took place there. Again, note that §1391(c) is irrelevant to this analysis, since it only defines the term "reside" for purposes of §1391(a)(1).

d. Here's one where the drafting of the statute may have gone awry. If you read s. 1391(a)(1) literally, venue would be proper in the Middle District of Tennessee: That section allows venue in a district where any defendant resides, if they both reside in the same state. Dixie and Calhoun do reside in the same state: they both reside in the Northern District of Georgia. So, venue is proper in a district where either resides. Dixie "resides" in the Middle District of Tennessee, under s. 1391(c), because it would be subject to personal jurisdiction there. So, the Middle District of Tennessee is a proper venue under s. 1391(a)(1)!

While this textual logic is unimpeachable, the evident purpose of s. 1391(a)(1) is to authorize venue in the state where both defendants reside — Georgia in this example. In light of this purpose, it seems likely that the courts won't read the statute literally, but confine venue to the state where both defendants reside. For a case rejecting this clever argument, see *Swanson v. Endres*, 2007 WL 1655230.

9. In this case Dixie is the plaintiff, so section 1391(c) does not apply. In addition, the claim is not based "solely on diversity," so §1391(b) applies. Venue is proper where Mead resides, in the Northern District, or in the districts where a substantial part of the events giving rise to the claim took place. Because the goods were distributed throughout Ohio, this would include both the Northern and the Southern districts.

By the way, trademark cases deal with a fairly specialized type of federal issue; perhaps Congress has seen fit to provide a specialized venue statute for them, as it has for copyrights and patents. In practice, you should be ever so careful to take a look for this. I took a quick look and didn't find a specialized venue statute for trademark cases, so I guess §1391 applies. If you bring a trademark case, look more carefully than I did.

10. This one is easy. Venue would be proper in the district within Oklahoma in which the accident occurred, under §1391(a)(2), since a "substantial part of the events giving rise to the claim" took place there. But the Supreme Court held in *World-Wide* that the Oklahoma court did not have personal jurisdiction over Seaway. Of course, without jurisdiction over Seaway, the plaintiffs will take little advantage from the fact that another ring, venue, is satisfied.

## Unlucky Number 11

11. The motion should be denied. Sumner brought suit in state court and chose one which was a proper venue under state law. Removal allows Davis to get the case out of the state court and into federal court, but it does not provide a means of avoiding trial in a state where suit was properly brought under the state rules.

    Put another way, 28 U.S.C. s. 1391, the federal venue statute, does not apply to cases removed to federal court: it only applies to cases *commenced* in federal court. The proper "venue" for a removed action is "the district court of the United States for the district and division embracing the place where such [state court] action is pending." 28 U.S.C. s. 1441(a). Thus, the proper venue for Sumner's removed action is the District of Massachusetts and only the District of Massachusetts.

    If defendants could do what Davis has tried to do here, it would give them a powerful means of avoiding trial in a state where they had properly been sued under state venue rules. Removal is meant to provide a federal forum only, not a means of avoiding the state in which the plaintiff has permissibly chosen to litigate.[5]

## Unlucky Number 12

12. Dixie's motion probably will be granted. A forum selection clause is an agreement between parties that suits between them will be filed in a particular court or state. Such clauses are fairly common in commercial contracts, and are generally enforced as long as they were fairly communicated to both parties, and are not otherwise commercially unreasonable. See generally 17 Moore's Federal Practice §110.01[4][b]. Here, Maryland is a logical choice for disputes arising from Dixie's operations, since it is Dixie's state of incorporation. As long as Mead had an opportunity to negotiate over the forum selection clause, and chose to accept it, the court will likely enforce it. Thus, while the Eastern District of Pennsylvania is a proper venue under §1391(a)(1), the case will likely be dismissed (or transferred under 28 U.S.C. s. 1404(a)), leaving Mead to litigate in the District of Maryland.

---

5. Once the case is in federal court, Davis could move for a change of venue under 28 U.S.C. §1404(a), and try to avoid Sumner's forum choice that way. However, this option is not radically different from his right to move in the state court for a forum non conveniens dismissal.

# Choosing a Proper Court

## The Three Rings Reconsidered

# INTRODUCTION

A major purpose of this book is to introduce procedural concepts, such as personal jurisdiction, subject matter jurisdiction, and venue, and to illustrate their operation through a variety of examples. However, an equally important goal is to help you to see the interrelatedness of things, to explore how these procedural doctrines interact to form a rather elegant system for adjudication of law suits. This chapter reconsiders the three rings analyzed in earlier chapters in order to emphasize how these separate constraints operate together to circumscribe the plaintiff's choice of a proper forum.

As a preliminary matter it is important to reemphasize that all three of these prerequisites must be satisfied in order to bring suit in a particular forum. It is no answer to an objection to personal jurisdiction that diversity (or some other basis for subject matter jurisdiction) is present or that the venue provisions of 28 U.S.C. §1391 are satisfied. Each of the three doctrines has a different legal source, serves a distinct purpose, and employs a different standard. The limits on federal subject matter jurisdiction are found in Article III, §2 of the Constitution, which authorizes federal jurisdiction over certain limited types of cases. Personal jurisdiction, on the other hand, arises from due process limitations in the Fourteenth Amendment and limits the power of states to require out-of-state defendants to defend suits in their courts. The third ring, venue, does not have a constitutional source: It is a statutory limit that imposes separate constraints on the place of trial to protect parties from inconvenient litigation.

While the three rings are distinct, the potential for confusing them is great because the standards that govern personal jurisdiction, subject matter jurisdiction, and venue are closely related. For example, the concept of domicile may be relevant to analysis of all three rings. Courts use domicile to determine the state citizenship of individuals (that is, natural persons) under 28 U.S.C. §1332(a)(1), the basic diversity provision. Domicile in the forum state is also a proper basis for exercising personal jurisdiction over an individual defendant. *Milliken v. Meyer*, 311 U.S. 457 (1940). Finally, domicile is relevant (with a twist) to venue because most courts have held that an individual "resides" under the venue statute in the judicial district where he is domiciled. Wright & Miller, Federal Practice & Procedure §3805. (The "twist" is that venue is only proper in the particular district within the state in which the individual has his domicile, not in the entire state.)

The concept of domicile, in the traditional common law sense of a place of residence where one intends to remain indefinitely, does not apply to corporations because they cannot have intent in the same sense that individuals do. However, the analogous doctrines of corporate citizenship or presence within the state are also relevant to all three rings. For the purpose of establishing subject matter jurisdiction on the basis of diversity, a corporation is deemed to be a "citizen" of the state of its principal place of business, as well as the state where it is incorporated. 28 U.S.C. §1332(c)(1). To establish personal jurisdiction over corporations, however, the courts invoke the separate but confusingly similar concept of general in personam jurisdiction. Under general in personam jurisdiction analysis, a corporation is subject to personal jurisdiction in states in which it conducts substantial and continuous business activities. See Chapter 1, pp. 5-7. The state in which a corporation is incorporated and the state of its principal place of business would almost certainly satisfy this standard, but other states may satisfy it as well.

For example, a major airline would be subject to general in personam jurisdiction in many states, due to the volume of flights it operates from those states and the facilities and employees it maintains there. Yet only one state will be its "principal place of business" for diversity purposes under 28 U.S.C. §1332(c)(1). Thus, both of these related inquiries consider the amount of business activity in the state, but the two standards do differ, and the states that meet the standards will overlap but may not be exactly the same.

Venue in suits against corporations requires yet another related analysis. Under 28 U.S.C. §1391(a)(1) or (b)(1), venue will lie in any judicial district in which a defendant "resides," if all defendants reside in the same state. For individuals, residence for venue purposes is generally equated with domicile, but, as explained above, corporations do not have a domicile in the common law sense of the term. Instead, corporate "residence" for venue purposes is defined in the venue statute. 28 U.S.C §1391(c). Under §1391(c), a corporate defendant resides for venue purposes in any judicial district in which its contacts would suffice to support personal jurisdiction.

Thus, corporate activity or presence in the district is relevant to determining venue in cases against corporate defendants, just as it is relevant to determining their state citizenship for diversity purposes and their amenability to personal jurisdiction. However, a much smaller quantum of corporate activity will satisfy the venue requirement than is needed to establish a corporation's "principal place of business" for diversity purposes, or "substantial and continuous activities" for general in personam jurisdiction. Under §1391(a)(1) and (c), for example, a district could be a proper venue based on a *single act* by a corporate employee in the district, if that act gave rise to the claim. Such a single act would support personal jurisdiction over the corporation for that claim, and therefore, under §1391(c), the corporation would "reside" in that district for purposes of the venue statute. But the corporation may also "reside" in a district under §1391(c) because it has *extensive* contacts there that would support general in personam jurisdiction. Sorting out these related, but different standards can admittedly be a bit trying.

# RELATION OF THE CLAIM TO THE FORUM

Another understandable source of confusion in applying the three-ring analysis is the fact that one of the rings may require a relationship between the state in which the suit is brought and the claim the plaintiff asserts, while that relationship is irrelevant to applying the other rings. Suppose, for example, that Santini, a California high-wire artist, sues Robinson Shows, Inc., a Virginia corporation with its principal place of business in Virginia. If Santini sues Robinson Shows in an Alabama federal court for a negligence claim that arose in Missouri, it is irrelevant to diversity analysis that the claim did not arise in Alabama. Diversity jurisdiction turns on a comparison of the citizenship of the opposing parties, not on the relationship between the parties or the claim and the forum state. So long as the parties are from different states (and the amount-in-controversy requirement is met) diversity is satisfied.

Similarly, the fact that Santini's claim did not arise in Alabama may be irrelevant to the venue and personal jurisdiction analysis. If the circus does sufficient business in Alabama, it will be subject to general in personam jurisdiction there. And, if that is true, venue will be proper in the Alabama district where the business activity takes place, under 28 U.S.C. §1391(a)(1) and (c), even though the claim does not arise out of the business done in that district. For example, if Robinson does extensive business in the Southern District of Alabama, that activity would support general in personam jurisdiction over Robinson, if the Southern District were a state, even though Santini's claim did not arise there. This suffices to make that district a proper venue under §§1391(a)(1) and (c).

Because venue in cases against corporations is proper where the corporation is subject to personal jurisdiction, under §1391(c), it should follow that wherever a corporation is subject to personal jurisdiction will also be a proper venue. Not quite true, unfortunately. First, of course, it would not suffice that it was subject to personal jurisdiction on some other claim unrelated to the case before the court. *Second*, the combination of §§1391(a)(1) [or (b)(1)] and (c) authorizes venue only in the particular districts within a state where the defendant has contacts. So a corporate defendant may be subject to personal jurisdiction in a state, but some districts in that state may still be improper venues. In Santini's case, for example, the Northern District of Alabama would not be a proper venue, if Robinson Shows has no contacts in that district, even though it is subject to personal jurisdiction in Alabama.[1]

The subtlety of these interrelations suggest that they were deliberately designed to intimidate first-year law students. However, the situation is not really so bad once you have worked with the related doctrines in the context of specific facts. The following examples will help you sort out the various rings. Assume, unless the example specifies otherwise, that the relevant long-arm statute is like California's (see supra p. 26), which authorizes the exercise of all constitutionally permissible jurisdiction, and that all suits are brought in federal court.

## Examples

### Into the Rings

1. Barnum, a citizen of Maine, sues Ringling Brothers, Inc. for injuries suffered when Kelly, a Ringling Brothers' clown, fails to secure the door on a lion cage while the train is refueling in Bangor, Maine, and Leo, a trained lion, escapes. Ringling Brothers is incorporated in Wisconsin with its principal place of business in Manhattan, in the Southern District of New York. The circus has its winter quarters in Florida, has permanent facilities for training performers in the Northern District of Ohio, and performs for two or three weeks each year in every state on the eastern seaboard. (For those whose geography is rusty, the eastern seaboard states include Maine, New Hampshire, Massachusetts,

---

1. In other cases, the district will not be a proper venue, even though the corporation is subject to personal jurisdiction there, because the other defendants do not reside in that state.

Connecticut, Rhode Island, New York, New Jersey, Delaware, Maryland, Virginia, North Carolina, South Carolina, Georgia, and Florida.)

   a. Could the suit be brought in federal district court in Maine? (Maine has only one judicial district.)

   b. Could the suit be brought in the Northern District of New York? (New York has Southern, Northern, Eastern, and Western Districts.)

   c. Could the suit be brought in any federal district court in Ohio?

   d. Could the suit be brought in any federal district court in New Jersey?

2. Barnum sues Ringling Brothers and Kelly, the clown who let the lion escape from the train. Kelly is domiciled in Florida.

   a. May Barnum sue in federal district court in Maine?

   b. May he sue in a Florida federal district court?

   c. May he sue in the Southern District of New York?

3. Barnum sues Ringling Brothers and Kelly in the Eastern District of Pennsylvania for the injuries Barnum suffered in Maine. Barnum serves the summons and complaint on Kelly and on T. Thumb, General Manager of Ringling Brothers, while the circus train is stopped just west of Philadelphia to feed the animals. Is the suit proper under the three rings?

## Juggling Acts

4. Suppose the circus sues Kelly, from Florida, and Rice, a Vermont citizen, for allowing Leo to escape. The circus alleges that Rice was negligent in failing to lock the cage when the train left Rutland, Vermont, and that Kelly was negligent in failing to check the lock when the train stopped to refuel in Bangor. The suit is brought in Maine.

   a. Will the Maine federal district court have subject matter jurisdiction over the action?

   b. Will the court have personal jurisdiction over the parties?

   c. Is Maine a proper venue?

5. Beatty, an Arizona citizen, sues the Bailey Circus Corporation for an injury suffered when Elmer, a willing but occasionally clumsy elephant, fell on him while Beatty was watching a circus performance in Phoenix, Arizona. When the accident occurred, in 2003, Bailey was incorporated in Delaware with its principal (and only) place of business in Phoenix. Since 2003, however, the circus has prospered. As of 2006, when suit was brought, its principal place of business was California, although it still performed extensively in Arizona as well. May Beatty bring suit in federal court in California?

## Procedural Acrobatics

6. In 2005, Beatty sues the Bailey Circus and Stenk, Elmer's trainer, for the circus accident. Suit is brought in the New Mexico District Court for

Guadaloupe County, the *state* court of general jurisdiction in New Mexico. Stenk is from New Mexico. Assume that the relevant New Mexico venue statute authorizes venue in the county where any defendant resides and that Stenk resides in Guadaloupe County.

a. Is the suit properly before the state court?

b. May the defendants remove to federal court?

## A Two-Ring Circus

7. A representative of Ringling Brothers visits Adler, a retired clown who lives in Cedar Rapids, Iowa, in the Northern District of Iowa. The agent explains that the circus wishes to get Adler's permission to use a famous poster of Adler in promoting the circus, for a small royalty. Adler agrees. Ringling Brothers uses the picture in advertising in New York but does not pay Adler. Adler decides to sue Ringling Brothers for breach of contract and federal copyright infringement. (Assume, contrary to fact, that the general venue statute applies to copyright claims.)

a. Can you think of a court or courts that would fall in the shaded area of Figure 9-1 (see p. 165), that is, in which personal jurisdiction and subject matter jurisdiction are satisfied but venue is not? (The relevant facts concerning Ringling Brothers' business activities are found in example 1.)

b. Assume that the contract involved was made in New York while Adler was visiting there, rather than in Iowa. Can you think of a court or courts that would fall in the hatched area of Figure 9-1, in which venue and subject matter jurisdiction are proper, but the court would not have personal jurisdiction over Ringling Brothers?

## Explanations

## Into the Rings

1. a. As pointed out in the Introduction, the suit may only be brought in those federal courts that satisfy all three rings of the analysis for choosing a proper court. There is clearly no problem with subject matter jurisdiction. Barnum is a Maine citizen, and Ringling Brothers is a citizen of Wisconsin (where it is incorporated) and New York (where it has its principal place of business) under 28 U.S.C. §1332(c)(1). As long as Barnum's claim is for more than $75,000 the requirements for federal subject matter jurisdiction based on diversity are met. The fact that Barnum is a citizen of the state where suit was brought is irrelevant to the diversity analysis; diversity is satisfied as long as he and Ringling Brothers are citizens of different states, regardless of which states those are.

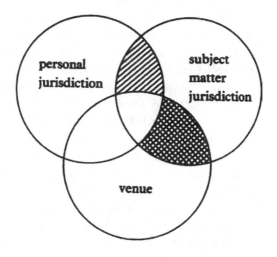

**Figure 9-1.**

The Maine court will also have personal jurisdiction over Ringling Brothers in this action. The claim arises out of a negligent act by its employee, which took place in the state and caused injury in the state. The defendant's negligent in-state conduct is sufficient to support specific in personam jurisdiction under the minimum contacts test, that is, jurisdiction over a claim such as Barnum's, which arises out of the in-state act itself. Venue is also proper in Maine.

Venue in diversity cases is governed by 28 U.S.C. §1391(a), which authorizes laying venue in the district where the defendants reside (§1391(a)(1)) or where a substantial part of the events giving rise to the claim took place (§1391(a)(2)). Venue is proper in the District of Maine under either §1391(a)(1) or (a)(2). Venue would be proper under §1391(a)(1) on the ground that Ringling Brothers "resides" in Maine for venue purposes. Under 28 U.S.C. §1391(c) a corporate defendant "resides" in every district in which it is subject to personal jurisdiction. Because the circus is subject to minimum contacts jurisdiction in the District of Maine for this claim, it "resides" there under 28 U.S.C. §1391(c). Venue is also proper under §1391(a)(2)) since a substantial part of the events giving rise to the claim took place in the district.

b. This case could not be brought in the Northern District of New York. The analysis of the court's subject matter jurisdiction is exactly the same as in example 1a. A diversity case is a diversity case is a diversity case: If the parties are from different states and the amount-in-controversy requirement is satisfied, any federal district court will have subject matter jurisdiction on the basis of diversity.

Personal jurisdiction over Ringling Brothers is proper in New York because it has its principal place of business there, which in virtually every case will establish the type of substantial and continuous contacts necessary to support general in personam jurisdiction over a corporation. Be careful, however, to distinguish this personal jurisdiction analysis from the diversity analysis. For personal jurisdiction, the question is whether Ringling Brothers' activities in the state are so substantial and continuous as to make it fair to subject it to personal jurisdiction for any claim. By contrast, whether the corporation is a citizen of the state for diversity purposes turns on whether that state is the *one* state in which the corporation's business activities are centered under the various tests for determining a corporation's principal place of, business. See Chapter 5, pp. 92-93.

Venue in Barnum's suit is analyzed under §1391(a), since it is a diversity case. Under §§1391(a)(1) and (c), Ringling Brothers "resides" in any New York district in which its contacts would suffice to subject it to personal jurisdiction. Once again, the analysis of the rings is similar but a little bit different. Since Ringling Brothers has contacts at its corporate offices in Manhattan, in the Southern District of New York, which would support personal jurisdiction over it (even for this claim, which arose elsewhere), venue would be proper in that district. However, the facts do not suggest that it has any contacts in the Northern District that would support jurisdiction over it there, nor did any events giving rise to the claim take place there. Nor does §1391(a)(3) apply, since it is a "fallback" provision that only applies if there is no other proper venue for the action. Since there is no basis for laying venue in the Northern District, the action may not be brought there; it comes up one ring short.

c. Suit would probably be proper in the Northern District of Ohio in Barnum's case. Subject matter jurisdiction is no problem since, as indicated above, the parties are just as diverse if suit is brought in Ohio as they are if suit is brought anywhere else. Note that Ringling Brothers is not a "citizen" of Ohio for diversity purposes even if it has substantial business activities there that would subject it to general in personam jurisdiction in that state.

General in personam jurisdiction would probably be proper over Ringling Brothers in Ohio because they have a substantial, continuous presence in the state, due to their permanent training facility there. Presumably, they own or rent property there and have regular employees in the state, contacts that frequently support general in personam jurisdiction.

Venue would also be proper in the Northern District of Ohio under §§1391(a)(1) and (c), as long as Ringling Brothers' contacts in that district, the permanent training facility, would suffice to subject it to general in personam jurisdiction there.

Even if Barnum has filed suit in a forum where all three rings intersect, it is still not certain that the suit will be heard there. The court has the power under 28 U.S.C. §1404(a) to transfer cases "for the convenience of parties and witnesses, in the interest of justice," including cases in which the plaintiff has properly chosen that court under the three-ring analysis. If Barnum brings suit in Ohio, the circus will have a good argument for transfer of venue under 28 U.S.C. §1404(a), since Barnum's claim did not arise in Ohio and the defendant's activities in the forum, though substantial, are completely unrelated to the claim before the court.

d. In this example, there is no basis for personal jurisdiction over Ringling Brothers in New Jersey for this claim. The claim does not arise out of any contacts of the defendant with New Jersey, so minimum contacts jurisdiction is not appropriate under *International Shoe*. Further, the two- or three-week tour that the circus makes in the state is unlikely to satisfy the substantial-and-continuous-contact requirement for general in personam jurisdiction. Since there is no basis for personal jurisdiction over Ringling Brothers, §§1391(a)(1) and (c) would not support venue there either. Nor would §1391(a)(2), since none of the events giving rise to this claim took place there.

2. a. This suit may properly be brought in Maine. Complete diversity is present: Barnum is a citizen of Maine, Kelly is a citizen of Florida, and Ringling Brothers is a citizen of New York and Wisconsin. Personal jurisdiction is proper over both defendants under minimum contacts analysis, based on Kelly's negligent act of allowing Leo to get loose. This is a minimum contact of Kelly personally, since she actually performed the negligent act in the state. It is also a minimum contact of the corporation because Kelly's negligence occurred in the course of her work for the circus, and the contacts of the corporation's agents while acting on its behalf will be attributed to the corporation.

Venue is also proper under §1391(a)(2), since a substantial part of the events giving rise to the claim took place in Maine. Note that §1391(a)(1) does *not* apply because Kelly does not "reside" in Maine, even though Ringling Brothers does (under §§1391(a)(1) and (c)). Nor does §1391(a)(3), the "fallback" provision, apply, since there are other proper venues under §§1391(a)(1) and (a)(2).

b. Barnum will also have the option to sue in at least one district in Florida under the three-ring analysis. Diversity is still present; here again it is irrelevant to diversity analysis that one of the parties

(Kelly) is from the forum state. Personal jurisdiction is also likely to be proper over both defendants in Florida. Kelly is subject to jurisdiction there because she is domiciled there, and the circus is probably subject to general in personam jurisdiction there since it has its permanent winter quarters in Florida.

Venue is also proper. Under 28 U.S.C. §1391(a)(1) venue is proper in the district where any defendant resides if they all reside in the same state. For venue purposes, Kelly "resides" in the district within the state where she actually lives. See Chapter 8, p. 143. If Kelly's home is in the Northern District of Florida, for example, she "resides" there for venue purposes but not in the Southern or Middle Districts. Ringling Brothers resides, under §§1391(a)(1) and (c), in whatever district its winter quarters is in, since this extensive and permanent contact would support general in personam jurisdiction. On these facts, venue would be proper in either the district where Kelly lives or the district in which Ringling Brothers' winter quarters are located. See §1391(a)(1) (the district "where any defendant resides, if all defendants reside in the same State"). If these are the same district, only that district will be a proper venue.

c. Suit will not be proper in the Southern District of New York because personal jurisdiction could not be asserted over Kelly in New York, under either minimum contacts analysis or general in personam analysis. Venue would also be a problem, since Kelly does not reside there and none of the events giving rise to the claim took place there.

3. a. The diversity analysis is unchanged here, but personal jurisdiction and venue are improper. Barnum may evidently obtain "transient" personal jurisdiction over Kelly by serving her with process while she is passing through the state. Burnham v. Superior Court of California, 495 U.S. 604 (1990). But this "gotcha" theory, based on physical presence within the state, applies to individual, warm-body defendants, not to corporations. They are not necessarily "in" the state just because someone who works for them is. See Wright & Miller at §1102. Because the claim arose in Maine, and the facts do not suggest any basis for general in personam jurisdiction over Ringling Brothers in Pennsylvania, the personal jurisdiction ring is not satisfied.

Nor is venue proper under §1391(a). Neither defendant resides there, and none of the events giving rise to the suit took place there. Nor does §1391(a)(3) apply, since there are other districts in which venue is proper under §1391(a)(1) or (a)(2).

## Juggling Acts

4. a. The Maine federal court, like any federal court, will have subject matter jurisdiction in this case, since there is complete diversity. Of course the amount-in-controversy requirement will have to be met, but my guess is that more than $75,000 goes into your basic trained lion. If Leo falls in love with a moose and never returns, the circus might recover more than that amount; that's all that's needed to meet the amount requirement.

   b. Personal jurisdiction presents a more difficult issue. Since neither defendant is domiciled in Maine, the circus will have to rely on specific jurisdiction, based on minimum contacts analysis. Kelly is clearly subject to jurisdiction in Maine under the *International Shoe* analysis because the claim arose from her negligent act (actually, her omission) in Maine. However, Rice's alleged negligence took place in Vermont, and it is doubtful that the mere foreseeability that the door would swing open in another state is sufficient to support jurisdiction over Rice there. Compare Chapter 1, example 4. Absent personal service in Maine or consent by Rice, the court will not have personal jurisdiction over her.

   c. Once again, this case should be analyzed under §1391(a), since jurisdiction is based on diversity. It appears that the District of Maine is a proper venue under §1391(a)(2), since a substantial part of the events giving rise to the claim took place there — Leo's escape. It is true that Rice did not do anything in Maine, but there would still be no claim against him if Leo had not escaped there, so subsection (a)(2) appears satisfied as to the claim against him and against Kelly.

      Some courts have analyzed venue separately against each defendant, holding that it must be satisfied independently as to each. See, e.g., *Schultz v. Ary*, 175 F. Supp. 2d 959, 965 (W.D. Mich. 2001) (where events giving rise to claim against one defendant arose in the district, but none giving rise to claim against the other, venue improper as to second defendant). However, there is a strong argument here that events giving rise to the claims against both Kelly and Rice took place in the District of Maine.[2]

      Of course, the fact that venue is proper is not enough to allow the court to hear the case. It must also have a basis for exercising personal jurisdiction over Rice, which, absent consent, appears unlikely in this case.

---

2. Other courts have applied a concept of "pendent venue" to claims against multiple defendants, finding venue proper so long as there is a basis for venue over one defendant. See, e.g., *Pacer Global Logistics v. National Passenger R.R. Corp.*, 272 F. Supp. 2d 784, 789-791 (E.D. Wis. 2003); see generally 14D Wright & Miller §3808.

5. The interesting aspect of this example is that none of the three rings would have been satisfied if Beatty had brought suit immediately after the injury. The parties were not diverse at the time of the accident, but became diverse by the time suit was brought, due to the change in Bailey's principal place of business. It is settled that diversity jurisdiction turns on the state citizenship of the parties when the suit is filed. See Chapter 5, example 6. Diversity jurisdiction is therefore proper in this case if the amount in controversy exceeds $75,000. In a case as weighty as this, that sounds likely.

   Similarly, Bailey would not have been subject to personal jurisdiction in California in 2003 for this claim. Because the claim arose in Arizona, Bailey was not (and still is not) subject to specific jurisdiction in California for this claim. Nor was Bailey subject to general in personam jurisdiction in California in 2003. Bailey had no contacts with California then; its continuous and substantial business in California has all developed since 2003. May it be sued there based on general in personam jurisdiction at the time suit is filed, even if it was not subject to such jurisdiction at the time the claim arose?

   Logically, it should not matter that the corporation was not subject to general in personam jurisdiction in California when the claim arose. No one was trying to assert jurisdiction over it then. The rationale underlying general in personam jurisdiction is that extensive corporate presence within the state reduces the inconvenience of litigation and affiliates the corporation with the state in such a substantial way as to make it fair to sue it there for any claim. If that presence exists at the time the suit is brought, the rationale for subjecting the corporation to jurisdiction is satisfied. In addition, any inconvenience to the corporation from litigating in the state occurs when the litigation takes place, and at that time Bailey had a substantial presence in the forum state.

   One court has held that, in general jurisdiction cases, the court "should examine a defendant's contacts with the forum state over a period that is reasonable under the circumstances — up to and including the date the suit was filed — to assess whether they satisfy the 'continuous and systematic' standard." *Metropolitan Life Ins. Co. v. Robertson-Ceco Corp.*, 84 F.3d 560, 569-570 (2d Cir. 1996). Under this approach, the California court could base general in personam jurisdiction over Bailey on its substantial contacts with California between the time of Beatty's accident and the time he files suit, even though it had few contacts there at the time of Beatty's accident.

   If this personal jurisdiction analysis is right, then venue will also be proper in those federal districts within California where Bailey does substantial business. Looking at those districts as though they were states, the contacts there would support general in personam jurisdiction over Bailey, even though the claim arose elsewhere; consequently Bailey "resides" in those districts under §§1391(a)(1) and (c).

## Procedural Acrobatics

6. a. This chapter deals primarily with the choice of a proper *federal* forum. The same three rings must also be satisfied if suit is brought in state court, but the standards for meeting those tests differ in a state suit. All states have a trial court that exercises broad subject matter jurisdiction over most types of claims, including negligence claims. In New Mexico, these courts of general jurisdiction are called district courts. They have subject matter jurisdiction over garden variety tort claims such as Beatty's, as well as a broad range of other common law and statutory causes of action. There is no need to consider the state citizenship of the parties, since the diversity requirements of 28 U.S.C. §1332 apply to subject matter jurisdiction of the federal courts, not that of the state courts.

   Venue analysis also differs in state court actions. Each state has its own statutes defining proper venue for claims brought in its courts, which may vary considerably from the federal venue provisions. Here, the New Mexico statute is satisfied since Stenk "resides" (whatever that may mean under the New Mexico statute) in the county where the suit is filed. By contrast, venue would not be proper in this example under 28 U.S.C. §1391, since the circus has no contacts there and the events giving rise to the claim took place elsewhere.

   Personal jurisdiction analysis, however, is likely to be the same whether the suit is brought in state or federal court. As indicated in Chapter 6, in most cases the federal courts exercise personal jurisdiction only to the extent that it would be exercised by the state courts of the state in which they sit, under Fed. R. Civ. P. 4(k)(1)(A). See pp. 113-114. In this case, jurisdiction would be proper over Stenk, on the basis of her New Mexico domicile, but not over Bailey, since the claim did not arise in New Mexico and the facts do not indicate that Bailey would be subject to general in personam jurisdiction there.

   b. By now you may wish you had run away and joined the circus instead of going to law school. Taming lions or swallowing swords might not be a bad alternative.

   The personal jurisdiction analysis will not be affected by the defendant's decision to remove, since both courts usually apply the same statutory and constitutional standards for exercising personal jurisdiction, unless a federal statute authorizes the federal courts to exercise broader jurisdiction. Fed. R. Civ. P. 4(k)(1). The defendants do not waive their right to object to personal jurisdiction by removing to federal court. See Chapter 7, example 21. Thus, Bailey could seek dismissal on this ground in the federal court after removal.

Venue and subject matter jurisdiction, however, require further analysis. Venue would not be proper under §1391 because all defendants do not reside in New Mexico, and the events giving rise to the claim did not take place there. *However,* the usual federal venue provisions do not apply in removed actions. For removed cases, the applicable provision is 28 U.S.C. §1441(a), which requires that the case must be removed to the district and division embracing the place where the state action was brought. See *Polizzi v. Cowles Magazines,* 345 U.S. 663, 665 (1953). Thus, as long as the defendants remove to the federal district that includes Guadaloupe County, venue will not be a problem.

The subject matter jurisdiction analysis requires a two-level inquiry. First, the removal statute requires that the case have been within the original subject matter jurisdiction of the federal court. 28 U.S.C. §1441(a). Assuming that suit was brought after Bailey moved its principal place of business to California, that requirement would be met, based on diversity. However, even if a case satisfies the basic diversity requirements, §1441(b) bars removal if any defendant is a citizen of the forum state. So, the short version of this long-winded answer is that the case cannot be removed, since Stenk is a citizen of New Mexico.

## A Two-Ring Circus

7. a. It appears that the Southern District of Iowa falls in this area. Federal subject matter jurisdiction would be proper if the suit was brought in that district, as in any other: Adler asserts a claim under the federal copyright laws, and supplemental jurisdiction will apply to his related breach of contract claim. (The court would also have independent jurisdiction over the contract claim on diversity grounds.) Personal jurisdiction is likely to be upheld in any Iowa court since the claim results, at least indirectly, from Ringling Brothers' deliberate contact in going to Iowa to make the royalty agreement with Adler. This would likely suffice for specific in personam jurisdiction under the *International Shoe* minimum contacts test.

   However, venue would not be proper in the Southern District of Iowa. This case is not founded solely on diversity, so the analysis must be under §1391(b). Ringling Brothers does not "reside" in the Southern District under §§1391(b)(1) and (c) because it has no contacts there if the district is viewed as a state, nor did a substantial part of the events giving rise to the claim take place there. Nor does §1391(b)(3) apply; like subsection (a)(3), it is a "fallback" provision that only applies if there is no district in which venue would otherwise be proper. Here, there are other districts in which venue is proper under §§1391(b)(1) and (2), so the third subsection does not apply.

There could be numerous other districts that fell in this area as well. In any state where the circus does enough business to support general in personam jurisdiction, the diversity and personal jurisdiction rings will be satisfied. However, if the circus does business in some districts of those states but not others, venue will only be proper in those districts where it does business. (Got that?)

b. The Northern District of Iowa might fall into this area on the diagram, depending on the interpretation of §1391(b)(2). Subject matter jurisdiction is proper based on the federal question and supplemental jurisdiction. Venue may be proper under §1391(b)(2) since the claim arises in part from an "omission" — Ringling Brothers' failure to pay Adler the agreed royalties — which arguably took place in the Northern District of Iowa. However, it is doubtful that the circus would be subject to personal jurisdiction in Iowa if the agreement was made in New York and the circus's only contact with Iowa was the failure to send the royalty checks to Adler there.

# PART II

## State Law in Federal Courts

# CHAPTER 10

# Easy *Erie*

## The Law of Rome and Athens

### *A Personal Fantasy*

It is December, and the pace of the first year of law school is picking up. Glannon sits numbly in Civil Procedure class. The professor is droning on, quite learnedly. Subject: the *Erie* doctrine. Glannon cowers as unobtrusively as possible in the middle of the class. All around him, students listen intently, with apparent comprehension. Glannon understands nothing.

Suddenly, the Archangel Gabriel appears, hovering resplendent above the class. No one else takes notice; the discussion moves on obliviously. Pointing a star-studded scepter at the object of his visit, Gabriel speaks. "Glannon," he declaims, "listen well, for you, *you* shall be called upon to explain the *Erie* doctrine to a future generation of students."

Astonished by the apparition and appalled at his message, Glannon streaks from the room. After a long convalescence and many setbacks, he takes a job watering flowers in a nursery.

# INTRODUCTION

Believe me, if old Gabe had really put in an appearance back then, I would surely have given the nursery job some serious thought. But even if I had stoically accepted the archangel's charge, I would never have contemplated calling anything about the *Erie* doctrine "easy." I certainly found it impenetrable then, and there is much about it that remains a mystery to me today. However, some aspects of *Erie* really are fairly straightforward, and, luckily, those are the aspects that it is particularly important for you to understand. This chapter deals with these comprehensible aspects of *Erie*.

The whole problem is really the Framers' fault. They decided to craft a federal form of government, in which most power would remain with the states, but certain limited powers would be delegated to the new national government. They spent a summer deciding what legislative powers the national government really had to have and set them forth in Article I, §8 of the Constitution. All other powers, anything they hadn't mentioned (or by fair implication "necessary and proper" to the exercise of these "delegated" powers), "are reserved to the States respectively, or to the people." U.S. Const., Amend. X.

At the same time, the Framers adopted Article III of the Constitution, which authorizes the creation of federal courts and defines their jurisdiction. In defining the federal judicial power, they authorized federal courts to hear claims that arise under federal law ("cases arising under this Constitution, the Laws of the United States, or Treaties made, or which shall be made, under their Authority"). Thus, when Congress makes law under its delegated powers in Article I, §8, and cases arise in which plaintiffs seek recovery under those laws, the federal courts have jurisdiction.

However, the Framers went further in Article III. They also created the diversity jurisdiction, which authorizes federal courts to hear cases that do not involve federal law at all. In fact, by definition a diversity case does not arise under federal law. If Plato, from Montana, sues Lucan, from South Dakota, for violation of the federal patent laws, the parties are diverse, but it is not a diversity case, since the claim arises under federal law. Plato's right to recover is created by federal law, a law Congress had the power to pass because the power to regulate patents is delegated to the federal government under Article I, §8. This is a federal question case; it is irrelevant that the parties are from different states.

On the other hand, if Plato's claim is for breach of contract, the federal court will have jurisdiction (if the amount in controversy is sufficient) based on diversity of citizenship. However, the substantive law that governs the claim cannot be created by Congress, since it has no delegated power to create a general law of contracts. The federal court has *judicial* power to hear the case, even though there is no federal *legislative* power to create the governing law. The question addressed in *Erie* — and in its infamous predecessor, *Swift v. Tyson*, 41 U.S. 1 (1842) — was what law should be applied in this anomalous situation.

# THE RULE OF *SWIFT V. TYSON*

There was no real reason why this had to be such a problem. The First Congress had considered the issue in 1789 and passed a statute to deal with it.

The Rules of Decision Act, 1 Stat. 92 (1789), provides:

> The laws of the several states, except where the constitution, treaties or statutes of the United States shall otherwise require or provide, shall be regarded as rules of decision in trials at common law in the courts of the United States, in cases where they apply.

The Rules of Decision Act (referred to herein as "the RDA") is still in force today, little changed from the original of 200 years ago. See 28 U.S.C. §1652.

Much controversy could have been avoided if the Supreme Court had simply interpreted the RDA differently in 1842, when Justice Story decided *Swift v. Tyson*. In *Swift*, the plaintiff, Swift, brought a federal diversity suit to collect on a bill of exchange. The bill had been given by Tyson to a third party, Norton, who endorsed it over to Swift in New York. As consideration for the bill, Swift had cancelled an antecedent debt owed him by Norton. Swift, a "holder in due course," was entitled to collect on the bill if he had given "a valuable consideration" for it. The less than earth-shaking issue in the case was whether Swift's cancellation of Norton's pre-existing debt constituted such consideration. 41 U.S. at 14-16.

Tyson, the defendant, argued that the RDA required the court to apply New York law to determine the validity of consideration, since the case involved a bill executed in New York and no federal statute applied. Under New York case law, Tyson contended, such consideration was insufficient. Justice Story doubted that the New York cases were so clear, but concluded that it didn't matter anyway. The RDA, he concluded, did not require the federal court to follow New York's view of this question of general commercial law. In Story's view, the phrase "the laws of the several states" in the RDA referred only to the statutes and certain established local usages of the state, not to judicial decisions interpreting general principles of common law.

If the federal court did not have to apply the common law decisions of the state in a diversity case, what law should it apply? In Story's view, the federal court should examine all the common law authorities — including cases from the state in which it sat, from other states, from federal courts, English courts, and the views of respected commentators — to ascertain the proper rule. The federal judge's job, Story believed, was the same as that of any other common law judge: to choose the right rule of consideration, rather than to follow a rule that some other judge deemed to be the right one.

## THE PHILOSOPHICAL UNDERPINNINGS OF *SWIFT*

It is not hard to see behind this conclusion a fundamental premise about the nature of law. The law, declared Justice Story, cannot be one thing in Rome and another in Athens. 41 U.S. at 19. The law is the Law, a body of absolute "right" rules, existing apart from a particular place, time, or judge. Under this "natural law" view (said to derive from Blackstone,[1] but doubtless more fundamentally from the Greek philosophers), the task of every judge was to look to all the available evidence to ascertain the ideal "right" rule on any common law question, such as the proper consideration for a contract or true duty owed to a trespasser on a railroad right of way:

> *Swift v. Tyson* rests on the philosophic premise that a court — specifically a state court — does not *make* the law but merely *finds* or declares the law, and so its decisions simply constitute evidence of what the law is, which another court is free to reject in favor of better evidence to be found elsewhere.

R. Jackson, The Rise and Fall of Swift v. Tyson, 24 A.B.A.J. 609, 612 (1938). In the lofty search for this "transcendental body of law,"[2] it is hardly surprising that one judge seeking the true rule of adequate consideration should not feel bound by a prior judge's perceptions. All looked to the same sources in their efforts to approximate the ideal outcome. The language of the pre-*Erie* opinions nicely reflects this premise. In *Swift*, for example, Story speaks of "the true result of the commercial law upon the question now before us." 41 U.S. at 19. In *Black & White Taxicab Co. v. Brown & Yellow Taxicab Co.*, 276 U.S. 518 (1928), the high-water mark of the *Swift* doctrine, the majority speaks of "the discovery" of common law principles and of looking to past cases as "evidence of the existing applicable rule." 276 U.S. at 529-530.

This natural law view ran into some problems along the way. First, it was clear that the law *could* be one thing in Rome and another in Athens, if the legislature so declared it. If the New York legislature passed a statute declaring that railroads owed a duty of due care to trespassers, that became the law of New York. There was no question that the RDA required the federal diversity court to apply that statute to New York cases. If Pennsylvania passed a statute declaring that the railroad need only avoid wilful or wanton negligence, the federal court sitting in diversity would have to apply that rule in a Pennsylvania case. The federal courts under *Swift*

---

1. W. Castro, The *Erie* Doctrine and the Structure of Constitutional Revolutions, 62 Tul. L. Rev. 907, 913 (1988).
2. *Black & White Taxicab Co. v. Brown & Yellow Taxicab Co.*, 276 U.S. 518, 533 (1928) (Holmes, J., dissenting).

also followed many so-called "local usages", such as established state common law rules concerning interests in land, for reasons of stability and predictability of titles.

*Second*, the Swift rule created potential for manipulation of the sort upheld in *Black & White Taxicab Co. v. Brown & Yellow Taxicab Co.*, 276 U.S. 518 (1928). In that case, the Brown & Yellow Taxicab Company sought to enforce a contract with the railroad, providing it the exclusive right to pick up and discharge passengers at a train station in Kentucky. Aware that the Kentucky state courts did not enforce such contracts, Brown & Yellow reincorporated in Tennessee, thus creating diversity between it and the defendant, Black & White. It then brought suit in *federal* court — in Kentucky, no less — to enjoin Black & White from interfering with its contract. The Kentucky federal court held, as other federal cases had, that the true rule was that the monopoly contract was enforceable, and enjoined the defendant from interfering with it. The Supreme Court upheld the decision on the ground that the federal court had the authority under *Swift* to reach its own conclusion on the common law issue of whether such exclusive contracts should be enforced. Even though Kentucky law would have been applied by a Kentucky *state* court, and would have barred enforcement of the contract, the Kentucky *federal* court enforced it. Thus, by invoking diversity jurisdiction, the plaintiff was able to choose a substantive rule of law that upheld rather than barred the contract.

# THE LEGAL REALIST ATTACK ON *SWIFT*

Justice Oliver Wendell Holmes wrote a marvelous dissent in *Black & White Taxicab*, in which he attacked *Swift's* basic philosophical premise about the nature of law. *Swift*, he wrote, was based on

> the impression that there is one august corpus, to understand which clearly is the only task of any Court concerned. If there were such a transcendental body of law outside of any particular State but obligatory within it unless and until changed by statute, the Courts of the United States might be right in using their independent judgment as to what it was. But there is no such body of law. The fallacy and illusion that I think exist consist in supposing that there is this outside thing to be found.

276 U.S. at 533.

If there is no "august corpus" of true rules of law, just what is the law anyway? The law, declares Holmes, is a set of rules laid down by those with the power to do so, to govern behavior in a given place at a given time:

Law is a word used with many meanings, but law in the sense in which courts speak of it today does not exist without some definite authority behind it. The common law so far as it is enforced in a State, whether called common law or not, is not the common law generally but the law of that State existing by the authority of that State.

Id. For Holmes, the rule that a railroad owes a duty of due care to a trespasser — or doesn't — derives its force not from its inherent "rightness," but from the fact that the authorities empowered to make such a rule have made it. The law *can* be one thing in Rome and another in Athens because the people who make Roman laws are different from those who make the Athenian laws. Since Athens is a different place, with different conditions and problems, its lawmakers may well choose different rules than the Romans do. And later Athenian lawmakers may choose different rules than their predecessors. Each rule may be "right" in the sense that it is appropriate to its time and place, but it is not "right" because it is the one true rule for all time on a particular issue.[3]

If this "legal realist" view of the judge's role is correct, what should a federal judge do in a case like *Black & White?* According to Holmes, he should ask what body has the authority to make rules governing the enforcement of contracts. The answer to that question is usually the states, since the Constitution delegates no general law-making authority over contracts to the legislative or judicial branches of the federal government. Whether the state speaks through its legislature or through its "other voice" (its courts), it must be heeded because it is the body with the authority to create the applicable law under our constitutional distribution of powers.

## THE *ERIE* DECISION

Justice Holmes died in 1935, so it fell to Justice Brandeis to sound the death knell for *Swift*. It was doubtless a task Holmes would have relished, since the Court in *Erie* dramatically repudiated the 100-year tradition represented by *Swift*.

The facts of the case were simple: Tompkins lost an arm when hit by a projection from an Erie Railroad train while walking on a pathway along the tracks. His injury was quite likely the result of negligence; however,

---

3. Holmes's language in *Black & White*, like that of the natural law judges, reflects his premise. He speaks of state courts "establishing," "declaring," or "adopting" rules of law, "say[ing] . . . that thus the law is and shall be." 276 U.S. at 534-535. His is not the language of discovery, but of creation.

there was no evidence that the railroad's employees had acted wilfully or wantonly in creating the danger, which was the standard for recovery under Pennsylvania law.[4] The federal district court, relying on *Swift*, concluded that it was not bound by the Pennsylvania decision and instead followed federal decisions, which held that railroads owed a duty of due care to users of lateral pathways along the track. Tompkins recovered in federal district court, though he would have lost if the case had been brought in state court.

Interestingly, no party argued that *Swift* should be overruled: The defendant in *Erie* argued instead that the federal court should have followed the Pennsylvania rule because it was a matter of "local usage" rather than general common law. I. Younger, What Happened in *Erie*, 56 Tex. L. Rev. 1011, 1025-1026 (1978). The *Erie* Court, however, dramatically rephrased the issue: "The question for decision is whether the oft-challenged doctrine of *Swift v. Tyson* shall now be disapproved." 304 U.S. at 69 (footnote omitted). To its own question, the Court answered "yes," for a number of reasons.

*First*, *Swift* had failed to achieve one of the main goals of its supporters. It was hoped that the gradual accumulation of "general common law" decisions by eminent federal judges would induce state judges to recognize the "rightness" of those decisions and fall into line, leading to broad uniformity in the common law throughout the nation. But state judges had the temerity to believe that they too could examine the "evidence" and "discover" true principles for themselves. Rather than docilely following federal cases, the state judges persisted in taking their own views. The result was a multiplicity of rules on recurrent issues, not only from different state courts, but also from federal and state courts within a single state.

*Second*, Justice Brandeis concluded, the federal practice of making common law had led to grave discrimination in the administration of justice. As *Black & White Taxicab* illustrates, it allowed an out-of-state plaintiff to choose a different rule of substantive law because he could choose federal court. While a local taxicab company would have to sue in a Kentucky state court, which would refuse to enforce exclusive contracts, a diverse plaintiff could go to federal court and get a more favorable outcome. Ironically, while diversity was created to prevent prejudice against out-of-staters — to assure a "level playing field," as they said in the 1980s — *Swift* had introduced discrimination in favor of the out-of-stater.[5]

---

4. All involved assumed that, if state law applied at all, Pennsylvania law would apply.

5. Arguably, there is no discrimination here between the parties to the case. After all, defendants get a choice of forum too: They can remove cases from state to federal court. But this is not true of in-state defendants. 28 U.S.C. §1441(b). Thus, in *Black & White*, if the Kentucky rule had been more favorable to the plaintiff than the "federal common law" rule, Brown & Yellow could have sued in state court, and the defendant would have been stuck in

*Third*, and most fundamentally, Justice Brandeis declared the *Swift* doctrine unconstitutional, since it authorized federal judges to "make" law in areas in which the federal government has no delegated powers. *Erie* emphatically adopts Holmes's view that, in choosing its rules of decision, the federal court must look to the body with the authority to make those rules. When it comes to common law matters not within the federal government's delegated powers, that body is the state, whether it speaks by statute or judicial decision. Thus, ignoring state common law rules invades rights reserved to the states under our federal system of divided powers:

> Notwithstanding the great names which may be cited in favor of the [*Swift*] doctrine . . . there stands, as a perpetual protest against its repetition, the constitution of the United States, which recognizes and preserves the autonomy and independence of the states, — independence in their legislative and independence in their judicial departments. Supervision over either the legislative or the judicial action of the states is in no case permissible except as to matters by the constitution specifically authorized or delegated to the United States.

*Erie*, 304 U.S. at 78-79, quoting from *Baltimore & Ohio R. Co. v. Baugh*, 149 U.S. 368, 401 (1893) (Field, J., dissenting).

I suggested earlier that Justice Story could have avoided the entire problem by interpreting the RDA a little differently. That act requires the federal courts to apply "the laws of the several States," unless the federal Constitution, treaties, or statutes require otherwise. If Story had concluded that the phrase "the laws of the several States" includes state common law decisions, the federal courts would have been required *by the RDA itself* to apply those decisions, and lofty questions of constitutional power to do otherwise would have been avoided. He didn't interpret it that way. In *Erie*, however, Justice Brandeis concluded that it would be unconstitutional to interpret it any other way. It was Justice Story's interpretation of the act, not the act itself, that the court rejected in *Erie*.[6]

---

state court. In addition, when the diverse plaintiff chooses federal court initially, the defendant is stuck with it, since there is no such thing as removal to state court. In *Black & White*, for example, the out-of-state plaintiff sued in federal court because the federal rule was more favorable, and the defendant was stuck with that court, and that rule.

Finally, there is another type of discrimination here, between out-of-state plaintiffs and in-state plaintiffs with similar claims against local citizens. A Kentucky taxi company who sued Black & White on a similar claim would not have had the same opportunity that Brown & Yellow had to choose the applicable law by choosing the "right" court.

6. Not everyone agrees that *Erie* is the best solution to the problem of state law in diversity cases. See, e.g., J. Coor, Thoughts on the Vitality of *Erie*, 41 Am. U. L. Rev. 1087 (1992), which rebuts Justice Brandeis's arguments for overruling *Swift*, argues that *Erie* has raised more problems than it has solved, and advocates returning to *Swift*.

## WHAT'S EASY ABOUT *ERIE*

Whatever its fascination may be as a triumph of legal realism or a constitutional landmark, the central command of *Erie* is basic. In diversity cases federal courts must apply the law that would be applied by the courts of the state in which they sit. They are not free to decide for themselves the "right" rule of consideration, the duty that a railroad owes to a trespasser, or the enforceability of exclusive contracts. Rather than create "general common law," their job in a diversity case is to *apply* state common law. In those broad areas where the law is largely judge-made, such as contracts, torts, probate, and property, state law reigns supreme because "there can be no other law," *Hanna v. Plumer*, 380 U.S. 460, 472 (1965).

In 97 percent of the cases, this is easy. Lawyers and federal courts apply *Erie* every day without the slightest difficulty because all parties recognize that state law provides the governing rules of decision and there is little question as to what the state law is. There's been a lot of fuss about some fringe case — we'll fuss over them ourselves in the next chapter — but in the overwhelming number of diversity cases *Erie* functions simply and effectively to determine the applicable principles of substantive law.

The following examples consider the basic mechanics of applying the *Erie* doctrine. In analyzing them, assume, unless otherwise specified, that all actions are brought in federal court on the basis of diversity. After the initial examples, we will consider a related question: How does a judge determine what the law of the state actually is?

### Examples

#### When in Rome . . .

1. Plato was injured in an accident in Minnesota when his car collided with those of Solon and Ovid. He sued Solon and recovered $200,000 in damages, which Solon paid. Solon then sued Ovid for contribution, that is, to get a judgment that Ovid, as a joint tortfeasor, must reimburse Solon for half of the damages he paid to Plato. The contribution action was brought in federal court in Minnesota.

    At the time of Solon's contribution suit, the law on contribution was in a state of flux throughout the United States. Most courts refused to order contribution between joint tortfeasors. A few courts, however, had adopted the opposite view, that a tortfeasor who had paid the plaintiff could require other negligent parties to pay their share of the loss. Several states had adopted statutes authorizing contribution. Minnesota had no statute on point, but its courts had followed the minority rule, allowing contribution.

    a. How should the federal district court decide the issue of Solon's right to contribution, if the case arose prior to *Erie?*

    b. How should the court decide the issue after *Erie?*

2. Assume that Solon's contribution action arose in 1925, before *Erie* was decided, and that most *federal* courts that had considered the issue had concluded that contribution should be allowed between joint tortfeasors. However, Judge Quintus, the federal trial judge in Solon's action for contribution, agreed with the reasoning of the courts that deny contribution. What should he do?

3. Assume that, prior to Solon's contribution action, Minnesota had passed a statute that authorized contribution among joint tortfeasors.

    a. How should the federal district court decide the contribution question, if the case arose before *Erie?*

    b. How should the court decide the issue after *Erie?*

4. Assume that Minnesota had a statute authorizing contribution among joint tortfeasors. Most states with contribution statutes had held that they are not intended to allow a party who acted wilfully or wantonly to seek contribution. However, assume that the Minnesota Supreme Court had construed the Minnesota statute to authorize a tortfeasor to seek contribution even if her conduct was wilful or wanton. If Solon seeks contribution, and Ovid argues that the statute does not authorize it because Solon's conduct was wilful or wanton, how should Judge Quintus rule if

    a. the case arose prior to *Erie?*

    b. the case arose after *Erie?*

## History Repeats Itself

5. Assume that Harry Tompkins III is walking on a lateral pathway along the tracks of the Erie Railroad in Pennsylvania in 2007. He is injured when hit by something projecting from a passing train. He sues the Erie Railroad in federal court under the Federal Interstate Railway Act, which (we will assume) authorizes suits for damages arising from railroad accidents. He also asserts a state law claim against the Erie for negligence. (The federal court has supplemental jurisdiction over this claim, under 28 U.S.C. §1367.) On the negligence claim, the railroad argues that Pennsylvania law does not allow trespassers on the right of way to recover damages, absent wilful or wanton negligence, but Tompkins argues that the court should apply the "more modern" due care standard to the negligence claim. What should the federal judge do, and why?

# ASCERTAINING STATE LAW

Because *Erie* requires federal courts to apply state law in diversity cases, federal judges obviously must decide what the state law is. In many cases that is easy because the issue has been clearly decided by the state's highest court. If there is a recent case from the Pennsylvania Supreme Court holding that railroads are only liable to trespassers for wilful or wanton conduct, the federal court knows its course and will dismiss a future *Tompkins* case if there is no evidence of such aggravated fault. Similarly, if the Kentucky decisions consistently refuse to enforce exclusive contracts like that in *Black & White*, the federal court in Kentucky will also refuse to enforce them.

Many cases, however, are not so squarely resolved by the case law. For example, there may be older cases from the Pennsylvania Supreme Court requiring wilful conduct but recent tort cases in related areas that suggest a trend to expand duties in tort cases generally. Or perhaps the Kentucky courts have refused to enforce exclusive contracts, but those cases are distinguishable because they involved matters of particular public interest. Or there may be no state supreme court case on the point, but there may be one from an intermediate appellate court. Or perhaps no appellate court from the state has decided the question in dispute, but a trial judge has. Or going one step further, perhaps there is absolutely no decision on point, though there are decisions on analogous tort issues.

The early post-*Erie* cases suggested that the federal court, in deciding what state law is, should follow any existing state precedent, without making creative predictions about how that precedent might be treated in a future case. In *West v. American Tel. & Tel. Co.*, 311 U.S. 223 (1940), for example, the Court held that, where there was no decision on point from the state supreme court, a decision of the state's intermediate appellate court was binding, "even though [the federal district court] may think that the state Supreme Court may establish a different rule in some future litigation." 311 U.S. at 238. The furthest extension of this approach came in *Fidelity Trust Co. v. Field*, 311 U.S. 169 (1940), in which the Supreme Court required the federal court to follow two trial court decisions on a question of New Jersey law, in the absence of any appellate cases on point, even though no other New Jersey judge would have been bound by those decisions. This led Judge Frank of the Second Circuit to complain that the federal judge was to woodenly follow existing state cases like a "ventriloquist's dummy." *Richardson v. Commissioner*, 126 F.2d 562, 567 (2d Cir. 1942).

The Supreme Court has since suggested, however, that federal judges have a bit more flexibility in determining state law under Erie. In *Commissioner v. Bosch*, 387 U.S. 456, 465 (1967), the Court held that a federal court construing state law should give "proper regard" to decisions of trial and intermediate appellate courts, but that its job is to apply the law as announced, or as it *would be announced*, by the state's highest court. Thus, the federal judge must predict how the issue before it would be decided by the state supreme court if that court decided the issue today. In making that prediction, the judge may look to all available data, including decisions from the state's lower courts, developing trends in the area of law that cast doubt on the earlier decisions, and dicta or legislative developments that weaken (or reaffirm) the existing precedents. The judge is not free to make up state law, but he is entitled to make an educated judgment on what rule the state supreme court would apply to the case *today*, rather than merely parroting what the rule was when the last case on point was decided. See generally Moore's §124.22[3].

The federal court may have an additional option in determining state law. Some states have "certification" procedures, which allow a federal court faced with a thorny state law issue to certify the issue to the state supreme court. See, e.g., Kan. Stat Ann. §§60-3201 to 60-3212; W. Va. Code §§51-1A-1 to 51-1-12. When the federal judge certifies the issue, a statement of the issue and the relevant facts is sent to the state court. The case then goes into the regular appellate pipeline: The parties brief and argue the issue before the state court as though it were a regular appeal from a lower state court. Ultimately, the state supreme court issues an opinion, much like that on any other appeal, resolving the issue. Then, armed with the answer to their question, the parties return to the *federal* court and pick up the litigation there.

While certification assures an accurate reading of state law (assuming the state court accepts the certification), a mere description illustrates why it can only solve the problem of ascertaining state law in a small percentage of cases. It is a lengthy and expensive diversion from the federal litigation. In addition, it creates the anomalous situation of federal courts determining the state supreme court's workload. For this latter reason, certification statutes usually give the state supreme court the power to accept or refuse the certification. Only those cases that the federal court chooses to certify and the state court accepts will lead to authoritative pronouncements of state law.[7]

---

7. Despite the complications it introduces, some federal cases continue to encourage use of certification "to avoid making unnecessary *Erie* 'guesses'" See, e.g., *Alltel Communications, Inc. v. City of Macon*, 345 F.3d 1219, 1225 (11th Cir. 2003); *Mosher v. Speedstar Div. of AMCA Intl., Inc.*, 52 F.3d 913, 916 (11th Cir. 1995).

## Examples

### ...Do As the Romans Do

6. Assume that the Minnesota Supreme Court, in *Aristotle v. Caesar*, a 1952 decision, refused to allow contribution between joint tortfeasors, reasoning that each tortfeasor who caused the plaintiff's injury may justly be made to pay the entire damages and that the legislature is the proper body to change this basic tort principle if it is dissatisfied with the common law no-contribution approach. In 2007, the issue comes before the Minnesota Court of Appeals, the *state* intermediate appellate court, in a new case, *Justinian v. Lycurgus*. It reviews the broad changes in many areas of tort law since 1952, including the very wide adoption by other states of the right of contribution. On balance, it concludes that if the state supreme court reconsidered the issue it would likely overrule *Aristotle* and allow contribution.

   a. What should the Minnesota Court of Appeals do in *Justinian v. Lycurgus*?

   b. Assume that, shortly *before* the mid-level appeals court's decision in *Justinian*, Solon brings an action against Ovid for contribution in federal court. Judge Quintus, the federal judge, reviews the 1952 *Aristotle* opinion, as well as the broad trend of tort law decisions in Minnesota, and concludes (as did the Court of Appeals in *Justinian*) that the Minnesota Supreme Court would overrule *Aristotle*. How should Judge Quintus rule on Solon's claim for contribution?

   c. Suppose that Solon sues Ovid for contribution in federal court after the Minnesota Court of Appeals (the intermediate state court) had predicted in *Justinian* that the Minnesota Supreme Court would overrule *Aristotle*. However, Judge Quintus, who is handling the *Solon* case, does not agree with the Court of Appeals' prediction. What should he do?

   d. If you represented Solon in the contribution action against Ovid, would you file suit in federal court or state court?

### Role Reversal

7. Justinian is held liable to Draco in a negligence action and sues Charondas in a Minnesota *state* court for contribution as a joint tortfeasor. Judge Ulpian, the state trial judge, prior to ruling on the right to contribution, researches the law on contribution and finds that there is no Minnesota case addressing the right to contribution between joint tortfeasors. However, in *Solon v. Ovid* (a diversity case applying Minnesota law), the Federal Court of Appeals for the Eighth Circuit had concluded that the Minnesota Supreme Court, if it considered the question, would allow contribution. How should Judge Ulpian rule?

8. Assume that Justinian's contribution action is brought in the *federal* district court for the District of Minnesota. Judge Quintus, the federal

district court judge, must decide whether Minnesota would allow contribution. His research uncovers *Solon v. Ovid* (described in the previous example) from the Eighth Circuit, which hears appeals from the federal District of Minnesota. How should Judge Quintus decide the contribution question?

## Preempted Predictions

9. Lucian sues Caesar for contribution in the federal district court for the District of Minnesota. At the time, it is unclear from the cases whether Minnesota recognizes a right to contribution among joint tortfeasors or not; the Minnesota Supreme Court has never decided the issue. Judge Quintus, the federal district judge, reviews the state law precedents in related areas and predicts that the Minnesota Supreme Court would not allow contribution. Consequently, he refuses to order contribution in Lucian's case, and enters a judgment dismissing it.

Eighteen months later, the Minnesota Supreme Court takes review in a state case raising the issue of the right to contribution, and holds that Minnesota law recognizes a right to contribution among tortfeasors. Now, Lucian moves for relief from judgment under Fed. R. Civ. P. 60 (b) in his federal contribution suit against Caesar, asking Judge Quintus to reopen the case and order contribution, since it is now clear that he had guessed wrong about the right to contribution under Minnesota law. What should Judge Quintus do?

## High Fidelity

10. The State of Illinois has not one, but five intermediate appellate courts. Each handles appeals from a separate geographical area of the state. See Figure 10-1. A case tried in Washington County, for example, in the Fifth District, would be appealed to the Fifth Judicial District of the Illinois Appellate Court. A case tried in Cook County goes on appeal to the First Judicial District. (Cook County is the only county in the First District because Chicago is located there and creates as much judicial business as many other counties put together.)

Assume that Gaius sues Draco in Cook County Circuit Court (the Illinois trial court of general jurisdiction) for contribution as a joint tortfeasor. Assume further that the Illinois Supreme Court has never decided whether contribution is available between tortfeasors. The Fourth and Second Districts of the Illinois Appellate Court have held that it is, but the First District has held that it is not.

a. What rule should the state trial judge in *Gaius v. Draco* follow?

b. Now, assume that the *Gaius* case is brought in Cook County but is removed to the federal district court for the Northern District of

**Figure 10-1**. Judicial districts of Illinois Appellate Court.
Source: www.state.il.us/court/AppellateCourt/Map.htm.

Illinois, which includes Cook County. What rule should the federal district judge apply?

## Explanations

### When in Rome . . .

1. a. If this case arose under the *Swift* regime, the federal judge would not be bound by the Minnesota decisions on the right to contribution. *Swift* authorized federal judges to make independent judgments as to what the proper rule should be on issues of "general common law." Contribution was a question of tort law, which had long been governed by the common law decisions of courts rather than by

statute. Thus, the judge was not bound to follow the Minnesota decisions, even though, had the suit been brought in a Minnesota state court, contribution would have been allowed.

Nor would he have been bound by the majority position of the other states: The rule was not necessarily "right" because it was more widely followed. The judge would look to all the cases and authorities, assess their reasoning, and reach the decision that, in his judgment, represented the proper rule on the issue.

b. After *Erie*, the judge would clearly be bound to follow the Minnesota rule, even though it is a judge-made common law rule rather than a statute. *Erie* held that the RDA requires federal courts to apply state law in diversity cases, whether judge-made or statutory, rather than following their own perception of the best rule. The rationale of *Erie* is that the grant of jurisdiction over diversity cases in Article III is not a grant of authority to displace state substantive rules of decision, but only to apply those rules in a federal, presumably neutral forum. Since only the state has the general power to make law on tort issues like the right of contribution among joint tortfeasors, the federal court must apply the state's law rather than creating its own law.

Note that the court must apply the Minnesota rule, not the rule that the majority of states would choose. Where the case is governed by Minnesota law, the issue is not how most state courts would rule, but how the Minnesota courts would.

2. This is an interesting dilemma for the judge under *Swift*. He was not bound by the state decisions — either those of Minnesota or of other states — but was he bound by the trend in the federal cases? One of the arguments for the *Swift* doctrine was that eventually uniform common law rules would evolve as a body of "general common law" decisions on similar issues accumulated. But the basic rationale of *Swift* is that each judge looks to the common law sources to reach an independent judgment as to the proper rule. Presumably, if a judge did that and concluded that the majority of his federal colleagues had reached the wrong result, he should not follow them any more than state judges who had missed the mark. Thus, he should not be bound by decisions from other federal district courts either. Although such decisions might be persuasive (just as the Minnesota decisions might be) he would make an independent judgment as to the proper contribution rule.

3. a. In this case the state rule is the same as in the previous examples, but it has been established by statute rather than by judicial decision. Even under *Swift* it was generally — though not always — held that the RDA required federal courts to apply state statutes in diversity cases. Moore's §124 App.01[2]. Thus, the federal court had to apply

the state rule if the legislature made it but was free to ignore it if the state supreme court did.

b. *Erie* held that the RDA must be interpreted to require federal courts to apply state common law decisions in diversity cases. It did not in any way impair the long-established view that the act required federal courts to apply state statutes in diversity cases. Indeed, under *Erie* this is not only the proper interpretation of the RDA, but the only permissible one. Since there is no general federal power to enact laws governing contribution among joint tortfeasors, state law must govern because "there can be no other law." *Hanna v. Plumer*, 380 U.S. 460, 472 (1965). Thus, after *Erie*, as before, the court would apply the Minnesota statute.

4. a. Here, there is a state statute on point, and the issue is the proper interpretation of it. Minnesota courts construe their statute one way, though other states construe similar provisions differently. Under *Swift*, the federal court had to follow state statutes in diversity cases, but did the federal court have to follow state court cases construing the meaning of those statutes?

Even under the *Swift* regime, the federal courts generally recognized that the issue in a case like this was what the Minnesota contribution statute meant, not what the "best" interpretation of similar statutes was. Most cases under *Swift* recognized that the Minnesota courts were the proper body to determine the meaning of the Minnesota statute, and therefore would follow the state cases interpreting it. Moore's Federal Practice, §124 App.01[2].

Ironically, however, some cases, particularly earlier ones, even refused to follow state courts' interpretations of their own state statutes. See R. Jackson, The Rise and Fall of Swift v. Tyson, 24 A.B.A.J. 609, 611-613 (1938). This seems even more of an affront to the state courts than the basic doctrine of *Swift*: It is one thing for the federal courts to take an independent view of what the common law rule of contribution *should* be. It is quite another for them to ignore the Minnesota court's conclusion as to what their own state statute *actually says*.

b. Under *Erie*, the federal court clearly should apply the Minnesota court's interpretation of the statute. The source of the applicable law is the state, since the question is not within the federal legislative authority. The federal diversity court must therefore follow the law of the state, as laid down in the statute and construed by the state court. This follows as a matter of *Erie* policy as well as constitutional division of powers. If the federal court were free to construe the statute differently, parties could invoke the diversity jurisdiction to get a more favorable substantive result, just as they did under *Swift*.

## History Repeats Itself

5. Strictly speaking, this case does not raise an *Erie* problem at all. The case is a federal question case rather than a diversity case, since Tompkins III has sued under the Federal Interstate Railway Act. However, as plaintiffs are wont to do, Tompkins has asserted a state law negligence claim as well.

   The state negligence claim would be properly before the federal court under supplemental jurisdiction, which authorizes a federal court to entertain related state claims that arise from the same facts as a federal claim. See 28 U.S.C. §1367; Chapter 16. However, supplemental jurisdiction is another example of a situation — like diversity — in which federal courts have jurisdiction to *hear* state claims but no power to *create* the governing law. Here, as in diversity cases under *Erie*, the court's job is to apply state law to the supplemental claim, not to make up its own rule. Thus, the judge should have his law clerk research Pennsylvania law to determine whether it requires a showing of wilful or wanton negligence. If it does, he must apply that rule to the supplemental claim.

   Obviously, the court would apply federal law to the interpretation of the Federal Interstate Railway Act claim. It may "make" law on that claim if necessary to decide the case, but it would have to follow state law, or predict it, on the state negligence claim. Thus, in many federal cases that are *not* diversity cases the court must engage in the same exercise of guessing at the content of state law that is required in diversity cases under *Erie*. Even if the foes of diversity jurisdiction ultimately achieve its repeal, ascertaining and applying state law will still be necessary in every case involving supplemental state law claims.

## . . . Do As the Romans Do

6. a. The Minnesota Court of Appeals is a mid-level appellate court, bound by the decisions of the highest court of the state. *Aristotle v. Caesar* is such a case, and it is directly on point. An intermediate appellate court would almost certainly consider itself bound by *Aristotle*. The role of the lower courts is to follow the law established by the highest court of the state, not to speculate about how that court might change it in the future. Unless *Aristotle* had been utterly eviscerated and effectively overruled by more recent Minnesota Supreme Court decisions, the Minnesota Court of Appeals would feel bound to follow *Aristotle* and deny contribution. The Court of Appeals might well write an opinion encouraging the state supreme court to review the case and change the law, but it cannot do so itself.

   b. In this case, the only Minnesota Supreme Court case on point denies contribution, but Judge Quintus (like the state Court of Appeals in the previous example) has strong grounds to believe, in light of other tort law developments, that the state supreme court would adopt a more liberal approach on this issue if it came before that court today.

The federal judge's role in a diversity case is to predict how the case would ultimately be decided if it wended its wobbly way through the state system and reached the highest court of the state. Judge Quintus may be very circumspect about predicting that *Aristotle* would be overruled, but if he is firmly convinced that the Minnesota Supreme Court would approve contribution today he should apply that rule.

c. The only difference in this scenario is that Judge Quintus, when he rules, has the benefit of the intermediate appellate court's prediction of what the state supreme court will do. That is certainly useful data in determining what Minnesota's highest court would say; indeed it is highly persuasive. But it is not absolutely dispositive. The federal judge's role is to predict what the Minnesota Supreme Court would do, not to follow what the Court of Appeals thinks its Supreme Court would do. See, e.g., *Dimidowich v. Bell & Howell*, 803 F.2d 1473, 1482 (9th Cir. 1986) (intermediate court decisions are data to be followed unless the court is convinced by other persuasive data that the state's highest court would decide otherwise). If Judge Quintus is convinced from his general review of the law in the area that the Minnesota Supreme Court would continue to follow *Aristotle*, he must do so.

d. If you had strong arguments that the Minnesota Supreme Court would change the rule, you might well file this case in federal court. In the state trial court you would likely lose on a motion to dismiss, since *Aristotle* is mandatory precedent, which the state trial judge must follow. Even if the case goes to the state Court of Appeals, you would still lose under *Aristotle*, since the intermediate appellate court will consider itself bound by that decision. Only if the Minnesota Supreme Court takes the case (a matter vested in its discretion, which is sparingly exercised)[8] will you have a chance of winning.

In federal court, on the other hand, if the trial judge is convinced that the state supreme court would adopt contribution, he may allow the case to go forward. This will keep the case alive. Maybe it will settle. If it goes up on appeal, the federal Court of Appeals will not be bound by *Aristotle*, if convinced it is a derelict waiting to be interred by its creator. Federal judges are not anxious to disregard state

---

8. Cf. *Abbott Laboratories v. Granite State Ins. Co.*, 573 F. Supp. 193, 198 & 198 n.5 (N.D. Ill. 1983), in which Judge Shadur argues that the chance of getting the Illinois Supreme Court's view on an issue of Illinois law is miniscule. For 1982, he notes, 706,893 cases were disposed of in the Illinois trial courts, but the Illinois Supreme Court only wrote 199 opinions.

supreme court decisions, but they can do it upon strong evidence, and sometimes it is pretty clear that the law will change.

The irony here is that the federal judge's freedom to predict what the law *will be*, rather than woodenly applying what it has been, opens up a narrow opportunity for diversity plaintiffs to choose more favorable substantive law despite *Erie*. Theoretically the ultimate result would be the same because the Minnesota Supreme Court, if the case got up there, would do what the federal court predicts it would. But, as a practical matter, the case probably won't get there. The result in state court is likely to be dictated by the (perhaps outdated) *Aristotle* case but might not be in federal court.

Perhaps because of this disparity some federal courts have expressed considerable reluctance to recognize new state law rights in diversity cases. See, e.g., *Tritle v. Crown Airways, Inc.*, 928 F.2d 81, 84-85 (4th Cir. 1991). These courts reason that the plaintiff who seeks recognition of new rights under state law should sue in state court:

> We have warned, time and again, that litigants who reject a state forum in order to bring suit in federal court under diversity jurisdiction cannot expect that new [state-law] trails will be blazed.

*Carlton v. Worcester Ins. Co.*, 923 F.2d 1, 3 (1st Cir. 1991) (quoting from *Ryan v. Royal Ins. Co.*, 916 F.2d 731, 744 (1st Cir. 1990); cf. *Spector Motor Service, Inc. v. Walsh*, 139 F.2d 809, 823 (2d Cir.) (Hand, J., dissenting), vacated 323 U.S. 101 (1944) (warning lower courts against "embrac[ing] the exhilarating opportunity of anticipating a doctrine which may be in the womb of time, but whose birth is distant").

## Role Reversal

7. Judge Ulpian should rule any way he wants to: He is not bound by the Eighth Circuit's conclusion that Minnesota law allows contribution. The Eighth Circuit under *Erie* cannot make the law of Minnesota, it can only predict what the Minnesota courts will do or follow what they have done. Minnesota judges are not bound by federal judges' predictions about Minnesota law, even federal appellate judges.

Although not bound by the Eighth Circuit's decision, Judge Ulpian is likely to give the opinion in *Solon v. Ovid* serious consideration in deciding Justinian's case. A panel of three august federal judges has looked at Minnesota tort law and concluded that the Minnesota Supreme Court would allow contribution. Judge Ulpian may not be bound to follow that conclusion, but he may well be persuaded by a well-reasoned opinion by judges who, though they do not make Minnesota law, are fully conversant with it. Put another way, *Solon v. Ovid* is persuasive authority, though not mandatory.

8. Federal district courts are normally bound to follow the precedents of their supervisory court of appeals. Certainly, if the Eighth Circuit Court of Appeals decided an issue of federal law, Judge Quintus would be bound to follow it. That's what the whole system of mandatory precedent means. However, in diversity cases, federal courts do not make the law, they just guess at it. Should the federal district judge be bound by the Eighth Circuit's guess as to what the Minnesota Supreme Court would do?

   As a practical matter, if Judge Quintus makes a different guess, the losing party will appeal, and the Eighth Circuit will overrule him based on its own guess announced in the *Solon* case. So it makes sense for the district court judge to follow the Eighth Circuit's conclusion even though the Eighth Circuit does not "make" Minnesota law.

   Suppose, however, that after *Solon* the Minnesota Supreme Court decided several cases in related areas that suggest that they would not change the rule on contribution. At this point, Judge Quintus may be convinced that the Eighth Circuit would no longer make the same prediction on Minnesota law that it did in *Solon* because the evidence as to what Minnesota law "is" has changed. In such cases, where the court is convinced that later developments render the federal appeals court's prediction obsolete, it may disregard it. See, e.g., *Scadron v. City of Des Plaines*, 734 F. Supp. 1437, 1451-1452 (N.D. Ill. 1990).

## Preempted Predictions

9. In this example, Judge Quintus did his best to ascertain what Minnesota's rule on contribution was, but his prediction on the matter simply turned out to be wrong. Once that becomes clear, should a party like Lucian be able to undo the judgment Quintus rendered 18 months before and proceed with his contribution action? A ruling that he may do so would arguably further the policies of *Erie*, since it would facilitate having the case come out the same way in federal court that it would in state court. But it would severely hamper another procedural value, the ability of litigants to rely on the finality of judgments.

   Several federal courts of appeals have confronted this problem. In *DeWeerth v. Baldinger*, 38 F.3d 1266 (2d Cir. 1994), the Second Circuit refused to reopen a diversity case, even though the federal judgment was based on an interpretation of state law that was later held wrong by New York's highest court:

   > The very nature of diversity jurisdiction leaves open the possibility that a state court will subsequently disagree with a federal court's interpretation

of state law. However, this aspect of our dual justice system does not mean that all diversity judgments are subject to revision once a state court later addresses the litigated issues. Such a rule would be tantamount to holding that the doctrine of finality does not apply to diversity judgments . . .

38 F.3d at 1273-1274. The Seventh Circuit similarly refused to reopen a diversity judgment in *McGeshick v. Choicair*, 72 F.3d 62 (7th Cir. 1995), though the court left open the possibility that "extraordinary circumstances" might support a different result.

These decisions, while obviously frustrating to the losing party, make sense. Ordinarily, if a judgment is entered and no appeal is taken, parties can rely on the fact that the case is over. If a diversity case could be reopened whenever the state court clarified state law down the line, the case would only be *provisionally* over. The parties would not be able to rely on the judgment, since it might be reconsidered at some indefinite future time. As has been said in another context, "sometimes it is more important that a judgment be stable than that it be correct." Friedenthal, Kane and Miller, p. 655. This is probably one of those situations. The risk of an erroneous prediction of state law is inherent in diversity jurisdiction after *Erie*. It is probably best to recognize that and let the chips fall where they may.

## High Fidelity

10. a. The Illinois Supreme Court has held that the trial courts within each judicial district must follow the rule established by the appellate court for that district, even though other appellate courts of equal stature have ruled otherwise. See *People v. Thorpe*, 367 N.E.2d 960, 963 (Ill. App. 2d 1977). Consequently, the judge in *Gains v. Draco* must follow the holding of the First District that contribution is not allowed between joint tortfeasors.

   Under this approach, if there is a split among the districts of the Illinois Appellate Court, the "law" of Illinois will differ from one part of the state to another until the Illinois Supreme Court takes a case on further review and resolves the split in the appellate decisions.

   b. The *Erie* doctrine requires the federal judge to follow the law of the state, but in this case, the "law" of the state differs, depending on which judicial district the case is filed in. What should the federal judge do?

   There are several possible answers in this situation. One, perhaps the most obvious in light of the earlier examples, is to predict how the Illinois Supreme Court would rule on the issue. The federal court's job, after all, is to predict what "the law" of Illinois is, not the law of the First Appellate District or the Third.

. . . Or is it? Judge Shadur of the Northern District of Illinois consistently ruled otherwise in a series of decisions applying *Erie*. He argued that the federal judge's job is to assure that the suit comes out the same way in federal court that it would in state court. See, e.g., *Abbott Laboratories v. Granite State Ins. Co.*, 573 F. Supp. 193, 196-200 (N.D. Ill. 1983). Allowing Gaius to avoid the First District's no-contribution rule by going to federal court, Judge Shadur argued, will undermine the *Erie* goal of uniformity and encourage choice of the federal court to obtain a "better rule of law." Consequently, he concluded that the federal district court must follow the rulings of the Illinois Appellate Court for the district in which the case was filed.

Most courts, however, have followed the "Supreme Court predictive approach," which asks how the state supreme court would decide the issue if the case got up that far. Judge Shadur found this rule unrealistic, because few cases *do* get to the state's highest court: For most parties "the law" is the rule of the mid-level appellate court for their judicial district. Thus, he argued, the "state supreme Court predictive approach" will often yield a result quite different from the one the parties would obtain in state court. See *Abbott Laboratories* at 198 & 198 n.5. For a good review of this problem, and the arguments both ways, see B. Mattis & B. Mattis, Erie and Florida Law Conflict at the Crossroads: The Constitutional Need for Statewide Stare Decisis, 18 Nova L. Rev. 1333, 1365-1376 (1994). However, the Seventh Circuit rejected Judge Shadur's approach in *Allstate Ins. Co. v. Menards, Inc.*, 285 F.3d 630, 637 (7th Cir. 2002): "[W]e adhere today to the general rule, articulated and applied throughout the United States, that, in determining the content of state law, the federal courts must assume the perspective of the highest court in that state and attempt to ascertain the governing substantive law on the point in question."

Like example 6, this example demonstrates that, despite the command of *Erie*, it is very difficult to assure absolute uniformity in treatment within the two court systems.

# CHAPTER 11

# Eerie *Erie*

## The Substance/Substance Distinction

---

## INTRODUCTION

As "Easy *Erie*" suggests, the *Erie* doctrine is applied without substantial difficulty in most diversity cases. *Erie* and the Rules of Decision Act (RDA) require the federal court to apply state law, and the court does. It uses the state rules governing the standard of care to a trespasser, enforceability of contracts, the validity of wills and property transfers, and myriad other state rules of law, whether pronounced by statute or by common law.

It sounds easy, and often it is easy. But not always. Lurking behind the majestic and simple truths of the *Erie* case were some complex implications, which, if not foreseen by the *Erie* justices, have certainly bedeviled their successors. These implications are so subtle and important to our ideas of federalism that they have fascinated law professors as well. Consequently, while they play a relatively minor part in the daily administration of diversity jurisdiction, they figure prominently in the first-year Civil Procedure course.

The most puzzling problem, of course, has been determining which issues are governed by the command of *Erie*. Clearly, *Erie* requires federal courts to apply state law to issues upon which there is no federal law-making power. For example, neither Congress nor the federal courts have any authority to establish the standard of care generally owed to trespassers. Thus, the RDA, as interpreted in *Erie*, requires the federal court to apply state law on this "substantive" issue. But it is doubtful that the Court ever thought that *Erie*'s command would require federal courts to follow state law on clearly *procedural* issues in diversity cases.

## THE EMERGENCE OF THE PROBLEM

It didn't take long for the substance/procedure problem implicit in *Erie* to begin to emerge. The very next term the Court decided *Cities Service Oil Co. v. Dunlap*, 308 U.S. 208 (1939), which raised an issue much closer to the line between substance and procedure than the tort issue in *Erie*: which party had the burden of proof on a question of title to land. Texas law placed the burden of proof on validity of title on the party challenging the title, but federal procedure placed it on the party who brought suit, in this case the holder of the record title. The federal Court of Appeals concluded that *Erie* did not require use of the state rule, since the issue was "a matter of practice or procedure and not a matter of substantive law." 101 F.2d 314, 316 (1939). However, the Supreme Court reversed, holding that the burden of proof issue "relates to a substantial right" so that *Erie* mandated application of state law. 308 U.S. at 212.

The *Dunlap* decision must have sent shock waves through the legal community. The decision suggested that *Erie* required diversity courts to defer to state law not only on "substantive" rules but also on matters of procedure that related to the enforcement of state rights. If the federal court had to apply state law on burden of proof in a diversity case, why not on the time for filing a complaint, the right to amend, or the admissibility of evidence? At its most extreme, this would mean that federal courts would have to abandon the Federal Rules of Civil Procedure in diversity cases and apply instead the entire *procedural* law of the state in which they sat. Federal courts would then operate under a dual system of procedure: the Federal Rules in federal question, admiralty, and other types of cases within federal subject matter jurisdiction, but state procedural law when jurisdiction was based on diversity.[1]

The next major post-*Erie* case did little to allay these concerns. In *Guaranty Trust Co. v. York*, 326 U.S. 99 (1945), the issue was whether a federal diversity court must apply the state statute of limitations to a claim,

---

1. This prospect was enormously ironic because until 1938 federal courts had followed state procedural rules in most cases. The Federal Rules of Civil Procedure took effect in 1938, the same year that *Erie* was decided. Prior to 1938 the Conformity Act of 1872 (17 Stat. 196) provided that federal courts should follow the procedural rules of the state in which they sat. Thus, under the Conformity Act the procedural rules differed from one federal court to another because each applied the procedure of the state in which it sat. The Federal Rules introduced a uniform, independent set of federal procedural rules for the first time . . . and the progeny of *Erie* promptly threatened to destroy it.

or whether it was free to apply its own more flexible "laches" doctrine to the case. The Court, speaking through Justice Frankfurter, refused to distinguish *Erie* on the basis that it involved state "substantive" law while *York* involved "procedure." Instead, the Court held that the state limitations statute must be applied, in order to implement the "policy" of *Erie* that

> in all cases where a federal court is exercising jurisdiction solely because of the diversity of citizenship of the parties, the outcome of the litigation in the federal court should be substantially the same, so far as legal rules determine the outcome of a litigation, as it would be if tried in a State court.

326 U.S. at 109. If following a federal practice that differed from state procedure might "significantly affect the result of a litigation" (id.), the court must apply the state rule instead, to prevent diverse parties from gaining unfair advantages simply because they can choose federal court. In *York*, this "outcome-determinative" test dictated use of the state limitations statute, since the claim was barred under that statute but might have been allowed to proceed under the federal laches doctrine.

In retrospect, it is clear that *York* and *Cities Service Oil* extended the *Erie* doctrine well beyond the area where application of state law was compelled by the United States Constitution. *Erie* required the lower federal court to apply the state duty of care because neither the federal courts nor Congress has constitutional authority to create rules of tort law.[2] However, *York* and *Cities Service Oil* involved situations in which there *was* federal authority to create a separate rule for the federal courts. The Constitution grants Congress the power to establish lower federal courts (Article III, §1), and to make laws "necessary and proper" for exercising that power. Article I, §8. Thus, there is constitutional authority to make federal procedural rules, even for diversity cases, presumably including the authority to provide a federal limitations period in a case like *York*, or a burden of proof rule for a case like *Cities Service Oil*. Despite this federal authority, *York*'s outcome determinative test required federal courts to apply state law, *as a matter of policy, not constitutional compulsion*, where using a separate federal rule could lead to a different outcome. Although the Court in *York* could have applied the separate federal laches rule, it concluded that uniformity of outcomes in state and federal court was more important than following a separate federal rule whenever it constitutionally could.

---

2. This is often, but not always, true. Various constitutional provisions may support federal power to enact tort legislation in some circumstances. For example, the interstate commerce power in Article I, §8, would doubtless support federal legislation dealing with products liability claims. And scholars have argued that Congress could have enacted a standard of care governing the *Erie* facts under the interstate commerce power because of its impact on interstate transportation. See, e.g., 19 Wright & Miller §4505 at text accompanying n.39.

Where *Erie* had commanded, "follow state tort law, because 'there can be no other law,' "[3] *York* pronounced, "follow state law, even where there can be federal law, if it will further the policy of uniform outcomes in state and federal court in diversity cases."

However, this uniformity policy clearly could have a drastic impact on federal procedure in diversity cases. Suppose that state law allows 30 days to answer a complaint and federal law only allows 20. If Clinton files suit in federal court, and Fisk answers on the twenty-fifth day, that difference could be outcome determinative. If Clinton serves Fisk by leaving the summons and complaint at his last and usual place of abode (see Fed. R. Civ. P. 4(e)(2)), but state law requires personal delivery to Fisk, that difference may be outcome determinative. If federal law allows Clinton to amend his pleadings to add new claims after the limitations period passes, but state law does not, that also may be outcome determinative. At its broadest, *York* would mandate use of the state rule in each of these cases, although there is federal constitutional authority to establish a different rule. If so, it should be clear that there would not be much left of the Federal Rules of Civil Procedure in diversity cases.

## THE PENDULUM SWINGS BACK . . . A LITTLE

Next in this intimidating line of post-*Erie* decisions is *Byrd v. Blue Ridge Rural Electrical Cooperative, Inc.*, 356 U.S. 525 (1958). The *Erie* issue in *Byrd* was whether the judge or the jury should determine the plaintiff's status as an "employee" of the defendant. State law left the question to the judge, but the practice in federal court was to send such issues to the jury.

Although *Byrd* is often viewed as a departure from *York*, the *Byrd* Court actually reaffirmed the holdings of both *Erie* and *York*. First, the Court reiterated that federal courts must honor the "definition of state-created rights and obligations by the state courts." 356 U.S. at 535. This is the constitutional prong of the *Erie* doctrine, exemplified by *Erie* itself, in which the rule at issue was a clearly "substantive" standard — duty of care to a trespasser — that the Constitution reserves to the states. In this category of cases, *Byrd* reaffirms, the federal court must follow state law because it has no power to create a separate federal rule. In *Byrd*, however, the South Carolina rule authorizing the judge to decide "employee" status was *not* "bound up with the definition of the rights and obligations of the parties," but "merely a form and mode of enforcing" the compensation scheme.

---

3. *Hanna v. Plumer*, 380 U.S. 460, 472 (1965).

356 U.S. at 536. Thus, the issue was a matter of procedure as to which the federal court was not constitutionally compelled to apply the state practice.

Having determined that *Erie*'s constitutional analysis did not require the federal court to apply South Carolina's rule, Justice Brennan next considered whether *York* did. He acknowledged that *York* evinced a "broader policy" than *Erie*, requiring federal courts to follow state practices even of "form and mode" (as opposed to clearly substantive law) if ignoring them would substantially affect the outcome of the litigation. 356 U.S. at 536. Thus, *Byrd* reaffirmed that, under *York*, federal courts should apply outcome-determinative state law even on procedural issues as to which there is federal constitutional authority to make its own rule. Brennan even conceded that, absent other considerations, the outcome determinative test would very likely require the court to apply state law to the judge-jury issue before it in *Byrd*. 356 U.S. at 537.

However, Justice Brennan went on to hold that, in deciding whether to follow state law in matters of "form and mode" (that is, the area in which the court follows state law as a matter of policy rather than constitutional command), the federal court must consider not only the York policy of uniform outcomes in diversity cases, but also any countervailing federal policies that arise from the federal court's status as an independent judicial system. In *Byrd*, the constitutional right to jury trial under the Seventh Amendment to the Constitution was at least tangentially implicated in making the choice between judge and jury. Given the importance of that right in the administration of federal courts, Justice Brennan concluded that the *Erie* policy of maximizing uniformity of outcome should yield to the federal policy of broad availability of jury trial. 356 U.S. at 538-539.

Because *Byrd* reaffirmed that state rules of form and mode should usually be applied if they might prove outcome determinative, it still appeared after *Byrd* that state procedural rules would often supersede the Federal Rules of Civil Procedure in diversity cases. It remained for the Warren Court to rescue the Rules in *Hanna v. Plumer*, 380 U.S. 460 (1965).

# THE RULES RESCUED: *HANNA V. PLUMER*

The issue in *Hanna*, like many of these post-*Erie* cases, was less than titillating. The plaintiff served process on the defendant, the executor of a Massachusetts estate, by leaving the summons and complaint at his home with "a person of suitable age and discretion," as required by Fed. R. Civ. P. 4(d)(1).[4] However, a Massachusetts statute required in-hand service

---

4. See now Fed. R. Civ. P. 4(e)(2)(B).

upon the executor. Mass. Gen. L. ch. 197, §9. While the issue was dull, the stakes were high: If service was valid, the case would go forward. If it was not, it would have to be dismissed, since the executor had not been served in hand within the limitations period. Validity of service turned thus on whether the federal court was required to apply the state service rule instead of Rule 4(d)(1).

The defendant made a seemingly airtight argument for application of the state rule: York says "use state law if doing so will affect the outcome." I win immediately if the state statute is applied, since service was not made within the limitations period. But the case goes forward if service was valid under the Federal Rule. Certainly, that difference is outcome determinative, so the state rule must be applied.

The argument was a good one, but Chief Justice Warren found several reasons for rejecting it. In the first part of the opinion (which I will call *Hanna* Part 1) he analyzed the conflict between the two service rules under a modified outcome-determinative test. Whether a federal procedure is outcome determinative, Warren concluded, must be viewed in light of the policies underlying *Erie*, to prevent forum shopping and inequitable administration of the laws. Not every difference between state and federal rules leads to those problems. It is very doubtful, for example, that a plaintiff would choose federal court over state court simply to avoid serving the defendant in person, since the effort required to do so is only marginally greater than that required to serve under the federal rule. Nor is the minor difference in litigation effort between "last and usual" service and in-hand service sufficient to be viewed as "inequitable administration of the laws." Thus, the Court concluded, the outcome-determinative test, viewed in light of the aims of the *Erie* doctrine, did not require the federal court to substitute the state rule for its own.

# *HANNA* PART 2: A DISTINCT ANALYSIS FOR FEDERAL RULES CONFLICTS

The major *Erie* cases, before *Hanna*, involved conflicts between federal judicial practices (that is, informal practices of federal judges not required by federal statute or Federal Rule) and state law. For example, *Erie* involved the practice of federal judges of "making" common law on tort issues, despite differing state common law. *York* involved the federal judicial practice of applying the laches doctrine, rather than state statutory limitations periods. *Byrd* involved the choice by federal judges, not commanded by statute or Rule, to send certain issues to the jury, which were determined by the judge under corresponding state practice. Thus, the

Court in these cases had no occasion to decide whether the standard for deferring to state law in a diversity case would be the same if the state law conflicted with a formal Federal Rule of Civil Procedure.

In *Hanna* Part 1, the Court analyzed the service issue before it *as though* it involved the typical "relatively unguided *Erie* choice" between an uncodified federal judicial practice and state law. It concluded that such conflicts should be addressed under a "modified outcome-determinative test" based on avoidance of forum shopping and inequitable administration of the laws. However, in the second part of *Hanna*, the Court noted that the service provision at issue (Rule 4(d)(1)) was a Federal Rule of Civil Procedure, recommended by the Advisory Committee on the Civil Rules, officially promulgated by the Supreme Court under the Rules Enabling Act (see 28 U.S.C. §2072, hereinafter referred to as the REA), and implicitly endorsed by Congress. In *Hanna* Part 2, the Court established an entirely different analysis for cases in which an official Federal Rule of Civil Procedure conflicts with state law.

The REA was enacted in 1934 and is still in effect. The first section of the REA authorizes the Supreme Court to "prescribe general rules of practice and procedure" for the federal courts.[5] Pursuant to this authority, an advisory committee appointed by the Supreme Court drafted the Federal Rules (and continues to revise them periodically). They were then promulgated by the Supreme Court and, as required by the REA, submitted to Congress for review before taking effect. See 28 U.S.C. §2074.

Thus there is both constitutional and statutory authority for the adoption of the Federal Rules. In *Hanna*, the Court held that Article III and the Necessary and Proper Clause provide broad *constitutional* authority to

> make rules governing the practice and pleading in [federal] courts, which in turn includes a power to regulate matters which, though falling within the uncertain area between substance and procedure, are rationally capable of classification as either.

380 U.S. at 472. This language suggests, as some have concluded, that Congress and the Court have broad constitutional authority to promulgate any rule that is "arguably procedural."[6]

---

5. The relevant provisions of the REA, as it presently reads, are as follows:

> §2072. (a) The Supreme Court shall have the power to prescribe general rules of practice and procedure and rules of evidence for cases in the United States district courts (including proceedings before magistrates thereof) and courts of appeals.
>
> (b) Such rules shall not abridge, enlarge, or modify any substantive right. . . .

6. See *Hanna*, 380 U.S. at 476 (Harlan, J., concurring) (describing the majority's test for validity as "arguably procedural, *ergo* constitutional").

The first section of the REA also provides broad *statutory* authority to promulgate "general rules of practice and procedure." In *Hanna* the court endorsed an equally broad construction of this statutory grant:

> The test must be whether a rule really regulates procedure — the judicial process for enforcing rights and duties recognized by substantive law and for justly administering remedy and redress for disregard or infraction of them.

*Hanna* 380 U.S. at 464 (quoting from *Sibbach v. Wilson,* 312 U.S. 1, 14 (1941)). Like *Hanna*'s broad definition of the constitutional grant, this somewhat tautological definition suggests that, in the REA, Congress has granted the Supreme Court authority to adopt any Federal Rule that is "arguably procedural." And, for what it is worth, Congress's acquiescence in the rules (by failing to intercept them after they are promulgated and submitted for review) provides a little extra dose of credibility. To invalidate one of the Rules, the Court would have to conclude that the Advisory Committee, the Supreme Court, and Congress had all erred in their judgment that the rule could validly be applied in federal court.

Given *Hanna*'s very broad construction of the federal constitutional and statutory authority to promulgate the Federal Rules, a party who argues that a Federal Rule is invalid because it is not "procedural" faces a very steep uphill battle. Suppose, for example, that the Court adopted a formal Federal Rule providing that the plaintiff shall bear the burden of proof in establishing title to property (the issue analyzed in *Cities Service Oil*). This rule, which governs the method of proof at trial of a civil case, is "arguably procedural." While it might not pass a *York* outcome determination test (perhaps even as modified by *Hanna* Part 1), it would survive scrutiny under the first subsection of the REA.

But wait! The second subsection of the REA (28 U.S.C. s. 2072(b)) opens another avenue of attack: It provides that "[s]uch rules shall not abridge, enlarge, or modify any substantive right." Thus, alas, the elusive substance/ procedure distinction also emerges in assessing the validity of Federal Rules under the REA. A Rule, though "procedural" under the first subsection of the REA, is invalid under the second if it impinges on "substantive rights."

Well, this is a little eerie: A federal judicial practice may not be applied in a diversity case, under *Hanna* Part 1, if it is "substantive" in the sense that it fails the modified outcome-determinative test. And a formal Federal Rule may not be applied if it impinges on "substantive" rights under the second subsection of the REA. However, "substance" must mean something different in the Federal Rules context than it does under the outcome-determinative test (hence the enigmatic title of the chapter) or there would be no need for separate analyses under *Hanna* Part 1 and *Hanna* Part 2.

# A FRAMEWORK FOR ANALYSIS

Although cases since *Hanna* have fine-tuned the analysis somewhat, *Erie*, *York*, *Byrd*, and *Hanna* provide the basic framework for determining when the federal court must defer to state law. What follows are some basic ground rules that should help you to identify the proper arguments to make in such cases.

There are four basic types of federal provisions that may conflict with state law. *First*, a federal constitutional provision might mandate a federal court procedure that differs from state law (as, for example, if the Seventh Amendment required a unanimous jury verdict, even though state law would allow a majority verdict). *Second*, a federal statute may govern federal practice but conflict with state law. An example might be a statute that requires federal courts to enforce arbitration agreements, even though the courts of a state would not. *Third*, a formal Federal Rule of Civil Procedure may conflict with state law, such as the conflicting service provisions in *Hanna*. *Last*, federal judges may develop judicial practices, that is, procedures applied as a matter of common practice not embodied in a Federal Rule or statute, which differ from state law (the situation discussed in *Hanna* Part 1). For example, federal judges may, as a matter of accepted judicial practice, comment to the jury on the evidence or allow alternate jurors to deliberate on cases or allow juries to decide certain issues, even though state practice is different. Each of these categories of conflicts requires a slightly different analysis.[7]

# A. Conflicts between a Federal Constitutional Provision and State Law

The United States Constitution is the "supreme Law of the Land." U.S. Const., Article VI, ¶ 2. Its provisions apply even if they conflict with state law, *substantive or procedural*, because we all agreed to that, by proxy, back in 1789, without any "ifs," "ands," "buts," or "outcome-determinative" modifiers. If the Constitution mandates a practice different from state law, the constitutional requirement prevails. For example, if the Seventh Amendment required unanimous jury verdicts, the federal court would apply that requirement in a diversity case even though state practice allowed majority verdicts, as some do. Indeed, if the Constitution were

---

7. This discussion owes much to the fine article by Westen and Lehman, Is There Life for Erie After the Death of Diversity, 78 Mich. L. Rev. 311 (1980). I highly recommend it to those who want to explore these issues further.

amended to bar trespassers from recovering from railroads, that provision would *also* trump state law, even though it establishes a clearly substantive rule.

## B. Conflicts between a Federal Statute and State Law

Federal statutes are also the supreme Law of the Land, if they are valid. So, if the conflict is between a federal statute and state law, the issue is whether Congress had the authority to enact the federal statute. *Hanna* holds that Congress has the constitutional authority to enact statutes governing procedure in the federal courts if, "while falling in the uncertain area between substance and procedure, [they] are rationally capable of classification as either." *Hanna*, 380 U.S. at 472. The duty-to-trespassers rule in *Erie* would fail this test, but most statutes related to the litigation process will not. If this "arguably procedural" test is met, the statute must be applied if it conflicts with state practice because Congress has the authority to enact the statute, and valid federal statutes are the "supreme Law of the Land" even if they conflict with state law. U.S. Const., Article VI, ¶ 2.

In *Stewart Organization, Inc. v. Ricoh Corp.*, 487 U.S. 22 (1988), the Supreme Court upheld application of 28 U.S.C. §1404 (a), the federal statute governing transfer of cases between federal district courts, on this reasoning. In *Stewart* the Court found a state practice refusing to enforce forum selection clauses in conflict with §1404(a), which calls for case-by-case discretion in deciding whether to transfer a case. Since the question of which federal court should hear a particular case is "arguably procedural," the Court concluded that Congress has the power to enact §1404(a). Thus, the statute is valid and applies in federal court even if the state court would apply a different rule.

## C. Conflicts between a Federal Rule and State Law

If a Federal Rule of Civil Procedure conflicts with state law, the Federal Rule applies if it is valid. *Hanna* Part 2. Congress has the constitutional power to authorize the Supreme Court to adopt a Federal Rule, *Hanna* concludes, if the Rule is "rationally capable of classification" as a procedural regulation. And the first section of the REA authorizes the Court to adopt the rule if it is procedural under the similarly broad definition in

*Sibbach,* that is, it "really regulates procedure — the judicial process for enforcing rights and duties recognized by substantive law and for justly administering remedy and redress for disregard or infraction of them." Virtually all Federal Rules will satisfy these broad tests. So the Federal Rules are valid, unless they "abridge, enlarge, or modify" a substantive right under the second subsection of the REA. (This exception is discussed further at pp. 212-214.)

# D. Conflicts between a Federal Judicial Practice and State Law

Federal judges have to run their courtrooms. That means they often make rulings resolving recurring issues that arise in the day-to-day administration of justice but are not addressed by the Constitution, federal statutes, or Federal Rules. Under *Erie* itself, such federal judicial practices are invalid if they purport to establish rules of primary behavior (like the duty to trespassers rule in *Erie*) which there is no federal constitutional power to make. In other cases, where the practice relates to the conduct of litigation (so that there is federal authority to make a separate rule), *Hanna* Part 1 indicates that a diversity court should generally apply the state rule if the difference between it and the federal practice could prove "outcome determinative," in the sense that following a separate federal practice could lead to forum shopping or inequitable administration of the laws. Whether the difference leads to those evils may be problematic in a particular case, but at least it is fairly clear that the argument should be framed under *Hanna* Part 1.

# PROBLEMS IN APPLYING THE *HANNA* ANALYSES

The principles above provide a framework for analyzing these eerie *Erie* problems. However, they do not answer the really hard questions which arise in working through the analysis. Here are some sticky parts:

- When is there a direct conflict between a federal statute or Rule and state law?

If a state statute, rule or procedure conflicts with a federal statute or Rule, a complex *Hanna* Part 2 analysis is necessary. However, if the state provision does not conflict with the federal statute or rule, the court can sometimes avoid the *Erie* problem entirely: It can simply apply the state provision because no federal law requires it to do otherwise. In several cases, the Court has avoided trouble by finding that there was no "direct conflict" between the state and federal provisions. In *Walker v. Armco Steel Corp.*, 446 U.S. 740 (1980), for example, the issue was whether the plaintiff had to file suit or serve process on the defendant within the limitations period. The plaintiff filed suit within the limitations period, but did not serve the defendant with the summons and complaint until well after. The Supreme Court avoided a difficult *Hanna* Part 2 clash by holding that Federal Rule 3, which provides that a suit is commenced by filing, is not intended to govern when the limitations period is tolled: It only prescribes the point for calculating various time requirements under the Federal Rules (such as the time for filing an answer, taking depositions, or sending interrogatories).

Similarly, the court in *Gasperini v. Center for Humanities, Inc.*, 518 U.S. 415 (1996), found no conflict between Federal Rule 59, which specifies that new trials may be granted in federal court for "the reasons for which new trials have heretofore been granted in actions at law in the courts of the United States," and a state statute which set a specific, stringent standard for review of damage awards. By contrast, the Court found a conflict between a state costs statute that required a penalty for certain appeals and Federal Rule 38, which gives appellate courts discretion to award costs for frivolous appeals. *Burlington Northern R.R. Co. v. Woods*, 480 U.S. 1 (1987).

These decisions don't provide consistent guidance. The easy cases will be those where the federal provision (whether a federal statute or a Federal Rule) and the state provision are directly contradictory. If a federal statute required unanimous verdicts and state law provided for majority verdicts, the two would require contradictory procedures and could not coexist. Probably, a conflict will also be found where federal law provides a discretionary standard to govern an issue, but state law requires a particular outcome, as was true in *Burlington Northern*. Beyond that, a conflict will likely be found where the relevant federal provision was meant to "occupy the field," or where applying the state rule would demonstrably impair the operation of the cognate federal provision.

- When does a Federal Rule, which is constitutionally valid and "procedural" under the first subsection of the REA, violate the second subsection because it "abridges, enlarges, or modifies" substantive rights?

This is a real toughie. A short answer is "seldom"; very few cases have invalidated a Federal Rule under this subsection of the REA. The Federal Rule will have to have a substantial impact on a state policy unrelated to litigation to be declared invalid under the second paragraph of the REA, given the heavy presumption of validity created by *Hanna*. The Court in *Burlington Northern R.R. Co. v. Woods*, 480 U.S. 1, 8 (1986), held that procedural rules which "incidentally" affect substantive rights are permissible under the second sentence of the REA, and rather casually concluded that Federal Rule of Appellate Procedure 38 passes muster because it "affects only the process of enforcing litigants' rights and not the rights themselves." 480 U.S. at 5, 8.

Various tests have been proposed to determine when a federal rule impermissibly trenches on "substantive" rights to this extent. One commentator suggests that a right is "substantive" in the REA sense if it is "granted for one or more nonprocedural reasons, for some purpose or purposes not having to do with the fairness or efficiency of the litigation process."[8] A House Report on amendments to the REA suggests that a Rule would interfere with substantive rights if it involved "lawmaking choices that necessarily and obviously require consideration of policies extrinsic to the business of the courts."[9]

A few illustrative cases may give a sense of the type of provision likely to pass muster — or not — under the second subsection of the REA. Doubtless, a Federal Rule barring trespassers from recovering damages would be struck down as substantive, or a provision barring enforcement of monopoly contracts. These examples govern primary rights outside the courtroom (though, of course, they must be enforced within one). On the other end of the spectrum, courts have applied Rule 42(a), which allows bifurcating a trial (for example, trying the liability and damages issues separately) in diversity cases even though state law requires a single trial.[10] Another case applied Federal Rule 32(a)(3), limiting use of depositions at trial in a diversity case in lieu of a more liberal state rule.[11] These examples deal directly with the administration of litigation in the courtroom, are not tied to any particular type of case, and do not necessarily favor one party over another. In between are the closer cases. For example, the right to claim the attorney-client privilege to avoid giving certain testimony is invoked in a courtroom, but clearly affects primary behavior — the communications between lawyer and client — outside the courtroom as well. Similarly, the right of a prevailing party to recover attorneys' fees in certain cases is administered in court, but has a substantial impact on the protection of the rights claimed in those cases. Very likely, a Federal Rule which contradicted state law in either of these two examples, though they

---

8. J. Ely, The Irrepressible Myth of Erie, 87 Harv. L. Rev. 693, 725 (1974).
9. House of Representatives Report 99-422 (1985) p. 22.
10. See, e.g., *Oulds v. Principal Mut. Life Ins. Co.*, 6 F.3d 1431, 1435-1436 (10th Cir. 1993).
11. *Frechette v. Welch*, 621 F.2d 11, 14 (1st Cir. 1980).

deal with issues "arguably procedural," would be held invalid under the second subsection of the REA.

- What differences are sufficient to lead to "inequitable administration of the laws" under *Hanna* Part 1?

Here again, the cases provide a framework for analysis but little clarity as to how the court will apply the relevant concepts. *Hanna* Part 1's modified outcome determinative test is certainly narrower than *York*'s, which required use of state law any time the difference could be outcome determinative. But it evidently requires more deference to state law than the second section of the REA, which bars Federal Rules which abridge, enlarge, or modify substantive rights. Some practices will pass muster if the Court and Congress formally require them, but not if federal judges simply adopt them as a matter of practice.

For example, *Walker* held that the state practice of tolling the limitations period upon service must prevail over a contrary federal judicial practice, but suggested that this difference would be upheld if the tolling-on-commencement rule were embodied in a formal Federal Rule, despite the effect on outcome. 446 U.S. at 753. Thus there is a tough "substance/substance distinction" between the analysis under *Hanna* Part 1 and *Hanna* Part 2. Probably such "inequitable administration" will be found where using the federal approach instead of the state rule would open up a significant difference in litigation opportunity, viewed not after the fact but prospectively.

- What is the current status of *Byrd*?

In *Gasperini v. Center for Humanities, Inc.*, 518 U.S. 415 (1996), the Supreme Court resurrected *Byrd* after several decades of neglect. The analysis in *Gasperini* is somewhat opaque — not all that legal academics had hoped for from Justice Ginsburg, a former civil procedure professor. But it is clear that the Court analyzed the case as a *Hanna* Part 1 conflict, and that it approved *Byrd*'s emphasis on the importance of the federal interests as a factor in making the "relatively unguided *Erie* choice" required under *Hanna* Part 1. Thus, where a federal statute or rule is not directly implicated, so that the choice between state and federal law involves the broader *Erie* policy of uniformity, *Byrd*'s admonition to weigh important federal policies against that uniformity policy remains a factor in the analysis.

This introduction may not suffice to "answer" all hard *Erie* problems. But hopefully the discussion and the following examples will provide a framework for analyzing these problems, so that you will understand which branch of the decision tree the court is likely to venture out upon and recognize the appropriate precedents to rely upon in arguing your client's position.

## Examples

## Collisions and Close Calls

1. Assume that Colorado's comparative negligence statute provides that the plaintiff's recovery in a negligence case is to be reduced in proportion to his own negligence but that the plaintiff may not recover at all if his negligence was "as great as" the defendant's. The statute also specifies that the jury shall be instructed that the plaintiff will not recover if his negligence is as great as (or greater than) the defendant's.[12] The evident purpose of this provision is to let the jury know that, if they find the plaintiff 50 percent or more at fault, he will take nothing.

   Morgan brings a diversity suit against Harriman in federal court for negligently causing a motor vehicle accident. The Colorado statute applies, but no one thinks to request the instruction on the effect of plaintiff's negligence. The jury is not so instructed and returns a finding that Morgan was 60 percent at fault. The judge enters judgment against Morgan, and he appeals, claiming a right to a new trial because the jury was not instructed in accordance with the statute.

   The Colorado courts hold that a plaintiff in these circumstances is entitled to a new trial (at which the required instruction is given), even if he did not request the instruction. However, Fed. R. Civ. P. 51(d) provides that a party may only appeal on the ground that the judge failed to give an instruction if that party properly requested the instruction at trial. Harriman argues that Rule 51 applies, while Morgan argues that *Erie* principles require the court to follow Colorado law and order a new trial.

   a. How would this issue be resolved under Justice Frankfurter's analysis in *York?*

   b. How do you think it would come out after *Byrd*, but before *Hanna?*

   c. If the case arose after *Hanna*, should the issue be analyzed under *Hanna* Part 1 or Part 2?

   d. How would the issue be resolved under *Hanna* Part 2?

   e. How would it come out if there were no Federal Rule on point, but federal judges followed a judicial practice of refusing to review errors that were not objected to below?

---

12. The Colorado comparative negligence statute contained such a provision for some years, but it has since been repealed. See Colo. Rev. Stat. §13-21-111(4), as amended by 1975 Colo. Sess. Laws 570, §1; repealed by 1986 Colo. Sess. Laws 679, §5.

2. Morgan sues Harriman for negligence in federal court. The relevant state negligence law recognizes contributory negligence of the plaintiff as a complete defense and provides that the plaintiff bears the burden of proving that he was not negligent. Morgan argues, however, that the defendant should bear the burden of proving that he (Morgan) *was* negligent because Fed. R. Civ. P. 8(c)(1) requires defendants to plead contributory negligence as an "affirmative defense." How should the court rule?

3. Recall the facts of *Guaranty Trust Co. v. York*: The federal courts typically applied the equitable laches doctrine in deciding whether a plaintiff had brought a certain type of claim too late, while state law enforced a two-year limitations period on that same claim. Plaintiff sued in federal court, and the question was whether the federal court could apply the laches doctrine or was bound to apply the state limitations period.

   a. If the *York* case arose shortly after *Hanna v. Plumer* was decided, would the court analyze the case under *Hanna* Part 1, or *Hanna* Part 2? How should the federal court rule?

   b. Assume that the Supreme Court promulgated Fed. R. Civ. P. 99, a formal Federal Rule providing that federal courts should use the laches doctrine in determining whether a claim was barred, instead of applying the state limitations period. If *York* arose after *Hanna*, should the federal district court apply Fed. R. Civ. P. 99 instead of the state limitations period?

   c. Assume that Congress passes the Federal Uniform Limitations Act of 2007, providing that no claim can be brought in federal court more than four years after the claim arose. York brings suit in federal district court, five years after his claim arose. Assume that state law provides a six-year limitations period for the claim. Would the claim be barred under the federal statute?

4. Assume that the judges in courts of the state of Aroostook, as a matter of judicial practice, give the jury instructions in writing, but that the federal judicial practice is to read the instructions to the jury without giving them a copy. Underwood sues Drew for negligence in federal court. Because jurisdiction is based on diversity, Aroostook law governs the underlying negligence claim. Must the federal judge instruct the jury in writing?

## The Ultimate Test

5. Assume that the Aroostook legislature has enacted a statute authorizing its supreme court to promulgate rules of procedure for the Aroostook courts, and it has adopted Aroos. R. Civ. P. 49(c), which requires the judge to give the jury a written copy of the instructions. Assume further

that federal judges, as a matter of judicial practice, instruct the jury orally. Underwood sues Drew for negligence in the federal court. Aroostook law again governs the underlying negligence claim. Must the federal judge instruct the jury in writing?

## Switching Tracks

6. Clinton brings a diversity suit in federal court against Fisk for negligence. To prove Fisk's negligence, Clinton offers two days of testimony by an eminent (and expensive) expert on accident reconstruction. Clinton wins at trial, and moves to collect as "costs" a $10,000 fee he paid to the expert to review the facts, perform experiments, and prepare for trial. The relevant federal statute, 28 U.S.C. §1920, provides that the prevailing party may recover certain limited types of costs of suit from the losing party. These costs include an attendance fee for witnesses who testify at trial, but include no provision for recovering an expert's fee for preparing for trial. By contrast, a state statute provides that the prevailing party in a negligence case may recover the full costs of retaining expert witnesses.
   a. Is there a conflict between the federal and state statutes?
   b. How should the judge rule on the motion?

7. The State of Aroostook, concerned by skyrocketing medical malpractice insurance premiums, passes a statute limiting recovery for intangible damages (such as pain, suffering, and emotional distress) in malpractice cases. The statute provides that recovery for intangible injuries from any incident shall not exceed $250,000 and that such damages shall be determined by the judge. Morgan sues Dr. Drew in federal court for medical malpractice. The trial judge concludes that, under the Seventh Amendment, the jury must determine the intangible damages in federal court and that it need not apply the cap in the Aroostook statute. The jury returns a verdict for Morgan, which includes $400,000 for pain and suffering.

   Dr. Drew appeals, arguing that the federal court should have followed the Aroostook statute, since its jurisdiction is based on diversity. Thus, the $250,000 cap on damages should apply, and the judge rather than the jury should assess the damages for intangible injuries. Morgan argues that the verdict should be upheld, since the Seventh Amendment mandates jury trial of factual issues such as the amount of the damages — which it does. How should the court rule?

## The Late Train

8. Morgan sues Harriman but discovers after the passage of the limitations period that it was actually Gould who was driving the car that hit him,

not Harriman. He seeks to amend his complaint to name Gould as a defendant. The relevant state law does not allow amendments to add a defendant who was not sued and served within the limitations period. Assume that Federal Rule 15(c), however, allows a plaintiff to amend the complaint to add a party if the party: 1) received notice of the action within the limitations period; and 2) knew that, "but for a mistake concerning the identity of the proper party," the action would have been against him. Assume that Gould was aware of the suit within the limitations period and that he was actually the intended defendant. Morgan argues that, since the requirements of Rule 15(c) are satisfied, the amendment should be allowed. Should the court allow the amendment?

9. Assume that the same version of Federal Rule 15(c) applies, but the state in which Morgan brings his action has a statute that provides:

> In any civil action, the court may, at any time, allow an amendment adding or changing a party, and allow any other amendment in matter of form or substance which may enable the plaintiff to sustain the action for the cause or recovery for which the action was intended to be brought. Such an amendment shall relate back to the time of the original pleading.[13]

After the passage of the limitations period, Morgan makes a motion in the federal action to name Gould as a defendant. Assume that Gould had no prior notice that Morgan intended to sue him. What rule should the court apply?

## A True Multiple-Choice Question

10. This multiple-choice example appears to have stumbled into the wrong book,[14] but I offer it for a reason.

---

**Take your choice.** The state of Acadia enacts Acadia Gen. Laws ch. 229, s. 17, as part of a "tort reform" initiative. This statute bars a plaintiff from seeking punitive damages in her original complaint. Instead, the plaintiff may only seek them by filing a motion to amend the complaint, and the judge may only allow the amendment if she finds that there is "a reasonable likelihood" that the plaintiff will prove facts at trial that would support an award of punitive damages. The apparent purpose of the provision is to discourage plaintiffs from making dubious demands for punitive damages.

---

13. This statute is an edited version of a Massachusetts statute, Mass. Gen. L. ch. 231, §51.
14. See J. Glannon, The Glannon Guide to Civil Procedure: Learning Civil Procedure Through Multiple-Choice Questions and Analysis.

Carnegie sues Frick in federal court in Acadia, on a tort claim. He includes in his complaint a demand for punitive damages. Frick moves to strike this demand, claiming it is barred by Acadia Gen. Laws ch. 229, s. 17. Carnegie argues that s. 17 should not apply in federal court, citing Fed. R. Civ. P. 8(a)(3) and 15(a)(2).

a. The court should analyze this under *Hanna* Part 2, because there is a direct conflict between the Acadia statute and Rule 8(a)(3).

b. The court should analyze this under *Hanna* Part 2, because there is a direct conflict between the Acadia statute and Rule 15(a)(2).

c. The court should analyze this under *Hanna* Part 1, because there is no direct conflict between the Acadia statute and either of these rules. Under this analysis, the court should apply the Acadia statute, to avoid forum shopping and inequitable administration of the laws.

d. The court should analyze this under *Hanna* Part 1, because there is no direct conflict between the Acadia statute and either of these rules. Under this analysis, the court should not apply the Acadia statute, because following federal procedure will not lead to forum shopping or inequitable administration of the laws.

## Explanations

### Collisions and Close Calls

1. a. In *York*, Justice Frankfurter concluded that federal courts should follow state rules if the difference between the state and the federal rules could be "outcome determinative." If *York*'s outcome-determinative test were applied to this example, there appears little doubt that the court would have to defer to state law. If the federal court sticks with its rule, Morgan loses because the appellate court will not consider the error. But if the federal court applies the Colorado approach, Morgan will get a new trial. At the new trial, the jury will be told the effect of finding Morgan more at fault and may well find him less faulty (say, perhaps, 49 percent?). Of course, we can't say Morgan will definitely win if he gets the new trial, just as the *York* court could not say for sure that the plaintiffs there would win if they were allowed to proceed to trial. However, applying the federal rule could make a difference, so the *York* test would require use of the state rule.

   b. The court in *Byrd* reaffirmed that the federal courts must follow state rules that define the "rights and obligations" of the parties. 356 U.S. at 535. This presumably refers to those clearly "substantive" rights, which (as *Erie* declared) the federal government has no authority to create. This matter of instructing the jury, however, seems more like a "matter of form and mode" for the conduct of the litigation itself, as to which there is federal authority to apply a separate rule. *Byrd* reaffirmed that the federal court should generally defer to state rules even in matters of "form and mode," if they are likely to be outcome determinative, in order to implement the policy of uniformity pronounced in *Erie* and reaffirmed in *York*. 356 U.S. at 536-537. Thus, unless affirmative countervailing considerations require application of the federal rule, *Byrd* would also support application of the state practice in this case.

A problem with the *Byrd* analysis is that it does not specify what federal policies will outweigh the *Erie/York* policy of assuring that diversity cases come out the same in state and federal court. Here, the federal objection rule is meant to assure that objections are presented to the trial court so they can be considered and resolved there, thus reducing errors and appeals. That is certainly a meaningful policy, aimed at increasing accuracy and efficiency of federal trials, but it is probably not such an overriding "countervailing consideration" as to outweigh *Erie*'s policy of uniformity. It certainly isn't as lofty a concern as the constitutional right to jury trial implicated in *Byrd*.

c. As the Introduction states, where there is a direct conflict between a state rule or statute and a Federal Rule of Civil Procedure, the court must analyze the problem under *Hanna* Part 2. Here the Colorado practice (ordering a new trial even if no instruction was requested) and Fed. R. Civ. P. 51 (barring reversal if no objection is made) are clearly incompatible. The court will affirm the verdict for the defendant if it follows the Federal Rule but will reverse if it follows state law. Thus, there is a direct conflict, and the REA analysis of *Hanna* Part 2 applies.

d. There can be little doubt about the Court's authority to promulgate Rule 51. On the constitutional level, it is "rationally capable of classification" as procedural, since it governs the process of instructing the jury at trial and reviewing those instructions on appeal. It also passes muster under the similar test of "procedurality" under the first subsection of the REA, since it relates to "the judicial process for enforcing rights and duties recognized by substantive law. . . ." Thus, it is valid unless it "abridge[s], enlarge[s], or modif[ies]" substantive rights: The second subsection of the REA prohibits enacting rules — even procedural rules — that alter substantive rights.

As discussed in the Introduction, it is at this stage that the analysis becomes murky. Professor Ely would ask whether the statute was enacted for any "nonprocedural" reason. Interestingly, the Colorado provision involved here was not found in Colorado's procedural code, but was part of the comparative negligence statute itself, suggesting a "nonprocedural" purpose. While it governs behavior in the courtroom, it is evidently aimed at affecting the substantive outcome of suits: More plaintiffs will win if juries know that they must be less than 50 percent at fault to recover.

Despite this argument, the case on which this example is based concluded (relying on Ely's article!) that following Rule 51 would not transgress the restriction in the second paragraph of the REA:

> This effect [denying review of the failure to give the instruction] however, is not an enlargement, abridgment or modification of the comparative negligence doctrine, which is the substantive rule of law at issue. It is rather a procedural directive, aimed at augmenting the fairness and efficiency of the litigation process in federal court.

*Platis v. Stockwell,* 630 F.2d 1202, 1206 (7th Cir. 1980). This reasoning, of course, is circular: The Rule does not abridge substantive rights because it is procedural. However, despite the Ely test, my sense is that most courts would reach the same conclusion, based on the heavy presumption of validity that *Hanna* accords to the Federal Rules, the fact that the Rule governs trial procedure, and the fact that the plaintiff can avoid any abridgement of the "right" involved by the simple expedient of asking for the instruction.

e. If the refusal to grant a new trial in the absence of an objection were a matter of federal judicial practice, rather than a Federal Rule, the analysis would proceed under *Hanna* Part 1. This may be an example of a rule that would be "substantive" under *Hanna* Part 1 although it does not affect "substantive" rights under *Hanna* Part 2. Under *Hanna* Part 1, the question would be whether the twin aims of *Erie* would be compromised by allowing the federal courts to ignore the state statute in favor of their usual practice. It is very clear that using the federal practice instead of the state statute would *not* lead to forum shopping. Any plaintiff who knows about the jury instruction rule would have no need to base his forum choice on the difference: He would simply be sure to ask for the instruction in either court, so the difference would make no difference!

However, it would arguably be "inequitable administration of the laws" for the federal court to refuse a new trial where a state court would be bound to grant one. Compare *Walker v. Armco,* in which the Court concluded that it would foster inequitable administration of the laws to allow a suit to go forward in federal court that would be barred in state court.[15]

---

15. Many differences look "inequitable" if viewed retrospectively, but not if viewed prospectively. The difference here, for example, hardly seems inequitable when viewed at the outset of the litigation: Any inequity can be avoided by careful trial planning. But looking back, after the plaintiff has failed to seek the instruction, the difference is crucial to his case.

The Court in *Hanna* Part 1 appeared to call for a prospective analysis. It emphasized that the prospective burden to comply with the two rules was not very different, though the plaintiff could no longer comply with the state rule at all at the time of the appeal. However, in *Walker* the Court appeared to revert to a retrospective approach, relying on the fact that the plaintiff would lose if the state rule applied but might win if allowed to proceed in federal court. 446 U.S. at 753.

2. The first issue here is whether there is a direct conflict between the state practice requiring the plaintiff to prove that he is free of negligence and Fed. R. Civ. P. 8(c). If there is such a conflict, the court must consider whether Rule 8(c) is valid under the REA. It certainly is "procedural" under the first sentence of the REA, since it regulates the process of proof at trial. However, it is a tough question whether the Rule would "abridge, enlarge, or modify" a substantive right under the second paragraph of the REA. The burden of proof can have a profound impact on the case, particularly where one or both of the parties is unable to produce evidence (as, for example, when one of two drivers is killed in the accident).

   In *Palmer v. Hoffman*, 318 U.S. 109 (1943), the Supreme Court nicely avoided tackling this REA issue by concluding that there is no direct conflict between Rule 8(c) and state burden of proof rules. The *Palmer* Court concluded that Rule 8(c) only addresses who must *plead* contributory negligence, not who bears the burden of proof on it. Based on this cramped reading of the Rule, the Court concluded that there was no conflict with state law, since federal law said nothing about who bore the burden of proof. Consequently, the state rule applied. As in *Walker v. Armco*, the Court construed the Rule narrowly to avoid a hard problem under the second section of the REA.

3. a. This example asks whether the *York* case would come out the same way under the modified outcome determinative analysis of *Hanna v. Plumer*. The conflict in *York* was between a state statute and a federal judicial practice, not a Federal Rule or federal statute. Thus, the Court would analyze it under the "relatively unguided" analysis of *Hanna* Part 1. The Court would consider whether allowing federal courts to use the laches doctrine instead of the state limitations period would lead to forum shopping or inequitable administration of the laws.

   Very likely, the Court would rule that the state limitations period must be applied, since ignoring the state limitations period in federal court would encourage both of these "twin evils." Clearly, a plaintiff whose claim was barred under the state statute would shop for the federal forum if the claim might not be barred under federal limitations principles. And, as the Court concluded in analogous circumstances in *Walker*, allowing such dramatic disparity in results would be inequitable:

   > There is simply no reason why, in the absence of a controlling federal rule, an action based on state law which concededly would be barred in the state courts by the state statute of limitations should proceed through litigation to judgment in federal court solely because of the fortuity that there is diversity of citizenship between the litigants.

   446 U.S. at 753.

b. If the Supreme Court were to mandate use of the laches doctrine through an official Federal Rule of Civil Procedure, the analysis would be under *Hanna* Part 2. The federal court would have to decide whether the Court (its boss!) had the authority under the REA to promulgate the rule, because it "really regulates procedure — the judicial process for enforcing rights and duties recognized by substantive law and for justly administering remedy and redress for disregard or infraction of them." *Hanna*, 380 U.S. at 464. Presumably, that standard of "procedurality" is met, since the Rule addresses the issue of when the claim may be litigated before the court.

However, even if fictional Fed. R. Civ. P. 99 is "arguably procedural," the second subsection of the REA bars adoption of rules that "abridge, enlarge or modify any substantive right." Very likely, this Rule would do just that. While the Court has not clearly articulated a standard for this proviso, ignoring state limitations periods would have a profound impact on the right itself. The period for recovering on a claim seems fairly closely "bound up" with the substantive claim itself. If applying the Federal Rule on laches could give longer life to the claim in federal court, that seems to significantly "modify" the underlying legal right itself. Very likely, a court would hold our hypothetical Fed. R. Civ. P. 99 invalid under the REA itself, because it does "abridge, enlarge or modify" substantive rights.

c. If Congress enacted a federal statute imposing a uniform limitations period for claims in federal court — including state law claims in diversity cases — the statute would be valid, if it regulates an issue that "while falling in the uncertain area between substance and procedure, . . . [is] rationally capable of classification as either." *Hanna*, 380 U.S. at 472. A federal limitations statute for federal courts would probably pass that lenient standard for "procedurality," since it relates to the process of litigation — when a claim can be prosecuted in a court. See Wright & Miller s. 4509, at text accompanying n.17. Thus, the statute would likely be upheld, though a Federal Rule of Civil Procedure mandating the same result would probably not. The difference is that Congress is only constrained by a broad requirement that the statute arguably govern a procedural issue, while the Supreme Court, in adopting rules, is constrained as well by the substantive rights proviso in the second subsection of the REA.

4. This case should be analyzed under *Hanna* Part 1, since the conflict is between a judge-made federal practice and state practice. The issue is whether the difference between written instructions and oral instructions will trigger the "twin evils" of forum shopping and inequitable administration of the laws. Neither seems at all likely from such a relatively minor discrepancy between state and federal practice. First, it

is unlikely that a litigant would choose federal court based on this procedural difference; if he wants to make sure that the jury clearly understands a particular instruction, he can ask the federal judge to instruct on it clearly and emphasize it in closing argument, rather than make the choice of forum turn on it.

Nor is there a substantial inequity in allowing this discrepancy between the administration of diversity cases in federal court and similar cases in state court. For one thing, it is not at all clear that it favors one litigant over the other, or (if it does) which one it will be in any particular case. Further, as suggested, any anticipated problem can probably be alleviated by careful argument to the jury. Thus, the federal court should apply this simple "housekeeping rule" despite contrary state practice, since doing so will not foster the "twin evils" discussed in *Hanna* Part 1.

## The Ultimate Test

5. If this example did not throw you off the track, you are well on your way to understanding the *Erie* doctrine. The analysis here is so straightforward that it's almost impossible to get it right.

In all of these cases, it *is the nature of the federal provision, not the competing state provision*, that determines the analysis. The issue is when *federal law*, whether made by the Framers, Congress, the Supreme Court, or federal judicial practice, is valid and therefore applies in federal court. If the federal provision is valid it prevails over a contrary state provision, whether found in the state constitution, a state statute or rule, or a state judicial practice.

A federal judicial practice is valid federal law if it governs the litigation process and passes the *Hanna* Part 1 test. The oral instruction rule here is valid, since the difference between the federal practice of giving oral instructions to the jury and the state written-instruction rule is unlikely to lead to forum shopping or inequitable administration of the laws. Consequently, the federal court may follow its own practice despite contrary state law. See example 4. It does not matter that the state provision is found in a formal Rule. The question is not whether a "higher" form of law (such as a constitutional provision, statute, or Rule) prevails over a "lower" one (such as a judicial practice). The question is whether the federal provision, from whatever source derived, is valid and applicable.

On the same analysis, a Federal Rule that passes muster under the constitutional and statutory analysis of *Hanna* Part 2 is valid federal law, which will apply despite a conflicting state provision, even if the state provision is found in a state constitution or statute. This is because federal law, made with the authority to make it, is the "supreme Law of the Land." See *Hanna* Part 2, in which the Court held that the Federal Rule prevailed over a state statute. See also *Hanna* Part 1, where the Court stated that the federal last-and-usual service provision would prevail over the state statute, even if it was a matter of judicial practice rather than a formal rule. 380 U.S. at 466-469.

## Switching Tracks

6. a. Clinton will probably argue that the two statutes are not in conflict. The federal statute only addresses the costs for a witness's testimony at trial; since it says nothing about fees for experts' preparation time, the matter is not covered by the federal statute, there is no direct conflict, and the issue should be analyzed under *Hanna* Part 1. This argument makes some sense, but was rejected by the Supreme Court. In *Crawford Fitting Co. v. J. T. Gibbons, Inc.*, 482 U.S. 437 (1987), the Court held that the statute, by specifying those items that may be recovered as costs, implicitly rejects taxing others, such as the expert's preparation fee. See 482 U.S. at 441-443 (§§1920 and 1821 "comprehensively addressed" the taxation of fees for litigant's witnesses, barring further fees for expert witnesses). Since the state statute allows full reimbursement for expert witness expenses, while the federal statute only authorizes minimal attendance fees, the Supreme Court concluded that the two are in direct conflict.[16]

   The cases don't always conclude that a narrow federal provision "comprehensively addresses" a problem. For example, Federal Rule 68 authorizes defendants to make offers to judgment, agreeing before trial to the entry of judgment for the offered amount. If the plaintiff rejects the offer, she must pay costs that accrue after the offer is made. But some state offer-of-judgment rules have mirror-image provisions, which allow *plaintiffs* to make offers of judgment as well as defendants. One might argue that these plaintiff-offer statutes cannot apply in federal court, since Rule 68 only allows defendants to make offers, impliedly rejecting plaintiffs' right to do so. Yet some cases have applied state plaintiff-offer provisions, arguing that "Rule 68 is limited to offers by defendants," and says nothing about plaintiff offers one way or the other. See, e.g., *S.A. Healy Co. v. Milwaukee Metropolitan Sewerage District*, 60 F.3d 305, 310 (7th Cir.), cert. denied, 516 U.S. 1010 (1995). So the fact that the federal provision governs some cases does not always lead to the conclusion the Court reached in *Crawford Fitting* — that other cases cannot be addressed by state law.

---

16. After *Crawford*, Congress enacted 42 U.S.C. s. 1988(c) which authorizes award of expert witness fees in civil rights cases.

    b. Assuming that there is a direct conflict between the state and federal statutes, the federal statute governs if it is constitutional, because the Constitution provides that federal statutes are the "supreme Law of the Land." U.S. Const., Article VI.

        The Court's discussion in *Hanna* certainly supports the conclusion that these cost statutes are constitutional under Article III and the Necessary and Proper Clause. *Hanna* concludes that Congress has power under those provisions to "regulate matters which, though falling within the uncertain area between substance and procedure, are rationally capable of classification as either." 380 U.S. at 472. A statute specifying which expenses in the conduct of a lawsuit may be collected by the winning party can rationally be classified as procedural. Thus, Congress had the power to enact this statute, and the statute applies despite the contrary state law.

        Note that the second paragraph of the REA is irrelevant to this analysis. That provision limits *the Supreme Court's rule-making authority*, not Congress's own power to enact procedural statutes. Only the Constitution limits that, and the constitutional authority (so says *Hanna*) is broad enough to encompass a statute of this sort, since it can rationally be classified as addressing a procedural issue.

7. Interestingly the analysis of this example doesn't have much to do with *Byrd*. In *Byrd* the "influence" of the Seventh Amendment lurked in the background, but it appears that it did not directly *require* that the jury decide the question. Here, by contrast, the Seventh Amendment directly conflicts with the state statute. That statute requires the judge to make the factual finding as to the amount of the intangible damages, while the Seventh Amendment requires factual questions such as the amount of damages to be decided by the jury in federal court.

        Because there is a direct conflict between the federal constitutional provision and the state statute, the analysis follows from the Court's discussion in Part 2 of *Hanna*. That analysis makes clear that if a federal statute or rule is valid and covers the issue, the federal court must apply it. A fortiori, if a federal constitutional provision applies, it will control despite a contrary state statute or practice. U.S. Const., Article VI, §2. Thus, since the assessment of Morgan's damages is an issue of fact, it must be decided by the jury if suit is brought in federal court.[17]

        However, the type and measure of damages recoverable in a tort case is a classically "substantive" issue, in the basic *Erie* sense. States are free to expand, define, or eliminate tort causes of action. See *Martinez v.*

---

17. The Seventh Amendment does not apply to the courts of the states. However, most state constitutions include a similar guarantee of jury trial. The statute hypothesized here might be unconstitutional under the Aroostook constitution but is still useful for illustration purposes.

*California*, 444 U.S. 277, 282 (1980). The Aroostook legislature could eliminate recovery for intangible damages entirely; it may also establish a cap on such damages instead. By doing so, the statute creates a state law "right" (or, better phrased, partial immunity), which must be honored under the command of *Erie* to follow state law on issues where the states have the authority to create it. Cf. *Gasperini v. Center for Humanities, Inc.*, 518 U.S. 415, 416 (1996) (state standard for reviewing size of verdict "substantive" under *Erie* analysis). Thus, the $250,000 limit on damages for intangible injuries will apply in Morgan's federal action. The judge should enter judgment on the jury's verdict but reduce the amount for intangible damages to $250,000.

## The Late Train

8. This is a direct conflict case: State law would bar the amendment, but Gould could be brought in if the version of Fed. R. Civ. P. 15(c) given in the example applies. Because the conflict is between a formal Federal Rule and a state practice, the analysis comes under *Hanna* Part 2. There appears to be little doubt that Rule 15(c) is within the "arguably procedural" arena, so that Congress may authorize federal courts to apply their own rules. There is also little doubt that it passes muster under the first subsection of the REA, since it regulates the "judicial process for enforcing rights and duties recognized by substantive law. . . ."

   The battleground in this case will be under the limiting language of the second subsection of the REA. Does the rule, which extends the right to sue a party beyond the limitations period, "abridge, enlarge, or modify" a substantive right? There is a nice analysis of this conflict in Westen and Lehman's article, 78 Mich. L. Rev. at 363-364. They argue that the "substantive" purpose of a limitation period is to provide notice to the defendant within the limitations period. Because the federal rule in the example only allows the amendment if the defendant has such notice and is aware that he is the intended target of the suit, this substantive purpose is not "abridged" and the assumed version of Rule 15(c) is valid. There is some difference in the state and federal approaches, but it is not sufficiently substantial to violate the REA limitation concerning substantive rights. In effect, there is a difference, but it does not significantly trench upon the policy underlying the state's approach, so (the authors conclude) it is a tolerable difference.

9. In this case, Rule 15(c) would not allow the amendment to relate back, since Gould did not have notice within the limitations period that anyone intended to sue him. See Fed. R. 15(c)(1)(C). But the state statute allows Morgan to amend to add Gould even if he had no notice of the action within the limitations period, so long as plaintiff had sued *someone* before the limitations period ran.

Clearly, Rule 15(c) is still "procedural" under the first subsection of the REA. However, there's a strong argument that disallowing the amendment would modify the substantive rights of the parties, under the second subsection. The state statute is meant to maximize litigants' ability to recover on their claims, even at the expense of the policy of repose underlying the statute of limitations. In this example, unlike example 8, Rule 15(c) draws a different balance between these policies, so that it might run afoul of the substantive rights proviso. See Marshall v. Mulrenin, 508 F.2d 39 (1st Cir. 1974). In 1991, the Rules were amended to eliminate this problem. Fed. R. Civ. P. 15(c)(1)(A) now provides that an amendment relates back if it would relate back under applicable state law, even if it would not relate back under Rule 15(c)(1)(C).

## A True Multiple-Choice Question

10. This eerie *Erie* problem has arisen in numerous cases, because at least eight states have enacted provisions like the Acadia statute. See R. Seamon, An *Erie* Obstacle to State Tort Reform, 43 Idaho Law Rev. 37, 47-48 (2006).

    If you chose a, you could cite *Cohen v. Office Depot, Inc.*, 184 F.3d 1293 (11th Cir. 1999), which refused to apply a similar Florida statute on the ground that Rule 8 governs the pleading of damages in federal court and contains no such restriction. If you chose b, you could cite *Dewick v. Maytag Corp.*, 296 F. Supp. 2d 905 (N.D. Ill. 2003), which ignored a similar Illinois statute on the reasoning in b. If you chose c, you could cite *Lowell v. Zurich Ins. Co.*, 1992 WL 212233 (D.N.D. 1992), in which the court applied North Dakota's statute under a "twin aims" analysis. If you chose d, you could cite *Berry v. Eagle-Picher*, in which the judge ruled that ignoring the state restriction was not "outcome determinative." For a very helpful analysis of the kaleidoscopic positions courts have taken on this (I've only described a few!), read Professor Seamon's fine article.

    So what is the lesson of this? That this is all slush, and the courts basically do what they want and couch it in appropriate terminology? Or that some *Erie* problems are just eerily intractable? I'd like to think — and actually believe — the latter. Law is language, and language, unlike math, connotes ambiguity. It is sometimes very difficult to apply verbal tests like "direct conflict" and "inequitable administration of the laws" with precision. Results won't always be uniform; there is room for disagreement and even some result-oriented manipulation. But in many, perhaps most, cases, the standards work well enough. For particularly difficult cases, higher courts can eventually provide an answer, if not an irrefutable one.

# Erie and State Choice of Law

## Vertical Uniformity and Horizontal Chaos

---

## INTRODUCTION

Chapter 10 suggests that the whole *Erie* problem was the Framers' fault, for creating a federal form of government. But that isn't really true. *Another* part of the problem is the colonists' fault because they settled in separate colonies. Those colonies developed more or less independently for 150 years before they became states and retain a great deal of autonomy under our constitution. This autonomy — from each other as well as from federal control — has some very interesting consequences for our judicial system.

A fundamental consequence, not generally appreciated, is that "the law" governing many types of claims can differ from state to state. The law of torts, for example, can be, and often is, one thing in Rome, Wisconsin, and another in Athens, Ohio. As "Easy Erie" explains, there is no general federal authority to "make" common law in areas such as tort law, so each state has to make its own. Also, there is nothing in the Constitution or in nature that says Wisconsin has to make the same tort law that Ohio does. Very frequently they don't, so that a tort case might come out differently if it were decided under Ohio law than it would if it were decided under Wisconsin law. The same is true in many other areas, such as commercial law, probate, contracts, and property. In this respect, the states are a little like independent countries, each of which has the authority to develop its own rules of law to apply to its own cases.

This phenomenon, that the 50 states may have 50 different rules on the duty of care to a trespasser, or the enforcement of exclusive contracts, is in itself surprising but tolerable. It is part of the price we pay for having a system of divided sovereignty, in which the states retain the power to make law in the many areas not delegated to the federal government. But this doctrine of state autonomy has a very unruly stepchild, the problem of "choice of law," which bedevils state courts as well as federal ones. This chapter explores the interaction of Erie's state law mandate with the curious quagmire[1] known as choice of law.

# THE DISMAL SWAMP: THE PROBLEM OF CHOOSING THE PROPER STATE LAW

The problem of choice of law is exactly what the phrase suggests, the need to choose a body of substantive law to apply to the dispute before the court. The Erie case itself involved a choice of law problem, since the Supreme Court had to determine whether federal courts in diversity cases were free to choose "federal common law" or were required to follow state law. But choice of law problems also arise when the plaintiff sues in *state* court, and the state court must choose whether to apply its own law to the claim or the law of another state.

The answer may appear obvious: The court should apply its *own* law, that is, the law of the state where the suit is brought. If Pogo sues Albert in Ohio for injuries suffered in a boat collision, the Ohio court should apply Ohio law. If he sues in Wisconsin, that court should apply Wisconsin law. Adopting this as the universal choice of law rule would have one great advantage: Everyone would know what law would be applied in each court, and there would be no litigation over choice of law.

Despite the simplicity of this choice of law rule, courts have not opted to apply their own substantive law in all cases, for several reasons. First, this approach would obviously encourage plaintiffs like Pogo to "forum shop" by suing in the state with the "best" (that is, the most Pogo-oriented) tort law. Suppose, for example, that Wisconsin applies contributory negligence, which would bar recovery if Pogo was negligent in any degree, but Ohio applies comparative negligence, which would allow him to recover but would reduce that recovery to account for his negligence. If Ohio always applied its own law, and Pogo was 10 percent at fault, he could sue in Ohio and recover 90 percent of his damages. However, if he brought

---

1. The "quagmire" and "dismal swamp" metaphors are from Prosser's famous quotation; see p. 232.

the suit in Wisconsin, he would get nothing.[2] That's a big difference. If Ohio's courts always chose to apply Ohio law, Ohio could become a magnet for tort cases that had no relation to that state or had more significant connections with other states.

In addition, as a matter of policy, it seems unwise to decide a controversy under a substantive rule completely foreign to the events in dispute. If Pogo lived in Wisconsin, the accident took place in Wisconsin, and Albert is a Wisconsin citizen, it would make little sense to apply Ohio law to the case, even if, for one reason or another, Pogo could sue in Ohio. The events and the parties had substantial connections to Wisconsin, but none at all to Ohio. At the time of acting, the parties had no expectation that Ohio law would determine the legal consequences of their conduct. In addition, Ohio has little interest in regulating or compensating this occurrence, but Wisconsin does. Pogo's choice of an Ohio court looks like a blatant attempt to avoid application of Wisconsin's contributory negligence rule to a Wisconsin accident between Wisconsin citizens. In such cases, where the case has little connection to the forum state but strong connections to another, many states would choose to apply the substantive law of the other state.

Similarly, suppose that Schulansky, from Massachusetts, goes to New Hampshire to meet with Ronan, a New Hampshire contractor. They negotiate there for the construction of an addition to her vacation home in Alton, New Hampshire, and enter into an agreement there for the work. If Schulansky has a problem with the quality of the work and sues Ronan in Massachusetts, the court would likely decide that the dispute has such significant ties to New Hampshire, and so few to Massachusetts, that it ought to be decided under New Hampshire contract law. Again, the result may be that a court in one state hears the suit but chooses to apply the substantive law of another.

# INTELLECTUAL QUICKSAND: APPROACHES TO CHOICE OF LAW

If courts do not always apply the law of the state in which they sit, they need to develop "choice of law" rules for deciding when they will choose the law of another state instead. They have done so, and the resulting rules are indeed a quagmire:

---

2. Whether Pogo can sue in Ohio (or Wisconsin, or Idaho, or any other state) depends on the three ring analysis explored in Part I. Often, Pogo will be able to satisfy the rings in a number of states, potentially giving him a choice of substantive tort rules as well as forums.

> The realm of the conflict of laws is a dismal swamp, filled with quaking quagmires, and inhabited by learned but eccentric professors who theorize about mysterious matters in a strange and incomprehensible jargon. The ordinary court, or a lawyer, is quite lost when engulfed and entangled in it.

W. Prosser, Interstate Publication, 51 Mich. L. Rev. 959, 971 (1953).

Stated less poetically, the various approaches that courts use for choosing the proper law in cases with connections to several states are complicated and in flux. The rules used to be fairly mechanical, based on "objective" connections between the claim and the state. See W. Richman and W. Reynolds, Understanding Conflict of Laws, pp. 180-197 (3rd ed. 2002) (describing the "vested rights" principles of the First Restatement of Conflicts of Laws). Under the First Restatement approach, tort cases were usually determined under the law of the place of injury ("lex foci delicti"), contracts cases under the law of the place where the contract was formed, and property cases under the law of the place where the property was located. It wasn't quite that neat, but that was the general idea. Under this approach Pogo's case would be decided under Wisconsin law (where the injury occurred), and Schulansky's under New Hampshire law (where, on the facts given above, the contract was made).

However, many courts have concluded that the First Restatement principles are too mechanical to yield satisfying solutions to choice of law problems. Led primarily by conflicts scholars, they have attempted to formulate choice of law rules that are more responsive to underlying policy considerations. One "modern" approach to conflicts of law weighs the interests of each affected state in applying its law to the case. See Richman and Reynolds at 241-251 (describing the "interest analysis" approach to conflicts). Suppose that Churchy and Howland, two Florida neighbors, decide to take a canoe trip in the Okefenokee Swamp, just over the Georgia border. A half mile into Georgia, the canoe swamps due to poor maintenance, causing serious injuries to Howland, who is hospitalized in Florida and permanently disabled. The First Restatement would require the court to apply the "lex loci delicti," the law of the place where the injury occurred, which is Georgia. However, a court that applies an "interest analysis" approach to conflicts might conclude that Florida has a greater interest in the case than Georgia, since the parties are domiciled there, the injured plaintiff was treated there, and the negligent maintenance, which caused the accident, took place there. Thus, "interest analysis" might lead the court to apply Florida law.

Another current approach to conflicts problems is to apply the law of the state with the "most significant relationship" to the case, in light of various policy considerations, including the expectations of the parties, the policy interests of the states with connections to the case, uniformity in enforcement, and others. See Richman and Reynolds at 206-214 (describing the approach of the Second Restatement of Conflict of Laws to torts, contracts and property issues). There are also other approaches and variations on all of them.[3] It is not crucial for our purposes to understand these theories, but rather to realize that *different approaches exist*, that they may lead the court in one state to choose different substantive law than another would apply to the same case, and that the selection of the applicable law will depend on the choice of law approach of the court in which the suit is filed.

## QUIRKS IN THE QUAGMIRE: FEDERAL COURTS CHOOSING STATE LAW

The situation is made even more complicated by the fact that the plaintiff often has the choice not only of state courts in different states, but also federal courts in each of those states. Suppose, for example, that Pogo becomes an Ohio citizen and sues Albert, from Wisconsin, for his injuries in the Wisconsin accident. Because the parties are diverse, Pogo may choose federal court and chooses the federal district court in Ohio. What law should that court apply? Clearly, the answer under *Erie* is "state law," since it is a diversity case. That is not the whole answer, however, because there are several states whose law might apply. Should the federal court choose Ohio law or Wisconsin law?

Three years after *Erie*, the Supreme Court addressed this question in *Klaxon Co. v. Stentor Manufacturing Co.*, 313 U.S. 487 (1941). In *Klaxon*, the Court held that the policy underlying *Erie* mandates the application of the forum state's choice of law rules as well as its substantive law:

> We are of opinion that the prohibition declared in *Erie R. Co. v. Tompkins*, 304 U.S. 64, against such independent determinations by the federal courts, extends to the field of conflicts of laws. The conflict of laws rules to be applied by the federal court in Delaware must conform to those prevailing in Delaware's state courts. Otherwise, the accident of diversity of citizenship would constantly disturb equal administration of justice in coordinate state and federal courts sitting side by side.

313 U.S. at 496 (footnote omitted). Under *Klaxon*, the federal court must do whatever the state court within that state would do. If an Ohio state judge

---

3. See *Ferens v. John Deere Co.*, 494 U.S. 516, 538 (1990) (Scalia, J., dissenting) (variety in state approaches to choice of law "has become kaleidoscopic"). Take the course in conflict of laws if you want to delve into these mysteries. It is a fascinating area and useful background for law practice.

would apply Ohio law to Pogo's case, so must the federal judge if the case is brought in an Ohio federal district court. If the Ohio state judge would choose Wisconsin law, the federal judge in Ohio must do so as well.

The *Klaxon* rule makes a certain amount of sense, as a matter of policy. *Erie* teaches that plaintiffs should not obtain an advantage due to the "accident of diversity" that they would not have in state court. If the state court would apply Ohio tort law to Pogo's case, but the federal court were free to choose Wisconsin's, the case could still come out differently simply because Pogo was able to invoke diversity jurisdiction. In the words of Judge Magruder, if federal diversity courts could follow their own choice of law rules, "the ghost of *Swift v. Tyson* . . . still walks abroad, somewhat shrunken in size, but capable of much mischief." *Sampson v. Channell*, 110 F.2d 754, 761 (1st Cir. 1940). The *Klaxon* rule puts the ghost to rest, since the federal court must again do whatever the state court would.

*Klaxon* has been met with some skepticism by the scholars. Although *Erie* clearly requires diversity courts to apply state law, it is certainly arguable that it is both constitutional and appropriate for a federal court to choose *which state's law* to apply in diversity cases. Choice of law involves the relations among the states, and the Framers might well have considered that a federal diversity court should be available to litigants as a neutral decision-maker in choosing the proper body of state law. See, e.g., H. Hart, The Relations Between State and Federal Law, 54 Colum. L. Rev. 489, 514-515 (1954) (arguing that *Klaxon* impedes development of conflicts law and promotes forum shopping).

Whatever the merits of these arguments may be, the Supreme Court continues to adhere to the *Klaxon* rule. The issue was raised again in *Day & Zimmerman v. Challoner*, 423 U.S. 3 (1975), a case involving strict liability claims for serious injuries to military personnel in Cambodia during the Vietnam War. The *Klaxon* approach required application of the Texas conflicts of law rule to the case, which in turn led to application of Cambodian law, under Texas' place-of-the-injury choice-of-law rule. However, Cambodian law did not recognize strict liability, so choosing its law would end the plaintiff's case. Despite these implications, the Supreme Court unanimously reaffirmed *Klaxon* in a brief per curiam opinion.[4]

Because *Klaxon* requires the federal court in a diversity case to apply the conflicts law that would be applied by the courts of the state in which it sits, the combination of *Klaxon* and *Erie* produces substantial "vertical

---

4. *Challoner* is a nice example of a situation in which interest analysis would yield a different result than the place-of-the-injury rule. The plaintiffs in *Challoner* were American servicemen. The defendant was an American corporation, and the shell that caused the injury was manufactured in Texas. As the Fifth Circuit pointed out in its opinion (reversed on other grounds by the Supreme Court), Cambodia had no interest in enforcing its fault requirement under the circumstances, while Texas had a substantial interest in applying its strict liability policy to the claim. See 512 F.2d at 80.

uniformity" between the state and federal courts within each state. However, a side effect of the two decisions is to destroy "horizontal uniformity" among the federal courts in different states. If Ohio would apply Ohio's comparative negligence principle to Pogo's accident, and Michigan would apply Michigan's contributory negligence law, the federal court in Ohio will apply a different rule than the federal court in Michigan would. Thus, *Erie* has not ended the game of forum shopping for a more favorable substantive law, it has just changed the rules of that game. Instead of choosing between federal and state court to obtain more favorable substantive law, plaintiffs may get the same result by choosing between federal courts in different states or between state courts in different states.

The following examples illustrate the effect of *Erie* and *Klaxon* on the law applied to the facts of the *Erie* case. Assume that all example cases arise after *Erie* and *Klaxon* were decided and that each case is based on diversity. After these examples, we will wade a little further into the quagmire by considering the implications of transfer of venue under 28 U.S.C. §1404(a).

## Examples

### Wading In

1. The unfortunate Harry Tompkins, Jr., a Pennsylvania citizen, is injured while walking on a track along the Erie Railroad near Hughestown, Pennsylvania, Evidently he was hit by an object, perhaps a door, projecting from the side of the train. He brings suit against the Erie Railroad, a New York corporation with its principal place of business in New York.

   Assume that, under Pennsylvania law, a trespasser like Tompkins is only entitled to recover if the railroad's conduct was wilful and wanton. New York law, on the other hand, holds railroads to a duty of due care to trespassers on a frequently used pathway along the tracks. Assume further that the Pennsylvania choice of law rule requires the court to apply the law of the place of the injury (lex loci delicti) in tort cases, and that the New York choice of law rule is the same.
   a. If Tompkins sues in a state court in Pennsylvania, what standard of care rule should the court apply?
   b. If Tompkins sues in a federal court in Pennsylvania, what standard of care rule should the court apply?
   c. If Tompkins sues in a state court in New York, what standard of care rule should the court apply?
   d. If Tompkins sues in a federal court in New York, what standard of care rule should the court apply?

2. On the same basic facts, assume that Pennsylvania tort law requires a showing of wilful and wanton conduct under the circumstances, and that it applies the place-of-the-injury choice of law rule. However, New York applies a due care standard to trespassers in Tompkins, Jr.'s position, and New York's choice of law rule involves a balancing of interests, which would lead to the application of New York law on the facts of Tompkins's case.

   a. If Tompkins sues in a state court in Pennsylvania, what standard of care rule should the court apply?

   b. If Tompkins sues in a federal court in Pennsylvania, what standard of care rule should the court apply?

   c. If Tompkins sues in a state court in New York, what standard of care rule should the court apply?

   d. If Tompkins sues in a federal court in New York, what standard of care rule should the court apply?

3. Tompkins, Jr., is injured near Hughestown and two weeks after the accident is transferred to a hospital in West Virginia. His wife moves to West Virginia to be near him. He is released three months later, is bedridden for nine more months, and does not recover fully for over two years. Mr. and Mrs. Tompkins decide to stay in West Virginia, and they bring a diversity suit against the Erie Railroad in federal court there. Mr. Tompkins seeks recovery for his injuries, and Mrs. Tompkins seeks recovery for loss of consortium, that is, for the interference with her relationship to her husband during the time he was incapacitated due to the injury. See *Hopson v. St. Mary's Hospital*, 408 A.2d 260 (1979) (loss of consortium includes the "'constellation of companionship, dependence, reliance, affection, sharing and aid'" which flows from marriage) (quoting from W. Prosser, Handbook of The Law of Torts, 881-332 (4th ed. 1971)). Assume that Pennsylvania law allows such claims, but West Virginia law does not. Assume also that West Virginia applies the place-of-the-injury choice of law rule in tort cases.

   a. What state's tort law should the West Virginia federal court apply to Mrs. Tompkins's claim?

   b. If the judge is unsure which law to apply, to which state court should she certify the issue?

## A Quagmire Quandary

4. Tompkins Jr. is injured near Hughestown, Pennsylvania, and decides to sue the Erie Railroad. He consults Webster, a local lawyer. Webster would like to sue "at home," of course, as most lawyers would. However, she is aware that Pennsylvania law requires wilful and wanton

conduct in cases like this, and that a Pennsylvania court would apply its own law to the case, under the lex loci rule.

In preparation for filing suit, Webster researches New York law on the duty of care to trespassers. She finds no case directly on point. Some older cases applied the wilful/wanton standard in analogous circumstances, but more recent New York cases have "modernized" some related doctrines of landowner liability.

Webster also researches New York conflicts of law doctrine, and finds (we will assume) that New York used to follow the mechanical conflicts rules of the First Restatement. A recent case rejected the First Restatement's approach to *contract* cases in favor of interest analysis, but no case has arisen asking the court to abandon the First Restatement's place-of-the-injury rule for tort cases. In short, it looks like change may be coming both in New York conflicts law for torts cases and in New York tort law, but it hasn't arrived yet, and may not arrive at all.

a. Should Webster sue in New York or Pennsylvania?

b. Should she choose state or federal court?

## The Procedure/Procedure Distinction

5. Assume that New York would choose Pennsylvania tort law in the Tompkins case under the place-of-the-injury approach. Webster decides to sue in *state* court in New York. She sues the Erie Railroad Company and also Hepzibah, the conductor in charge of the train that hit Tompkins. Webster learns that Hepzibah lives with her mother in Queens, New York, and serves process on Hepzibah by delivering the summons and complaint to her mother at the house. Hepzibah moves to dismiss for improper service, on the ground that New York law requires service in hand upon her personally. Assume that New York law does indeed require in-hand service but that leaving it at the house with Hepzibah's mother would suffice under Pennsylvania law.

a. How should the court decide the motion?

b. If Webster had sued in federal court in New York, how would that court have ruled? See Fed. R. Civ. P. 4(e)(2)(B).

6. Two-and-a-half years after his accident, Tompkins goes to see Webster. Assume that the statute of limitations on tort claims in New York is four years, but that it is two in Pennsylvania. Assume further that New York choice of law rules would lead to the application of Pennsylvania tort law to the case. Webster files a diversity suit in federal district court in New York against the Erie Railroad. The Erie brings a motion for summary judgment on the ground that the claim is barred due to passage of the limitations period. What should the federal court do?

# TOTALLY SWAMPED: THE IMPACT OF TRANSFER

All of this is exquisitely complex. So let's make matters worse by considering another procedural wrinkle, transfer of venue under 28 U.S.C. §1404(a). Because the basic federal venue rules provide a wide choice of venues (see Chapter 8), the plaintiff will often have the right to bring suit in courts that have little connection to the events in suit. Section 1404(a) provides federal courts with the discretionary authority to transfer a case to another federal district "for the convenience of parties and witnesses, and in the interest of justice," where the plaintiff has chosen one district but it makes more sense to litigate the case in a different district.[5] If a case is based on diversity, and if the judge transfers it to another district, even more elaborate complications arise in determining the applicable law.

An example may help to explain the problem. In *Van Dusen v. Barrack*, 376 U.S. 612 (1964), the plaintiffs were the personal representatives of passengers who died when an airplane crashed upon takeoff from a Boston airport, en route to Philadelphia. They brought a diversity action in federal district court in Pennsylvania against the airline, the manufacturer of the plane, and other defendants. The defendants moved for transfer to the District of Massachusetts under §1404(a).

There were some good practical reasons for the court to grant the motion. The site of the accident and many witnesses and documents were in Massachusetts. In addition, other actions arising from the crash had been filed there; if the Pennsylvania suits were transferred, they could be consolidated with those and litigated more efficiently, which is presumably "in the interest of justice."

However, the defendants' motion may have been motivated less by these practical factors than by several significant substantive differences between the wrongful death statutes of Massachusetts and Pennsylvania. The Massachusetts statute limited damages to $20,000 per decedent, while Pennsylvania law did not. Liability under the Massachusetts statute turned on the culpability of the defendant (so that even the $20,000 figure was limited to egregious conduct), while Pennsylvania law viewed wrongful death damages as purely compensatory. Because of these differences, recovery under Pennsylvania law might be substantial in each case, while

---

5. The factors to be considered in deciding whether a transfer is appropriate include the private interests of the parties, such as their residences, access to sources of proof, ability to subpoena witnesses, the need for a view of premises involved in the litigation, whether a judgment can be enforced in the forum, and others. There are also systemic interests involved, including appropriate distribution of cases among the federal districts, local decision of local cases, distribution of the burden of jury service, and the trial court's familiarity with the applicable law. See *Gulf Oil Corp. v. Gilbert*, 330 U.S. 501, 508-509 (1947).

recovery under Massachusetts law might not even equal the expenses of litigation.

In *Van Dusen* much turned, then, on what law the Massachusetts federal court (called the "transferee court") would apply if the case were bounced up there. If the defendants could convince the Pennsylvania federal court to transfer, and the transferee court applied Massachusetts law, *they could forum shop too*. After the plaintiffs chose a federal court in Pennsylvania to have the case decided under Pennsylvania's more favorable wrongful death statute,[6] the defendants could trump that choice with a strategic coup of their own, by seeking transfer to a court that would apply the stingy Massachusetts wrongful death remedy.

The Supreme Court refused to take the gambit. In *Van Dusen* the Court held that a transfer of venue under §1404(a) should effect a change of court but not a change of law. That is, the transferee court should apply the law that the transferor court would have applied if the case had not been transferred. On the *Van Dusen* facts, if the case were transferred to the Massachusetts court, that court should choose whatever law the Pennsylvania federal court would have applied (based on *Klaxon*'s mandate to mimic a Pennsylvania state court), because the plaintiffs had the right to file suit there and had done so. Put a bit more cynically, the transferee court should honor the plaintiffs' forum-shopping choice, rather than allowing the defendants to displace it through transfer.

The combination of *Erie*, *Klaxon*, and *Van Dusen* places the federal judge in a transferred case in a position wondrous to contemplate. Under *Van Dusen* and *Klaxon*, she must determine what the choice of law rules of the transferor state are, and what state's law the courts of the transferor state would have chosen under that choice of law rule. Then, under *Erie*, she must determine what the substantive law of *that* state is and apply it. As Judge Friendly wryly observed in a related context:

> Our principal task, in this diversity of citizenship case, is to determine what the New York courts would think the California courts would think on an issue about which neither has thought.

Nolan v. Transocean Airlines, Inc., 276 F.2d 280, 281 (2d Cir. 1960). The following examples illustrate some of the complexities engendered by the combination of *Erie*, *Klaxon*, and *Van Dusen*.

---

6. This assumes, of course, that the Pennsylvania courts would have applied Pennsylvania law, while the Massachusetts courts (and therefore the Massachusetts federal court, if bound to do the same) would have applied Massachusetts law to the case. It is entirely possible, under current choice of law principles, that this would have happened on the *Van Dusen* facts.

## Examples

### Games People Play

7. Assume for the purposes of this example the same facts concerning Tompkins, Jr.'s accident. Tompkins goes to see Webster two-and-a-half years after the accident, inquiring about suing the railroad and wishing to sue at home. Webster researches the law and learns that Pennsylvania tort law would allow Tompkins to recover on a showing of simple negligence, but New York law would require him to prove wilful or wanton conduct. She also learns that New York applies the place-of-the-injury choice of law rule to tort cases. Last, she finds that Pennsylvania has a two-year limitations period for tort claims, but that New York's limitations period for tort claims is four years.

   a. Tompkins brings suit in state court in New York. The Erie Railroad moves to transfer the case to Pennsylvania, arguing that the accident took place there, the plaintiff and all the witnesses are there, and that Pennsylvania law will apply, so it makes more sense to litigate the case in Pennsylvania. What will the court do?

   b. Tompkins sues in federal court in the Southern District of New York, based on diversity. The Erie Railroad then moves to transfer the case to the Middle District of Pennsylvania, where the events in suit took place. If the court grants the motion, what law will be applied to the limitations question and to the merits?

   c. Suppose that Tompkins sues in the Southern District of New York, and then *he* moves to transfer to the Middle District of Pennsylvania. If the court grants the motion, what law will apply to the limitations question and to the merits?

## Explanations

### Wading In

1. a. This case has some connections to both New York and Pennsylvania, since it involves a New York corporation and a Pennsylvania citizen, and the accident occurred in Pennsylvania. In such cases a court must choose which state's law to apply. Pennsylvania's choice of law principles (the example assumes) require its courts to apply the law of the place of the injury in tort cases, so the Pennsylvania state court will apply Pennsylvania law to this case. Tompkins will lose unless he can prove wilful and wanton conduct.

   b. If this case is brought in federal court in Pennsylvania, the federal district judge must, under *Klaxon*, apply Pennsylvania choice of law rules to determine the applicable tort standard. She must first decide which state's tort law Pennsylvania courts would apply, and then she must decide what the law of the chosen state is on the tort issue. Here, because Pennsylvania applies the place-of-the-injury choice of law rule to tort cases, the federal judge must do so as well. Under Pennsylvania's place-of-the-injury approach, she will select Pennsylvania tort law, since the accident took place there. Under Pennsylvania law (the example assumes) the railroad is only liable for wilful or wanton conduct toward a trespasser, and the federal court must apply this standard. *Klaxon* assures "vertical uniformity" within Pennsylvania, because Tompkins, Jr., will be stuck with the same rule in Pennsylvania federal court that would apply in the state court.

c. If Tompkins sues in a state court in New York, that court must use its choice of law rules to determine what state's substantive law to apply. Since New York applies the place-of-the-injury choice of law rule (the example assumes), New York will apply the tort law of Pennsylvania to this case. Since Pennsylvania law requires a showing of wilful and wanton conduct to recover, the New York state court will do so as well. Even though a plaintiff injured in a similar accident in New York would be entitled to recover on a showing of simple negligence, the "lex loci" choice of law rule means that the New York court will apply another state's law to the case.

An interesting consequence of this scenario is that the New York state court will end up doing the same kind of exercise that federal courts do in diversity cases, making its best guess at the content of another state's substantive law. New York courts cannot "make" Pennsylvania tort law, so when they choose to apply Pennsylvania tort law to a case, they have to engage in an Erie-type analysis of what the Pennsylvania law is on the point.[7]

d. The federal judge in New York must apply the same choice of law rule that a state court in New York would apply. Since the state court would look to Pennsylvania law, the New York federal judge must do so as well. Thus, the combination of *Klaxon*, New York choice of law doctrine and Pennsylvania tort law again leads to application of the wilful/wanton rule.

In this example the case comes out the same way in all four courts because the choice of law principles in all four courts point to application of the same state's law. If all states used the same choice of law rules, all cases would theoretically be decided under the same substantive law no matter where suit was brought, since the choice of law rules would always direct the court—whatever court it

---

7. It would be interesting to know whether state courts use the same kind of predictive approach in this context that the federal courts use under Erie or whether they try to act like a trial court of the other state in following any binding precedent on point.

was — to the same law.[8] That would eliminate forum shopping for more favorable substantive law.

The First Restatement rules aspired to this legal nirvana, but exceptions and idiosyncratic application made uniformity elusive. The more recent approaches, because they are based on judgmental balancing of interests and policies unique to each case, are less likely to lead courts in different states to apply the same state's law. Consequently, they create greater opportunities for forum shopping. However, because modern choice of law "rules" involve an ambiguous (one might even say, slushy) balancing of policy considerations, it is also harder to predict what state's law the forum court will choose. Thus, plaintiffs can only try to forum shop; they may end up mired in a different state's law because the court drew the balance differently than they predicted.

2. a. The Pennsylvania state court judge will apply Pennsylvania choice of law doctrine, which points to Pennsylvania tort law. As in example 1a, the result is application of the wilful/wanton rule.

   b. The Pennsylvania federal judge, under *Klaxon*, will also choose Pennsylvania's wilful/wanton rule, as in example 1b.

   c. The New York state judge will apply New York's balancing of interests approach to conflicts law, which leads (the example assumes) to the conclusion that New York tort law should apply to the case. This is a realistic possibility under modern choice of law principles. A number of factors, such as the residence of the parties at the time of the accident, the interests promoted by application of a particular tort principle, the place of the negligence that led to the accident, and the place in which the effect of the injuries is felt, might lead a court to apply its own law even though the accident took place in another state.[9]

   If New York does choose its own law in this case, Tompkins will be able to recover by showing that the railroad was negligent, even though he would have to show wilful or wanton conduct in a Pennsylvania court. He will have exactly the choice of two different substantive rules that the Court decried in *Erie*. However, the result arises because *different states* apply different tort law, not because the results differ between the state and federal courts within the same state, as was true under *Swift*.

   d. Once again, *Klaxon* requires the New York federal judge to achieve "vertical uniformity" by applying the same law that the New York state judge would. Therefore, the federal judge, following

---

8. Unless, of course, the choice of law rule was to always apply forum law.
9. See, e.g., the Fifth Circuit's opinion in *Challoner*, discussed in note 3.

New York's interest analysis choice of law rule, will apply the New York simple negligence rule. "Horizontal" uniformity is lost because the New York federal court applies different law than the Pennsylvania federal court would. Compare example 2b. The Court in *Klaxon* acknowledged that its decision would destroy horizontal uniformity among the federal courts:

> Whatever lack of uniformity this may produce between federal courts in different states is attributable to our federal system, which leaves to a state, within the limits permitted by the Constitution, the right to pursue local policies diverging from those of its neighbors.

313 U.S. at 496. The different results in these examples are illustrated in Figure 12-1. Note that in each scenario, there is "vertical uniformity" between the federal court and the state court in which the federal court sits — both will apply the same law to the case. However, in example 2 this vertical uniformity leads to horizontal disuniformity: The federal courts in Pennsylvania and New York apply different standards of care to the case because the state courts of those states would too.

3. a. *Klaxon* requires the West Virginia federal court to apply the choice of law approach of West Virginia courts, which is the lex loci delicti (place-of-the-injury) rule. The problem, however, is in

|  | Pennsylvania | New York |
| --- | --- | --- |
| ***Example 1*** | | |
| State Court: | Chooses Pa. law, wilful/wanton rule applies | Chooses Pa. law, wilful/wanton rule applies |
|  | ↕ | ↕ |
| Federal Court: | Chooses Pa. law, wilful/wanton rule applies | Chooses Pa. law, wilful/wanton rule applies |
| ***Example 2*** | | |
| State Court: | Chooses Pa. law, wilful/wanton rule applies | Chooses N.Y. law, negligence rule applies |
|  | ↕ | ↕ |
| Federal Court: | Chooses Pa. law, wilful/wanton rule applies | Chooses N.Y. law, negligence rule applies |

**Figure 12-1.** Choice of courts and choice of law.

determining whether Mrs. Tompkins's consortium injury took place in Pennsylvania, where her husband was injured, or in West Virginia, where they lived during most of the time that her relationship with him was impaired by his injury. Or did part of her "injury" take place in Pennsylvania (where she suffered two weeks of consortium losses) and part in West Virginia?

The First Restatement had a mechanical solution for this problem. Under Section 377 the court looked to "the state where the last event necessary to make the actor liable for the alleged tort takes place." Presumably, this would be Pennsylvania, since the Erie Railroad became liable to Mrs. Tompkins as soon as she started to suffer consortium losses. If West Virginia followed the First Restatement approach, it would choose Pennsylvania law on the loss of consortium claim. Thus the federal court would do so as well, and apply Pennsylvania tort law to her loss of consortium claim. But it is hardly self-evident that the law of Pennsylvania should govern this injury, which primarily affects Mrs. Tompkins in another state. Such rigidities led to a revolt against the First Restatement, which is still going on.

b. The ambiguity here is not as to the content of the tort law of either state, but rather as to how a West Virginia court would identify the "place of the injury" in applying its choice of law rule. Because the federal judge in West Virginia must apply the place-of-the-injury rules as the West Virginia court would, it should certify the issue to the West Virginia Supreme Court, if it has a certification procedure.

Suppose that the judge were unsure whether West Virginia's choice of law rule would point to Pennsylvania law *and* whether Pennsylvania tort law allowed recovery for loss of consortium. To get definitive answers to these questions, the judge would have to certify the choice of law issue to the West Virginia court and (if it determined that Pennsylvania law should apply) then the substantive law issue to the Pennsylvania court!

## A Quagmire Quandary

4. a. This is a quandary indeed. Several important strategic considerations point to suing at home: The witnesses will likely be available in Pennsylvania; it is convenient for Tompkins; and it is convenient for Webster. It is *not* so convenient for the Erie Railroad, which will have to hire local counsel and monitor litigation in another state. However, the wilful/wanton rule looms as a serious stumbling block to recovery, and one certainty in the case is that the wilful/wanton rule will apply if Webster sues in Pennsylvania.

On the other hand, suing in New York is inconvenient for Tompkins, who wants to sue at home and wants Webster to do it. In addition, important witnesses may be beyond the subpoena power of the New York court. Yet suing in New York has some important potential advantages. If the court decides to apply New York law, and if New York tort law would allow recovery based on simple negligence, Tompkins's case looks a good deal stronger on the merits. Naturally, Tompkins has a strong interest in the merits.

This is a difficult tactical decision because the advantage New York offers turns on several contingencies. First, Webster must convince the New York court that the lex loci delicti rule has effectively been overruled by recent New York choice of law decisions adopting interest analysis for contract cases, so that it should apply interest analysis to tort cases as well. *Second*, if the court applies interest analysis to the case, Webster must also demonstrate that that approach supports application of New York law to this accident. Just because the court applies a different choice of law *rule* does not necessarily mean it will choose New York tort law. The court might assess the interests of the parties and the states involved and conclude that they weigh in favor of Pennsylvania law anyway. *Last*, if she convinces the New York court to look to New York law, she must still convince that court that New York tort law now allows recovery based on simple negligence.

All of this is a little chaotic, isn't it? It is hard to give up the home forum on the speculative chance that all those decisions will go your way in a distant court. These contingencies will certainly act as a check on forum shopping in many cases. Webster's decision will turn on how strong her arguments are on these legal issues and, conversely, how weak her case would be if she sued in Pennsylvania and had to meet the wilful/wanton standard.

b. If Webster does choose to sue in New York, she might be well advised to choose a federal court in New York. If New York law — both tort law and conflicts law — is in the process of change, the federal court may have more flexibility to anticipate those changes than the state trial court would. Presumably, the federal diversity court must apply New York conflicts law in the same way it would apply New York substantive law; that is, it must ask what the state's highest court would do if the issue were before it today. If the case law strongly suggests that the highest court would no longer apply the place-of-the-injury rule, the federal court may be more willing to reject it than a state trial court, which will feel bound by the highest court's past precedents unless they are clearly eviscerated by later holdings. See Chapter 10, example 6.

## The Procedure/Procedure Distinction

5. a. This example raises the issue of whether the New York court, when it chooses the law of another state, must apply the whole law of the other state, including matters of procedure. Sound familiar? It is akin to the dilemma explored in "Eerie Erie," as to when the federal court must select state law and when it may apply its own procedures. In the "horizontal" choice of law context, as in the *Erie* context, things get dicey because, generally speaking, state courts apply their own procedural law even if they have chosen the substantive law of another state under their choice of law rules. Moores, §124.30 [4].

It isn't hard to see why this dichotomy has long been accepted in the horizontal choice of law context. Just as federal diversity courts would have to abandon the Federal Rules entirely if *Erie* required them to exactly imitate the state court, the New York court would have a very difficult task if, once it chose to apply Pennsylvania tort law, it *also* had to apply Pennsylvania procedural law. The problem would be even worse than the federal judge's under *Erie*. Since New York courts might choose the law of many different states in different cases, the New York judge would have to learn the procedural quirks of many states. Effectively, she would be forced to run her courtroom under 50 different procedural systems instead of one. See G. Gelfand and H. Abrams, Putting *Erie* On the Right Track, 49 U. Pitt. L. Rev. 937, 963 (1988). That is insupportable; to avoid it, the substance/procedure distinction has emerged in conflicts of law doctrine as it has under *Erie*. Thus, the New York court would require compliance with its in-hand service of process rule, even though Pennsylvania would not.

   b. If Webster sued in federal court in New York, the court would deny the motion to dismiss. While *Erie* mandates application of state law in diversity cases, it does not require wholesale abandonment of federal procedure. Where a valid Federal Rule covers an issue, it may be applied in a federal diversity case despite contrary procedure in the state court. *Hanna v. Plumer*, 360 U.S. 460 (1965). Here, Fed. R. Civ. P. 4(e)(2)(B) provides that leaving the papers at Hepzibah's home with a person residing therein is sufficient. The federal court need not ask (under *Erie*) what New York law would require, nor must it ask (under *Klaxon*) whether New York would look to Pennsylvania law. It may apply the Federal Rule.

6. You don't know enough to "answer" this example, but you do know enough to see the quizzical problem it poses. The case is in federal court. Under *Erie*, the judge must look to state law on "substantive" issues — "substantive," that is, in the *Erie* sense of the term. In *Guaranty Trust Co. v. York*, the Supreme Court concluded that the state limitations

period for a claim was "substantive" for *Erie* purposes, so that state law applied. So, the judge has to apply the state limitations period.

That much is easy, but only gets us part of the way. There remains the question as to *which* limitations period should be applied, New York's or Pennsylvania's? Well, that's easy too: *Klaxon* requires the federal court to do what the New York court would do. That turns on whether a New York court would apply the Pennsylvania limitations period or its own longer one.

If the issue is "substantive" (see *Guaranty Trust Co. v. York*), presumably the New York court would apply the Pennsylvania limitations period. Unfortunately, it very well might not. The line between substance and procedure has been drawn differently in the horizontal choice of law cases than it has in the vertical choice of law cases under *Erie*. Limitations periods are an example. While the statute of limitations issue is "substantive" for *Erie* purposes, many courts still apply their own limitations law to a case even if their conflicts of law rules mandate application of the substantive law of another state. See *Sun Oil Co. v. Wortman*, 486 U.S. 717 (1988) (approving application of Kansas limitations period to claim even though Kansas lacked sufficient connections to the case to apply its own substantive law); Richman and Reynolds at 296 (stating and criticizing this approach). Thus, New York might apply its limitations period to the claim, because it is "procedural" for choice of law purposes, while the federal court would be required to make the same choice because it is "substantive" for *Erie* purposes![10]

## Games People Play

7. a. The one thing that the New York state court will *not* do is transfer the case. A New York state court has no authority to send a case to a Pennsylvania court; these are different, autonomous court systems, which decide for themselves which cases they will hear.[11] The situation is different in federal court, because all federal courts are "branches" of the same federal court system and are required under

---

10. Another area that has been subject to this schizophrenic classification is burden of proof. See *Sampson v. Channell*, 110 F.2d 754 (1st Cir. 1940), in which the First Circuit held that *Erie* required a federal court to apply state law on the issue of burden of proof. However, it chose to apply the burden of proof rule of the state in which suit was brought (Massachusetts) rather than the rule of the state where the accident had occurred (Maine). The court concluded that the Massachusetts court would have viewed burden of proof as "procedural" for horizontal choice of law purposes, and therefore applied its own rule. Consequently, the court held (anticipating *Klaxon*) that the federal court should do the same.
11. There is a model state statute, the Uniform Transfer of Litigation Act, which, if adopted, would allow such transfers between state courts. However, as of 2007, no state had adopted this model act.

§1404(a) to entertain cases transferred from other branches of the same system.

That leaves the state court with several options. It could dismiss under "forum non conveniens." The forum non conveniens doctrine is based on a premise similar to §1404(a) that sometimes cases that are properly filed under the three ring analysis still logically belong somewhere else. Under forum non conveniens, which is recognized in many states, the court may dismiss a case where the interests of justice indicate that it should be litigated elsewhere.[12]

If the court dismisses Tompkins's case he will lose: If he refiled in Pennsylvania, the Erie Railroad would plead the two-year statute of limitations as a complete defense. That prospect is likely to convince the New York court not to dismiss for forum non conveniens. So the court is likely to take the alternative course of entertaining the action. If, as a good many courts do, New York applied its own limitations statute (see example 6), Tompkins would get the benefit of the four-year limitations period and—since New York looks to Pennsylvania tort law under the place-of-the-injury choice of law rule—the simple negligence standard of care.

b. Tompkins gets a pretty good result under the first scenario, but he would still have to go to New York to litigate. Maybe he can do better by suing in federal court in New York. Since the federal court under *Klaxon* must act like the New York state court, it will apply New York's longer limitations period (see example 6) and Pennsylvania's simple negligence rule. In addition, if the federal court transfers the case to the Middle District of Pennsylvania under §1404(a), he will get the best of both worlds. The suit will be litigated in Pennsylvania, and, under *Van Dusen*, the court will apply New York limitations law and Pennsylvania tort law.

In the forum-shopping business, this is the highest form of art: The plaintiff shops for New York law on some issues and Pennsylvania law on others . . . maybe it should be called "issue shopping." In this case there will be a good argument for transfer, since the accident took place in Pennsylvania, most of the witnesses are likely to be there, Tompkins is there, and Pennsylvania law will apply to the case.

Even this scenario is chancy, however. The railroad may not move to transfer, since it is from New York and will have the

---

12. The doctrine is also applied in the federal courts when the appropriate forum is in another country. Just as a New York court cannot order a Pennsylvania court to hear a case, a United States court cannot order a court in another country to do so. If, therefore, the case clearly should be litigated in another country, the federal court's only option is to dismiss under forum non conveniens.

advantage of litigating at home. Even if it does, the court may deny the motion.

c. This is the ultimate in chutzpah: Tompkins sues in New York and then asks the court to send the case to his home forum, taking the New York statute of limitations — but not New York tort law — with it. *Van Dusen* was not quite this egregious, since the defendants sought the transfer.

The scholars had predicted that the Supreme Court would discourage this game by holding that the law of the *transferee* forum would apply if the plaintiff sought transfer. In Tompkins's case, that would mean that the Pennsylvania court would apply its own two-year limitations period (which would mean, in turn, that Tompkins wouldn't seek the transfer). However, in *Ferens v. John Deere Co.*, 494 U.S. 516 (1990), the Supreme Court perplexed the prognosticators by holding (by a 5-4 majority) that the *Van Dusen* rule applies even where the plaintiff seeks transfer. The reasons are complicated, and the arguments on both sides of the issue are close. Read the case if you can. The bottom line, however, is that Tompkins could sue in the inconvenient forum, get back into Pennsylvania, obtain the benefit of Pennsylvania tort law, and invoke the longer New York limitations period.

If this isn't chaos, it certainly is a peculiar form of order.

# PART III

# The Scope of the Action

# Sculpting the Lawsuit

## The Basic Rules of Joinder

## INTRODUCTION

A great deal of time is spent during the first year of law school analyzing decided cases, doing postmortems on past lawsuits. But every lawsuit also has a beginning, and at the beginning someone must make important tactical decisions about the scope of the lawsuit, that is, whom to sue and which claims to assert. The traditional rule in American courts has been, and largely still is, that "the plaintiff is master of his claim," that it is up to the plaintiff (or his lawyer) to decide who the parties to the suit will be and which claims will be asserted in the action.

An example may help to frame the problem. Assume that Wright is the main contractor on a construction job. The electrical subcontractor is Edison Electric. While driving an Edison truck to the construction site, Edison's site manager, Volt, collides with Wright's cement truck, as well as with a private vehicle driven by Ellsworth. All three drivers are injured, and the two trucks are heavily damaged.

If Volt decides to bring suit against Wright to recover for his injuries, he will have to decide whether to sue alone or to bring a combined action along with Edison Electric, which will seek to recover for the damage to its truck. Ellsworth may also wish to join as a plaintiff to recover for her personal injuries and property damage. Alternatively, Volt may wish to sue both Wright and Ellsworth on the theory that each was negligent or, for whatever reason, to sue one tortfeasor but not the other.

Volt's options as to which defendants he may sue and which potential plaintiffs he decides to sue with are defined by the rules of "joinder of parties." In the federal courts, initial joinder of parties is governed by Fed. R. Civ. P. 20(a)(1), which authorizes plaintiffs to sue together if they assert claims arising out of the same transaction or occurrence (or series of transactions or occurrences) and their claims against the defendant or defendants will involve a common question of law or fact. In Volt's suit, for example, Volt and Edison may join as plaintiffs because their claims arise out of the same accident, and the factual issue of whose negligence caused the accident is common to both their claims.

Similarly, Rule 20(a)(2) allows the plaintiff to sue multiple defendants in a single action if the same criteria are met. Volt could sue Ellsworth and Wright as codefendants in the same action, since he claims relief from each arising from the same accident and there will be a common question as to whose negligence caused the accident. Here are some configurations that would be permissible under the rule:

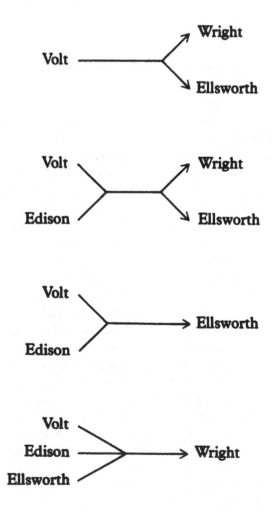

It makes good sense to allow parties to join as plaintiffs or to sue defendants jointly in a single action if the criteria in Rule 20(a) are met. When a number of claims involve a single transaction or occurrence, and the same issue or issues will have to be litigated to resolve each claim, it is more efficient to litigate those issues once in a combined action, rather than repeatedly in separate suits. In addition, resolving those issues in a single action avoids the possibility of inconsistent judgments on the same issue. For example, if Volt sues Ellsworth and recovers, but Edison sues Ellsworth and loses, the two juries must have disagreed on whether Ellsworth was negligent (barring any contributory negligence defense). Such inconsistent results reflect unfavorably on the judicial system and are best avoided where possible. If Volt's and Edison's claims are tried together there will be no inconsistent verdicts, since there will be only one finding on Ellsworth's negligence.

Interestingly, however, Rule 20(a) does not *require* parties to be joined whenever the criteria in the rule are met. At least initially, the joinder decision is left to the plaintiffs. If they choose to sue some but not all defendants in one action, they may sue the others in a separate action or never sue them at all. If they choose not to join in a suit by other plaintiffs against the defendant, they remain free to pursue their own claims in separate suits.

## An Early but Sensible Question

1. Since it promotes efficiency and consistency to litigate related claims such as Volt's and Edison's together, why doesn't Rule 20(a) *require* joinder of parties where the two criteria in the rule are met?

# COUNTERCLAIMS AND CROSS-CLAIMS

You should be careful to distinguish Rule 20, which governs joinder of *parties*, from Rules 18 and 13, which authorize parties, once they are properly joined in a law suit, to assert additional *claims* against opposing parties. Rule 13 authorizes a defending party in a suit to assert claims back against a party who has claimed against him. Such counterclaims come in two shapes, compulsory (Rule 13(a)) and permissive (Rule 13(b)). If the defending party's counterclaim arises from the same transaction or occurrence as the claim against him, it is compulsory, which essentially means that he must assert it in the original action or lose it. For example, if Volt sues Ellsworth for his injuries arising out of the accident and Ellsworth suffered injuries in the same accident, which she attributes to Volt's negligence, Rule 13(a)(1) requires Ellsworth to assert her claim for these injuries in Volt's action. This rule makes sense; it forces parties who are already adversaries to litigate all claims arising from the same set of facts in a single action.

## Another Impromptu Question

2. Under Rule 20(a), the parties are never forced to bring parties into a particular suit. Rule 13(a)(1), by contrast, compels a party to assert some claims at a time and place not of his choosing. Why did the rulemakers choose to force parties to assert compulsory counterclaims?

Defending parties may also assert counterclaims that are completely unrelated to the original claim, under Rule 13(b). This cannot be justified on efficiency grounds, since (by definition) a permissive counterclaim will involve different events from the main claim, and the court will almost certainly order separate trial of the permissive counterclaim. See Rule 42(b). But the rule at least allows a defendant, once brought before the court, to settle all his claims against his opponent without having to file a separate lawsuit.

Yet another type of claim is addressed in Rule 13(g), which provides for assertion of *cross-claims* arising out of the same transaction or occurrence as the main claim. A cross-claim is a claim asserted by one party against a co-party; that is, someone on the same side of the "v" as the claimant. Suppose that Volt sues Wright and Ellsworth for injuries suffered in the accident. If Wright suffered injuries as well and believes that the accident was Ellsworth's fault, she may cross-claim against Ellsworth for her injuries. This is called a cross-claim rather than a counterclaim because it is asserted by one defendant against a co-defendant, not against an opposing party.[1] The configuration would look like this:

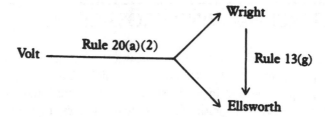

**Figure 13-1.** Volt joins Wright and Ellsworth as defendants under Rule 20(a)(2); Wright cross-claims against Ellsworth under Rule 13(g).

Here again, allowing assertion of these claims in the main action promotes efficiency and consistency because the same underlying facts will be litigated on the main claim and on the cross-claim. Yet here again, the

---

1. Of course, once Wright asserts the cross-claim against Ellsworth, they become opposing parties. But they weren't before that.

rule makes joinder optional, leaving Wright free to sue separately on her claim against Ellsworth if she prefers to do so.

The various joinder rules may also work in tandem. For example, the counterclaim rules, Rules 13(a)(1) and (b), both authorize "a pleading" to assert a claim against an "opposing party." Once again the rulemakers have chosen the language of the rule with care. This language authorizes any defending party — not just an original defendant — to assert counterclaims against a party who has claimed against him. In the last diagram, once Wright cross-claims against Ellsworth, she becomes an "opposing party" on Wright's cross-claim. Rule 13 applies to any claim she may have against Wright. If she has a claim against Wright for her injuries in the collision, she must assert it as a compulsory counterclaim once Wright has asserted a claim against her. Fed. R. Civ. P. 13(a)(1). If she has any unrelated claims against Wright, she may assert them, but is not required to, under Rule 13(b).

## JOINDER OF CLAIMS UNDER RULE 18(A)

Rule 18(a) is the broadest of the basic joinder rules. Unequivocally, it provides that a party seeking relief from an opposing party may join with his original claim any additional claims he has against that opposing party. Suppose, for example, that Volt exchanges words with Wright after the accident and a fight ensues. Rule 18(a) allows Volt to assert his claim for assault in the same action with the negligence claim. It would also allow Volt to add a completely unrelated claim against Wright for libel, trespass, or anything else. Unlike Rule 20(a), there is no common transaction or occurrence requirement in Rule 18(a).

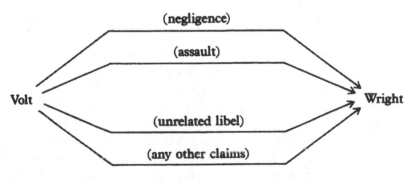

(Rule 18(a) authorizes joinder of all these claims, related and unrelated)

Rule 18(a), like Rule 13, authorizes "a pleader" to assert as many claims as he has against an opponent. This applies not only to the original plaintiff, but also to any party seeking relief against another party, whether on a counterclaim, a cross-claim, or a third-party claim. Suppose, for example, that Volt sues Ellsworth and Wright for negligence, based on the collision at the construction site, and Ellsworth cross-claims against Wright for her damages arising out of the accident. Rule 18(a) authorizes Ellsworth, as a party seeking relief, to add on any claim, related or unrelated, that she may have against Wright:

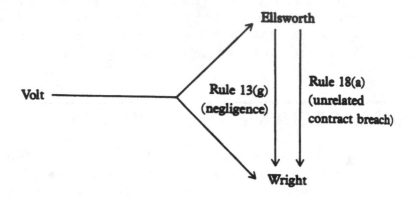

Note that Ellsworth could not have asserted this unrelated contract claim as a cross-claim if it were the only claim she had against Wright: Rule 13(g) only allows cross-claims that arise out of the same transaction or occurrence as the main claim. However, once Ellsworth asserts a proper cross-claim against Wright, Rule 18(a) kicks in, allowing her to add on totally unrelated claims as well.

A cautionary note is in order here, however. The fact that the Rules authorize joinder of multiple claims, or claims against multiple parties, does not confer subject matter jurisdiction on the court to hear those claims. For every claim, subject matter jurisdiction must be analyzed separately; at times, the joinder rules will authorize the joinder of a claim, but the court will not have jurisdiction to hear it. These two requirements are compared and distinguished in Chapter 17, entitled "Joinder vs. Jurisdiction: The Difference between Power and Permission."

In puzzling out the following examples, start by identifying the party asserting the claim as a plaintiff or defendant and then consider, given the particular posture of the claim, which of the rules applies. Assume that all suits are brought in federal court.

## An Artistic Disaster

3. Morisot and Cassatt hire Van Gogh and Renoir to paint their studio. Van Gogh and Renoir hire Pissarro as an assistant. Pissarro goes for coffee, leaving the electric paint remover on, and burns the studio to the ground. Morisot breaks her leg jumping from the third-story window, three of Cassatt's priceless masterpieces are burned, and Renoir suffers second-degree burns. Everyone is mad.

   a. Suppose that Morisot and Cassatt are co-owners of the studio. May they join as plaintiffs to sue Pissarro for the damages to the studio from the fire?

   b. Suppose that Cassatt owns the studio on her own. May she and Morisot join as plaintiffs to sue Pissarro for his negligence, if Cassatt seeks recovery for damage to the building and Morisot seeks damages for her broken leg?

   c. Assume that Van Gogh and Renoir are liable for the negligence of Pissarro under the law of respondeat superior, if he acted in the scope of his employment in leaving the heat gun on. May Morisot sue Van Gogh, Renoir, and Pissarro in a single action to recover for her broken leg?

   d. Could Cassatt sue Van Gogh and Renoir for breach of contract for burning down her studio in the process of painting it, and Morisot join as a coplaintiff asserting a negligence claim against the same defendants for the injury to her leg?

   e. Change the facts a little: Assume that either Pissarro or Gauguin, another employee, left the paint remover on, and Cassatt is unsure which it was. Can she sue them both under Rule 20(a)(2)?

   f. If Cassatt sues Renoir for breach of contract, may Renoir assert claims against Pissarro and Van Gogh in the same suit for negligently causing his injuries? (In considering this example, compare Rule 20(a) with Rule 14(a)(1).)

4. If Cassatt chooses to sue Renoir alone, may she assert both negligence and breach of contract claims against Renoir for her losses in the fire?

5. If Cassatt sues Renoir and Van Gogh for breach of contract, do the rules authorize her to add a claim against Renoir for breach of a separate contract to paint her house in another village?

6. Cassatt sues Renoir for breach of the studio painting contract. Later, after losing on that claim, she sues Renoir for a previous breach of the unrelated contract to paint her house. Can she do that?

## The Tables Turned

7. Assume that Morisot owned the studio and contracted with Renoir and Van Gogh to paint it. Morisot sues Renoir and Pissarro for negligence and breach of contract as a result of the studio fire. Renoir asserts a claim against Morisot in the same action for payment for the painting work that had been completed before the building burned.
   a. Is Renoir's claim properly joined?
   b. What would happen if Renoir did not assert this claim in Morisot's suit, but sued on it separately in a later action.

8. Following up on the last example, assume that Renoir also has a claim against Morisot for injuries suffered in an auto accident two months after the fire but before the suit was commenced. Can he assert this claim as well?

9. Suppose on the same facts that the only counterclaim Renoir had against Morisot was for the unrelated auto accident. Could he assert it in this action?

10. If Morisot sues Renoir for her fire losses, may Renoir assert his claim against Morisot for breach of the studio painting contract and also bring in Cassatt (a co-signer of the contract) as a codefendant on that claim?

## Acting at Cross-Purposes

11. Suppose that Cassatt sues Renoir, Van Gogh, and Pissarro jointly. She seeks recovery from Pissarro for his negligence and from Renoir and Van Gogh as Pissarro's employers, under the doctrine of respondeat superior. Renoir wishes to assert a claim against Pissarro for indemnification (that is, reimbursement for any damages he — Renoir — must pay if he is found liable to Cassatt) since it was Pissarro's negligence that actually caused the damage to the studio.
    a. May Renoir assert this claim against Pissarro in the same suit?
    b. Why is this claim not a counterclaim?

12. On the facts of example 11, could Renoir assert a claim against Pissarro for his own injuries suffered in the fire?

13. If Cassatt sues Renoir and Van Gogh for their negligence in burning the studio, may Renoir assert a claim against Van Gogh for his failure to pay him half of the money they earned on another paint job?

14. Another variation: Suppose that Cassatt sues Renoir and Van Gogh, and Renoir wishes to assert claims against Van Gogh for his own injuries due to the fire and for the money owed him for the other paint job. May he do so?

15. Assume that Van Gogh and Renoir do not agree as to who was negligent in causing the fire. Van Gogh claims that it was Renoir's negligent instructions to Pissarro that caused the blaze. Renoir claims that Van Gogh failed to cut the power to the paint remover when Pissarro left for his break. When Cassatt sues Van Gogh and Renoir, Renoir cross-claims against Van Gogh for indemnification for any damages he must pay Cassatt on the main claim. May Van Gogh assert a claim against Renoir for injuries he suffered in the fire?

## Last Impressionists

16. One final example to make a particular point. Suppose Morisot (from Massachusetts) sues Renoir (from Maine) and Van Gogh (from Massachusetts) in federal court for their negligence in burning down the studio. Is the suit proper?

## Explanations

### An Early but Sensible Question

1. While it would serve several goals of our procedural system to force all parties to join in a single action if their claims arise out of the same events, it would raise other serious procedural difficulties. Suppose that Volt and Ellsworth want to sue in federal court, but Edison prefers the state court? Suppose that Volt prefers to sue in Maine, but the others prefer New Hampshire? What if Edison wants to bring suit immediately, but Volt prefers to attempt a settlement first? Will Volt's lawyer represent all parties, or will each have her own lawyer? Who will plan litigation strategy? What if they can't agree? Suppose that some of the potential plaintiffs are also potential defendants: Who will decide which side of the "v" to put them on?

   In addition to these possible differences of opinion as to tactical choices, the jurisdictional problems would be even more serious. The right to join parties under the Federal Rules does not confer subject matter jurisdiction on the court. Fed. R. Civ. P. 82. For example, suppose that Volt is from Maine, Ellsworth from New Hampshire, and Wright, the intended defendant, from Maine. If Volt and Ellsworth were forced to sue together, the suit could not be brought in federal court because there would not be complete diversity. Under the permissive language of Rule 20(a)(1), if Ellsworth prefers federal court she may preserve the option to sue there by not joining as a co-plaintiff with Volt. Alternatively, assume that Volt wishes to sue Wright, from Maine, and Ellsworth, from New Hampshire, for damages that took place in a Pennsylvania accident. Under Rule 20(a), which allows Volt to sue each defendant separately, he will at least be able to sue Wright at home in Maine because the Maine court will have personal jurisdiction over Wright on the basis of her domicile. If Volt were forced to join both defendants, he would have to sue in Pennsylvania, the one state where he could obtain personal jurisdiction over both defendants.

Obviously, a compulsory joinder rule would raise a host of procedural problems, which could undermine rather than further the goal of efficiency. The federal rulemakers chose to stick with the old adage that "the plaintiff is master of his claim," rather than to create a whole new set of procedural complexities.[2] However, despite these problems, the time-honored principle of plaintiff autonomy has had its critics. In this era of scarce judicial resources and managerial judging, broader suggestions for limiting plaintiff autonomy have also been floated. Professor Richard Freer, for example, suggests that the court should play a greater role in determining the scope of party joinder. See R. Freer, Avoiding Duplicative Litigation: Rethinking Plaintiff Autonomy and the Court's Role in Defining the Litigation Unit, 50 U. Pitt. L. Rev. 809 (1989). "A plaintiff is entitled to due process, but has no right to sole possession of center stage; we need to tell the prima donna of the legal world that she must work with some co-stars." Id. at 819.

For some years New Jersey experimented with a doctrine which rejected Rule 20(a)(2)'s plaintiff autonomy rule. Under New Jersey's "entire controversy" doctrine, a plaintiff who brought suit on a transaction or occurrence was required to join all parties who might be liable to him for that transaction or occurrence in the action, or lose his claims against the omitted parties. See *Cogdell v. Hospital Center at Orange*, 560 A.2d 1169 (N.J. 1989). The premise of the doctrine was that parties have an obligation to facilitate efficient resolution of cases, and that joining all defendants in the first action would facilitate that goal. In practice, however, the rule led to confusion as to when parties had to be joined. It also led to assertion of questionable claims simply to prevent forfeiting those claims by operation of the rule. New Jersey later abandoned this aspect of the entire controversy doctrine in favor of a more modest requirement that plaintiffs notify the court of potential claims against other parties, allowing the court to order such parties joined in some circumstances. See New Jersey Rules 4:5-l, 4:29-1(b).

## Another Impromptu Question

2. Although forcing joinder of parties raises many problems, most of these do not apply to the joinder of an additional claim between parties who

---

2. One exception, however, is Fed. R. Civ. P. 19, which requires joinder of certain persons under limited circumstances. Rule 19 is analyzed in Chapter 15.

are already properly before the court. The subject matter jurisdiction problems referred to in the analysis of example 1 will not arise in the compulsory counterclaim situation because there is usually supplemental jurisdiction over compulsory counterclaims. See Chapter 16, example 4. Nor will personal jurisdiction bar assertion of the claim: The plaintiff, by initiating suit, submits to jurisdiction for counterclaims arising out of the transaction or occurrence that is the subject of his claim. 6 Wright & Miller at §1416. Nor does compulsory joinder of the counterclaim pose uncertainties as to who must be joined, since no new parties are brought into the suit by the assertion of the counterclaim.

The only substantial argument against making counterclaims compulsory is that it violates the longstanding common law principle that the plaintiff (or, in this case, the defendant) is master of his claim, free to choose where and when to assert any claim he may have. The federal rule makers evidently concluded that this was insufficient to outweigh the obvious advantage of litigating the same facts and issues between the same parties in a single action. Some state rulemakers have weighed these policies differently, however, and refused to make any counterclaims compulsory. See Friedenthal, Kane, and Miller at 370 n.15.

## An Artistic Disaster

3. a. This is the simplest example of parties who wish to join as coplaintiffs in a single lawsuit. Rule 20(a)(1) allows it, so long as they are asserting claims arising out of the same transaction or occurrence and their claims will involve at least one common question of law or fact. These criteria are met here because Morisot and Cassatt both seek relief arising out of the fire and both claims involve a common question of fact, whether Pissarro was negligent.[3]

   b. The only difference between this example and the last is that the two plaintiffs seek compensation for different injuries. However, that does not affect their right to sue together. Rule 20(a)(1) does not require that the plaintiffs seek recovery for exactly the same injuries or on a joint interest. In fact, the rule specifically provides that any one plaintiff "need not be interested in obtaining . . . all the relief demanded." It only requires that the underlying transaction or occurrence be the same and that the two plaintiffs' claims share a common question of law or fact. Those criteria are met here, and joinder is proper under the rule.

---

3. Indeed, as joint owners they may even be required to join as plaintiffs, under Fed. R. Civ. P. 19(a).

This result is appropriate, given the efficiency and consistency goals of Rule 20(a). As long as the claims will require resolution of common issues, joint litigation in a single suit will save time for the parties, the witnesses, and the court.

c. Rule 20(a) applies not only to plaintiffs bringing suit together, but also to one or more plaintiffs bringing suit against multiple defendants. See Fed. R. Civ. p. 20(a)(2). Here, Morisot seeks relief from all three defendants on claims arising out of the same fire, and her right to recover on each claim will require litigation of the common negligence issue. Joinder is proper.

d. This example involves multiple plaintiffs and defendants. While Rule 20(a) does not explicitly authorize suit by multiple plaintiffs against multiple defendants, it does authorize suits by multiple plaintiffs (Rule 20(a)(1)) and (in Rule 20(a)(2)) against multiple defendants. It is a fair inference that both types of joinder may be used in the same suit. It is proper, therefore, for some or all of the potential plaintiffs to join to sue all of the potential defendants or to sue selected defendants.

The other difference in this example is that the two plaintiffs are proceeding on different theories: Cassatt for breach of contract and Morisot for negligence. Compare example 3b, in which the plaintiffs proceeded on the same theory but for different damages. Nothing in Rule 20(a) requires the plaintiffs to proceed on the same theories in order for joinder to be proper. The idea behind the joinder rule is that there is efficiency and consistency to be gained from litigating the same facts in a single action. These goals are served by joinder criteria that allow a single action even though the plaintiffs are proceeding on different theories.

However, the criteria of Rule 20(a) must still be met. In this case the "same transaction or occurrence" test clearly is met since all claims arise out of the fire. The "common question of law or fact" requirement will likely be met as well: Both Morisot and Cassatt will have to prove that Pissarro's acts caused the fire in order to recover from Van Gogh and Renoir on their respective theories. So long as some such common question exists, joinder is proper, even though many issues (for example, the damages suffered by each plaintiff) will be different.

e. In this example, one of the defendants — but not both — will be liable to Cassatt. However, she may still sue them as codefendants under Rule 20(a)(2). She has a legitimate claim against each of them, though she will presumably only win against one or the other. Her claims against both defendants arise from the fire, and they both involve the common question of who caused it. Where these two requirements are met, Rule 20(a)(2) expressly allows joinder, even though relief is sought against the defendants "in the alternative."

f.  In this case, it is the defendant who has joined multiple parties in the action, not the plaintiff:

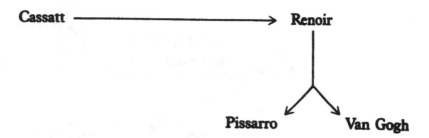

The general language of Rule 20(a)(2), if read in isolation, might be interpreted to allow a defendant to join new parties as "defendants" in the original action. However, a look at Rule 14(a)(1) indicates that this type of situation, a defendant bringing new parties into the suit (whom the plaintiff did not choose to sue), is separately dealt with in that rule, which allows joinder only in much more limited circumstances than Rule 20(a). See Chapter 14. The Rule 14(a)(1) requirement for impleading Pissarro and Van Gogh would not be met on these facts.

By contrast, Rule 20(a) only applies to joinder of parties by the original plaintiffs. The rulemakers' meticulous language confirms this: Rules 20(a)(1) and 20(a)(2) speak specifically of "plaintiffs" and "defendants" rather than "parties claiming a right to relief" or similarly general language. Compare Rules 18(a) and 13, which are deliberately phrased more generally in order to apply more broadly.

4.  This example is typical of the myriad cases in which a plaintiff asserts a number of claims against a single defendant for the same injuries but bases those claims on different theories of relief. The question here is joinder of claims, not parties, since Cassatt is seeking relief from a single party on two separate claims. Rule 18(a) establishes a refreshingly broad rule for joinder of claims: Once Cassatt decides to sue Renoir, she may join whatever claims she has against Renoir in the suit. Thus, joinder of the negligence and contract claims is proper. It would also be proper if they were totally unrelated.

5.  The answer to this question involves application of both Rules 20 and 18. Rule 20(a)(2) allows Cassatt to sue Renoir and Van Gogh together for breach of the studio-painting contract. Compare example 3c. Rule 18(a) allows Cassatt, once she has properly asserted a claim against Renoir, to assert her unrelated contract claim against Renoir as well,

even though it arises out of a completely separate incident. Visually, the case looks like this:

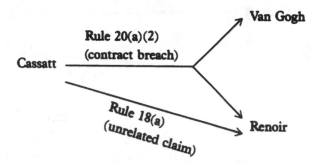

This compound effect of the rules is confusing. It seems to contradict the limitations on joinder established in Rule 20(a)(2), since it allows Cassatt to inject into the case a claim that is completely unrelated to the transaction or occurrence that gave rise to the joint claim she has against the two defendants. After all, if she sued Van Gogh on the studio claim, she could not add Renoir on the unrelated claim under Rule 20(a)(2), could she?

That is true, but the Rules take the position that once you *have* properly gotten the two of them into court, you may add any claims you have against either defendant, related or unrelated. Presumably, the theory is that once the parties become proper adversaries in a lawsuit they ought at least to have the opportunity to resolve all their differences in one suit.

6. This example is meant to emphasize one point about Rule 18(a): It is permissive. Cassatt may assert unrelated claims against Renoir under Rule 18(a) but is not obligated to do so. Thus, she could bring separate actions against Renoir on these two unrelated contract claims in whatever order she chooses.

One note of caution should be added. While Rule 18 may not force a plaintiff to join all his claims against a defendant in a single action, the rules of res judicata will (at least under federal res judicata principles) if the claims arise out of a single transaction or occurrence. If Morisot has claims for breach of contract and negligence against Renoir and both arise from the studio fire, these would constitute a single "claim" for res judicata purposes that must be litigated in one action, despite the permissive language of Rule 18(a). See Chapter 27, which compares the joinder rules with the principles of res judicata, especially example 2, which specifically addresses the Rule 18 issue. However, because the two claims asserted here are completely unrelated, separate suits will be permissible under res judicata analysis as well as under Rule 18(a).

## The Tables Turned

7. a. Morisot's joinder of Renoir and Pissarro as co-defendants is proper here under Rule 20(a)(2). Renoir's claim against Morisot is a counterclaim under Rule 13(a)(1), that is, a claim by a defending party against the party suing him. Not only do the rules authorize Renoir to assert this claim, they require him to do so. Rule 13(a)(1) provides that a defending party's pleading "must" state as a counterclaim any claim he has that arises out of the same transaction or occurrence as the main claim. Here, Renoir's claim arises out of the performance of the same paint job that gave rise to Morisot's claims. It is therefore a compulsory counterclaim under Rule 13(a)(1).

   b. If Renoir did not assert this compulsory counterclaim in Morisot's action, but brought a separate suit later for the payments, the court would dismiss it. Rule 13(a)(1) requires the counterclaim to be joined in the original suit. As a logical implication, courts hold that the defendant waives a compulsory counterclaim if she fails to assert it in the original case. See Moore's Federal Practice s. 13.14. Obviously, this approach is necessary to give teeth to the rule. In litigation practice, lawyers tend to ask not only, "what does the rule require?" but also "what will happen if I don't do what it requires?" The spectre of waiving the claim encourages compliance with the rule.

8. Rule 13 provides for the assertion of both compulsory (13(a)(1)) and permissive (13(b)) counterclaims. In this example, Renoir has properly asserted one of each: the compulsory claim against Morisot based on the painting contract and the permissive counterclaim arising out of his auto accident with Morisot. The difference between the two is the source of the claim: The contract claim, which arises out of the same transaction as the original claim, is compulsory, while the claim arising from unrelated events is permissive.

9. Yes, Renoir is free to assert his unrelated counterclaim, even though it is the only claim he has against Morisot. Rule 13(b) authorizes the assertion of unrelated counterclaims without restriction.

   This may seem illogical. Why drag claims into the lawsuit that will have no factual relation to the main claim? It hardly seems likely to promote efficiency to join the painting contract claim with the auto accident claim, which will present completely different factual and legal issues. The rules allow joinder of such claims, however, on the theory that a defendant, once forced into court by the plaintiff, at least ought to have the option to settle all disputes with that plaintiff in a single action. That way, the defendant can save the cost of filing a new action and serving process again, and perhaps lower the cost of discovery as well. Also, in terms of fairness, Rule 13(b) gives defendants the same broad authority to join unrelated claims that plaintiffs have under Rule 18(a). If a single trial does not make sense, the court may order a separate trial of the unrelated counterclaim. Fed. R. Civ. P. 42(b).

10. Here Renoir asserts a counterclaim against Morisot and wants to add Cassatt as an additional party to the counterclaim. Although the plaintiff is ordinarily "master of his claim," to include or exclude possible parties, this is a situation where the defendant also gets some control over the parties. Under Rule 13(h), Renoir is authorized to bring in an additional party on the counterclaim, so long as his claims against the added party and the original plaintiff meet the requirements of Rules 20(a)(2)(A) and 20(a)(2)(B), that is, both claims arise out of the same transaction or occurrence and share a common question of law or fact. These prerequisites are met here, so the joinder of Cassatt as an additional party to the counterclaim against Morisot is proper.

## Acting at Cross-Purposes

11. a. This is the first example in which one defendant seeks to recover against a codefendant. Rule 13(g) authorizes assertion of such "cross-claims" against a coparty if they arise out of the same transaction or occurrence as the original claim. Renoir's claim qualifies because it arises out of the fire.

   b. Be careful to distinguish cross-claims from counterclaims. Counterclaims are asserted against a party who has asserted a claim against you. Cross-claims are asserted against a coparty, that is, a party to the action who is on the same side of the "v" as the cross-claimant. Renoir's claim is not a counterclaim since Renoir is not claiming against Cassatt, who sued him, but against Pissarro, his codefendant.

12. This is also a valid cross-claim under Rule 13(g). It differs from the last example because the cross-claimant here seeks recovery for his own injuries, not indemnification for damages he may have to pay the plaintiff. Either type of claim is permissible so long as it arises out of the transaction or occurrence that gave rise to the main claim. The

second sentence of Rule 13(g) specifically allows cross-claims for indemnification, such as Renoir asserted in example 11. But the broad language of the first sentence clearly authorizes any cross-claim that arises from the same underlying events as the main claim in the action.

13. This attempt at joinder is improper. As already stated, Rule 13(g) requires that the cross-claim arise out of the same transaction or occurrence as the main claim; this completely unrelated claim is therefore improper. Under the efficiency rationale of the joinder rules, this result is appropriate. There will be little efficiency gained from litigating the unrelated claim in this suit because it involves a completely separate transaction. In addition, litigating these claims separately poses no risk of inconsistent judgments because the judgments rendered on them will not involve the same issues.

14. After the last example, you may be somewhat frustrated by the answer to this one: Joinder of both claims is proper here. Renoir's claim for his own injuries is a proper cross-claim (as in example 12). And, once a proper crossclaim has been asserted against Van Gogh, Renoir may add on any other claims he has against Van Gogh, under Rule 18(a).

It is crucial to understand the differing roles of Rule 18(a) in these two cases. Although Rule 18(a) appears on its face to authorize any party to assert any claim he has against an opposing party, the rule actually requires a party to assert one claim that is proper under the other joinder rules before he can add others to it under Rule 18(a). Thus, once Renoir has properly asserted a cross-claim against Van Gogh under Rule 13(g), he may add others under Rule 18(a). Similarly, if Renoir asserted a proper third-party claim against Pissarro under Rule 14(a)(1), he could add others under Rule 18(a). But Rule 18(a) is not a general hunting license to assert any claim against any party; if it were, all the other rules discussed in this chapter would be unnecessary.

Admittedly, it does not seem logical to allow Renoir to assert the unrelated claim if he asserts a related one (as here), but not if he asserts it alone (as in example 13). Yet, that is just what the Rules do. The apparent rationale is that once Renoir and Van Gogh become adversaries by the assertion of a proper cross-claim, they might just as well resolve all their differences in a single suit. Once again, the court has the discretion to order a separate trial of the unrelated claim if there is no efficiency to be gained from joint litigation.

15. Not only may Van Gogh assert this claim, he must do so under Rule 13(a)(1). When Renoir claims against him, Van Gogh becomes an

"opposing party" subject to the counterclaim rules of 13(a) and (b). Visually the case looks like this:

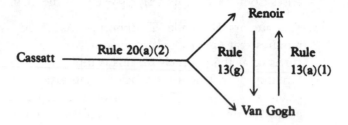

Remember that the counterclaim rules are written in general language to apply to all defending parties, not just original defendants. Since Renoir had made Van Gogh an opposing party by asserting a cross-claim against him, and Van Gogh's claim against Renoir arises out of the same transaction or occurrence as Renoir's cross-claim, it is a compulsory counterclaim. It must be asserted in this action or lost.

## Last Impressionists

16. The point of this example is so important that I have devoted an entire chapter to it. See Chapter 17, which explores the distinction between "power" (subject matter jurisdiction) and "permission" to join claims under the Rules. The problem here is that Morisot has properly joined Van Gogh and Renoir as co-defendants under Rule 20(a)(2), but the court lacks subject matter jurisdiction because there is neither complete diversity nor a federal claim. The joinder rules *do not provide a basis for subject matter jurisdiction;* they only govern who may properly be made parties when all jurisdictional rules are satisfied. Thus, this case is not properly before the court, even though the joinder rules authorize joinder.

# Into the Labyrinth

## Joinder of Parties under Rule 14

---

## INTRODUCTION

A persistent civil procedure theme explored in the earlier chapters is the right of the plaintiff or plaintiffs to sculpt the lawsuit by their choice of the forum and their initial decisions to join parties as plaintiffs or defendants. An equally persistent theme, however, is the various ways in which the plaintiff's well-laid plans may go awry. For example, she may end up in a different court if the defendant removes or seeks a change of venue; or she may end up *defending* a claim if another party asserts a cross-claim or counterclaim against her.

Rule 14 provides another example of the complexities that await the unwary plaintiff who disregards Dickens's famous advice.[1] Rule 14(a) gives a defendant a limited right to implead (that is, bring into the suit) new parties against whom she has claims related to the main action. Under the rule the defendant may bring in a person not yet a party to the suit who may be liable to her, the defendant, for all or part of any recovery the plaintiff obtains on the main claim.

In many tort cases third parties are impleaded for *contribution*, that is, to obtain a judgment that the third party is liable to pay the main defendant part of the damages she is ordered to pay the plaintiff. For example, suppose that Napoleon sues Wellington for negligently injuring him

---

1. "Suffer any wrong that can be done you rather than come [to the courts of chancery]," Charles Dickens, Bleak House 7 (Norton ed. 1977).

during a polo match. Wellington claims that the negligence of Robespierre, riding a third horse, also caused the accident. Under many states' rules of contribution among joint tortfeasors, Wellington would be entitled to recover from Robespierre part of any damages Wellington pays Napoleon,[2] if he can prove that Robespierre was also negligent. On these facts Wellington may implead Robespierre under Rule 14(a)(1) since he may be liable to Wellington for part of any damages that Wellington is ordered to pay Napoleon. The case looks like this:

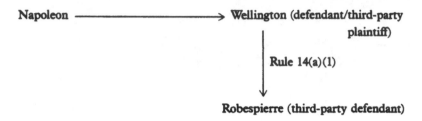

In other cases the defendant may claim that the third party is liable to her for all damages that she may have to pay the plaintiff. For example, consider Ronan Construction's third-party complaint against Jones in the Schulansky case. Ronan's last claim for relief (see infra p. 636) alleges that, if it is liable to Schulansky for the damage to the house caused by Jones's back-hoe work and pays for that damage, it should be reimbursed by Jones. Under tort law, this is often true: Ronan, as the general contractor, would be liable for the negligence of a subcontractor but, if the subcontractor's negligence caused the harm, would have a right of full indemnification from the negligent subcontractor. On this theory, Ronan may implead Jones to recover "all" of its liability to Schulansky.

Another common example of a proper impleader claim is a claim for indemnity against an insurer. In Napoleon's case against Wellington, for example, suppose that Wellington has liability insurance with Lloyds of London, but Lloyds denies that the policy covers the claim. Wellington may implead Lloyds under Rule 14(a)(1), seeking indemnity for any judgment Napoleon recovers against him. In both these examples, the defendant seeks to pass on all of his liability, not just a part as in the contribution example. This also satisfies the requirement in Rule 14(a)(1) that the impleaded party may be liable to the defendant for "all or part" of the plaintiff's claim against the defendant.

---

2. In some jurisdictions, Wellington would recover half of the judgment from Robespierre. In others, the extent of Robespierre's liability for contribution would depend on the percentage of negligence the jury attributed to him in causing Napoleon's injury. In states which have abandoned joint and several liability, however, contribution is not allowed. See Glannon, The Law of Torts: Examples and Explanations 552-554 (3rd ed. 2005).

It is crucial to distinguish these cases from situations in which the defendant contends that another person is liable directly to the plaintiff but not to her. Suppose that Wellington's polo match took place in a jurisdiction that did not allow contribution between joint tortfeasors. In that case Robespierre might still be liable to Napoleon directly, but Wellington could not implead him because Robespierre would not be liable to Wellington at all. He can't offer up Robespierre as an alternate defendant to Napoleon, saying, "Here, Napoleon, you sued me, but you really should have sued us both, so here's Robespierre; go at him." That would allow the defendant to dictate to the plaintiff whom to sue where, in defiance of the conventional doctrine that the plaintiff is master of her claim.

To further illustrate this point, assume that a police officer assaults Dillinger in the course of arresting him for robbery. Dillinger sues Officer Hayes, a six-foot-two, red-headed policeman, for the assault. Hayes claims mistaken identity: It was actually Officer Kelly, another six-foot redhead, who arrested Dillinger. Hayes cannot implead Kelly. He has no claim that Kelly is liable to him. Either one or the other assaulted Dillinger; one or the other will be solely liable to him. Hayes contends of course that Dillinger should have sued Kelly instead of him, but this gives him no right to substitute another defendant or to add one under Rule 14. That rule does not allow defendants to suggest new targets for the plaintiff. Rather, it allows defendants to bring in targets of their own if they may be able to pass on liability (either some of it or all of it) to the impleaded party.[3]

It follows from this central requirement of Rule 14(a)(1) that the third-party defendant's liability will depend on the outcome of the main claim. If Napoleon does not recover from Wellington, Wellington will have no right of contribution against Robespierre. Robespierre can hardly be asked to contribute if Wellington doesn't have to pay; nor would Lloyds be liable to indemnify Wellington unless Wellington has to pay a judgment; nor Jones to pay Ronan if Schulansky loses on the main claim. The impleaded party may escape liability by defeating either the plaintiff's original claim or the defendant's derivative claim against her. Consequently, the rule allows her to assert defenses to both. See Rule 14(a)(2)(A) (defenses to third-party

---

3. At one time Rule 14 did allow defendants to add new parties who might be liable directly to the plaintiff. That provision created serious problems that led to the elimination of this option:

> [I]n some cases plaintiff declined to press his claim against the third-party defendant and could not be compelled to amend his complaint in order to do so. When that occurred, the third-party action would have to be dropped since no one had alleged a claim against the third-party defendant. In other cases, an amendment to assert a direct claim against the third-party defendant, if allowed, would have destroyed diversity of citizenship as the basis of federal jurisdiction. For these reasons the rule was amended in 1948 to eliminate defendant's right to implead persons directly liable to plaintiff.

6 Wright & Miller at §1441 at n.8.

claim) and 14(a)(2)(C) (defenses to the plaintiff's claim against the original defendant).

The impleader claim is treated like an original suit for pleading, service, and other purposes. The defendant, as "third-party plaintiff," must file a third-party complaint against the impleaded "third-party defendant." The complaint must comply with the pleading requirements of Rules 8 through 11 and must be served under Rule 4. See Chapter 34, p. 680, for an example of a third-party complaint in the *Schulansky* case. The third-party defendant must respond under Rule 12 and has the same options to answer or move to dismiss. The third-party defendant may also file counterclaims against the third-party plaintiff (Rule 14(a)(2)(B)) and may implead further parties under Rule 14(a)(5). The rule also allows the plaintiff and the third-party defendant to assert claims against each other if they arise out of the same transaction or occurrence as the main claim. See Rule 14(a)(2)(D), (a)(3).

Under Rule 14(a)(1) the defendant may implead a third party within ten days of answering the complaint, without obtaining leave of court. This automatic impleader provision suggests that the court must hear the third-party claim if it is filed within the ten-day period. However, the cases establish that it is always within the court's discretion to refuse to entertain the impleader claim. See generally Moore's Federal Practice §14.20. Factors favoring impleader include the efficiency of hearing the related claims together and avoidance of repeated suits or inconsistent judgments. Factors suggesting denial of impleader include undue delay in seeking it, complication of the issues in the main action, and potential prejudice to the plaintiff from impleading a sympathetic third party. In some cases the court may be able to address these concerns by allowing the impleader but separating the main suit and the third-party suit for trial. See Rule 14(a)(4).

Two further points should be mentioned concerning the relation of impleader claims to the three-ring analysis in the earlier chapters. First, impleading a third-party defendant does not affect the court's jurisdiction over the original claim. Suppose, for example, that Napoleon is from Maine, Wellington from Connecticut, and Robespierre from Maine:

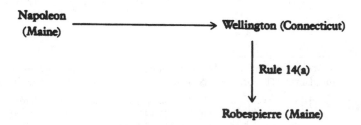

The original case between Napoleon and Wellington is a proper diversity case. Wellington's decision to implead Robespierre does not affect the court's jurisdiction over the original claim, even though Robespierre is from Maine. If the citizenship of the third party did affect jurisdiction over the initial claim, it would allow defendants to manipulate jurisdiction by impleading third-party defendants to destroy diversity.

However, there must still be a basis for subject matter jurisdiction over the impleader claim. Here, there may be diversity jurisdiction, if the amount-in-controversy requirement is met, since Wellington and Robespierre are from different states. If there isn't, there will usually be "supplemental jurisdiction" over a proper impleader claim, under 28 U.S.C. s. 1367(a). See Chapter 16, example 7b.

Second, the third party is also disregarded in determining whether venue is proper. For example, the case in the illustration could properly be brought in the District of Connecticut, where Wellington resides, under 28 U.S.C. §1391(a)(1), despite the fact that the third-party defendant resides in Maine, not Connecticut. Wright & Miller §1445, at n.9 ff. Here too, if the third-party defendant's residence were considered in applying the venue statute, defendants would be able to defeat federal jurisdiction in many cases in which the plaintiff had properly invoked it, simply by impleading defendants from the right (that is, the wrong) states.

The examples below may help to dispel some of the darkness that engulfs this murky rule. In considering them, assume that all cases are brought in federal court and that subject matter jurisdiction is proper in each case. In addition, focus on whether the claim would satisfy the requirements of Rule 14, not whether the court (assuming the rule is satisfied) would exercise its discretion to hear the impleader claim.

## Examples

### Pleaders and Impleaders

1. Ali sues Bellefonds, the engineer on a canal construction project, for negligence arising out of faulty engineering calculations in planning the canal. May Bellefonds implead Le Pere, another engineer whom he claims was also negligent in making the calculations?

2. Ali sues Bellefonds for his faulty engineering calculations. Bellefonds impleads Le Pere, alleging that it was actually Le Pere who did the calculations. Is the impleader proper?

3. France sues DeLesseps, a general contractor, for faulty canal construction. DeLesseps claims that if there was a breach it was actually the fault of Said, the subcontractor he hired to do the dredging work on the canal, and that Said should therefore bear the loss. Can he implead Said?

4. Suppose that DeLesseps is unclear as to whether the defective construction work resulted from Said's dredging work or faulty concrete work done by another subcontractor, Ismail. May he implead both?

5. Assume that France sues DeLesseps on the canal contract, and Delesseps wishes to recover from Said, his subcontractor, for certain camels Said took away when he left the job. May he implead Said?

6. In the same contract action, could DeLesseps implead Said and assert both the indemnification claim described in example 3 and the camel-trover claim in example 5?

7. DeLesseps is sued by France, and impleads Said, claiming that his sub-contract work caused the problem, so that he should indemnify DeLesseps if he is held liable to France. Said moves to dismiss the third-party claim, arguing that DeLesseps has no valid claim against him at this point, since his right to recover indemnification from Said does not accrue until he incurs a judgment to France and pays it. What should the court do?

8. France sues DeLesseps for the faulty canal construction. DeLesseps does not implead Said. France recovers a judgment from DeLesseps and DeLesseps pays the damages. May he now sue Said for indemnification?

## Heads of the Hydra

9. Suppose that DeLesseps is sued by France for breach of the canal contract. He impleads Said for faulty subcontract work, and Said wants to assert a claim against France, the plaintiff, for intentional interference with his subcontract with DeLesseps. May he do so?

10. Note that the language of the Rule (always so carefully chosen by the Solomons of civil procedure) does not call Said's claim against France in the last example a counterclaim. Why isn't it a counterclaim?

11. Think of three ways in which a counterclaim could insinuate itself into this suit.

12. Assume that DeLesseps impleads Said for indemnification on the theory that his faulty dredging work caused the contract breach. Said claims that his insurer, Cairo Casualty and Indemnity Co., has a duty to pay any damages resulting from his breach. May Said assert a claim against Cairo in the same action?

13. If Said is impleaded, may France assert a claim against Said for shoddy construction on an unrelated job Said did for France?

## Another Unlucky Number 14

14. Assume that France is from California, Delesseps from Texas, and Said from Arizona. The canal work was done in Colorado. France sues DeLesseps in Texas, and DeLesseps impleads Said based on his faulty subcontract work. Is the impleader proper?

15. Suppose that DeLesseps counterclaims against France, to collect the contract price for the canal work. May France implead Disraeli, who cosigned the contract along with France and is, therefore, also contractually bound to pay DeLesseps for the contract work?

## Explanations

### Pleaders and Impleaders

1. Here, Bellefonds seeks to implead Le Pere, not yet a party to the suit, to recover part of any judgment Ali recovers from Bellefonds. Assuming that the relevant state law authorizes contribution among joint tortfeasors, this is a proper impleader claim. Le Pere is a new party who "is or may be liable to it [the defendant/third-party plaintiff Bellefonds] for all or part of the claim against [Bellefonds]". If Bellefonds is found liable to Ali and Le Pere is also found negligent, Bellefonds will be entitled to recover from Le Pere part of the damages Bellefonds pays Ali. Note that at the time he impleads Le Pere, it is not clear that Le Pere will be liable to contribute. That depends on whether Bellefonds is found negligent, whether Le Pere is found negligent, and whether Bellefonds pays more than his share of the judgment. But the rule only requires that Le Pere "may" be liable to Bellefonds; Le Pere's liability need not follow automatically from Bellefonds's, nor must Bellefonds have already been adjudged liable before he can implead Le Pere.

2. As stated in the introduction, impleader under Rule 14 cannot be used to foist alternate defendants on the plaintiff. Ali chose to sue Bellefonds, not Le Pere. If Bellefonds didn't do the faulty calculations, Ali will lose his suit against him. Maybe Ali will then sue Le Pere or maybe he won't. That is his choice. But Bellefonds may not bring Le Pere in on the mere allegation that Le Pere is liable to Ali. Bellefonds may only implead Le Pere to recover from him all or part of the damages Bellefonds must pay Ali. If liability is an either/or proposition, Bellefonds has no such claim against Le Pere, and impleader should be denied.

   Ali could have chosen to join Bellefonds and Le Pere as codefendants under Rule 20(a)(2). See Chapter 13, pp. 254-255. Alternatively, Bellefonds may defend against Ali's claim on the ground that Le Pere was the offending party instead of him. But he can't use Rule 14 as a backdoor means of forcing Ali to sue Le Pere, which Rule 20(a)(2) allows, but does not require Ali to do.

3. This is a proper impleader claim. Under contract law, DeLesseps, as the general contractor, will be liable to France if the work does not meet the contract specifications, even though it was a subcontractor's negligence that caused the breach. However, DeLesseps will surely have a

contractual right under his separate contract with Said (and probably a right under negligence law as well) to indemnity for damages caused by Said's faulty subcontract work. Thus, Said "may be liable to [the third-party plaintiff DeLesseps] for all . . . of the claim against [DeLesseps]," and DeLesseps may properly implead Said under Rule 14(a)(1).

4. In this case DeLesseps is unclear as to whether he should be indemnified by one subcontractor or the other or both. Although the rule is not explicit on the point, there is no reason why a defendant should have to limit his impleader claims to one third party when several may be liable to him. As long as the provisions of Rule 14(a)(1) are satisfied, a defendant may implead multiple third-party defendants, claiming either joint or alternate liability.

5. This is not a proper impleader claim. Here, DeLesseps has a claim against Said, arising out of the same transaction (the construction of the canal) as the main claim, but Said's liability to DeLesseps is not derivative of the main suit. DeLesseps has a totally independent claim against Said, which he could assert whether France wins or loses on the main claim or never sues at all.

   It might make sense to design the rules of procedure to allow the defendant to expand the lawsuit in this way, but it would certainly introduce many tangential claims sharing few witnesses or factual or legal issues with the main claim. That would be the case here, since the claim for the missing camels is clearly distinct from the faulty construction claim. The rule-makers decided to confine the defendant's options more narrowly, by use of the "may be liable to it [the third-party plaintiff] for all or part of the claim against it" language.[4] But see, with some perplexity, the following example.

6. Curiously, despite the previous answer, Rule 18(a) expressly allows DeLesseps, once he has forced Said into the suit on a proper impleader claim, to add on this independent claim. Presumably the rationale for

---

4. There is nothing inevitable about the strict limit Federal Rule 14 imposes on impleader claims. Some state rules are much more liberal. See, e.g., Pa. R.C.P. No. 2252(a), which authorizes a defendant to join a party who "may be

> (1) solely liable on the underlying cause of action against the joining party or . . . (4) liable to or with the joining party on any cause of action arising out of the transaction or occurrence or series of transactions or occurrences upon which the underlying cause of action against the joining party is based."

Subsection (4) clearly would allow DeLessep's camel claim in example 5.

this is that once the third-party defendant is in the case the Rules might as well allow the defendant to settle all her differences with the third-party defendant in a single action. Visually the suit looks like this:

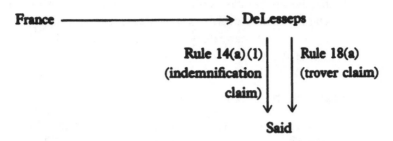

However, Rule 18(a) alone does not allow DeLesseps to bring Said into the suit. To do that, DeLesseps must first assert a claim complying with Rule 14. Rule 18 only allows him to add related (or unrelated) claims once he has properly impleaded Said under Rule 14.

7. The court should deny the motion. The point of Rule 14 is to allow the main claim to be determined jointly with other claims that may be triggered by it. Thus, although Said is not yet liable to DeLesseps, he "may be," if France wins on the main claim, and the trier of fact determines that DeLesseps has an incipient right of indemnification from Said, *and* if DeLesseps pays the judgment. Impleader allows DeLesseps to "accelerate" the indemnification claim, so that it can be litigated jointly with the main claim. This promotes efficiency in litigation and eliminates the possibility that two juries will make inconsistent findings about the cause of the damage. It also allows Said, once he is impleaded, to assert any defenses that DeLesseps has to France's claim against him. See Fed. R. Civ. P. 14(a)(2)(C). After all, if DeLesseps wins on the main claim, Said will win on the third-party claim: DeLesseps will not need indemnification if he isn't held liable to France.

If France wins on the main claim, and DeLesseps wins on the impleader claim, the judge can enter a conditional judgment, ordering Said to indemnify DeLesseps only after DeLesseps pays the judgment against him.

8. This example makes a single important point, that a defendant is not forced to implead a third party under Rule 14, even if the third party may be liable to reimburse the defendant for all or part of the plaintiff's claim. The rule says the defendant "may" implead a third party, which clearly implies that he has a choice. If DeLesseps chooses not to, he will not be barred from suing Said in a separate action to recover indemnification for the judgment he paid.

A mandatory impleader rule might make sense, from an efficiency perspective. However, it would cause problems if the third party was not subject to personal jurisdiction, and it would override the deference that the system has traditionally paid to DeLesseps's choice of when and where to sue Said. In an era of scarce judicial resources, the system may move toward mandatory joinder in situations like this, but has not yet arrived there.

## Heads of the Hydra

9. In this example, Said has been properly impleaded and seeks to assert a related claim against the original plaintiff. Rule 14(a)(2)(D) explicitly authorizes Said to do so. The suit now looks like this:

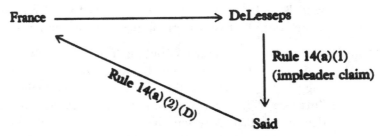

But Said cannot assert any claim he has against France. Under Rule 14(a), his claims against the plaintiff are limited to those that arise out of the same transaction or occurrence as the main claim. Assuming the court takes a reasonably broad view of that test, this claim will satisfy it.

10. A counterclaim is defined in both Rules 13(a)(1) and (b) as a claim against an "opposing party." Before Said asserts a claim against France they are not opposing parties. France has a claim against DeLesseps, not Said. Although France and Said are locked in the same litigious dance, they are not yet partners.

11. Counterclaims may be asserted by any defending party against her opponent. Rule 13(a). Obviously, DeLesseps may have some counterclaims against France. Said, once impleaded, may assert counterclaims against DeLesseps. See Rule 14(a)(2)(B). Indeed, Said *must* assert them if they satisfy the Rule 13(a)(1) test for compulsory counterclaims. For example, he may have a claim against DeLesseps for the subcontract price for his services. This claim arises out of the same transaction as DeLesseps's claim against him and must be asserted in the impleader action under Rule 13(a)(1).

Finally, once Said has asserted a claim against France, they become opposing parties as well. If France has any claim against Said arising from the canal construction, he must assert it.[5] If he has any other claim against Said, he may assert it as well under Rule 13(b). Thus, hydra-like,[6] the suit may grow:

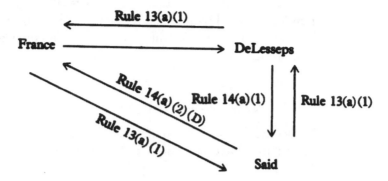

12. Said may implead Cairo under Rule 14(a)(5), which allows the third-party defendant to assert such telescoping claims against any further party "who is or may be liable to the third-party defendant for all or part of the claim against it." The suit now looks like this:

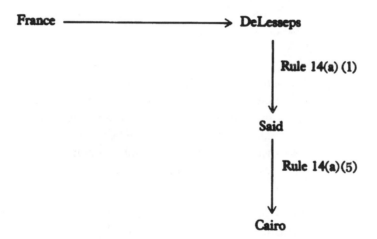

Imagine the title of Cairo's answer to this claim: "Fourth-Party Defendant's Answer to the Third-Party Defendant/Fourth-Party Plaintiff's Fourth-Party Complaint"![7]

---

5. Although Rule 13(a)(1) would require France to assert this claim the court may not have subject matter jurisdiction over it under 28 U.S.C. §1367(b). See Chapter 16, ex. 8.
6. The hydra, a Greek beast, was reputed to sprout two heads for each lopped off by its unfortunate adversary.
7. For a case taking these antics to the sixth power, see *Bevemet Metais, Ltd. v. Gallie Corp.*, 3 F.R.D. 352 (S.D.N.Y. 1942).

13. France's claim here does not arise out of the same transaction or occurrence as the main claim. Rule 14(a)(3) authorizes joinder of claims the plaintiff has against the third-party defendant if those claims satisfy the same transaction or occurrence test. By implication, the rule excludes unrelated claims, so this one fails. This limits the introduction of unrelated matters into the action, lest it become completely unmanageable.

## Another Unlucky Number 14

14. The fact that you were given the states for each party should have tipped you off that there is some jurisdictional problem here. It can't be diversity: As the Introduction points out, the third party's citizenship is irrelevant to determining diversity, and besides, there is complete diversity anyway. It can't be venue either: The third party is also disregarded in determining proper venue. Here, at least one district in Texas is a proper venue, since DeLesseps resides there, although Said, the third-party defendant, does not.

   It must be personal jurisdiction. Indeed it is, or may be. *Whenever* a party is brought into a suit, whether as an original defendant, a third-party defendant, an additional party to a counterclaim, or whatever, the court must have the power to require that party to appear and defend in that state. Said's due process rights would be as clearly abridged if he were forced to defend a third-party action in a forum with which he lacks contacts as if he were forced into such a court as the original defendant. If Said objects to personal jurisdiction, the court will have to consider whether Said has minimum contacts with Texas or is subject to personal jurisdiction there for this claim on some other basis. Compare Jones's motion to dismiss in *Schulansky v. Ronan*, p. 693.

15. This is an example of a plaintiff, now a defendant on a counterclaim, impleading a party who may be liable to her (the plaintiff) for all or part of a judgment the counterclaiming defendant obtains from her. Since Disraeli is a co-obligor on the contract, France may be entitled to pass on to him part of the contract price. Thus, impleading Disraeli is explicitly authorized by Rule 14(b).

# Essentials and
# Interlopers

Joinder of Parties under Rules 19 and 24

## INTRODUCTION

The last two chapters analyzed the basic rules governing joinder of claims and parties in federal court. Under those rules, the plaintiff is generally "master of her claim." She decides the initial shape of the lawsuit, by choosing who to sue and what claims she will assert against those defendants. Later, other parties may end up expanding the suit, by adding counterclaims or cross-claims. They may also bring additional parties into the case, by asserting third-party claims under Rule 14 or by adding parties to a counterclaim or cross-claim under Rule 13(h).

This chapter deals with two additional rules that may expand the lawsuit beyond the plaintiff's initial design. First, under Fed. R. Civ. P. 19, certain persons not sued by the plaintiff may be ordered joined in the suit, if they need to be made parties to fairly adjudicate the case. Second, in certain situations, absentees — again, not sued by the plaintiff — may "intervene" in the case, that is, move to become parties on one side or the other, under Fed. R. Civ. P. 24. Although such redesign of the plaintiff's case is unusual, it may sometimes be appropriate or necessary. Rules 19 and 24 describe the circumstances in which it may happen.

# JOINDER UNDER RULE 19(A): PARTIES TO BE JOINED IF FEASIBLE

Rule 19 provides a three-step process for analyzing whether a party should be added to the lawsuit. The first step in the analysis under Rule 19(a) is to consider whether some person who was not joined in the original action should be made a party to it. The rule describes three situations in which such an absentee should be made a party "if feasible." A person should be added to the case if, in the person's absence, "the court cannot accord complete relief among existing parties." Fed. R. Civ. P. 19(a)(1)(A). Second, the absentee should be made a party if she has an interest in the subject matter of the action and her ability to protect that interest will be impaired if she does not participate in the litigation. Fed. R. Civ. P. 19(a)(1)(B)(i). Third, Rule 19 counsels joinder of the absentee if she has an interest in the subject matter of the suit and adjudicating the case without her might leave one of the existing parties exposed to multiple or inconsistent obligations. Fed. R. Civ. P. 19(a)(1)(B)(ii). The best way to understand these situations is to describe some situations in which each subsection might apply.

## Parties to Be Joined under Rule 19(a)(1)(A)

Rule 19(a)(1)(A) addresses situations in which the court cannot adequately provide redress to the parties who *are* before the court, unless an absentee is also brought into the case. Here are some examples in which the court would likely hold that a person should be made a party under this provision.

- Menendez enters into a contract to purchase a business from Adams and Vincenzo. He subsequently learns that they had misrepresented the financial condition of the business and sues Adams to rescind the contract.
  - Naturally, complete relief cannot be accorded to Menendez unless Vincenzo is also made a party to this case. An order of rescission against Adams would leave the sale rescinded as to one seller but not as to the other. Vincenzo should be joined if feasible under Rule 19(a)(1)(A).
- Tower Financial leases an office building from General Leasing Corporation and then subleases three floors to Affiliated Products. After taking possession, Affiliated discovers that the electrical service is insufficient for its power needs and asks Tower to increase the service. Tower Financial is required under the sublease to accommodate such

reasonable requests for alterations, but cannot make them without the consent of the owner. Tower refuses to make the alterations, because General Leasing refuses to consent. Affiliated sues to enforce its sublease. Tower moves to join General Leasing as a party to the action.

— Here, too, the court cannot provide the plaintiff with full relief unless the absentee is joined. It could order Tower Financial to increase the electrical service, but Tower would be unable to do so without the consent of the building owner. Thus, it makes sense to join General Leasing in the case, so that complete relief can be granted between the original parties to the case.[1]

# Parties to Be Joined under Rule 19(a)(1)(B)(i)

Rule 19(a)(1)(B)(i) addresses a second situation in which an absentee should be made a party to the case "if feasible." It provides that a person who claims an interest related to the subject matter of the case should be made a party if proceeding without that person might impair her ability to protect that interest. Sometimes, litigation has practical impacts on strangers to the case, even though they are not directly subject to orders entered in the litigation. Rule 19(a)(1)(B)(i) provides that such absentees should be brought in, so that this collateral effect of the case can be considered or reduced. Here are some examples of cases in which the absentee "should be joined if feasible" under Rule 19(a)(1)(B)(i).

- Haas and Glueck buy 250 shares of stock in Acme Corporation. The shares are held in Haas's name, but Glueck claims that they were to be jointly owned by the two investors. Later, Haas gets in financial difficulties and threatens to use the stock to pay some of his creditors. Glueck sues Acme Corporation, to get the stock reissued jointly to himself and Haas.
  - In this situation, if the court concludes that the stock is jointly owned and orders it reissued, that order would clearly affect Haas's interest — especially if he disagrees about the nature of his agreement with Glueck. Thus, Haas is a person whose interest in the subject matter of the dispute — the stock — may be impaired if the court enters an order without his participation. Under Rule 19(a)(1)(B)(i), he should be joined in the case if it is feasible to do so.[2]
- Pursuant to a treaty, a federal agency allocates fishing quotas in a river basin among twenty-three Indian tribes. The Makah Tribe, one

---

1. Cf. *Associated Dry Goods Corp. v. Tower Financial Corp.*, 920 F.2d 1211 (2nd Cir. 1990).
2. See *Haas v. Jefferson National Bank of Miami Beach*, 442 F.2d 394 (5th Cir. 1971).

of the tribes that signed the treaty, sues the federal agency, claiming that its quota is inadequate under the standards in the treaty.

— In this case, an increase in the Makah's allotment will automatically decrease the allotments of the other tribes. Since an order in the Makah Tribe's suit might, as a practical matter, impair the other tribes' ability to protect their interests in their fishing rights, they should be joined in the initial action if feasible.[3]

## An Early Question

1. In cases like these, in which an absentee should be made a party to effectively adjudicate a case, why might it *not* be "feasible" to join the absentee in the case?

# Parties to Be Joined under Rule 19(a)(1)(B)(ii)

Rule 19(a)(1)(B)(ii) provides for joinder of an absentee if adjudicating the case without her would expose one of the original parties to a risk of multiple or inconsistent obligations. The Makah Tribe case illustrates a situation in which this provision might apply. If the court orders the federal agency to increase the Makah's fishing allotments in the tribe's action, the other tribes' allotments would be reduced. The agency might then be sued by other tribes claiming that their allotments were inadequate. In those cases, the court might order increased allotments inconsistent with the judgment in the Makah's action. Thus, the agency would be whipsawed, subject to conflicting orders in two actions that could not both be implemented.

Here's another example in which Rule 19(a)(1)(B)(ii) might counsel joinder of the absentee to avoid inconsistent obligations.

- Carena sells a parcel of real estate to Jaquith. The First National Bank holds $20,000 of the proceeds from the sale in escrow. The funds are to be released to Carena if she completes certain repairs to the premises by January 1. Carena sues the First National Bank, alleging that she completed the repairs and is entitled to the funds. However, Jaquith claims the repairs are unsatisfactory, so the funds should be released to her instead.
  - If the court in Carena's action orders the Bank to pay the funds to Carena, the Bank faces the likely prospect of a second action by Jaquith claiming she is entitled to the funds. The court in that action might order the funds paid to Jaquith, subjecting the Bank

---

3. See *Makah Indian Tribe v. Verity*, 910 F.2d 555 (9th Cir. 1990).

to inconsistent obligations. Unless the claims are adjudicated together, the Bank may have to violate one court order or pay twice. The wisest course in such a case is to join Jaquith in Carena's suit. That way, whatever judgment enters will bind all the interested parties.

# THE ROLE OF RULE 19(B): WHAT TO DO IF THE ABSENTEE SHOULD BE JOINED BUT CANNOT BE

So, Rule 19(a) provides standards for deciding whether strangers should be added to the lawsuit. If proceeding without the absentee does not pose any of the problems detailed in Rule 19(a)(1), there is no need to bring the absentee into the case, and it will proceed without her. If the absentee should be joined, and there is no jurisdictional impediment to doing so, she will be made a party, usually a defendant.

The more difficult problem is what to do if the absentee *should* be joined under Rule 19(a), but cannot be. There are only three choices, really. The court could go forward anyway, without the absentee. Or, it could dismiss the case because it would be improper to proceed without the absentee. Last, it could go forward, but try to craft the judgment to provide appropriate relief to the parties before the court despite the inability to join the absentee. Rule 19(b) provides guidance to the trial judge in choosing among these alternatives.

Cases predating Rule 19 tended to take a fairly mechanical approach to the problem of parties who should be joined, but could not be: If a party was held necessary to the action, but could not be brought in, the action would be dismissed. Now, Rule 19(b) counsels a more nuanced approach to this problem. The judge need not automatically dismiss the case if a Rule 19(a) party cannot be joined. Instead, she should "determine whether in equity and good conscience the action should proceed among the parties before it, or should be dismissed." The second sentence of the Rule specifies factors the judge should consider in making this discretionary decision:

- to what extent a judgment rendered in the person's absence might be prejudicial to the person or those already parties
- the extent to which protective provisions in the judgment may be used to avoid or lessen the prejudice to the absent party
- whether a judgment rendered without the absent person will be adequate [among the parties before the court]
- and last, whether the plaintiff will have an adequate remedy — presumably in another court — if the action is dismissed due to the inability to join the absentee

Rule 19(b) recognizes that the circumstances of every case are unique, that there are no bright-line solutions to the problem of the effect of litigation on absentees, and that the problem is best dealt with by granting guided discretion to capable trial judges. If the absentee should be brought in but cannot be, Rule 19(b) directs the court to evaluate the impact of proceeding without the absentee, as well as possible methods of crafting the judgment to avoid adverse effects on the parties or the absentee.

Often, the court will be able to do substantial justice between the current parties even though an absentee should be made a party but cannot be brought into the case. In some situations, however, the court will conclude that the case cannot fairly proceed without the absentee, so that the case must be dismissed. Traditionally, if a person should be joined, but could not be, and the case could not proceed without her, the absentee was labeled "indispensable," and the case dismissed. The 2007 revision of Rule 19 drops the word "indispensable" from the Rule, but the court may still conclude, balancing the factors in Rule 19(b), that a case must be dismissed because the absentee cannot be made a party.

The following examples illustrate the application of Rule 19. We then take up Rule 24, which involves the related concept of intervention.

## Examples

### Rule 19: The First Step

2. Paredes, a New York City landlord, sues the New York City Housing Department, claiming unreasonable delays in processing applications for refunds of excess housing tax payments. He seeks an order from the court mandating prompt processing of his applications. The Department claims that state law bars it from granting refunds until it completes an audit of the landlord's rent history, which it cannot do until it receives relevant documents from the State Housing Division. What is the argument that the State Housing Division is a person to be joined if feasible? What subsection of Rule 19(a) would you cite in support of the argument?

3. Ramirez, from Colorado, sues Bryan, from Montana, for injuries in a three-car auto collision. The suit is for negligence and is brought in a court that applies joint and several liability in tort cases — that is, each party who is found to have negligently caused the plaintiff's injury is liable to her for her full damages. Bryan moves to dismiss the case for failure to join Grayson, a citizen of Colorado. He argues that Ramirez should have joined Grayson as a co-defendant, because Grayson drove a third car involved in the accident and may have also been negligent.
   a. As a fussy technical matter, what is wrong with Bryan's motion?

    b. Would the joinder rules authorize Ramirez to sue Grayson as a co-defendant with Bryan in the initial action?

    c. Is Grayson a person to be joined if feasible under Rule 19(a)(1)(A)?

    d. Suppose that Grayson was also injured in the accident. If Grayson is not joined in Ramirez's suit and later brings suit for her own injuries in the collision, couldn't Bryan be subject to "multiple obligations" under Rule 19(a)(1)(B)(ii)?

    e. Isn't it possible, if Grayson is not joined in Ramirez's action, that the jury will find Bryan not negligent in Ramirez's action, but a later jury will find that he was negligent in a later action by Grayson for her injuries? Isn't that a risk of "inconsistent obligations"?

    f. Suppose that Grayson is not joined and that the jury finds that Bryan was not negligent and, therefore, is not liable to Ramirez. Wouldn't this decision "as a practical matter impair [Grayson's] ability to protect" her interest in recovering damages for her injuries in the accident (Rule 19(a)(1)(B)(i)), since Bryan has been found blameless in the first case?

    g. Suppose that Bryan has $100,000 in auto liability coverage and no personal assets to satisfy a judgment. What subsection of Rule 19(a)(1) might now apply to make Grayson a person to be joined if feasible?

4. Minority firefighters bring a race discrimination case against the Town of Rangeley in federal court. They claim that the Town has historically discriminated against minorities in the promotion of firefighters and seek an injunction requiring that forty percent of all future promotions go to minority firefighters until the percentage of minority lieutenants in the department reflects the percentage of minorities in the town.

    a. The Town moves to join the non-minority firefighters in the department as defendants in the case. Are they parties to be joined if feasible under Rule 19(a)? If so, what subsection applies?

    b. Suppose several plaintiffs brought suit against the Town for discrimination in failing to hire minority firefighters. What problem would you foresee if the Town moved to join absentees under Rule 19? How might it be resolved?

5. Xavier, a Wisconsin citizen, brings a diversity action against Apex Corporation. Xavier claims that Belinsky, an Apex employee, negligently injured him while driving a truck for Apex, so that Apex is liable for his negligence. Apex is incorporated in Delaware, with its principal place of business in Illinois. It moves to join Belinsky, a Wisconsin citizen, as a party in the action, claiming that Belinsky has an interest in the case because his negligence will be adjudicated. Is Belinsky a person to be joined under Rule 19(a)?

6. Schutten, a Louisiana citizen, sues Shell Oil Company in federal court. Schutten claims that he owns certain land from which Shell is pumping oil and is entitled to royalties on the oil. Shell (a citizen of states other than Louisiana) claims that it does not owe any royalties to Schutten, since it acquired the mineral rights on the land from the Orleans Levee Board, the true owner of the land, which is entitled to the royalties. Shell moves to join the Orleans Levee Board (a Louisiana public district) in the action under Rule 19(a).

   a. Is the Levee Board a person to be joined if feasible under Rule 19? If so, which section applies?
   b. If the Levee Board should be joined, can the court order it joined?
   c. If it does not order the Board joined as a party, what should it do, considering the factors in Rule 19(b)?

# THE RELATED CONCEPT OF INTERVENTION

Rule 19 instructs the court to consider whether a person who was not made a party to the initial action should be made a party to it. Rule 24, by contrast, authorizes an absent party who learns of an action to become a party to the litigation. Although it seems unlikely that bystanders would seek to become parties to lawsuits, it actually happens with surprising frequency. Rule 24(a) specifies circumstances in which the absentee has a right to become a party to a case. Rule 24(b) provides for "permissive intervention," that is, situations in which the court may, in its discretion, allow an interested person to become a party.

## Intervention as of Right

Rule 24(a)(1) allows a person to intervene as of right if a statute authorizes the party to do so. A surprising number of statutes, both state and federal, create rights to intervene in particular types of cases. Frequently, statutes authorize a government agency to intervene in cases in which it may have an interest. See, e.g., 42 U.S.C. s. 2000h-2 (right of United States Attorney General to intervene in certain civil rights actions); 15 U.S.C. s. 1071(b)(2) (Director of Patent and Trademark Office entitled to intervene in certain patent and trademark appeals); and 28 U.S.C. s. 2403(b) (authorizing intervention by state attorneys general in cases that challenge the constitutionality of state statutes). Some statutes also authorize private parties to intervene in particular types of cases. See, e.g., 42 U.S.C. 3612(o)(2) (aggrieved party entitled to intervene in Fair Housing Act case brought by attorney general).

Rule 24(a)(2) further authorizes a person who is not a party to a case to intervene if three conditions are met:

- the person claims an interest relating to the property or transaction that is the subject matter of the action
- that interest may, as a practical matter, be impaired if the person is not allowed to participate in the case, and
- the absentee's interest is not adequately represented by those already parties to the action.

Note the similarity in the standard for joinder under Rule 19(a)(1)(B)(i) and intervention under Rule 24(a)(2). Both concern a person, not a party to a suit, whose interests may be affected by it. Rule 19(a)(1)(B)(i) provides that such a person should be made a party if feasible. Rule 24(a)(2) entitles such a person to take the initiative, by moving to intervene and become a party. The two rules were drafted together and are both meant to achieve the same purpose: to allow absentees with important interests to participate in on-going litigation before the court.

Here are some examples in which an absentee would likely have a sufficient interest to support intervention under Rule 24(a)(2).

- Newton, an inventor, assigns his interest in a patent on widgets to Apex Corporation, in exchange for the right to receive a royalty on each widget sold. Apex is then sued by Prima Corporation, claiming that Newton's patent is invalid. Newton moves to intervene as a defendant in the action.
  - If the court holds in Prima's suit against Apex that the patent is invalid, Apex would stop making royalty payments to Newton. Thus, Newton has an interest in the subject matter of the action (the patent) that may be impaired if he doesn't participate. True, res judicata would not bar Newton from suing separately to uphold the validity of the patent, but "as a practical matter" the judgment in the first suit would affect his patent rights. Thus, Newton probably has an interest that would support intervention under Rule 24(a)(2).
- After a boating accident, the insurance company that insured the boat brings an action for a declaratory judgment against the owner, Greaves. The insurer seeks a ruling that the insurance policy covering the boat is invalid, due to misrepresentations made by Greaves in obtaining the insurance. Taylor, a passenger seriously injured in the accident, moves to intervene to argue that the policy was not fraudulently obtained and therefore provides coverage for the accident.
  - In this case, the declaratory judgment action is between the insurer and the policy holder. Taylor, the injured party, is not a

beneficiary of the policy nor has he sued Greaves, though he intends to. In the case on which this example is based,[4] the court held that the tort plaintiffs had an interest in the subject matter of the action (the insurance coverage). It also held that their interest would be impaired, as a practical matter, if they were not allowed to intervene. Because the policy holder had few other assets, any claim would be worthless if there were no insurance to pay the judgment. The plaintiff was allowed to intervene under Rule 24(a)(2).

Rule 24(a)(2) does not create an automatic right to intervene if the absentee meets the standard. First, the motion to intervene must be "timely." Rule 24(a)(2). If a party tries to get in long after it is aware of its interest, or at a time when adding parties will significantly disrupt the litigation, the court has discretion to deny intervention. The Rule also provides that intervention will be allowed "unless existing parties adequately represent that interest." The exception gives the court discretion to deny intervention if the absentee is likely to make the same arguments as an original party, or to represent the same interest. "The applicants must show that they bring something to the litigation that otherwise would be ignored or overlooked if the matter were left to the already-existing parties." Moore's Federal Practice, s. 24.03[4][a][i]. Here are several cases in which the court found that the absentee's interests were not adequately represented.

- In *Georgia v. United States Army Corps of Engineers*, 302 F.3d 1242 (11th Cir. 2002), the State of Georgia brought an action against the Corps of Engineers to compel the Corps to increase local water releases from a Georgia reservoir. The State of Florida, which also drew water from the reservoir, sought to intervene to assure that its interests would be considered in allocating releases. The court held that the Corps, which controlled releases from the reservoir, did not adequately represent Florida's interest, since it had no stake in any particular formula for allocating releases.
- An environmental group sued the United States Department of Transportation, seeking to have the court vacate approval of a regional transportation plan they claimed did not comply with the Clean Air Act. A trade organization representing private builders, transportation companies, and other development interests sought to intervene to uphold the plan. Because the government, which represents the interests of the public as a whole, might not

---

4. *New Hampshire Ins. Co. v. Greaves*, 110 F.R.D. 549 (D.R.I. 1986).

adequately represent the private interests of this trade group, the court held that the group should be allowed to intervene. *Utahns for Better Transportation v. U.S. Dept. of Transportation*, 295 F.3d 1111 (10th Cir. 2002).

Here are several cases in which the court concluded that the person seeking intervention had an interest that might be affected by the action, but that the interest was adequately represented by those already parties.

- A law firm representing the plaintiff in a breach of contract action was discharged. It held a lien against any recovery in the action for the fees it had earned prior to being discharged and sought to intervene in the suit, to assure aggressive litigation of the underlying claim, so as to maximize the recovery and assure payment of its fee. The court saw no reason to conclude that the client and the new law firm would not vigorously prosecute the action. Since they would adequately represent the first firm's interest, the court denied the right to intervene even though the original firm had an interest in the recovery. *Butler, Fitzgerald & Porter v. Sequa Corp.*, 250 F.3d 171 (2d Cir. 2001).
- A developer sued a town, challenging a municipal ordinance limiting commercial structures outside the town's business district. A group trying to preserve the rural nature of the town sought to intervene as a defendant, to support the validity of the ordinance. The court held that the town adequately represented the group's interest; the group was denied the right to intervene. *Great Atl. and Pac. Tea Co. v. Town of East Hampton*, 178 F.R.D. 39 (E.D.N.Y. 1998).

## Permissive Intervention

Even if a party has no right to intervene under Rule 24(a), they may be permitted to intervene under the much broader standard in Rule 24(b)(1)(B). That section broadly authorizes intervention of any person who has a claim or defense "that shares with the main action a common question of law or fact." This liberal standard may be met in myriad circumstances. Clearly, it allows intervention in cases that go far beyond the standards in Rule 24(a)(2), including cases that will not have a direct effect on the legal rights of the intervenor. For example, in *Kootenai Tribe v. Veneman*, 313 F.3d 1094 (9th Cir. 2002), an Indian tribe and numerous other organizations sued to enjoin the Department of Agriculture from implementing a "roadless rule" in large areas of national forest. A number of environmental organizations were allowed to intervene under Rule 24(b)(1)(B). These organizations sought to intervene as defendants to urge the court to uphold the roadless rule. The court held that these organizations sought to raise defenses to the action that involved questions of law or fact common to those asserted by the Department, so that the district court had properly allowed them to intervene to support the rule.

Similarly, in *McNeill v. New York City Housing Authority*, 719 F. Supp. 233 (S.D.N.Y. 1989), low-income tenants facing eviction brought suit to challenge certain policies of the city housing authority. Other tenants who were also facing eviction sought to intervene as co-plaintiffs to challenge the same policies. The court upheld permissive intervention, since the intervenors' claims raised the same issues about the constitutionality of the housing authority's policies as the main claim, and litigating them together would not delay the litigation. Here again, the intervenors would not have been directly affected if they were not allowed to become parties to the case, but they shared an interest that made it efficient and helpful to have them participate as parties.

While the standard in Rule 24(b)(1)(B) is broad, the liberality of the rule is tempered by two limitations. First, the request must be "timely." Rule 24(b)(3) expressly requires the court to consider whether allowing intervention will "unduly delay or prejudice the adjudication of the original parties' rights." Courts often deny permissive intervention because it is sought at a point when it would delay resolution of the case, would require reopening of discovery, or because the intervenor did not attempt to intervene sooner. Second, even if the motion to intervene is timely, the court has discretion not to allow it. See Rule 24(b)(1) ("the court *may* permit" intervention [italics added]). The court may deny intervention on various grounds, sensitive to the facts and litigation history of each case. Intervention is more likely to be granted if the party seeking it can show that it brings a special expertise or a different perspective to the controversy than the original parties, or if refusing intervention may lead to other suits litigating the same issues.

In addition, the court may allow intervention for limited purposes or authorize intervenors to participate in limited ways. For example, the court might allow an absentee to intervene to litigate only a single claim or defense, or allow the intervenor to file briefs and argue motions, but not to take discovery or present witnesses. In one case, the court allowed a citizens group to intervene in a hazardous waste cleanup case, subject to the conditions that it could not (1) assert any claim for relief not already requested by one of the original parties; (2) intervene in the cleanup costs claim; or (3) file motions or conduct its own discovery unless it first conferred with all the original parties and obtained the permission of one of them. See *Stringfellow v. Concerned Neighbors in Action*, 480 U.S. 370, 373 (1987).

Interestingly, Rule 24(b)(1), unlike Rule 24(a)(2), does not expressly provide that intervention may be denied if the absentee's interest is adequately represented by one of the original parties. However, the cases make clear that this is an important factor in the discretionary decision to grant or deny permissive intervention.

## Examples

### All Aboard

7. Suppose a case brought by a natural gas pipeline company, seeking a license to build a pipeline across the corner of a town.
    a. Which of the following interested spectators would have the weakest argument for intervention under Rule 24(a)(2) in the case?
       - Homeowners whose land is likely to be taken by eminent domain for construction of the pipeline.
       - A local public utility that will purchase gas transported through the pipeline.
       - A local oil company whose business will be hurt if a new pipeline creates competition from the gas company.
       - Homeowners a mile from the proposed pipeline who believe it will lower property values in the town.
       - An environmental organization that seeks to lessen global warming by encouraging use of alternative fuels.
       - A citizen of a nearby town who fears that escaping gas could pose an explosion hazard.
    b. Why not let all of these bystanders intervene? If they are interested, why shouldn't they participate?

8. In an important affirmative action case, *Grutter v. Bollinger*, 188 F.3d 394 (6th Cir. 1999) *reversed in part on other grounds by Gratz v. Bollinger*, 539 U.S. 244 (2003), white students rejected by the University of Michigan brought suit challenging the University's affirmative action policies, which allowed consideration of race as a factor in admissions to the University. Such policies are often defended on the ground that they provide a remedy for past discrimination based on race and that they assist in achieving a diverse student body that provides a vital learning environment. Minority students who planned to apply to the University moved to intervene as defendants in the action to argue in support of those policies.
    a. Would the intervening students satisfy the standard for intervention in Rule 24(a)(2)?
    b. How might the minority students argue that their interests were not adequately represented by the University itself?
    c. Were these potential applicants persons to be joined if feasible under Rule 19(a)? If so, was it feasible to join them? If not, what should the court do?

9. Weninger, a Vermont citizen, suffers from a condition that she believes to be a side effect from taking Sindox, a drug manufactured by Apex Pharmaceuticals. She sues Apex for resulting damages in federal court. Garriega, who took the same drug in Utah a few months later and suffers from the same condition, reads about Weninger's lawsuit in the papers.

   a. If he had known about Weninger's plan to sue Apex, could Garriega have joined as a co-plaintiff in her suit against Apex, under Rule 20(a)?
   b. Could Garriega intervene as a plaintiff in Weninger's suit?

## A Financial Interest

10. Maroney brings a tort action against Massoud for serious injuries suffered in an accident. Paramount Insurance Company, Maroney's health insurer, moves to intervene as a co-plaintiff, to recover $175,000 it paid for Maroney's medical treatment as a result of the accident. Under its health insurance contract with Maroney, Paramount has a contractual right to be reimbursed for these payments from any tort judgment Maroney recovers from Massoud. Does Rule 24(a) authorize Paramount to intervene?

11. Suppose, on the facts of the previous question, that Paramount applied to intervene to obtain an order that Maroney reimburse it for its medical payments out of any settlement or judgment collected from Massoud? Should it be allowed to intervene?

12. Vohra is fired by Smithson University and brings suit against the University, claiming discrimination based on national origin. After extensive litigation, the parties agree to settle and file a settlement agreement with the court. At the request of the parties, the court seals the agreement, making it inaccessible to the press and the public. The *Nashville Gazette*, a local paper, moves to intervene to challenge the court's decision to seal the agreement. Is intervention authorized by Rule 24?

13. Yost, from South Carolina, worked for the Torrington Company (incorporated in Virginia with its principal place of business there). When hired, he signed an agreement not to work on any competing projects for another company for two years and not to reveal trade secrets. He subsequently resigned and went to work for INA, a Virginia competitor. Torrington sued Yost for breach of the agreement, seeking an injunction barring him from working for INA.

   a. Is INA a person to be joined if feasible under Rule 19(a)? Under which subsection?
   b. Can it be joined?

c. Suppose that INA had moved to intervene. What would the court have ordered?

## Explanations

### An Early Question

1. A number of jurisdictional issues might prevent joinder of the absentee in the case. She might not be subject to personal jurisdiction in the state in which the suit was brought. Or, adding the absentee might "destroy diversity," because she is from the same state as an opposing party in the action. Third, adding the absentee might make venue improper. The added party might also be immune from suit in federal court for one reason or another. For example, in *Makah Indian Tribe v. Verity*, 910 F.2d 555 (9th Cir. 1990), on which the fishing rights example is based, the action was dismissed because the competing Indian tribes were parties to be joined under Rule 19(a), but could not be brought into the action due to tribal sovereign immunity from suit.

### Rule 19: The First Step

2. The argument in support of joining the State Housing Division here is that any order the judge may enter against the City Housing Department will be inadequate to resolve the dispute between the parties. Since state law requires the Department to base its decision on the documentation from the state, it will be unable to comply with a court order requiring prompt resolution of refund requests. The only way that the court can provide meaningful relief to the plaintiff is to get the state Housing Division into the case as well, so that it can consider the delays resulting from the state auditing process and enter an order that will bind the Division as well as the City Housing Department. Thus, the Division is a person to be joined if feasible under Fed. R. Civ. P. 19(a)(i)(A): In the absence of the State Division, it will be very difficult for the court to fashion effective relief between Paredes and the City Housing Department.

3. a. This is technical: Bryan's motion should be a motion to join the party, not a motion to dismiss the case. The court will then consider whether Grayson should be joined under Rule 19(a), and, if she should be, whether to dismiss the action if she cannot be for one of the reasons discussed in example 1.

   b. Yes, Ramirez could have sued Grayson as a co-defendant with Bryan under Fed. R. Civ. P. 20(a)(2). Ramirez has a claim against her arising from the same occurrence as the claim against Bryan, and there will be a common question of fact as to which driver's negligence caused the accident. But Rule 20(a) does not require him to join Grayson, and Ramirez has designed the suit to his liking, leaving Grayson out. Rule 19 presents the question whether Bryan can force him to sue Grayson as well.[5]

c. While Grayson could have been sued along with Bryan, Rule 19(a)(1)(A) does not require that he be brought in to adjudicate the case. Ramirez can obtain complete relief for his injuries in the suit against Bryan without adding Grayson to the case. If Bryan is found to have negligently caused Ramirez's damages, the court can enter a judgment against Bryan for his full damages: Under joint and several liability, any tortfeasor found liable to the plaintiff is liable for the plaintiff's entire damages. So if Ramirez wins, he can obtain full compensation for his injuries from Bryan.

d. It is certainly possible that Bryan will incur multiple *judgments*: If he is found liable in Ramirez's case, he will owe him damages. And, if he is found liable to Grayson in a separate suit, he will owe her damages as well. But this is not the type of situation that Rule 19(1)(B)(ii) is meant to address. After all, Bryan could incur multiple judgments to Ramirez and Grayson *even if they do join* in the first action, if his negligence caused both their injuries. Instead, Rule 19(a)(1)(B)(ii) applies to situations in which the non-party may be subject to contradictory or inconsistent court orders if he is not joined in the action, such as an order in the original suit to renew a tenant's lease, and in a later action to grant the lease to a competing business. In those situations, the party is being whipsawed between two orders and can't comply with both. In this example, if Bryan is held liable to two injured plaintiffs in two different suits, he can pay them both. He may not like it, but he can do it.

e. Yes, there is a risk, if the two cases against Bryan are tried separately, that the two juries will make contradictory findings on Bryan's negligence. However, this does not make Grayson a person to be joined under Rule 19(a). Rule 19(a)(1)(B)(ii) refers to multiple or inconsistent "obligations," not inconsistent judgments. Bryan here is not subject to inconsistent obligations: He has not been ordered to do something under Judgment #2 that he has been ordered not do to under Judgment #1. He has just been found liable to one plaintiff but not the other.

The fact that a tortfeasor might be sued by other parties injured in the accident does not mandate joinder of those other potential plaintiffs. While the injured parties could choose to join together

---

5. While Rule 20 would allow joinder here, there would be subject matter jurisdiction problems, since Grayson and Ramirez are both from Colorado.

under Rule 20(a)(1), they may bring their own separate actions if they choose. See Advisory Committee to the Civil Rules, Note to 1966 Amendment to Rule 19 (amended rule "not at variance with the settled authorities holding that a tortfeasor with the usual 'joint-and several' liability is merely a permissive party to an action against another with like liability. . . . Joinder of these tortfeasors continues to be regulated by Rule 20 . . .")

f. Grayson certainly has an "interest" in establishing Bryan's liability in her own action against him. However, Grayson's right to do so should not be affected by a finding in the Ramirez/Bryan lawsuit that Bryan was not negligent. Grayson would be free to relitigate the issue of Bryan's negligence, since she was not a party to the first case. Bryan cannot impose the no-negligence finding from the first action on Grayson, because Grayson has not had her chance to litigate that issue. Under due process analysis, Grayson has the right to her own day in court to try to establish Bryan's negligence. See Chapter 29, example 1.

g. If Bryan has limited insurance coverage, there is a real likelihood that Grayson's ability to protect her interest in recovering damages from Bryan will be impaired if she is not made a party in Ramirez's action. If Ramirez sues Bryan and recovers a large judgment, the insurance will be exhausted. Grayson's ability to recover will "as a practical matter" be defeated if she isn't joined in the first case, since Bryan has no other funds with which to pay a judgment. In this scenario, Rule 19(a)(1)(B)(i) makes Grayson a person to be joined if feasible, so that she can protect her interest in recovering at least partial damages.

In this scenario, however, it isn't clear that either Ramirez or Bryan will move to join Grayson in the suit. Ramirez has no interest in moving to join her, which can only reduce the funds available to satisfy any judgment he recovers. Bryan might have an interest in moving to join her, *if she can't be joined*, because that might lead the court to dismiss the action under Rule 19(b). But if Grayson can be joined, why would Bryan move to do it, thus becoming the target of two plaintiffs instead of one?

Perhaps in this situation the judge would raise the issue on her own motion if she recognizes Grayson's interest at an appropriate time. Alternatively, Grayson is likely to find out about the suit; as a witness to the accident, she will probably be deposed by Ramirez or Bryan. When she finds out about the suit, she will have the opportunity to move to intervene under Rule 24, arguing that she should be allowed in to recover part of the limited insurance available. See Rule 24(a)(2).

4. a. Very likely, both Rule 19(a)(1)(B)(i) and Rule 19(a)(1)(B)(ii) apply to this case. If the court orders preferential promotion of minority firefighters, to remedy past discrimination, this will likely mean fewer or later promotions for non-minority firefighters. Thus, the decree is likely to have an adverse impact, "as a practical matter," on non-minority firefighters' interests in promotion. Fed. R. Civ. P. 19(a)(1)(B)(i).

   In addition, if the court orders minority preferences, without participation by the non-minority firefighters, the town is likely to face a separate suit by the non-minority firefighters who lost chances for promotion as a result of the first decree. The court in that suit might order racially neutral promotion policies, so that the Town would find itself subject to inconsistent obligations — preferential hiring under the first decree and race-neutral hiring under the latter. This predicament can be avoided if all interested groups are made parties to the initial case.

   b. If the original claim were for discrimination in hiring, it would be difficult or impossible to identify the absentees who should be made parties. Presumably, an order for racial preferences to remedy past discrimination would limit future hiring of non-minority firefighters. Yet it would be very difficult to identify those future applicants for positions, in order to join them in the action. Thus, it may be impossible to join the absentees, not due to jurisdictional problems, but because of uncertainty as to who they are or (in a case against a large municipality) because of the large number of potential absentees who might be affected by the decree.

   The court might address the problem in several ways. It might be able to identify some absentees who will be affected — for example, applicants who have recently taken the civil service exam for entry-level firefighter positions. Perhaps a union representing the current firefighters could be joined to represent the interests of future applicants. Joinder of these parties might provide participation by some absentees whose interest may be impaired by preferential hiring. If so, the court might conclude, considering the factors in Rule 19(b), that the case could still go forward, even though all absentees who might be affected had not been joined.

5. One might wonder about Apex's motive for seeking to join Belinsky in this action. It may be trying to get Belinsky, a non-diverse defendant, into the case so it can argue that the case should be dismissed for lack of subject matter jurisdiction.

   Whatever Apex's motive, the court will not find that Belinsky is a party to be joined under Rule 19(a). Although Belinsky's negligence will be litigated in the action, Apex is the defendant, not Belinsky. Under res judicata principles, Belinsky cannot be bound by a finding that he was negligent if he was not a party to the case. Although his conduct is being litigated in the action, that does not in itself mandate his joinder under Rule 19.

> The mere fact . . . that Party A, in a suit against Party B, intends to introduce evidence that will indicate that a non-party, C, behaved improperly does not, by itself, make C a necessary party. Given the vast range of potential insults and allegations of impropriety that may be directed at non-parties in civil litigation, a contrary view would greatly expand the universe of Rule 19(a) necessary parties.

*Pujol v. Shearson American Express, Inc.*, 877 F.2d 132, 136 (1st Cir. 1989).

6. a. Rule 19(a)(1)(A) probably does not apply. If, in Schutten's case against Shell, the court finds that Schutten is the owner, it can order Shell to pay him royalties. If it finds Schutten does not own the land, it can dismiss his claim. Either way, it can resolve the case between the current parties.

   However, the Levee Board clearly satisfies the Rule 19(a)(1)(B)(ii) standard for joinder. If it is not joined, Shell might be ordered to pay royalties to Schutten as the owner and then, in a later suit by the District, be ordered to pay the same royalties to the Board. This would require Shell to pay the same royalties twice, the type of "double" liability referred to in Rule 19(a)(1)(B)(ii).[6]

   Arguably, Rule 19(a)(1)(B)(i) would also apply. Although the Levee Board could bring its own suit against Shell if it stopped paying royalties, the Board would certainly suffer a disruption of payments before it could reassert its right to them.

   b. No, it can't. If the Levee Board is joined, it would be aligned as a defendant along with Shell, since they both oppose Schutten's claim to ownership. This would place Louisiana citizens on both sides of the "v," defeating complete diversity.

   c. In *Schutten v. Shell Oil Co.*, 421 F.2d 869 (5th Cir. 1970), on which this example is based, the court concluded that the Board should be joined but couldn't be. Consequently, it proceeded to consider, under the factors in Rule 19(b), whether the case could proceed without the District. It concluded under Rule 19(b)(1) that the Board would suffer prejudice, as a practical matter, if the court decided the case without joining the Board, since a finding that Schutten owned the land would impair its title. It further held that this prejudice could not be avoided (Rule 19(b)(2)) by any limitations it might impose on the relief in Schutten's case. "We are unable to envision a decree which would effectively settle [the title

---

6. Distinguish example 3(c). There, Bryan was at risk of incurring judgments to both injured parties, but for their *separate injuries*, not for the same loss.

dispute] without doing substantial practical injury to the Levee Board's unassertable claims." 421 F. 2d at 874. Last, it considered whether Schutten could obtain an adequate remedy if the case were dismissed. This factor favored dismissal, since all parties could be joined in a single action in the Louisiana state courts, which could then render a decision on the title that would bind all parties. Consequently, the court dismissed the action for failure to join the District.

## All Aboard

7. This example is inspired by one in an article by Professor David Shapiro, *Some Thoughts on Intervention Before Courts, Agencies, and Arbitrators*, 81 Harv. L. Rev. 721, 724 (1968). Each of these potential intervenors can claim an interest in this case, since the pipeline could have broad social and economic impacts. A great deal depends on how the court construes the concept of an "interest" under Rule 24(a)(2). Clearly, an applicant can have a protectable interest even though it will not be bound by the outcome of the original action and does not claim direct ownership of property in dispute. Beyond this accepted premise, courts have struggled to articulate a definition of the interest needed to support intervention. For example, in *Kleissler v. U.S. Forest Service*, 157 F.3d 964, 972 (3d Cir. 1998), the court held that the intervenor must have "an interest that is specific to them, is capable of definition, and will be directly affected in a substantially concrete fashion by the relief sought. The interest may not be remote or attenuated."

Such general formulas don't provide clear answers to this example or most cases. Perhaps the weakest claim in this case is that of the environmental organization, which asserts a generalized social interest rather than an individualized impact from the project in suit. In an era of climate change, however, it is hard to brush aside the legitimacy of this interest just because it affects us all. The distant homeowners who fear an adverse impact on property values would also likely be denied intervention, on the ground that their interest is too remote. Yet abutters making the same argument would very likely be allowed to intervene. Although Rule 24(a)(2) — unlike Rule 24(b) — does not explicitly confer discretion on the trial judge, broad concepts like "interest" and "impairment" inevitably leave much leeway to the trial judge to reach a practical decision on motions to intervene, influenced by the nature of each applicant's interest, the likelihood that its interest will be affected, and the extent to which those already parties will represent that interest.

It will frequently be necessary to determine facts in order to assess the interest of an applicant for intervention. For example, a hearing on the out-of-towners' concern about explosions might reveal that such concerns are far-fetched, suggesting that they lack sufficient interest to intervene. The same might be true for the cross-town owners' worries about property values. Thus, the decision about whether these absentees get to litigate may itself involve significant litigation, diffusing the focus on the underlying claims. Such litigation *about intervention* is one of the costs of allowing parties to seek participation.

b. Although it seems nice to be inclusive, expanding the scope of litigation comes at a significant cost. When new parties are added to a case, litigation becomes more expensive and time consuming. Additional parties will want to take discovery, adding expense to the case. They will likely be entitled to argue all motions, present evidence, and cross-examine witnesses at hearings and trials. They will file pleadings, briefs, and memos that judges have to read and consider. When additional parties are added, the original parties lose a measure of control over the case — consequently, it is not uncommon for the original parties to oppose intervention, even by those who are arguably aligned on their side.

All of this exacts an administrative price that ought only to be paid if there is value added. Efficiency concerns must be balanced against the potential impact on the applicant for intervention. Where the interest of the applicant is speculative or indefinite, the court will likely deny intervention, limiting participation to those with a direct protectable interest in the dispute. Even if the applicant can demonstrate an interest under Rule 24(a)(2), the court may deny intervention if the positions likely to be advanced by the intervenor are already being pressed by parties similarly situated. The decision "involves an accommodation between two potentially conflicting goals: to achieve judicial economies of scale by resolving related issues in a single lawsuit, and to prevent the single lawsuit from becoming fruitlessly complex or unending." *Shuck v. Hobson*, 408 F.2d 175, 179 (D.C. Cir. 1969).

8. a. Certainly, these students have an interest in seeing the University's affirmative action policy upheld. They planned to apply to the University and might benefit from that policy if it were still in place, in terms of both their own admission and the racial make-up of the student body. And, as a practical matter, their interest would likely be impaired if that policy were ordered discontinued. Even if they could bring their own action to have it reinstated, that action would not likely be resolved in time to affect their admission or their college experience.

b. Very likely, the University will support its affirmative action program on the ground that it promotes a diverse student body and a vital learning environment. It is less likely to argue aggressively the other rationale for such programs: to remedy past discrimination by the institution. To do so, the University must impeach its own past practices. In *Grutter*, the court recognized that these arguments were likely to be downplayed by the University, so that the intervenors would bring a different perspective to the case. 188 F.3d at 400-401. Intervention was granted.

Many cases hold that the applicant's burden to show that his interest is not adequately represented by existing parties is "minimal." See, e.g., *Trbovich v. United Mine Workers of America*, 404 U.S. 528, 538 n.10 (1972). Despite this language, a good many cases still deny intervention based on the adequacy of existing parties to represent the intervenor's interest, where the applicant asserts basically the same position as an existing party and will likely make the same arguments for the same result.

c. Perhaps they were. As the previous explanation indicates, they certainly had an interest in the case that could be impaired if they were not joined. But how does one find and join all those who might apply to a large university in the coming year? If one of the parties argued that all minority applicants should be made parties under Rule 19(a)(1)(B), the court would consider, under Rule 19(b), whether to proceed in light of the fact that they cannot be joined. Very likely, it would conclude that it should proceed. Although it is impractical to get all interested parties before the court, it might attempt to join *some* potential applicants to represent these parties. Rule 19(b) does not mandate dismissal if all parties cannot be joined; it invites a practical decision by the trial judge to proceed with whatever measures may lessen the impact of doing so on absentees who may be affected by the judgment.

9. a. Rule 20(a)(1) allows multiple plaintiffs to sue together if their claims arise out of the same transaction or occurrence — or series of transactions or occurrences — and their claims will involve a common question of law or fact. Here, it is doubtful that Garriega and Weninger could sue as co-plaintiffs. Their two claims, although arising from taking the same drug, do not arise from a single transaction — they bought Sindox independently and took it at different times and places. They might argue that their separate acts of taking the drug constitute a "series of transactions or occurrences," but this seems a stretch. If their separate acts constitute a series, then the claim of every other Sindox user would be part of the same series of transactions or occurrences. The discrete events of each party's claim seem too diffuse to be part of a series. Their claims are really united by a common issue — was Sindox defective? — but that is only half of the test for joinder under Rule 20(a)(1).

b. If Weninger sues, Garriega could move to intervene under Rule 24(b)(1)(A). The standard for permissive intervention is met, since his claim against Apex shares a common question of fact with Weninger's: Did Sindox cause the side effect they both suffered. This gives the judge authority to allow joinder of parties with interests similar to those of the original parties or with similar claims that do not meet the same-transaction-or-occurrence test.

Weninger's case could be expanded exponentially if many patients who took the drug sought to intervene. That could have significant benefits to the system, since the central issue in the case, whether Sindox causes the condition the various patients claim, would be litigated once instead of many times. But if many patients are allowed to intervene, deciding Weninger's case will be delayed, and she never asked to litigate on behalf of others, she just wants her own case decided. There will be management problems, jurisdictional issues, and other complexities to be addressed. Rule 24(b), by providing that the court "may" permit intervention if there is a common question of law or fact, gives the trial judge discretion to limit joinder to those situations in which litigation values such as efficiency, consistency, and manageability favor joint litigation.

## A Financial Interest

10. Paramount certainly has an interest in the transaction that is the subject matter of Maroney's suit, since it can only recover its payments if Maroney wins. And its interest will certainly be impaired if Maroney does a poor job of litigating the case and loses or settles for less than Paramount has paid out. Thus, it can make an argument for intervention as of right. However, its interest is exactly the same as Maroney's, to obtain as large a recovery as possible. It does not want in to provide a different point of view, to press a different claim, or to argue for different relief, but just to make sure that Maroney's lawyer does a good job of advocating the same position it would assert if allowed to intervene. Thus, the court is likely to conclude that its interest is adequately represented by an existing party—Maroney. In many tort cases, there will be entities like Paramount who claim a right to reimbursement out of the settlement. If they were routinely allowed to intervene, plaintiffs would be represented not by one lawyer, but by two.

11. This motion would be much more likely to be granted. First, Paramount is not seeking to litigate the tort claim here. It seeks intervention for a limited purpose, to assure that it will participate in the distribution of the proceeds of the action. Thus, its intervention will

not interfere with the progress of the litigation; it will only participate on one limited issue, the distribution of the proceeds of the judgment. Second, it has a clear interest in the "property" — the judgment — that is the subject of the action, since it is entitled to recover its payments from it. And third, if the judgment is paid to Maroney, there is a real risk that he will dissipate it or distribute it to other creditors, impairing Paramount's right to reimbursement. So this motion will have less impact on the litigation, while protecting a legitimate interest of the intervenor.

12. In this case, the newspaper seeks to intervene for a limited purpose, to obtain access to a document filed in the case. It does not seek to litigate the underlying claim in the case (Vohra's discrimination claim) or to assert any defense on the merits. Very likely, it lacks "an interest in the property or transaction that is the subject matter of the action" that supports intervention as of right under rule 24(a)(2). However, it does have a claim that shares an issue of fact with the parties to the case: whether the court properly sealed the settlement agreement from the public. A number of courts have allowed permissive intervention by the media in such cases, to challenge denial of public access to court documents. See, e.g., *Jessup v. Luther*, 227 F.3d 993, 996-999 (7th Cir. 2000). Similarly, courts have allowed permissive intervention in other circumstances where the intervenor had no direct interest in the underlying lawsuit, but objected to a particular order of the court. See, e.g., *United Nuclear Corp. v. Cranford Ins. Co.*, 905 F.2d 14274 (10th Cir. 1990) (permissive intervention by parties to other lawsuits seeking access to discovery materials filed in case against insurer).

13. a In the case on which this example is based,[7] the court held that INA was a party to be joined if feasible under Rule 19(a). It had an interest in Yost's continued employment, which would be impaired if Yost were barred from working for INA. Thus, it should be joined under Rule 19(a)(1)(B)(i). In addition, if INA were not joined, and Yost were ordered not to work for INA, he would be subject to inconsistent obligations: to work for INA under his contract with it, and not to, under the court order. Thus, the standard in Rule 19(a)(1)(B)(ii) also applies.

b. INA could not be joined. If it were, it would clearly be aligned as a defendant along with Yost. But then there would be Virginians on both sides of this diversity case, destroying subject matter jurisdiction.

---

7. *Torrington v. Yost*, 139 F.R.D. 91 (D.S.C. 1991).

c. INA very likely would be entitled to intervene under Rule 24(a)(2), for the same reason that it should be joined under Rule 19(a)(1)(B) — it has an interest in Yost's continued employment that would be impaired if he is ordered not to work for INA. However, if it intervened, it would intervene as a defendant, which would again raise subject matter jurisdiction problems. See 28 U.S.C. s. 1367(b), which bars supplemental jurisdiction over claims by plaintiffs against intervenors under Rule 24. In *Yost*, the court concluded that it could not adequately decide the case without INA's participation. Since Torrington Company had a practical alternative, suing INA and Yost together in state court, the federal court dismissed the case.

# Jurisdictional Fellow Travelers

## Supplemental Jurisdiction

## INTRODUCTION

The preceding chapters on the federal joinder rules describe a highly flexible system that liberally allows parties to expand the litigation by joining claims in a single action. However, permission under the joinder rules to assert a claim, while necessary, is not sufficient to allow the court to hear it: From early on, we have seen that the court must always have subject matter jurisdiction over a claim if it is to proceed. As you have already read — and you will hear it repeated ad nauseum for the rest of your professional life — the subject matter jurisdiction of the federal courts is limited to the categories of cases enumerated in Article III, §2, of the Constitution.

These two principles, broad joinder under the Rules of Civil Procedure and the need for subject matter jurisdiction over every claim, are on something of a collision course. Frequently, the rules will authorize joinder of claims over which there is no independent basis of subject matter jurisdiction. Such cases pose a dilemma for the courts: The efficiency goals of the Rules favor inclusion of related claims, but the ineluctable need for subject matter jurisdiction appears to bar the court from hearing them.

## EXAMPLES OF THE PROBLEM

The problem can arise in a number of contexts. The simplest is the case in which the plaintiff asserts two claims against a nondiverse defendant, one arising under federal law and one under state law. Assume, for example, that Byron brings suit in federal court against Rossetti (a fellow resident of Wisconsin) for violation of a federal age discrimination statute and also claims that the dismissal constitutes a breach of contract. Visually, the case is illustrated as follows:

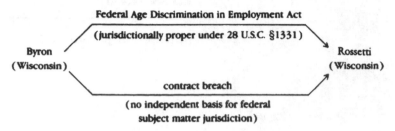

These claims are properly joined under Rule 18(a). Also, the court clearly has jurisdiction over the federal law claim. But nothing in Article III authorizes jurisdiction over the breach of contract claim: The parties are not diverse, and the claim does not arise under federal law. If Byron sued solely on the contract claim, the federal court would have to dismiss it. Yet the efficiency and consistency goals of the Rules favor hearing Byron's two claims together, since they involve the same occurrence — the dismissal. Doubtless, the witnesses will be the same on both claims, and much of the same evidence will be relevant to both claims. If the federal court is to litigate this case, it would surely be desirable for it to hear the *whole* case, including the federal claim and the related state law claim.

Here is another example: Byron brings his dismissal action against Rossetti under the federal statute, and Rossetti counterclaims against Byron for assault, claiming that at the time of the firing Byron threatened to kill her for firing him. The case now looks like this:

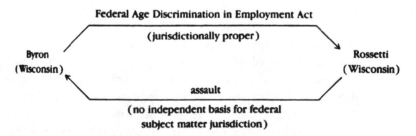

This is a compulsory counterclaim under Rule 13(a), since it arises from the same occurrence as Byron's claim. However, it is again a state law claim between parties from the same state. If Rossetti sued Byron on this claim alone, the federal court would not have the power to hear it, since nothing in Article III, §2, or the United States Code gives the federal district courts subject matter jurisdiction over state law claims between parties from the same state.

One more frequent example: Burns, from Wyoming, sues Cowper, from Utah, for injuries suffered in an auto accident. Cowper impleads a third driver, Hunt (also from Utah) under Rule 14(a)(1), claiming that Hunt was also negligent and is therefore liable to him for contribution:

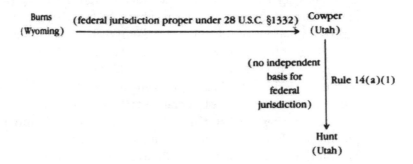

Again, this is proper under the Rules; and again, the existence of common issues argues for allowing the third-party claim to be heard with the main claim. But, once again, there is no independent basis for subject matter jurisdiction: Cowper's claim is a state law claim between two citizens of the same state.

## ESSENTIAL HISTORY, PART I: PENDENT JURISDICTION

Historically, two doctrines evolved to support jurisdiction over such related claims in federal court. The first, *pendent jurisdiction*, involved the configuration in the first diagram above, in which the plaintiff asserted a jurisdictionally proper claim against a nondiverse party and added on a related state law claim. In *United Mine Workers v. Gibbs*, 383 U.S. 715 (1966), the Supreme Court established guidelines for the exercise of jurisdiction over such "pendent" claims.

In *Gibbs* the plaintiff asserted a federal claim against the defendant under the Labor Management Relations Act and a second claim under state law for interference with contractual relations. Both claims were based on the same dispute, concerning the opening of a particular mine. Because there was no diversity between the parties in *Gibbs* and the interference claim arose under state law, there was no independent basis for subject matter jurisdiction over the interference claim. Yet the *Gibbs* Court held that the federal court had pendent jurisdiction over the state law claim because it was joined with the federal labor law claim.

The Court concluded Article III grants jurisdiction over entire "cases," not just over particular claims or issues in a case. If a case includes a claim that is jurisdictionally proper under Article III, the argument goes, the court has constitutional power to hear the *entire dispute* between the parties, not just the claim that is expressly provided for in Article III, §2. Thus, so long as the plaintiff asserts a proper claim based on federal law, diversity, or some other federal ground, the federal court has the power—at least the *constitutional* power—to hear other claims arising out of the same "common nucleus of operative facts."[1] In *Gibbs*, for example, the case was properly before the federal court because the plaintiff asserted a claim under the federal labor laws. The constitutional "case," however, was broader than the federal claim, encompassing all of Gibbs's claims arising out of the same nucleus of operative facts, the opening of the new mine.

This holding in *Gibbs*, that a "case" includes not simply the plaintiff's jurisdictionally sufficient claims, but all claims that arise from the same set of historical facts, is one of the Court's most sensible and enduring procedural decisions. Further, it is consistent with the intent of the Framers, who would hardly have contemplated that the federal courts would be required to dissect a single dispute and limit their jurisdiction to certain strands of a logically interrelated set of claims. The language of Article III, §2, after all, speaks in terms of "cases" and "controversies," not of individual theories or causes of action.

While the *Gibbs* Court concluded that the federal courts had the *power* to hear claims that arose from the same nucleus of facts as the jurisdictionally proper claim, it did not *require* the federal court to entertain the related claims. Wisely, the Court provided a second step in the analysis. Once the judge ascertains that he has power to hear the related claim, because it is part of the same "case," he must then determine whether it makes sense to exercise that jurisdiction. See *Gibbs* at 726-727. This discretionary decision depends on a variety of factors in each case, such as whether the state law claim predominates, whether it would require the court to decide sensitive or novel issues of state law, whether hearing the claims together might confuse the jury, and whether the federal issues are resolved early in the case, leaving only a state law claim for decision. These factors might lead the court to conclude that, while it had power under the first part of *Gibbs* to entertain the pendent claim, it should refuse, in its discretion, to do so.

---

1. Chief Justice Marshall is a little more explicit on the point in *Osborn v. Bank of the United States*, 22 U.S. 738 (1824):

> [W]hen a question to which the judicial power of the Union is extended by the constitution, forms an ingredient of the original cause, it is in the power of congress to give the [federal courts] . . . jurisdiction of that cause, although other questions of fact or of law may be involved in it.

If it does decline jurisdiction over the state law claims, and therefore dismisses them, they may then be brought in a separate suit in state court.

## ESSENTIAL HISTORY, PART II: ANCILLARY JURISDICTION

The courts evolved a similar approach, under the rubric of *ancillary jurisdiction*, to deal with cases like those in the last two diagrams above, in which related claims were asserted by defendants or other additional parties after the initial complaint. In *Moore v. New York Cotton Exchange*, 270 U.S. 593 (1926), the plaintiff sued the defendant under the federal antitrust laws, and the defendant asserted a compulsory counterclaim against the plaintiff under state law. The Court upheld jurisdiction over the state law counterclaim, even though the parties were not diverse and there was no other basis for independent federal jurisdiction over the counterclaim. The Court's discussion in *Moore* is terse, but it did emphasize that the counterclaim (like all compulsory counterclaims) arose out of the same transaction as the main claim. Thus, the decision appears to turn, as did *Gibbs*, on the conclusion that the close connection between the original, jurisdictionally proper claim and the added claim made them part of a single "constitutional case."

From the seed of the *Moore* case, courts extended ancillary jurisdiction to many claims asserted by defending parties that bore a "logical relationship" to the main claim. Third-party claims like that in the figure on p. 311 were consistently held ancillary, since they are by definition "logically related" to the main claim: The third-party plaintiff can only recover from the third-party defendant if the plaintiff recovers from the third-party plaintiff. Fed. R. Civ. P. 14(a)(1). On a similar rationale, ancillary jurisdiction was extended to cross-claims under Rule 13(g) and to intervention as of right under Rule 24(a). But the same logic dictated denial of ancillary jurisdiction for permissive counterclaims. By definition, such claims arose from different events (see Rule 13(b)) and therefore lacked a close logical relation to the main claim. See generally Friedenthal, Kane, and Miller 4th ed. at §2.12, pp. 70-71.

## ESSENTIAL HISTORY, PART III: STATUTORY LIMITS ON JURISDICTION

All of this was complex enough, but the Court multiplied these woes in three major cases by introducing a more sophisticated analysis of the limits of such supplemental jurisdiction. In *Aldinger v. Howard*, 427 U.S. 1 (1976), *Owen Equipment & Erection Co. v. Kroger*, 437 U.S. 365 (1978), and *Finley v. United States*, 490 U.S. 545 (1989), the court reiterated the basic principle that federal jurisdiction is not only limited by the Constitution but also must be conveyed to the federal district courts by Congress in a jurisdictional statute. (Recall Judge Sirica's well-phrased comments on the "Article III storehouse," supra p. 69.)

In *Aldinger* the plaintiff was dismissed from her county job and brought suit against Howard and other individual defendants under a federal statute, 42 U.S.C. §1983. She also asserted a state law claim based on the same incident, against Spokane County. The case looked like this:

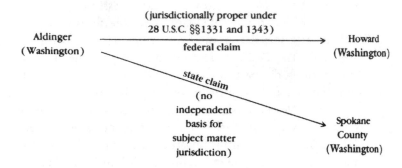

This was an attempt to exercise "pendent party" jurisdiction, that is, to add a jurisdictionally insufficient claim against one defendant to a jurisdictionally proper claim against the other. The claim against Howard was proper, since Aldinger asserted a right to relief under §1983, a federal statute. However, the claim against the county was based on state law and, thus, not jurisdictionally proper in itself. *Aldinger* at 5. The Court concluded that even though the claim could be viewed as part of a single constitutional case under the first part of *Gibbs*, allowing a state law claim against the county would be inconsistent with the apparent intent of Congress to bar federal civil rights claims under §1983 against counties.[2] Thus, there was no *statutory* grant of jurisdiction over the pendent party claim.

The second case, *Kroger*, involved an interesting twist on the established types of supplemental jurisdiction. In *Kroger*, the plaintiff sued the Oklahoma Public Power District (OPPD), a diverse defendant, which then impleaded Owen, a corporation. Owen, it turned out, was not diverse from either

---

2. At the time *Aldinger* was decided, counties were not considered "persons" subject to suit under §1983. *Monroe v. Pape*, 365 U.S. 167, 187-191 (1961). After *Aldinger* was decided, however, the Supreme Court overruled this aspect of *Monroe*. See *Monell v. Department of Social Services*, 436 U.S. 658, 690-691 (1978).

original party. The plaintiff, Kroger, then asserted a direct claim against Owen, as Rule 14(a)(1) allows. The configuration of the parties was as follows:

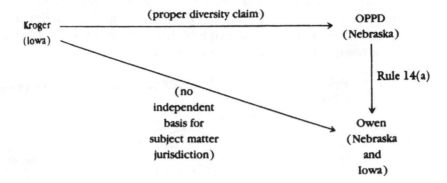

The issue posed was whether the court had jurisdiction over Kroger's claim against Owen.

The *Kroger* Court assumed that, under the constitutional analysis in *Gibbs*, Kroger's claim against Owen was part of the same "constitutional case" as the main claim against OPPD, since it arose out of the same accident. 437 U.S. at 371 n.10. However, the Court went on to consider whether the relevant jurisdictional *statute*, 28 U.S.C. §1332, indicated congressional intent to grant federal courts ancillary jurisdiction over a related claim asserted by the plaintiff against a nondiverse third-party defendant. The Court held that extending ancillary jurisdiction to this claim would be inconsistent with the long-standing interpretation of §1332, requiring complete diversity between the parties. Since Mrs. Kroger could not have sued OPPD and Owen together originally, it would ignore the statutory limits on jurisdiction to allow her to do the same thing indirectly after Owen was brought in as a third-party defendant.

However, the *Kroger* Court's discussion suggested that ancillary jurisdiction could be exercised over compulsory counterclaims, cross-claims, and third-party claims. The opinion implied, for example, that jurisdiction over OPPD's claim against Owen would be proper, even though it also abridges the complete diversity requirement. The court emphasized the difference between the claim of a defending party, brought in against its will, and a plaintiff, who presumably had the choice to sue all parties jointly in state court. 437 U.S. at 375-377.

The third important background case, *Finley v. United States*, involved pendent party jurisdiction. The plaintiff, Finley, sued the United States under the Federal Tort Claims Act (FTCA). Jurisdiction over this claim was proper under Article III, §2, because the United States was a party. It was also authorized by 28 U.S.C. §1346(b), which gives the federal district courts exclusive jurisdiction over claims against the United States under the FTCA. However, Finley also asserted related state law claims against other defendants in the action. There was no diversity between the plaintiff and these defendants; instead she asked the court to take jurisdiction over them on the basis of "pendent party" jurisdiction. The configuration of the parties looked much like that in *Aldinger*, in which the court had previously refused to allow pendent party jurisdiction:

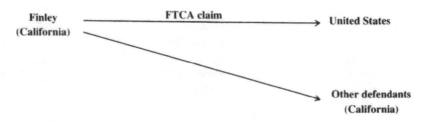

Although the pendent party claims in *Finley* arose from the same nucleus of facts as the jurisdictionally proper claim against the United States, the *Finley* Court reiterated that jurisdiction must be granted not only by Article III, but also by statute. The Court found no indication in §1346(b) that Congress meant to convey jurisdiction over any claims other than those against the United States. Consequently, it held that the district court had no jurisdiction over the pendent party claims. As the Court acknowledged, this meant that Mrs. Finley would have to bring two lawsuits, one in federal court against the United States and a second state court action against the other defendants. But that, the court opined, was not a reason to ignore the statutory limits on the federal court's subject matter jurisdiction. 490 U.S. at 555-556.

# A STROKE OF THE PEN

All of this case law is now history, albeit very important history. In 1990 Congress enacted 28 U.S.C. §1367, which for the first time provides a statutory basis for "supplemental jurisdiction" in the federal courts. With a stroke of the pen, Congress substantially clarified the authority of the federal courts to entertain claims that are related to proper federal claims, but are not jurisdictionally proper in themselves.

Let's take §1367 one section at a time. Section 1367(a) provides:

> Except as otherwise provided in subsections (b) and (c) or as expressly provided otherwise by Federal statute, in any civil action of which the district courts have original jurisdiction, the district courts shall have supplemental jurisdiction over all other claims that are so related to claims in the action within such original jurisdiction that they form part of the same case or

controversy under Article III of the United States Constitution. Such supplemental jurisdiction shall include claims that involve the joinder or intervention of additional parties.

Under this section, if the plaintiff brings a proper federal claim or diversity claim, so that the federal court has "original jurisdiction," the court may hear all the claims that are part of the same "case or controversy under Article III. . . . " While the section does not explicitly define what claims come within a single case or controversy, this phrase has been held to have the same meaning in §1367 that it was given in *United Mine Workers v. Gibbs. Chicago v. Int'l College of Surgeons*, 522 U.S. 156, 165-166 (1997). Congress was aware of the widespread use of the *Gibbs* test for a single "constitutional case" in pendent and ancillary jurisdiction cases. Since it chose the same concept in defining the limits of supplemental jurisdiction, the natural inference is that it meant to adopt the same standard. See 13B Wright & Miller §3567.3 (§1367 "ratifies and incorporates" the constitutional analysis in *Gibbs*). Thus, it appears that the section (with certain exceptions discussed below) authorizes the courts to hear all claims that arise out of the same nucleus of operative facts as the proper federal claim. This includes additional claims asserted by the plaintiff, but also those asserted by other parties as well, such as cross-claims and counterclaims.

If *Gibbs* already defined a single constitutional case in those terms, why did Congress pass the statute? Well, in *Aldinger, Kroger*, and *Finley*, the Supreme Court emphasized that it was not enough that the court has constitutional power to hear the related claim. These cases required statutory authority to exercise that jurisdiction as well. By enacting §1367, Congress *provided the necessary statutory authority to hear the related claims*. The Court in its recent cases had said, "Congress, we can't exercise jurisdiction, even if it would be proper under Article III, unless you give it to us as well." And Congress responded by saying, "Okay, federal courts, you say we have to give you statutory jurisdiction to hear the related claims, so here it is." The authority Congress gave is very broad indeed, reaching in most situations to the outer bounds of the "constitutional case" before the court. Thus, today, the statute, not the "essential history" cases reviewed above, provides the governing law. For example, the exercises of pendent party jurisdiction held improper in *Finley* and *Aldinger* would be upheld under §1367. See 28 U.S.C. §1367(a) last sentence.

## LIMITS ON SUPPLEMENTAL JURISDICTION: SECTION 1367(B)

While Congress granted supplemental jurisdiction in very broad terms in §1367(a), it hedged a little in §1367(b). That section provides that supplemental jurisdiction shall not extend to certain claims by plaintiffs in diversity cases, even if the claim is within the broad grant in §1367(a). Specifically, the court may not hear

> . . . claims by plaintiffs against persons made parties under Rule 14, 19, 20, or 24 of the Federal Rules of Civil Procedure, or over claims by persons proposed to be joined as plaintiffs under Rule 19 of such rules, or seeking to intervene as plaintiffs under Rule 24 of such rules, when exercising supplemental jurisdiction over such claims would be inconsistent with the jurisdictional requirements of section 1332.

This provision must also be read in light of the "essential history" reviewed above. Section 1367(b) obviously responds to *Kroger*, in which the Supreme Court rejected jurisdiction over Mrs. Kroger's claim because it contradicted the complete diversity requirements of §1332. In §1367(b), the drafters tried to catalogue various joinder possibilities under the Rules that would allow the plaintiff to circumvent the limits of the *Strawbridge* rule, and specified that supplemental jurisdiction would not extend to joinder in those circumstances if it allowed an end run around those limits.[3] The scholars have suggested that the drafters — some other scholars — did a clumsy job here,[4] but their basic idea in drafting §1367(b) was to preserve the limits on ancillary jurisdiction suggested in *Kroger*.

Finally, in §1367(c), Congress codified the second holding in *Gibbs*: Section 1367(c) authorizes the court to decline jurisdiction over supplemental claims for any of four reasons, similar to but not quite the same as those discussed in the second half of the *Gibbs* opinion.

## AN ATTEMPTED SYNTHESIS

The *Aldinger/Kroger/Finley* trilogy suggested that pendent and ancillary jurisdiction were coalescing into a single doctrine. Congress has confirmed this by adopting a single term, "supplemental jurisdiction," to describe claims that would previously have been classified as either pendent or ancillary. Under §1367 supplemental jurisdiction requires a three-part analysis:

---

3. In several respects, §1367(b) also restricts jurisdiction previously available under case law. For example, prior to the new statute, claims by intervenors as of right under Fed. R. Civ. P. 24(a) were considered ancillary, even if the intervenor destroyed complete diversity. This anomaly has been eliminated by §1367(b), which bars claims by non-diverse plaintiff intervenors in diversity cases.
4. See, e.g., R. Freer, Compounding Confusion and Hampering Diversity: Life after *Finley* and the Supplemental Jurisdiction Statute, 40 Emory L.J. 445 (1991).

*First*, the court must determine whether there is *constitutional power* under Article III, §2, to hear the supplemental claim. This analysis has nothing to do with §1367: Congress cannot determine by statute what claims the Constitution authorizes a court to hear. This analysis stems from *Gibbs*, which held that the constitutional power to hear the related claim exists if there is a proper claim within the jurisdiction of the federal court and the related claim arises from the same nucleus of operative facts. This level of the analysis is no different now than it was before §1367 was enacted.

*Second*, the court must determine whether there is a *statutory grant* of jurisdiction over the related claim. Now, that grant is provided in most cases by §1367 itself. Because §1367(a) grants jurisdiction over all related claims that are part of the same "case," the answer to the statutory question is much simpler than it was under *Kroger* and *Finley*. As long as the federal court has a basis for original jurisdiction over the case, §1367(a) broadly grants statutory authority to hear related state law claims that meet the *Gibbs* constitutional test. However, under §1367(b), certain claims in diversity cases, which would contradict the limits on jurisdiction in §1332, are excepted.

*Third*, Congress has codified the second half of the *Gibbs* analysis in §1367(c). Once the court determines that it has constitutional and statutory authority to hear the related claims, it must decide, based on the various discretionary factors in that section, whether to do so.

To properly analyze the following examples, it would help to read *Gibbs* and *Kroger*, as well as §1367. It will also help to draw quick diagrams of the configuration of the parties and claims in the examples. Then consider whether the constitutional test of *Gibbs* and the statutory requirements in §1367 are met. (Disregard for the moment the third, discretionary prong of the analysis.) Assume that all cases are brought in federal court.

# Examples

## Simple Addition

1. Keats, from Minnesota, is arrested by Shelley, a Minnesota police officer, for disturbing the peace. During the arrest, Shelley forcibly restrains Keats, and Keats resists. Keats claims that Shelley used excessive force in making the arrest and sues Shelley under the federal civil rights statute, 42 U.S.C. §1983. Keats also seeks to recover from Shelley on a state law claim for battery based on the scuffle that took place during the arrest.
   a. Does the court have constitutional power to hear the battery claim?
   b. Does the court have statutory authority to hear the battery claim?
   c. Assume that the court concluded that it lacked power to hear the battery claim. What should it do with the §1983 claim?

    d. Assume that the court declined in its discretion to hear Keats's battery claim. What would happen to the §1983 claim?

    e. Assume for this example only that there were no statutory authority to exercise supplemental jurisdiction. What would Keats have to do in order to recover on both of his claims?

2. Apparently there was some prior history to the Keats/Shelley altercation; Shelley owed Keats $500 at the time of arrest as payment for work that Keats had done on his house. Keats was upset because he had not been paid and tempers flared, leading to the arrest. Keats therefore asserts a third claim for the debt in his action against Shelley. Does the court have the power to hear it?

3. Browning, Blake, and Wordsworth are involved in a three-car collision. Browning, a New Yorker, sues Blake and Wordsworth, both from Ohio, for $80,000 for her personal injuries. Blake asserts a cross-claim against Wordsworth for his own injuries arising from the collision. Does the court have jurisdiction over the cross-claim?

4. Suppose, on the facts of example 3, that Blake (Ohio) asserts a counterclaim against Browning (New York) for $35,000 for his injuries. Does the court have jurisdiction to hear the counterclaim?

5. May Blake assert a $25,000 counterclaim in the accident case against Browning for Browning's trespass on Blake's property four months prior to the accident?

## Important Example, Requiring Thought

6. Please reconsider example 3, in which Browning sued Blake and Wordsworth for her injuries in an auto accident. In that case could Blake (Ohio) assert a counterclaim against Browning (New York) for an unrelated infringement of a patent Blake holds? Assume that the counterclaim is for $30,000 in damages.

7. Suppose that Browning (New York) sues Blake (Ohio) for her injuries from the collision, and Blake impleads Wordsworth (Ohio) for contribution if he is found liable to Browning

    a. Is there independent subject matter jurisdiction over the impleader claim?

    b. Is there supplemental jurisdiction over it?

## Complex Equations

8. If Blake (Ohio) impleads Wordsworth (Ohio), and Browning, the New York plaintiff, then asserts a claim directly against Wordsworth, will the court have the power to hear it?

9. Blake (Ohio) impleads Wordsworth (Ohio) as a third-party defendant, and Wordsworth asserts a claim against Browning, the New York plaintiff, for $25,000 for his own injuries in the accident.
   a. Will the court have supplemental jurisdiction over the claim?
   b. Assume that, after Wordsworth asserts his claim against Browning, Browning then asserts a claim against Wordsworth for $15,000 for property damage to her car in the same accident. Will the court have supplemental jurisdiction over the claim?

10. Browning, from New York, sues Blake, from Ohio, for $100,000 as a result of her injuries in the auto accident. Coleridge, a New York passenger in Browning's car, joins as a plaintiff, seeking $25,000 for his injuries.
    a. Does the court have the constitutional power to hear Coleridge's claim?
    b. Is there supplemental jurisdiction over it under §1367?

11. Assume that Browning sues Blake for $60,000, and Coleridge joins with him to assert a claim for $40,000. Does the court have jurisdiction over the case?

12. Byron (Wisconsin) sues Rossetti (Wisconsin) for patent infringement, arising out of Rossetti's manufacture of inverse roto-turnbuckles on which Byron claims he holds a patent. Byron also asserts a claim against Hunt, a former employee and Wisconsin citizen, for breach of contract, for assisting Rossetti in making the devices. Is there supplemental jurisdiction over Byron's claim against Hunt under §1367?

## Unlucky Number 13

13. Suppose, on the facts of question 10, that Browning and Coleridge join as co-plaintiffs to sue Blake and Wordsworth as co-defendants, seeking recovery for their injuries in the auto accident. Browning's claim against each defendant is for $100,000 and Coleridge's is for $25,000. Does the court have supplemental jurisdiction over Coleridge's claims under 28 U.S.C. §1367?

## Impenetrable Number 14

14. Suppose that Browning, from New York, sues Blake, from Ohio, for his injuries in the accident. He seeks $100,000 in damages. Cowper, an Ohio citizen, joins as co-plaintiff, seeking $100,000 in damages for

her injuries in the action. How would you argue that the court has supplemental jurisdiction over Cowper's claim?

## Explanations

### Simple Addition

1. a. This is a straightforward example in which the plaintiff asserts a claim under federal law and a related state law claim against the same defendant. It is exactly analogous to *Gibbs*, and clearly satisfies *Gibbs*'s criteria for a single constitutional case: The plaintiff has asserted a proper claim under federal law (the §1983 claim), and the state law battery claim arises out of the same "nucleus of operative facts," the scuffle during the arrest. Thus, there is constitutional power to hear the battery claim.

   b. Before Congress enacted §1367, the court would have had to analyze the statute granting jurisdiction over §1983 claims to determine whether Congress intended to allow pendent claims in §1983 cases. Now, however, Congress has answered that question in §1367: If the federal claim and the related claim are part of the "same case or controversy under Article III," the court has supplemental jurisdiction to hear the related claim. Because the "same case or controversy" requirement in §1367(a) means essentially the same thing as a single "constitutional case" under *Gibbs*, the court has supplemental jurisdiction, since the battery claim arises from the same nucleus of operative facts as the §1983 claim. Nor does §1367(b) bar this claim; that subsection only applies to cases based solely on diversity.

   c. If the court lacked jurisdiction over the related state law claim, it would have to dismiss it. But it could not dismiss the federal claim. The court has jurisdiction over that claim, and (absent some extraordinary situations not discussed here, such as federal abstention) it has a duty to exercise that jurisdiction by hearing and deciding the §1983 claim.

   d. The same result follows if the court concludes that it has jurisdiction over the battery claim but declines to hear the claim as a matter of discretion under §1367(c). Keats is still entitled to a federal forum on his federal claim even though the related state claim will be heard in state court. If the court dismisses the state law claim, Keats may end up litigating the same facts in state and federal court at the same time.

   e. If there were no statutory authority to hear related state claims, Keats would not be able to join his battery claim in the federal suit. He would then have two choices. He could bring two lawsuits, one in federal court on the §1983 claim and the other in state court on the battery claim. Alternatively, he could bring a single action in state court seeking relief on both claims, since state courts have concurrent jurisdiction over federal claims unless Congress makes federal jurisdiction exclusive. If he chose the latter course, the state court would decide Keats's §1983 claim, and, of course, it would decide his state law claim as well.

These alternatives for Keats illustrate the importance of supplemental jurisdiction. Without it, a plaintiff like Keats would have a strong incentive to sue in state court in order to have his entire case resolved in one proceeding. Many federal law cases would be heard in state rather than federal courts, even though a primary purpose of federal courts is to expound and develop federal law. Thus, supplemental jurisdiction assures that plaintiffs in Keats's position who prefer the federal forum will have full access to it.

2. This example fails at the first level of the analysis, the same-constitutional-case requirement established in *Gibbs*. Under *Gibbs*, jurisdictionally insufficient claims are part of the same case (and therefore within the Article III grant of federal jurisdiction) if they arise out of the same nucleus of operative facts as the federal claim. Here, the assault claim does arise out of the same set of facts, but the debt claim does not. Although there may be a causal relationship between the debt and the eventual arrest, it is probably too attenuated to make them part of the same nucleus of facts. Thus, the court lacks supplemental jurisdiction over the debt claim. (It would also fail the "same case or controversy" test of §1367(a), for the same reason.)

3. This case, illustrated below, involves a cross-claim by a defending party against another defendant arising out of the events that gave rise to the original claim. There is no independent basis of federal jurisdiction over this state law cross-claim, since both parties are from Ohio.

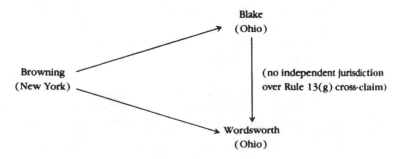

Prior to §1367 the courts routinely took "ancillary" jurisdiction over cross-claims. Because a cross-claim must arise out of the same transaction or occurrence as the main claim (see Rule 13(g)), it was considered part of the same constitutional case.[5] And, because cross-claims are asserted by a defendant, "hauled into court against his will," *Kroger* suggested that they would not be barred even if they abridged the complete diversity requirement of §1332. 437 U.S. at 376.

Now, a statutory basis for supplemental jurisdiction over Blake's cross-claim is provided by §1367(a), which authorizes the court to hear all related claims that arise from the same set of facts as the main claim. Since Blake's claim arises from the same accident as the proper diversity claim, this requirement is met.

Although §1367(b) limits the broad reach of supplemental jurisdiction in diversity cases, that subsection only bars certain claims by plaintiffs in diversity cases. Here a defendant asserts the related claim, so §1367(b) does not bar supplemental jurisdiction over it.

4. This is the classic ancillary jurisdiction situation addressed in *Moore v. New York Cotton Exchange*, 270 U.S. 593 (1926). Blake's counterclaim is compulsory because it arises from the same accident as the main claim. Yet the court lacks independent jurisdiction over it because it is based on state law and does not satisfy the amount-in-controversy requirement.

Under the *Gibbs* analysis, the court has constitutional power to hear the added claim since it arises out of the same incident as the main claim. Further, the court has statutory authority to hear the claim because §1367(a) authorizes supplemental jurisdiction over all claims that meet the *Gibbs* standard. The exceptions in §1367(b) do not apply, since the claim is not asserted by the plaintiff,

5. There is no independent basis for subject matter jurisdiction over the counterclaim in this case, since it does not meet the amount-in-controversy requirement of 28 U.S.C. §1332(a). Further, because this permissive counterclaim does not arise out of the same events as the main claim, there is no basis for supplemental jurisdiction over it. It founders on the *Gibbs* constitutional analysis, which only allows the court to hear claims that arise from the same nucleus of operative facts as the main claim. Consequently, there is no basis under Article III to append it to the other claim.

---

5. It is not clear whether the reach of a "common nucleus of operative facts" is exactly the same as the "same transaction or occurrence test" used in the federal joinder rules. One scholar suggests that since the transaction or occurrence test was well established when *Gibbs* was decided, the court must have meant something different — and probably broader — when it formulated the common nucleus test in *Gibbs*. See Matasar, A Pendent and Ancillary Jurisdiction Primer: The Scope and Limits of Supplemental Jurisdiction, 17 U.C. Davis L. Rev. 103, 130 (1983). It is probably safe to assume that the *Gibbs* test is satisfied if the related state claim arises out of the same transaction or occurrence as the federal claim but that it might also be satisfied in some more loosely related situations. See generally Moores Federal Practice §106.25[1].

Since this claim fails at the constitutional level of analysis, there is no need to consider whether §1367 provides a statutory basis for jurisdiction over the claim. However, it clearly does not: Section 1367 defines the statutory reach of supplemental jurisdiction by the same test as the outer reach of constitutional authority under *Gibbs*. Because the constitutional test is not met, the statutory test isn't either.

## Important Example, Requiring Thought

6. This example isn't that hard, but it is very important. This case is like example 5, except for one crucial difference. In this case there is an independent ground for jurisdiction over the unrelated counterclaim. While the court could not take supplemental jurisdiction over the claim under §1367 (because it is not part of the same case or controversy as the main claim) it has *original* jurisdiction over the patent claim since it arises under the federal patent laws. 28 U.S.C. §§1331, 1338.

   Always remember that "supplemental" jurisdiction provides a basis for jurisdiction over claims that do not otherwise support federal jurisdiction. It is a "fill-in" that may allow related claims to be heard in an action in federal court because of their relation to another, jurisdictionally proper claim. Where there is original jurisdiction over a claim, as there is here under 28 U.S.C §1331, there is no need to bootstrap the patent claim into federal court based on a relation to another claim in the action. Here, Blake could have sued Browning on this claim alone in federal court, and the court would have had jurisdiction. Thus, there is no need to invoke supplemental jurisdiction based on a relationship to Blake's diversity claim.

7. a. The point here is fundamental, but by no means obvious. The impleaded third party, Wordsworth, is diverse from the plaintiff but not from the defendant who impleaded him. Whom do you count in measuring diversity over the third-party claim?

   The third-party action by Blake against Wordsworth must be viewed as a separate claim for purposes of determining subject matter jurisdiction over it. If the court would not have jurisdiction over this claim as a separate suit, it lacks independent jurisdiction when it is brought as a third-party claim as well. Since Blake and Wordsworth are from the same state, there is no independent ground for jurisdiction over the impleader claim. The fact that Wordsworth is diverse from Browning avails him not. Conversely, if Wordsworth were from New York there would be independent subject matter jurisdiction over the impleader claim (assuming the amount requirement is met) even though he was not diverse from the plaintiff.

b. This claim is analogous to the Power District's third-party claim against Owen in *Kroger*, in which the Power District impleaded Owen as a third-party defendant for contribution. Impleader claims must arise from the same set of facts as the main claim to satisfy the requirements of Fed. R. Civ. P. 14. Thus, they will meet the common nucleus test of *Gibbs* and the statutory test of §1367(a) for supplemental jurisdiction.

Section 1367(b) does not prevent the court from exercising supplemental jurisdiction here. That section bars some "claims against persons made parties under Rule 14(a)," but only such claims *brought by plaintiffs*. This claim is not asserted by the plaintiff, so the general supplemental jurisdiction authority under §1367(a) applies.

## Complex Equations

8. If you diagrammed this case, you will have noticed that it is the same configuration as *Kroger*, with the plaintiff asserting a claim against the third-party defendant. Although it arises from the same set of facts (and therefore satisfies the *Gibbs* constitutional test), *Kroger* clearly held that there was no jurisdiction over such a claim in a diversity case. And Congress took the same position in §1367(b), which bars supplemental jurisdiction over claims brought by plaintiffs against parties brought in under Rule 14.

However, in this case there may be *independent* subject matter jurisdiction over the claim. The plaintiff and the third-party defendant here are diverse; if Browning's claim is for more than $75,000 the court will have jurisdiction over it without regard to supplemental jurisdiction. If it is for less, the court will not have jurisdiction over it.

9. a. This configuration, the reverse of *Kroger*, is a claim by the third-party defendant against the plaintiff, now authorized by Rule 14(a)(2)(D). There is no independent jurisdiction over the claim because the amount-in-controversy requirement is not satisfied. But it is part of the same "constitutional case," since the claim arises from the same accident as the main diversity claim. Consequently, the court has both constitutional power to hear the claim under *Gibbs* and supplemental jurisdiction over it under §1367(a), unless it is excepted by §1367(b). Since Wordsworth is a defendant, not a plaintiff, §1367(b) does not apply. Ironically, supplemental jurisdiction is proper here, even though it was not in example 8 when the plaintiff asserted the claim.

b. Of course this had to be the next example. Here, the third party has claimed against the plaintiff, and that makes the plaintiff a

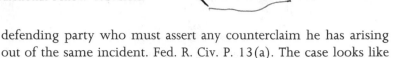

defending party who must assert any counterclaim he has arising out of the same incident. Fed. R. Civ. P. 13(a). The case looks like this:

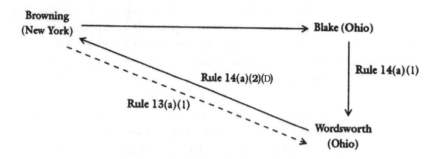

Since Browning's claim arises from the original accident, it is a compulsory counterclaim, and also satisfies the single "constitutional case" test of *Gibbs* and the basic §1367(a) test for supplemental jurisdiction. Thus, the court has jurisdiction unless it is barred by the exception in §1367(b).[6]

This is an interesting one: Section 1367(b) bars "claims by plaintiffs against persons made parties under Rule 14." Browning is a plaintiff and his claim is against Wordsworth, who was made a party under Rule 14 when Blake impleaded him. So the claim appears to fall within the §1367(b) exception. This makes little sense: Rule 13(a) requires Browning to assert the claim, and much efficiency will be gained by hearing it in the federal action. Yet the plain language of §1367(b) precludes the court from hearing it. Perhaps the courts will blink at the language to achieve a more sensible result.

However, at least one court has refused to do so in analogous circumstances, while expressing the wish that it could. See *Guaranteed Systems, Inc. v. American National Can Co.*, 842 F. Supp. 855 (M.D.N.C. 1994) (where plaintiff sued on counterclaim, no supplemental jurisdiction over its impleader claim against a third party under §1367(b)). The court in *Guaranteed Systems* stated that, if it could, it would construe §1367(b) to allow jurisdiction, but that "such a construction would reach beyond the limits of Section 1367(b)." Id. at 857.

---

6. Although Browning and Wordsworth are diverse, Browning's claim does not meet the amount-in-controversy requirement. If it did, this would be a proper diversity claim on its own, and there would be no need for supplemental jurisdiction. Remember that we only need to consider supplemental jurisdiction for claims as to which there is no direct basis for jurisdiction.

10. a. In this case, there is complete diversity, but Coleridge's claim does not meet the amount-in-controversy requirement. That of course is irrelevant to satisfying the constitutional requirements for diversity jurisdiction: There is no amount-in-controversy requirement in Article III, §2. Since both plaintiffs are diverse from the defendant, there is proper diversity jurisdiction under Article III.

    b. There's little doubt that jurisdiction over this claim is authorized by 28 U.S.C §1367(a). Coleridge's claim arises from the same nucleus of facts as Browning's, and §1367(a) expressly authorizes jurisdiction over such claims, even if they involve joinder of additional parties. So we need to drop down to §1367(b), to see whether it makes an exception for this claim. If you read that section carefully, you will not find anything taking away jurisdiction over this claim. Coleridge's claim is a claim by a plaintiff, but it is not against a party joined under Rule 14, 19, 20,[7] or 24.

       Before enactment of the supplemental jurisdiction statute, the traditional rules for aggregation of claims in diversity cases would not have allowed this claim. The case law consistently held that each plaintiff had to satisfy the amount requirement independently. *Clark v. Paul Gray, Inc.*, 306 U.S. 583 (1939). The legislative history of §1367 suggests that the drafters did not intend to change this result, but the Supreme Court recently concluded that the language of §1367 does change it. The broad grant of jurisdiction in §1367(a) authorizes jurisdiction over Coleridge's claim. And, §1367(b) doesn't have any exception for claims by "plaintiffs joined under Rule 20(a)." See *Exxon-Mobil Corp. v. Allapattah Services, Inc.*, 545 U.S. 546, 558-565 (2005). Thus, Coleridge may bootstrap his claim onto Browning's, even though it does not independently meet the amount-in-controversy requirement. This may have been a drafting mistake, rather than an intentional change in the aggregation rules. If so, the *Exxon-Mobil* Court held, "it is up to Congress rather than the courts to fix it." 545 U.S. at 565.

11. Section 1367(a) requires that the court have "original jurisdiction" over *some claim* in the case before supplemental jurisdiction can be invoked to add other claims. Here, neither Browning nor Coleridge has a claim sufficient to confer diversity jurisdiction on the court. Since there is no claim that is properly before the court on its own, there is nothing to add other claims *to* under §1367. Thus, there is no jurisdiction over either claim in cases like this, where neither plaintiff meets the amount in-controversy requirement.

---

7. Although he is a defendant, Blake is not "joined under Rule . . . 20." That rule deals with the joinder of multiple plaintiffs or defendants, not claims against a single defendant.

12. This "pendent party" case is closely analogous to *Finley*. The plaintiff asserts a proper federal claim against Rossetti. (In fact, Byron must take this claim to federal court since federal courts have exclusive jurisdiction over patent claims. 28 U.S.C. §1338(a).) Byron then seeks to add a state law claim against Hunt, a nondiverse party. There is no independent jurisdictional basis for this claim.

However, it appears clear that Congress intended to authorize supplemental jurisdiction over this type of claim. "Such supplemental jurisdiction shall include claims that involve the joinder or intervention of additional parties." 28 U.S.C §1367(a). This language suggests that, if the court has jurisdiction based on a proper federal claim, the court's supplemental jurisdiction extends to claims by or against other parties, *even if the plaintiff has not asserted any jurisdictionally sufficient claim against the added party*. For example, this language seems to authorize jurisdiction on the facts of *Finley*. Nor does any exception in §1367(b) apply, since §1367(b) does not apply to cases in which the jurisdictionally proper claim is a federal question claim.

The same result would apparently follow if Arnold, another plaintiff, joined with Byron to assert a state law claim for damages for the same acts. Even if there were no independent basis for federal jurisdiction, the quoted language would allow the added party to sue with Byron. Once again, §1367(b) would not apply since it is not a diversity case.

## Unlucky Number 13

13. I hope you're ready for this. Let's start with §1367(a). It authorizes supplemental jurisdiction over Coleridge's claims, even though they don't meet the amount-in-controversy requirement, because they arise out of the same set of facts as Browning's claim. Section 1367(a) authorizes supplemental jurisdiction over such claims, even if they are brought by an additional party, as they are here. So the broad grant in §1367(a) applies.

But in this case, §1367(b) makes an exception. It bars supplemental jurisdiction in diversity cases over "claims by plaintiffs against persons made parties under Rule . . . 20." This is a diversity case, and Blake and Wordsworth are made parties under Rule 20, which authorizes joinder of multiple defendants. By its terms, §1367(b) bars Coleridge's claim. So Coleridge can join to assert his claim if he and Browning sue one defendant, but not if they sue two or more. That doesn't make much sense, but it appears to follow from the language of §1367(b) and the Court's reasoning in *Exxon-Mobil*.

Assuming this is correct, Browning and Coleridge will probably manage to litigate all their claims in federal court despite the prohibition in §1367(b). They could bring two separate suits, one against Blake and one against Wordsworth, in the same federal court. Each of these suits would have only one defendant, so the court would have supplemental jurisdiction over Coleridge's claims. See Explanation 10b. Since the two suits arise from the same events, the court would likely consolidate them under Fed. R. Civ. P. 42, so the parties would litigate them together anyway.

## Impenetrable Number 14

14. Here's the argument: The court has to have "original jurisdiction" over some claim before supplemental jurisdiction applies. 28 U.S.C. §1367(a). Browning has a proper diversity claim against Blake, since they are diverse and Browning's claim is for more than $75,000. So, that gives the court original jurisdiction. Then, Cowper piles on under §1367. Her claim satisfies the §1367(a) requirement for supplemental jurisdiction, since it arises from the same accident as Browning's. And §1367(b) doesn't take it away, since there is no reference to claims by plaintiffs joined under Rule 20. So, voilà! the court has jurisdiction over the whole case.

If this analysis worked, it would overrule *Strawbridge* v. *Curtiss*, 7 U.S. 267 (1806), which requires complete diversity between all plaintiffs and defendants. And why shouldn't it work? If it's OK to use supplemental jurisdiction to add a plaintiff who doesn't meet the amount requirement, why shouldn't it be OK to add one who doesn't meet the basic diversity requirement?

In *Exxon-Mobil* the Supreme Court held that it isn't OK. The majority held that a federal court doesn't have diversity jurisdiction *over any claim in the action* unless there is complete diversity between all plaintiffs and defendants. 545 U.S. at 552-554. You can't break the case down, find "complete diversity" between Browning and Blake, and then use the supplemental jurisdiction statute to add other non-diverse parties. So, there is no supplemental jurisdiction over Cowper's claim in this case . . . in fact, there is no jurisdiction over any claim in it, as long as Cowper remains a plaintiff.[8] By this finesse, the Court preserved the complete diversity rule, even though it held that §1367 changed the rules for applying the amount-in-controversy requirement.

---

8. In *Exxon-Mobil*, there was complete diversity between the parties. The only jurisdictional problem was that some plaintiffs did not satisfy the amount-in-controversy requirement.

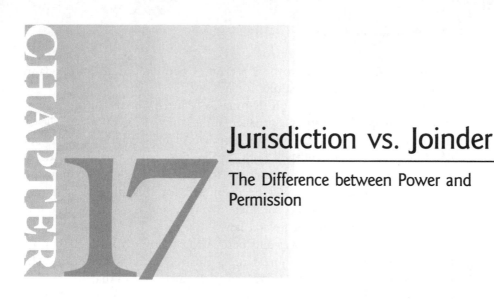

# Jurisdiction vs. Joinder

## The Difference between Power and Permission

---

## INTRODUCTION

Concepts such as supplemental jurisdiction and joinder of parties are difficult enough to grapple with individually. Yet these doctrines do not exist in isolation; they interact to create a system[1] that lawyers must understand as a whole in order to litigate effectively. The real challenge (and fascination) of civil procedure is to try to see how the various pieces of the puzzle fit together into an interrelated, consistent framework for adjudication.

The preceding chapters have separately analyzed the rules governing joinder of claims and parties, on the one hand, and the doctrine of supplemental jurisdiction on the other. However, a particular suit is proper only if both the joinder rules and the jurisdictional requirements are met. This chapter will explore the interrelations of these affiliated doctrines.

As the earlier chapters on joinder demonstrate, no party may assert a claim against another party in the federal courts unless one of the joinder rules — Rules 13, 14, 18, 19, 20, or 24 — authorizes assertion of that claim. However, the fact that the Rules authorize joinder of a particular claim is not sufficient to assure that the federal court may hear it. The court must also have a basis for exercising subject matter jurisdiction over the claim. The federal courts have only limited jurisdictional power; if there is

---

1. Some lawyers, those unfortunates who have never been captivated by the symmetry and logic of it, might call it a maze, a net, or a trap.

no basis in Article III, §2, to hear a claim, "permission" to join a claim under the Rules cannot substitute for it.

An example may help. If Nimitz is injured in an auto accident involving two other drivers, Spruance and Halsey, Rule 20(a)(2) allows him to sue them both in a single suit. Nimitz's claims against both arise out of a single occurrence and will both involve the common factual issue of whose negligence caused the accident. However, if Halsey and Nimitz are both from Texas, the suit will be dismissed for lack of subject matter jurisdiction since there is no complete diversity and the suit (a basic tort claim) does not arise under federal law.

This need for both power and permission follows from basic constitutional doctrine. All federal jurisdiction must be found in the "Article III store-house," and it is up to Congress to confer all or part of that jurisdiction on the lower federal courts. See Judge Sirica's comments, p. 69. The Federal Rules, on the other hand, are promulgated by the Supreme Court. While the Court has the power to make rules to assure the orderly conduct of business in the federal courts (see 28 U.S.C. §2072), it may not use its rule-making power to expand their jurisdiction. Thus, though the Court has broadly authorized joinder of claims and parties under the Federal Rules, the need for subject matter jurisdiction provides an implicit limitation on joinder in every case. The Court itself reaffirmed this limitation in Fed. R. Civ. P. 82, which provides that "[t]hese rules shall not be construed to extend or limit the jurisdiction of the United States district courts."

Although joinder cannot substitute for jurisdiction, it would often make life easier if it could. As we saw in the last chapter, there is a tension between the Rules, which encourage broad joinder of related claims to promote efficiency, and the strict Article III limits on federal court jurisdiction. In cases such as the Halsey example, it would make eminent good sense to hear the claims against Spruance and Halsey together, since the witnesses and much of the evidence will be the same, the legal issues will overlap, and the plaintiff is the same in both claims. The joinder rules encourage and sometimes even require such sensible litigation practice, but good sense may be thwarted at times by the limitations on federal subject matter jurisdiction.

Similarly, in *Owen Equipment & Erection Co. v. Kroger*, 437 U.S. 365 (1978), joinder of Kroger's claim against Owen, the third-party defendant, was permissible under Rule 14. It certainly would have made sense to hear that claim in the same action with the main claim and the third-party claim. The parties were all before the court already, much of the evidence would have been the same, and the judge was already familiar with the case. But the Court balked at extending ancillary jurisdiction to provide a basis for subject matter jurisdiction over the claim. Absolutes are absolutes, and subject matter jurisdiction is as absolute as you get in the civil procedure business.

In many cases supplemental jurisdiction under 28 U.S.C. §1367 will provide a jurisdictional base for additional claims. By granting broad authority to hear related claims, Congress acknowledged the good sense of allowing those related claims to be settled in a single action. In other cases, where supplemental jurisdiction does not authorize the additional claims, there may be an independent basis for subject matter jurisdiction. For example, in the *Kroger* case, if Kroger had been from Colorado, there would have been independent diversity jurisdiction over her claim against Owen. Since joinder was proper under Fed. R. Civ. P. 14(a), both power and permission would have been proper. Yet other cases may fall between the cracks, either for lack of jurisdiction or, conversely, because the joinder rules do not authorize assertion of the claim.

The examples below will help you grasp the distinction and the interrelations between these two problems — permission to join the claims under the Federal Rules and power to hear them under subject matter jurisdiction. In analyzing these cases, assume that all are brought in federal court and that personal jurisdiction is proper. To help with the analysis, draw diagrams of the parties and claims in each example.

## Examples

### Some Basics

1. Nimitz, a citizen of Texas, sues Bradley, from Missouri, and Patton, from California. Nimitz claims that each defendant libeled him, though on different occasions. He claims $100,000 in damages from each. Is the case properly before the court?

2. Nimitz (Texas) sues Bradley (Missouri) for the libel claim and an unrelated breach of contract. He seeks $55,000 in damages on the contract claim and $40,000 on the libel claim. Can the court entertain the claims?

3. Nimitz (Texas) brings suit against Bradley (Missouri) and Clark, a Texas citizen. Nimitz asserts that the two defendants violated his federal civil rights by arresting him under an invalid warrant. Does the federal court have power and permission to hear the claims?

4. Suppose that Nimitz (Texas) sued Clark (Texas) only on the federal civil rights claim and on a state law battery claim arising from the same arrest. Are power and permission both present?

### Mixing Apples and Oranges

5. Assume that Nimitz (Texas) sues Clark (Texas) and Bradley (Missouri). He asserts a federal civil rights claim against Clark for using excessive force in

the course of arresting him and a state law battery claim against Bradley, arising from the same arrest. Is the case properly before the court?

6. Suppose, on the facts of the last example, that Clark counterclaims against Nimitz for $90,000 due on a loan he made to Nimitz six months prior to the arrest. Does the court have both power and permission to hear the claim?

7. Instead of counterclaiming against Nimitz, Clark (Texas) cross-claims against Bradley (Missouri) to recover on a $90,000 loan to him. Is the claim properly before the court?

8. Nimitz (Texas) sues both Bradley (Missouri) and Gavin, also from Missouri, for violation of his federal civil rights. Could the federal court entertain a cross-claim by Bradley against Gavin, alleging that Gavin assaulted him (Bradley) in the course of the arrest?

## A Few Mazes, Nets, or Traps

9. Halsey, a New Jersey citizen, brings a negligence action against MacArthur, from Arkansas, seeking $95,000 for injuries arising out of a boating accident. MacArthur impleads Spruance, from Arkansas, who was piloting a third boat involved in the collision. In his impleader complaint, MacArthur seeks contribution from Spruance on any damages he must pay Halsey for the boating injuries, as well as recovery for libel arising out of a newspaper article in which Spruance deprecated his leadership skills. Can a federal district court in Arkansas entertain the entire suit?

10. Suppose on the facts of example 9, that MacArthur (Arkansas) impleaded Spruance (Arkansas) for contribution, and Halsey, the New Jersey plaintiff, then asserted a $90,000 libel claim against Spruance. Is Halsey's claim against Spruance properly before the court?

11. Assume that Halsey (New Jersey) sues MacArthur (Arkansas) alone on his claim arising out of the boating accident, and MacArthur counterclaims against Halsey and Spruance (Arkansas) for his own injuries in the collision. Can the federal court hear the counterclaims?

12. Halsey (New Jersey) sues MacArthur (Arkansas) for his injuries in the accident, and Spruance (Arkansas) intervenes in the suit to assert a claim against MacArthur for his injuries. May the court hear Spruance's claim?

## Three More Quick Tricks

13. a. Halsey, from New Jersey, sues Old Navy Corporation, a corporation incorporated in Delaware with its principal place of business in

New Jersey, for firing him. His claim against Old Navy is based on the Federal Age Discrimination in Employment Act. He also sues Turner, from Illinois, in the same action, claiming that Turner, a co-worker, misrepresented the quality of his work, leading to his discharge. His claim against Old Navy is for $120,000; his claim against Turner is for $60,000.

b. Halsey, from New Jersey, sues New Army Corporation, a corporation incorporated in Delaware with its principal place of business in New York, for breach of contract, for firing him from his job. In the same action, he sues Turner, from Illinois. He claims that Turner, a co-worker, misrepresented the quality of his work, leading to his discharge. His claim against New Army is for $120,000; his claim against Turner is for $60,000.

c. Halsey, from New Jersey, sues New Army Corporation, a corporation incorporated in Delaware with its principal place of business in New York, for breach of contract, for firing him from his job based on a dispute over policy. In the same action, Phillips, a Utah citizen, joins as a co-plaintiff in the action, claiming that he was demoted for taking Halsey's part in the dispute. Halsey's claim against New Army is for $120,000; Phillips's is for $60,000.

## Explanations

### Some Basics

1. Power:   Yes      Permission:   No

This case in its present form would have to be dismissed. Jurisdiction is proper in the action since there is complete diversity and the amount in controversy exceeds $75,000 against each defendant. However, Nimitz's joinder of Patton and Bradley is improper under the joinder provisions of the Federal Rules. Rule 20(a)(2), which governs joinder of multiple defendants, only authorizes joinder if the plaintiff's claims against both defendants arise out of the same transaction or occurrence. Nimitz alleges libel stemming from two separate incidents; although his theory of liability is the same against each, his claims are based on separate historical occurrences. Thus, joinder under the Rules is not satisfied, though jurisdiction is proper.

Although Nimitz's case can't be heard in its present form, it need not be dismissed in its entirety either. Under Fed. R. Civ. P. 21, the court may drop either Patton or Bradley from the action, eliminating the joinder problem. Nimitz will presumably then file a separate suit against the dropped defendant, perhaps in the same court, which will proceed independent of the original case.

2. Power:   Yes       Permission:   Yes

The court in this case has an adequate basis for joinder and juris-diction. Rule 18(a) authorizes a single plaintiff to join any claims she has against an opposing party, regardless of whether they arise from a single transaction or occurrence. Rule 18(a) is the ultimate in permis-siveness: Whatever claims you have, based on the same or separate historical events, may be joined, so long as the various claims are asserted against a single defendant.

Jurisdiction is also satisfied here because the parties are diverse, and the amount-in-controversy requirement is satisfied by aggregation of Nimitz's two claims against Bradley. A single plaintiff like Nimitz may aggregate claims — including totally unrelated claims — against a single defendant to meet the amount requirement, but not against multiple defendants. See Chapter 5, p. 98.

3. Power:   Yes       Permission:   Yes

This case may properly be brought in federal court. Joinder is proper here, unlike in example 1, because the same transaction or occurrence requirement of Rule 20(a)(2) is met; Nimitz seeks damages against both defendants based on the same underlying real-world event. The second requirement of Rule 20(a)(2), that Nimitz's claims against the two defendants share a common question of law or fact, is also met since Nimitz must presumably prove many of the same facts (for example, the invalidity of the warrant) to prevail on both claims.

Jurisdiction is also satisfied in this suit since Nimitz asserts a federal claim against each defendant. 28 U.S.C. §1331. The lack of complete diversity is therefore irrelevant.

4. Power:   Yes       Permission:   Yes

This is an easy case. Rule 18(a) authorizes joinder of the two claims, even though they are based on different sources of law. It would similarly authorize joinder of any other claims that Nimitz's creative genius (tempered by the ethical constraints of Rule 11) might come up with, regardless of whether they arose from the arrest or any other incident.

Jurisdiction over the federal civil rights claim is proper under 28 U.S.C. §1331. Jurisdiction over the state law claim is also proper. This is a classic "pendent claim," a jurisdictionally insufficient claim that arises from the same nucleus of operative facts as the proper federal claim. Prior to the enactment of the supplemental jurisdiction statute it would have been proper (though discretionary) under *United Mine Workers v. Gibbs*. See Chapter 16, pp. 311-312. It is now authorized by §1367(a), since that statute authorizes the court to hear claims that are part of the same case or controversy as the jurisdictionally sufficient claim. See Chapter 16, example 1.

## Mixing Apples and Oranges

5. Power:   Yes        Permission:   Yes

The problem here is clearly not on the joinder issue; Rule 20(a)(2) authorizes joinder of these claims since they both arise out of the same arrest and will likely involve common questions of fact, such as which injuries were caused by Clark and which by Bradley.

Jurisdiction is more difficult. Jurisdiction is proper over Nimitz's claim against Clark because it arises under federal law. However, his claim against Bradley is based on state law; it must have a separate basis for federal jurisdiction. Nimitz and Bradley are diverse . . . but Nimitz and Clark are not. However, since there is a separate basis for jurisdiction over Clark, his citizenship need not be considered in measuring diversity, even though he is a party to the action. See Chapter 5, example 4. Consequently, Clark does not destroy diversity. If Nimitz seeks more than $75,000 from Bradley the suit is proper.

Even if there were no diversity between Nimitz and Bradley (or if the amount-in-controversy requirement was not met), the supplemental jurisdiction statute would provide a basis for jurisdiction over Nimitz's claim against Bradley. Section 1367(a) authorizes jurisdiction over claims that are part of the same case or controversy as the main claim, including such claims against additional parties. This provision would presumably apply here, since Nimitz's claim against Bradley is part of the same "case" as his claim against Clark, which is properly before the federal court as a claim arising under federal law.[2] Prior to the enactment of §1367, this would have been referred to as "pendent party" jurisdiction and would have required a complex analysis. See the discussion of "essential history" in Chapter 16, pp. 314-316.

6. Power:   No        Permission:   Yes

Here, the federal court lacks power to hear the counterclaim, although the Rules grant permission to join it. Clark's counterclaim is permissive because it arises from a transaction unrelated to the main claim. Rule 13(b) authorizes (but does not require) Clark to assert it in this action.

However, there is no independent basis of subject matter jurisdiction over this claim because it is a state law claim between nondiverse parties. Clark would have to rely on supplemental jurisdiction to support this claim. As discussed in Chapter 16, however, the courts will apply the "common nucleus of operative fact" test in determining whether the added state law claims are part of the same case or controversy as the jurisdictionally sufficient claim. Since the loan

---

2. The limit on such supplemental claims in §1367(b) does not apply, since the case is not "founded solely on §1332," the diversity statute.

counterclaim does not arise out of the same nucleus of operative facts as the arrest claim, it is not part of the same case, so it fails both the *Gibbs* test and the similar "case or controversy" test for supplemental jurisdiction under §1367(a). Presumably, this will always be true of Rule 13(b) permissive counterclaims, since, by definition, they are unrelated to the main claim.

7. Power:   Yes      Permission:   No

Clark will have to save this claim for another day as well. Jurisdictionally, the claim passes muster since there is diversity between Clark and Bradley (the opposing parties on the cross-claim) and the amount in controversy is sufficient. But the Rules don't authorize assertion of this claim in the Nimitz lawsuit: Rule 13(g) limits cross-claims to those arising out of the same transaction or occurrence as the main claim.

This result makes good sense. There is no relationship between the factual or legal issues relevant to the arrest claim and those relevant to the loan cross-claim and, therefore, no efficiency to be gained from allowing them to be heard in the same suit.

8. Power:   Yes      Permission:   Yes

This is a nice contrast to example 7. Here, unlike example 7, joinder is proper under Rule 13(g), since the cross-claim arises out of the same incident as the main claim. There is no independent basis for subject matter jurisdiction, but jurisdiction is supplied by §1367(a), the supplemental jurisdiction statute, because the cross-claim arises out of the same nucleus of facts as the main claim.

Because cross-claims can only be asserted under Rule 13(g) if they arise from the same set of events as the main claim, they should always satisfy the test for supplemental jurisdiction. But see 28 U.S.C. §1367(b), which may sometimes deny supplemental jurisdiction to cross-claims brought by plaintiffs.

## A Few Mazes, Nets, or Traps

9. Power:   In part      Permission:   Yes

The Rules authorize joinder in this case, but jurisdiction is only proper over part of the case. First of all, I asked whether an *Arkansas* federal district court could hear the action. Really, this was just to blow a little smoke. Personal jurisdiction and venue are satisfied because both the defendant and third-party defendant are domiciled in Arkansas. *Milliken v. Meyer*, 311 U.S. 457 (1940); 28 U.S.C. §1391(a)(1). And the particular federal district in which the suit is brought is irrelevant to determination of subject matter jurisdiction. See Chapter 5, example 1a.

Joinder is proper in this action under Rules 14 and 18. MacArthur properly brought in Spruance under Rule 14(a)(1), since he is seeking to recover from Spruance part of any damages that Halsey recovers from him, MacArthur. MacArthur's claim for contribution satisfies this requirement because he is asking Spruance to pay him half of any judgment Halsey wins, by way of "contribution" to the judgment. MacArthur's libel claim is also proper: Under Rule 18(a) MacArthur may assert any additional claims he has against Spruance, once he has asserted one claim against him that is proper under Rule 14(a)(1). MacArthur could not have impleaded Spruance on the basis of the libel claim since it is an independent claim that does not satisfy the "may be liable to the third-party plaintiff for all or part of the plaintiffs claim" requirement of Rule 14(a). But once he impleads Spruance on a proper Rule 14(a) claim, he may pile on any claims he has against Spruance. See A. Greenbaum, Jacks or Better to Open: Limitations on Co-Party and Third-Party Joinder, 74 Minn. L. Rev. 507, 531-534 (1990).

So much for permission. The claims must also be analyzed individually as to jurisdictional power. There is supplemental jurisdiction over MacArthur's contribution claim against Spruance since it arises from the same nucleus of operative facts as Halsey's jurisdictionally sufficient claim against MacArthur. But supplemental jurisdiction does not extend to the libel claim since it is unrelated to the main claim and therefore not part of the same case or controversy under §1367(a). Nor is there an independent basis for subject matter jurisdiction since it is a state law claim between non-diverse parties.

10. Power:   Yes     Permission:   No

This example involves a state law claim somewhat similar to Kroger's claim against Owen, the third-party defendant. Supplemental jurisdiction would not apply, because it does not arise out of the same events as the main claim, but since the claim is between diverse parties and is for more than $75,000, it is within the court's independent diversity jurisdiction. Supplemental jurisdiction is unnecessary where there is a direct basis for jurisdiction over a claim, as there is here.

However, the Rules do not authorize joinder of this claim. Claims by plaintiffs against third-party defendants are authorized by Rule 14(a)(3), which limits such claims to those arising from the same transaction or occurrence as the main claim. Halsey's claim is independent of the boating accident and therefore must be sued upon separately.

Curiously, if Halsey asserted a claim against Spruance for injuries arising from the boating accident, he could then pile on the unrelated libel claim under Rule 18(a). Jurisdiction and joinder would both be satisfied, and the court would be able to entertain the claim. However, it would likely be severed under Rule 21 and proceed effectively as a separate action anyway.

11. Power:   Yes     Permission:   Yes

Both joinder and jurisdiction are satisfied in this case. Joinder is proper under Rule 13(a) and (h); MacArthur has asserted a compulsory counterclaim against Halsey, and added Spruance (who destroys diversity) as an additional party to it, which is authorized by Rule 13(h). Visually the case looks like this:

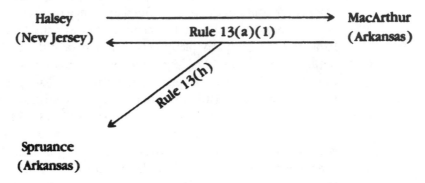

As to the power question, supplemental jurisdiction will provide a basis for jurisdiction. Section 1367(a) is apparently intended to reach these claims, since they arise from the same dispute over the boating accident. Even though MacArthur has added a new party to the compulsory counterclaim, §1367(a) expressly states that supplemental jurisdiction includes "claims that involve the joinder or intervention of additional parties." Further, the exceptions in §1367(b) do not apply, since the party asserting the added claims is not a plaintiff. Thus, even though complete diversity is lacking, the court may hear the counterclaims.

The irony here is that MacArthur may assert a counterclaim that he could not have asserted as an original claim: If he had sued Halsey and Spruance together, the case would have been dismissed for lack of diversity. While this result is ironic, it is not completely illogical. Prior to the enactment of §1367 the courts had given defendants hauled into court against their will broad opportunities to settle all claims arising out of the events that gave rise to the litigation. See *Kroger*, 437 U.S. at 375-377 (distinguishing jurisdictionally insufficient claims by defendants from those by plaintiffs on this basis). In §1367, Congress has preserved this defendant bias by barring claims by plaintiffs that are inconsistent with complete diversity, but allowing similar claims by defending parties.

12. Power:   No        Permission:   Yes

Permission to join Spruance's claim is provided here by Rule 24(b)(1)(B), which allows a party to seek intervention if her claim shares a question of fact or law with the main claim. Here, Spruance and Halsey will both seek to prove that MacArthur was negligent, thus satisfying the Rule 24(b) standard. Of course, Spruance would need to seek leave to intervene, since permissive intervention under Rule 24(b) is always at the discretion of the court.

However, Congress has barred supplemental jurisdiction over this claim in 28 U.S.C. §1367(b). That section bars supplemental jurisdiction over claims by persons "seeking to intervene as plaintiffs under Rule 24 of such rules, when exercising supplemental jurisdiction over such claims would be inconsistent with the jurisdictional requirements of section 1332." Allowing Spruance to intervene here would be inconsistent with the requirements of §1332, since it would allow a claim by one Arkansas citizen against another, based on state law. If Spruance were allowed to intervene in this case, it would allow him to evade the complete diversity requirement. Instead of suing with Halsey, which would be improper under *Strawbridge v. Curtiss*, 7 U.S. 267 (1806), he could simply allow Halsey to start the suit and then achieve the same result by intervening. Obviously, Congress adopted the view of the Supreme Court, expressed in *Kroger*, that, supplemental jurisdiction should not provide a means of evading the complete diversity requirement. Cf. *Exxon-Mobil Corp. v. Allapatta Services, Inc.* 545 U.S. 546, 560-567 (2005) (supplemental jurisdiction cannot support jurisdiction over case based on minimal diversity).

This case presents a situation in which it would make good litigation sense to take jurisdiction. The claims arise out of the same nucleus of operative facts, thus satisfying the constitutional test for a single case. In terms of efficiency there is as much justification for hearing this claim as there is for hearing a third-party impleader claim, or MacArthur's counterclaim against Spruance in example 11. But without a statutory basis, the court can't exercise jurisdiction over the claim, and here Congress has withheld the authority to do so.

## Three More Quick Tricks

13. a. Power:   Yes        Permission:   Yes

Let's start with subject matter jurisdiction. Halsey has sued Old Navy, a non-diverse defendant. But he has sued it under federal law. Jurisdiction over this claim is proper under 28 U.S.C. §1331, as a claim arising under federal law. There's no need for the parties to be diverse in such a case. And supplemental jurisdiction applies to his claim against Turner, since it arises out of the same set of facts. Section 1367(a) applies, even though Halsey has no independently proper claim against Turner; see the last sentence of §1367(a). Nor does §1367(b) bar the claim; it only applies to diversity cases.

Joinder is proper too. Halsey sues the two defendants on claims arising out of the same underlying event, his discharge. The fact that they are based on different legal theories does not matter. Doubtless there will be some common question of fact involved, such as the reason that he was fired. So the requirements for joinder under Rule 20(a)(2) are met.

b. Power: In part     Permission:   Yes

Joinder is proper here under Rule 20(a)(2), just as it was in the last example. Halsey sues two defendants for claims arising from the same discharge, which will doubtless raise at least one common question of law or fact.

The jurisdictional analysis is more perplexing. There is complete diversity between Halsey and the defendants, which is a good start; Exxon-Mobil clearly requires that even in light of the supplemental jurisdiction statute. And, in Exxon-Mobil, the Supreme Court held that §1367 can provide jurisdiction over claims that, like Halsey's, fail to meet the amount-in-controversy requirement. However, oddly, the text of §1367(b) appears to bar this claim, since it is a claim by a plaintiff against a party joined under Rule 20. See Chapter 16, example 13.

c. Power: Yes     Permission:   Yes

Once again, joinder is proper here under Rule 20(a), since the two plaintiffs' claims arise from the same underlying events and will pose at least one common question (e.g., was the policy disagreement the cause of the adverse employment actions?).

Here, however, jurisdiction is proper, according to the Supreme Court's interpretation of §1367. There is complete diversity between the plaintiffs and New Army. Further, Halsey's claim exceeds $75,000, so it is a claim that, on its own, gives the court "original jurisdiction." Since there is one such claim, all other claims that are part of the same case or controversy get swept in under §1367(a) . . . unless excluded by §1367(b). As Exxon-Mobil holds, nothing in §1367(b) bars supplemental jurisdiction over claims by multiple plaintiffs against a single defendant. So the court has jurisdiction over Phillips's claim as well.

# PART IV

## Steps in the Litigation Process

# CHAPTER 18

# The Bearer of Bad Tidings

Service of Process in the Federal Courts

## INTRODUCTION

Some of the most profound protections of our constitutional system are astoundingly simple. "Due process of law" under the Fourteenth Amendment, for example, guarantees parties the basic right to notice of a court's intention to adjudicate their rights and an opportunity for those parties to be heard before the court proceeds to do so. "An elementary and fundamental requirement of due process in any proceeding which is to be accorded finality is notice reasonably calculated, under all the circumstances, to apprise interested parties of the pendency of the action and afford them an opportunity to present their objections." *Mullane v. Central Hanover Bank*, 339 U.S. 306, 311 (1950). In civil suits, this requirement is fulfilled through service of process.

The term *service of process* is often used to refer to the delivery to a party or witness of various court orders required by the relevant rules of law to be served upon him, including subpoenas, writs, and other orders that are entered in the course of litigation. However, in a stricter sense the term is used — as we will use it here — to refer to service of the initial notice to the defendant of the filing of a lawsuit against him. Service of this initial summons both notifies the defendant that he has been sued and informs him that the court intends to proceed to adjudicate his rights. The summons in the *Schulansky* case, for example (infra p. 640), specifically warns the defendants that they must respond to the plaintiff's complaint, or judgment by default will be entered against them.

345

All courts, state and federal, have elaborate provisions governing service of this initial notice to defendants. State service provisions may be found in statutes (see, e.g., N.Y. Civ. Prac. Law §§305-318) or in court rules (see, e.g., Mass. R. Civ. P. 4, set forth on pp. 352-353 for use in this chapter). This chapter explores the intricacies of Rule 4 of the Federal Rules of Civil Procedure, which governs service of process in the federal courts, as an example of service provisions.

Rule 4 specifies in detail what documents must be served on the defendant (Rule 4(c)(1)), the contents of the summons (Rule 4(a)), how the papers must be served (Rules 4(e)-(j)), when they must be served (Rule 4(m)), who must serve them (Rule 4(c)(2)), and how the requirement of service may be waived (Rule 4(d)). For example, if you look at Form 3 of the Federal Rules Forms, which follows the Federal Rules of Civil Procedure, you will see that the summons there complies with each of the requirements in Rule 4(a) as to the contents of the summons. It provides for the signature of the clerk and the seal of the court, identifies the court and the parties, provides the name of the plaintiff's attorney, states the time within which the defendant must respond, and that default judgment will enter against him if he fails to do so. Compare the summons in the *Schulansky* case (infra p. 640), drawn to comply with similar provisions as to form in Mass. R. Civ. P. 4(b).

---

# METHODS OF SERVICE OF PROCESS

Rule 4 contains detailed provisions for service of process on various categories of defendants, including individuals, corporations and other business entities, the United States, and other governmental defendants. Fed. R. Civ. P. 4(e) to (j). These provisions apply, whether the defendant is served in the district where suit is pending, or in other federal districts. However, Rules 4(f) and 4(h)(2) contain special provisions for service on individuals and corporations in other countries.

## Methods of Service on Individuals

Fed. R. Civ. P. 4(e) governs service of process on an individual defendant, that is, a person. It provides five different methods for serving process on individual defendants in federal suits. The three traditional methods are found in Rule 4(e)(2), which authorizes service by personally delivering the summons and complaint to the defendant, or by leaving copies of the summons and the complaint at his dwelling or usual place of abode with a person of suitable age and discretion residing therein, or by delivering the papers to an agent appointed by the defendant to receive service of process on his behalf.

Until 1983 service by personal delivery on a defendant had to be made by a United States marshal or a person specially designated by the court to serve process. This provision frequently led to delays in service or motions to the court for appointment of special process servers because the marshals were too busy with other duties to serve process promptly. Now, however, Rule 4(c)(2) provides that personal service may be made by any person who is over 18 years of age and not a party to the action. In most cases, plaintiff's counsel will hire a constable or professional process server to serve the papers.

The plaintiff's fourth option is to serve individual defendants under the provisions governing service on individuals in the courts of the state where the federal court sits. Fed. R. Civ. P. 4(e)(1). The plaintiff in an action in the federal district court in Massachusetts, for example, may use any methods for service of process on individuals that apply in the Massachusetts Superior Courts; that is, any of the methods provided in Mass. R. Civ. P. 4(d)(1) (see infra p. 353). If the suit were brought in federal court in Maine, the plaintiff would look to the service rules of the Maine courts. Note that service under the state rules pursuant to Rule 4(e)(1) is an *alternative* to service under the other methods provided in Rule 4(e)(2); the plaintiff may choose whichever he prefers.

Rule 4 also authorizes a fifth method of serving process on individual defendants who are served *outside* the state where the action is pending. Rule 4(e)(1) authorizes service pursuant to the law of the state where the defendant is actually being served. Suppose, for example, that Vaughan brings suit in the federal district court for the District of Massachusetts against Spenser, who lives in Maine, and wishes to serve process on Spenser there. Rule 4(e)(1) authorizes Vaughan to use any method for service on an individual defendant authorized by the *Maine* service rules, since that is the "state . . . where service is made."

# Methods of Service on Corporations and Other Entities

Methods of service of process on corporations or other entities (such as partnerships or unincorporated associations) are specified in Rule 4(h). If the defendant is served anywhere in the United States ("in a judicial district of the United States"), Rule 4(h)(1) applies. If the defendant is served outside the United States ("at a place not within any judicial district of the United States"), Rule 4(h)(2) applies.

Under Rule 4(h)(1), the available methods parallel the methods for service on individuals under Rule 4(e). Service may be made by delivery of a copy of the summons and complaint to an officer, managing or general agent of the defendant, or to an agent authorized to receive service of process. Alternatively, service may be made by one of the methods prescribed in Rule 4(e)(1), which includes service by a method prescribed by the law of the state where the federal court sits or by a method prescribed by the law of the state in which process is to be served on the defendant. (Presumably, however, this means a method prescribed by the state's law for service *on a corporation*; it does not make methods for service on individuals under state law applicable to corporations.)

To illustrate these options, assume that Vaughan sues the Sidney Corporation, a corporation incorporated in Maine and conducting most of its business there, in the federal district court for the District of Massachusetts. Under Rule 4(h)(1)(B), he could serve process on Sidney by delivering the papers to an officer, managing or general agent of Sidney, or an agent authorized to receive service of process for Sidney. Alternatively, he could serve Sidney under any of the provisions for serving process *on a corporation* available under the Massachusetts rules for service of process. See Rule 4(h)(1)(A) In addition, to serve process in Maine, he could also use any method available under the Maine rules for serving process on a corporation.

# WAIVER OF SERVICE OF PROCESS

Rule 4(d) also provides an alternative to the various methods of service of process described above. It authorizes the plaintiff to solicit a waiver of all these technicalities by sending the defendant the complaint, two copies of a notice of the action and a request that the defendant waive formal service of the summons and complaint upon him. The defendant is supposed to return the request, thus waiving formal service.

Rule 4(d) contains several provisions intended to give defendants an incentive to waive formal service. First, Rule 4(d)(1) creates a duty to avoid "unnecessary expenses of serving the summons" — presumably by agreeing to waive service. Second, under Rule 4(d)(2)(B), the court must impose the costs of service on a defendant who refuses to waive service without good cause. Third, Rule 4(d)(3) offers defendants a tempting reward for waiving service: It gives them 60 days, rather than the usual 20, to respond to the complaint. For busy defense counsel, this carrot may be more persuasive than the relatively mild threat of paying the costs of service if they refuse to waive it.

# THE RELATION OF SERVICE OF PROCESS TO PERSONAL JURISDICTION

It is crucial to distinguish the concept of service of process from the related concept of personal jurisdiction. In many cases, particularly older cases, challenges to personal jurisdiction have been framed in terms of "insufficient service of process," although the actual basis of the defendant's objection was insufficient contact between the defendant and the state to support personal jurisdiction. In modern phraseology, a challenge to service of process (a motion to dismiss for insufficiency of service of process under Fed. R. Civ. P. 12(b)(5)) attacks the adequacy of the method used by the plaintiff to give the defendant notice of the action (the subject of this chapter), not the power of the court to exercise personal jurisdiction over him, which would be raised by a motion to dismiss for lack of personal jurisdiction under Fed. R. Civ. P. 12(b)(2).

It is not surprising that the *Pennoyer*-era cases blended the two concepts. When *Pennoyer* was decided, service of process on the defendant within the forum state was the predominant means of obtaining jurisdiction, as well as giving notice to the defendant of the suit. Thus, under *Pennoyer*, if service was not made properly (that is, delivered personally to the defendant within the state), personal jurisdiction was not obtained. The two requirements were thus frequently discussed as though they were interchangeable; but today the two are quite distinct, and either may be satisfied though the other is not.

For example, suppose that Drayton is injured when Lovelace, a vacationing Marylander, hits him on the street in Salt Lake City, Utah. He sues Lovelace in Utah and serves process on Lovelace by publishing notice of the suit in a Salt Lake City newspaper. On these facts, the Utah court would have the constitutional power to exercise personal jurisdiction over Lovelace, based on the in-state contact of causing tortious injury in the state. However, service would be improper, since in most cases publication is not a constitutionally adequate means of informing a defendant that he has been sued. In this example, a Rule 12(b)(2) motion would not be granted, but a Rule 12(b)(5) motion would.

By contrast, suppose that Drayton sued Lovelace in Alaska for the Utah accident, and served the summons and complaint on Lovelace by personal delivery to him at his Maryland home. On these facts, the Alaska court would lack personal jurisdiction over Lovelace, assuming that he has no contacts with Alaska. However, service of process in the action would be proper under Fed. R. Civ. P. 4(e)(2); personal service is as good as it gets as a means of informing a defendant of the suit. On these facts, the action could not proceed. Proper service is not a substitute for a basis for the court to exercise personal jurisdiction: *Both* requirements must be met in order for the suit to proceed. While historically intertwined, these two due process requirements are distinct, and should always be analyzed separately.

# THE FEDERAL "LONG-ARM STATUTE" IN RULE 4

Most of Rule 4 deals with the mechanics of service, that is, how the defendant is actually informed that a lawsuit has been filed against him. However, Rule 4 also contains a "long-arm statute" for the federal courts. Rule 4(k), entitled "Territorial Limits of Effective Service," specifies when a federal court may assert personal jurisdiction over a defendant served under Rule 4. In this sense, it is like a state long-arm statute, by which a state legislature specifies the circumstances in which personal jurisdiction may be exercised by its courts.

When suit is brought in a federal court, just as when it is brought in a state court, two questions must be asked to determine whether that court can assert jurisdiction over the defendant. First, has the relevant legislature authorized the jurisdiction, and second, if it has, would it be constitutional for the court to exercise jurisdiction in the circumstances of the particular case? See Chapter 2, which analyzes state grants of jurisdiction in long-arm statutes, and the examples in that chapter, which compare the reach of long-arm statutes to constitutional limits on personal jurisdiction.

In federal suits, the first question, the legislative authority for federal courts to exercise personal jurisdiction, is addressed in Rule 4(k).[1] That rule provides that service of process "is effective to establish jurisdiction over the person of a defendant" in four circumstances. First, the federal court is authorized to assert jurisdiction if the courts of the state in which the federal court sits could assert jurisdiction over the defendant. Rule 4(k)(1)(A). In other words, if the *state* long-arm statute authorizes jurisdiction in the circumstances of the case, and it would be constitutional for the *state* court to assert jurisdiction under Fourteenth Amendment analysis, then the federal court may do so as well. In most cases, this subsection of Rule 4(k) will apply, because the other three subsections cover fairly limited situations. Under it, the reach of personal jurisdiction in a federal court is *the same as the reach of personal jurisdiction in the courts of the state in which it sits.* An Arizona federal court will exercise jurisdiction to the same extent that an Arizona state court would; a Michigan federal court will exercise jurisdiction to the same extent that a Michigan state court would; and so on.

---

1. Although Rule 4 was promulgated by the Supreme Court rather than Congress, the Court promulgates the Rules under congressional authority in the Rules Enabling Act. Thus, Rule 4(k) is analogous to a legislative grant of the power to exercise personal jurisdiction.

In addition, Rule 4(k) authorizes federal courts to take jurisdiction in certain other limited situations, including impleaded parties served within 100 miles of the courthouse (Rule 4(k)(1)(B)), parties subject to interpleader jurisdiction (Rule 4(k)(1)(C)), and in federal question cases, over parties who have sufficient contacts with the United States as a whole to constitutionally support jurisdiction, but whose contacts would not suffice to support personal jurisdiction in the courts of any state. Rule 4(k)(2). Last, service will support jurisdiction if some other federal statute provides that service suffices to support jurisdiction for a particular type of case. Rule 4(k)(1)(C).

As with state long-arm statutes, the fact that Rule 4(k) authorizes the assertion of jurisdiction will not always mean that it is constitutional to exercise it; the second prong of the analysis must always be considered as well. However, recall that the constitutional constraints on a *federal court's* exercise of personal jurisdiction are found in the Fifth Amendment due process clause, not in the Fourteenth Amendment. The Fifth Amendment has usually been held to require only that the defendant have minimum contacts with the *United States as a whole* to support jurisdiction, not with any particular state. See Chapter 6, pp. 113-114; see generally R. Casad, Personal Jurisdiction in Federal Question Cases, 70 Tex. L. Rev. 1589, 1599-1606 (1992).

Despite the fact that the *Fifth Amendment* due process clause defines the limits of a federal court's power to exercise jurisdiction, in most cases a federal court will actually look to the *Fourteenth Amendment* to determine the limits on its power to exercise jurisdiction over the defendants. This is because in most cases Fed. R. Civ. P. 4(k)(1)(A) applies. That rule tells the federal judge to apply the limits on personal jurisdiction that would apply in the local state court, including both the local long-arm statute and Fourteenth Amendment constraints that would limit state court jurisdiction. Thus, the *Rule*, not the *Constitution*, requires the federal court to look to the Fourteenth Amendment. The Constitution would frequently allow the court to exercise a broader reach of personal jurisdiction.[2]

Several other mechanical aspects of service should be mentioned. First, the person making service must make proof of service (often called "return of service") by promptly filing an affidavit with the court setting forth the manner in which service was made. Fed. R. Civ. P. 4(l). Proof of service is often inserted on the summons itself. See the Schulansky summons (infra p. 640), which contains a printed form for proof of service.

---

2. This has the salutary effect of neutralizing the reach of personal jurisdiction as a forum-shopping factor between the state and federal courts. Since the federal court will generally be bound by the state limits on jurisdiction, under Rule 4(k)(1)(a), plaintiffs will not choose federal court in order to obtain broader personal jurisdiction over defendants.

*Second*, Rule 4(m) specifies that service of process must be made within 120 days of filing the complaint, or the action may be dismissed. Earlier versions of Rule 4 did not specify a time limit for service, and in some cases service was upheld long after the complaint was filed, so long as there was no unreasonable delay on the plaintiff's part in attempting it. Under Rule 4(m), the court must dismiss the action if the plaintiff fails to show "good cause" for failure to make service within the 120-day period. This time limit for service of the summons and complaint is separate from and in addition to the requirements of any applicable statute of limitations. The fact that an action is *filed* within the limitations period (which, in many cases, will satisfy the statute of limitations) does not affect this additional requirement in Rule 4(m) to *serve* the complaint within the 120-day period.

*Third*, as noted earlier, many other papers get "served" on parties and witnesses in law suits in addition to the original complaint. All motions, pleadings (other than the complaint), discovery requests, and other papers filed with the court must be served on each party to the action; all parties have a right to notice of subsequent filings in the case, as well as notice of the commencement of suit. However, virtually all such papers may be served under the more flexible provisions of Fed. R. Civ. P. 5, which authorizes service of papers subsequent to the complaint by mailing them to the party's attorney. See the certificate of service at the end of the answer in the *Schulansky* case, infra p. 667) and the accompanying note (p. 673).[3] The complaint is singled out for special treatment because it is the first notice the defendant receives of the filing of the suit. If he does not receive this notice, he may never learn of the action at all. Once he *has* been properly informed of the suit, however, the law presumes that he will keep an eye on the docket and eventually learn of any paper that was served by mail under Rule 5 but, for one reason or another, never reached him.

In analyzing the following examples, assume that all actions are brought in the federal district court for the District of Massachusetts. Because Federal Rule 4 incorporates state provisions for service of process in some circumstances, you will have to consider the methods of service provided in Mass. R. Civ. P. 4, as well as those in Federal Rule 4. The relevant portions of Massachusetts Rule of Civil Procedure 4 are as follows:

> **(c) By Whom Served.** Except as otherwise permitted by paragraph (h) of this rule, service of all process shall be made by a sheriff, by his deputy, or by a special sheriff; by any other person duly authorized by law; by some person specially appointed by the court for that purpose; or in the case of service of process outside the Commonwealth, by an individual

---

3. Rule 5 now authorizes service of subsequent filings by electronic means, if the parties consent to it. Fed. R. Civ. P. 5(b)(2)(E). Courts are increasingly developing methods of electronic filing and service, which will likely become the norm in the near future.

permitted to make service of process under the law of this Commonwealth or under the law of the place in which the service is to be made, or who is designated by a court of this Commonwealth. A subpoena may be served as provided in Rule 45. Notwithstanding the provisions of this paragraph (c), wherever in these rules service is permitted to be made by certified or registered mail, the mailing may be accomplished by the party or his attorney.

**(d) Summons: Personal Service within the Commonwealth.** The summons and a copy of the complaint shall be served together. The plaintiff shall furnish the person making service with such copies as are necessary. Service shall be made as follows:

(1) Upon an individual by delivering a copy of the summons and of the complaint to him personally; or by leaving copies thereof at his last and usual place of abode; or by delivering a copy of the summons and of the complaint to an agent authorized by appointment or by statute to receive service of process, provided that any further notice required by such statute be given. . . .

(2) Upon a domestic corporation (public or private), a foreign corporation subject to suit within the Commonwealth, or an unincorporated association subject to suit within the Commonwealth under a common name: by delivering a copy of the summons and of the complaint to an officer, to a managing or general agent, or to the person in charge of the business at the principal place of business thereof within the Commonwealth, if any; or by delivering such copies to any other agent authorized by appointment or by law to receive service of process, provided that any further notice required by law be given. . . .

**(e) Same: Personal Service outside the Commonwealth.** When any statute or law of the Commonwealth authorizes service of process outside the Commonwealth, the service shall be made by delivering a copy of the summons and of the complaint: (1) in any appropriate manner prescribed in subdivision (d) of this Rule; or (2) in the manner prescribed by the law of the place in which the service is made for service in that place in an action in any of its courts of general jurisdiction; or (3) by any form of mail addressed to the person to be served and requiring a signed receipt; or (4) as directed by the appropriate foreign authority in response to a letter rogatory; or (5) as directed by order of the court.

## Examples

## A Comedy of Errors

1. Marvell brings a pro se[4] diversity action against Donne for breach of contract. He serves Donne by having a copy of the complaint delivered to Donne personally at his summer home on Cape Cod, in Hyannis, Massachusetts. Is service proper?

---

4. A pro se action is one brought by a party who is not represented by a lawyer.

2. The court upholds Donne's objection to the original service and orders Marvell to re-serve Donne properly. Marvell takes a copy of the complaint and summons, drives to Hyannis, and serves them personally on Donne. Donne moves again to dismiss for improper service of process. Why will the motion be granted?

3. Disgusted with the whole process (no pun intended), Marvell retains Herbert to represent him. Herbert promptly serves process on Donne by having Marple, an investigator from his office, deliver copies of the summons and complaint to Donne in Hyannis. Donne is not there when the investigator arrives, so she pushes the papers under the front door. Donne renews his objection to the method of service. Is the objection valid?

4. Herbert changes tactics and orders Marple to serve the summons on Donne at his year-round residence in Boston. Since the elusive Donne is not at home, Marple serves copies of the summons and complaint by leaving them with Donne's sister, who lives in Texas but is visiting Donne to run in the Boston Marathon. Though not to be found at home, Donne reappears faithfully in court to object once again to the manner of service. Has Herbert cured the defect?

5. If Donne is elusive, Herbert is tenacious. He sends the sheriff to Donne's house in Boston to serve the papers. As the sheriff knocks on the front door, Donne leaves by the back for a pressing appointment. The sheriff slips the papers under the front door and leaves. Is service finally proper?

6. Assume that Herbert decides to try to get Donne to waive service instead of using the methods in the prior examples.
   a. How should he solicit the waiver of service from Donne?
   b. Suppose he follows the required waiver procedure, but receives no waiver back from Donne. What should he do next?

## At Your Service

7. Herrick sues Marlowe for personal injuries arising out of an accident while visiting Marlowe's truck repair garage in Revere, Massachusetts. The action is again brought in the federal district court for the District of Massachusetts. Herrick serves copies of the summons and complaint by having them delivered in hand to Daniel, Marlowe's service manager, at the garage. Is service proper?

8. Herrick sues both Marlowe and Daniel for his injuries arising out of the accident at the shop. He serves the complaint by having his

investigator, Poirot, deliver a copy of the complaint and summons to Marlowe at the shop. Is service proper?

9. Herrick sues Marlowe in Massachusetts federal district court for the injuries suffered in the accident at the shop, and Marlowe decides to implead Daniel under Fed. R. Civ. P. 14, on the theory that Daniel, who actually caused the injury, should indemnify him for any judgment Herrick obtains in the main action. Marlowe serves the complaint on Daniel under Fed. R. Civ. P. 5, by mailing a copy to him at his home in Boston. Is service proper?

10. Assume that Marlowe has incorporated his business in Massachusetts, as Poetic Truck Repair, Inc., with himself as president. Herrick decides to sue the corporation for injuries he suffered on its premises.
    a. He serves the complaint by having Poirot take the papers to Marlowe's house and leave them there with Marlowe's wife. Is service proper?
    b. He serves the complaint by having Poirot deliver copies of the summons and complaint to Daniel at the shop. Is service proper on the corporation?

## Process and Due Process

11. As the Introduction explains, service of process is a separate requirement from personal jurisdiction. The fact that service was properly made on the defendant does not mean that the court has the power to require the defendant to defend in the forum state. Conversely, the fact that it would be permissible, under due process analysis, to require the defendant to defend the action in the forum state does not eliminate the need to provide adequate notice of the action. Consider whether the two requirements have been met in the cases below.

    Davies sues the Holland Corporation, a corporation incorporated and doing business only in Florida, in federal district court for the District of Massachusetts, for injuries suffered in an accident in Florida. She serves process on Holland by mailing a copy of the summons and complaint, certified mail, return receipt requested, to Chapman, the president of Holland Corporation, at the corporate headquarters in Florida.
    a. Is service proper?
    b. Does the court have personal jurisdiction over Holland Corporation?

12. In the same case, Davies sues Holland Corporation in Massachusetts federal court and serves process on Chapman, Holland's president, while he is visiting his daughter in Boston.

    a. Is service proper?

    b. Does the court have personal jurisdiction over Holland Corporation?

13. Sidney, a New Hampshire contractor, does occasional business in the town of Pepperell, just over the border in Massachusetts. He builds a garage for Chapman in Pepperell and Chapman, unhappy with the work, sues Sidney in federal court in Massachusetts. She serves process on Sidney by delivering a copy of the summons and complaint to the Pepperell town clerk under Mass. Gen. L. ch. 227, §5A, which provides that a person who does business in a city or town of the Commonwealth appoints the town clerk as his agent for service of process for suits arising out of that business.

    a. Is service proper?

    b. Does the court have personal jurisdiction over Sidney?

14. Suppose on the facts of example 13 that Chapman serves Sidney by having the sheriff slip the summons and complaint under the front door at his home in Peterborough, New Hampshire. Sidney's housekeeper picks the papers up along with the newspaper, and later absent-mindedly throws them out. Sidney does not learn of the suit and default judgment enters against him.

    a. Is the judgment valid?

    b. If you represented Sidney, what would you do?

## Unlucky Number 15

15. National Assurance Corporation, an insurer, brings an action under the federal interpleader act, 28 U.S.C. §1335, against a number of defendants, to determine who is entitled to the insurance proceeds on a building that was destroyed by fire in Atlanta, Georgia. The action is brought in the federal district court for the District of Massachusetts. A special service statute, 28 U.S.C. §2361, applies to actions under the interpleader act. It authorizes service of process anywhere in the nation in interpleader cases and provides that service shall be "addressed to and served by the United States marshals for the respective districts where the claimants reside or may be found." National's counsel serves process on Drayton, a co-owner of the building and one of the defendants, by mailing the summons and complaint, certified mail, return receipt requested, to Drayton at his home in Louisiana. Drayton has no contacts with Massachusetts.

    a. Is service proper?

b. Does the court have personal jurisdiction over Drayton Corporation? See Fed. R. Civ. P. 4(k)(1)(C).

## Explanations

### A Comedy of Errors

1. Service is improper because Marvell has only delivered a copy of the complaint itself. Rule 4(c)(1) requires both the summons and the complaint to be served on the defendant.

   This requirement makes sense. The complaint is simply the plaintiff's introductory pleading, stating the nature of the case and the relief sought. It is designed to inform the defendant of the events that gave rise to the plaintiff's claim and the nature of his claim. The summons, on the other hand, is an official court document, issued by the court and signed by the court clerk (see Fed. R. Civ. P. 4(a)), commanding the defendant to respond to the accompanying complaint and telling him the time within which it must be done. The Schulansky summons, for example, warns the defendant that "[y]ou are hereby summoned and required to serve . . . an answer to the complaint which is herewith served upon you." It is the court itself, not the plaintiff, that has the authority to compel the defendant to respond to the complaint, and it is the summons by which the court exercises that power.

2. This time Marvell has served the right documents but has done it in the wrong manner. Presumably, he is proceeding under Fed. R. Civ, P. 4(e)(2), which authorizes service by delivering the papers to the defendant. However, Rule 4(c)(2) provides that service of process may be made by any person who is not a party and is not less than 18 years of age. Marvell is a party; the rule bars him from serving the summons and complaint himself, perhaps on the theory that such service might lead to immediate (but distinctly nonjudicial) settlement of the parties' differences.

3. Technicalities, technicalities. Herbert has apparently relied again on Federal Rule 4(e)(2) but has not fulfilled the requirements of that subsection. First, it is doubtful that Donne's summer house constitutes his "dwelling or usual place of abode"; it is apparently a vacation home. Second, the rule requires the process server to leave the summons and complaint with a person of suitable age and discretion residing therein. Herbert has clearly failed to meet this requirement.

   Herbert might claim that service was proper under Mass. R. Civ. P. 4 (d)(1). Remember that Fed. R. Civ. P. 4(e)(1) allows Marvell to serve Donne under the state service rules. Mass. R. Civ. P. 4(d)(1), unlike its federal counterpart, does not require that the summons and complaint be left with anyone. However, it does require them to be left at the "dwelling or usual place of abode," which arguably does not include a seasonal home. In addition, under the Massachusetts rule, service must be made by a sheriff or other official process server. Mass. R. Civ. P. 4 (c). Service is therefore improper under either rule.

4. It is difficult to fault Marple here, but Donne will probably win this round too. Here again, Herbert has apparently tried to comply with Rule 4(e)(2) of the Federal Rules. That rule allows him to leave the summons with a person other than the defendant but only if that person is of suitable age and discretion *and* resides at the defendant's dwelling house or usual place of abode. Presumably, Sister Donne has just flown in for the marathon and would not be held to "reside" at Donne's Boston home.

You well might ask, "How is Marple to know that Sister Donne doesn't live in the house?" Perhaps Sister will tell her if she asks; most people are fairly trusting and not expecting the process server. If not, Marple risks another motion to dismiss under Rule 12(b)(5) by serving in this manner.

Some cases have been more obedient to the spirit than the letter of the "resides there" requirement in Rule 4(e)(2). In *Churchill v. Barach*, 863 F. Supp. 1266, 1270-1271 (D. Nev. 1994), for example, the court found this requirement satisfied when service was made on a doorman in an apartment building who, though he regularly took messages and packages for residents, didn't live there. Compare *Edes v. Fredson*, 344 F. Supp. 2d 209, 211 (D. Me. 2004) (refusing to follow *Churchill*).

5. He who laughs last laughs best. Although Herbert's latest attempt is insufficient under Fed. R. Civ. P. 4(e)(2) (because not left with a person of suitable age, etc.), that is not his only option. Rule 4(e)(1) authorizes service under the Massachusetts provisions as well. Mass. R. Civ. P. 4(d)(1) allows service by leaving a copy of the summons and complaint at the defendant's last and usual place of abode. The state rule does not include a requirement that it be left with a family member or with any person at all. Thus, having the alternative of service under state law proves useful to effect service on an elusive defendant such as Donne.[5]

Service is proper here, unlike in example 4, because the papers were left at the defendant's last and usual place of abode, and they were served by the sheriff. The Massachusetts rule may be more liberal on the

---

5. While it is clear that leaving copies of the summons and complaint at the last and usual abode is sufficient under Mass. R. Civ. P. 4(d)(1), it is questionable whether such service is constitutionally sufficient in all cases. See *Greene v. Lindsey*, 456 U.S. 444, 452-456 (1982) (service in eviction proceeding by posting on door of apartment invalid under due process clause).

methods of delivery, but it is more restrictive on the issue of who delivers it. This is certainly appropriate if service is to be allowed without personal delivery. A sheriff or constable is a neutral party with a professional reputation to protect. His or her certification that service was actually made by leaving the papers at the last and usual place of abode is more trustworthy than that of a party or someone working for a party.

6. a.  Federal Rule 4(d) sets forth the procedure for obtaining a waiver of service. Herbert should send a notice of the action addressed to Donne, with a request that Donne waive service of process. Rule 4(d)(1). The notice must identify the court in which suit has been filed, be accompanied by a copy of the complaint (Rule 4(d)(1)(C)) and must be sent by first class mail "or other reliable means." Rule 4(d)(1)(E). It must inform the defendant of the consequences of waiving service, and of not waiving service. Rule 4(d)(1)(D). It must also include the date on which the request is sent (Rule 4(d)(1)(E)), provide the defendant at least 30 days to respond (Rule 4(d)(1)(F)), and include an extra copy of the notice and request with a prepaid means of responding (such as an envelope with a stamp on it!). Forms sufficient to comply with Rule 4(d)(1) are provided in the Appendix to the Rules. See Forms 5 and 6.

   b.  Donne has a duty under Rule 4(d)(1) to "avoid unnecessary costs of serving the summons," but what if he doesn't do his duty? The clear implication of the rule is that Donne must then be served through one of the regular methods in Rule 4(e). The court may impose costs on Donne for his non-compliance (see Rule 4(d)(2)), but Donne still must be served in order to be properly brought before the court.

      In some states, the date for determining whether the statute of limitations has been satisfied runs from the date of *service on the defendant*, rather than the date of filing of the complaint. See, e.g., *Walker v. Armco*, 446 U.S. 740 (1980) (applying Oklahoma law). Rule 4(d)(4) provides that, where the waiver procedure is used, service shall be deemed effected on the date of filing of the waiver of service (that is, filing with the court). Plaintiffs who file suit shortly before the expiration of the statute of limitations should not use the waiver procedure, since they may not receive it back for at least 30 days — or may not receive it at all — and mailing the waiver form does not toll the limitations period.

## At Your Service

7. Since nothing in this example indicates that Marlowe's business is incorporated, we will assume that he is doing business as an individual and that Herrick is suing him individually. Herrick's argument here

must be that service is proper under Fed. R. Civ. P. 4(e)(2) because Daniel, as manager at Marlowe's shop, is his agent for service of process. The argument fails, however, because 4(e)(2) (and its Massachusetts counterpart) only permit service on an agent "authorized by appointment or by law to receive service of process." Daniel may act generally for Marlowe in the shop, but this general authority to conduct his business is not the same as being specifically appointed to receive service of process.

This provision is meant to reach cases in which the defendant has specifically empowered another person to accept notice of suits. It does not apply to an employee who acts generally as the defendant's agent in the conduct of his business. See Moore's at §4.93. Specific appointments to accept process are sometimes made in contracts, where one of the parties seeks to insure that he will be able to sue the other in a particular state. See, e.g., *National Equipment Rental v. Szukhent*, 375 U.S. 311 (1964) (approving service on agent for service appointed in contract between the parties). They may also occur by operation of law. For example, Massachusetts law provides that a nonresident who does business in any Massachusetts city or town appoints the clerk of that city or town his agent for service of process in actions arising out of business conducted there. Mass. Gen. L. ch. 227, §5A. In such a case, service on the city clerk would satisfy the provision in Federal Rule 4(e)(2) for service on an agent "authorized . . . by law to receive service of process."

8. This raises a fairly obvious issue but one that is not explicitly answered by the rule. Service is proper on Marlowe in this case, under Fed. R. Civ. P. 4(e)(2), but not on Daniel. Every defendant is entitled to direct notice of suits against him, under the provisions of Rule 4. Just as the law refuses to presume that a general agent of Marlowe would inform him of a suit, it also refuses to rely on one defendant to inform others (who, in many cases, he may not even know) that they have been sued. Each defendant is entitled to proper service under the Rules. Herrick will have to serve Daniel separately under one of the provisions of Rule 4.

9. By now you may be wondering how these rules can be so intricate yet leave so many questions unanswered. In this case, the defendant has brought in a new party, who clearly must be informed of the suit. It appears that Rule 4 should apply since it governs service of summonses and complaints, and Rule 14(a) requires the impleading party to serve a summons and complaint on the third party. However, Rule 5(a) provides that "every pleading subsequent to the original complaint"

shall be served on all parties, and Rule 5(b) authorizes such service by ordinary mail, which is insufficient under Federal Rule 4.[6]

While the Rules themselves are not explicit on the point, the policies that underlie service support the conclusion that the third-party complaint, like an original complaint, should be served under Rule 4. The purpose of Rule 4 is to insure adequate notice to parties who do not yet know that they have been sued. Rule 5, by contrast, is designed to provide a simple method for exchange of the many subsequent pleadings and papers that are filed in the case. It trades a little bit of certainty (under the stricter procedures of Rule 4) for a great deal of efficiency (under the ordinary mail provision of Rule 5). The rationale for doing so is that the defendant is already aware of the suit and presumably will stay in touch with subsequent developments. That rationale does not apply to the new third-party defendant. As to him, the third-party complaint is his first notice of the action, and he has the same right to notice of it under the due process clause as an original defendant. See *Adams Dairy Co. v. National Dairy Products Corp.* 293 F. Supp. 1164, 1165 (W.D. Mo. 1968) (Rule 4 makes exclusive provision for service of all summonses and complaints, including third-party complaints); Moore's at §14.22.

10. a. In this case, it appears that Herrick has used the Rule 4(e)(2) procedure for service of process on an individual, by leaving the papers at Marlowe's house with a person of suitable age and discretion residing therein. Unfortunately, he is not serving Marlowe as an individual defendant. Herrick is serving Marlowe as an officer of the corporation in order to effect service on the corporation, Poetic Truck Repair. It is certainly proper to serve the president of Poetic, under Rule 4(h)(1), but that rule says nothing about leaving the papers with someone else. It speaks of "delivering [the papers] to an officer . . . ," suggesting that they must be served directly on the officer to comply with the rule.

   Herrick's attempted service on Poetic is also improper under Mass. Rule 4(d)(2), since it also requires personal delivery to the officer. In addition, under the Massachusetts service rules the papers must be delivered by an official process server. Mass. R. Civ. P. 4(c).

   b. Service on corporations is governed by Rule 4(h)(1), which authorizes service on a "managing or general agent" of the corporation as well as various officers or appointed agents. Therefore, whether service on Daniel will suffice turns on whether his functions as service manager for Poetic make him a managing or

---

6. Though it may be sufficient under state law.

general agent. This will depend on the specifics of Daniel's duties, but it is likely that he will satisfy this requirement. The rationale for allowing service on a general agent for a corporation is that an employee with general responsibilities is likely to realize the importance of the summons and complaint and inform the appropriate officers of the corporation of service. A service manager (again, no pun intended) for a business that solely does repair work is likely to have that kind of general responsibility and awareness.

Note that under Rule 4(h)(1) service on a managing agent is sufficient, although example 7 indicates that it is not under Rule 4(e). This distinction reflects the policy of the rule that when an individual is sued, service should be made on him personally (or on a member of his household) unless he has specifically consented to service on another on his behalf. A corporation, however, is not a flesh-and-blood defendant; it cannot be "personally" informed of the action. Instead, the Rule authorizes service on corporate employees sufficiently highly placed to make it probable that the corporate officers who must respond to the suit will learn of it.

Service on Poetic in this case might also be proper under Mass. R. Civ. P. 4(d)(2). Use of state procedure is proper for service on corporations as well as individuals: Federal Rule 4(h)(1) incorporates the provisions of Rule 4(e)(1), which allows service under state law. Mass. R. Civ. P. 4(d)(2) authorizes service on a domestic corporation by service on a managing or general agent, or on the person in charge of the corporate business at its principal place of business in the state. Depending on the particular facts, Daniel might well satisfy this provision. However, under the Massachusetts service rules, an official process server must serve the papers, which was not done in this case.

## Process and Due Process

11. Service:   Yes       Personal Jurisdiction:   No
   a. In this case service was properly made on Holland under the combination of Federal Rule 4 and the Massachusetts rules. Federal Rule 4(h)(1) authorizes use of the procedures available under Fed. R. Civ. P. 4(e)(1), which in turn authorizes service under the Massachusetts rules. Mass. Rule 4(e)(3) authorizes service on an out-of-state party by any form of mail requiring a signed receipt. (Mail service would also be proper if it were authorized by the Florida rules for service on corporate defendants.)
   b. Personal jurisdiction is not proper in this case, since the defendant has no contacts with Massachusetts. It is not incorporated there, does not do business there (which might support general in

personam jurisdiction), and the claim arises from contacts with Florida, not Massachusetts.

12. Service:   Yes     Personal Jurisdiction:   No
    a. Here again, service is proper. Personal delivery of the summons and complaint to the president of the corporation is proper under Fed. R. Civ. P. 4(h)(1)(B); it's hard to imagine a better way of letting Holland Corporation know it has been sued.
    b. Personal jurisdiction is still not sufficient here. Although *Burnham v. Superior Court*, 495 U.S. 604 (1990), reaffirmed that service of process in the state may confer jurisdiction over an *individual* defendant, it does not suggest that a corporation is subject to personal jurisdiction in a state simply because an officer is served while there for an unrelated purpose.

13. Service:   No     Personal Jurisdiction:   Yes
    a. The answer to this one is a little bit tricky. Service here was proper in the sense that Federal Rule 4 authorized Chapman to serve process as she did. Rule 4(e)(2) authorizes service on an agent appointed by law to receive service, and the town clerk has been appointed by law — specifically, by Mass. Gen. L. ch. 227, §5A — to receive service on Sidney. However, compliance with the service rules is not enough to make service proper. It must also comply with the constitutional requirement in *Mullane v. Central Hanover Bank* that it be "reasonably calculated . . . to apprise interested parties of the pendency of the action . . ." 339 U.S. at 311. Simply delivering the papers to the town clerk will not satisfy that standard, since it provides no assurance of actual notice of the action to Sidney.

        An earlier version of §5A was held invalid for failure to require actual notice to the defendant. *Impoco v. Lauro*, 129 F. Supp. 543 (D. Mass. 1955). Subsequently, the following sentence was added to the statute: "When legal process against any such person is served upon such clerk, a copy of such process shall forthwith be sent by registered mail with a return receipt requested by the plaintiff to the defendant at his last known address." Under this provision the plaintiff must give the required notice by mail; if he does, service will be proper under Mass. Rule 4(e)(2) and constitutionally sufficient under *Mullane*.
    b. Clearly, personal jurisdiction is not a problem in this case, since it arises from the defendant's contracting work done in the forum state. This would suffice to allow the Massachusetts court to assert jurisdiction under the "transacting business" provision of a long-arm statute and under *International Shoe*. Since the Massachusetts court could require Sidney to appear, the federal court in Massachusetts could do so as well, under Federal Rule 4(k)(1)(A).

14. a. This is a tough question, which sometimes gets a tough answer. Here, Chapman has used a method of service that is authorized by Mass. R. Civ. P. 4(d)(1), and that is reasonably calculated to inform Sidney that he has been sued. However, it still went awry, and Sidney never found out about the case. Is the resulting judgment valid?

       Most courts would hold that it is. Under *Mullane*, Chapman must use a method of service that is reasonably calculated actually to inform Sidney of the action. *Mullane* does not hold that the defendant must *actually find out about the suit* for notice to be adequate. See Restatement (Second) of Judgment, §2, comm. c. (where procedure used was reasonably likely to provide notice, valid judgment may be entered though the defendant does not actually learn of the action). Here, delivery to Sidney's home is sufficient under the *Mullane* standard, so the judgment is probably valid though Sidney never learned of it and therefore never had a chance to present his defense. (But see the next answer.)

    b. If I were Sidney, I would move for relief from judgment under Rule 60(b). That rule gives a judge discretionary power to undo the finality of a judgment for various reasons, including "inadvertence, surprise, or excusable neglect" (Fed. R. Civ. P. 60(b)(1)) and "any other reason that justifies relief" from the judgment. Rule 60(b)(6). Although lack of actual notice may not render the judgment void, it certainly should satisfy the standard for reopening the case. The purpose of Rule 60(b) is to allow the court to relieve a party from the effect of a judgment — even a valid judgment — where fairness supports reopening the case. Sidney will have a good argument that this purpose would be served in his case, since he has never had an opportunity to respond to the claim.

       However, in some cases the equities might lead to denial of the motion for relief from judgment. Suppose, for example, that the suit involved an action to quiet title to land, that a judgment declaring Chapman the owner had entered, and the land had been sold to a third party after the judgment entered and a factory built on it. On those facts, allowing the judgment to be reopened would upset the legitimate expectations of third parties, and a judge might refuse to do it.

## Unlucky Number 15

15. Service:  No     Personal Jurisdiction:   Maybe
    a. In this case, National's counsel has used a method of service that is proper under the Massachusetts rules for serving an individual outside the state. Ma. R. Civ. P. 4(e)(3). Ordinarily, this would be

authorized by Fed. R. Civ. P. 4(e)(1), which allows use of state service methods. However, §4(e) begins with the loaded caveat, "except as otherwise provided by federal law." Here, federal law provides otherwise: It requires service by the federal marshals, for reasons unknown to me. If a federal statute mandates another method of service, the methods in Rule 4(e) do not apply,

b. Interestingly, personal jurisdiction may be proper here, even though Drayton has no contacts with Massachusetts, The court would not obtain personal jurisdiction through Rule 4(k)(1)(A), which allows a federal court to exercise jurisdiction if the local state court could. State court jurisdiction is limited by the Fourteenth Amendment due process clause, and it would be unconstitutional under the Fourteenth Amendment due process clause for a Massachusetts court to assert jurisdiction over Drayton, who has no contacts with Massachusetts.

However, Rule 4(k)(1)(C) allows the federal court to assert jurisdiction in interpleader cases without regard to the limits on the state court's jurisdiction. Because jurisdiction is being asserted by a federal court rather than a state court, the constitutional restriction on its exercise of personal jurisdiction is found in the Fifth Amendment due process clause, not in the Fourteenth Amendment. Most courts have held that, under the Fifth Amendment due process clause, a federal court may exercise personal jurisdiction over a defendant who has contacts with the United States as a whole. Drayton certainly has such contacts, based on his ownership of the building in Georgia and his residence in Louisiana.

On this rationale, the court might find jurisdiction over Drayton proper. But some federal courts have held that the Fifth Amendment due process clause also imposes a fairness limit on where a suit may be brought, similar to the limit on minimum contacts jurisdiction under *International Shoe*. See, e.g. *Peay v. Bellsouth Medical Assistance Plan*, 205 F.3d 1206 (10th Cir. 2000) ("where jurisdiction is invoked based on nationwide service of process, the Fifth Amendment requires the plaintiff's choice of forum to be fair and reasonable to the defendant"). A court which takes this view would probably not find that suit in Massachusetts, against a Louisiana citizen for a claim arising in Georgia, comports with this due process limit.

And you thought you wanted to be a litigator.

# CHAPTER 19

# Getting Off Easy

## The Motion to Dismiss

---

## INTRODUCTION

The defendant usually responds to the plaintiff's complaint by filing an answer as provided in Fed. R. Civ. P. 12(a). (For an example, see the answer to the Schulansky complaint, Chapter 33.) However, the rules provide a second option in limited circumstances: If the defendant has certain preliminary objections to the suit, she may avoid answering immediately by filing a motion to dismiss the complaint instead under Fed. R. Civ. P. 12(b). See Jones's motion to dismiss in the *Schulansky* case, infra p. 693.

Two important points about such "pre-answer motions" should be made at the outset. First, filing a pre-answer motion under Rule 12(b) is an *alternative* to answering the complaint. A defendant who moves to dismiss under Rule 12(b) need not answer the complaint until after the motion is decided. See Rule 12(a)(4). If she prevails on the motion, she may never have to answer. This can be a strong tactical advantage since filing an answer may require the defendant to admit damaging allegations in the complaint or undertake substantial factual investigation.

*Second*, filing a pre-answer motion is entirely optional. Defendants are not required to use it to raise the defenses listed in Rule 12(b); each may be raised in the answer instead. See Fed. R. Civ. P 12(b), which provides that the listed defenses "may" be raised by pre-answer motion. What, then, is the point of providing a separate device for raising these particular defenses?

Essentially, the Rules provide this device in order to short-circuit the usual litigation process in cases in which the defendant has a valid defense, evident from the outset, to the court proceeding with the case. These defenses are of two kinds. Some of the 12(b) defenses are immediately fatal to the plaintiff's case. For example, if the court lacks subject matter jurisdiction over the action (Rule 12(b)(1)), it has no power to render a valid judgment; it would be a useless charade for it to go any further with the action. The same is true if the court is not a proper venue (Rule 12(b)(3)) or lacks personal jurisdiction over the defendant (Rule 12(b)(2)). A defendant should not even be required to answer the allegations in the complaint if the case has been brought in the wrong court. To protect the defendant from such inappropriate suits, Rule 12(b) provides an avenue to secure immediate dismissal in cases where the court is powerless to do anything else.

Other defenses under Rule 12(b) raise defects in the procedure by which the plaintiff has initiated the action. The defense of insufficient service of process (Rule 12(b)(5)), for example, attacks the manner in which the complaint was served. Similarly, the Rule 12(b)(7) defense of failure to join an necessary party asserts a defect in the scope of the suit as the plaintiff has framed it. Generally, these are curable defects that will not require dismissal of the suit but will have to be remedied before the case proceeds. If service of process was insufficient, for example, the court will order proper service of the complaint before proceeding. Similarly, if an absentee should be joined under Fed. R. Civ. P. 19, the court will order her joinder if possible. If the absentee cannot be joined — for example, if her joinder would destroy diversity — the court will determine whether the case can proceed without the absentee, dismissing only if the absentee is "indispensable." In these cases the Rule provides a mechanism to flush out preliminary problems and resolve them before getting into the substantive work of the lawsuit.

The 12(b)(6) dismissal, unlike the other pre-answer defenses, challenges the substantive merits of the complaint. The defendant who moves to dismiss "for failure to state a claim upon which relief can be granted" asserts that even if the plaintiff were to prove all the allegations in the complaint, she would still not be entitled to any relief. It hardly makes sense for the court to entertain the action and decide the facts if the law will not provide any relief to the plaintiff even if she proves everything alleged in the complaint. An example would be a suit for negligent infliction of emotional distress in a jurisdiction that does not recognize a right to recover for emotional distress unless the plaintiff also suffers physical injury. If physical injury is required, and the plaintiff cannot allege it, the court might just as well dismiss at the outset since the plaintiff will not be entitled to relief if she is allowed to proceed with the suit.

Although the 12(b)(6) motion is unique in attacking the substantive merits of the plaintiff's claim, it is akin to the "fatal" defenses under 12(b)(1), (2), and (3), in that it can lead to dismissal if it is upheld by the court. However, a plaintiff whose *complaint* has been dismissed under Rule 12(b)(6) will virtually always be given at least one opportunity to amend the complaint to state a compensable claim, before her *case* is dismissed.[1] If the plaintiff has grounds to plead all the elements of a proper claim, but had simply failed to include them all in the original complaint, she can amend the complaint to state a compensable claim once the defect is brought to her attention. (For example, a plaintiff who had suffered a physical injury, but had simply failed to allege it in her complaint for emotional distress, could amend to add an allegation of physical injury.) On the other hand, if the plaintiff is unable to amend to state a compensable claim because the facts do not support a necessary element of the claim, then the case will be dismissed. The Rule 12(b)(6) motion is explored in more detail in Chapter 23.

## WAIVER OF DEFENSES UNDER RULE 12

So much for the consequences of raising Rule 12(b) defenses. The more puzzling aspect of the rule is the consequences of *not* raising them. Rules 12 (g) and (h), which govern those consequences, appear Byzantine at first but are more easily understood once their rationale is clear. Essentially, those subsections of the rule, read together (very carefully), provide that four of the 12(b) defenses will be waived if not raised in the defendant's first response to the complaint. If the defendant objects to personal jurisdiction, venue, the form of the process, or the method of service of process, she must raise those defenses in the pre-answer motion or (if she does not make a pre-answer motion) in the answer. If she fails to raise one of these four "disfavored" defenses in her initial response, she has waived the omitted defense for all time.

This result, hard though it may be to extract from the language of these subsections, makes good sense. If the defendant has suffered any prejudice from these preliminary defects, she should become aware of it when the complaint is served upon her. For example, if the suit is filed in a state that has no personal jurisdiction over the defendant, she should be able to tell that from the caption of the complaint (indicating where the suit has been filed) and the facts alleged in it, which indicate what events gave rise to the claim. Thus, it is not unreasonable to put the burden on the

---

1. Some circuits hold that the plaintiff has an absolute right to amend under Fed. R. Civ. P. 15(a). See e.g., *Car Carriers, Inc. v. Ford Motor Co.,* 745 F.2d 1101, 1111 (7th Cir. 1984). Others allow such amendments as a matter of discretion. *Triplett v. Leflore County, Oklahoma,* 712 F.2d 444, 446 (10th Cir. 1983). See generally Moore's §15.12.

defendant to raise these defects right away. If the rule did not require these objections to be raised immediately, the court and the parties might proceed to adjudicate the suit, only to learn down the road that the court had no right to do so. A defendant might even keep procedural objections in her back pocket and spring them on the court and the plaintiff later on if things go badly on the merits. To avoid such tactics and wasted judicial resources, the rule provides that the defendant must raise these defenses immediately or waive them by her failure to do so.[2]

## An Early Question

1. Presumably, if the complaint fails to state a claim upon which relief can be granted, the defendant should be able to tell that from the complaint alone. Why, then, did the rulemakers not provide that the Rule 12(b)(6) defense is also waived if it is left out of a pre-answer motion?

These rules may seem fussy and technical to you, but it is well worth your while to learn them now. Many a lawyer has re-read Rule 12 in a cold sweat to find out if she has unwittingly waived her client's rights. It is one thing to lose a case by doing the wrong thing, but it is all the more embarassing to lose it by doing nothing. Under Rule 12 the decision to do nothing is fraught with consequences for your client.

## Examples

### Traps for the Unwary

2. David files a complaint for assault against Goliath. Goliath files a timely motion to dismiss for insufficient service of process. Several months later, the judge denies the motion to dismiss and so notifies the parties.
    May Goliath, after being notified of the denial of his motion:
    a. answer the complaint, responding on the merits to its allegations?
    b. move to dismiss for lack of personal jurisdiction?
    c. answer, including the defense of lack of personal jurisdiction in the answer?
    d. move to dismiss for failure to state a claim upon which relief can be granted?

---

2. While a defending party waives "disfavored" defenses by failing to raise them by pre-answer motion or in the answer, asserting those defenses under Rule 12 may not suffice to preserve them. The party must also press these defenses *after* raising them. See *Hamilton v. Atlas Turner, Inc.*, 197 F.3d 58 (2d Cir. 1999) (although defendant asserted personal jurisdiction defense in its answer, it forfeited the defense by failing to press it over four years of litigation).

   e.  answer, including the defense that the complaint fails to state a claim upon which relief can be granted in the answer?

   f.  move for a more definite statement under Rule 12(e)?

   g.  move to dismiss for lack of subject matter jurisdiction?

3. After the court denies his motion to dismiss for insufficient service of process, Goliath answers the complaint. May he include in his answer:

   a.  a defense of improper venue?

   b.  a claim that the court lacks subject matter jurisdiction over the action?

   c.  a defense that David has given him a signed release from liability on all claims arising out of the alleged assault?

4. Suppose that Goliath decides to answer David's complaint instead of filing a Rule 12(b) motion to dismiss or any other pre-answer motion. May he include in his answer:

   a.  a defense of insufficient service of process?

   b.  a defense that the complaint fails to state a claim upon which relief can be granted?

   c.  a motion for a more definite statement under Rule 12(e)?

   d.  a defense that the court lacks subject matter jurisdiction over the action?

5. Assume that Goliath's first response to the complaint is to move for a more definite statement under Rule 12(e). The judge grants the motion and orders David to file a clearer complaint within ten days. David complies. After Goliath receives the more definite statement, may he:

   a.  move to dismiss for insufficient service of process?

   b.  move to dismiss for failure to state a claim upon which relief can be granted?

   c.  answer, raising the defense of insufficient service of process?

   d.  answer, raising the defense of failure to state a claim upon which relief can be granted?

6. If Goliath responds to the complaint by moving to dismiss for insufficient service of process, may he move at the same time to dismiss for improper venue and lack of personal jurisdiction?

7. What is the difference between the defense of insufficient service of process (Rule 12(b)(5)) and insufficient process (Rule 12(b)(4))?

8. Suppose that Goliath does not raise any objections by pre-answer motion. He simply answers the complaint, denying the substance of the plaintiff's claims. Three months later, he files a motion to dismiss for lack of personal jurisdiction. What will the court do?

### Permutations

9. Assume that Goliath answers the complaint and includes in his answer a counterclaim against David, seeking damages from David for calling him a bully. David contends that the counterclaim does not state a claim upon which relief can be granted. What should he do?

10. David files his claim for assault. Goliath moves to dismiss it under Rule 12(b)(3). Four months later, while the motion is pending, David decides to amend his complaint to add a claim for battery. May he do so without leave of court? (Consider Rule 15(a)(1)(A) and Rules 7(a) and 7(b) in analyzing this example.)

11. David sues Goliath in state court. Five days later Goliath files a notice of removal in the appropriate federal district court. Three days after that he files a Rule 12(b)(2) motion to dismiss for lack of personal jurisdiction in the federal court. Is the motion proper?

12. One more variation, and then we will banish David and Goliath back to antiquity. David sues for assault, and Goliath files an answer, denying that he intentionally assaulted David. Several months later Goliath realizes that the court lacks personal jurisdiction over him and seeks to amend his answer, with leave of court under Rule 15(a), to raise this defense. May he do so?

# A PERENNIAL PUZZLER — SPECIAL APPEARANCES AND RULE 12(B)(2)

In many of the classic personal jurisdiction cases, the defendant challenged personal jurisdiction by filing a "special appearance." See, e.g., *International Shoe Co. v. Washington*, 326 U.S. 310 (1945); *Shaffer v. Heitner*, 433 U.S. 186 (1977); *World-Wide Volkswagen v. Woodson*, 444 U.S. 286 (1980). I find that students are frequently confused by the relationship between this traditional method of challenging jurisdiction and the pre-answer motion under Fed. R. Civ. P. 12(b)(2).

The "special appearance" was a common law procedural motion that allowed a defendant, sued in the courts of another state, to appear and challenge personal jurisdiction without submitting to the court's authority. The device was technical and tricky: a defendant who filed a special appearance had to be very careful to challenge only the authority of the court to exercise personal jurisdiction over him. If he carefully limited his appearance to that one objection, the court would decide it, and dismiss the case if it lacked personal jurisdiction. However, if the defendant in any way went beyond objecting to jurisdiction, he was regarded by the court as appearing "generally" to defend the case. The rationale for this technical rule was that, by asserting defenses other than jurisdiction, the defendant acknowledged the authority of the court to adjudicate the case, thereby submitting to its jurisdiction.

For example, in *Davis v.Eighth Judicial Dist. of the State of Nevada*, 629 P.2d 1209 (Nev. 1981), the defendants appeared and objected to personal jurisdiction, but also opposed the plaintiff's motion to amend the complaint. The *Davis* court held that the defendants, by litigating an issue other than personal jurisdiction, had made a "general appearance and submitted themselves to the jurisdiction of the district court." Id. at 1212. Similarly, in *Manning v. Furr*, 66 F.2d 807 (D.C. Cir. 1933), the defendant referred in his special appearance to "other matters apparent on the face of the record." He was held to have raised issues going beyond jurisdiction, thereby appearing generally and waiving his objection to jurisdiction.

Civil procedure rules in a few states still require the defendant to challenge personal jurisdiction by entering a special appearance. See, e.g., Tex. R. Civ. P. 120(a). In federal court, however, Fed. R. Civ. P. 12(b) now governs such objections. Rule 12(b) is a good deal more flexible than the common law approach. First, it allows a defendant who objects to personal jurisdiction to assert other defenses at the same time: "No defense or objection is waived by joining it with one or more other defenses or objections in a responsive pleading or motion." Fed. R. Civ. P. 12(b). This language squarely eliminates the trap for the unwary that ensnared the defendants in *Davis* and *Manning*. Under Rule 12(b) a defendant who joins her objection to personal jurisdiction with other defenses does not abandon the objection by doing so. *Second*, the rule allows the defendant to raise her objection to personal jurisdiction in her answer to the complaint. Obviously, the defendant who places the jurisdictional objection in the answer asserts it along with other defenses on the merits. This is permissible under the Federal Rules, though it would waive the jurisdictional objection under the special appearance approach.

While the Rule 12(b) approach to objections to jurisdiction is more flexible than the special appearance approach, federal practice resembles the common law in one important respect: As under the special appearance approach, the defendant must assert the objection to jurisdiction right away, or waive it by failing to do so. As the earlier examples illustrate, the defendant must raise the Rule 12(b)(2) objection in her pre-answer motion, if she makes one, or in her answer if she does not make a pre-answer motion. If she does not raise it, she waives the objection. Fed. R. Civ. P. 12(h).

The courts in a few states still apply the common law special appearance approach to raising challenges to jurisdiction. In federal courts, however, Rule 12(b)(2) supersedes the special appearance, providing a more flexible method of asserting the objection. In addition, a majority of states, somewhere around thirty-five, have adopted rules closely modeled on the Federal Rules. In these states, the special appearance has also been superseded by the motion to dismiss for lack of personal jurisdiction.[3]

Consider these illustrations.

## Procedures, Procedures

13. David sues Goliath in the Superior Court of West Dakota, a state that retains the special appearance approach to challenging personal jurisdiction.
    a. Goliath answers the complaint, setting out his admissions and denials and affirmative defenses, and objecting to the court's power to exercise jurisdiction over him for the claim. Has he waived his objection to personal jurisdiction?
    b. Goliath makes a special appearance to challenge personal jurisdiction. A week after making the special appearance, he moves to dismiss the complaint for failure to state a claim upon which relief can be granted. Has he waived his objection to personal jurisdiction?
    c. Goliath appears in the action and moves to dismiss it for failure to state a claim upon which relief can be granted. The judge denies the motion. Goliath now answers the complaint, including an objection that the court lacks jurisdiction over him. Is the objection proper?

14. Instead, David sues Goliath in the federal district court for the District of West Dakota.
    a. Goliath moves to dismiss under Fed. R. Civ. P. 12(b)(2) for lack of personal jurisdiction and under Fed. R. Civ. P. 12(b)(6) for failure to state a claim upon which relief can be granted. Has he waived his objection to personal jurisdiction?
    b. Goliath answers the complaint, including in his answer an objection to personal jurisdiction. Has he waived his objection to personal jurisdiction?
    c. Goliath moves to dismiss under Fed. R. Civ. P. 12(b)(6) for failure to state a claim upon which relief can be granted. The judge denies

---

3. Nevada, which applied the special appearance doctrine in the *Davis* case, has since adopted the Federal Rules approach. See *Hansen v. Eighth Judicial District Court*, 6 P.3d 982 (Nev. 2000).

the motion. Goliath answers the complaint, including in the answer an objection to personal jurisdiction. Is this proper?

## Explanations

### An Early Question

1. It is true that a defendant should be able to tell that a complaint is legally insufficient from the complaint itself, so that it would be arguably justifiable for Rule 12 to provide for waiver of the Rule 12(b)(6) defense unless it is asserted immediately. However, the defense of failure to state a claim is a fundamental challenge to the merits of the plaintiff's claim. If the defendant really has committed no legal wrong, she should not be held to waive this basic defense by the mere failure to raise it at the beginning of the suit. If this were the rule, we would be back to the rigidities of the common law, which forced the parties to stick to their original pleadings even if subsequent investigation uncovered basic defenses or theories that went to the merits of the dispute. The four disfavored defenses are distinguishable since these involve procedural objections, which should be apparent to the defendant as soon as she receives the summons and complaint.

In addition, it may not always be easy to determine whether a complaint fails to state a claim at the outset. It may be clear enough in a case like my emotional distress hypo, but imagine a securities fraud case involving alleged violations of complex statutory filing and disclosure requirements. It might be very difficult to determine at the outset whether such a claim is legally sufficient. On balance, the system properly favors preservation of this basic objection over the efficiency gained from forcing defendants to raise it immediately.

### Traps for the Unwary

2. a. Of course he can, and must. Rule 12(b) allows Goliath to assert certain preliminary defenses by motion. Some of these, if valid, would end the case, so that Goliath would never have to answer the substantive allegations in the complaint. If the pre-answer motion is denied, however, the defendant must then file an answer. See Fed. R. Civ. P. 12(a)(4)(A), which provides that the defendant's answer is due within ten days after he receives notice of the denial of the pre-answer motion.

   b. No. Rule 12(g)(2) provides that a defendant who chooses to make a pre-answer motion may not later make a second one asserting other pre-answer objections. Here, Goliath must have known, if he received the complaint at all, that he was being ordered to appear before a court that might not have jurisdiction over him. Since the personal jurisdiction defense was "available" to him at the time he filed his first motion to dismiss, it could have been consolidated in the first motion. Rule 12(g)(1). Because Goliath omitted it, Rule 12(g)(2) provides that he cannot make a second motion to dismiss on this ground.

This provision prevents the defendant from nickel and diming the plaintiff to death by repeated motions to dismiss on different grounds. Otherwise, Goliath might make three or four successive motions, each on a single ground, and unduly delay the proceedings.

c. No again. Here Goliath seeks to raise in his answer a defense that he could have included in his pre-answer motion. Rule 12(g) does not address this; it only bars Goliath from making a second pre-answer motion on this ground. However, Rule 12(h)(1)(A) does prevent him from raising it because he made a pre-answer motion but omitted this defense from it. Goliath does not have to file a pre-answer motion to dismiss at all, but if he decides to, the combination of Rule 12(g) and (h) forces him to put all four of these defenses in the motion or waive the ones he omits.

Don't be fooled by Rule 12(h)(1)(B)(ii), which appears to imply that these four defenses can be raised in either the motion to dismiss or the answer. True, they may be raised in either response, but if a defendant makes a pre-answer motion, she can't raise some in the pre-answer motion and reserve others for the answer. Subsection (h)(1) provides that these defenses are waived if the defendant makes a pre-answer motion and leaves them out (Rule 12(h)(1)(A)), or answers instead, and leaves them out. Rule 12(h)(1)(B)(ii). The rule does not authorize the defendant to leave some out of a motion and then insert them in her answer.

d. Probably not. Since Goliath has made a pre-answer motion to dismiss, Rule 12(g) requires him to include in that motion all 12(b) defenses then available to him. Under Rule 12(g)(2) he cannot make a new pre-answer motion based on such defenses.

This does not mean, however, that Goliath has waived his right to raise this defense entirely. As example 1 indicates, this objection is too fundamental to be subject to any rigid early waiver requirements. Rule 12(g)(1) only prevents Goliath from *making another pre-answer motion* on this ground. Rule 12(h)(2) allows him to raise it in his answer or by another motion after pleading or at the trial on the merits.

I said above that Goliath would "probably not" be allowed to move to dismiss on this ground. It is possible that his objection to service of process was that no copy of the complaint was served on him. If that were the case he would not have known what the complaint alleged and could not have had grounds to dismiss under Rule 12(b)(6) when he filed his first motion. On those facts Goliath *would* be able to file a second pre-answer motion raising this defense since the 12(b)(6) defense was not "available" to him when he filed the first one. The fact that the judge denied the first motion makes this unlikely, however.

e. Yes. The 12(b)(6) objection may be raised in the answer, even though it was omitted from an earlier pre-answer motion. Rule 12(h)(2)(A) expressly provides that this defense may be raised "in any pleading allowed or ordered under Rule 7(a)." An answer is clearly allowed (indeed, required) by Rule 7(a).

f. Probably not. The motion for a more definite statement raises the defense that the complaint is so unclear that the responding party cannot frame a meaningful response to it. This defense is "available" to the pleader as soon as the complaint is served on her. Because the objection that the complaint is too vague to respond to was "available" to Goliath as soon as he received the complaint, Rule 12(g)(2) required him to assert it in his first pre-answer motion.

There is a possibility, as in example 1d, that Goliath never received a copy of the complaint. If so, then he could hardly be expected to know that it would be incomprehensible when he did get it. If this were the case, the defense would not have been available to Goliath when he filed his first pre-answer motion, and he would be allowed to file a second motion on this ground.

g. The language of 12(g)(2) would support an argument that this motion is barred. That rule provides that a party who makes a pre-answer motion may not make a further pre-answer motion on any ground that was available at the time she made the first one. However, Rule 12(b)(3) requires the court to dismiss "at any time" that it determines that subject matter jurisdiction is lacking. Although there is no explicit authority to make a second pre-answer motion, this reference to dismissal "at any time" suggests that lack of subject matter jurisdiction may be raised by such a motion. Because no court can act beyond its subject matter competence, a court will dismiss whenever the lack of jurisdiction is called to its attention.

3. a. No. As soon as the complaint was served on Goliath, he was in a position to object to venue. Here Goliath made a pre-answer motion, and Rule 12(g) allowed him to include his objection to venue in his pre-answer motion. Because he did not include it in his first response to the complaint, it is lost, waived, gone forever. Rule 12(h)(1)(A).

It may not always be that easy for defendants to determine from the complaint that they have an objection to venue or to personal or subject matter jurisdiction. It may not be possible to tell from the complaint, for example, whether a corporate defendant is subject to personal jurisdiction in a district for purposes of 28 U.S.C. §1391(c) or whether all defendants reside in the same state. See 28 U.S.C. §1391(a)(1), (b)(1). Yet the rule requires immediate assertion of the defense. Clearly, if there is doubt as to the propriety of venue the defense should be raised, subject to the ethical restraints on pleading in Rule 11. If more time is needed to investigate before responding, counsel may move for an extension of time to file a response under Fed. R. Civ. P. 6(b).

b. Yes. As previously stated in example 2g, Rule 12(h)(3) authorizes either party to raise this defense at any time.

c. Yes. This is not one of the preliminary defenses singled out in Rule 12(b) for special treatment. It is an affirmative defense on the merits to the plaintiff's claim, which properly should be raised in the answer. Indeed, it could not be raised in a pre-answer motion even if Goliath wished to: Rule 12(b) (first sentence) provides that all Goliath's defenses, except the seven listed in Rule 12(b) itself, must be presented in the answer. Since this defense may not be raised before answering, it is certainly appropriate to put it in the answer.

4. a. Yes. Rule 12 does not require Goliath to raise his defense of improper service in a pre-answer motion. It only requires that *if he makes such a motion*, he include all his preliminary defenses in it. He may simply file an answer including this defense, and it will be considered by the court in the same manner as if it had been raised by pre-answer motion. (See the answer in the *Schulansky* case, infra at p. 665, which asserts an objection to personal jurisdiction that could have been presented by pre-answer motion under Rule 12(b)(2) instead.) The real difference is a tactical one: If Goliath answers, he must respond to the substantive allegations in the complaint. He must make his admissions and denials under Rule 8(b), raise his affirmative defenses under Rule 8(c), and assert his counterclaims under Rule 13. If he moves to dismiss, he may avoid, at least temporarily, the need to answer the plaintiff's allegations.[4]

b. Yes. As in the previous answer, Goliath has a choice to raise this in the answer instead of by pre-answer motion. Indeed, he may raise it

---

4. Filing a Rule 12(b) pre-answer motion does not, however, suspend the litigation. Absent a stay by the court, the parties may engage in discovery for example, even while a motion is pending that challenges the court's authority to hear the case. See, e.g., *SK Hand Tool Corp. v. Dresser Industries, Inc.*, 852 F.2d 936, 945 (7th Cir. 1988); cf. *Chadusama v. Mazda Motor Corp.*, 123 F.3d 1353, 1367 (11th Cir. 1997) (encouraging district courts to defer discovery and rule on Rule 12(b)(6) motion where motion may terminate a dubious claim).

in the answer even if he omitted it from a pre-answer motion. See example 2d.

c. No. The purpose of the motion for a more definite statement is to provide the defendant with a sufficiently clear statement of the plaintiff's allegations so that the defendant can meaningfully respond to them, either by filing a pre-answer motion or by answering the complaint. Consequently, Rule 12(e) requires the defendant to make this motion "before filing a responsive pleading."

d. Yes. Rule 12(b) allows this to be raised by motion but Rule 12(h)(3) makes clear that whether or not a pre-answer motion was made, this basic defense may be raised in the answer or at any other time as well.

5. a. No. The defense of insufficient service challenges the manner in which the complaint and summons were served upon the defendant. Goliath should have been aware of any defects in the method of service as soon as the papers were served upon him, even if the complaint itself was indecipherable. Since the defense was available to him when he filed the motion for a more definite statement, he should have joined it in that motion. See Rule 12(g)(1), (2). Rule 12(h)(1)(A) says that the defense is now waived.

b. Yes. This defense was presumably not "available" to Goliath when he filed his motion for a more definite statement because he couldn't figure out what the plaintiff's complaint was alleging. It is only after Goliath receives the clearer complaint that he is able to ascertain whether the plaintiff's allegations state a claim. Because this defense was not previously available, Rule 12(g) does not preclude Goliath from subsequently asserting it in another pre-answer motion, despite the usual command of Rule 12(g) that all pre-answer defenses be raised together.

c. No. Goliath should have been aware of defects in the method of service at the time he was served with the complaint. This defense was available to him when he filed the earlier Rule 12(e) motion, and Goliath waived the defense by failing to raise it there.

d. Yes. First, this defense was not available at the time the first motion was made. See example 5b. Second, this defense can be raised in the answer even if it was omitted from a pre-answer motion. Rule 12(h)(2)(A).

6. I threw this question in to see if you would stick to your guns and answer "absolutely." The defendant is not required to stake his case on one of these defenses if others may also be available to him. Not only may he assert multiple objections in a pre-answer motion under Rule 12(b), he must do so to avoid waiving them. That is the purpose of Rule 12(g) and (h).

7. The Rule 12(b)(4) motion challenges the adequacy of the summons itself, the court document served on the defendant that orders her to respond to the complaint. Rule 4(a) details the requirements of a summons. (For an example of a summons, see Chapter 31, p. 640.) A motion to dismiss under Rule 12(b)(4) might allege that some requirement of that rule was omitted, such as the clerk's signature or the court seal.

   By contrast, the Rule 12(b)(5) motion for insufficient service of process challenges the manner in which the complaint and summons were delivered to the defendant. See Chapter 18 concerning proper methods of serving process in the federal courts. A Rule 12(b)(5) motion by Goliath might be based, for example, on the ground that it was not left at his cave with a person of suitable age and discretion (see Rule 4(e)(2)(B)) but at a neighbor's instead.

8. The court will refuse to entertain the motion. Goliath has waived the personal jurisdiction defense by failing to raise it in his response to the complaint. The whole point of the complexities of Rule 12(g) and (h) is to provide for the automatic waiver of the four disfavored preliminary objections, unless they are brought forth in the first response to the complaint. Goliath did not include this defense in his answer (his first response to the complaint), and so it is waived by operation of the rule.

## Permutations

9. Rule 12(b) governs not only an original defendant's options in responding to a complaint, but also those of other defending parties. See Rule 12(b), first sentence (referring to defenses to "any pleading"). Here, David, as a defending party on Goliath's counterclaim, has the same options for responding to the counterclaim that Goliath had in responding to the original complaint. David may present his defense of failure to state a claim by a pre-answer motion to dismiss or in his answer to the counterclaim, just as the original defendant may. The same would be true of a defendant responding to a cross-claim or a third-party complaint.

10. Rule 15(a)(1)(A) allows a party to amend her pleading once "as a matter of course" — that is, without leave of court — before her opponent files a responsive pleading. Is Goliath's motion to dismiss a responsive pleading? No. Rule 7(a) enumerates possible pleadings, including complaints, answers, and replies; motions are provided for in a separate subsection (7(b)). See *Car Carriers, Inc. v. Ford Motor Co.*, 745 F.2d 1101, 1111 (7th Cir. 1984). Since a motion is not a pleading, Goliath has not yet filed a responsive pleading, and David is free to

amend once without the court's permission. Indeed, if the court is slow to decide the motion, this period for an amendment as of right may go on for some time.

11. In cases like this my students sometimes respond that Goliath has waived his right to object to personal jurisdiction because he did not include the objection in his first response to the complaint—the notice of removal. However, if you analyze Rules 12(g) and (h) carefully, you will conclude that Goliath's removal does not waive his right to object to personal jurisdiction. Rule 12(g)(2) does not bar the motion, because Goliath has not made a previous pre-answer motion. And Rule 12 (h) (1) does not bar the motion, because the objection was not left out of a previous Rule 12 motion or answer.

Filing a notice of removal is not a response to the complaint—it simply moves the case from the state to the federal court. It does not affect the right to raise Rule 12(b) defenses by pre-answer motion once you get there. Once the case has been removed, the defendant must respond to the complaint by motion or answer. See Fed. R. Civ. P. 81(c)(2), which provides that, after removing, the defendant must "answer or present other defenses or objections under these rules . . ." (i.e., move to dismiss under Rule 12(b)) within a specified number of days.

12. Goliath's train of thought here is obvious. He has run afoul of the rule by failing to include the jurisdictional defense in his answer. Under Rule 12(h)(1)(B)(ii), therefore, he has waived the personal jurisdiction defense. When Goliath realizes his oversight, he tries to get the defense into the answer by amendment under Rule 15, asking the court to accept the amendment and treat it as though it had been included in the original answer. (See Rule 15(c)(1)(B), which provides that an amendment "relates back" to the date of the original pleading if certain requirements are met.)

If this worked, it would provide an easy end-run around the waiver provisions of Rule 12, at least if the judge granted the motion. It won't work though. Rule 12(h)(1)(B)(ii) provides that the defense is lost if it is left out of a pre-answer motion, a responsive pleading, "or an amendment allowed by Rule 15(a) as a matter of course." As usual, the rule-makers thought about this possibility and impliedly rejected Goliath's tactic by limiting amendments to cure such omissions to those filed as a matter of course. Goliath only had 20 days to amend as a matter of right (Rule 15(a)(1)(B)); since several months have elapsed, he has waived his objection to personal jurisdiction. Even if the judge was willing to grant leave to amend, it would be inconsistent with the limitation in Rule 12(h)(1)(B)(ii) to allow the defendant to do so. *Morgan Guaranty Trust Co. of New York v. Blum,* 649 F.2d 342, 345 (5th Cir. 1981); 5A Wright & Miller §1391 at n.30.

## Procedures, Procedures

13. a. Yes. Under special appearance practice, the defendant waived the objection to personal jurisdiction if he asserted other objections or defenses along with the objection to personal jurisdiction. In answering the complaint, Goliath asserts his defenses on the merits of the complaint. He has exceeded the limits of a special appearance, impliedly submitting to the court's jurisdiction to consider the merits of the case.

   b. Yes. By taking other steps to litigate the case, such as moving to dismiss for failure to state a claim, Goliath "appears generally" and waives his objection to personal jurisdiction. The fact that he made the second motion after entering his special appearance would not change the result. He has still joined issue on a substantive issue in the suit, impliedly accepting the court's authority to hear and decide the substance of the case.

   c. No, the objection is not proper. By appearing and making the motion challenging the legal sufficiency of the complaint, Goliath has joined issue on the merits of the case, thus waiving his objection to personal jurisdiction.

14. a. No, he has not waived the objection. Rule 12(b) clearly states that he may assert the jurisdictional objection along with other defenses, even ones, like the Rule 12(b)(6) objection, that challenge the merits of the claim. The result here is clearly different from special appearance practice.

   b. No, he has not waived it. Rule 12(b) allows a defendant to make a pre-answer motion, but does not require it. See Rule 12(b), second sentence, which states that the listed objections "may" be raised by motion. The Rule clearly contemplates that the objection to personal jurisdiction may be raised in the answer, if the defendant does not choose to make a pre-answer motion. Here too, the result differs from the result in a jurisdiction that still follows the special appearance rule.

   c. No. As the earlier examples explain, a defendant who makes a pre-answer motion must include her Rule 12(b)(2) objection in the motion or waive it. Fed. R. Civ. P. 12(h)(1)(A). This result is similar to that under special appearance practice. A defendant who comes in and responds to the complaint without asserting the jurisdictional objection waives it.

# When Justice So Requires

Amendments to Pleadings under the
Federal Rules

---

## INTRODUCTION

Under the Federal Rules of Civil Procedure, parties commence litigation by filing their initial pleadings — the complaint and the answer. The plaintiff starts the action by filing the complaint (Fed. R. Civ. P. 3) and serving it on the defendant. In most cases, the defendant responds by filing an answer. Fed. R. Civ. P. 12(a)(1)(A). These pleadings set forth the basic positions of the parties about the dispute, the claims and defenses they hope to establish at trial.

Naturally, when the parties file the original complaint and answer, their understanding of their claims and defenses will be incomplete. They will certainly have done some investigation, and given serious thought to their legal theories and positions on the disputed facts. Indeed, Rule 11 requires them to do so. See Fed. R. Civ. P. 11(b)(2), (3). But at the time the complaint and answer are drafted, much of the detailed development of the case lies ahead. Parties are not entitled to engage in discovery — the process of forced disclosure of information by other parties and witnesses — until the case has been filed. And, given human nature, the intense focus of many litigators is not on embryonic cases that are at the pleading stage, but mature ones that are about to go to trial.

When the parties do get into the details, through post-pleading factual investigation, discovery, preparation of expert witnesses, and legal research on theories of claim and defense, their understanding of their positions may change. They may, in light of their evolving understanding of the case, wish to add or change the *legal theories* in their pleadings. Perhaps the plaintiff pleaded breach of contract in the original complaint, but begins to doubt that the contract is enforceable. Consequently, she wants to assert a claim for recovery on a quantum meruit theory. Perhaps she pleaded a claim based on strict products liability, but learns that the court is unlikely to apply strict liability for one reason or another, and wishes to add a negligence claim. Perhaps the defendant learns facts in discovery that would suggest that the plaintiff had waived performance of a requirement of the contract, and wants to amend to add that affirmative defense to his answer.

Preparation of the case may also lead parties to want to change the *factual allegations* asserted in their original pleadings. Perhaps the plaintiff pleaded that she was arrested by Officer Rivera, only to learn through discovery that the arresting officer was O'Brien. Perhaps she pleaded that she was arrested by officers of the Bedford Falls police department, but learns through discovery that officers from Pottersville also took part. Perhaps the defendant, in a false arrest case, pleaded in its answer that a clerk had seen the plaintiff steal merchandise before she was detained, but later learns that it was a customer who made the allegation.

For these and many other reasons, parties to litigation will frequently wish to change the positions in their pleadings as the case proceeds. In federal court, their opportunities to do so are governed by Rule 15 of the Federal Rules of Civil Procedure. Rule 15(a) addresses two types of amendments: those filed "as a matter of course" and those allowed by leave of court (or consent of the adverse party).

---

# AMENDMENTS "AS A MATTER OF COURSE" UNDER RULE 15

Rule 15(a) gives all parties the opportunity to amend once as a matter of course, that is, of right, without having to make a motion and have it granted by the judge. The first part of Rule 15(a)(1) provides, "A party may amend its pleading once as a matter of course at any time before being served with a responsive pleading. . . . " This provision generally applies to plaintiffs' right to amend, because in most cases the complaint is the only pleading that requires a "responsive pleading" — an answer. The quoted provision authorizes the plaintiff to amend, once, without leave of court before she receives the answer to her complaint.

Under this provision, if Mary files a complaint against Potter on March 1, 2005, she would have the right to amend it, without asking the court's permission or consent of the defendant, at any time before the answer to the complaint is served on her. The Rules require the defendant to serve an answer to the complaint (again, in the usual case) within twenty days (Fed. R. Civ. P. 12(a)(1(A)(i)), so Mary will probably have a couple of weeks to rethink her complaint and file a new, amended one to take its place. She might add more claims, or add some and drop some, change some factual allegations, or file a completely revised complaint. She need not file a motion to amend; the very point of an amendment "as a matter of course" is that you have a *right* to do it. You don't have to ask anybody, you just file it.

## An Early Question

1. Gower, a lawyer, calls his student law clerk, Violet, into the office and asks her, "I filed a complaint in federal court today against Potter. I had to file it in a hurry. How long do I have to amend it without having to make a motion to the judge?" Violet looks up the rule and responds, "twenty days." Gower fires Violet. Why?

Ordinarily, no further pleading is required in response to an answer; in the typical two-party case the complaint and the answer are the only pleadings filed. See Fed. R. Civ. P. 7(a). The defendant's answer to the complaint "closes the pleadings." However, Rule 15(a)(1)(B) also allows a defending party a chance to amend as a matter of course, within 20 days after serving its answer to the complaint. This provides defending parties with a twenty-day window after serving the answer to file an amended answer, without seeking permission from the court or the adverse party.

# THE STANDARD FOR AMENDMENTS WITH LEAVE OF COURT

After the period for an amendment as of right has gone by, a party must obtain the court's permission or consent of the adverse party to amend its pleading. See Fed. R. Civ. P. 15(a)(2), which provides that the court "should freely give leave when justice so requires." This is a very liberal standard, which tells judges to be flexible in allowing parties to amend their pleadings. At least early in the litigation, there is a presumption in favor of allowing amendments, unless the opposing party provides a substantial reason for denying them.

To appreciate the reason for such a liberal standard for amendments, consider how cases would be tried if parties were not allowed to amend the pleadings. A party would only be able to recover by proving exactly what she pleaded in the original complaint. Suppose that Martini sued

Potter for an accident on Main Street, alleging that Potter deliberately ran a red light and plowed into Martini. Suppose further, that during discovery Potter's chauffeur testified that he did not deliberately run the light, but his brakes failed because they had been inadequately maintained. At this point, Martini would of course want to change his position, to allege negligent maintenance by Potter as the cause of the accident. If the system did not allow such changes in the allegations, Martini would lose his case, even if Potter's negligence had caused the accident. The common law at its most formalistic apparently took this rigid approach. Parties were forced to plead one version of their claim, and to prove that at trial. A "variance" from the initial pleading could prove fatal to the case, even if the plaintiff could prove facts that merited relief. See J. Koffler & A. Reppy, Handbook of Common Law Pleading, 145.

The Federal Rules reject such technical impediments to reaching the merits — the true facts — of the case. The liberal amendment standard in Rule 15(a)(2) reflects the view that parties should not be barred from proving a claim or defense simply because they had not pleaded it on the first day of the law suit. If, in the development of the case, counsel develop a new legal theory, or become aware of new facts that might support recovery, they should be able to restate the positions in their pleadings, so that the trial can be based on this fuller understanding of their cases. The merits should rule the pleadings, rather than the pleadings constraining the merits. "The thrust of Rule 15 is . . . that cases should be tried on their merits rather than the technicalities of pleadings." *General Elec. Co. v. Sargent & Lundy*, 916 F.2d 1119, 1130 (6th Cir. 1990). Otherwise, in the words of one critic of common law procedural technicality, "substance [would be] secreted in the interstices of procedure."[1]

Here are some representative examples of cases in which courts, under Rule 15(a)(2)'s liberal standard, have held that a motion to amend should be granted, even though the amendment was offered well into the litigation.

- In *King v. Cooke*, 26 F.3d 720, 723-724 (7th Cir. 1994), an amendment was allowed to change admissions to denials, where the course of the litigation indicated that the defendants had contested the allegations during the litigation and the plaintiff had not relied on the admissions or changed its conduct based on the admissions.
- In *Harrison v. Rubin*, 174 F.3d 249, 252 (D.C. Cir. 1999), the Court of Appeals held that it was an abuse of discretion to deny an amendment where the claims and defenses under the amended claim required essentially the same proof as under the original pleading.

---

1. Sir Henry Maine, Dissertations on Early Law and Custom, 389 (Arno Press 1975).

Since the proof would be the same, the opposing party would suffer no prejudice from the delay in offering the amendment.

- In *Material Supply Intern. v. Sunmatch Industries*, 146 F.3d 983, 991 (D.C. Cir. 1998), it was held an abuse of discretion to deny an amendment to add a statute of limitations defense. Although the amendment was offered after close of discovery and just prior to trial, the plaintiff was on notice of the defense from defendant's argument in an earlier memo, and no discovery was needed to prepare to try the limitations issue.

- In *Rachman Bag Co., Inc. v. Liberty Mutual Ins. Co.*, 46 F.3d 230, 234 (2d Cir. 1995), it was held proper to allow an amendment to plead fraud, despite the passage of four years, where the amending party had pleaded fraud before, but the court had redirected parties to focus on other issues, and no showing was made of prejudice to the opposing party or bad faith.

- In *Security Ins. Co. of Hartford v. Kevin Tucker & Associates, Inc.*, 64 F.3d 1001, 1009 (6th Cir. 1995 ), it was held an abuse of discretion to deny an amendment where the case had been dormant during most of the period of delay in seeking amendment. The case remained in the early stages of discovery, and no cut-off for discovery or trial date had been set.

# COUNTER-ARGUMENTS: FACTORS SUPPORTING DENIAL OF LEAVE TO AMEND

Although the standard for granting amendments is generous, amendments are not invariably granted. A judge's attitude toward motions to amend will change as the case moves toward trial. At the outset, before parties have planned their discovery and hired their experts, there seems little reason to deny an amendment. However, if an amendment is sought later in the process, the argument for denial becomes considerably stronger. Suppose, for example, that Ernie, injured by a lawn mower made by Wainwright Corporation, sues Wainwright for fraud, claiming that Wainwright employees represented it as safe for certain uses. At the close of discovery, however, having failed to obtain any convincing evidence of fraud, he moves to amend the complaint to allege a claim based on strict product liability.

Here, the amendment may well be denied. First, if Ernie was injured by the product, his lawyer should surely have considered asserting a products liability claim from the beginning. Any personal injury lawyer should recognize that such a claim may be warranted in a case involving injury from a product. Second, if the amendment is allowed, Wainwright will have to start from scratch in formulating its defense. It will have to hire experts on product design, depose witnesses again, and engage in other discovery relevant to the new theory. Thus, there is little reason why this amendment could not have been offered earlier, and granting it would substantially prejudice Wainwright's ability to defend the case. Indeed, the last-minute motion smacks of manipulation — a strategic move to spring a new claim on Wainwright at the last minute.

Courts will also deny amendments that assert legally insufficient claims, for example, where the added claim fails to state a claim upon which relief could be granted, or would be barred by the statute of limitations. Amendments may also be denied where there is clear prejudice to the opposing party, due to delay or loss of evidence, or where the judge has reason to conclude that the party seeking to change the pleading has acted in bad faith, for example, by waiting to add the claim until it will be difficult for the opposing party to hire an expert or prepare to try the issue. Fourth, a judge will consider whether the party has already had opportunities to amend and failed to add an available claim or defense in an earlier amendment.

Here are some examples of cases in which courts have *denied* motions to amend, despite the liberal standard in the rule.

- In *Davis v. United States*, 961 F.2d 53, 57 (5th Cir. 1991), an amendment was properly denied where the plaintiff sought to add claims that would have required joinder of additional parties and complicated the litigation.
- In *Cleveland v. Porca Co.*, 38 F.3d 289, 297 (7th Cir. 1994), the trial court properly denied a motion to amend to add a new claim for relief where defendant had already filed witness and exhibit lists for trial and the deadline for amendments had passed.
- In *Janicki Logging Co. v. Mateer*, 42 F.3d 561, 566 (9th Cir. 1994), the trial court properly denied the amendment where the plaintiff was aware of its claims against the additional defendant years before, where allowing the added party would deprive the court of subject matter jurisdiction, and where plaintiff had failed to assert the additional claim earlier for strategic reasons.
- In *Jones v. Childers*, 18 F.3d 899, 909 (11th Cir. 1994), the Circuit Court upheld the trial judge's denial of the defendant's motion, made a week before the pretrial conference, to amend to add "a host of new affirmative defenses which would have further complicated an already complex case and likely delayed the trial by necessitating the reopening of discovery."

- In *Moore v. State of Indiana,* 999 F.2d 1125, 1128 (7th Cir. 1993), the court denied amendments to add claims against parties who could not be sued in federal court under the Eleventh Amendment, and against whom the limitations period had already expired.
- In *Bell v. Allstate Life Ins. Co.,* 160 F.3d 452, 452 (8th Cir. 1998), the Court of Appeals held that the trial judge had not abused her discretion by denying an amendment that would have added new theories after the deadline for motions, that involved new factual and legal issues, and would have necessitated extending discovery deadlines.

The judge's decision under Rule 15(a)(2) to allow or to deny an amendment requires a close exercise of judgment influenced by many factors unique to the particular case. Consequently, appellate courts review amendment decisions with deference to the trial judge's on-the-spot feel for the case; they will only reverse such decisions for "abuse of discretion." Thus, the battle over an amendment generally must be won or lost in front of the trial judge. If she grants the motion, very likely she will not be overruled. If she denies it, that decision will probably not be overruled either.

# RELATION BACK OF AMENDMENTS UNDER RULE 15(C)

Rule 15(c)(1) provides that an amendment to a pleading "relates back to the date of the original pleading" if it arises from the conduct, transaction or occurrence set forth in the original pleading. This means that the claim asserted in the amended pleading will be treated as though it had been asserted in the original pleading. Why do we care whether an amendment "relates back"?

This "relation back" provision addresses the common situation in which a party adds a claim by amendment after the limitations period for that claim has passed. To illustrate, suppose that Ernie sues Violet for breach of contract, after she sells him some worthless stocks. The sale took place on April 3, 2002. Ernie brings the action on April 1, 2005, two days before the three-year statute of limitations expires. Four months later, Ernie's counsel concludes, based on further investigation of the claim, that Ernie may also be able to recover from Violet for fraud in selling him the stock. (Assume that the fraud claim also has a three-year limitations period.) On August 9, 2005, he moves to amend the complaint to add the fraud claim as a second claim for relief. Figure 20-1 illustrates the sequence of events.

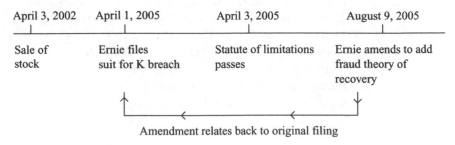

| April 3, 2002 | April 1, 2005 | April 3, 2005 | August 9, 2005 |
|---|---|---|---|
| Sale of stock | Ernie files suit for K breach | Statute of limitations passes | Ernie amends to add fraud theory of recovery |

Amendment relates back to original filing

**Figure 20-1.**

In this case, Ernie asserts the fraud claim against Violet after the limitations period has run out on that claim. If he had not sued Violet before, and sued her for fraud on August 9, 2005, Violet would have pleaded the statute of limitations as a defense, and the case would have been dismissed because he did not bring it in time.

But that's not what happened in our example: rather, Ernie sued Violet for the sale of stock within the limitations period, and now wants to seek relief for that sale on an additional theory. He wants to tack the new fraud claim — based on the same underlying events — onto the original claim, and treat it as though it had been in the case all along.

In this typical scenario, it doesn't seem unreasonable to allow Ernie to assert the new theory of relief against Violet. The purpose of a limitations period is to provide notice to the defendant, within a prescribed period of time, that the plaintiff has brought an action against her arising out of a given set of events. In our example, Violet received that notice, before the three-year limitations period elapsed. She knew, within the prescribed three years, that Ernie had filed a suit seeking relief from her for the stock sale. True, she wasn't placed on notice of a *fraud* claim, only a breach of contract claim. But she knew she'd been sued *for the sale*, and that's the main thing. Once she knows that, she can go about finding witnesses and preserving evidence about the sale. As long as she has notice within the limitations period that she has been sued for this sale of stock, she shouldn't be unduly surprised if Ernie's lawyer, after filing suit, thinks up some more bad names to call her conduct. It seems reasonable to allow the fraud claim to "relate back" to the filing of the initial complaint, even though the limitations period has now passed.

This is basically what Rule 15(c)(1)(B) allows. It provides that, once you have sued the defendant for particular conduct, or a certain transaction or occurrence, any amendment to add new claims based on the same conduct, transaction or occurrence will be treated, for statute of limitations purposes, as though it had been in the original complaint. In Ernie's case, his fraud claim will be treated as though it had been included in his original complaint, filed on April 1, 2005, before the limitations period on the fraud claim expired. Thus, the statute of limitations will not bar the claim, even though, in fact, it was asserted in the amended pleading filed after the limitations period had run.

### Another Early Question

2. Suppose that Ernie moved to amend his complaint to add the fraud theory, and the judge denied the amendment. Consequently, Ernie filed a separate suit against Violet, on November 14, 2005, asserting a right to recover for the sale of stock on a fraud theory. How would Violet respond, and what would the judge do?

---

# THE REAL KICKER: RELATION BACK OF AMENDMENTS AGAINST NEW PARTIES

Rule 15(c)(1)(B) determines when an amendment to add a new claim "relates back" to the date of the original action. Rule 15(c)(1)(C) determines when an amendment that adds a new party to a suit will relate back to the initial filing, that is, when the amendment will be treated as though it was filed on the date of the original complaint.

Suppose that Clarence sues Potter in January 2005 for a breach of contract that took place in February 2002. Assume that Crevins, a business associate of Potter's, had warned Potter not to do business with Clarence, leading to the breach. In September 2005, Clarence learns of this and decides to add Crevins as a second defendant, claiming that Crevins intentionally interfered with his contract with Potter. (Assume that the statute of limitations is three years for both claims.) If Clarence sued Crevins in a separate action, Crevins would plead the limitations period as a defense and get the case dismissed. Can he instead move to add Crevins as an additional defendant to his suit against Potter, and have it "relate back" to the date of filing of that suit? Here's the scenario:

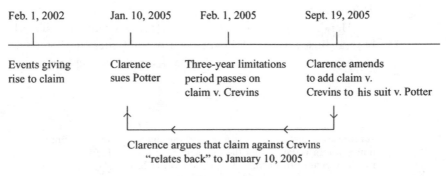

Figure 20-2.

Here, if the amendment to add Crevins were allowed to "relate back" to the filing of the original complaint on January 10, 2005, Crevins would doubtless cry "foul." While Clarence sued Potter before the limitations period ran, Crevins presumably did not have any notice within the three-year period that Clarence was asserting a claim against him. The fact that Potter sued Clarence within the limitations period doesn't make it fair to sue Crevins later, does it? Isn't Crevins entitled to notice within the limitations period?

He is entitled to notice within the limitations period,[2] and, under Rule 15(c)(1)(C), this amendment would not relate back to the filing of the original complaint. Under that subsection, the amendment to add a party will only relate back if three requirements are met:

- the claim against Crevins to be added by amendment arises from the same conduct, transaction or occurrence as the original claim against Potter (that is, that Rule 15(c)(1)(B) is satisfied);
- Crevins had notice, within the period for delivery of the original complaint to Potter, that the action against Potter had been filed;
- Crevins knew or should have known that, but for a mistake as to the identity of the proper party, the original action would have been against him.

In the example, the claim against Crevins would only relate back (i.e., be treated as though it had been filed on January 10, 2005, within the three-year limitations period) if all three of these requirements are met. On the facts of Clarence's action, two of the Rule 15(c)(1)(C) requirements are not met. First, Clarence did not sue the wrong party due to a mistake. He still claims a right to relief against Potter, but wants to assert an additional claim against Crevins as well. Second, this is not a situation in which Crevins should realize that he was meant to be the defendant instead of Potter. Clarence might have valid claims against them both; the fact that he sued Potter does not put Crevins on notice that Clarence will, or meant to sue him. Thus, even if the judge allows the amendment, it will not relate back to the initial complaint. It will be treated as filed on September 19, 2005, which is too late.

Here's a case in which Rule 15(c)(1)(C) likely *would* allow relation back against a new defendant. Wainwright sues the Pottersville Bank for misrepresentation, claiming that bank employees represented to him that a

---

2. More accurately, he is entitled to have the suit filed within the limitations period, and to notice within 120 days after the suit is filed, under Fed. R. Civ. P. 4(m). See p. 393, below, for discussion of this confusing provision in Rule 15(c)(1)(C).

loan he took out was interest-free, but then charged him 37% interest. Suit is filed on May 7, 2005, and the complaint is served that day on Lionel Potter, president of the Bank. Potter is aware of the transaction, since he had put his employees up to the misrepresentation. Five months later (after the limitations period has passed) Wainwright's counsel checks the records in the Secretary of State's office, and discovers that the corporation that runs the bank is actually the Pottersville Corporation. He moves to amend to change the defendant from "Pottersville Bank" to "Pottersville Corporation."

In this case, the requirements of Rule 15(c)(1)(C) are met. Here, Pottersville Corporation, through its president, was on notice when it received the original complaint, that suit had been filed, and Potter doubtless was aware that, but for Wainwright's mistake as to the proper defendant, the suit would have named Pottersville Corporation as the defendant. Consequently, the proper defendant received notice, before the limitations period ran out, that the suit had been filed and that it was the real target of the action. Here, the purpose of the limitations period — making sure the "real" party knows about the suit within the proper period — is satisfied. Thus, it is appropriate to treat the amended complaint against Pottersville Corporation as though it had been filed when the original complaint was. This amendment satisfies the criteria in Rule 15(c)(1)(C) and would relate back.

# NOTICE "WITHIN THE PERIOD PROVIDED BY RULE 4(M)..."

Rule 15(c)(1)(C) does not say that the "real" defendant must receive notice of the action within the limitations period. Instead, it requires that the defendant to be added by amendment receive notice of the action "within the period provided by Rule 4(m) for serving of the summons and complaint" [on the original defendant]. This is more than a little confusing.

The rule makers had to account for a quirk in the law here: In many cases, the original defendant might be sued within the statute of limitations, but not know it. In federal question cases filed in federal court, a plaintiff meets the limitations period if she *files* the complaint before the statutory period passes. But the defendant still may not know that she has been sued, because Fed. R. Civ. P. 4(m) gives the plaintiff 120 days *after* filing the complaint to find the defendant and serve the complaint upon her. Consider Figure 20-3.

| July 6, 2003 | July 2, 2005 | July 6, 2005 | Sept 26, 2005 | Nov. 1, 2005 |
|---|---|---|---|---|
| Events giving rise to claim | Annie files suit against Potter | Two-year limitations period runs | Annie serves complaint on Potter | Period for service expires |

**Figure 20-3.**

In this example, Potter does not actually find out that he has been sued within the limitations period: he finds out more than two months later when he is served with the complaint. But the limitations period is satisfied, because the complaint was *filed* within the two-year period.

So, under Fed. R. Civ. P. 4(m), the original defendant won't necessarily know of the suit within the limitations period, but will know within 120 days thereafter. The drafters of Rule 15(c)(1)(C) concluded that an amendment to add a new defendant should relate back if the new defendant receives notice of the suit within this same, slightly longer period. If she does, she becomes aware of it within the same period that she would have if she been the original defendant.

To summarize relation-back principles, amendments to change factual or legal allegations against the *original* parties to a suit will relate back as long as the new allegations arise from the same litigation events as the original pleadings. But an amendment to add a new party will relate back only in the unusual case where the plaintiff, due to a mistake about the identity of the proper party, sues the wrong one, but the proper party learns of the suit within the period for service of the complaint and realizes that it was actually meant to be the defendant. The examples should help to sort these provisions out.

# ULTIMATE LIBERALITY: AMENDMENTS AT TRIAL

One last provision of Rule 15 will be mentioned, but not analyzed in detail. Rule 15(b) allows the court to treat issues as presented by the pleadings, even though they are not. How's that for judicial indulgence! The point of this provision is that sometimes everyone assumes that an issue is being tried, even if it was not actually pleaded. For example, in a products liability case, a plaintiff might plead that the product was defectively designed, but not allege failure to warn of a danger in the product. Yet, the plaintiff and the defendant may conduct discovery on the warnings issue, hire experts on it, list it as one of the issues in dispute in a pre-trial order, and present and rebut evidence at trial concerning the warnings provided. In other words, everyone assumes that it is in issue, and litigates it fully, even though it is not in the complaint. In such cases, where issues "are tried by express or implied consent of the parties," the court may treat them as though they were pleaded, since everyone clearly understood that they were being litigated.

In order to treat an issue as though it had been pleaded, the court must find that the issue really was tried by "express or implied consent" of the parties. In many cases, parties present evidence relevant to an issue but it is not clear that they are seeking relief on that basis. In a products liability case, for example, evidence of warnings might be relevant to the issue of defective design: a defendant might argue that the design was not defective because a warning of a particular risk was provided, and sufficed to make the product safe. The key to treating issues as litigated by consent is that the course of the litigation clearly put all parties on notice that the issue was asserted as a basis for recovery or defense. If that is true, the Rule favors allowing the case to turn on the issue. But if it is not clear that the issue was really being contested at trial, treating it as though it was would prejudice the party who did not clearly understand that the unpleaded issue was in the case.

## Examples

### The Price of Cooperation

3. Here's a fascinating scenario, which gave rise to an unfortunate action for legal malpractice. Smith was the defendant in a property case, sued by Jones for failure to convey an easement he had contracted to convey. Shortly after the suit was brought, Jones moved to amend the complaint to add an additional claim against Smith under the state Consumer Protection Act. Jones's lawyer called Smith's counsel, Lincoln, and asked him to consent to the amendment to add the Consumer Protection Act claim. Lincoln consented to the amendment. When the case reached trial, Jones recovered several hundred thousand dollars — on the Consumer Protection Act claim only.

   Smith then sued Lincoln for legal malpractice, claiming that he was negligent for consenting to the amendment, and that, if the amendment had been denied, he would not have incurred the resulting judgment under the Consumer Protection Act.

   a. Why would Lincoln consent to the amendment?
   b. What would he argue to avoid liability for doing so?

## As a Matter of Course?

4. Billy sues Potter for interference with advantageous relations, after Potter gets him fired from his job at the Bedford Falls Savings & Loan by insinuating that Billy is incompetent. Potter responds by filing a Rule 12(b)(6) motion to dismiss the claim for failure to state a claim upon which relief can be granted, arguing that the state does not recognize the cause of action for interference with advantageous relations. Three months later, while the motion to dismiss is still pending, Billy files an amendment to his complaint to add a claim for slander. He does not seek leave to amend from the court. Is the amendment proper? To answer the question, compare Fed. R. Civ. P. 7(a) and (b).

## Better Late Than Never?

5. Billy sues Potter for interference with advantageous relations, after Potter gets him fired from his job at the Bedford Falls Saving & Loan by insinuating that Billy is incompetent. Six months after Potter answers the complaint, and four months before the period set by the judge for discovery has ended, Billy's counsel moves to amend the complaint to add a claim for slander, claiming that Potter's statements were slanderous, and undermined his reputation in the banking world. Potter's counsel opposes the amendment, on the ground that Billy's lawyer should have realized that the statements he alleged in the original complaint were slanderous, and therefore included the slander claim in the original complaint. Assuming that this is true, how should the judge rule on the motion to amend?

6. In Billy's action against Potter for interference with advantageous relations, Billy moves to amend his complaint, three weeks before the close of discovery, to add a claim for punitive damages. When Billy filed his suit, the only authority on the right to punitive damages was *Abbott v. Pottersville Bank*, from the state's mid-level appellate court, which had held that punitive damages may not be recovered in commercial cases. However, a week before Billy filed his amendment, the state supreme court had overruled *Abbott*, holding that punitive damages may be recovered for interference with advantageous business relations. Should Billy's motion to amend be granted?

7. In Billy's action against Potter, Billy's counsel moves to amend his complaint, a month before the date set for trial, to add a claim for slander. He bases his motion on new evidence he obtained three days before, when he interviewed Billy's nephew and colleague, George Bailey. In the interview, Bailey, an upright citizen, told Billy's counsel that, at the time of the events giving rise to the suit, Potter made

several slanderous statements about Billy's drinking habits and banking incompetence. Should the judge grant the motion?

8. Assume that Billy sues Potter for slander, that the statute of limitations on the claim is three years, and that Billy brings his action a year and a half after it arises. The discovery deadline is one year from filing. A month before the deadline expires, Billy moves to amend his complaint to add a claim for slander against Perry, who he has just learned (from his interview with George Bailey) also slandered him during the meeting with Potter. The judge denies the amendment, since it is offered so late in the litigation. Could Billy bring a separate action against Perry?

9. Assume, on the same facts, that the statute of limitations on the slander claim was two years, so that it had passed on the claim against Perry when Billy sought the amendment to make him an additional defendant. Could the judge (if she were so inclined) grant an amendment to add Perry as a defendant in the action against Potter?

## Relation Way Back

10. Burt sues Potter on April 1, 2005, for defamation, a claim that has a three-year limitations period under applicable law. The claim is based on a heated argument that Burt had with Potter on April 3, 2002. On August 9, 2005, he moves to amend the complaint to add a claim for intentional infliction of emotional distress. This claim arises from the same argument as the defamation claim. The judge grants the motion to amend to add the distress claim. The limitations period for the emotional distress claim is two years. Potter then moves to dismiss the emotional distress claim, on the ground that it is barred by the statute of limitations. Burt argues that the claim relates back under Rule 15(c)(1)(B). How should the judge rule?

11. Martini sues Potter for usury, for charging him 65 percent interest on a loan he made to Martini on September 22, 2002. The suit is filed on July 1, 2005. On July 15, 2005, Potter answers the complaint, denying that he is liable under the usury statute, and asserting a counterclaim to collect on the loan, on which Martini defaulted one week after taking it out. On December 4, 2005, Potter moves to amend his answer to add a second counterclaim against Martini for fraud, based on the same loan transaction. The limitations period on the fraud claim is three years. Martini opposes the amendment, claiming that it would be pointless to allow it, since the fraud claim is barred by the three-year limitations period. Is that true?

## No Relation?

12. Assume the same basic facts: Martini sues Potter for usury, for charging him 65 percent interest on a loan he made to Martini on September 22, 2002. The suit is filed on July 1, 2005. On July 15, 2005, Potter answers the complaint, denying that he is liable under the usury statute. On December 4, 2005, Potter moves to amend his answer to add a counterclaim against Martini for misrepresentation about his assets when he took out the loan. The limitations period on the misrepresentation claim is three years. Martini opposes the amendment, claiming that it would be pointless to allow it, since it is barred by the three-year limitations period. Is that true?

13. Clarence sues Potter for breach of contract on August 15, 2004. The events giving rise to the claim took place on February 1, 2002. On January 7, 2005, he files and serves on Crevins a motion to add Crevins as a second defendant, claiming that Crevins intentionally interfered with his contract with Potter. Assume that the limitations period on the intentional interference claim is three years. Assume further that Crevins was unaware of the suit against Potter. The judge allows the amendment to add Crevins. Does the amendment relate back? Should the claim against Crevins be dismissed?

14. Ernie, driving to the movies with his date Violet, was in an accident with Potter. Potter sued him, claiming that his negligent driving caused the accident. The three-year limitations period passes. After it does, Potter's counsel deposes Ernie, who testifies that, just before the accident he and Violet were fooling around in the front seat, Violet had playfully grabbed the wheel, and his car then swerved into Potter's car. Violet had learned of the suit the day that Ernie received service of process in the action. She was afraid she would be sued too once the facts came out. Potter's counsel moves to amend to add Violet as a second defendant. If the court grants the motion, will the claim against Violet relate back to the filing of the original complaint?

## Identity Crisis

15. Potter is arrested for avarice by four officers of the Bedford Falls police department. In the course of the arrest, he is roughed up. He sues for violation of his civil rights, naming Burt, the only officer he recognized at the time, and three other defendants, John Does #1, #2 and #3, three unknown members of the Bedford Falls Police Department. He files the suit a month before the statute of limitations runs. He then takes Burt's deposition, learns the names of the other three officers — Tom, Mary, and Jane — and amends his complaint to substitute their names for the John Does. Tom, Mary, and Jane move to dismiss based

on the statute of limitations. Assuming that Tom, Mary and Jane found out about Potter's suit when he filed it, does the amendment to name them relate back?

## Explanations

### An Early Question

1. Violet got off to a good start by *looking at the rule*. The Rules answer so many questions in civil procedure, if lawyers and students would only read 'em! So often, when I ask a question in class, the student looks at the wall; she looks at her notes; she looks into space; she looks at me. But I find that students have a stubborn aversion to looking at the one source where the answer is likely to be found, the Rule itself. I was probably the same way when I was in law school.

   Although Violet looked in the right place, she came up with the wrong answer. Rule 15(a)(1)(A) does not give a plaintiff twenty days to amend as a matter of course. It allows such an amendment as of right "before being served with a responsive pleading." True, a responsive pleading to a complaint — that is, the answer — must be filed within twenty days. Fed. R. Civ. P. 12(a)(1)(A)(i). But it might be filed sooner. Maybe Potter's been expecting the complaint, and will whip up an answer and serve it the next day. That's not likely, but it is quite possible that an answer will be served sooner than twenty days. The point is that you don't have twenty days to amend a complaint as a matter of course, you have the period of time before the answer is served on you, however long that turns out to be.[3] And, since you don't know when the defendant will serve her answer, you don't know how long you have to amend as of right. Best to be safe and amend quickly!

### Another Early Question

2. If the judge denied the amendment to add the fraud claim, and Ernie brought a separate action on the fraud theory, Violet would move to dismiss it, on the ground that it was filed after the limitations period had passed. And the judge would grant that motion, since it was filed more than three years after the events giving rise to the claim. So at this point Ernie couldn't recover on this claim in an independent action. His only way to get recovery on it is to convince the judge to allow him to add it to his pending action for breach of contract. If the amendment is

---

3. Frequently, defendants seek extensions of time to file an answer, either by consent of the plaintiff or from the court. If the period is extended, the period for amendments as of right continues.

allowed, Rule 15(c)(1)(B) will avoid the limitations defense. Clearly, the judge's decision on the "procedural" motion to amend will have a profound substantive impact on Ernie's case; indeed, that decision to allow or deny the amendment is now life or death to the fraud claim.

## The Price of Cooperation

3. a.  In this case the amendment was offered shortly after the pleadings were filed. Because an answer had been served, Jones could not amend to add the additional claim as of right. However, at this very early point in the litigation, the judge would almost certainly allow an amendment to add the additional claim. None of the arguments against granting leave to amend suggest themselves: there hasn't been delay in offering the amendment, there's still plenty of time to prepare to meet the claim; there's no reason to suspect strategic behavior or bad faith by plaintiff's counsel.

Since the judge will grant the motion anyway, refusing to consent to it will look like unreasonable intransigence by Lincoln. Litigation is a long process that involves continuous interaction between opposing lawyers. Lincoln is likely to need the cooperation of Jones's lawyer in the future, and digging in his heels on this slam-dunk amendment issue would not bode well for cooperation later in the litigation. It would also annoy the judge, who doesn't want to be bothered by a motion with an obvious outcome. So, while it seems like "giving something away" to the other side, it is a reasonable and common occurrence for counsel to consent to such amendments. Rule 15(a) expressly authorizes amendments by consent.

b.  Lincoln has several arguments to avoid liability. First, legal malpractice is a negligence claim. Smith will have to prove that Lincoln failed to act with due care in consenting to the amendment, and that his negligence caused harm to Smith. Lincoln will argue that, for the reasons just given, his exercise of professional judgment in consenting to the amendment was not malpractice, but a reasonable strategic judgment.

Second, Lincoln can argue that, even if his decision was negligent, it did not cause any harm to Smith, his client. In the actual case, Lincoln argued that, given the liberal standard in Rule 15(a)(2), the court would have granted the amendment anyway, so Smith lost nothing by Lincoln's decision to consent to it. On this logic, the jury brought in a verdict for Lincoln.

An interesting issue in the case was whether, in the legal malpractice case, the judge or the jury should decide whether the amendment would have been granted if Lincoln had not consented to it. If a motion to amend had been made in the underlying case, the judge would obviously have decided whether to allow it. But in the malpractice case, this becomes a factual issue on the tort requirement of causation: whether consent to the amendment had caused any harm to Smith. The court sent this issue to the jury, after testimony by experts on the standards for amendment under Rule 15.

Although Lincoln won the malpractice case, the message of the case is truly unfortunate, isn't it? It suggests that litigators should never give an inch, never consent to anything, litigate every issue, in order to avoid the risk of a malpractice action down the road. Most lawyers would not agree that such "scorched earth" litigation practice serves their clients' best interests. Reasonable cooperation generally reduces the cost and the stress of litigation and facilitates processing of cases to a fair resolution.

## As a Matter of Course?

4. Billy's amendment is proper, even though his counsel did not obtain leave of court to amend the complaint. Under Rule 15(a)(1)(A), a plaintiff may amend the complaint once as a matter of course (without leave of court) before the responsive pleading is served. A motion to dismiss is not a responsive pleading. See Fed. R. Civ. P. 7(b) (providing for motions), and compare Fed. R. Civ. P. 7(a) (listing permissible pleadings). When a pre-answer motion to dismiss under Rule 12 is filed, it suspends the time for filing an answer (which is a responsive pleading) until the motion is decided. Fed. R. Civ. P. 12(a)(4). So no responsive pleading has been filed, and Billy may amend — once — without leave of court.

It is not unusual for a complaint to go unanswered for a considerable period of time, where some pre-answer motion is made and not acted upon immediately by the court. When that is true, the period for amendments as a matter of course ticks along unchecked. A defendant might actually *choose to file an answer* before it is due under Rule 12(a)(4), in order to terminate the as-of-right period for amendments.

## Better Late Than Never?

5. In this example, Billy's counsel should have realized that he had a slander claim when he filed the original complaint. The statements he alleged there should suggest to any competent lawyer that a slander claim could be pleaded as well. However, even if Billy's lawyer was negligent, the court will likely allow the amendment anyway. The spirit

of the rules is to allow cases to be litigated on the merits, not to rigidly confine the parties to their original pleadings. Fed. R. Civ. P. 15(a)(2) (amendments should be freely granted "when justice so requires"). The court is unlikely to foreclose Billy from recovering on a potentially valid claim just to punish Billy for his counsel's mistake. Since discovery is still going on, adding the new theory should not prejudice Potter's ability to prepare a defense. Very likely, the discovery already done will reveal the facts relevant to both theories. If it does not adequately address the slander claim, Potter's counsel can seek further information through further interrogatories or reopening depositions.

While the court is likely to allow the amendment, it may require Billy (or his counsel) to pay the costs Potter incurs as a result of the amendment. Moore's Federal Practice, §15.17[2]. For example, if Potter's counsel has to redepose witnesses, the additional costs may be shifted to Billy, whose failure to assert the claim in a timely manner has led to the extra expense.

6. This seems like a strong case for granting the amendment. When Billy filed the action, state law appeared to bar punitive damages. Billy moved to add the claim as soon as the state supreme court held that they are permissible. True, it is at the close of discovery. But here there is no showing of bad faith or dilatory motive; Billy has a good reason for seeking the amendment when he does. If Potter needs more time to prepare a defense to the punitive damages claim, the court can extend the discovery period. But he may not even need that. The right to punitive damages generally turns on how egregious the defendant's conduct was. Presumably, the parties were already litigating that on the basic interference claim. The added claim may not require much information that has not already come to light in discovery.

Potter might argue that Billy should have foreseen the possibility that *Abbott* would be overruled, and asserted the punitive damages claim from the beginning. If the court accepted that argument, however, it would suggest that parties should routinely plead claims unsupported by current law, on speculation that they might be recognized later. This approach would put plaintiffs' counsel between a rock and a hard place, given the ethical limits on pleading. Consequently, Potter's argument is unlikely to carry the day.

7. This motion should be denied. While Billy's counsel only discovered his grounds for adding the slander claim three days before seeking the amendment, he *should have* discovered it long before. He can hardly excuse his failure to interview direct witnesses to the events in the suit until this late in the game. Since George Bailey is likely a favorable witness, he need not even have deposed him; he could have interviewed

him informally at an earlier stage of the case. Very likely the motion to amend will be denied.

One might argue that the consequence of his counsel's neglect in preparing the case should not be visited on Billy. However, it very likely will be in this instance. If this argument invariably prevailed, judges would have to allow many belated amendments that could facilitate the merits but result from delay, neglect of counsel, or bad faith. Likely, Billy's recourse will have to be an action for malpractice instead.

That is not to say that judges are insensitive to the effect of denying an amendment on the requesting lawyer's client. In close cases, this is likely to weigh heavily, since the thrust of the rules is to facilitate decision on the merits rather than on procedural missteps. But this is not a close case, and clients are ultimately responsible for their choice of counsel.

8. Yes, he could. The statute of limitations has not passed, and the fact that he has sued Potter in one action does not bar him from suing Perry separately in another. Federal Rule 20(a)(2) allows, but does not require, the joinder of defendants based on a single transaction. And res judicata only bars suit against a party who was sued before. Since Billy can do this anyway in a separate action, shouldn't the judge serve the goal of efficiency by allowing him to add Perry to his suit against Potter?

Although it is generally more efficient, and avoids inconsistent judgments, to litigate claims against multiple defendants together, the judge's denial of the motion is still appropriate. Billy's action against Potter is ready for trial, and will certainly be delayed if Perry is added. Perry will need time to do discovery to prepare for trial, perhaps considerable time. Adding another defendant will affect Potter's trial strategy as well. It will likely require him to renew discovery and rethink his trial preparation. Even though Billy can still sue Perry separately, it makes sense not to disrupt the progress of the suit against Potter at this late stage of the litigation.

9. Perhaps you answered "no" to this question, based on Rule 15(c)(1)(C). However, Rule 15(c)(1)(C) doesn't bar the grant of an amendment, it only deals with whether the amendment "relates back" to the date of filing of the complaint. The judge could grant the amendment, under Rule 15(a)(2), but is likely to deny it as "futile" if Perry argues the limitations defense. The Rule 15(c)(1)(C) requirements would not be met in this case, since nothing indicates that Perry knew about the action before the period for service of process ran, or that he is being added due to a mistake about the proper defendant. On the contrary, Billy simply seeks to add an additional claim against another alleged tortfeasor. Under these circumstances, an amendment will not relate back, so the

claim, if allowed by amendment, would face the bar of the statute of limitations. Consequently, the judge will likely deny it.

## Relation Way Back

10. The judge should grant the motion to dismiss the claim. It is very important to understand why. Perhaps drawing the case out will help to make the point:

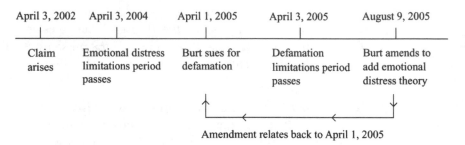

Figure 20-4.

In this example, Burt filed suit just before the three-year limitations period for defamation passed. His defamation claim is timely. Four months later, he amends to add his emotional distress claim. Under Rule 15(c)(1)(B), the emotional distress claim will "relate back" to the date of filing of the original complaint, that is, it will be treated as though it had been included in the original complaint. However, if the emotional distress claim *had* been in the original complaint, it *would still have been too late*: the two-year limitations period for that claim had passed almost a year before! Rule 15(c)(1)(B) does not provide that any added claim will be timely; it provides that it will be treated as though it had been filed when the original complaint was filed. If the limitations period on the added claim had already passed on that date, Rule 15(c)(1)(B) will not resuscitate the claim.[4]

11. In this example, Potter has answered before the limitations period passed, asserting a counterclaim. He now wants to add a second counterclaim. If the judge allows his motion, Rule 15(c)(1)(B) will apply: It provides that an amendment of *a pleading* (not just of a complaint) relates back to the original pleading if it asserts a claim arising from the same conduct, transaction or occurrence. Since Potter's second counterclaim arises from the same default on the loan

---

4. Potter should have argued the limitations issue in opposition to the motion to amend to add the claim. Had he done so, the judge would likely have recognized that the claim was barred and denied the amendment, as discussed in Example 9.

as his original pleading (his answer and counterclaim), it will be treated as though it had been filed on July 15, 2005, which was well within the three-year limitations period applicable to the fraud claim. Thus, it will (constructively) have met the three-year limitations period.

Of course, Potter will still have to convince the judge to allow the amendment. Rule 15(c)(1)(B) provides that the amended pleading will relate back if it is *allowed*. It does not alter the Rule 15(a)(2) requirement that the judge grant permission to amend to add the counterclaim.

## No Relation?

12. The interesting thing about this example is that, prior to Potter's amendment, Potter had not asserted *any* claim against Martini. In the typical added-claim scenario, a party asserts one claim against a party, and then adds another, arising from the same events, after the limitations period runs. In the last example, Potter asserted a counterclaim in the original answer, so Martini was on notice that relief was being sought from him within the limitations period. He has notice that he may have to defend a claim based on the default, and the amendment to add another counterclaim just adds insult to injury. But here, Potter did not seek any relief against Martini before the three years passed. He isn't adding a claim, he's asserting his first claim after the passage of the limitations period.

    Despite this, interpreting Rule 15(c)(1)(B) to allow the amendment adding the counterclaim to relate back to the date the answer was filed seems fair. Martini himself has commenced litigation on the loan transaction. He should not be surprised that a defendant may also have claims arising from that transaction; thus he has adequate notice to gather his evidence both to prove his own claim and to defend against counterclaims that arise from the transaction as well.

13. In this example, the requirements in Rule 15(c)(1)(C) are not satisfied, since Crevins did not have notice of the action within the period for service of the original complaint. Consequently, the amended claim against Crevins will not relate back to August 15, 2004, when the original complaint was filed. It will be treated as filed on January 7, 2005, when it actually was filed and served.

    But who cares? January 7, 2005 is still within three years of the events giving rise to the claim, so the claim against Crevins is timely even though it does not relate back. If Clarence had filed an original action against Crevins on January 7, 2005, Crevins would have no statute of limitations defense. So the fact that he doesn't meet the requirements of Rule 15(c)(1)(C) is irrelevant. That rule simply determines when an amendment to add a party will be treated as though it had been included in the original filing. An amendment — like this one — may still be timely even though it *does not* relate back! The action should not be dismissed based on the statute of limitations.

14. In this case, Potter moves to add Violet as a second defendant. If the judge grants the motion, the question will be whether the suit is barred by the statute of limitations, which passed before she was brought into the case. It will be barred, unless the claim against Violet relates back to the date when the suit was filed against Ernie. That turns on Rule 15(c)(1)(C), which allows a claim against a new party to relate back if the added[5] party received notice of the action within the time for service of the original complaint, and knew that, but for a mistake concerning the identity of the proper party, the action would have been brought against her.

While the example states that Violet knew about the suit before the limitations period ran, it is very doubtful that the second requirement is met here. Potter has sued Ernie for negligence. Now, it appears that Violet may have been negligent too — or, perhaps have been the sole negligent party. But Potter did not make a mistake about who he meant to sue. He meant to sue Ernie and he did. There is a difference between a mistake as to who committed the negligent act and a mistake as to the identity of a party. Here, Potter knew who the driver was, and sued him, claiming he was negligent. He may lose, if Ernie wasn't at fault, but that doesn't mean he made a mistake as to the identity of the proper party. In other words, a mistake about who was negligent is different from a mistake about "identity."

Compare this case, in which an earlier version of Rule 15(c)(1)(C) was held to authorize relation back: In *Meredith v. United States*, 41 F.R.D. 34 (S.D. Cal. 1966), the plaintiff was injured in a near collision between a commercial jet and a military plane. She sued the United States for negligence of the pilot of the military plane. However, it turned out that the plane was being tested by Lockheed Aircraft Corporation, and a Lockheed pilot was flying the plane. The plaintiff amended to add Lockheed as a defendant. The court held that Lockheed was on notice of the plaintiff's claim from a government investigation of the incident, and knew that, if the plaintiff had known the true facts, it would have been sued instead. The amendment was therefore held to relate back.

---

5. While Rule 15(c)(1)(C) refers to an amendment that "changes" the party against whom the claim is asserted, it has been interpreted, quite sensibly, to apply as well when a party is added to the suit but the original defendants remain in the case as well.

Ernie's case would be similar if Potter had alleged that Ernie was driving, but Violet actually was. Then, Violet would presumably be on notice that she would have been sued instead of Ernie if Potter's counsel knew the true facts. See, e.g., *Leonard v. Parry*, 219 F.3d 25 (1st Cir. 2000) (allowing relation back on similar facts). On the facts given in the example, however, Violet only knows that Potter might have grounds to sue her as well as Ernie, but hasn't done so.

## Identity Crisis

15. This example also turns on the meaning of Rule 15(c)(1)(C). The example states that Tom, Mary, and Jane had notice of the action before the limitations period ran, so the interpretive problem is whether they "knew or should have known that, but for a mistake concerning the identity of the proper party," the suit would have been against them.

Most courts have held that Rule 15(c)(1)(C) does not authorize relation back in this situation, since the plaintiff has not made a "mistake" about the identity of the defendants, but rather simply didn't know who they were until discovery revealed their names. See, e.g., *Jacobsen v. Osborne*, 133 F.3d 315, 320 (5th Cir. 1998); *Cox v. Treadway*, 75 F.3d 230, 240 (6th Cir. 1996). The Third Circuit has taken a more flexible approach, opining that the amendment should relate back in these circumstances. *Singletary v. Pennsylvania Dept. of Corrections*, 266 F.3d 186, 200-202 (3d Cir. 2001). The Third Circuit notes the difficulty of the plaintiff's position in these cases if the majority approach applies: if she doesn't know the names of those involved in her injury, she must sue well before the limitations period runs, learn the identities of the "Doe defendants" through discovery, and move to amend before the period runs. The *Singletary* court suggests that the Advisory Committee consider amending Rule 15(c) to clearly authorize relation back in such cases. Id. at 201 and 201 n.5. This result seems fair, where the Doe defendants learn within the limitations period that the action has been brought, and that they were meant to be made defendants.

# The Scope of Discovery

## The Rules Giveth, and the Rules Taketh Away

---

# INTRODUCTION

The big news in civil procedure over the last century has been the demise of pleading and the rise of discovery. In the early common law, pleading played a central role in defining the issues and the factual contentions of the parties. Plaintiffs learned as much as they could about their cases before commencing suit, and then pleaded their cases based on their best guess as to what they would be able to prove. Once the pleadings were closed, the shape of the case was settled; it only remained to be seen whether the parties could prove what they had alleged.

Modern civil practice turns this approach on its head. Under our current notice pleading rules, the complaint and the answer provide a tentative view of the parties' positions, based on preliminary research and investigation. Once issue is joined, full development of the parties' positions evolves through the process of discovery, the court-mandated production of information from other parties and non-party witnesses. As discovery puts flesh on the bare-bones case presented in the pleadings, the parties may usually amend those pleadings to conform to their evolving understanding of the dispute.

The major tools of discovery include interrogatories under Fed. R. Civ. P. 33, requests for production of documents under Fed. R. Civ. P. 34, oral depositions under Fed. R. Civ. P. 30, and automatic disclosure under Rule 26(a). These tools are discussed in detail in the next chapter; this one addresses more general issues concerning the permissible scope of discovery under the Federal Rules of Civil Procedure.

Perhaps the most fundamental point about discovery is that it is conducted by the parties, not by the court. Interrogatories and requests for production are sent by counsel for the parties to each other, and responses are sent back by counsel. Depositions are scheduled and conducted by counsel. The judge is not present at the depositions, nor does she screen interrogatories and document requests before they are sent. She is there to assist in scheduling discovery and resolving disputes that arise during the exchange, but does not directly participate in the exchange herself.

However, the devices of discovery, established by court rule and enforceable by the court, give counsel for the parties powerful mechanisms for demanding the production of evidence from those who have it. Through discovery requests, counsel may force opposing parties and other witnesses to give oral testimony on any issue in the case, and can force opponents to produce even the most damaging "smoking gun" documents lurking in their confidential files. In most cases, it is effective use of these expansive discovery tools, not trial, that determines the value and the outcome of cases:

> Most cases settle, and victory is not in the scathing cross, but in the tedious review of documents. Success is in the details, the expertly drafted interrogatories or request for records, and in the ingenious strategy to obtain the statement allegedly protected by privilege. For it is Discovery which we do. The motions, the papers, the depositions. This is the numbing, ditch digging work that determines the winner. . . ."[1]

This expansive — and intrusive — approach to pre-trial discovery, followed in most American courts in civil cases, is remarkable and unusual. In most court systems around the world, the development of the case rests primarily in the hands of the judge. Even here, discovery is much more limited in criminal cases than it is under the civil rules.

# THE RULES GIVETH: THE BASIC TEST OF RELEVANCE

The rules of discovery are powerful not only because they compel the production of evidence, but also because of the broad scope of the evidence that must be produced. The scope of discovery is governed by Rule 26(b)(1):

---

1. Discovery, 1997 A.B.A. Sec. Litig. 23, quoted in S. Subrin, Discovery in Global Perspective; Are We Nuts?, 52 DePaul L. Rev. 299, 299-300 (2002).

> Parties may obtain discovery regarding any nonprivileged matter that is relevant to any party's claim or defense—including the existence, description, nature, custody, condition, and location of any documents or other tangible things and the identity and location of persons who know of any discoverable matter. For good cause, the court may order discovery of any matter relevant to the subject matter involved in the action. Relevant information need not be admissible at the trial if the discovery appears reasonably calculated to lead to the discovery of admissible evidence.

This provision, which allows parties to obtain virtually any information relevant to the claims or defenses raised in the case, seems about as broad as it could be. Interestingly, however, until recently the scope of discovery under Rule 26(b)(1) was even broader: Until 2000 the standard allowed discovery of "any matter, not privileged, relevant to the subject matter involved in the pending action." Under this broader language the Supreme Court had held that a party could

> discover any matter that bears on, or that reasonably could lead to other matter involved that could bear on, any issue that is or may be in the case. . . . Consistently with the notice pleading system established by the Rule, discovery is not limited to issues raised by the pleadings, for discovery itself is designed to help define and clarify the issues.

*Oppenheimer Fund, Inc. v. Sanders*, 437 U.S. 340, 351 & n. 12 (1978). The Advisory Committee on the Civil Rules recommended the somewhat narrower "relevant to any party's claim or defense" language in an effort to rein in excessive discovery at the outer bounds of relevance. Under this revised provision, discovery will be limited to the issues framed by the parties' pleadings. However, it remains to be seen whether discovery will really be more restricted under the new standard; the new rule may be narrower than the anything-goes standard of the prior rule, but it is still extremely broad.[2]

While the presumptive reach of discovery is broad under Rule 26(b)(1), information is not automatically subject to production if it meets the broad relevance standard. Rule 26 provides that relevant information is discoverable unless "otherwise limited by court order." A party who receives a discovery request may seek a "protective order" from the court limiting discovery—even of information clearly within the relevance standard in Rule 26(b)(1)—"to protect a party or person from annoyance, embarrassment, oppression, or undue burden or expense." Fed. R. Civ. P. 26(c)(1).

---

2. Clearly, the rule makers *intended* the new standard to be more restrictive: The second sentence of the new rule allows the court to expand discovery to the reach of the old standard where necessary. There would be no point to this provision if there were no difference in the two standards.

The court may enter a protective order limiting discovery for various reasons, including the burden and expense of producing the information, the potential for revealing intimate facts which should remain private, the potential for use of discovery to annoy or intimidate an opponent, to protect proprietary business information, or for other reasons.

# THE RULES TAKETH AWAY: PRIVILEGE OBJECTIONS TO DISCOVERY

Although Rule 26 creates a broad presumption in favor of discovery of all relevant evidence, it also taketh away through several important exceptions to discovery. Rule 26(b)(1) itself limits discovery to information that is "nonprivileged." Courts have long recognized that some evidence, even though relevant to litigation, should be protected from disclosure in a lawsuit. Despite the general principle that "the law is entitled to every person's evidence," courts have created privileges where some policy favoring confidentiality is judged to be more compelling than access to the evidence. "Their warrant is the protection of interests and relationships that, rightly or wrongly, are regarded as of sufficient social importance to justify some sacrifice of availability of evidence relevant to the administration of justice." McCormick on Evidence, 5th ed. 1999 §72, p. 114.

The classic example is the attorney-client privilege, which bars inquiry into communications between a client and her counsel in the course of legal representation. The rationale for the privilege is that effective representation requires full and frank communication between lawyer and client. See *Upjohn v. United States*, 449 U.S. 383, 389 (1981). Such communication will be inhibited if opposing counsel could essentially "listen in" on these communications by asking about them at trial — or in discovery. If Murrow sends an interrogatory to Pyle, asking him whether he admitted to his lawyer that he ran the red light at the time of the accident, Pyle's counsel may respond "The defendant objects to Interrogatory #7 on the ground that the requested information is protected by the attorney-client privilege." Although Pyle's conversations with his lawyer about the accident are relevant to Murrow's claim under the broad standard in Rule 26(b)(1), the policy of confidentiality underlying the attorney-client privilege is deemed to outweigh the opponent's need for this information.

A variety of other privileges are also recognized by the courts. For example, many states recognize a privilege for communications between priest and penitent, between doctor and patient, between psychotherapist and patient, and between husband and wife. In recent years, more exotic privileges have been claimed and sometimes recognized, such as a news reporter's privilege to keep sources confidential, a scholar's privilege to protect confidential sources, a teacher-pupil privilege, and others. See generally McCormick on Evidence §76.2 (5th ed. 1999) 219. Such privileges may be created by state or federal common law or statute or — as in the case of the privilege against self-incrimination — in the U.S. Constitution. The important point for our purposes is not to analyze privileges in detail, but to recognize that courts may choose to protect information despite its relevance, and that where they do, the information need not be disclosed in discovery.

# THE RULES TAKETH AWAY: "WORK PRODUCT" OBJECTIONS

A second major exception to the broad scope of discovery under Rule 26(b)(1) is the so-called work product privilege, which bars production of certain materials developed in anticipation of litigation. The work product privilege was recognized in *Hickman v. Taylor*, 329 U.S. 495 (1947), in which plaintiff's counsel in a wrongful death case sought discovery of defense counsel's notes of interviews with various witnesses to the tugboat sinking that caused the deaths. He also requested, through interrogatories, the substance of other interviews that Fortenbaugh (the defendant's lawyer) had conducted but had not written down. In other words, he wanted Fortenbaugh to write out his memory of the interviews in response to the interrogatories.

Fortenbaugh balked at producing either his written notes of the interviews or information on the interviews that had not been recorded. He argued that allowing this discovery would improperly interfere with the privacy of his trial preparation.

## Some Early Questions

1. a. Does the information sought in *Hickman* satisfy the general standard for discovery in Rule 26(b)(1)?
   b. Why couldn't Fortenbaugh raise the attorney-client privilege to avoid producing the requested materials?
   c. Two types of statements were sought in *Hickman*: those in writing, and the content of those that were taken orally. Which is more intrusive, and why?
   d. How could plaintiff's counsel have obtained the requested information without getting it from Fortenbaugh?
   e. Since the information was available by other means, why did plaintiff's counsel seek it from Fortenbaugh instead?

When *Hickman* was decided, Rule 26 provided no explicit basis for an exception to discovery for "trial preparation materials." However, the plaintiff's efforts to "secure the production of written statements and mental impressions contained in the files and the mind of the attorney . . . " (329 U.S. at 509) troubled the Supreme Court for several reasons. First, allowing such discovery would interfere with the confidentiality of trial preparation. Opposing counsel would be able to "psych out" her adversary's strategy by learning through discovery who she had interviewed and what issues she had pursued in those interviews. It would be very difficult to separate factual information in trial preparation materials from the thought processes of the lawyer who developed them; if such discovery were allowed, it could reveal much about an adversary's legal theories, evaluation of witnesses, and plans for trial and settlement. If such discovery were routinely allowed, lawyers would become reluctant to keep written records, an approach hardly calculated to improve the quality of representation.

Second, the Court expressed concern that allowing discovery of trial preparation materials would allow lawyers to ride on their adversary's coattails in preparing for trial, by letting opposing counsel do all the work, and then obtaining the results through discovery. That might not be a good way to prepare for trial — indeed, it certainly would not be — but it would be a temptation that the system ought not to encourage. Third, the *Hickman* Court expressed concern about the prospect of lawyers ending up as witnesses in their own cases if the statements they produced contradicted other testimony from the same witness.

Based on these concerns, the *Hickman* Court denied production of the requested information. However, the Court did not categorically bar production of all such "attorney work product," Instead, the Court indicated that written statements given by witnesses might be subject to discovery if the party seeking discovery made a sufficient showing of need for the material and inability to obtain it through other means. 329 U.S. at 511-512. At the same time, the Court expressed considerable doubt that an attorney's mental impressions or personal notes on a witness interview would ever be subject to discovery.

Some twenty years after *Hickman*, the federal rule makers partially codified the "work product" doctrine in Fed. R. Civ. P. 26(b)(3). That subsection provides that "documents and tangible things . . . prepared in anticipation of litigation or for trial by or for another party or its representative" can only be obtained in discovery if the requesting party demonstrates that she has substantial need for the materials and cannot obtain substantially equivalent information through other means without undue hardship. Rule 26(b)(3) further provides that, *even where such a showing is made*, the "mental impressions, conclusions, opinions, or legal theories of a party's attorney or other representative" shall be protected from disclosure. Fed. R. Civ. P. 26(b)(3)(B).

Thus, today, claims of "work product privilege" regarding documents or other tangible items are analyzed under Rule 26(b)(3). The rule creates three categories of work product. First, as to documents prepared in anticipation of litigation that contain information that can reasonably be obtained through other means, discovery is barred. For example, on the facts of *Hickman*, where the witnesses involved were available for plaintiff's counsel to interview or depose herself, discovery of statements made by those witnesses to the defendant's counsel would be denied. Second, if the requesting party demonstrates that she has a substantial need for materials developed in anticipation of litigation, and that similar information cannot be obtained through other means without substantial hardship, the court may order production of the materials. Third, opposing counsel's thought process in preparing a case, such as legal theories or litigation strategy (often called "opinion work product"), cannot be discovered under the rule.[3]

---

# THE RULES GIVETH AND TAKETH AWAY: DISCOVERY OF EXPERTS

Most witnesses testify as to facts relevant to the action, such as who entered the intersection first, how many tons of sand were delivered to the worksite, or whether the defendant made harassing comments to the plaintiff. In many cases, however, parties also offer the testimony of "expert" witnesses on issues in the case. An expert witness is a person whose testimony, because of her specialized knowledge, skill, experience, training, or education, will assist the trier of fact in understanding the facts and reaching conclusions on the contested issues. Fed. R. Evid. 702.

An expert may be used to provide important background information to help the trier of fact understand the case, such as how a hip replacement operation is performed, the proper procedure for supporting a bridge, or the manner in which electronic fund transfers are accomplished between banks. Experts may also offer *opinions* on issues critical to the case. An epidemiologist may testify as to whether a chemical released by the defendant caused the

---

3. Opinion work product may not be absolutely protected in all cases. Occasionally, opinion work product may actually be a factual issue in a case. *Holmgren v. State Farm Mutual Ins. Co.*, 976 F.2d 573 (9th Cir. 1992), was an action brought against an insurer for bad faith failure to settle a claim. In *Holmgren*, the claims adjuster's memorandum, explaining his opinion of the value of the claim, was relevant to the issue of the insurer's good faith in failing to make a reasonable settlement offer. Although the memo was opinion work product of an agent of the defendant (and thus presumptively protected by Rule 26(b)(3)(B)), discovery of the memo was upheld, since the insurer's valuation of the claim was a core factual issue in the case.

plaintiff's illness. A psychiatrist may testify as to whether psychiatric care was provided in accordance with professional standards. A medical actuary may testify as to the likely cost of operations the plaintiff will require at various times in the future. Where the issues require experts to assist the jury, both sides will likely offer expert testimony.

In addition to such "testifying experts," parties often hire experts to help them understand the issues in a case, even though they do *not* plan to use experts as witnesses at trial (or plan to use a different expert at trial). In a complex construction case, for example, counsel might hire an experienced construction manager to help her understand the proper sequence of construction, the propriety of change orders demanded by the contractor, and whether materials used complied with the contract specifications. In a surgical malpractice case, counsel might retain a surgeon experienced in the type of procedure in issue, to analyze whether the procedure was performed properly and whether it caused the plaintiff's injury. In this chapter, I will refer to these experts as "non-testifying experts."

There is little doubt that the knowledge experts can provide about complex issues in a case is relevant to the claims or defenses in the case, so that their testimony is within the presumptive scope of discovery under Rule 26(b)(1). However, the Federal Rules (and similar state rules) contain special provisions restricting the right to obtain pre-trial discovery from other parties' expert witnesses. Under Federal Rule 26(a)(2), parties are required to disclose the names of their *testifying* experts at least 90 days before trial, together with a report concerning their opinions and the bases of those opinions, their qualifications, compensation, and other information. After disclosure, testifying experts may be deposed as well. Rule 26(b)(4)(A). This broad right under the Rules to discovery from testifying experts culminates a long trend toward liberal discovery based on the recognition that experts cannot be effectively cross-examined at trial without the opportunity to conduct discovery concerning their opinions and the bases for those opinions. See Wright & Miller §§2029-2031.1.

Non-testifying experts, however, are treated quite differently. Rule 26(a) does not require disclosure of the identity or opinions of non-testifying experts, and Rule 26(b)(4)(B) provides that a party may only seek discovery concerning non-testifying experts upon a showing of "exceptional circumstances." This protection echoes the similar protection for work product under Rule 26(b)(3)), and for similar reasons. Non-testifying experts are fully involved in the preparation of a case for trial, including educating counsel on the procedures and lore of a specialized profession, developing theories of recovery, sifting relevant testimony, producing exhibits, and preparing witnesses to testify. Allowing discovery from these experts would allow counsel to delve deeply into her opponent's trial strategy, and would stultify open exchange between counsel and her own experts.

It is useful to analyze problems concerning the scope of discovery in much the same sequence as they are discussed in this introduction. That is, ask first whether the information is within the broad presumptive scope of discovery under Rule 26(b)(1), and then whether one of the exceptions to discovery of relevant information applies. In analyzing the following examples, assume that the Federal Rules apply.

## Examples

### The Rules Giveth: Relevance

2. Liebling was injured using a pair of electric hedgeclippers manufactured by the Miller Manufacturing Company. He sues Miller, alleging that it negligently designed the hedgeclippers, by leaving a bare wire inside that caused an electric shock. During discovery, he sends a Rule 34 request for production of documents that includes a request for all written warnings provided with the clippers concerning risks that the clippers posed to users. Miller objects to this request on the ground that it is relevant to a negligent failure to warn or strict liability theory, and Liebling has only pleaded a different theory, that the hedgeclippers were negligently designed. Is the objection valid?

3. When Liebling files suit. Miller Corp. responds by filing a motion to dismiss under Fed. R. Civ. P. 12(b)(2) for lack of personal jurisdiction.
   a. Liebing sends interrogatories to Miller inquiring about its business contacts with the forum state and the manner in which the offending clippers entered the state. Must Miller answer the interrogatories?
   b. While the motion is pending, Liebling sends interrogatories to Miller asking questions about the design of its hedgeclippers and complaints from consumers about injuries using them. Must Miller answer the interrogatories?

4. Liebling sends interrogatories to Miller requesting information on any changes it had made to the design of its clippers "from the date of the accident to the present." Miller objects, on the ground that changes after the date of the accident are irrelevant to Liebling's claim, and would be inadmissible at trial under Fed. R. Evid. 407, which bars use of evidence that the defendant took "subsequent remedial measures" to improve the product after an accident to show that the product was negligently designed at the time of the accident.[4] Is the objection proper?

---

4. The rationale for this evidentiary rule is that, if such evidence could be used at trial, it would discourage parties from making changes that increase the safety of their products, for fear that such changes would be used to prove that they were negligent in the first place.

## The Rules Giveth and Taketh Away:
## Balancing Relevance and Burden

5. Liebling claims in his action that he has been disabled from performing his former job as a landscaper, and seeks damages for loss of earning capacity. Miller sends a request for production of documents to Liebling seeking his tax returns for the five years before the injury and the two years that have passed since the injury. Must Liebling produce them?

6. Murrow Corporation brings an antitrust action against the Pyle Company, a menswear company that brought out a new line of shirts in 1999. Murrow claims that Pyle has engaged in illegal price fixing arrangements with various retailers concerning marketing of the shirts. Murrow sends a Rule 34 Request for Production of Documents, requesting all documents relating to pricing of the company's menswear products between 1989 and 2005. Pyle's counsel replies that it "objects to the Plaintiff's Request for Production on the ground that it is unduly burdensome and seeks information irrelevant to the claims or defenses in this case." Is the objection justified? If Murrow's counsel believes the objection is not justified, how should she proceed?

7. Gellhorn sues Jones for sexual harassment, claiming that Jones harassed her over a period of months, and then fired her from her job as a waitress at a bar because she refused to engage in sexual conduct with him. Jones contends that he actually fired Gellhorn because she was using her job to pick up men at the bar.

   During discovery, Jones's counsel sends interrogatories seeking the names of all men with whom Gellhorn has had sexual relations in the last five years.
   a. Does the information requested satisfy the relevance standard in Rule 26(b)(1)?
   b. How should Gellhorn's counsel respond to this interrogatory?

## The Rules Taketh Away: Privilege

8. Shirer sues Tubbs for injuries suffered in an accident. He claims that Tubbs was drunk at the time of the accident. Tubbs retains Severeid to represent him. At their first meeting, Tubbs says, "Look, you're my counsel and I'm entitled to speak with you in confidence. The fact is that I had been drinking at Fred's Bar and Grill for two hours before the accident, had seven beers, and was pretty well around the bend when I left Fred's. But you're not going to tell them that, are you? How do you think we should play this?"

Subsequently, Shirer sends interrogatories to Tubbs asking whether he had been drinking before the accident, if so where, and how many drinks he had had. What should Severeid do in responding to the interrogatories?

9. At Tubbs's deposition, Shirer's counsel asks him, "Didn't you tell your lawyer that you had had seven beers before the accident?" Severeid objects based on the attorney-client privilege. Does the privilege apply?

10. Suppose that at the deposition Severeid instructs Tubbs not to answer a question, on the basis of the attorney-client privilege. Shirer's counsel does not believe the information he has asked for is privileged, since he thinks that Severeid did not represent Tubbs at the time of the conversation. What should Shirer's counsel do?

11. Consider again example 8, in which Gellhorn sues Jones for sexual harassment. Unfortunately, Gellhorn has no witnesses to Jones's alleged harassment, which took place in his office for obvious reasons. However, she knows that Jones is in psychotherapy, and from comments he made she believes that Jones has discussed his actions with his therapist. Gellhorn's counsel, while acknowledging that Jones's communications with his therapist are privileged, moves for an order granting discovery of the therapist's notes, arguing that, even though the records are privileged, the only way he can make a case against Jones is through access to them. How should the court rule?

## The Rules Taketh Away: Work Product Limits on Discovery

12. Irwin Coal Company supplies coal to Mauldin Corporation's factory under a two-year contract. Early in the course of the contract, a dispute arises as to whether the coal Irwin is supplying meets the contract specifications, which require delivery of "first quality coal." Irwin delivers Grade AB coal, but Mauldin claims this does not constitute "first quality" coal. Mauldin threatens to refuse further deliveries if Irwin continues to deliver AB coal. Irwin counters by threatening to recall coal already en route if Irwin does not accept grade AB.

Irwin's president asks Crane, the sales representative who negotiated the contract with Mauldin, to write out in detail the sequence of negotiations leading to the contract, to determine whether Mauldin's position is justified. Crane drafts a long memorandum detailing the negotiations and the various statements he made during three meetings with Mauldin employees. He attaches his personal notes of the meetings.

Later, Mauldin cancels the contract and Irwin sues to collect. Mauldin's counsel sends interrogatories to Irwin seeking all "notes, records, letters, memoranda, or other communications concerning the contract in issue."

    a. May Irwin invoke Rule 26(b)(3) to avoid producing Crane's memorandum?

    b. May it protect Crane's original notes of his meetings with Mauldin employees under Rule 26(b)(3)?

13. Irwin sues Mauldin for breach of the coal contract. Assume that Hersey, the employee who negotiated the contract for Mauldin, has since moved to Abbu Dhabi and cannot be found, and that Hersey left no memos detailing the negotiations for the contract. Irwin's counsel sends an interrogatory to Mauldin's president asking him to "relate the substance of any interviews you and/or your counsel conducted with Hersey concerning the contract involved in this action." Mauldin's lawyer had in fact interviewed Hersey, though he did not record or take notes at the interview. Does Rule 26(b)(3) protect this information from discovery.

14. Assume that Mauldin's lawyer took extensive notes at his interview with Hersey. The notes include factual statements made by Hersey about the course of the negotiations, and evaluative comments concerning the credibility of Hersey's statements, other evidence that might contradict it, and problems with admissibility of the evidence. Irwin's interrogatories seek production of "any notes, memoranda, recordings, or other records of discussions with Hersey concerning the events in suit." Are the notes protected under Fed. R. Civ. P. 26(b)(3)? (Assume, for purposes of the example, that the attorney-client privilege does not protect these documents.)

15. Irwin sends an interrogatory to Mauldin asking whether, at the time of the negotiations for the contract, Hersey had given assurances to Irwin's employees during the negotiations that Grade AB coal would suffice under the contract. Hersey had admitted to Mauldin's counsel that he had said that Grade AB was satisfactory. Mauldin's counsel refuses to answer, on the ground that the information is protected by the "work product privilege." Does Rule 26(b)(3) apply?

## The Rules Giveth and Taketh Away: Discovery from Experts

16. Sherrod is injured in a mining accident and sues Gold Mining Company for his injuries. The parties begin discovery. Consider the following problems, in light of Rule 26(b)(4).

    a. Bigart is a metallurgist who consults for mining operations, periodically testing the effects of stress on various metals used in shoring up mine shafts, and testing supports involved in mining accidents. Before the accident, Bigart had performed stress tests on several supports that collapsed during the accident. Sherrod's counsel notices Bigart's deposition. Gold objects, claiming that he is a non-testifying expert, and therefore cannot be deposed absent exceptional circumstances under Fed. R. Civ. P. 26(b)(4)(B). Is the objection valid?

  b. Suppose that, after the accident, Gold retained Bigart as a non-testifying expert to assist in preparing to defend Sherrod's case. May Sherrod's counsel depose him?

  c. After the accident, Gold, anticipating a lawsuit, consults Mydans, another metallurgist, and asks her to review the specifications for the mine structure and test the supports that collapsed. Gold pays Mydans a fee for this service. Mydans sends a short report concluding that the structural members were improperly placed, given the unusual configuration of the mine shaft. Gold decides not to retain Mydans to assist with the litigation. Sherrod's counsel sends an interrogatory seeking the identity of all experts Gold has consulted with regard to the accident. How should Gold respond?

  d. Gold, a sophisticated corporation with lots of knowledge about mining, begins to organize its defense shortly after the accident. Its counsel learns that there are only three experts on the particular type of engineering involved in the accident, one of whom is not well reputed. It hires the other two, one as a testifying expert, the other as a non-testifying expert. Three months later, after getting out of the hospital, Sherrod hires counsel, who looks for an expert. She locates the same three, and contacts them, only to find that the two good ones have been sewed up by the opposition. What can she do about it?

## Explanations

### An Early Question

1. a. The statements requested in *Hickman* clearly satisfy the broad relevance standard in Rule 26(b)(1) — even the amended standard of 2000. All were from witnesses to the accident or to the subsequent repairs on the tug, and would have shed light on events in suit, such as how the accident happened or the decedent's injuries. Certainly, this would be relevant to the plaintiffs' claims for personal injury damages.

  b. The attorney-client privilege did not apply, since the interviews did not involve confidential communications with Fortenbaugh's client, but rather discussions with non-party witnesses to the events. Even if the witnesses may have believed they were meeting with

Fortenbaugh "in confidence," this belief would not protect their statements from court-ordered discovery.

c. It is one thing to seek written statements taken from a witness. It is quite another to conscript opposing counsel to write out the details of an oral interview with a witness. True, both would force a lawyer in Fortenbaugh's position to assist in developing her opponent's case, but the latter enlists him even more in that effort, since it requires him to recall what was said at an earlier interview and write it out for the plaintiff's benefit.

On the other hand, if Fortenbaugh were ordered to produce the substance of oral statements, he could at least protect his own mental evaluations of the testimony by producing only *factual* statements the witness had made. If he were forced to produce the notes he had taken on earlier interviews, he would be revealing both factual statements and his own interpretive or evaluative comments at the same time.

d. Plaintiff's counsel had an unusually comprehensive opportunity to learn the nature of the witnesses' testimony. First, they had all appeared and given testimony at a public hearing about the accident. See *Hickman*, 329 U.S. at 498. Second, plaintiff had inquired concerning the facts in interrogatories to Fortenbaugh's client. Any information about the accident gleaned from the witness interviews would have to be revealed in answering those interrogatories. Finally, plaintiff's counsel could presumably have called these witnesses for depositions under Fed. R. Civ. P. 30 and compelled them to testify fully about the events in suit.

e. Plaintiff's counsel claimed that he wanted the information only to cover all the bases — to make sure he hadn't missed anything in his own preparation. 329 U.S. at 513. However, he may not have been fully candid about his reasons for seeking the information from Fortenbaugh rather than by other means. He may have been trying to limit his expenses by getting these statements from the witnesses without the expense of deposing them or obtaining transcripts of the public hearing. In addition, he may have believed that these witnesses were likely to be more candid in speaking "off the record" to Fortenbaugh than they would be at a public hearing or a recorded deposition, and hoped to catch them in inconsistencies or revelations unavailable through these other avenues.

## The Rules Giveth: Relevance

2. This is an interesting question, and it is rendered more interesting by the 2000 amendment to Rule 26(b)(1). That Rule now authorizes discovery of any information "relevant to any party's claim or defense."

If the word "claim" refers to the "claim" asserted in Liebling's complaint, there is a strong argument that this information is not discoverable. The "claim" in Liebling's complaint is for negligence in the design of the hedgeclippers, not for failure to warn of the risks involved in using the clippers. Arguably, this is a different claim, not yet raised by any party, and therefore not within the scope of discovery.

In fact, isn't it likely that Liebling is seeking this information in order to ascertain whether there is a factual basis for adding a new "claim" for negligent failure to warn? At the time he filed the complaint, he may not have had enough facts to support a failure to warn claim, and therefore left that theory out of his complaint to avoid Rule 11 problems. Now he would like to use discovery to gather the information necessary to decide whether to amend the complaint to add a failure-to-warn claim. Under the new wording of Rule 26(b)(1), it appears that he may not be able to use discovery to probe this alternative theory.

If the rule is interpreted to refer only to the "claims" — that is, the legal theories — already pleaded, counsel will be under great pressure to plead multiple theories, even if they have little or no evidentiary support for some of them. To obtain access to discovery on those theories under Rule 26(b)(1), counsel would have to plead them first. This could create considerable tension between the need for discovery to develop a case and the strictures in Rule 11 on unsupported pleadings.

Under the prior version of Rule 26(b)(1), this tension was avoided. The documents concerning warnings may not be relevant to negligent manufacture (the "claim" Liebling pleaded initially), but they would be discoverable under the standard in Rule 26(b)(1) prior to 2000, because they are relevant to the "subject matter involved in the pending action" — the hedgeclipper accident. Under that standard, Liebling was able to seek discovery of information relevant to the underlying litigation events even if he had not yet pleaded a "claim" for failure to warn.[5]

3. a. Strictly speaking, Liebling's interrogatories are relevant to the court's jurisdiction, not to the merits of the personal injury claim itself or any substantive defense to it. However, it is not much of a stretch to argue that the information sought is relevant to Miller's jurisdictional

---

5. The amended version of Rule 26(b)(1) does give Liebling another option: He can make a motion for an order expanding the scope of discovery to the broader limits under the prior version of the rule. See Rule 26(b)(1), second sentence (authorizing the court, upon a showing of good cause, to allow discovery of any matter relevant to the subject matter of the action). However, it is doubtful that judges are going to be very enthusiastic about such motions. If the litigant's only ground for the motion is that she would like to see what she can find, the motion could be made in every case and looks like mere disagreement with the new rule rather than an individualized ground for a waiver in particular circumstances.

"defense," and therefore within the scope of discovery under Rule 26(b)(1). Clearly, the jurisdiction question is relevant to whether the court can adjudicate Liebling's claim *at all*, and Liebling should be entitled to find out the jurisdictional facts so that he can litigate the motion. Consequently, courts generally held that jurisdictional issues were within the scope of discovery under the prior version of Rule 26(b)(1). See Moore's, s. 26.41[11][b]. They will almost certainly continue to do so under the amended rule. See, e.g., *Commissariat A L'Energie Atomique v. Chi Mei Optoelectronics Corp.*, 395 F.3d 1315 (Fed Cir. 2005) (granting jurisdictional discovery under amended Rule 26(b)(1)).

b. Liebling's interrogatories are clearly within the scope of discovery under Rule 26(b)(1), since they seek information relevant to his claim that the hedgeclippers were negligently designed. Miller, however, may argue that it should not have to respond to these interrogatories at all, since it is not subject to the jurisdiction of the court where Liebling has filed suit.

Generally, the fact that a defendant raises a jurisdictional objection to an action does not suspend the right of parties to take discovery on the merits. However, Miller could move for a protective order, asking the court to stay discovery on the merits of the claim until its jurisdictional objection has been resolved. Miller's position is that it should not have to litigate in the forum at all; it seems appropriate that, if the objection is substantial, discovery on the underlying personal injury claim should be suspended until the court determines whether it has the power to adjudicate the merits. The court might grant the stay, if it thinks the jurisdictional objection may prevail. However, if the jurisdictional facts are intertwined with the merits, or the court views the objection as dubious, it also might not.

4. No, it is not proper, because discovery is not limited to information that would be admissible under the rules of evidence. Information "need not be admissible at trial" (Rule 26(b)(1)) to be discoverable, if it is relevant and "appears reasonably calculated to lead to the discovery of admissible evidence." Id. Here, evidence of changes in the design will certainly help Liebling to locate witnesses with information about the design, and may help her to prove that other designs could have avoided the danger. Thus, the evidence would assist Liebling in examining Miller's witnesses about the negligence issues, and is discoverable.

## The Rules Giveth and Taketh Away:
## Balancing Relevance and Burden

5. Miller has a good case for obtaining information about Liebling's income through discovery. A major issue in the case is whether the accident has affected Liebling's earnings. His tax returns from before and after the accident are an excellent source of proof on that issue; thus, they are clearly relevant to Liebling's claim for damages.

   Liebling, of course, will be reluctant to produce his tax returns, which contain much confidential information besides his income. However, there is no blanket "tax return privilege" that bars their production, and litigation often compels parties to share information that is otherwise private with opponents in the suit.

   On the other hand, Miller's legitimate need for discovery can be accommodated while still protecting Liebling's privacy interest in his tax returns. To meet Liebling's claim of lost earning capacity, Miller needs to know Liebling's *earned income* prior to the accident. There is no need to produce his entire tax returns to provide this information to Miller: It is available from his wage statements or self-employment tax forms. Producing these will meet Miller's legitimate discovery needs while preserving the privacy of other aspects of Liebling's returns. See Wright & Miller §2019 at nn.31-33.

   If Miller requests the returns themselves, Liebling's counsel will likely respond by offering the wage statements instead. Miller will likely acquiesce in this, because he probably won't be able to convince the court that he needs anything more.

6. Pyle's objection here is to the breadth of the material requested. The suit relates to pricing of shirts, but the request is much broader, extending to all marketing documents concerning any of Pyle's products. In addition, the line of shirts at issue in the case only came out in 1999, while the request seeks documents going back to 1989. On the other hand, the test for discovery is broad, and it is arguable that Pyle's general pricing practices are relevant to Murrow's claim here. If Pyle has engaged in price fixing on other products, information concerning their methods may assist Murrow in proving that they did the same thing with their new shirts.

   There is simply no bright line "yes or no" answer to the proper scope of discovery here. The documents become less relevant as we go further back in time and move to other lines of products, but are still of some relevance. This is the type of practical, ambiguous discovery dispute that counsel ideally work out during discovery. Perhaps they can agree to some limits on the time period, the products involved, or the method of identifying relevant documents to satisfy the plaintiff's discovery need without undue burden, expense, or intrusion on the defendant's business. For a good case discussing the judge's discretion in resolving disputes involving burdensome discovery, in a straight-forward factual context, see *Surles Ex Rel. Johnson v. Greyhound Lines, Inc,* 474 F.3d 288, 304-306 (6th Cir. 2007).

Both parties' lawyers have an incentive to work out such discovery disputes. Murrow's counsel wants to get the information, without the hassle of going to court to do so. Pyle's counsel, while he objects to the breadth of this request, doubtless realizes that some subset of the information is relevant and important. If Murrow files a motion to compel production of the documents, Pyle will be ordered to respond to some extent, and the judge will be irked if he takes up court time by inflexibly resisting production. In addition, Pyle's counsel will be seeking discovery too; if he digs in his heels on this one, he can expect corresponding resistance to his requests as well.

The rules now require the parties to attempt to resolve problems like this before seeking an order from the court compelling production of the information. Under Rule 37(a)(1) the party moving to compel production must certify that he has "in good faith conferred or attempted to confer with the person or party failing to make disclosure or discovery in an effort to obtain it without court action." If the parties cannot resolve the issue, the court will have to decide. Since Pyle has refused to produce the documents, Murrow will have to seek an order from the court compelling production, or accept Pyle's refusal. If the information is likely to be marginal, Murrow may let the matter go, given the time and expense of the motion to compel.

If Murrow moves to compel and Pyle's objection is held insufficient, the court may award the costs of the motion (including Murrow's attorney's fees) to Murrow. Fed. R. Civ. P. 37(a)(5)(A). In a case where the objection is arguable, however, (as it probably is here), the court may refuse to do so, even if it orders production of some or most of the documents requested.

7. a. Arguably, evidence of at least some of Gellhorn's past sexual conduct is relevant to Jones's defense that Gellhorn was using her position to "pick up" men at the bar. For example, if Gellhorn identifies her past sexual partners Jones might learn of men whom she had picked up at his bar, which would corroborate his version of the events in suit.

b. Gellhorn should respond by objecting to the interrogatory based on the private nature of the information sought, or moving for a protective order barring production of this information. Even if evidence is relevant, it is not necessarily discoverable: The court has a role to play in limiting discovery where disclosure may not be justified. Rule 26(c) allows the court to enter protective orders limiting discovery *even* if the requested information meets the broad relevance standard in Rule 26(b)(1). See also Rule 26(b)(1), (relevant evidence is discoverable "unless otherwise limited by court order . . .").

Here, there is a strong argument that Gellhorn should not be compelled to produce such intimate information. In *Priest v. Rotary*, 98 F.R.D. 755, 761 (N.D. Cal. 1983), on which this example is loosely based, the court granted a protective order barring such inquiries, noting that "[d]iscovery of intimate aspects of plaintiffs' lives as well as those of their past and current friends and acquaintances, has the clear potential to discourage sexual harassment litigants from prosecuting lawsuits such as the instant one." Although intimate information must often be produced in discovery, the marginal value of the information requested here is outweighed by the intrusion on Gellhorn's privacy.

## The Rules Taketh Away: Privilege

8. To say the least, Tubbs has placed Severeid in a very delicate position. He has told him facts that, if revealed in the litigation, will clearly hurt Tubbs's case. While he evidently assumed that the attorney-client privilege would protect his candid comments from disclosure, he is seriously mistaken about the limits of the privilege.

The attorney-client privilege only protects *the communications between lawyer and client* from discovery. The privilege does *not* protect a party from responding to discovery of facts about the case just because those facts have been told to an attorney.

> The protection of the privilege extends only to *communications* and not to facts. A fact is one thing and a communication concerning that fact is an entirely different thing. The client cannot be compelled to answer the question "What did you say or write to the attorney?" but may not refuse to disclose any relevant fact within his knowledge merely because he incorporated a statement of such fact into his communication to his attorney.[6]

A moment's thought makes it obvious that this distinction must be made. Otherwise, Tubbs could immunize everything he knows from discovery simply by telling those facts to his lawyer. Thus, in answering the interrogatories, Severeid cannot disregard facts he knows about the case, even though Tubbs told him those facts "in confidence." Although the factual responses to interrogatories are signed by the client, not the lawyer (see Rule 33(b)(5)), Severeid cannot

---

6. *Upjohn v. United States*, 449 U.S. 383, 395-396 (1981) (quoting from *City of Philadelphia v. Westinghouse Electric Corp.*, 205 F. Supp. 830, 831 (E.D. Pa. 1962)).

facilitate perjury by filing answers that he knows to be untrue. A.B.A. Model Rules of Professional Conduct, 3.3(a)(3). The system is predicated on lawyers hewing to their ethical obligations, and, in the long run, you will fare better in the profession by taking those obligations seriously. Severeid will have to explain to Tubbs that (absent some *other* privilege, such as the Fifth Amendment privilege against self-incrimination) he must reveal what he has been told, or else withdraw from representing Tubbs.[7]

The irony here, of course, is that the attorney-client privilege purports to encourage full and open communication between lawyer and client. See, e.g., *Fisher v. United States*, 425 U.S. 391, 403 (1976) (purpose of privilege is to "encourage clients to make full disclosures to their attorneys"). But a client like Tubbs may feel sandbagged by the unexpected consequences of his candor. At the least, the example suggests that lawyers should explain to clients at the outset the limits on the protection the attorney-client privilege provides.

9. The privilege is validly raised here. Tubbs's conversations with Severeid in the course of the representation are protected by the privilege, lest he be discouraged from consulting counsel. Thus, Shirer's counsel cannot inquire about what Tubbs told Severeid to determine whether he may have told him a different story than he told at some other time.

10. The party requesting information through discovery need not roll over and play dead just because opposing counsel objects to producing the information. The obvious first response is to ask opposing counsel the basis for the objection. Perhaps Severeid can be convinced that his objection is not well grounded under the circumstances. If not, the discussion will at least elicit the ground of the objection more specifically, so that Shirer's counsel can decide whether to accept the objection or press for an answer. Rule 26(b)(5) requires a party claiming the privilege to "describe the nature of the documents, communications or tangible things not produced or disclosed — and do so in a manner that, without revealing information itself privileged or protected, will enable other parties to assess the claim."

---

7. If this answer seems naive, there may be other sufficient reasons for facing the music in a situation like this rather than playing fast and loose with the facts. If Tubbs really was drinking at Fred's, one way or another this fact is likely to surface. If it does, and Tubbs has denied it under oath, his credibility with the jury on other issues in the case will suffer grievously.

Some lawyers suggest that you should make sure that this situation never arises, by signaling to the client one way or another what you don't want to hear. To the extent this is true, it is ironic, because such signals obviously undermine the professed goal of open communication between lawyer and client.

If Shirer's lawyer considers the information important, and is still convinced that it is not privileged, she will have to file a motion to compel Tubbs to answer under Rule 37(a)(1). The court will then decide whether the privilege applies and, if it does not, order Tubbs to respond.

11. Here, the psychotherapist/patient privilege applies to protect Jones's communications with his therapist from disclosure. But, argues Gellhorn, I *really need* the privileged material; without it I simply cannot make a case.

This is not strictly true, of course — Gellhorn can testify herself to the harassment in Jones's office, and that may suffice to make a prima facie case. But the evidence is obviously of great importance to her case. However, even if the testimony is essential, its importance will generally not override the claim of privilege. The creation of a privilege represents a judgment by a court or legislature that it is more important to protect the communication from disclosure than it is to give litigants access to it. Thus, absent some constitutional issue, a claim of privilege will usually prevail even if the information withheld is crucial. Compare, however, the more limited protection under Rule 26(b)(3) for trial preparation materials.

## The Rules Taketh Away: Work Product Limits on Discovery

12. a. Crane's memo is clearly relevant to Irwin's claim, so it is presumptively discoverable under Rule 26(b)(1). However, Irwin will argue that it is "work product" subject to the limits on discovery in Rule 26(b)(3).

There are several problems with Irwin's argument. First, Crane's memo was created by an Irwin employee for another Irwin employee; no lawyer was involved at all. (Compare *Hickman*, in which the materials involved were prepared by counsel for the defendant). Can it still be work product?

Yes it can; the rule expressly applies to documents or tangible things "prepared by or for another party" or by or for that party's representative (such as his lawyer). This makes sense; lawyers are not the only ones who prepare for trial; parties do too. The rule protects the privacy of their preparation as well as counsel's. Indeed, in many cases it will be hard to separate materials prepared for the party from those prepared for counsel. The rule protects them both.

However, there is a second problem with Irwin's work product claim. At the time Crane drafted his memo, no lawsuit was pending between the parties. They were involved in a dispute, but no one had threatened suit or retained counsel to file one. They were simply at odds on interpretation of a contract, a very common commercial occurrence. Thus, there is a very substantial question as to whether the memo was "prepared in anticipation of litigation" as Rule 26(b)(3) requires.

Materials certainly can be "prepared in anticipation of litigation" even if no suit has been filed. In many cases it will be clear that suit is imminent and the documents are for use in the case, so that the work product privilege will apply. In others, however, documents relating to a dispute will be prepared in the regular course of business (such as an accident report or investigation) or in order to *avoid* litigation. One test used in the cases protects materials under Rule 26(b)(3) if they are prepared "'because of the prospect of litigation.'" *United States v. Adlman*, 134 F.3d 1194, 1202 (2nd Cir 1998) (quoting from Wright & Miller, s. 2024). This test would probably not apply to Crane's memo, which was evidently prepared to resolve the dispute with Mauldin rather than to prosecute a lawsuit. Another test found in the cases, whether the document was prepared primarily to aid in litigation (see Moore's at 26.70[3][a]), is even more restrictive and would clearly not be met in this case.

b. It might be argued that every record a business creates these days is "in anticipation of" litigation: It certainly is common enough for commercial transactions to end up in court. But accepting this argument would allow the exception (work product protection from discovery under Rule 26(b)(3)) to swallow the rule (broad access to relevant information under Rule 26(b)(1)). Instead, Rule 26(b)(3) restricts work product protection to those documents prepared for use in litigation. Crane's notes of the meetings with Mauldin were created before the dispute concerning the terms of the contract arose, at a time when neither party contemplated litigation, and presumably for general record-keeping purposes. They are not protected under Rule 26(b)(3).

13. Actually, Rule 26(b)(3) does not apply here at all; that rule only applies to "documents and tangible things." Here, Irwin has asked Mauldin's lawyer to relate the substance of conversations which he had with Hersey, but never wrote down. Admittedly, these are "mental impressions" of the lawyer, which, if revealed, may disclose his legal theories or conclusions. They merit protection, but Rule 26(b)(3), read literally (or even liberally), doesn't provide that protection.[8]

---

8. Although Rule 26(b)(3)(B) protects a lawyer's mental impressions, conclusions, opinions, or legal theories, it only applies to "those materials," that is, the "documents and tangible things" referred to in Rule 26(b)(3)(A). Rule 26(b)(3)(B) does not provide general protection for mental impressions beyond those contained in documents and tangible things.

While Rule 26(b)(3) doesn't apply, the court would doubtless fall back on the common law protection of *Hickman* itself to bar the discovery Irwin has requested. Requiring Mauldin's counsel to reconstruct interviews with witnesses would raise all the concerns that troubled the *Hickman* Court. Rule 26(b)(3), because of its limitation to "documents and tangible things," only *partially* codifies *Hickman*, but the same concerns would very likely lead a court to protect attorney mental impressions in other circumstances as well. See, e.g., *In re Sealed Case*, 856 F.2d 268, 273 (D.C. Cir. 1988) (deposition questions that would have required attorney testimony on mental impressions of their witness interviews protected under *Hickman*).

14. The notes requested here are documents prepared in anticipation of trial, since Mauldin's counsel interviewed Hersey in preparing his defense of the contract claim. Thus, the notes enjoy qualified protection under Rule 26(b)(3). However, the court still might order production of at least parts of the notes on motion by Irwin's counsel. Rule 26(b)(3) creates a limited right to obtain trial preparation materials on a showing of substantial need and inability to obtain equivalent information through other means. That showing might well be made here, since Hersey's testimony will be crucial but cannot otherwise be obtained.

However, even if such a showing is made, Rule 26(b)(3) protects Mauldin's counsel's "mental impressions, conclusions, opinions or legal theories" from discovery. His notes concerning admissibility of the evidence, Hersey's credibility, and other evidence in the case are all protected "opinion work product." If the court orders production of the notes on Hersey's testimony, it should allow Mauldin's counsel to produce a "redacted" version of the notes, with all this evaluative material stricken out.

15. In this example, Irwin has asked Mauldin a *factual question*, whether Hersey made a particular statement about Grade AB coal during the negotiations. Mauldin's counsel knows that he did, and his knowledge of that information is imputed to his client, since Mauldin's lawyer acts as its agent in conducting the litigation. Even though counsel knows this information as a result of his work in preparing for litigation, he still must reveal it. The work product doctrine does not protect *facts* from being discovered, even if they are learned through trial preparation. Most of the facts are learned that way.

Suppose, for example, that Mauldin's lawyer had discussed the case with various Mauldin employees, to determine who had information regarding the contract, and was then faced with an interrogatory asking for "the names of all persons with information relevant to the events in suit." He cannot protect such information under the work product privilege, even though his knowledge of the names of witnesses is a "mental impression" and was acquired in the course of trial preparation. The privilege protects documents produced in the course of case preparation, and opinions of counsel, but does not allow counsel to refuse proper discovery requests for factual knowledge about the issues.

## The Rules Giveth and Taketh Away: Discovery from Experts

16. a. Gold's objection is not valid. While Bigart rendered specialized services for Gold, at the time he was not retained in anticipation of litigation. The facts indicate that he routinely performed such tests for Gold. Although Bigart is an "expert" in the sense that he has specialized information relevant to the case, his knowledge comes from his testing of the structural members in the ordinary course of his employment. As to this information, acquired prior to the litigation and for general business purposes, Bigart is a fact witness, not an expert hired to offer an opinion in a lawsuit, and is subject to full discovery.[9]

   This is a very important distinction. In most complex cases there will be witnesses with specialized knowledge of the facts who are not experts in the litigation. For example, in a fraud case, a bank's systems analyst, who understands how transactions are processed through the computer system, can provide valuable testimony about how the system was programmed and the sequence of steps in completing a particular type of transaction. However, this is factual evidence about the case, which the expert acquired independent of the litigation in the normal course of business. Counsel is entitled to inquire into such information, whether the analyst is an "expert" or not. Similarly, General Motors doubtless has highly trained, "expert" employees who run its crash testing program. But the Rule 26 discovery limits on experts would not bar a plaintiff from deposing those employees about how the crash testing program is conducted or how the car in issue was designed to meet crashworthiness standards.

   b. Even though Bigart is now an "expert specially employed in anticipation of litigation," under Rule 26(b)(4)(B), Sherrod's counsel

---

[9]. Nor would Bigart's test results be protected as trial preparation materials under Rule 26(b)(3), since they were not prepared in anticipation of litigation, but as part of normal company quality control procedures.

could still depose him to learn any information he had about the case *as a fact witness*. Gold should not be able to immunize facts Bigart knows about the litigation events from discovery by paying him a fee to help with the defense. Even though Rule 26(b)(4)(B) refers to "facts known" by the expert, this must refer to facts known through preparing the case, not facts known independently as a witness to the litigation events.

c. You can see why Sherrod would like to have Mydans's name, and why Gold would prefer not reveal it. If Sherrod finds out that Gold had consulted Mydans, and that she had offered an opinion that the supports were defective, he might hire Mydans himself.

Rule 26(b)(4)(B) doesn't expressly address whether Sherrod can learn Mydans' name through discovery. First, it isn't clear whether Mydans was "retained or specially employed . . . in anticipation of litigation" by Gold. She was paid a fee for an initial consultation, but only with a view to determining whether to retain her as a non-testifying expert. Since her opinion was not helpful to the defense, Gold decided not to retain her further.

Even if she is a non-testifying expert under Rule 26(b)(4)(B), Gold may not have to reveal her name. That rule only allows discovery of "facts known or opinions held" by such experts "in exceptional circumstances." This suggests that, without a very substantial showing of need, you can't get any discovery from these experts. They are private consultants, whose participation in the litigation is intimately tied to work product and trial strategy. Counsel should be able to prepare the case with them, free of concerns that the other side will learn of their discussions. Thus, most of the cases hold that even the identity of consulting experts is protected from discovery. See Wright & Miller, §2032. The Advisory Committee note to the 1970 Amendment to Rule 26(b)(4) states that "the subdivision precludes discovery against experts who were informally consulted in preparation for trial but not retained or specially employed." Moore's Federal Practice, §26 App.05[2]. Thus, Gold is probably free to "expert shop" without fear that Sherrod will obtain the names of its rejected experts through discovery.

d. This is a "real world" litigation problem that Sherrod's counsel probably can't do much about. Nothing in the Rules bars Gold from hiring good experts, even if there aren't many of them. And the rules seriously limit Sherrod's ability to obtain discovery from Gold's experts. Absent "exceptional circumstances," Sherrod cannot get discovery from the retained expert at all (Rule 26(b)(4)(B)), and must wait until shortly before trial (under Rule 26(a)(2)) to depose the testifying expert.

**433**

This situation might constitute "exceptional circumstances" under Rule 26(b)(4)(B)(ii), allowing Sherrod to seek discovery from Gold's non-testifying expert. See Wright & Miller §2032 at n.24 (such discovery may be proper where one party has "corner[ed] the market" on experts). Even if Sherrod is allowed some discovery from Gold's retained expert, however, the fact remains that the best experts have been co-opted by the defense, leaving Sherrod to use the third stringer to make his own case.

# Tools of the Trade

## The Basic Methods of Discovery

---

## INTRODUCTION

The last chapter considered broad conceptual issues raised by the right of discovery in civil litigation. This chapter addresses more practical, "how-to" issues that arise in using the rules of discovery to develop the facts of cases.

As the previous chapter indicates, modern procedure, unlike traditional practice, is premised on wide access to information possessed by adversaries and third parties *before* trial. Under the federal discovery rules, parties may obtain almost all information in the other side's hands before the case is tried. Ideally, broad discovery makes trial a matter of clear, orderly presentation of evidence known to all litigants. It also encourages settlement by educating the parties about the strengths and weaknesses of their cases.

The discovery process is conducted by counsel for the parties with the court sitting as a referee to adjudicate disputes that arise during the exchange. Under the original Federal Rules, the process was driven entirely by discovery requests; that is, counsel had to ask for information or testimony; if they didn't ask for an item, they didn't get it. If an appropriate request was made, the opponent generally had to respond, but there was no provision for automatic exchange of information. This basic premise was changed by the 1993 amendments to the Federal Rules, which introduced some "automatic disclosure" requirements for the first time. Fed. R. Civ. P. 26(a). For the most part, however, discovery remains an antiphonal process, under which a litigant who wants information sends a request for discovery to her adversary, who either provides the necessary information or raises an objection to doing so.

The basic devices for seeking discovery in federal court are interrogatories under Fed. R. Civ. P. 33, requests for production of documents under Fed. R. Civ. P. 34, and oral depositions under Fed. R. Civ. P. 30. Each of these is discussed in turn below. Although state practice may differ, the federal rules provide a representative example of a discovery system.

# INTERROGATORIES

Interrogatories are probably the most frequently used form of discovery. Plainly put, they are questions propounded by one party to another, seeking information relevant to the issues in dispute. In practice, of course, they are not written by the parties; they are drafted by counsel for the requesting party, who is experienced at framing interrogatories to extract the required information as fully as possible.

The great advantage of interrogatories is that they are an inexpensive means of getting information from other parties. However, interrogatories are often less effective than one might expect. Although Rule 33(b)(3) requires the responding party to answer each interrogatory under oath (unless she has an objection), interrogatories are seldom answered spontaneously by regular people — the answers will be drafted by the opposing party's lawyer after consultation with the client. In an adversarial system, the answers are often crafted to reveal as little as possible, to avoid embarassing admissions, and to place the facts in a light favorable to the client.[1] Objections based on the discovery limits and privileges discussed in the previous chapter are also frequently raised. (See p. 465 for a set of interrogatories and responses in the *Schulansky* case, which illustrate both the use and the frustrations of interrogatories.)

Thus, interrogatories are probably most effective for obtaining basic background information, like the names and addresses of witnesses, the location and nature of records and other evidence, the names of treating physicians, itemization of bills, and similar information. They are also useful to force an opponent to specify the grounds of the general claims raised in a complaint or answer, through so-called "contention interrogatories." Many lawyers recommend using interrogatories early in the case, to help develop a plan for further discovery through document requests and depositions.

---

1. "[L]awyers who craft the responses [to interrogatories] seem to assume that it is their professional responsibility to be as stingy and self-serving in the answers they write as a strained view of the English language and the proper bounds of legal ethics permit." *McCormick-Morgan, Inc. v. Teledyne Ind., Inc.*, 134 F.R.D. 275 (N.D. Cal. 1991).

# REQUESTS FOR PRODUCTION OF DOCUMENTS

Rule 34, the second common discovery rule, dramatically illustrates the Federal Rules' premise that litigation should be based on open access to all relevant information. It authorizes a party to require an opponent to produce designated documents or things in its control for inspection and copying. In essence, the rule requires the opponent to open her files, or at least cull through them for documents relevant to the issues in suit, and produce them for the other side to review in preparing for trial.

It is not hard to imagine how intrusive many litigants find this process, even if they have nothing to hide. Naturally, the client who *does* possess potentially damaging documents — as most litigants will in cases of any size — finds it even more objectionable. The lawyers are caught in the middle, between clients pressing to minimize disclosure, and the Rules, which clearly mandate very broad production of documents. This can lead to great pressure on counsel to resist document requests. "The difficulties surrounding requests for documents can resemble those that might be encountered in a large library staffed by hostile librarians who respond to research queries only if asked precisely the right question." Yeazell, Civil Procedure (6th ed. 2004), p. 422. Parties resist document requests by construing them narrowly and by liberally invoking the privileges and other objections discussed in the previous chapter. If such objections are asserted without a substantial basis, the responding party may be sanctioned under Rule 37. In many cases, however, the objections do not so clearly transgress permissible bounds as to court the risk of sanctions.

Because the receiving party need only produce documents that are within the scope of the request, parties serving requests for production under Rule 34 tend to draft them broadly to snare as much information as possible. Often, requests will be introduced by a tedious list of definitions, intended to assure that opposing counsel cannot construe the request narrowly to avoid revealing a critical document. Here, for example, is an introductory definition of the term "document" that might be routinely spewed out of a litigator's word processor to preface a Rule 34 request:

> The word "documents" means all writings of any kind, including the originals and all non-identical copies, whether different from the originals by reason of any notation made on such copies or otherwise, including without limitation, correspondence, memoranda, notes, diaries, statistics, letters, telegrams, minutes, contracts, reports, studies, checks, statements, receipts, returns, summaries, pamphlets, books, interoffice and intraoffice communications, notations of any sort of conversations, telephone calls, meetings, or other communications, bulletins, printed matter, computer printouts, teletypes, telefax, invoices, worksheets, all drafts, alterations, modifications, changes and amendments of any of the foregoing, graphic or oral records or

representations of any kind, (including, without limitations, photographs, charts, graphs, microfiche, microfilm, videotapes, recordings, motion pictures), and any electronic, mechanical or electric records or representations of any kind (including, without limitations, tapes, cassettes, discs, recordings, and computer memories).[2]

Lawyers draft dismal passages like this to make sure that the opposing party cannot avoid discovery by narrowly construing the request. For example, absent a definition of this sort, a request for "all documents concerning a meeting held on April 27, 1997, at company headquarters" might be construed not to extend to a tape recording of the meeting or an e-mail concerning it. However, it is debatable whether such tedious edicts actually do much to assure full discovery.

Parties responding to Rule 34 requests may simply offer to open their records as they are kept in the ordinary course of business for examination by the requesting party. See Fed. R. Civ. P. 34(b)(1)(B). This can often impose a greater burden on the requesting party to cull through the records than it would on the responding party. For example, it may be a great deal easier for Ace Corporation to review its records to locate "all documents relating to recall decisions for Ace roto-turnbuckles manufactured between January 1, 1998, and December 31, 2002," than it would be for the plaintiff, unschooled in Ace's business or its recordkeeping methods, to unearth such information from voluminous computer records or files organized under unknown methods. At a minimum, the responding party should indicate how the records are organized, what sets of records respond to which requests, and any other information necessary to locate requested items. Fed. R. Civ. P.34(b)(2)(E); see also Fed. R. Civ. P. 33(d) (allowing party to respond similarly to interrogatories that require search of records).

Extensive Rule 34 requests often give rise to disputes over who is going to search for relevant documents — and who is going to pay for it. Ideally, counsel work these issues out between themselves, without resort to the judge, who invariably believes that she has better things to do with her time. In most cases, the producing party will pay the costs of the search initially, though these costs may be taxable to the losing party if the case goes to trial. The presumption is that virtually any document that fits the broad relevance standard of Rule 26(b)(1) must be produced. A party who objects will have the burden on a motion to compel production to convince the court that she has a good reason to refuse.

Rule 34 is not limited to requests for documents. It also authorizes inspection of tangible things, such as a car involved in the disputed accident or a urine sample alleged to have tested positive for drugs. Counsel

---

2. R. Haydock and D. Herr, Production of Results under Rule 34, 5 Am. J. Trial Advoc. 253, 261-262 (1981).

can also inspect places under Rule 34, such as the assembly line where the plaintiff's accident took place, or even conduct tests on relevant items of evidence, such as stress tests on a metal girder involved in a platform collapse. See Rule 34(a)(1) (authorizing production for testing and sampling as well as entry upon land for testing and other purposes).

# DISCOVERY OF ELECTRONIC DOCUMENTS

An increasingly complex litigation problem involves discovery of information stored in electronic form. These days, about ninety percent of documents are never written down; they exist only as stored electronic information. R. Marcus et al. *Civil Procedure: A Modern Approach*, 377 (4th ed. 2005). They are on employees' computers, main server hard drives, CD-ROMs, backup tapes, and other arcane electronic devices. "A typical discovery phase of a trial involving a large corporation might turn up hundreds of CD-ROMs of material, each containing the equivalent of 30,000 to 40,000 printed pages." ABA Journal, March 2005, p. 60. In addition, much information will be found in e-mails sent from individuals on their own computers. This information is likely to be stored for a time on a main server (whatever that is; I majored in poetry in college). Eventually, much of this material may get "deleted" — that is, overwritten — but may be mystically subject to resurrection if you know how to do it. Evidently, instant messaging also has archives. Cell phone and voice-messaging systems also preserve data, as well as an array of other high-tech devices. Many electronic files also include "metadata," information about when a file was produced, when earlier drafts were written, and to whom it was sent.

Older data will likely be found on backup tapes, which are copies periodically made of the information on a main computer. These backups may be in an obsolete language, or may have deteriorated over time, but sometimes can be retrieved by advanced (and expensive) computer techies. In one recent commercial case, the defendant estimated that the information from its 800 backup tapes could be retrieved . . . for between 1.5 and 1.9 million dollars. *Toshiba Am. Elec. Components, Inc. v. Superior Court of Santa Clara County*, 21 Cal. Rptr. 3d 532, 535 (Cal. App. 2004). Unfortunately, computers don't think like file clerks, so the information is not found in any particular order on the tapes. "The difficulty with backup data is that the media (usually backup tapes) hold a large amount of data that is only loosely organized. Consequently, finding relevant data requires restoring a tape, viewing its directories, and searching within the directories for specific files. If the file is not on the tape, the process must be repeated for each backup tape." *Toshiba* at 538.

The process of reviewing and producing such records can be enormously complicated and expensive. Imagine that you represented a large corporation and received a request for all documents relevant to a major transaction or product line. Finding all the relevant information in the myriad places such data might be stored would be a huge technical task. In addition, it would require considerable diplomatic skill to obtain the cooperation of all the employees and experts who would have to help in finding, preserving, and producing it, all for the humiliating purpose of handing it over to an adversary in a lawsuit

Not surprisingly, the producing party often resists discovery, arguing that little relevant information will be found, that the material is irretrievable, that the burden to do so is excessive, or that the requesting party should assume the cost of exhuming the data. The Federal Rules were amended in 2006 to address some of the issues raised by widespread electronic discovery in litigation.

- The definitions in Rules 33 and 34 were amended to make clear that electronically stored information is discoverable. See Fed. R. Civ. P. 33(d); 34(a)(1)(A).
- Rule 26(b)(2)(B) provides a process for addressing disputes over electronically stored information that is "not reasonably accessible" because of the expense of locating, reviewing, or reproducing it. This rule allows the producing party to object to producing information that it identifies as not reasonably accessible. The requesting party may then move for its production, and the court will consider whether to order production, deny it, or order production with restrictions. The court also may decide which party will pay for the costs of retrieving such "not reasonably accessible" information.
- Electronic discovery leads to production of such massive amounts of material that it is hard for the producing party to be sure that it has not mistakenly produced privileged information. After producing electronic records, the producing party may discover that one or more contains some privileged material and seek its return.

   Under Rule 26(b)(5)(B), a party may notify an opponent of such "inadvertent disclosure." The receiving party must then destroy, return, or hold such inadvertently disclosed documents, pending adjudication of the privilege issue by the court. In addition, Rule 16 (b)(5)(B)(iv) authorizes the parties, during scheduling conferences, to consider agreements that inadvertent production of privileged documents will not waive the privilege or that such documents will be returned.
- Many computer systems automatically delete or overwrite information periodically, pursuant to routine "document retention" programs. Rule 37(e) was added to the Rules to make clear that

sanctions may not be imposed for the destruction of electronic information through "routine good faith operation of an electronic information system."

However, this rule will not protect a party from sanctions if the party had a duty to stop the automatic deletion of electronic information relevant to litigation. Once it becomes clear that litigation is pending — and perhaps even before it is actually filed — a party may have a duty, under state law, ethical rules, or other regulations, to preserve relevant evidence. If so, the party will need to initiate a "litigation hold" to assure that routine document deletion procedures are suspended, so that documents relevant to the case are preserved. Failure to do so would seldom meet the "good faith" standard in Rule 37(e).

# ORAL DEPOSITIONS

The third common method of discovery is the oral deposition under Rule 30. A deposition is the taking of testimony from a witness under oath. Counsel for both parties sit down with the witness, and the attorney requesting the deposition questions the witness. Because the witness is sworn, her testimony is subject to the penalties for perjury. Fed. R. Civ. P. 30(c)(1). The testimony is recorded, usually by a court stenographer.

Such live testimony is, without doubt, the most effective means of obtaining detailed information from witnesses before trial. First, counsel gets to *see* the party or witness. There is nothing like looking the crucial witnesses in the eye to evaluate how effective they will be as trial witnesses. A deposition may well be counsel's only opportunity to do so prior to trial.

Second, because the witness is required to answer questions spontaneously, uncoached by counsel (at least, at the deposition itself), the deposition provides a much better preview of the witness's trial testimony than sanitized interrogatory answers can. Third, examining counsel can frame follow-up questions at a deposition based on previous answers, and explore in detail issues that arise during the examination. Fourth, the deposition gets the deponent "on the record," that is, it commits her to a detailed version of the relevant events. If the witness later changes her testimony, excerpts from the deposition can be used to impeach that testimony.

The major drawback of the deposition is the time and expense of conducting it. Taking an effective deposition requires a full understanding of the case, including the legal issues, elements of proof, likely defenses, testimony of other witnesses, and the relevant documents *before* taking the deposition. Developing this understanding takes time. In addition, the deposition itself takes time, from several hours for a short deposition to several days or more for an extensive one. The cost of the court reporter is also substantial. Reporters are usually paid by the page for providing transcripts of the deposition. Transcripts may cost $3.00 per page or more; a deposition might run anywhere from seventy-five to several hundred pages or more. Thus, between the deposing lawyer's time, witness fees, and the reporter's fee, a short deposition could easily cost more than $500, and many will cost a good deal more than that.

# TAKING DEPOSITIONS: TIMING AND MECHANICS

Because counsel should have a thorough understanding of her case before taking depositions, the conventional wisdom is that they should come after interrogatories, which reveal general information and positions of the opponent, and after requests for documents, which produce the documents needed to examine the deponent effectively. In addition, because of their expense, it may be wise to postpone depositions until it is clear that trial is likely. Thus, depositions are frequently taken toward the end of the discovery phase.

However, taking an early deposition sometimes makes tactical sense. For example, counsel may wish to pin down an opponent to a version of the facts or a particular legal position before she (or her counsel) have conducted extensive discovery or educated themselves about the case. A deponent's untutored, spontaneous testimony early in the case may be more damaging than it would be after she becomes familiar with contradictory evidence.

Rule 30(a)(1) allows counsel to take the deposition of "any person, including a party." Thus, persons who are not parties, such as witnesses to the events in suit, treating physicians, or the custodians of relevant records, may be deposed. If the deponent is a party, counsel initiates the deposition by sending a notice of deposition to all parties in the action, stating the time and place of the deposition. Fed. R. Civ. P. 30(b)(1). If the person to be deposed is not a party, she must also be "subpoenaed" for the deposition under Fed. R. Civ. P. 45. A subpoena is a court order to appear and give testimony. If deposing counsel wishes a non-party deponent to produce records or other tangible evidence for the deposition, she must serve a subpoena (now functioning as a "subpoena duces tecum" to command the production of the requested items) with the notice of deposition, specifying the documents or things to be brought to the deposition.

As a practical matter, the time and place of depositions will usually be arranged informally between counsel. In most cases, they are taken at deposing counsel's office, unless there is reason, such as the location of voluminous files or physical evidence, to take a particular deposition elsewhere.

At the deposition, the witness is sworn, and may be examined by deposing counsel on any issues within the scope of discovery. Counsel representing the deponent may object to questions on a number of grounds, such as irrelevance. However, unlike at trial, the witness is usually required to answer the question even if she has an objection to it. See Fed. R. Civ. P. 30(c)(2) (when objection is made, it shall be noted on the record but "the examination still proceeds; the testimony is taken subject to any objection").

This approach avoids many battles over arguably objectionable deposition questions. Most evidentiary objections are aimed at keeping evidence from being introduced at trial. Thus, answering objectionable questions in a deposition does not prejudice the objecting party as long as her counsel can still object to use of the evidence at trial. Ninety to ninety-five percent of cases don't go to trial, so these objections generally don't have to be resolved, saving a great deal of court time ruling on objections which ultimately don't have to be decided.[3]

However, where an objection is based on a *privilege* not to reveal information, such as the attorney-client privilege, counsel for the deponent may instruct her not to answer the question. Fed R. Civ. P. 30(d)(2). The whole point of a privilege is to protect information from disclosure *at all*, not just disclosure at trial. Obviously, the privilege would be eviscerated if the privileged testimony had to be revealed at deposition, even if its use at trial could still be contested later on.

At the deposition, counsel for the deponent (and for other parties as well) have the right to cross-examine after deposing counsel has finished examining the deponent. Generally, there is little reason for counsel "defending the deposition" to cross-examine, since she can talk to her own witnesses privately. However, counsel may want to cross-examine at times to clarify statements made during the direct examination. For example, if the witness gives adverse testimony because she was confused by the question, or gives testimony that could be misinterpreted, it may be important to clarify it right away, rather than try to explain later at trial if the answer is used to impeach the witness.

Opposing counsel would also cross-examine fully if the deposition is a "trial deposition" rather than a "discovery deposition." A trial deposition is one that will be used at trial in *place* of the witness's live testimony. The evidence rules allow this if the witness cannot be subpoenaed to testify in the trial district or if the witness is unable to testify in person. Where the

---

3. In practice, counsel frequently stipulate at the beginning of the deposition that they will save all objections, except as to the form of the question or as to privilege, until the time of trial.

deposition may be so used, counsel taking the deposition will prepare and conduct the deposition much differently than if it is simply to obtain the witness's story. And opposing counsel will want to cross-examine fully, since the deposition will provide her only opportunity to do so.

# PHYSICAL OR MENTAL EXAMINATIONS AND REQUESTS TO ADMIT

The Rules authorize two other important methods of discovery, the physical or mental examination under Rule 35 and request for admissions under Rule 36.

Under the Rules, parties are required to respond to most discovery requests without court intervention. Rule 35, which authorizes physical or mental examination of parties whose condition is at issue in the case, is an exception to this principle. Due to the intrusive nature of such examinations, parties must obtain a court order for a physical or mental exam, which will only be granted "for good cause." Fed. R. Civ. P. 35(a)(2). The rule is most commonly invoked to allow the defendant to obtain an independent medical examination of the plaintiff in cases involving claims for physical injury. In almost all such cases, the fact that the plaintiff is claiming substantial injuries will justify an order for an exam. Because a physical will likely be ordered in such cases, the parties often arrange it without the required court order.

If a party does obtain an examination of another party under Rule 35, she must provide a copy of the independent examiner's report to the examined party if she requests it. Fed. R. Civ. P. 35(b)(1). In response, the party who has submitted to the exam must provide copies of any reports she has from her examining physician. Fed. R. Civ. P. 35(b)(3). These reports will provide a preview of the medical testimony for both sides, as well as a basis for deposing each side's medical witnesses.

The request for admissions under Rule 36 is not really a discovery device at all, but a means of narrowing the scope of trial by eliminating uncontested issues. The rule authorizes a party seeking admission of certain facts to send a request to an opponent to admit those facts. The receiving party is required to admit or deny the truth of the statements, or raise an objection to the request. Admissions can be used to narrow the scope of proof at trial, since matters that are admitted are deemed established for purposes of the case. Fed. R. Civ. P. 36(b).

Unfortunately, it is not always possible to rely on admissions to remove issues from dispute. First, opponents will usually go as far as ethical constraints allow in refusing to admit damaging facts. In addition, if the admitting party has not thoroughly prepared for trial, she may learn later that she had grounds to contest facts previously admitted, and move to withdraw the admissions. Judges will often grant such requests if the admitting party has good ground to contest the facts: Naturally they prefer to see cases resolved on the evidence rather than on mistaken concessions of counsel. Thus, the motion to withdraw admissions may be granted, leaving the opponent in the frustrating position of litigating an issue that her opponent had previously withdrawn from contention.[4]

# AUTOMATIC DISCLOSURE

In 1993, the Federal Rule makers introduced a requirement that parties automatically disclose certain information to their adversaries at the outset of the case, without a discovery request. Fed. R. Civ. P. 26(a)(1). The logic for automatic disclosure is that certain basic information about the case will inevitably be requested, so why not mandate its disclosure without a request? Under Rule 26(a), as amended in 2000, the required disclosure is limited to discoverable information and witnesses the party "may use to support its claims or defenses." This formulation does not force a party to disclose damaging information — even though within the scope of discovery under Rule 26(b)(1) — if the party does not intend to present it at trial. This eliminates the awkward obligation in the 1993 rule to automatically disclose unfavorable witnesses and information. In addition, eight categories of cases in which discovery is infrequently used are now exempted from the disclosure requirement. Fed. R. Civ. P. 26(a)(1)(B).

Limiting disclosure to information "the disclosing party may use to support its claims or defenses" makes disclosure less controversial, since it is much narrower than the anything-relevant standard in the 1993 disclosure rule. However, because of this narrower standard, disclosure can never substitute for use of the other discovery tools: Under the amended rule, it is only through interrogatories, document requests, and depositions that a party will obtain information *unfavorable* to the responding party.

Rule 26(a) also includes other disclosure requirements, which have not been substantially altered by the 2000 amendments. As trial approaches, parties must disclose the identity and reports of experts (Fed. R. Civ. P. 26(a)(2)), the names of witnesses to be called at trial, and documents and depositions each party expects to offer in evidence at trial. Fed. R. Civ.

---

4. Frequently, stipulations at the pre-trial conference provide a more effective means of removing issues from dispute. See Fed. R. Civ. P. 16(c)(2)(C) (consideration should be given at pre-trial conference to obtaining admissions and stipulations).

P. 26(a)(3). To facilitate disclosure, Rule 26(f) requires the parties to confer about disclosure and the subsequent course of discovery. Until this meeting, parties are barred from traditional discovery by interrogatories, requests for documents, and depositions. Fed. R. Civ. P. 26(d)(1).

---

# DISCOVERY: COURT SUPERVISION AND SANCTIONS

Unfortunately, litigators who use the discovery rules every day almost inevitably begin to think about procedural issues like this: "The Rules require me to do X, but what will happen if I don't do X?" It's a dirty little secret that frequently the roof doesn't fall in if you fail to comply with the rules. Often, indeed, nothing happens.

The consequence of failure to comply with a request for discovery depends on your opponent. A refusal to provide requested discovery puts the ball in the requesting party's court. If the information is of marginal importance, she may not pursue it, or may make informal efforts to force compliance but not go beyond that. If the information is important, however, she will likely move for an order to compel discovery under Fed. R. Civ. P. 37.

Under Rule 37(a)(1), a party who believes an opponent has failed to comply with a proper discovery request must first confer informally with the opponent, to see if the dispute can be resolved without resort to the court. If informal means don't resolve the matter, the requesting party must move to compel disclosure or discovery under Fed. R. Civ. P. 37(a)(3). If the motion is granted, the court may order the noncomplying party to pay the moving party's expenses and fees for the motion to compel. Fed. R. Civ. P. 37(a)(5). The court may also enter protective orders defining the scope of required discovery. Fed. R. Civ. P. 37(a)(5)(C). If the court grants a motion to compel, but the party still does not respond adequately, Rule 37(b) authorizes a variety of sanctions, such as striking claims, taking disputed facts or claims as established (or barring the recalcitrant party from establishing them), excluding evidence, dismissing the action, or ordering payment of the fees and expenses caused by the refusal to comply.

Too often, parties deliberately drag their feet in the discovery process, leading to frustration, reciprocal stonewalling, and consequent discovery battles. While counsel for each party may believe that her position is supported by the rules, many discovery issues are ambiguous and complex. Going to court tends to absorb the parties' resources, irritate the judge, leave counsel feeling unsupported by the court, and yield compromise solutions that satisfy no one. Thus, while the threat of court sanctions lurks in the background, the vast bulk of discovery disputes are resolved (or left unresolved) by the parties. If it were any other way the system would break down very quickly.

The following examples explore the basic discovery devices, the tools of the modern litigator's trade.

## Examples

### Gone Fishin'

1. Alewife sues Dr. Perch for injuries allegedly caused by Perch's negligence in the course of back surgery. Her lawyer obtains a copy of the surgical notes that indicate that Trout, a nurse, assisted at the operation. She contacts Trout to interview him about the case, but Trout refuses to speak to her.
   a. Is Trout within his rights to refuse to speak with Alewife's lawyer?
   b. Since Trout refuses to cooperate, Alewife sends a set of interrogatories to him. Must Trout respond to the interrogatories?
   c. Advise Alewife as to how she can best obtain evidence from Trout.

2. You represent Dr. Perch. You have received a set of interrogatories for Perch to answer. Interrogatory #12 asks "State whether, prior to commencing the surgical incision in the operation in suit, you examined the x-rays of the plaintiff's back in her medical records."

   In preparing answers to the interrogatories, you sit down with Dr. Perch and ask her whether she examined the x-rays prior to the surgery. She replies, "Well, between you and me, I didn't. It was a hectic morning, we had an emergency surgery right before hers, and I just didn't do it. I knew what had to be done anyway." As a medical malpractice defense lawyer, you know that this testimony will severely damage Perch's case, since any expert will testify that good medical practice requires full review of the x-rays prior to back surgery. How do you answer the interrogatory?

### Refusing to Take the Bait

3. Assume, on the facts of example 2, that Perch had examined the x-rays two days before surgery. Could you answer "yes" to interrogatory #12?

4. In the same set of interrogatories, the plaintiff asks the names of every person who conducted any investigation of her surgical incident. Dr. Perch tells you that she thinks someone from the hospital did an investigation, but she has no idea who it was.
   a. How should you respond to the interrogatory?
   b. Suppose you represented the hospital as well. How should you respond?

5. Assume that Dr. Perch is unaware that an investigation was conducted of the incident and answers the interrogatory in example 4 stating that there was none. Later, at the deposition of one of the nurses, Perch's counsel learns that the hospital did conduct an inquiry. Does she have a duty under Fed. R. Civ. P. 26(e)(1) to supplement or retract her earlier response to the interrogatory?

6. Interrogatory #9 in Alewife's interrogatories to Dr. Perch asks her to state the substance of any discussions she has had with her counsel concerning the possible causes of Alewife's injury. As counsel for Perch, you conclude that this information is privileged. How should you respond?

7. Salmon is injured when his hand is caught in a stamping machine manufactured by Puffer Corporation. He brings a product liability action against Puffer for his injuries. One of his interrogatories asks Puffer to list all complaints it has received over the past ten years concerning safety guards on any of its machines. The company, which manufactures some 20 types of machines, has a complaints file that is not broken down by product. Any one of the 4,000 or so complaints in the file could be responsive to the interrogatory.

   Puffer responds to the interrogatory as follows: "The information requested in Interrogatory #7 is contained in the company's complaints file, located in its administrative offices at 731 Angel Drive, San Francisco, California, in the custody of Mr. Robert Guppy, Secretary of the Corporation. The records are organized by the year in which the complaint was filed. The records will be made available to plaintiff's counsel for inspection and copying at a mutually agreeable time to be arranged with Mr. Guppy."

   Is Puffer's response proper? See Rule 33(d).

## Keeping the Sharks at Bay

8. Snapper is the plaintiff in a negligence suit against Blue based on an auto accident. Blue requests production under Rule 34 of "all medical records pertaining to any treatment Snapper has received, from any medical provider or other health care professional, which the plaintiff alleges was required as a result of injuries suffered in the accident that is the subject of this action." Snapper responds that he does not have these medical records, which are retained by the doctors or hospitals that have treated him. Is this response proper?

9. Assume that you represent Sword, a company that has recently marketed a new line of shirts. Several competitors have complained to Sword that its pricing of the shirts may constitute price fixing, but have not threatened to sue. Should you advise the corporation to go through and destroy all documents that might contain damaging evidence relating to its pricing practices?

10. In Snapper's case against Blue, Snapper learns that the car Blue was driving was owned by Herring, and that Herring plans to junk the car because it was totalled in the accident. You, as Snapper's counsel, want to inspect and test it first. What should you do?

## On the Hook

11. You are the newest associate in the firm of Capelin & Menhaden, which represents Blue in the accident case. A partner asks you to prepare all the necessary documents to bring in Minnow, the driver of a third car involved in the accident, for a deposition and to obtain any relevant documents Minnow may have. You never had to do that in law school.
    a. Where should you start in determining what documents to prepare?
    b. What documents should you prepare?
    c. Who should you send them to?
    d. How should they be served on the deponent?

12. On the appointed date, Minnow shows up for the deposition. (Hey, it really worked!) However, he does not bring counsel with him. Can the deposition proceed?

## Lines of Inquiry

13. Assume that Snapper's counsel deposes Minnow early in the case. At the time, her theory of the case is that Blue was distracted by something in his car, and swerved, causing him to collide with Snapper's and Minnow's cars. Later, however, she learns from another witness that Minnow may have swerved before the accident, and wants to get Minnow's testimony on this. What should she do?

14. Gold sues Puffer Corporation in federal district court in South Dakota for sexual harassment by Tiger, her former supervisor at Puffer. She tells you that Shad, who worked with her at the time of the alleged harassment, will corroborate her testimony about various instances of harassment. Through interrogatories, you learn that Shad left Puffer Corporation (which is located in South Dakota) a year ago for a job in Tucson, Arizona. You manage to trace her down and would like to depose her. How can you do that? Consider Rules 45(a)(2)(B) and (b)(2).

15. To build the case against Puffer, Gold's counsel would like to depose whoever keeps the records and investigates complaints of harassment by supervisors at Puffer. However, she does not know who that person is. How should she proceed?

16. At Gold's deposition, Puffer's counsel asks her if she has ever been unfaithful to her husband. What should Gold's counsel do?

## An Embarrassment of Riches

17. Patagonia Corporation is involved in a large commercial case against MicroChip Corporation. During discovery, it assembles a large number of documents in electronic form and provides them to MicroChip's lawyers pursuant to a Rule 34 request for production of documents. Four months later, in preparing for trial, Patagonia's lawyers discover that a letter from counsel to a vice president of Patagonia, advising her about the legal implications of the disputed transaction, was attached to one of the electronic files it produced. Patagonia's lawyers claim that the attached file is subject to the attorney-client privilege.

    a. What should Patagonia's lawyers do about the problem?
    b. What should MicroChip's lawyers do with the document if they are notified of the privilege claim?
    c. Suppose that Patagonia's lawyers make a motion for return of the document. What will the court do if it determines that the document is privileged?

## Explanations

## Gone Fishin'

1. a. It is generally true that "the law is entitled to every person's evidence," but that does not mean that private citizens have to provide information just because someone — even a party to a lawsuit or her lawyer — asks them for it. Very frequently, witnesses — particularly favorable witnesses — will cooperate with counsel, and it generally makes sense to ask them to give a statement voluntarily. However, a non-party witness is generally within her rights to tell you to get lost; if she does, some type of court-ordered discovery will be necessary to get her evidence.

    b. Rule 33(a) authorizes serving interrogatories on "any other party" to be answered by the party served. The rule uses this language deliberately: It establishes a means for parties to the action to obtain information from other parties, but does not authorize sending interrogatories to non-party witnesses. Trout is not a party, has never been brought before the court, and is consequently not required to answer the interrogatories.

    c. The only way to force Trout to give testimony is to subpoena him for a deposition: Rule 30(a)(1) authorizes a party to take the deposition of "any person, including a party."

       Although this clearly authorizes Alewife to take Trout's deposition, it may be frustrating to have to get Trout's story this way. For one thing, Trout may be put off by being served with a subpoena, which means he will come in reluctantly and perhaps predisposed against the deposing party. In addition, Trout might not have much relevant information once you get him there, so that the effort and expense of deposing him may turn out to be unproductive. It certainly would be nice if you could just sit down and talk with Trout, like two normal people, instead of going through all this formality. However, since witnesses like Trout need not cooperate, it will often be necessary to subpoena them to get them to talk to you at all. In other cases, it may be important to "get the witness on the record" by taking her deposition even if she is willing to talk informally.

2. This is a tough one, isn't it? Your client appears to be a decent, hardworking professional. You represent her; she is *your client*. You know full well that answering "no" to this interrogatory will harm her defense. What do you do?

The rules, and an attorney's ethical obligations to the court, leave no doubt as to what you must do. Hard as it is in a system that is designed to be adversarial, you bite the bullet and tell the truth. As an officer of the court, an attorney cannot misrepresent the facts in litigation. See ABA Model Rules of Professional Conduct 3.3(a)(1).

But wait: The *factual responses* to interrogatories are signed by the client; the lawyer only signs as to the legal objections. Fed. R. Civ. P. 33(b)(5). If the client wants to put herself on the hook by giving false information, perhaps that is her problem?

Not under the rules of professional conduct. Interrogatories are to be answered "under oath." Fed. R. Civ. P. 33(b)(3). Obviously, the rule contemplates telling the truth, and lying under oath, in answering an interrogatory just as on the witness stand, constitutes the crime of perjury. No lawyer can assist or countenance such a fraud on the court by his client. ABA Model Rules of Professional Conduct 3.3(a)(3) (lawyer shall not offer evidence that the lawyer knows to be false).

So, Perch's counsel is in a box. One way out might be a quick settlement, before answering the interrogatories. There is no ethical restraint on settling a case that you think will go badly, nor is there any bar on settling while a discovery request is pending. Another is to answer truthfully, but add explanatory information that will cushion the effect of this admission, such as the fact that Perch had read the x-rays the day before, or been fully briefed by the assisting surgeon, or whatever.

## Refusing to Take the Bait

3. This is a very tempting way out of the dilemma above, isn't it? There is some ambiguity in the interrogatory, as there will be in many. By liberally construing it to mean "at any time before surgery," you may

be able to answer "yes" and mask the fact that Perch didn't check the x-rays that morning. Perhaps it will never come out that it was 48 hours before, rather than ten minutes.

A law professor might argue that the interrogatory clearly means "*immediately* prior to commencing the surgical incision," so that counsel here should answer "no." Many litigators, however, would seize on this ambiguity to answer "yes," based on the earlier review of the x-rays. It is, after all, an adversarial system. Perch's counsel would have to answer to Perch for being overly conscientious: Like most clients, Perch may malign the legal profession for cutting it close to the line but demand that her own counsel do just that at every opportunity. And, as a litigator, Perch's counsel may feel that her opponent deserves what she gets for poor drafting: She could easily have averted the problem by adding the simple phrase "and if so, when?"

It seems a pity that the judicial search for truth should foster such scholastic jousting. The system pays a large price for its adversarial premise.

4. a. A party answering interrogatories has no duty to go out and conduct a detailed investigation of facts beyond her control in order to respond. James, Hazard & Leubsdorf, Civil Procedure (5th ed. 2001) 296. It is sufficient to respond with information you know or that is within your control. Here, for example, it would be proper to respond that "The defendant believes that an investigation was conducted by employees of the City General Hospital shortly after the surgery. The defendant does not know the names of the person or persons who conducted that investigation, other than Dr. Hilda Kildare, Chief of Surgery."

   b. If the hospital were a defendant, and were asked this interrogatory, counsel clearly would have a duty in responding to provide information about the incident known by the hospital's employees, since information they possess is within the hospital's control. Thus, if the Chief of Surgery were answering the interrogatories on behalf of the hospital, she would have an obligation to find out which employees conducted the investigation and answer accordingly.

   This provides an interesting contrast with deposition practice. If the Chief of Surgery were deposed, she would only answer from personal knowledge, or records she had brought with her. In responding to interrogatories, however, parties must conduct a reasonable investigation to provide facts within their control. See Moore's Federal Practice §33.102[2].

5. Rule 26(e)(1) provides that a party has a duty to supplement a discovery response that she later learns is incorrect or incomplete. However, Perch hasn't learned of it . . . her counsel has. Well, this puts too fine a gloss on the Rule. Perch's counsel acts as her agent in the

discovery process: Whatever she learns will be imputed to Perch. Thus, if counsel learns that earlier discovery responses are incomplete or inaccurate, she should send supplemental responses to correct them.

However, under Rule 26(e)(1) prior responses need only be supplemented if the information "has not otherwise been made known to the other parties during the discovery process or in writing." The example here indicates that the information came out in a deposition, which was doubtless attended (perhaps even conducted) by Alewife's counsel. Thus, Perch probably has no duty to supplement since the information was "made known" to Alewife's agent (her counsel) through the deposition.

6. Discussions between counsel and a party about possible causes of the injury would clearly fall within the attorney-client privilege. Such information does not have to be revealed, even if within the broad relevance standard in Rule 26(b)(1).

A party who believes that information requested is not subject to discovery may object to the interrogatory and state the specific ground for the objection. Fed. R. Civ. P. 33(b)(4). Where an objection is interposed, the party need not answer. However, Fed. R. Civ. P. 26(b)(5)(A) requires the objecting party to expressly claim the privilege and describe the nature of the documents or communications withheld. Perch's counsel might respond as follows: "The defendant refuses to answer Interrogatory #9 on the ground that it requires her to reveal the contents of oral discussions with her counsel concerning the cause of the injury in suit, which are protected from discovery by the attorney-client privilege."

Note that Perch's *counsel* signs the interrogatories as to any legal objections raised in the response. Fed, R. Civ. P. 33(b)(5). Obviously, it is counsel, not the client, who decides to raise legal objections such as privileges. The signature requirement reminds counsel, as the person raising the objection, that she stands behind that decision and takes the risk of sanctions if a motion to compel is granted.

7. Under Rule 33(d), a party may respond by specifying the records from which the relevant information can be ascertained and inviting the requesting party to conduct the search herself. However, you can't just say "come and get it"; the response must identify the nature and organization of the records sufficiently to allow the requesting party to "locate and identify [the records] as readily as the responding party could." Fed. R. Civ. P. 33(d)(1).[5]

---

5. "Here is the room, here is the pile, open the drawers and see all the files" will not do under Rule 33. R. Haydock, D. Herr & J. Stempel, Fundamentals of Pretrial Litigation (3rd ed. 1994), p. 357.

Rule 33(d) provides a tempting means for counsel to avoid a potentially burdensome discovery request. "Here, Salmon, you want it, you do it." However, the rule authorizes this response only in situations where the burden of extracting the information is "substantially the same" for both parties. In many cases, this will not be so, since the party keeping the records will be familiar with the content and organization of the records, and better positioned to retrieve specific items.

Even if the burden is substantially the same, Puffer still might not invoke Rule 33(d). It may not want Salmon mucking around in its files, for various good reasons. No large operation would want strangers, who don't know the system and don't ever have to find anything from it again, pawing around in ten years' worth of records. In addition, while culling through all those files may be burdensome, it will give Salmon's counsel a thorough education concerning complaints about the company's products, including much information that might not come to light if Puffer had searched the records for the exact items requested. Providing access to the records may also waive the attorney-client privilege as to the materials examined by an adversary.

Aside from all of this, Puffer, or its counsel, will eventually end up going through these records anyway. Even if it allows Salmon to search them, it will surely want to know what Salmon found about the product in order to prepare an effective defense. Consequently, in most cases the wiser course will be for the responding party to search the records itself rather than open them to opposing counsel.

## Keeping the Sharks at Bay

8. This is a bogus objection. Rule 34(a)(1) authorizes requests for production of documents "in the party's possession, custody or control." Surely Snapper's medical records are within her "control"; as the patient, she is entitled to obtain them and should do so in response to the request, or send Blue's counsel a release allowing her to get them directly. An objection like this will only make Snapper's counsel look like an obstructionist in the eyes of the court. Reasonable cooperation is expected in discovery and this does not qualify. In many cases such obviously crucial records would be forwarded to the defense without any formal request.

9. The first question here is whether Sword's counsel has an ethical obligation as an attorney not to advise the destruction of information that may be relevant to future litigation. She would have such an obligation if suit had been filed, or, perhaps if it were clearly impending. See. e.g., ABA Model Rules of Professional Conduct, 3.4(a) (lawyer shall not "unlawfully" obstruct another party's access to evidence); *Capellupo V. FMC Corp.*, 126 F.R.D., 545, 550-551 (D. Minn.

1989); *Alliance to End Repression v. Rochford*, 75 F.R.D. 438, 440 (N.D. Ill. 1976) (imposing sanctions for document destruction where suit was clearly about to be filed).[6] However, there is no ethical bar on a general policy of periodic document destruction simply because documents might be relevant to some future lawsuit. See Note, Legal Ethics and the Destruction of Evidence, 88 Yale L.J. 1665, 1666-1674 (1979). Indeed, many companies have adopted company-wide "document retention policies" that establish standards for deletion of documents after a certain period. Consistent application of comprehensive policies on retention of documents tends to defuse the argument that the company has deliberately destroyed potentially harmful evidence. See Fed. R. Civ. P. 37(e) (barring sanctions for loss of electronically stored information lost through routine, good-faith operation of an electronic information system).

As a practical matter, advising Sword to destroy the documents would not be wise. If the organization is large, it may be hard to purge all copies of the unfavorable documents. Even if Sword manages to do so, it cannot purge the knowledge of these documents from its employees' memories. Unless those employees lie under oath, existence of the documents is likely to come out in depositions. At that point, the fact that they cannot be found looks very suspicious. Indeed, if asked, the employees who destroyed the documents would have to admit to doing it, which could be pretty devastating evidence at a future trial. At the same time, the substance of the documents will probably be pieced together from the witnesses anyway, so that destroying the documents may well turn out only to be counterproductive. For these reasons, playing it straight may well be the most practical as well as the most ethical approach.

10. If Herring were a party to the suit, Rule 34 would clearly authorize inspection and testing of the car. See Rule 34(a) (authorizing requests to a *party* to produce documents and tangible things for inspection, copying, or testing). However, since Herring has not been sued, he is not yet subject to the court's authority, and must be subpoenaed to produce the car. See Fed. R. Civ. P. 34(c), 45. Snapper would have to subpoena Herring under Rule 45(a)(1)(D) to produce the car. Although Rule 45(a) now authorizes issuance of a subpoena solely to examine or test things, Snapper might decide to subpoena Herring for a deposition too, so that she can establish ownership and other relevant facts about the car from Herring at the time of the inspection.

---

6. A party destroying evidence might also be subject in some situations to a suit for spoliation of evidence. See I. Johnston, Federal Courts' Authority to Impose Sanctions For Prelitigation or Pre-Order Spoliation of Evidence, 156 F.R.D. 313, 314 (1994).

## On the Hook

11. a. Students often resist the idea, but the *rules* really are the place to start in analyzing many procedural issues, especially those involving discovery. In this case, Rules 30 and 45 pretty much chart your course, describing the proper steps for "noticing" the deposition and subpoenaing the witness to appear.

    b. Rule 30(b) provides that a notice of deposition must be served on the other parties to the action and specifies all the information that must be in it. The notice must state the time and place of taking the deposition, the name and address of each person to be examined (Fed. R. Civ. P. 30(b)(1)), and the method by which the examination will be recorded. Fed. R. Civ. P. 30(b)(3). If records are to be produced for inspection at the deposition, the notice must also specify the documents to be produced. Fed. R. Civ. P. 30(b)(2). Figure 22-1 is an example of a notice of deposition that would meet the requirements of the rule.

    Here, Minnow, the deponent, is not a party to the action. Thus, he is not yet under the court's authority, and must be ordered to appear and give evidence. A subpoena is a court order that commands a non-party to appear and produce evidence or give testimony. In practice the court in which the action is pending will issue blank subpoenas, signed by the court clerk, to attorneys. Fed. R. Civ. P. 45 (a)(3). Counsel sending the subpoena will then fill in the details (names, places, documents requested, nature of the hearing or deposition, and so forth) and serve it on the deponent. Thus, while the court "issues" the subpoena, and may enforce compliance with it, the attorneys carry the laboring oar in filling it out and serving it. In most cases, the court will not even know that it has been served and may never have to know as long as discovery proceeds without incident.

    The subpoena must include the name of the issuing court, the title of the action, the name of the court in which the case is pending, and the civil action number of the case, and it must command the person to whom it is directed to appear and give testimony. Rule 45(a)(1). If documents are requested, it must also command the deponent to produce the documents designated for inspection or copying. Id. The subpoena must also set forth in full the text of Rule 45(c) and (d), which explain the rights of witnesses and the means of raising objections to the subpoena. Since in many cases subpoenas are directed to persons who are not parties, and are not represented by counsel, this assures that the person subpoenaed will be informed of her rights and obligations in responding to it. Fed. R. Civ. P. 45(d). Figure 22-2 is an example of a subpoena drafted to comply with the requirements of Rule 45.

UNITED STATES DISTRICT COURT
DISTRICT OF WEST DAKOTA

| | |
|---|---|
| PHILLIP R. SNAPPER, | CIVIL ACTION NO. 07-1074 |
| Plaintiff | |
| v. | NOTICE OF DEPOSITION |
| MARIE P. BLUE, Defendant | |

TO:    Rebecca Remora
       Attorney for Plaintiff
       191 Federal Center
       Bridger, West Dakota 50422

Please take notice that, pursuant to Rules 26 and 30 of the Federal Rules of Civil Procedure, the Defendant in the above entitled action will conduct a deposition of Milton L. Minnow, commencing at 10:00 a.m. on the seventh day of April, 2007, and continuing from that time until complete, at the law offices of Pollock & Hake, 3 First Avenue, Badlands, West Dakota 60417.

The deposition shall be by oral examination, with a written record made thereof, before a notary public or before some other officer authorized by law to administer oaths. A copy of the designation of materials to be produced by the witness at the deposition is attached.

Date: March 21, 2007

*Frederick C. Pollock*

Frederick C. Pollock
Pollock & Hake
3 First Avenue
Badlands, West Dakota 60417
(904) 522-9804

**Figure 22-1.**

---

UNITED STATES DISTRICT COURT
DISTRICT OF WEST DAKOTA

| | |
|---|---|
| PHILLIP R. SNAPPER, <br> Plaintiff <br><br> v. <br><br> MARIE P. BLUE, <br> Defendant | CIVIL ACTION NO. 07-1074 <br><br> SUBPOENA TO TESTIFY <br> AND PRODUCE DOCUMENTS |

TO:   Milton L. Minnow
      84 Pleasant Street
      Badlands, West Dakota 60417

You are hereby commanded to appear at <u>3 First Avenue</u> in the city of <u>Badlands</u> on the <u>seventh</u> day of <u>April, 2007,</u> at <u>10:00</u> a.m., to testify on behalf of <u>defendant Blue</u> at the taking of deposition in the above entitled action pending in the _____ District of <u>West Dakota,</u> and to bring with you for inspection and copying the documents (and things) described in the attachment to this subpoena entitled "Attachment to Subpoena Duces Tecum."

This subpoena has been issued by the United States District Court for the _____ District of <u>West Dakota</u>. You must appear, give testimony, and produce all of the materials described in this subpoena and its attachments, for inspection and copying at the time and place set out in this subpoena. Your failure to do so may be punished as a contempt of court.

[Here, the subpoena should set forth the full text of Fed. R. Civ. P. 45(c) and (d).]

Date: <u>March 21, 2007</u>

*Elizabeth Smith*
Clerk of Court

*Harold Hake*
Harold R. Hake

Attorney for
Address:

Telephone:

<u>Marie P. Blue</u>
<u>3 First Avenue</u>
<u>Badlands, West Dakota 60417</u>
<u>(904) 522-9804</u>

Figure 22-2.

c. The subpoena must, of course, be sent to Minnow, the party to be deposed: It is the official command of the court to appear and give evidence. The notice of deposition should be sent to "every other party." Rule 30(b)(1). Other parties are entitled to notice so that they can exercise their right to be present, object, and cross-examine at the deposition. In practice, both documents are routinely sent to all parties and to the deponent. Sending a copy of the subpoena to other counsel in the case indicates that the witness has been subpoenaed, as required by law.

d. A non-party who is subpoenaed to testify is not yet before the court, and may not even know that an action is pending. Service of the subpoena provides notice of her duty to respond and also asserts the court's jurisdiction over her. Thus, it is important that it be served in a manner likely to inform her of the obligations it imposes. Rule 45(b)(1) requires subpoenas to be served in person on the person to be deposed. This is even stricter than the service provisions for complaints under Rule 4. And, as the new associate, don't forget that the subpoena must be served with the fees for a day's attendance and mileage to the place of deposition. Rule 45(b)(1).[7] The partner will be duly impressed if you present her with the subpoena, the notice of deposition, and the checks together. She will be correspondingly irked if you omit them. Without the checks, the subpoena could perhaps be ignored with impunity.

The notice of deposition, like virtually all papers exchanged among parties to the action, may be served on other parties to the action under Rule 5, which authorizes service by mail. Rule 5(b)(2)(C).

12. Persons subpoenaed for a deposition will frequently appear without counsel. There is no requirement that non-party witnesses be represented by counsel at a deposition. It is bad enough to have to give up a day of work to appear and be grilled by two humorless adversaries, without having to pay a lawyer for the privilege of doing so. The deposition can proceed.

---

7. How do you know how much to make these checks out for? I spent a half hour in the library running this down. It turns out that 28 U.S.C. §1821 specifies the fees. The daily attendance fee is $40. 28 U.S.C. §1821(b). The mileage fee is more complicated. Section 1821(c)(2) states that the travel allowance if the deponent is to travel by private vehicle (and how do you know *that?*) is "equal to the mileage allowance which the Administrator of General Services has prescribed, pursuant to section 5704 of title 5, for official travel of employees of the Federal government . . . " I didn't bother to try to run that down. As a practical matter, someone in your firm is likely to know the current rate. If you hang out your own shingle, this is only one of a multitude of minutiae calculated to drive the sole practitioner berserk.

## Lines of Inquiry

13. Naturally, Snapper's counsel would like to depose Minnow again, but opposing counsel or the witness may well object to being called for a second deposition. Rule 30(a)(2)(A)(ii) now provides that, unless the parties agree that Minnow can be called again (the rule says nothing about Minnow's feelings on the matter!) Snapper's counsel must obtain leave of court to do so.

   Counsel might try to avoid the strictures of this provision by "suspending" depositions rather than terminating them. This technical distinction leaves counsel free to recall the witness at a later date to finish. However, opposing counsel will doubtless object if this is routinely done without good cause. This suggests one reason for taking depositions late in the discovery process. After the facts and theories of recovery have been developed fairly clearly, counsel will be able to plan depositions to cover all the bases, avoiding the expense and disputes likely to arise from requests for a second deposition.

14. First, remember that Shad, as a non-party, is under no obligation to talk to Gold's counsel. Even if she is willing to, counsel may want to depose her anyway: If Shad is unavailable for trial in South Dakota, her deposition will be admissible instead. See Fed. R. Civ. P. 32(a)(4). Thus, she should be subpoenaed for a deposition. However, under Rule 45(a)(2) and (b)(2), a federal district court can only subpoena witnesses within that district or within 100 miles of the place within the district where the deposition is taken. This is intended to protect witnesses like Shad from having to travel long distances to be deposed. Thus, the South Dakota court will not be able to subpoena Shad for the deposition.

   If Gold's counsel really needs Shad's testimony then, he has several options. First, he can go to Arizona to depose her. The *Arizona* federal district court for the district where Shad resides has the authority under Rule 45(a)(2) and (b)(2) to subpoena her to testify in Arizona, even though the *lawsuit* is pending in South Dakota. Thus, Gold's counsel could obtain a subpoena from the federal district court in Arizona and take the deposition there. See Friedenthal, Kane, and Miller, p. 425.

   This isn't going to be cheap. Gold's counsel will have to fly down there to take the deposition. So will Puffer's counsel, if she chooses to attend. The clock is running and the expenses mounting for both sides. (Although Gold will not initially pay for Puffer's counsel to attend the deposition, if Puffer wins at trial some of this expense may be taxed to Gold as part of the costs of suit.)

   There are some cheaper alternatives. If Shad would like to visit old friends, Gold might pay for her to fly back to South Dakota, thus saving both attorneys' travel time and one airfare. The rules also now authorize a deposition to be taken by telephone or other electronic means. Fed. R. Civ. P. 30(b)(4). Counsel could arrange to question Shad by telephone and have her answers videotaped in Arizona. Last, Rule 31 authorizes depositions on written questions. Under this rule, the witness is brought before an authorized officer (in practice a court reporter), and asked questions drafted by counsel. The witness's answers are recorded by the reporter and forwarded to counsel for the parties.

15. Gold could use interrogatories to learn who within the defendant's corporate structure has this information. Alternatively Rule 30(b)(6) allows her to send a notice of deposition to the defendant, describing the matters to be examined, and requesting that the defendant designate the person or persons best able to testify as to those matters. Gold will then depose that person on the matters specified.

16. Naturally, counsel should object, on the ground that Gold's marital fidelity is irrelevant to her harassment claim against Puffer. But what do you do when Puffer's counsel smugly quotes to you from Rule 30(c)(2), which provides that objections at a deposition shall be noted, but the answers taken subject to the objection?

   Well, that may be true as a general matter, but there must be some limit to counsel's ability to embarrass the deponent by wide-ranging inquiry into irrelevant matters. That limit is provided in Rule 30(d)(3)(A), which authorizes a party to move to suspend or limit the scope of the deposition where "the examination is being conducted in bad faith, or in a manner that unreasonably annoys, embarrasses, or oppresses the deponent or party . . ." See also Rule 30(c)(1), which authorizes defending counsel to instruct a deponent not to answer "to present a motion under Rule 30(d)(3)." Gold's counsel should instruct her not to answer and indicate her intent to make a Rule 30(d)(3) motion. At that point, Puffer's counsel will likely withdraw the question rather than try to justify this indefensible line of inquiry to the court.

## An Embarrassment of Riches

17. a. Patagonia's lawyers should notify MicroChip's lawyers of the inadvertent disclosure in writing and request return of the privileged document. The notice should identify the materials for which a privilege is claimed with sufficient specificity to allow MicroChip's lawyers to assess the privilege claim.

b. Rule 26(b)(5)(B) provides that MicroChip's lawyers must "return, sequester or destroy" the document. Even if they have read the document, they must not use any information derived from it until the claim of privilege is adjudicated by the court. As a practical matter, it will be hard for MicroChip's lawyers to expunge from their heads any strategic insight they have gained from reading the document. But they could not frame discovery requests or deposition questions, for example, based on the document while the privilege issue is being decided by the court.

Even if MicroChip's lawyers agree that the designated material is subject to a privilege or is trial preparation material (also protected under the rule), they may refuse to return it, arguing that the privilege was waived by producing the material. Rule 26(b)(5)(B) does not provide for automatic return of privileged materials that were inadvertently disclosed. It just bars use of the material until a claim of privilege is resolved by the court. Nor does the rule address the underlying question of whether inadvertently producing protected materials waives the privilege.

c. When MicroChip's lawyers are notified of the privilege claim, they might return the materials, presumably accepting the claim and agreeing not to make any use of the information. Alternatively, they may present the material to the court for a ruling on whether it is privileged and (if so) whether producing the material waived the privilege. Alternatively, Patagonia's lawyers may move for return of the material based on their privilege claim. The court will then have to determine whether the document is privileged and, if it is, whether the privilege has been waived by disclosure.

Federal courts have taken three distinct positions on whether inadvertent disclosure waives an evidentiary privilege. Some hold that inadvertent disclosure waives any privilege that would otherwise protect the material, because the information has been revealed, which typically does waive a privilege with regard to it. See, e.g., *International Digital Sys. Corp. v. Digital Equip. Co.*, 120 F.R.D. 445, 450 (D. Mass 1988). Some hold that inadvertent disclosure does not waive the privilege, on the theory that no waiver was intended. See, e.g., *Mendenhall v. Barber-Greene Co.*, 531 F. Supp. 951 (N.D. Ill. 1982). Many courts have taken a middle ground, employing a multi-factor test to determine whether the privilege has been waived, including the precautions taken to avoid inadvertent disclosure, the time it took to discover the error, the scope of the production, the extent of the material inadvertently disclosed, and general considerations of fairness. See, e.g., *Alldread v. City of Grenada*, 988 F.2d 1425, 1433 (5th Cir. 1993); see generally A. Perlman, Untangling Ethics Theory from Attorney Conduct

Rules: The Case of Inadvertent Disclosures, 13 George Mason L. Rev. 767, 775-776 (2005).

While a balancing approach to the waiver issue may be appropriate, it provides another collateral issue for lawyers to litigate at their clients' expense. In many cases, lawyers — recognizing the unwieldy task of reviewing a massive number of documents for privilege claims — will deal with the problem early in the case through so-called "clawback" agreements, agreeing to return inadvertently disclosed materials. See also Fed. R. Civ. P. 26(f)(3)(D) (parties' discovery plan must cover possible agreements relating to privilege issues).

# A PRACTICAL PERSPECTIVE: SAMPLE INTERROGATORIES, ANSWERS, AND COMMENTS

It may be helpful after all this theory to see an actual set of interrogatories and responses. The sample that follows is based on the facts of *Schulansky v. Ronan*, the example case explored in more detail in Chapters 31 to 35.

The plaintiff in *Schulansky*, Deborah Schulansky, met with Richard Ronan, of Ronan Construction Company, to discuss putting an addition on her historic vacation house in Alton, New Hampshire. Allegedly, he represented to her that he was a specialist in such work. After some discussions, they signed a short agreement (the "proposal and estimate") and Ronan proceeded with the work. While the cellar was being excavated, Schulansky visited the site to check on the work. The house had an old foundation made of loose stones. While she was there she saw that Jones, the bulldozer operator, had dislodged some of the stones. She asked Ronan if the old foundation was adequate to support the addition, and he allegedly said it was, but that he would reinforce it with concrete if necessary. A major dispute in the case involves exactly what he had agreed to do to repair the old foundation (if anything) and whether Schulansky waived any agreement to rebuild it during their conversation at the job site.

After the work was mostly done, Schulansky visited again and noticed cracks in several rooms of the old part of the house. She had an engineer look at the house, and he concluded that the old foundation was settling, causing structural damage. After trying to get Ronan to address the problem, Schulansky sued Ronan and his company, Ronan Construction Company, for damages. (For more detail on the facts, see Chapters 31 and 33.)

Figure 22-3 is a set of answers to interrogatories sent by Schulansky's lawyers to Ronan. Note that Ronan's response includes each original interrogatory, followed by Ronan's answer to it. Following are some explanatory comments about them.

## Comments on the *Schulansky* Interrogatories and Answers

1. Many of Schulansky's interrogatories seek the identity of witnesses and records relevant to the action. Once Schulansky learns the names of relevant witnesses, they can be interviewed (if they are willing to be) or deposed (if they are not). The answers regarding records can be followed up with a Rule 34 Request for Production of Documents. As the Introduction explains, automatic disclosure of supporting witnesses and records is now required under Federal Rule 26(a).

   Counsel often combine interrogatories with a request to produce the documents that are identified in the answers to interrogatories. For example, Schulansky's counsel could add a request after Interrogatories #5 and #6 that all records identified be produced for inspection and copying pursuant to Rule 34.

2. The interrogatories are addressed to defendant Richard L. Ronan, not to both defendants together. Under Rule 33(a), court permission is required to serve more than 25 interrogatories on "any other party." Presumably, Ronan Construction Company is a different "party," even though it is Ronan's company, so Schulansky can presumably still serve 25 *more* interrogatories on it.

   Placing a limit on the number of interrogatories may lead counsel to resort to questions with sub-parts. See, for example, Interrogatories #15 and #22. This can lead to tedious battles (at lawyerly rates) over whether such sub-questions are really separate questions that should count toward the limit.

3. Interrogatories and responses must be served on all other parties to the action (not just the responding party). Rule 5(a)(1)(C). This keeps all parties fully informed of what has occurred in the action. Most discovery materials are not filed with the court, however, unless they are used in litigating a motion or at trial. Fed. R. Civ. P. 5(d). This saves the courts a great deal of filing space.

4. Interrogatory #19 seeks discovery on the issue of the court's jurisdiction to hear the case rather than the merits. Discovery on jurisdictional issues is proper, since they obviously pertain to the adjudication of the dispute. *Oppenheimer Fund, Inc. v. Sanders*, 437 U.S. 340, 351 n.13 (1978); Chapter 21, ex. 3.

---

UNITED STATES DISTRICT COURT
DISTRICT OF MASSACHUSETTS

CIVIL ACTION NO. 06-6719

DEBORAH SCHULANSKY,

Plaintiff

v.

RICHARD L. RONAN,
RONAN CONSTRUCTION
COMPANY,
Defendants

DEFENDANT'S ANSWERS TO
PLAINTIFF'S FIRST SET OF
INTERROGATORIES UNDER
FED. R. CIV. P. 33

The defendant Richard L. Ronan responds to the plaintiff's first set of interrogatories as follows:

1. Please list each occasion on which you or anyone acting on behalf of you or Ronan Construction Company discussed the terms or performance of the contract in issue in this action with the plaintiff.

Answer: I met with the plaintiff twice in early March of 2006 to discuss the work. She also visited the site in early May during the construction. She called me twice late in May to discuss alleged damage resulting from the work.

2. For each conversation identified in Interrogatory #1, please state in detail the substance of that conversation, stating in chronological order what was said by each of the parties.

Answer: At the first meeting, we discussed generally the nature of the work to be done, my experience on similar jobs, and when I would be able to do the work.

At the second meeting, we went over specifics concerning dimensions, materials, excavation, subcontracting electrical work, and landscaping. We agreed to a price and I agreed to send a Proposal and Estimate for Ms. Schulansky to sign. During the conversations in late May, the plaintiff expressed concern about some stress cracks in several rooms of the house. I explained that these cracks did not result from the addition work, but were there when we began the job. They result from settling over the two hundred odd years since the house was built.

3. Please identify the name and address of each person who was present during each and every conversation between yourself and the plaintiff, prior to, during, and after the execution of the contract at issue in this action.

Figure 22-3.

<u>Answer:</u> Deborah Schulansky, 219 Parker Street, Plymouth, MA 02360, and Richard L. Ronan, 3 Carleton Drive, Nashua, NH 04125.

4. Please identify the name and address of each person who has any knowledge of the facts concerning the negotiations, execution, or performance of the contract that is at issue in this action.

<u>Answer:</u> Deborah Schulansky and Richard L. Ronan. As to performance, Arlen Jones, 14 Prescott Place, Canterbury, NH 03316; Marie Shepard, 62 Summer Street, Laconia, NH 03329; Renee Dufresne, 19 Third Ave, Nashua, NH 03325; and T. J. Argento, 414 Piper Lane, Nashua, NH 03327 (office address) as well.

5. Please identify each and every document, letter, memorandum, or other record, whether in electronic or other form, of which you have knowledge, whether or not it is in your custody, possession or control, that contains information concerning the negotiations, execution, or performance of the contract in issue in this action.

<u>Answer:</u> Proposal and estimate attached to plaintiff's complaint: letter agreement dated April 8, 2006, between Ronan Construction Company and Arlen Jones.

6. Please identify each and every document, brochure, information sheet, advertisement, or other writing that describes the nature of the construction services offered by Ronan Construction Company, or its expertise or experience in restoring or working on historic properties.

<u>Answer:</u> occasional advertisements in Manchester Union Leader, Old House Journal, Lowell Sun over the last three years. Specific dates not known.

7. For each document identified in response to Interrogatory #5, please state whether such document is within your possession, custody, or control, and if not, state to the best of your knowledge who does have possession, custody, or control of such document.

<u>Answer:</u> Advertising copy may be available from publisher of each paper specified in answer to Interrogatory #6.

8. Please state whether any documents relating to the events alleged in this action have been lost or destroyed. If the answer is "yes," please state for each such document the nature and content of the document, the person creating the document, and the circumstances surrounding the loss or destruction of that document.

<u>Answer:</u> None.

9. Please list the names and addresses of all persons who performed any services related to the work that forms the basis of this action.

<u>Answer:</u> Richard L. Ronan, Arlen Jones, Marie Shepard, Renee Dufresne. Also T. J. Argento (electrical contractor).

For addresses see response to Interrogatory #4.

10. For each person identified in Interrogatory #9, please specify the nature of the services performed, the manner in which such person was compensated (whether by the job, hourly, weekly, or otherwise), the amount of compensation provided to such person for this job, whether a contract was entered into for the services rendered by such person, and the number of other jobs on which such person has rendered services for either of the defendants during the last two years.

Answer: The defendant objects to this interrogatory as burdensome and calling for information that is irrelevant to the issues in suit. Without waiving this objection, the defendant responds that Arlen Jones conducted the excavation pursuant to a letter agreement dated April 8, 2006, for a fixed price of $3,000.

11. Please identify each and every contract or other agreement, whether in writing or not, concerning the addition work that is the subject of this action, which either defendant entered into with the plaintiff, with Arlen Jones, or with any other persons who rendered services on the contract that is the subject of this action.

Answer: Proposal and estimate attached to plaintiff's complaint; letter agreement dated April 8, 2006, between Ronan Construction Company and Arlen Jones.

12. Please identify, by giving the address of the property and the name and address of the owner, each and every structure in excess of 100 years old on which you or your company have rendered construction services during the last six years.

Answer: The defendant objects to this interrogatory as burdensome and calling for irrelevant information beyond the proper bounds of discovery.

13. For each property identified in Interrogatory #12, please state whether any dispute arose concerning the terms or performance of the work, and if so, whether any legal action was threatened or initiated against either you or Ronan Construction Company as a result of such dispute.

Answer: The defendant objects to this interrogatory as burdensome and calling for irrelevant information beyond the proper bounds of discovery. Without waiving this objection, the defendant states that neither he nor Ronan Construction Company has been sued for any claim arising out of his construction business during the past six years.

14. Please state whether either of the defendants has made an investigation into the allegations upon which the complaint in this action is based.

Answer: Yes.

15. If the answer to Interrogatory #14 is "yes," please state for each such investigation

a. the names and addresses of each person who has made such investigation.

Answer: Richard L. Ronan

b. the dates of each such investigation.

Answer: June 1, 2006.

c. identify all reports, summaries, witness statements, photographs, estimates, opinions or other documents, whether in written or electronic form, that have been created as a result of such investigation, including any specifications or estimates of damages to the original house or addition at the Alton property.

Answer: None.

16.  Please describe, step by step, in detail and in chronological order, exactly what you or your servants or agents or subcontractors did to rebuild or reinforce the old part of the foundation exposed during the excavation for the addition that is the subject of this action, or to ascertain the sufficiency of that foundation to support the addition at issue in this action.

Answer: The rock foundation was solid and did not require any reconstruction. At the plaintiff's request, we poured concrete into several open spaces among the rocks during the work.

17.  Please identify by name and address each person who was present during any part of the work that is the subject of Interrogatory #16.

Answer: Richard L. Ronan, Deborah Schulansky, Arlen Jones, Marie Shepard, Renee Dufresne, T. J. Argento.

18.  Please state each and every fact upon which you rely in support of your contention in the Fourth Defense in your Answer to the complaint, alleging that the plaintiff waived performance of the contractual obligation to reinforce the foundation prior to construction of the addition.

Answer: When the plaintiff visited the site on April 17, 2006, the foundation was exposed and she asked whether it was sufficient. I said it was, but I would fill in any holes in the foundation with concrete. She agreed that this would be satisfactory.

19.  Please state each and every fact upon which you rely in support of your contention in the Second Defense in your Answer that the defendants are not subject to personal jurisdiction in this action.

Answer: This action arises out of work done in New Hampshire. The defendant Richard L. Ronan is domiciled in New Hampshire and has not been served with process in Massachusetts. Ronan Construction Company is a New Hampshire corporation with offices in New Hampshire. None of the services rendered under the agreement in suit were rendered in Massachusetts, nor has either defendant consented to suit in Massachusetts on this claim.

20. Please state each and every fact upon which you rely in support of your contention in the Third Defense in your Answer that the Proposal and Estimate for the work involved in this action constitutes the entire agreement of the parties and does not require reconstruction of the foundation.

Answer: The parties signed the Proposal and Estimate, which includes all the terms of the contract between them. There was no other agreement requiring reconstruction of the foundation nor does the written contract require it.

21. Please state the name and address of each expert you expect to call to testify at the trial.

Answer: The defendant will make disclosure of its expert witnesses in accordance with Fed. R. Civ. P. 26(a) (2) at least 90 days prior to the anticipated date of trial.

22. For each expert identified in Interrogatory #21, please specify
    a. his or her professional qualifications;
    b. the subjects upon which the expert is expected to testify;
    c. the substance of the opinion to which the expert is expected to testify;
    d. the grounds upon which the expert bases his or her opinion.

Answer: The defendant will make disclosure of its expert witnesses in accordance with Fed. R. Civ. P. 26(a) (2) at least 90 days prior to the anticipated date of trial.

Signed Under the Penalties of Perjury This 21st Day of November 2007.

_____
Richard L. Ronan

Signed as to objections

_____
Arthur Ackerman
Ackerman, Sloan & Cariotis
59 State Street
Boston, MA 02114
(617) 228-6301

5. Interrogatories #18-20 ask Ronan to state all the facts upon which he bases various defenses raised in the answer. These are known as "contention interrogatories," because they ask the opponent to lay out the factual basis for contentions raised more generally in the pleadings.

   For many years, the courts were split on whether contention interrogatories were permissible. In 1970, Rule 33(c) was added (See now Rule 33(a)(2)), which provides that an interrogatory is not objectionable "merely because it asks for an opinion or contention that relates to fact or the application of law to fact." This amendment clearly approves use of contention interrogatories to probe the factual basis for allegations, and also to narrow the issues by revealing what is not contended. Here, for example, Ronan's answer to Interrogatory #18 shows that he relies on the conversation at the worksite as the ground for his waiver argument. This will assist Schulansky in preparing to meet this defense at trial.

   Sometimes parties will not be able to respond effectively to contention interrogatories until they have conducted most of their own discovery. To obviate this problem, Rule 33(a)(2) allows the court to order that such interrogatories not be answered until other discovery is completed.

6. Although Rule 33 does not require parties responding to interrogatories to restate each interrogatory before the response, this obviously makes the responses much easier for all parties to review. Some local rules require setting forth the interrogatory before each response.

7. These interrogatories look so comprehensive and detailed that you would expect them to yield a great deal of useful information. When you compare the answers, however, the reality doesn't live up to their promise. Some answers are too general to be really helpful. Others seem to reflect stonewalling or laziness. Still others indicate that Ronan has no information on the matter. (This, it turns out, can be *very* helpful, since Ronan will be bound by this representation; he cannot later bring forth evidence at trial which he has denied having in answering the interrogatories.)

   For example, Ronan's answer to Interrogatory #2 seems minimally responsive: It does not provide details of who said what, in what order, even to the best of Ronan's memory. Schulansky might move for further answers, but the court probably won't be impressed. Interrogatories like this tend to invite summary answers. To get precise details, counsel should ask very specific questions ("At your meeting on February 23, 2006, did you tell the plaintiff that you would tear out the old foundation and rebuild it?" or "State exactly what you told the plaintiff at the February 23, 2006, meeting that you would do to the old foundation"). Or, better still, she should depose Ronan so she can ask precise follow-up questions.

8. Ronan has objected to Interrogatory #10 as burdensome and irrelevant. These details do seem pretty peripheral to the issue of the sinking foundation, so the objection is at least arguable. And Ronan has made his position look more reasonable by providing the one item that Schulansky probably would press for, the agreement between Ronan and Jones, which is relevant on the question of whether Jones was a Ronan employee or an independent contractor. Schulansky's counsel probably won't press the point.

9. Presumably Schulansky has included Interrogatories #12 and #13 to determine whether Ronan, who represented to her that he was an expert at working on historic houses, had had problems on other such jobs. This might, I suppose, lead to other admissible evidence (see Rule 26(b)(1)), but it is pretty much of a fishing expedition. By objecting, Ronan puts the burden on Schulansky to give up on this or move to compel production. And, by responding that he hasn't been sued on any jobs, Ronan lets her know that she at least won't find that if she pushes the point. (Notice that he did not say there had been no disputes, just that there had been no suits.)

   It is common for parties to state an objection to an interrogatory, but then to provide some responsive information anyway, both to appear cooperative and to reduce the opponent's incentive to file a motion to compel further answers.

10. Schulansky's counsel asked for any reports of investigations by Ronan, but did not consider the possibility that he investigated but didn't write anything down. Now she will have to ask supplemental interrogatories as to his findings or explore this at Ronan's deposition.

11. Interrogatories #21 and #22, requesting information concerning expert witnesses, may not be appropriate. Rule 26(a)(2) requires automatic disclosure of information concerning the qualifications, compensation, and opinions of trial experts 90 days before trial. Here, Ronan has taken the position that Rule 26(a)(2) governs disclosure of experts, so that he does not have to provide information about them until that rule requires it.

12. As discussed in the examples, Ronan has signed the interrogatories, but Ronan's counsel has signed separately as to the objections, indicating that he has considered the objections raised and deems them legally justified.

# Defective Allegation or Insufficient Proof?

Dismissal for Failure to State a Claim Compared to Summary Judgment

---

## INTRODUCTION

One major theme of the civil procedure course is "The Perils of Plaintiff" or "all the ways you can bring a lawsuit and never get to trial." We have already explored a variety of purely *procedural* defects that may bring the suit to an untimely end, such as lack of jurisdiction, improper venue, and improper service of process. However, there are also several devices that defendants may use to challenge the *merits* of the plaintiff's case before trial, which may foreclose a trial if the court agrees with the defendant's objections. The principal devices for such pretrial resolution are the motion to dismiss for failure to state a claim upon which relief can be granted, or "Rule 12(b)(6) motion," and the motion for summary judgment under Rule 56. This chapter will examine these two motions in turn and offer some examples to help you distinguish them.

---

## THE RULE 12 (B) (6) MOTION

Under Rule 12(b)(6) of the Federal Rules (and the similar "demurrer" device in code pleading jurisdictions) a defendant may move to dismiss the plaintiff's complaint on the ground that it fails to state a claim that entitles the plaintiff to any form of relief. The gist of the defendant's objection in making the motion is that the "wrong" that the plaintiff describes in his

473

complaint is not recognized as a violation of any legal rights. If that is true, the court would not be able to grant damages or other relief to the plaintiff even if he proved all the facts alleged.

Suppose, for example, that Ferraro sues Gramm for voting Republican, after he promised Ferraro that he wouldn't. The law does not currently recognize a right to have promises performed unless consideration, estoppel, or some other additional acts make the promise binding. Even if Ferraro proves that Gramm made the promise, a court could not grant her any relief for Gramm's failure to keep it. Since there is no right to relief on Ferraro's claim, it would simply place a pointless burden on the court and the parties to proceed with the action. On these facts Gramm could move to dismiss the complaint for failure to state a claim upon which relief can be granted.

Because the purpose of the Rule 12(b)(6) motion is to test whether the plaintiff's allegations (assuming they can be proved) state a claim for which a court might grant relief, the only question posed by the motion is whether the complaint itself states a legally sufficient claim. Consequently, the court does not consider any other pleadings or evidence in deciding the motion. Nor does the court consider or determine whether the facts alleged in the complaint are true; for purposes of the motion, it assumes that the facts alleged *are* true. The motion only addresses a purely legal question: whether, if the plaintiff proves the allegations in the complaint, he will have established a cause of action entitling him to some form of relief from the court. In cases like Ferraro's, dismissal on the basis of the complaint alone is appropriate under this test. Since Ferraro's complaint does not state a legal wrong for which the court could grant her redress, allowing her to litigate the allegations through discovery and trial would be a waste of both the parties' and the court's time.

Dismissal of a suit for failure to state a claim is a drastic measure. If the court dismisses, the plaintiff will never have the opportunity to present his case to a jury, or to gather evidence through the discovery process that might demonstrate that he has suffered a legally cognizable injury. Consequently, courts give every benefit of the doubt to the plaintiff in deciding the motion. The court may not consider the likelihood that the plaintiff will be able to prove his factual allegations; it must assume for purposes of deciding the motion that the plaintiff will prove them.

In considering the motion, the pleadings must be liberally construed in favor of sustaining the complaint. Thus, if the allegations in the complaint are susceptible of two constructions, one of which would support relief while the other would not, the court must construe the complaint in favor of the pleader. For example, a complaint that alleges that the defendant "swerved and ran into me on Bleecker Street" might be construed to allege either negligent driving or an unavoidable accident. In deciding the Rule 12(b)(6) motion, the court would likely infer that the plaintiff (who is suing the defendant, after all) is alleging that the collision resulted from the defendant's negligence.

In cases like Ferraro's, a complaint will be vulnerable to dismissal under Rule 12(b)(6) because the plaintiff has sought relief for acts that are simply not proscribed under current law. In other cases, however, the complaint may be defective because the plaintiff (or his lawyer) has simply failed to allege the necessary elements of a claim that, if properly pleaded, would state a sufficient claim. Suppose, for example, that Berlin sues Porter for malicious prosecution, alleging that Porter filed a criminal complaint against him without cause, and that as a result he suffered damage to his reputation. To recover for malicious prosecution a plaintiff must prove that the original proceeding (in this example, the criminal case) was brought without probable cause, that it was terminated in his favor, that the defendant acted with an improper purpose, and that the plaintiff suffered resulting harm. See Restatement (Second) of Torts §653. If Berlin's complaint does not allege favorable termination, Porter may move to dismiss for failure to state a claim, on the ground that Berlin has failed to allege all the necessary elements of a claim for malicious prosecution.

Now, Berlin's failure to plead favorable termination may simply be an oversight. If so, the court will allow Berlin to amend the complaint to add this allegation, and the suit will proceed.[1] However, Berlin may not be able to allege favorable termination. For example, he may have been convicted, or entered into a plea bargain. If that is the case, his complaint is fatally defective and cannot be rescued by an amendment. Since an essential element of the complaint cannot be alleged, the claim may be dismissed under Rule 12(b)(6).

Before comparing the Rule 12(b)(6) motion with the motion for summary judgment, a few examples may help to clarify the function of the motion to dismiss for failure to state a claim. In considering the examples, assume that all actions are brought as diversity actions in federal court, that personal and subject matter jurisdiction are proper, and that state substantive law applies. (The explanations begin on p. 482.)

## Examples

### Threshold Challenges

1. While Gershwin and his wife, Comden, are jogging in Central Park in New York City, a car driven by Hart negligently careens off the road and hits Gershwin. Comden is not hit herself but suffers severe emotional distress from seeing Gershwin seriously injured. She sues Hart, alleging

---

1. When a complaint is dismissed, the court will ordinarily give the plaintiff at least one opportunity to amend to cure defects in the original complaint. See 3 Moore's at §12.34[5].

the above facts in her complaint and claiming a right to damages for negligent infliction of emotional distress. Hart moves to dismiss under Rule 12(b)(6).

a. How would you phrase the issue posed by Hart's motion?

b. Assume that New York law does not recognize a right to relief for negligent infliction of emotional distress unless the plaintiff also suffered direct physical injury from the defendant's negligence; that is, she was hit by the car too (or, perhaps, flying debris). Will Hart's motion be granted?

2. Assume that Comden makes the same allegations but also includes in her complaint an allegation that there is a right to relief under New York law for negligent infliction of emotional distress even if the plaintiff suffered no physical injury. Hart moves to dismiss for failure to state a claim. Should the motion be granted?

3. Assume, for purposes of this example only, that the right to recover for negligent infliction of emotional distress under New York law is not quite so clear. Early cases rejected such recovery, but recent appellate cases have allowed recovery for intentional infliction of emotional distress without physical injury. Comden can make a fair argument that the recent cases effectively overrule prior law and recognize a right to relief for negligently inflicted emotional injuries as well. Is a motion to dismiss for failure to state a claim a proper means for Hart to challenge the complaint?

## Void for Vagueness?

4. Assume that New York law bars recovery for emotional injuries without accompanying physical impact but that Comden words her complaint more generally. She alleges that Hart negligently drove his automobile in Central Park on the day in question and that Hart's negligence proximately caused personal injuries to her, for which she claims damages. Hart moves to dismiss for failure to state a claim. Will the motion be granted?

5. Jones is arrested for vagrancy by Rogers, a police officer of the Town of Broadway. Rogers books Jones and places him in a cell. An hour later, Jones is found hanging from the bars of the cell, an apparent suicide. Kern, the administrator of Jones's estate, sues Broadway for wrongful death, claiming that the town is liable for the failure of Rogers and other officers to take precautions to prevent Jones from taking his own life. Under applicable tort law, the Town would be liable if its employees, acting in the scope of employment, failed to take precautions to protect Jones from suicide, provided they knew or had reason to know of the particular risk that Jones might attempt suicide.

The complaint alleges that Rogers arrested and booked Jones, that neither he nor the other officers took any precautions to assure Jones's safety, that Jones committed suicide in the cell, and that the Town is therefore liable to the estate for damages. Broadway moves to dismiss the complaint for failure to state a claim upon which relief can be granted. Should the motion be granted?

6. Assume, on the facts of example 5, that Kern files an amended complaint, which properly alleges the necessary elements of the claim, including the requirement that the officers should have known of the risk that Jones would attempt suicide. Broadway answers the complaint, denying that its officers had any reason to know that Jones might attempt suicide. The Town then files a motion to dismiss for failure to state a claim, on the ground that its officers had no reason to know this risk.

   a. Can Broadway make the motion at this point?
   b. Will the motion be granted?

## SUMMARY JUDGMENT DISTINGUISHED

The first part of this chapter suggests that the plaintiff does not bear a heavy burden in avoiding dismissal under Rule 12(b)(6). He need not prove any facts nor even allege them in detail so long as the court can infer that he is alleging the elements of a proper claim. The motion offers no assistance in weeding out cases in which a proper cause of action has been alleged but the plaintiff cannot prove his claim.

The motion for summary judgment under Fed. R. Civ. P. 56 is designed to allow early resolution of cases in which the plaintiff meets the minimal burden to plead the elements of a compensable claim, but cannot *prove* one or more of those elements. *Summary* judgment means entry of judgment by the court in favor of either the plaintiff or the defendant without trial. Such resolution of the case (or a part of it) by the judge is appropriate only if the evidence before the court demonstrates that there are no disputed issues of material fact to be tried and that the moving party is entitled to judgment on the undisputed facts. Fed. R. Civ. P. 56(c).

Suppose, for example, that Berlin, the malicious prosecution plaintiff introduced above, properly alleges that Porter brought a criminal action against him, that he had no probable cause, that it was brought without a proper purpose, and that it terminated in his favor. However, Porter knows that the case was "continued without a finding" by the court, rather than dismissed.[2] If this disposition does not constitute "favorable termination," Berlin cannot win his malicious prosecution case. Under Rule 56, Porter may challenge Berlin's ability to prove favorable termination by moving for summary judgment, supported by evidence to prove that the case was continued without a finding and a memorandum arguing that the continuance is insufficient to meet the "favorable termination" element of a malicious prosecution action.

Porter's motion challenges Berlin's ability to prove an essential element of his claim. Berlin cannot recover without showing that the criminal case was resolved in his favor; Porter has produced evidence that it was not. When the motion is made and adequately supported, Berlin must respond by producing admissible evidence that tends to prove the challenged element. Fed. R. Civ. P. 56(e). He might, for example, submit evidence that there were two charges against him and that one was continued but the one on which he relies was dismissed. He might submit evidence that the continuance the defendant relies on was simply to postpone the hearing and that the case was subsequently dismissed. Such evidence would demonstrate that there is a "genuine issue of material fact" as to whether the prior proceeding was terminated in Berlin's favor.

If Berlin produces such countervailing evidence, summary judgment must be denied. Summary judgment is not meant to try the facts but only to determine whether there are genuinely contested issues of material fact. Thus, the burden of the party opposing summary judgment is only to show that he has legally competent evidence upon which a jury could resolve the factual issues in his favor. If there is a genuine dispute as to the relevant facts, it is the jury's role to resolve it. The judge's role on summary judgment is only to determine whether the parties' evidence reveals such a factual dispute.

If Berlin does not produce countervailing evidence, he has not demonstrated that there is a factual dispute for the jury to try. If his action against Porter were allowed to go to a jury without any evidence to prove that the original action had terminated in his favor, the jury would have no legitimate basis upon which to find for Berlin. A verdict for him could only reflect irrational decision-making. Summary judgment avoids this risk, as well as the delay and expense of trying unprovable cases.[3]

---

2. In some states, criminal cases may be "continued" for a period of time rather than dismissed or tried. Under this procedure the court can impose conditions on the defendant in exchange for suspending the prosecution, but the defendant does not plead guilty or acquire a criminal record. Since this practice is routinely used in cases in which the defendant's guilt is clear, it is doubtful that the court would hold that such a continuance constitutes "favorable termination" under the common law of malicious prosecution. At least one case has held that it does not. *Van Arsdale v. Caswell*, 311 S.W.2d 404 (Ky. 1958).
3. A recent article argues that summary judgment is unconstitutional, on the ground that it conflicts with the right to jury trial guaranteed by the Seventh Amendment. S. Thomas, Why Summary Judgment Is Unconstitutional, 93 Va. L. Rev. 139 (2007). The argument

## Some Interim Questions

7. Assume that Berlin has alleged that the prior suit was terminated in his favor but has no evidence to prove it. Could Porter obtain dismissal of Berlin's claim under Rule 12(b)(6) at the outset of the case?

8. Why might Berlin have filed the action if the case was continued indefinitely rather than dismissed? Isn't he wasting his time and money and flouting the ethical constraints on pleading in Rule 11?

Summary judgment also provides a needed avenue for resolution of another category of cases, in which the parties agree on the underlying facts but disagree as to the legal implications of those facts. In Berlin's case, for example, the parties may agree that the case was decided by a continuance without a finding but disagree as to whether that disposition constitutes "favorable termination" for purposes of an action for malicious prosecution. If so, Porter might move for summary judgment, supported by evidence that the case was continued without a finding. If Berlin admits that the case was continued, he will not respond with countervailing evidence but instead make the legal argument that the continuance satisfies the "favorable termination" element of a malicious prosecution claim. On these facts, the motion has framed a single, dispositive legal issue for the court. If it concludes that the continuance suffices for favorable termination, it will deny summary judgment and allow the case to proceed. If it concludes that it does not satisfy the favorable termination requirement, it will enter judgment for Porter because he is "entitled to judgment as a matter of law."[4]

The motion can also be used to resolve individual claims in a multi-claim lawsuit. Fed. R. Civ. P. 56(c), (d). Or, claims by or against one party might be resolved on summary judgment, leaving others for trial. For example, Hart might get summary judgment on the emotional distress claim alleged by Comden in example 1, but still have to go to trial on Gershwin's physical injury claim.

Rule 56 provides that a motion for summary judgment may be supported by affidavits, depositions, answers to interrogatories, admissions,

---

starts from the premise that the Seventh Amendment "preserves" the right to jury trial. Thus, if summary judgment was not available when the Amendment was adopted in 1791, using it thereafter would not preserve the right to have the jury determine the facts. Courts have summarily rejected constitutional challenges to the use of summary judgment. "The function of a jury is to try the material facts; where no such facts are in dispute, there is no occasion for jury trial. Thus the right to trial by jury does not prevent a court from granting summary judgment." *Plaisance v. Phelps*, 845 F.2d 107, 108 (5th Cir. 1988). Professor Thomas's article may provoke a further look at this issue by the courts.

4. Often the parties will stipulate to the relevant facts and submit the case for decision on "cross motions" for summary judgment, each arguing that he should get judgment as a matter of law on the undisputed facts.

and admissible documents. Fed. R. Civ. P. 56(c), (e). These materials are not always admissible at trial themselves, but they demonstrate that the party has evidence that would be admissible. For example, an affidavit of Hart concerning the Central Park accident is a sworn evidentiary statement based upon personal knowledge. If the case went to trial, Hart could come into court and give the same testimony. So the affidavit shows that Hart *has* admissible evidence to support his claim. The same is true for depositions, admissions, and answers to interrogatories, all of which represent sworn statements of parties or witnesses. Many documents, if shown to be authentic, are also admissible under the rules of evidence and therefore may also be used to support or oppose a summary judgment motion. In the Broadway case, for example, the police booking records would be admissible evidence. However, allegations in the pleadings, which represent the parties' *assertions* as to what they can prove, are not admissible evidence and therefore may not be used as supporting evidence on a summary judgment motion.

## Another Interim Question

9. Why must the evidence presented in support of or in opposition to a motion for summary judgment be evidence that would be admissible at trial?

The function of the summary judgment motion is similar to that of the Rule 12(b)(6) motion, but there are important differences. The following examples should help you to understand summary judgment and its relationship to the motion to dismiss for failure to state a claim.

## Examples

### No Genuine Issue

10. Recall example 4, involving Comden's claim against Hart for negligent infliction of emotional distress. In that example Comden pleaded generally that she had suffered "personal injuries" and the complaint therefore survived a motion to dismiss.
    a. If New York law did not recognize a right to relief for negligent infliction of emotional distress without direct physical injury, could Hart obtain judgment on a motion for summary judgment?
    b. If he seeks summary judgment, what supporting materials might he submit?

11. Suppose, on the same facts, that Hart moves for summary judgment on Comden's claim, supported by an excerpt from Comden's deposition in which she admits that she suffered no direct physical injury. Comden responds with an affidavit stating in detail the emotional

injuries she sustained and the lost earnings that resulted from her emotional reaction to the accident. She also submits authenticated bills for resulting psychiatric care. Should the motion be granted?

12. Consider again Berlin's case against Porter, in which he sought recovery for malicious prosecution. Assume that the original criminal action was tried, and Berlin was found not guilty. After suing Porter for malicious prosecution, and alleging favorable termination, Berlin files a motion for summary judgment, attaching a copy of the court docket that shows the not-guilty finding and subsequent dismissal of the criminal case. If Porter produces no countervailing evidence, what order should the court enter?

13. In Kern's action against Broadway arising from the jail suicide, assume that Kern's complaint properly alleges the elements of the claim. Broadway answers, denying that Rogers or the other officers knew or should have known of Jones's suicidal tendencies. It then moves for summary judgment, supported by an affidavit of Rogers, the booking officer, in which he testifies that Jones was sullen and uncommunicative when arrested, that he never made any statement indicating an intent to take his life, and that Jones was strongly intoxicated and never said a word during the entire booking process. Kern opposes the motion, but does not submit any evidentiary materials with his opposition. Should the motion be granted?

## Point/Counterpoint

14. Broadway moves for summary judgment, supported by affidavits of all the police officers involved in the arrest and booking of Jones. Each testifies that Jones behaved normally during the process, cooperated with the officers, did not appear depressed, and made no statements suggesting that he might attempt suicide.
    a. Assume that Kern submits no opposing affidavits or evidence. How does the judge know that the officers are telling the truth in their affidavits? If she doesn't, how could she grant summary judgment for Broadway?
    b. Kern submits no opposing evidence but argues in opposition to the motion that he has alleged in his complaint that the officers knew or should have known that Jones was suicidal, thus placing that fact in dispute. Should the motion be granted?
    c. Kern submits his own affidavit in opposition to the motion, in which he states under oath that Officer Rogers "knew or should have known from Jones's behavior that Jones was depressed and suicidal." Should the motion be granted?

d. Kern submits an opposing affidavit that states that Jones called him shortly after his arrest and was crying and threatening suicide on the phone. He also submits an affidavit from a witness to Jones's arrest, who states that Jones was irrational and made suicidal statements when Officer Rogers arrested him. Should the motion be granted?

e. In responding to the police officers' affidavits described in the beginning of the example, Kern submits an affidavit in opposition to the motion stating that the officers failed to take Jones's belt away from him, and that Jones hung himself with the belt. Broadway responds with a further affidavit of Rogers stating that Jones was not wearing a belt at the time of his arrest. Should the motion be granted?

## Baring the Burden

15. Broadway moves for summary judgment. In support of the motion, it submits Kern's answer to an interrogatory asking him to "state all facts upon which you base your allegations that the police officers knew or should have known that Jones was suicidal." Kern's response to this interrogatory states that Jones had told him several days earlier that he wanted to die, and that Jones was in desperate financial circumstances and had just separated from his wife. Broadway also submits an excerpt from Kern's deposition, in which he is again asked what facts he relies on to establish the officers' knowledge that Jones might attempt suicide. Kern's response was, "It was obvious; he had been depressed for months, often talked of suicide, and was out of a job. Don't your officers have any common sense?" Broadway does not submit any evidence from its own witnesses but argues that this record demonstrates that Kern cannot support his claim that the officers knew of the risk of suicide. Kern offers no affidavits of his own. Should the motion be granted?

## Explanations

### Threshold Challenges

1. a. The issue posed by the motion is whether a party who suffers emotional distress from witnessing negligently caused injury to another, but suffers no direct physical injury himself, has a right to recover damages for emotional distress from the negligent party. Note that the issue is not whether Comden actually suffered the emotional distress or whether Hart was negligent but only whether, assuming all the pleaded facts to be true, the law authorizes an award of damages for such injuries.

b. On the assumption given, this motion should be granted. It is clear from the allegations in Comden's complaint that she was not hit by Hart's car; she is claiming relief based solely on emotional distress from seeing Gershwin injured. If New York law does not recognize a right to relief for acts that only cause emotional distress to a defendant, Comden has asked for relief that the court cannot grant. If the court allowed Comden to proceed to trial, and Comden proved at trial that Hart was negligent, that his negligence caused physical injuries to Gershwin, and that Comden suffered emotional distress as a result, the court would still be unable to grant Comden's demand for damages. The claim Comden has alleged is simply not recognized under the applicable law as a legal wrong entitling her to compensation. If that is true, there is no reason to proceed to trial. In such cases, the court can short-circuit the process by dismissing the case at the outset. That's what Rule 12(b)(6) is designed to do.

2. Comden's train of thought here is creative, though unavailing. If the court must assume the truth of the allegations in the complaint, why not allege that the law allows relief for emotional distress without physical injury? Unfortunately, Comden is singing the wrong tune. The court only accepts the *factual* allegations of the complaint as true for purposes of the motion. The legal issue of whether her allegations state a claim is exactly what the motion is intended to resolve. Rule 12(b)(6) would be useless if the plaintiff could simply allege that he has stated a compensable claim and thereby prevent the court from deciding whether he has.

3. In this example it is difficult to determine whether Comden has stated a claim for relief because the state of the law on the crucial issue in the case is not definitively settled by the cases. If the recent cases have effectively overruled the old doctrine, Comden has stated a compensable claim and must be allowed a chance to prove her allegations. If, on the other hand, the old rule remains valid (perhaps because the recent cases limited the right to recover to emotional distress caused by intentional acts) Comden has not stated a claim.

Although the motion here requires close analysis of the relevant case law, Hart's motion to dismiss is still a proper means to challenge the sufficiency of Comden's complaint. The Rule 12(b)(6) motion is available to resolve difficult issues of law as well as clear ones, and whether Comden has stated a claim depends on a question of law. If the court concludes that the recent New York cases have established a right to recover for negligent infliction of emotional distress without physical injury, it should deny the motion and allow Comden to go to trial. On the other hand, if the court concludes that the recent cases are limited to intentional acts, it should dismiss since Comden's allegations are based solely on negligence.

Admittedly, some courts may be reluctant to grant motions to dismiss if the state of the law is unsettled. The court may sense that the issue is a close one that could be better decided on a full record after discovery or trial. The judge might therefore allow the case to proceed to trial and allow the appellate court to clarify the law on appeal after a verdict. But if the court is convinced that the case law does not allow recovery, it has the power to dismiss under Rule 12(b)(6) since the issue, though difficult, is one of law for the court.

## Void for Vagueness?

4. Comden has phrased her allegations so generally here that the court cannot tell from the complaint that the "personal injuries" she has suffered are solely emotional. You and I may know it from the facts described in example 1. Hart may know it since he knows that his car only hit Gershwin. But for purposes of the motion to dismiss, the court only "knows" what is in the complaint. In deciding the Rule 12(b)(6) motion, the court must ask whether the plaintiff, on the allegations of the complaint, could prove facts that would entitle her to relief. On these general allegations, Comden might prove that the "personal injuries" she suffered were direct physical injuries, clearly compensable under traditional negligence law. Thus, the complaint may state a claim upon which relief may be granted, and the motion must be denied.

If this tactic will avoid dismissal, and pleading this generally is sufficient under *Conley v. Gibson*, why would plaintiffs ever plead a questionable cause of action more specifically? One answer is that a more specific complaint is more helpful to the court and also will trigger more specific responses from the defendant in his answer. See Chapter 33, p. 668. In addition, the plaintiff may prefer to put the difficult legal issue on the table from the beginning. After all, if the case will ultimately turn on the legal question, it may be desirable to resolve it at the outset rather than vigorously litigating the truth of the factual allegations only to discover down the line that proving them will still leave the plaintiff without any right to relief.

On the other hand, in many cases plaintiffs do plead their claims very generally, in order not to reveal weaknesses in their cases or simply to avoid giving the opposing party any "free discovery." In some cases such generality may at least postpone the day of reckoning, but as we shall see, the defendant will likely use the summary judgment motion to flush out such weaknesses anyway.

5. This complaint is insufficient for several reasons. To begin with, the Town is only liable if the police officers acted in the scope of employment, but Kern has not alleged that they did. However, most judges would not dismiss the complaint on this basis. Although the complaint does not explicitly include the scope-of-employment allegation, the complaint alleges that the police officers acted at the jail, performed acts that are part of ordinary police procedure, and that the Town is liable. It is a fair inference that the estate bases its claim on the fact that the officers acted in the scope of their employment for the Town. In ruling on the motion to dismiss, the court must resolve any ambiguities in the pleadings in favor of the nonmoving party. If the court, looking at the complaint, can reasonably infer that the plaintiff has stated a valid cause of action, it must deny the motion to dismiss. In this case, there is enough there for a court to conclude, taking all inferences in favor of the plaintiff, that the estate may have a compensable claim. Perhaps a judge who loves his rules will require the estate to amend to allege that the officers acted in the scope of employment, but the court should not dismiss the action on this ground.

The other defect, however, is substantive. Kern has not alleged that the officers had any reason to know that Jones was suicidal. Under the applicable tort law, the duty to take precautions arises once the officers in charge of Jones have reason to know that he might try to injure himself. If they didn't know or have reason to suspect that, the Town is not liable, even if they could have prevented the suicide by greater vigilance. Unless Kern alleges that they had reason to believe there was a risk of suicide, he has not alleged a necessary element of the cause of action.

It may be that Kern's counsel simply neglected to allege this element clearly in the complaint. If so, he will certainly be allowed to amend to cure the defect. However, if he didn't allege it because he has no reason to believe it is true, he will not be able to amend to make the allegation. If that is so, the complaint may be dismissed under Rule 12(b)(6) because, without such an allegation, there is no right to relief.

6. a. The timing of Broadway's motion is procedurally proper. Rule 12(h)(2) authorizes the defendant to raise the objection of failure to state a claim in any pleading, by motion for judgment on the pleadings[5] or even at trial. The rules allow this objection to be

---

5. A judgment on the pleadings is authorized by Fed. R. Civ. P. 12(c). It may be used either as a delayed motion to dismiss, that is, a challenge to the sufficiency of the complaint standing alone, or as a challenge to the sufficiency of the complaint in light of particular defenses raised in the answer. See generally Moore's Federal Practice at §12.38.

At this stage, the motion still challenges the legal sufficiency of the complaint, but it is technically not a "Rule 12(b)(6) motion"; that Rule applies to pre-answer motions only.

raised throughout the suit because it is pointless for a court to proceed if it cannot ultimately provide the plaintiff with any relief for the claim he asserted.

b. Be careful to distinguish the issue of the legal sufficiency of the plaintiff's allegations from the factual issue of whether the allegations are true. Here, Broadway does not deny that Kern could recover, if he proved that its police officers should have known of the risk of Jones's suicide. Rather, Broadway denies that the officers had any reason to know of that risk. Thus, Broadway's motion really challenges the truth of this allegation in the complaint, not its legal sufficiency.

At this stage of the case the court has no basis to determine whether the officers knew of the need to take precautions to protect Jones. Kern has alleged that they did, and Broadway has denied it. But at this point *there is absolutely no evidence before the court on the issue*. All it has before it is Kern's allegations and Broadway's denial. The motion to dismiss for failure to state a claim, whether made before or after the defendant answers the complaint, still challenges only the legal sufficiency of those allegations. Broadway's denial in its answer that the officers had reason to know that Jones might attempt suicide disputes the truth of that allegation, but does not change the fact that Broadway may be liable if Kern proves that they did. Whether its officers should have realized the risk and taken precautions is a factual issue, which cannot be resolved based on the allegations in the pleadings.

## Some Interim Questions

7. Even if he knows that Berlin cannot prove his claim for malicious prosecution, Porter will not be able to obtain dismissal under Rule 12(b)(6). On a 12(b)(6) motion the court only considers whether the plaintiff has alleged the elements necessary to state a claim. Here, Berlin alleged all the elements of malicious prosecution in his complaint, including that the original action terminated in his favor. The court cannot look beyond the plaintiff's allegations in deciding the Rule 12(b)(6) motion; therefore, such a motion would have been denied, since Berlin has alleged all the elements of the claim. To get the case dismissed, Porter needs to "pierce the pleadings," that is, go beyond the allegations in the complaint in order to convince the court that although Berlin has *alleged* a proper claim for malicious prosecution, he cannot *prove* the favorable termination element of his claim.

8. People file lawsuits for many reasons. Berlin may have been unclear as to the necessary elements of the claim, or he may have had grounds to

believe that under the applicable law a continuance is sufficient to satisfy the favorable termination requirement. He may have hoped to induce Porter to settle the claim, despite doubt as to its legal sufficiency. He may even have had little hope of winning, yet filed suit as a means of venting his anger or embarrassing the defendant. In some cases such suits may violate the ethical limitations on pleading in Fed. R. Civ. P. 11 or the Code of Professional Responsibility, as a misuse of court process. In others, however, they may simply reflect the uncertainties inherent in the application of general legal principles to particular cases.

For whatever reason, many suits are filed that, when tested on the merits, prove fatally defective. Summary judgment provides a means to probe for such defects without going to trial on all issues in the case.

## Another Interim Question

9. When a party presents his case to the jury, he must present "admissible" evidence before the jury on each element of his claim or defense. Admissible evidence is evidence that is deemed sufficiently reliable, under established rules of evidence, for a jury to hear and consider in reaching its decision on the facts.

Since the point of the summary judgment motion is to see if there is any evidence on the challenged allegation for the jury to consider, it follows that the evidence used to support the motion should be evidence that the jury could hear at trial. If the party opposing summary judgment has no admissible evidence on one or more elements of his claim, the jury would have no evidentiary basis upon which to find that he had proved that element of his case. The summary judgment motion tests whether this is so by challenging the opposing party to produce such admissible evidence in opposition to the motion.

## No Genuine Issue

10. a. This is exactly the type of situation in which summary judgment allows parties to obtain judgment without trial, despite the fact that the plaintiff's complaint alleges a proper claim for relief. Here, Hart knows that Comden cannot prove a compensable claim under New York law, but Hart has to show the court that this is true by demonstrating that Comden cannot prove physical injury, an essential element of her claim. By moving for summary judgment supported by admissible evidence that Comden suffered no physical injuries, Hart will flush out the fatal weakness in Comden's case. Presumably, Comden will be unable to counter Hart's evidence since it is true. The motion will therefore demonstrate that

there is "no genuine issue" (Fed. R. Civ. P. 56(c)) as to whether Comden suffered physical injuries and that Hart is entitled to judgment as a matter of law, since solely psychic injuries do not give rise to a right to recover under applicable law.

Note that here, as on the motion to dismiss under Rule 12(b)(6), the case ultimately boils down to a legal issue. However, in the procedural posture of this case, a 12(b)(6) motion would have been denied because Comden had alleged a compensable claim (due to the generality of her complaint), even though she cannot prove a crucial element of it. The summary judgment motion allows Hart to demonstrate this fatal weakness in Comden's case.

b. Hart may use any materials that demonstrate that he has admissible evidence to support his motion. A party's answers to interrogatories, for example, are sworn statements that the party could testify to at trial. Hart could send interrogatories to Comden asking whether she suffered direct physical injury in the accident. Comden would presumably answer "no," and that answer could be submitted in support of the motion. Hart could offer similar testimony from Comden's deposition or his own affidavit stating that his car did not hit Comden, that he observed Comden after the accident, and that she had no physical injuries. Sworn affidavits of other witnesses or a certified police report in which Comden stated that she suffered no physical injury would also constitute proper supporting evidence.

11. Assuming that New York law does not allow recovery for purely emotional injuries, Comden's claim will again end on a sour note. Hart has submitted admissible evidence in support of his motion showing that Comden did not suffer direct physical injury. Comden has filed an opposing affidavit, but the affidavit does not demonstrate that there is any issue as to whether she suffered physical injury. Her evidence goes to prove the severity of her psychic injury, but that is not enough to entitle her to take her case to a jury. She may be totally incapacitated and prove it by the testimony of 20 unimpeachable witnesses, but she will still not be entitled to relief if the law requires accompanying physical injury.

This example illustrates an important point. It is not enough to show that there is a dispute in the evidence on *some* fact; the dispute must be on an issue that is material to the right to recover. Here, Comden's opposing affidavits indicate that she can prove facts, but facts that are irrelevant under the governing law. Thus, there is no dispute of *material fact* (see Fed. R. Civ. P. 56(c)), and Hart is entitled to judgment as a matter of law.

Actually, Rule 56 is very confusing on this point. Rule 56(c) provides that summary judgment can only be granted if there is "no genuine issue as to any material fact," but in many cases summary judgment is granted even though there are many hotly disputed, clearly material issues in the case. Suppose, for example, that Simon sues Hammerstein for damages in an auto accident, and there is lots of contradictory evidence as to whether his injuries resulted from the accident or a preexisting condition. However, Simon has no evidence that Hammerstein was negligent in causing the accident. Here, there is a genuine issue for trial as to damages, but Hammerstein would still be entitled to summary judgment if Simon has no evidence of negligence. In other words, the "no-dispute-of-material-fact" language means that there is no factual dispute concerning the *particular element of the claim that is challenged by the motion.* There may be genuine disputes in the evidence on every other element, but a chain is only as strong as its weakest link: If Simon has no proof of negligence, he must lose.

12. Since Porter has not shown the existence of any factual dispute concerning favorable termination, the judge should enter an order granting *partial* summary judgment for Berlin on his allegation that the criminal prosecution was terminated in his favor. However, this does not mean that Berlin automatically wins the case; it simply establishes one element of Berlin's claim. He will still have to prove all the other elements, including lack of probable cause, that Porter acted with an improper purpose, and damages.

    Compare the converse situation, in which the judge grants summary judgment for Porter after Berlin produces no evidence of favorable termination. Berlin can only win if he proves each element of his claim; if the proof fails on any one of them, he cannot recover. So Porter's successful challenge on the favorable termination element will lead to summary judgment for him on the entire claim; the whole case will be dismissed. But summary judgment for the *plaintiff* may simply establish one element of the claim, leaving him to shoulder the burden on the other elements at trial.

13. You may have concluded that Broadway's motion should be granted on the purely procedural ground that Kern has filed no affidavits or other evidence in opposition to the motion. Rule 56(e)(2) appears at first blush to require this result, since it provides that a party opposing summary judgment may not simply rest on the allegations in his pleading but is required to come forward with evidence in support of those allegations.

    That conclusion, while understandable from an initial reading of Rule 56(e), is wrong. Summary judgment should only be granted under Rule 56(e) "if appropriate." It is never "appropriate" to grant the motion if the moving party's evidence itself raises doubts as to the relevant facts. It is only where the moving party's materials would suffice to establish that party's version of the facts that the burden shifts to the opposing party to introduce contrary evidence.

In this example, Roger's testimony indicates that Jones never stated that he intended to commit suicide, but surely that is not the only behavior that would put police officers on notice of such a risk. Maybe his sullenness, refusal to talk, and intoxication should be sufficient in themselves to suggest depression and reduced impulse control, factors commonly associated with suicide. This affidavit hardly suffices to eliminate the possibility that the officers were on notice of the risk. In deciding the summary judgment motion, the court will view the evidence submitted in the light most favorable to the party opposing the motion. If the evidence offered on the summary judgment motion could give rise to two inferences, one of which would support the opposing party's case, the court should assume that the jury would make that inference and deny summary judgment. *Anderson v. Liberty Lobby, Inc.*, 477 U.S. 242, 255 (1986). Thus, Broadway's supporting evidence does not demonstrate that there is no genuine issue of fact as to whether the officers knew of Jones's suicidal tendencies. Since Broadway's own materials do not entitle it to summary judgment, the motion should be denied even if Kern does not file opposing materials.

Of course, it is hardly advisable for Kern to rest solely on the argument that there is ambiguity in Broadway's evidence. Kern should also respond with positive evidence to support his contention that the officers knew or should have known of the risk, rather than stake his case on the argument that Broadway has failed to meet its initial burden to adequately support the motion.

## Point/Counterpoint

14. a. The judge *doesn't* know that the officers are telling the truth; they may be lying through their teeth. But the purpose of the summary judgment motion is not to determine whether the officers are telling the truth: that would be finding the facts, a role reserved for the jury. Instead, the motion tests whether the party opposing summary judgment — Kern, in this case — has any meaningful evidence to prove her allegation that they were on notice of Jones's suicidal tendencies. The defendant has produced evidence that they weren't on notice; if Kern doesn't have any evidence that they were, how can she ever prove that essential allegation at trial? And if she can't prove an essential allegation, how can she win? If the case went to trial, and

Kern submitted no credible proof on the knew-or-should-have-known allegation, the judge would have to order judgment for Broadway based on Kern's lack of proof. The summary judgment motion thus tests whether the plaintiff has sufficient evidence on the challenged element of the claim to make a trial necessary. If she doesn't, the case must be dismissed on summary judgment, whether the officers are telling the truth or not.

b. Kern's response here is insufficient to keep the show on the road. Rule 56(e) specifically provides that a party may not avoid summary judgment by resting on contrary allegations in the complaint. All that Kern has done here is to say, "All right, you have evidence to prove that the officers didn't suspect that Jones was suicidal, but I say they did." This is mere persistence, not proof. The court knows that is Kern's position, but a summary judgment motion challenges him to show that he has evidence to prove it, not just allege it.

c. Once again, Kern is whistling Dixie. He has simply taken the knew-or-should-have-known allegation in his complaint and restated it in his affidavit. If Kern cannot avoid summary judgment by resting on the allegation in his complaint, it hardly seems appropriate to let him achieve the same result by simply repeating the same allegation in an affidavit. This is not admissible evidence as to facts, but simply the unsupported opinion of an interested party as to how the factual issue should be resolved. If parties could avoid summary judgment by this tactic, it would hardly be an effective device.

If a party moves for summary judgment and properly supports the motion with admissible evidence, the opposing party must respond with countervailing evidence in order to avoid the entry of judgment against him. Fed. R. Civ. P. 56(e)(2). It is not sufficient for the opposing party to respond by simply reiterating that he disagrees with the evidence proffered by the moving party. At the summary judgment stage the court wants to see what evidence the parties have to put before the jury if a trial is held, not a rehash of their positions in the pleadings. See *Street v. J. C.Bradford and Co.*, 886 F.2d 1472, 1478 (6th Cir. 1989) (summary judgment motion challenges opponent to "put up or shut up" on a critical issue). Otherwise, the motion would simply occasion a renewed swearing match between the parties, which would not probe their ability to prove their cases.

d. This is an entirely different situation. Here Kern has offered admissible evidence, his own testimony and that of another witness to relevant events, as to *facts* that tend to prove that the officers should have been aware that Jones might attempt suicide. These affidavits do not absolutely establish that awareness, but they do raise a question of fact on the issue. Summary judgment should be denied here because the evidence is contradictory, thus posing a triable issue of fact as to whether the officers were on notice of Jones's suicidal tendencies. In this case, the show must go on.

e. The parties' affidavits here certainly raise a factual issue as to whether Jones was wearing a belt. But the issue is not *material* to the cause of action alleged by Kern. His claim is that they should have taken precautions to protect Jones because they were aware that he might attempt suicide. The duty to take such precautions is premised on knowledge of the risk; absent that knowledge, the fact that they didn't take appropriate precautions, such as taking the belt away, is irrelevant. Unless Kern can prove notice of the risk, failure to avert it is legally irrelevant.

As Kern's lawyer, you would probably argue (as my students do when we study the case on which these examples are based)[6] that it is negligent not to take belts away from *all* prisoners, regardless of any reason to anticipate a risk of suicide. Maybe it is (though it was not held to be in the actual case), but that is a different theory of the case than the one alleged in Kern's complaint. If Kern wants to argue this, he should plead that the officers were negligent in their general booking procedures, as well as in failing to take special precautions because of their awareness of Jones's condition. If he pleaded that theory, the conflict in the evidence on the belt issue *would* be material to that theory, and would keep his case alive even if his claim based on their knowledge of Jones's suicidal tendencies failed on summary judgment.

## Baring the Burden

15. In this example, Broadway has not submitted any evidence to *disprove* Kern's allegation that its officers knew of Jones's suicidal tendencies. Instead, it has submitted materials to show that Kern cannot meet his burden to prove that they did. Broadway is saying, "Hey, Court, look at this record. I've used the discovery tools the way they're supposed to be used, to probe the other side's case, and look what he's got: nothing. His statements in his deposition and answers to interrogatories do not contain any evidence to show that the police officers knew or should have known that Jones was suicidal. On this record, it is clear that the plaintiff has nothing whatsoever to prove that we knew of Jones's suicidal tendencies. Kern cannot prove that element of his case, so we win. Throw this case out."

Broadway is right on this record. Kern's answers do not show that the officers had any reason to take special precautions to protect Jones.

---

6. *Slaven v. Salem*, 386 Mass. 885 (1982).

The facts that he was depressed, out of work, and separated tend to prove that he might be suicidal, but do not prove that the officers *knew or should have known* it. Whether the motion should be granted turns, then, on whether the moving party can get summary judgment by pointing out that the party with the burden of proof lacks adequate evidence to meet that burden, without producing any evidence of its own to disprove the alleged facts.

In *Celotex Corp. v. Catrett*, 477 U.S. 317 (1986), the Supreme Court held that a party can support a summary judgment motion with materials that show that the party who has the burden of proof on an essential fact cannot prove that fact. In *Celotex*, the issue was whether the plaintiff's decedent had been exposed to the defendant's asbestos products. The record suggested that the plaintiff had no proof of such exposure. The Court held that, if the defendant demonstrated that there was no evidence in the record to support the plaintiff's claim of exposure, and the plaintiff did not produce evidence tending to prove exposure, the defendant could get summary judgment without presenting any evidence to show lack of exposure. Celotex would be "entitled to judgment as a matter of law" because the plaintiff, who held the burden of proof on the issue, had no evidence to carry that burden.

This holding makes some sense: You can't very well carry the burden of proof at trial without any evidence. At the same time, however, it puts plaintiffs like Kern in a very difficult position. Broadway can move for summary judgment, supported by the interrogatory showing that Kern has no evidence to prove that the officers knew or should have known of the risk. The burden would then fall on Kern, in opposing the motion, to produce some evidence of that knowledge. If he can't, he will lose, even if they knew of the risk all along.[7]

Thus, after *Celotex*, Kern must aggressively develop the evidence before the motion, perhaps by taking the depositions of the officers to determine what they knew or suspected. If he doesn't, he may lose, not because his claim lacks merit, but because he has not yet gathered the evidence necessary to prove it. The moving party, on the other hand, can force his opponent (usually the plaintiff) to this effort without tipping his own hand as to the contrary proof he will produce

---

7. It is sometimes said that summary judgment is not appropriate on issues involving state of mind, such as the officers' awareness of the risk of suicide in Kern's case, because they are subjective questions, which turn on credibility and difficult inferences about what people intend or know. However, summary judgment may be proper if there is no evidence from which those inferences can be made. In *Slaven*, for example, the court granted summary judgment because there was no evidence in the record to support the allegation that the officers were on notice of the decedent's suicidal tendencies.

at trial if the plaintiff avoids summary judgment by producing admissible evidence on the issue.

Plaintiffs in this position will doubtless have recourse to Rule 56(f), which allows the court to grant continuances to allow the opposing party to develop his case. However, relief under Rule 56(f) is discretionary; the party seeking it should always be ready to specify exactly what further discovery is necessary in order to properly respond to the defendant's "*Celotex* motion."

# The Judge and the Jury, Part One

Judgment as a Matter of Law
(Directed Verdict)

---

## INTRODUCTION

Every good citizen knows that the Constitution guarantees "the right to trial by jury." However, a good part of the civil procedure course is devoted to studying various hurdles that stand between the litigant who demands jury trial and actual jury decision of the merits of her case. As the last chapter demonstrates, the plaintiff's case may be cut short by a motion to dismiss under Rule 12(b)(6), which allows the judge to enter judgment for the defendant on the ground that the plaintiff's complaint does not state a legal claim for relief. If the plaintiff's case survives a Rule 12(b)(6) challenge, it may still meet an early demise on a motion for summary judgment if the judge concludes that there is "no genuine issue of material fact" for the jury to consider.

Although these two motions may preclude the parties from obtaining a jury trial, they are justifiable, since both are based on the premise that there is really nothing for the jury to do. It comes as more of a surprise to students to learn that even after the beginning of trial and the presentation of evidence the judge may still snatch the case from the jury or even more invasively, allow the jury to render a verdict and then enter judgment for the party who lost the jury verdict. This chapter and the one that follows are intended to help you understand several devices that the judge may use to control the jury's decision-making process: judgment as a matter of law and new trial.

# THE PLAINTIFF'S BURDEN OF PRODUCTION

In order to understand these devices, it helps to have a preliminary understanding of the plaintiff's burden to produce evidence at trial in support of her claim, Figure 24-1[1] represents varying degrees of evidence in support of the plaintiff's claim. At the extreme left is the case in which the plaintiff produces no evidence to prove her claim; as you move to the right along the line the strength of the plaintiff's evidence increases. The X line on the diagram indicates the point at which the plaintiff has produced evidence that is sufficiently persuasive that a jury, acting rationally, could find that she has proved each element of her case. If the plaintiff's evidence crosses this line, she is said to have satisfied her *burden of production*. Even though the judge may consider the plaintiff's evidence weak or less persuasive than the defendant's, if the evidence is sufficient to cross the X line the case falls in the realm of legitimate difference of opinion and must go to the jury for decision.

The Z line on the diagram represents the point at which the evidence is evenly balanced; that is, evidence of equal probative value supports the plaintiff's position and the defendant's. In a civil case the plaintiff's *burden of proof* is to establish that her version of events is more probably true than the defendant's — that is, that a simple preponderance of the evidence favors the plaintiff's version of events. In terms of the diagram, her evidence must fall to the right of the Z line to carry her burden of proof. The Y line represents the point at which the plaintiff's proof becomes so strong that any reasonable jury would have to conclude that the plaintiff has proved her case.[2]

Between the X and Y lines lies the arena for legitimate differences of opinion as to the proper outcome — and hence the arena for jury decision. Even though the judge concludes that the evidence falls at point Q, well to the left of the point where the balance of the evidence favors the plaintiff, she must allow the jury to decide the outcome. If the judge could take the case from the jury when the proof lies between X and Y, she could essentially usurp the role of the jury by substituting her own judgment for that of the jury at any time. General practice (and the constitutional right to jury trial) denies the judge such power: If reasonable minds can differ as to the result, the case is for the jury, not the judge.

1. A similar diagram in Landers and Martin, Civil Procedure (1981) was used, with permission, as the basis for this diagram.
2. In a criminal case, the state's burden of proof falls near if not on the Y line since the state must prove the defendant's guilt beyond a reasonable doubt.

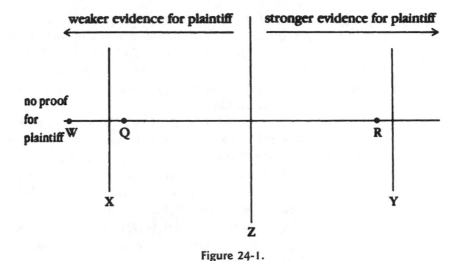

**Figure 24-1.**

Similarly, if the judge concludes that the balance of the evidence fells at point R on the spectrum, where the plaintiff's evidence substantially outweighs the opposing evidence (but is not so persuasive that the only reasonable verdict is for the plaintiff), the case must also go to the jury. Even though the judge believes that the balance tips in the plaintiff's favor, at this point on the spectrum that conclusion is legitimately debatable, just as it is at point Q. If the jury could rationally find for the defendant, it must be given the opportunity to consider the case, even though the judge believes that the preponderance of the evidence favors the plaintiff.

## OLD WINE IN NEW BOTTLES: THE MOTION FOR JUDGMENT AS A MATTER OF LAW

The courts have long provided a procedural means for judges to take cases away from the jury if the plaintiff's evidence docs not reach the magical X line. If the judge concludes that the plaintiff's case[3] is so weak that no jury, acting rationally on the evidence before it, could find for her, allowing the case to go to the jury simply invites irrational decision-making based on irrelevant or prejudicial factors. The judge has traditionally had the authority

---

3. The motion may be granted for plaintiffs as well as defendants (if the plaintiff's evidence is so strong as to pass the hypothetical Y line), though for reasons discussed below this is much less common than directed verdicts for defendants.

to guard against such flawed verdicts by refusing to send cases to the jury if there is no legitimate doubt as to which side should prevail. See *Rutherford v. Illinois Central R.R.*, 278 F.2d 310, 312 (5th Cir.) cert. denied, 364 U.S. 922 (1960) (court's power to take case from jury provides "a method for protecting neutral principles of law from powerful forces outside the scope of law — compassion and prejudice.")

The traditional device for taking the case from the jury has been the "motion for a directed verdict." Under early procedure, the judge actually did "direct" the verdict: If she concluded that the evidence was too weak to support a verdict for the plaintiff, she ordered the jury to go out and come back with a verdict for the defendant.[4] Eventually, this pro forma (if not demeaning) procedure was dropped; instead, the judge would "direct the verdict" for the defendant herself, and the case would not go to the jury at all.

In truth, this practice does not involve a "verdict" at all, which connotes a jury's finding of facts. However, the motion is still called a motion for a "directed verdict" in most state courts. The "directed verdict" terminology was also used in the federal courts until 1991, when the federal rule-makers changed the name without altering the substance of the motion. Now, in the federal courts, a party seeking to have the judge take the case from the jury on the ground that the evidence is too weak to support a verdict makes a "motion for judgment as a matter of law." Fed. R. Civ. P. 50(a)(1)(B). This is a good name for the motion for several reasons. First, it eliminates any implication that the jury has a role in the decision: As under directed verdict practice, if the judge grants the motion, the jury is discharged without deliberating or deciding anything. Second, the new name emphasizes that the judge, in theory, does not resolve factual issues when he withdraws the case from the jury but makes a legal judgment that the evidence is so lopsided that there really is no meaningful factual dispute for a jury to consider.

However, the change in terminology will create some confusion. The federal courts have developed a good half-century of "directed verdict" case law. Lawyers — like you — who will practice under the current rule must understand that the motion for judgment as a matter of law really is old wine in a new bottle. The rulemakers have not changed the *substance* of

---

4. See W. Blume, The Origin and Development of the Directed Verdict, 48 Mich. L. Rev. 555, 582 (1950). For a curious example of this practice, see *Cahill v. Chicago, Minneapolis & St. Paul Ry. Co.*, 74 F. 285 (7th Cir. 1896), in which the judge ordered the jury to return a verdict for the defendant and one juror refused to do it. The court of appeals was not pleased with such recalcitrance:

> The conduct of the juror in this instance was in the highest degree reprehensible, and might well have subjected him, and any who encouraged him to persist in this course, to punishment for contempt. His conduct was in violation of law, subversive of authority and obstructive of the orderly administration of justice.

74 F. at 290. (Really, court, lighten up a little!)

Rule 50(a). They did not change the fact that the judge makes the decision, rather than the jury. They did not change the *standard* for taking the case away from the jury. Thus, the case law under prior Rule 50(a) is still authoritative on most aspects of the motion. In addition, the change in terminology in Rule 50(a) only applies to the federal courts. State courts allow the judge similar latitude to control the jury, but most still use the "directed verdict" terminology. Thus, you will have to adjust to the schizophrenic need to make the same motion in federal court under one name and in state court under another. In this chapter I will generally use the term "judgment as a matter of law," since much of the discussion focuses on the federal rule, Fed. R. Civ. P. 50(a).

# THE TIMING OF THE MOTION

As Figure 24-2[5] indicates, the plaintiff in a civil case presents her evidence first at trial. She has the burden during her case-in-chief to produce enough evidence on each element of her claim to pass the X line and reach the jury. Typically, the defendant will move for judgment as a matter of law at the close of the plaintiff's evidence, on the ground that that evidence does not cross the X line, that is, it does not satisfy the plaintiff's burden to produce credible evidence in support of each element of her claim. If the judge agrees that the plaintiff has not produced enough evidence to support a rational verdict in her favor, she may withdraw the case from the jury by entering judgment as a matter of law for the defendant at this point.

If the judge denies the motion, the defendant will present her evidence to rebut the plaintiff's case or to establish affirmative defenses. After the defendant rests she may move again for judgment as a matter of law. When the motion is made at this point it challenges the sufficiency of all the evidence, both plaintiff's and defendant's, to support a verdict for the plaintiff. As the diagram indicates, the plaintiff may also move for judgment as a matter of law at this point, though not at the close of her own case.

## Two Fundamental Questions

1. Why may the defendant, but not the plaintiff, move for judgment as a matter of law at the close of the plaintiff's case?

---

5. The diagram and the accompanying discussion are a bit oversimplified. For example, after the close of the defendant's case, the court will often allow the plaintiff to re-open her case to offer rebuttal testimony.

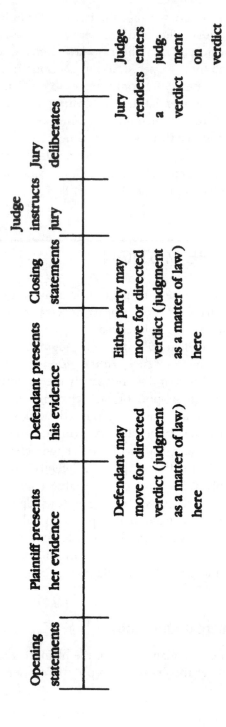

Figure 24-2. Sequence of trial.

2. What will happen next if the judge grants the defendant's motion at the close of the plaintiff's case?

---

# THE STANDARD FOR ENTERING JUDGMENT AS A MATTER OF LAW

Because the judge risks encroachment on the role of the jury in taking the case away from it, it is important to have a clear picture of just where the X and Y lines fall. Unfortunately, while it is easy to draw diagrams conceptualizing the parties' burdens of production, it is a great deal harder to articulate a clear and workable *standard* for deciding when the evidence crosses those lines. Federal Rule 50(a)(1) specifies that judgment as a matter of law may be entered when there is "no legally sufficient evidentiary basis to find for" the nonmoving party. However, this really just poses the question of when the evidence is legally sufficient, rather than providing an answer.

A few state courts hold that a case should go to the jury if there is even "a scintilla" of evidence to support the opposing party's case. Under this test, if the plaintiff has any evidence to support the elements of her claim, she will get to the jury. This standard places point X almost on top of point W in Figure 24-1. See, e.g., Brown v. Turner, 497 So. 2d 1119, 1120 (Ala. 1986) (case goes to jury if there is "'a mere gleam, glimmer, spark . . . or a scintilla'" in support of complaint). Obviously this rule stretches the area between X and Y, giving the greatest latitude to the jury but at the expense of effective judicial control of irrational jury decision-making.

Another suggested standard requires the judge to consider only the evidence that supports the case of the nonmoving party (usually the plaintiff). Under this standard, the judge must assume the truth of all evidence offered by the nonmoving party (usually the plaintiff), take all the inferences from the evidence in the light most favorable to that party, and enter judgment as a matter of law only if that evidence would not support a verdict for the nonmoving party; see *Reeves v. Sanderson Planting Products, Inc.* 530 U.S. 133, 150 (2000). *Wilkerson v. McCarthy*, 336 U.S. 53, 57 (1949). In passing on the motion, the judge applying this test may not determine the credibility of witnesses; the issue of which witnesses to believe is classically a jury decision. The test is not whether the judge believes the plaintiff's witnesses, but whether the jury, if it chooses to believe those witnesses, would have sufficient evidence to support a verdict for the plaintiff.

Suppose, for example, that Pavarotti sues Sills for negligence after he is hit by a car on Maple Street in Cleveland, Ohio. He presents evidence that Sills lives three blocks from the scene of the accident and owns a red

Chevrolet bearing the license number 301-LJM. One of Pavarotti's witnesses testifies that she saw a red Chevrolet leave the intersection after the accident, driven by a blonde woman (assume that Sills is blonde) and read the first three numbers of the license number as 311. Although this evidence is hardly overwhelming, it may be sufficient to allow a jury to make a rational inference that Sills was the driver. Under the "plaintiff's evidence" standard, the judge would probably allow this case to go to the jury, regardless of the evidence Sills presented in rebuttal.

A third standard for taking the case from the jury requires the judge to consider the nonmoving party's evidence in its most favorable light (just as in the second test) but also to consider any evidence put forward by the moving party that is not impeached or contradicted by the opposing party's evidence. *Reeves*, 530 U.S. at 150. If, considering all of that evidence, "there can be but one reasonable conclusion as to the verdict" (Moore's Federal Practice, s. 50.60[1]), the judge should enter judgment as a matter of law for the moving party. A frequent statement of the rule is as follows:

> [T]he court should consider all of the evidence — not just that evidence which supports the non-mover's case — but in the light and with all reasonable inferences most favorable to the party opposed to the motion. If the facts and inferences point so strongly and overwhelmingly in favor of one party that the Court believes that reasonable men could not arrive at a contrary verdict, grant of the motions is proper. On the other hand, if there is substantial evidence opposed to the motions, evidence of such quality and weight that reasonable and fair-minded men in the exercise of impartial judgment might reach different conclusions, the motions should be denied, and the case submitted to the jury.

*Boeing Co. v. Shipman*, 411 F.2d 365, 374 (5th Cir. 1969). The federal courts apply this standard under Fed. R. Civ. P 50(a). For easy reference, I will call it the "federal standard," although this approach is widely followed in state courts as well.

To illustrate the operation of this standard, assume that Sills (after the plaintiff, Pavarotti, presents the evidence described above) offers the undisputed testimony of two eyewitnesses to the accident that she was not the driver of the car and documentary evidence that indicates that she was performing in an opera in Minneapolis at the time of the accident. On this state of the evidence, her motion for judgment as a matter of law at the close of all the evidence should be granted under the federal standard. The plaintiff produced enough evidence to support a legitimate (but not compelling) inference that Sills had hit him. But that inference is negated by the defendant's uncontradicted, unimpeached evidence to the contrary and leaves the jury without a reasonable basis to conclude that Sills is liable. By contrast, if Sills's case consisted of her own testimony that she was having lunch at the time of the accident at a restaurant two miles away, issues of credibility would be posed, and judgment as a matter of law would be denied.

The examples that follow should help you to get a sense of the court's role in controlling jury action by entering judgment as a matter of law. The examples are based on one of the classic cases on directed verdicts, *Pennsylvania R.R. Co. v. Chamberlain*, 288 U.S. 333 (1933). The relevant evidence in *Chamberlain* is set forth immediately below, but you may want to read *Chamberlain* before considering the examples.

Chamberlain's suit sought recovery for her husband's death. She alleged that negligence of other employees of the railroad caused him to fall under a train while he was sorting railroad cars in a switching yard. Here is the court's description of the circumstances:

> The lead track crossed a "hump," and the work of car distribution consisted of pushing a train of cars by means of a locomotive to the top of the "hump," and then allowing the cars, in separate strings, to descend by gravity, under the control of hand brakes, to their respective destinations in the various branch tracks. Deceased had charge of a string of two gondola cars, which he was piloting to track 14. Immediately ahead of him was a string of seven cars, and behind him a string of nine cars, both also destined for track 14. Soon after the cars ridden by the deceased had passed to track 14, his body was found on that track some distance beyond the switch. He had evidently fallen onto the track and been run over by a car or cars.

288 U.S. at 335-336. The plaintiff's theory was that the railroad's employees negligently caused the string of cars Chamberlain was riding to collide with the following string of nine cars, throwing him under the train.

## Examples

### The Plaintiff's Case

3. In *Chamberlain* the plaintiff offered the following evidence as to the cause of the accident:

> The plaintiff's only witness to the event, one Bainbridge, then employed by the road, stood close to the yardmaster's office, near the "hump." He professed to have paid little attention to what went on, but he did see the deceased riding at the rear of his cars, whose speed when they passed him he took to be about eight or ten miles. Shortly thereafter a second string passed which was shunted into another track and this was followed by the nine, which according to the plaintiff's theory, collided with the deceased's. After the nine cars had passed at a somewhat greater speed than the deceased's, Bainbridge paid no more attention to either string for a while, but looked again when the deceased, who was still

> standing in his place, had passed the switch and onto the assorting track where he was bound. At that time his speed had been checked to about three miles, but the speed of the following nine cars had increased. They were just passing the switch, about four or five cars behind the deceased. Bainbridge looked away again and soon heard what he described as a "loud crash," not however an unusual event in a switching yard. Apparently this did not cause him at once to turn, but he did so shortly thereafter, and saw the two strings together, still moving, and the deceased no longer in sight. . . . Until he left to go the accident, he had stood fifty feet to the north of the track where the accident happened, and about nine hundred feet from where the body was found.

288 U.S. at 336-337

Assume that the plaintiff in *Chamberlain* presents the evidence quoted above to prove that her husband's death was caused by negligence of the railroad's employees. She then produces uncontradicted evidence of her damages and rests her case.

a. Assume that, after the plaintiff rests her case, the railroad moves to dismiss the case for failure to state a claim upon which relief can be granted. How should the trial judge rule on the motion?

b. Assume instead that, after the plaintiff rests her case, the defendant moves for judgment as a matter of law, on the ground that the plaintiff has not established a submissible case on negligence. If the court applies the "plaintiff's evidence" standard, should it grant the motion?

c. Assume that the case is tried instead in a court that applies the federal standard, which also allows consideration of the moving party's uncontradicted, unimpeached evidence. Should the railroad's motion at the close of the plaintiff's case be granted under that standard?

## Counselor Fudd's Motion

4. Assume that, after Chamberlain presents the evidence just described, the railroad's lawyer (coincidentally named Fudd) moves for judgment as a matter of law, arguing that Chamberlain has not carried her burden of proof on the issue of whether her husband's death was caused by negligence of the railroad's employees. What is wrong with Attorney Fudd's argument?

5. Suppose that Bainbridge was again the only witness and gave the same testimony but that he had made his observations while riding on a third string of cars following the nine-car string. If the railroad moved for judgment as a matter of law at the close of the plaintiff's case, should the court grant the motion? Assume that the "plaintiff's evidence" standard applies.

6. Assume that the *Chamberlain* case involved extensive evidence on damages (such as pain and suffering, medical costs, and lost earnings), as well as on liability. At trial, the plaintiff's evidence for liability is the same, again based on Bainbridge's testimony. After she presents her case on liability, but before she offers her evidence on damages, the railroad moves for judgment as a matter of law. Is the motion proper?

## The Defendant's Case

7. If the federal standard applies, should the railroad be allowed to move for judgment as a matter of law at the close of all the evidence if it failed to do so at the close of the plaintiff's case?

8. Suppose that the plaintiff in *Chamberlain* rests her case after offering the evidence described, and the railroad rests its case without offering any evidence. The plaintiff moves for judgment as a matter of law. Should it be granted?

9. Assume that the court refuses to enter judgment for the defendant in *Chamberlain* at the close of the plaintiff's evidence. Therefore, the railroad proceeds to present its case. (See Figure 24-2 supra.) As the case report indicates, the railroad's case was as follows. "Three employees, riding the nine-car string, testified positively that no such collision occurred. They were corroborated by every other employee in a position to see, all testifying that there was no contact between the nine-car string and that of the deceased." 288 U.S. at 336.
   a. After presenting its case, the railroad moves for judgment as a matter of law. Should the motion be granted under the plaintiff's evidence standard?
   b. Should the motion be granted under the federal standard?

## A Few Variations

10. Suppose that Bainbridge offered the same testimony as above, but there were only two trains, the two-car string and the nine-car string, in the yard at the time. How should the court rule if the railroad offers the same evidence as above and then moves for judgment as a matter of law at the close of all the evidence? Assume that the federal standard applies.

11. Suppose again that Bainbridge's testimony was the same, but that there was only one witness for the defendant, the railroad yardmaster. Assume that he was standing near the spot where the decedent was found and testified unequivocally that no collision occurred. Could the judge enter judgment as a matter of law for the railroad?

12. Assume once again that the plaintiff offered the same proof, through Bainbridge, and in rebuttal the railroad called only one witness, the brakeperson riding on the nine-car string following the decedent's. She testifies that she braked the nine-car string as it descended from the hump, followed the two-car string at a distance, and that the two strings never collided. At the close of the evidence, the railroad moves for judgment as a matter of law. Should the motion be granted under the federal standard?

## Trial and Error

13. Assume that the *Chamberlain* case was tried to the judge instead of a jury. (Parties are entitled to a jury trial in most tort cases, but may opt for a judge trial if they prefer it.) The defendant's counsel rises at the close of the plaintiff's case and moves "for judgment as a matter of law under Rule 50(a), on the ground that no reasonable jury could find for the plaintiff." What two grievous errors did defendant's counsel make?[6] See Fed. R. Civ. P. 52(c).

## A Retrospective

14. Let's back up a minute and assume that the railroad moved for summary judgment before trial and submitted affidavits in support of the motion from its employees. The affidavits all state that no collision took place between the two strings. The plaintiff submits an opposing affidavit of Bainbridge, stating his testimony as it is given in example 3. Should the railroad's motion be granted?

# Explanations

## Two Fundamental Questions

1. Due process of law entitles every litigant to an opportunity to be heard before a court adjudicates her rights. If the court could enter judgment as a matter of law for the plaintiff at the close of her case, the defendant would be deprived of the opportunity to present evidence, either to refute the plaintiff's proof or to establish an affirmative defense. Even if the judge concludes that the plaintiff's evidence has crossed the Y line, the defendant may well produce countervailing evidence that would leave legitimate doubt as to the facts, making the case an appropriate one for the jury. Thus, no matter how strong the plaintiff's evidence may be, the defendant will be given a chance to rebut it.

---

6. Your humble author made both of these mistakes in a case involving a large Boston pothole. Learn from his mistakes!

2. The judge may only grant judgment as a matter of law for the defendant if she concludes that the plaintiff has not produced enough evidence to support a rational verdict in her favor. If the judge concludes that the plaintiff has not produced adequate evidence on each of the elements of her "prima facie case," there is no need to go on and hear the defendant's evidence. The judge will enter judgment for the defendant on the basis of the insufficiency of plaintiff's proof.

## The Plaintiff's Case

3. a. The judge should deny the railroad's motion. A motion to dismiss for failure to state a claim asserts that the plaintiff's allegations, even if true, do not support a right to relief under recognized law. Chamberlain's widow alleges that negligence of the railroad's employees caused her husband's death. Clearly, the law of negligence does support recovery of damages for negligently causing death. Chamberlain's complaint asserts a valid negligence claim. Her problem is with *proving* that the negligence of railroad's employees caused her husband's death, meeting her burden to produce credible evidence from which reasonable jurors could find that the railroad's employees were negligent. The proper way for the railroad to challenge that, at trial, is by a motion for judgment as a matter of law, arguing that the evidence of its employees' negligence is too weak to support a rational verdict.

   b. Under the plaintiff's evidence standard, the motion should be denied if the jury, considering only the evidence supporting the plaintiff's case, could reasonably infer that the accident resulted from the railroad's negligence. Although the plaintiff's evidence that the two strings collided (thus indicating negligence by the railroad) is less than compelling, it is probably sufficient to support a rational inference that a collision caused the accident. If the jury credits Bainbridge's testimony, it would have evidence that the sound of a crash was heard, that the nine-car string was moving considerably faster than the two-car string before the crash, and that the two strings subsequently were seen moving in tandem. In addition, the fact that the decedent had fallen from the train supports the inference that a collision had knocked him off. If such an inference could rationally be made, the jury should be allowed to make it (or reject it). The defendant's motion should probably be denied.

   c. The result at this stage of the case should be the same under the federal test. At the close of the plaintiff's case the only evidence before the court is that offered by the plaintiff. Thus, the defendant's motion at this point will usually be based on the position that the plaintiff's evidence is insufficient to cross the X line, that is, it does not satisfy her burden to produce evidence that would rationally support the conclusion that the accident resulted from the railroad's negligence. As indicated above, the plaintiff's evidence in *Chamberlain* was probably sufficient to defeat this motion.

It is conceivable that the railroad's attorney would elicit evidence from the *plaintiff's* witnesses that would foreclose a verdict in the plaintiff's favor. For example, the railroad might get Bainbridge to admit on cross-examination that he is unable to see farther than 25 feet without his glasses, which he was not wearing at the time. This evidence would be considered under the federal standard and, if not impeached or contradicted by other evidence for the plaintiff, it could force the plaintiff's case back over the X line and lead to a directed verdict (judgment as a matter of law) for the railroad even before it presents its own case. Absent such impeachment, however, the result should be the same under either standard at this point.

## Counselor Fudd's Motion

4. Counselor Fudd has confused the burdens of proof and production here. The trial judge can only grant judgment as a matter of law if Chamberlain has failed to meet her burden of *production*, that is, if she has not produced enough credible evidence to cross the X line on the left of the diagram. Fudd has argued that the judge should enter judgment for the railroad if Chamberlain has failed to meet the burden of *proof*, that is, if her evidence fails to pass the Z line in the middle of the diagram. This would usurp the jury's role in all cases in which (in the judge's view) the evidence falls between X and Z. Essentially, if she didn't think the plaintiff should win she could take the case from the jury.

5. Although the judge is required to view the case in the light most favorable to the plaintiff, there comes a point where the unlikely fades into the impossible. As the case report indicates, Bainbridge apparently viewed the moving trains from a three-degree angle if he was standing *beside* the track. If he were actually on a train following the nine-car string (and there were no bend in the track) it would be impossible for him to observe a collision 900 feet in front of him on the same track. On this evidence the reasonable judge could reasonably conclude that only an unreasonable jury could find for the plaintiff.

It is true that the judge, by taking the case from the jury on these facts, exercises some judgment as to the strength of the plaintiff's case. In this sense, the term "judgment as a matter of law" is a bit of a misnomer because the judge has made a factual judgment here that the evidence is too farfetched to justify a finding for the plaintiff. But a line must be drawn somewhere between the inherently incredible and the unlikely-but-possible. If the court abdicates the responsibility of doing so, the jury becomes the unrestrained arbiter of the parties' rights regardless of the inadequacy of their proof.

6. The motion is proper even though Chamberlain has not yet presented her evidence on damages. The railroad's position here is that the evidence on damages is legally irrelevant if Chamberlain has not proved liability. Why should the parties and the court waste their time on lengthy damage evidence if Chamberlain has not met her burden of production on the liability issue? To reach the jury, the plaintiff must present credible evidence on each element of her claim; if proof fails on *any one*, the defendant is entitled to judgment as a matter of law.

While motions for a directed verdict are usually made after the plaintiff presents her entire case (see Figure 24-2), it may sometimes be appropriate to try a dispositive issue first and determine the legal sufficiency of the evidence on that issue. If Chamberlain has not passed the X line on the liability element of her claim, there is no need to hear the damages evidence. The Advisory Committee notes to Rule 50(a) emphasize that a motion for judgment as a matter of law may be appropriate "as soon as a party has completed a presentation on a fact essential to that party's case." Advisory Committee note to the 1991 revisions to Rule 50(a), fifth paragraph. This suggestion is in line with the modern tendency to encourage judges to aggressively manage cases in order to speed their disposition. See, e.g., Fed. R. Civ. P. 16 (authorizing discovery and pretrial conferences to streamline the trial process).

Under this approach, a judge might even order that an affirmative defense be tried first, if it appeared that the defense might be decisive. For example, if a defendant in a negligence case claims that the plaintiff gave him a release of the claim, and the evidence on the issue is strong, the judge might order this issue tried first, to determine whether there is a jury question as to whether the claim was released. If she concludes that the release defense is established as a matter of law, the case will be dismissed without trying the plaintiff's basic negligence case at all.

Some lawyers feel that this managerial approach unfairly encroaches on their traditional prerogative to present their cases in their own way. In the example, Chamberlain's counsel would doubtless prefer to put in her entire case, hoping that the judge's decision on the motion would be colored by the compelling evidence of Chamberlain's damages. Many courts will still defer the decision to the end of the plaintiff's evidence, but there is a marked tendency, especially in the federal courts, to curtail counsel's autonomy in litigation procedure in the interest of efficient resolution of cases. The federal rulemakers, in revising Rule 50, have given judges a green light to extend this tendency to directed verdict practice as well.

## The Defendant's Case

7. Yes. There is no requirement that a defendant move for judgment as a matter of law at the close of the plaintiff's case in order to preserve her right to do so at the close of all the evidence. Nor should there be; as stated in the Introduction, the motion raises distinct issues depending upon when it is made. When the defendant makes this motion at the close of the plaintiff's case the issue is whether the plaintiff has produced so little evidence that no reasonable jury could conclude that she has carried her burden of proof. The defendant's motion at the close of all the evidence may, if the federal standard applies, be based on the argument that the plaintiff had initially presented a strong enough case to go to the jury, but the unimpeached and uncontradicted evidence that she has presented forces the case back to the left of the X line in Figure 24-1, where the judge must enter judgment from the defendant. If that is true, then it would be improper to take the case from the jury at the close of the plaintiff's case, but appropriate at the end of all the evidence under the federal standard.

8. A plaintiff's motion for judgment as a matter of law at the close of the case asserts that the uncontradicted, unimpeached evidence in support of her case is so strong that the proof falls to the right of the Y line, where no reasonable jury could reach a verdict for the defendant. In passing on the plaintiff's motion, the court must assume that the jury would believe all of the defendant's evidence and reject all evidence for the plaintiff that had been contradicted or impeached. If, upon these assumptions, the only rational conclusion is that the plaintiff has proved each element of her case, the verdict may be directed.

On the *Chamberlain* facts, the motion should be denied. Even though the railroad offered no evidence, it does not follow that the plaintiff has established her case beyond doubt. The jury would still have to infer from Bainbridge's circumstantial evidence that a crash occurred between the two-car string and the nine-car string. Reasonable jurors might make that inference, but they also might not. The evidence is strong enough to support a verdict for Chamberlain but not strong enough to compel it.

As a practical matter, the judge seldom orders judgment as a matter of law for plaintiffs because they bear the burden of proof as to each element of their claim. Most cases turn at least in part on the credibility of witnesses. If the credibility of the plaintiff's witnesses has been challenged, the court will have to assume for purposes of the motion that the jury will disbelieve them. If their testimony is necessary to establish any element of the plaintiff's claim, and there is any basis for doubting that testimony, the motion will be denied.

9. a. The analysis of example 3b suggests that the plaintiff's evidence, taken alone, was sufficient to place the *Chamberlain* case in the middle area of the diagram, between the X and Y lines, where the jury must decide the contested issues of fact. If the plaintiff's evidence standard is applied here, the court must disregard all of the railroad's opposing testimony, and the same result will follow in this case even though the defendant has introduced very strong contrary evidence.

   b. If the federal standard is applied, the court must consider not only Bainbridge's testimony for the plaintiff but also the uncontradicted and unimpeached testimony for the defendant. The crucial question is whether the defendant's witnesses, who testify directly that no crash occurred (and therefore no negligence and no ground for recovery), are contradicted or impeached by the plaintiff's evidence.

   The Court holds, and I think rightly, that Bainbridge's and the defendant's versions of the incident are not contradictory. Bainbridge's testimony indicates that there was a crash and that the trains were moving along at the same speed after the crash. A jury could infer from this that the nine-car string collided with the two-car string. Alternatively, they could infer that a collision took place someplace else in the yard, and that these two strings were moving at the same speed because each had been braked to the same speed. The defendant's witnesses do not contradict Bainbridge; their testimony that the nine-car and the two-car strings did not collide simply eliminates one of the two possible inferences from his testimony. Unless the jury has some rational basis for rejecting their testimony, it is no longer possible to infer from Bainbridge's circumstantial version of events that these two strings actually collided.

   It might be argued that the jury could reject the testimony of the defendant's witnesses because they were all employed by the railroad and thus could be biased. The argument has some force, but the Court concluded in *Chamberlain* that the mere fact of employment by the defendant was insufficient to impeach their testimony. See also *Chesapeake & Ohio Railway Co. v. Martin*, 283 U.S. 209, 216-220 (1931). The case would likely be different if only one employee testified for the railroad and the evidence indicated that he was promoted the week after the accident.

   Needless to say, application of these standards for taking the case from the jury is hardly scientifically precise. In *Chamberlain*, the trial judge directed a verdict for the railroad. The court of appeals reversed, in a two-to-one decision, on the ground that the case should have been left to the jury. The eminent Judge Learned Hand wrote for the majority, and Judge Swan, another respected jurist, registered a strong dissent. 59 F.2d 986 (1932). The Supreme Court then unanimously reversed the court of appeals. Clearly, reasonable judges may differ about when reasonable jurors may differ. Yet the fact that there are close cases does not change the fact that the motion provides needed control of irrational jury behavior.

## A Few Variations

10. This change in the facts introduces a direct contradiction between the plaintiff's and the defendant's evidence. Bainbridge testifies that he heard a crash of the type made by trains colliding, and there only were two in the yard. If you believe Bainbridge, the only possible inference is that those two strings of cars collided. Unlike the facts of the actual case, this testimony would directly contradict the testimony of the defendant's witnesses. Although there were six or seven witnesses for the defendant and only one, Bainbridge, for the plaintiff, the court may not pass on issues of credibility in ruling on a motion for judgment as a matter of law. If there is a legitimate conflict in the evidence, the jury must resolve it. If the jury believes Bainbridge over the railroad's employees, it could reasonably find for the plaintiff and should be given the opportunity to do so.

11. As suggested above, practice in this area is heavily fact-specific and unscientific. Consequently, distinctions that are conceptually clear do not always dictate results. In this case, the state of the evidence has not changed much when evaluated under the federal standard for taking the case from the jury. The plaintiff's case is still built upon inference, and it is still directly contradicted by evidence that the jury has little or no reason to discredit.

    Yet many courts would not direct the verdict on these facts. There is not the same level of certainty about the defendant's case as there was in the real case, in which six or seven witnesses unanimously denied a collision. A single witness might be unbiased but simply wrong. The argument for bias is stronger here as well since there is more incentive for a managerial employee of the railroad to testify falsely than for lower-level yard workers to do so.

12. Here, the motion should be denied. Not only is there only one witness who denies a collision, but that witness has a strong incentive to deny the collision even if it happened. No one wants to admit that she committed a negligent act, especially if it led to the death of a co-worker. Such an admission would expose the railroad to substantial

liability and the employee to likely dismissal. Thus, the jury could reasonably disbelieve her self-serving denials and infer from Bainbridge's testimony that the strings did in fact collide. Since the jury has a rational basis for disregarding the employee's testimony, they should be given the chance to decide whether or not to do so. See Wright & Miller §2527 (jury may often disbelieve even unimpeached, uncontradicted testimony of interested witness).

## Trial and Error

13. The railroad's attorney has made two mistakes here, one technical but the other substantial. *First*, he should not have sought judgment under Rule 50(a) at all. That rule addresses the judge's power to enter judgment in a case tried to a jury. See Rule 50(a)(1) ("If . . . during a jury trial . . ."). Here, the case was tried to the judge, so Rule 50(a) is not relevant; the proper motion would have been for a judgment of dismissal by the court under Fed. R. Civ. P. 52(c).

*Second*, and more important, the railroad's attorney has inappropriately asked the judge to apply the standard for withdrawing a case from the jury to a case in which *the judge is the factfinder*. In a jury case the judge's role is to act as a gatekeeper, keeping obviously inadequate cases from the jury. However, when the defendant in a nonjury trial moves for judgment at the close of the plaintiff's case, the judge *is* the factfinder. The issue is not whether the evidence is strong enough that a reasonable jury could find for the plaintiff (i.e., whether it has passed the X line on the diagram), but rather whether the judge, as the factfinder, believes that the plaintiff has proved the elements of her cause of action by a preponderance of the evidence (i.e., whether the plaintiff's evidence has passed the Z line). If the plaintiff has not satisfied that standard, the judge may enter judgment without hearing the defendant's evidence, since the plaintiff has had a full opportunity to make her case and has not carried her burden of proof. See Fed. R. Civ. P. 52(c).

In determining whether the plaintiff has carried her burden of proof, the judge may also consider the credibility of the witnesses. She is not deciding whether the jury *could* believe plaintiff's witnesses but rather whether she, the judge acting as the factfinder, *does* believe them. In other words, in a judge-tried case, the motion for a finding allows the judge to determine whether the plaintiff has carried her burden of *proof*, while in a jury case the judge acts as a gatekeeper to prevent the jury from hearing insubstantial cases, and must confine herself to considering whether the plaintiff has carried her burden of production.[7] Compare example 4.

## A Retrospective

14. Summary judgment is only appropriate if there is "no genuine issue of material fact" to be resolved by the jury. It is often said that if the evidence is so one-sided that a judge would be required to enter judgment as a matter of law at trial, then no genuine factual issue exists and summary judgment is appropriate. See, e.g., *Anderson v. Liberty Lobby, Inc.*, 477 U.S. 242, 250 (1986). Under this analysis, the difference between the Rule 50(a) motion and the summary judgment motion under Rule 56 is essentially procedural: The Rule 50(a) motion is raised during the trial and decided on the basis of the testimony and documentary evidence offered at trial, while the summary judgment motion is made before trial and determined solely on the basis of documentary evidence such as depositions, interrogatories, business records and affidavits. See *Anderson*, 477 U.S. at 251.

While this is conceptually consistent, many courts are more reluctant to grant summary judgment than judgment as a matter of law under Rule 50(a). Although in theory the judge asks the same question in passing on both motions — whether the party opposing the motion has offered enough evidence that a reasonable factfinder could find in her favor — the context of the motions is strikingly different. In most cases summary judgment motions are decided on the basis of affidavits and other documentary evidence. The opposing party may submit her own evidentiary materials but will not have the benefit of cross-examination. In addition, the motion often comes fairly early in the litigation, before the parties have exhaustively developed their cases. If the judge senses that the case will turn on questions of fact that are not fully elucidated by the record, she will likely conclude that the parties should have a full opportunity to present their evidence at trial before a decision is made to withdraw the case from the jury.

---

7. The analogy in a jury case would be if the judge sent the jury out after the plaintiff rested her case to determine whether the plaintiff's evidence had moved the case over the Z line (that is, satisfied the plaintiff's burden of proof) and dismissed the action if the jury concluded that the plaintiff had not. I suppose jury trials could be run that way: The jury would deliberate twice, once after the plaintiff's case to determine whether she had carried her initial burden of proof by a preponderance of the evidence; and a second time after the defendant's evidence to determine if she had pushed the case back over the Z line. Such a system would break the flow of the evidence and confuse the jury as well. But the judge *can* do this in a nonjury trial, since she is used to dealing with the concept of burdens of proof and can more easily break up the presentation of the evidence to consider the motion.

In considering a motion for summary judgment, the district court must give the benefit of the doubt to the party who asserts he can prove a dubious proposition at trial. In considering a motion for a directed verdict, in contrast, the district court has had the benefit of seeing what the parties alleged they could prove prior to trial tested in the crucible of open court. Accordingly, the district court is entitled to grant a directed verdict even though some evidence supports the opposite position.

*Kim v. Coppin State College*, 662 F.2d 1055, 1059 (4th Cir. 1981). Consequently, it is not unusual for the court to deny summary judgment but subsequently grant judgment as a matter of law at trial for the same party.

In the *Chamberlain* case there is ample ground for a court to conclude that full trial of the issues might reveal a submissible case for the plaintiff. The evidence was largely testimonial; cross-examination might have revealed inconsistencies in the defendant's witnesses' testimony, or impeached their credibility. In such cases judges tend to give the party opposing summary judgment the benefit of the doubt by allowing the case to proceed. See Field, Kaplan, and Clermont, Civil Procedure (8th ed. 2003) at 698 (motion for directed verdict "comes at a later stage in the litigation with lesser worry of prematurely interceding, and it is decided upon a more complete and effective airing of the evidence. The result is a practical difference in standards, with the test for directed verdict being slightly easier to meet"). Even if (as here) the judge ultimately takes the case from the jury, such forbearance gives the parties the fullest opportunity to satisfy their burden of production (and thus get to the jury) in close cases.

# The Judge and the Jury, Part Two

## Whose Case Is This, Anyway?

---

## INTRODUCTION

A misguided minority of law students think that civil procedure is dull, but in truth it is full of surprises. You may well have been surprised to learn from the last chapter that a judge may snatch a case from the jury in the middle of trial by entering judgment as a matter of law. It is perhaps even more surprising that the judge may actually allow the jury to deliberate and reach its verdict on the evidence but refuse to enter judgment on the verdict rendered. At first blush this seems the ultimate affront to the jury system, for the judge to allow the jury to go through the entire trial process and reach its decision, and then disregard or reverse it. Yet, as we shall see, there are good reasons to allow the judge to do so.

Traditionally, the judge has had the authority to displace the jury's verdict by entering a "judgment notwithstanding the verdict," or j.n.o.v.[1] The j.n.o.v. motion is essentially a delayed (or, more accurately, renewed) motion for a directed verdict. The standard for granting the j.n.o.v. motion is the same as that for directing a verdict: Either motion will be granted if the opponent's evidence is so weak that no reasonable jury could have reached a verdict for him. Of course, when the losing party moves for j.n.o.v. after the jury's verdict, a jury *has* found for the opposing party. Thus, the j.n.o.v. motion asserts that the jury acted irrationally, in

---

1. J.n.o.v., or judgment "*non obstante veredicto*," is Latin for judgment notwithstanding the verdict. The two terms are used interchangeably in practice.

disregard of the evidence in reaching a verdict for the party opposing the motion.

The j.n.o.v. motion has long been a fixture of trial practice in both the state and federal courts. However, the 1991 amendments to the Federal Rules changed the name of the j.n.o.v. motion: It is now called a motion for judgment as a matter of law, the same as the Rule 50(a) motion made during trial to take the case away from the jury. See Fed. R. Civ. P. 50(b). Again, the change in the name makes sense because it emphasizes that the motion after verdict asks the judge to do exactly the same thing that the motion during trial does: take the case from the jury to prevent an irrational result. Again, as with the earlier motion, the new wine really is the same vintage as the old. The motion for judgment as a matter of law after verdict is the functional equivalent of a motion for j.n.o.v. And, again, the j.n.o.v. terminology persists in most state courts, so you will have to use both terms in practice. In this chapter, I will use the federal terminology. However, because the new name refers to both the pre-verdict and post-verdict motion, I will indicate in parentheses whether I am referring to a motion made before the case goes to the jury (d.v.) or after the verdict (j.n.o.v.).

# RATIONALE FOR ALLOWING THE RENEWED MOTION

You may well wonder what purpose is served by allowing the motion for judgment as a matter of law after the verdict (j.n.o.v.). If the standards for granting the motion before the jury deliberates (d.v.) and after (j.n.o.v.) are the same, why not simply grant the motion before the jury deliberates? This will save the jury the trouble of unnecessary deliberations and avoid the affront of having their findings disregarded.

If the decision to take the case from the jury was cut and dried, this argument would have considerable force. However, reasonable judges may differ — and often do — about whether a given case is strong enough to go to a jury. Because the decision that the evidence is too weak to go to the jury is often debatable, the judge's entry of judgment as a matter of law before the jury deliberates (d.v.) will frequently be appealed. If the appellate court concludes that the evidence *was* sufficient to send the case to the jury,[2] it will reverse the judge's entry of judgment and order a new

---

2. Because the decision to grant a directed verdict motion is based on the conclusion that the evidence is too weak as a matter of law to support a verdict for the other party, it is reviewed de novo by the appellate court under the same standard used by the trial judge. See Moore's §50.92 [1].

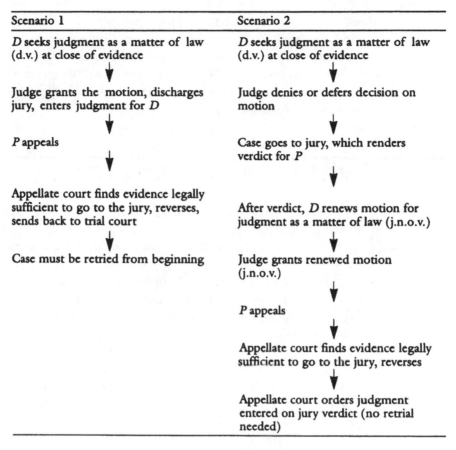

| Scenario 1 | Scenario 2 |
|---|---|
| D seeks judgment as a matter of law (d.v.) at close of evidence | D seeks judgment as a matter of law (d.v.) at close of evidence |
| Judge grants the motion, discharges jury, enters judgment for D | Judge denies or defers decision on motion |
| P appeals | Case goes to jury, which renders verdict for P |
| Appellate court finds evidence legally sufficient to go to the jury, reverses, sends back to trial court | After verdict, D renews motion for judgment as a matter of law (j.n.o.v.) |
| Case must be retried from beginning | Judge grants renewed motion (j.n.o.v.) |
| | P appeals |
| | Appellate court finds evidence legally sufficient to go to the jury, reverses |
| | Appellate court orders judgment entered on jury verdict (no retrial needed) |

**Figure 25-1.**

trial. Since the jury never rendered a verdict in the first trial, this will then require a wasteful repetition of the entire trial. See scenario 1 in Figure 25-1.

If, instead, the judge withholds decision on the sufficiency of the evidence by denying the motion for judgment as a matter of law (d.v.) at the close of the evidence, this scenario can be avoided. In most cases, where the evidence is weak enough to lead the judge to consider directing the verdict, the jury will agree that the case is too weak and return a verdict for the moving party anyway. This is the best possible result: It avoids any apparent intrusion on the right to jury trial, leads to a verdict that the judge finds supportable on the evidence, and avoids the appeal that would likely have followed if the judge had taken the case from the jury.

If, on the other hand, the jury returns a verdict for the party (usually the plaintiff) against whom the judge considered directing the verdict, the judge can still enter judgment as a matter of law (j.n.o.v.) for the other party. Here again, the party whose verdict has been taken away will frequently appeal on the ground that the evidence was strong enough to support a rational verdict in his favor. If the appeals court agrees and reverses the judge's order for entry of judgment as a matter of law (j.n.o.v.), it can simply order judgment entered on the jury's verdict. Thus, the need to retry the case is avoided by waiting until after the verdict to decide whether the case is jury-worthy. See scenario 2 in Figure 25-1.

---

# PREREQUISITES TO THE RENEWED MOTION

There are several important limitations on the right to seek judgment as a matter of law (j.n.o.v.) after the verdict. Under Fed. R. Civ. P. 50(b) (and many state rules modeled on it) the motion must be filed within ten days of the entry of judgment on the jury's verdict.[3] In addition, a party may only move for judgment as a matter of law (j.n.o.v.) after the verdict if he made the same motion (d.v.) before the verdict. See Fed. R. Civ. P. 50(b) (party who made motion for judgment as a matter of law at the close of all the evidence may file a "renewed" motion after verdict).

There are two reasons for this second requirement, one historical and rather silly, the other policy-based and entirely sensible. The historical reason has to do with the Seventh Amendment to the United States Constitution, which provides that "no fact tried by a jury, shall be otherwise reexamined in any Court of the United States, than according to the rules of the common law." Early cases held that it was unconstitutional for the judge to allow the jury to decide the facts and then "reexamine" them through the j.n.o.v. motion. *Slocum v. New York Life Ins. Co.*, 228 U.S. 364 (1913). However, the Supreme Court retreated from this position in *Baltimore & Carolina Line, Inc. v. Redman*, 295 U.S. 654 (1935). In *Redman* the Court held that it was permissible for the trial court to grant judgment notwithstanding the verdict if the moving party had sought a directed verdict before the jury deliberated and the court had reserved decision on the motion.[4] The first sentence of Rule 50(b) embodies the *Redman* fiction

---

3. Entry of judgment occurs when the court clerk enters a notation of the judgment on the case docket. See Fed. R. Civ. P. 58, 79(a). It is also permissible to seek j.n.o.v. after the verdict but before entry of judgment. Rule 50(b) merely requires that the motion be filed "no later than" ten days after entry of judgment.

4. This was regarded as permissible, despite the "reexamination" clause in the seventh amendment, because the court was deemed to have the power to direct the verdict for the defendant without ever sending the case to the jury. If the judge could do that, the *Redman* court reasoned, he should also be allowed to submit the case subject to a subsequent decision on the directed verdict motion. Instead of "reexamining" the jury's verdict, the judge is simply "examining" the sufficiency of the evidence for the first time, but a little late.

that the judge who denies a directed verdict has simply delayed decision upon it, rather than "reexamined" the jury's findings.

The second reason for requiring a pre-verdict motion as a prerequisite for granting judgment as a matter of law (j.n.o.v.) after the verdict is more substantial. A party who moves for judgment as a matter of law at the close of the evidence must state his grounds for concluding that the case should not be submitted to the jury. Fed. R. Civ. P. 50(a)(2); see also Fed. R. Civ. P. 7(b)(1)(B). Thus, the motion will alert the court and the opposing party to the defects in that party's case before the jury has gone out, while there is still time to offer further evidence to cure the defect. Suppose, for example, that the plaintiff sues an employer for negligence of its employee, but fails to put on evidence that the employee was acting in the scope of employment at the time of the accident. If the employer moves for judgment as a matter of law, it will have to specify that the ground for the motion is the lack of evidence of scope of employment, a crucial element of the claim. Doubtless, the judge will then allow plaintiff to reopen her case to submit evidence on the scope-of-employment question. If the lack of evidence was due to inadvertence, plaintiff will cure it. If, however, it is because plaintiff has no such evidence, she won't, and the motion will be allowed, either before or after the case goes to the jury.

Thus, by requiring the motion before the jury goes out in order to preserve the right to move for judgment after the verdict, the rule prevents a party from "sandbagging" his opponent by raising defects in the opponent's evidence after the jury has been discharged, when it is too late to cure those defects. It may be frustrating to a careful lawyer to be forced to help a less perceptive opponent make his case by pointing out those defects. However, remember that the entire thrust of the Rules is to ensure that suits are determined on the merits, not on the procedural skills of counsel.[5]

# NEW TRIAL DISTINGUISHED

The judge may also deprive a party of a verdict by granting a new trial under Fed. R. Civ. P. 59. Unlike the motion for judgment as a matter of law, which leads to a judgment for the moving party, the grant of a new trial does not end the case but leads to a second trial on all or part of the case.

---

5. Despite this reasoning, many states do not follow the federal practice of requiring a directed verdict motion to preserve the right to seek j.n.o.v. See Friedenthal, Kane, and Miller, p. 581.

There are two general categories of cases in which the courts have traditionally granted new trials. The first is for errors in the trial process. Every litigant is entitled to "due process of law," including a fair trial procedure before his rights are determined. Any number of mistakes may be made in the course of trial, such as the improper admission or exclusion of evidence, improper instructions by the judge as to the legal principles the jury must apply, or juror contacts with witnesses outside the court-room. Errors of this sort may taint the jury's decision-making process, leading it to consider inappropriate information in reaching a verdict or to use the wrong rules of law in assessing liability or damages. See generally James, Hazard & Leubsdorf (5th ed. 2001) at §§7.25-7.27.

If the losing party moves for a new trial on the basis of such errors immediately after trial,[6] Rule 59 allows the judge to vacate the verdict and order the case retried in order to assure the parties a fair trial procedure. If the judge refused to grant a new trial despite substantial errors at the trial, the party prejudiced by the error would doubtless appeal, the appellate court would reverse, and a new trial would be ordered anyway, after much additional effort and expense. The judge can save this effort and expense by ordering the new trial himself if he is convinced that there was prejudicial error in the first trial.

In addition to new trials for procedural errors, the trial judge has traditionally had the power to grant a new trial if he believes the trial *process was fair but the result is clearly wrong*. The federal cases suggest various (but quite similar) standards for granting a new trial based on a dubious outcome. It is said that the judge may grant a new trial if the jury's verdict is "against the 'clear weight,' 'overwhelming weight,' or 'great weight' of the evidence" (*Goldsmith v. Diamond Shamrock Corp.*, 767 F.2d 411, 416 (8th Cir. 1985)); when it is "quite clear that the jury has reached a seriously erroneous result" (*Lind v. Schenley Industries, Inc.*, 278 F.2d 79, 89 (3d Cir. 1960)); or when a new trial "is necessary to prevent injustice" (*Whalen v. Roanoke County Board of Supervisors*, 769 F.2d 221, 226 (4th Cir. 1985)); see generally Wright & Miller §2806 nn.23, 24. Under such formulas the judge cannot displace the verdict simply because he disagrees with the jury. But he may order a new trial in cases in which the evidence is strong enough to rationally support the jury's verdict, but he believes that verdict is seriously erroneous (represented, perhaps, by point Q on the diagram in the last chapter, p. 497. The difference in the judge's role in passing on motions for new trial and motions for judgment as a matter of law is illustrated in Figure 25-2 on p. 523.

---

6. The motion for new trial, like the Rule 50(b) motion for j.n.o.v., must be filed within ten days of entry of judgment. Fed. R. Civ. P. 59(b).

| Evidence Evenly Balanced | | | | | |
|---|---|---|---|---|---|
| ← weaker evidence for plaintiff | | | stronger evidence for plaintiff → | | |
| Judge's assessment of the evidence | Evidence too weak to support a rational verdict for plaintiff | A verdict for plaintiff is supportable, but against clear weight of the evidence | Judge does not agree with jury, but cannot say verdict for plaintiff is against clear weight of the evidence | Judge and jury concur that preponderance of the evidence favors plaintiff | A verdict for defendant is supportable but against clear weight of evidence | Judge concludes that evidence is so compelling that no reasonable jury could find for defendant (rare — see infra pp. 610-611 |
| Judge's disposition of the case | Judge may enter directed verdict or j.n.o.v. for defendant | Judge may order new trial | Judge will order entry of judgment on the jury's verdict | Judge will order entry of judgment on the verdict for plaintiff | Judge may order new trial | Judge enters directed verdict or j.n.o.v. for plaintiff |
| | X | | Z | | Y |

**Figure 25-2.** The judge's power to displace the jury's verdict: a schematic.

In passing on the new trial motion, the judge *may* consider the credibility of the witnesses. Compare the motion for judgment as a matter of law, which, in both its incarnations, requires the judge to assume the truth of the evidence for the nonmoving party. Thus, the judge in passing on the motion for a new trial acts to some extent as a "thirteenth juror," making an independent assessment of the evidence. The judgment to be made is not whether the verdict was totally irrational but whether the judge is convinced that it is so strongly suspect that it would serve the ends of justice to have another jury hear the case.

Arguably, the judge's power to grant a new trial on this ground is even more intrusive than the power to take the case away from the jury, since the standard for granting a new trial is less stringent than that for entering judgment as a matter of law. However, it may be defended on the ground that a new jury, not the judge, will reconsider the case if the motion is granted. In fact, if a new trial is granted, the next step in the case will be to hold the second trial, at least in federal court. Under federal procedure, the party who won the verdict may not immediately appeal the judge's new trial grant, since parties are only entitled to appeal when the case is over in the trial court. When the judge enters an order to retry the case, there is no "final decision" from which to take an appeal. See 28 U.S.C. §1291; Moore's at §59.50[1]. Some state systems, however, allow an "interlocutory" (i.e., immediate) appeal from the grant of a new trial. G. Shreve and P. Raven-Hansen, Understanding Civil Procedure (3rd ed. 2002) 439 n.334.

The judge may also grant partial new trials in appropriate cases. If, for example, the jury's verdict on liability is clearly supportable but the damages greatly exceed the losses reflected in the evidence, the judge may order a new trial as to damages only.[7] In other cases, the judge may find the verdict against one defendant clearly supported by the evidence but not against another and grant a new trial solely on the claims against the second defendant.

An important difference between new trials for trial error and for verdicts against the weight of evidence is the standard of appellate review. Questions concerning the admission or exclusion of evidence or the proper instructions to the jury often involve issues of law, which can be reviewed de novo (that is, from scratch, without any deference to the trial judge's decision on the point) by the courts of appeals. Appellate judges, after all, are specialists in such legal questions. However, whether the verdict goes against the great weight of the evidence is a delicate decision that requires a

---

7. In cases where the verdict is excessive, the judge may also offer the plaintiff a remittitur. Under remittitur practice, the court agrees to enter judgment for the plaintiff if he will accept a lesser sum than the jury's verdict. If the plaintiff refuses to accept the remittitur, the judge orders a new trial. See generally Wright & Miller §2815.

balancing of evidence, usually including live testimony, which only the trial judge has had a full opportunity to observe. Consequently, it is rare for appellate judges to second-guess the trial judge's on-the-spot judgment that a new trial is warranted on this ground. Early federal cases suggested that the grant of a new trial on this ground was "unreviewable," that is, committed completely to the discretion of the trial court. See *Fairmount Glass Works v. Cub Fork Coal Co.*, 287 U.S. 474, 481-482 (1933). The trend, however, has been for the courts of appeals to review new trial grants — rather gingerly — under an abuse of discretion standard. This trend was approved by the Supreme Court in *Gasperini v. Center for Humanities, Inc.*, 518 U.S. 415 (1996).

The first examples that follow illustrate the relationship between motions for judgment as a matter of law before the verdict (d.v.) and after the verdict (j.n.o.v.), and new trial. The second part of the chapter explores the procedural complexities of joint motions under Rule 50(c) and (d). Assume that all actions are brought in federal court.

## Examples

### Never Say Die

1. Milne brings an action against Potter for infringement of a copyright Milne holds on a book about a bear. The case is tried to a jury. Potter moves for judgment as a matter of law (d.v.) at the close of Milne's evidence. The motion is denied. Potter renews the motion after presenting her own evidence. The motion is denied again. The jury is instructed, deliberates, and returns a verdict for Milne. May Potter now move again for judgment as a matter of law (j.n.o.v.)?

2. Potter, the defendant, moves for judgment as a matter of law (d.v.) at the close of the evidence. The motion is denied. The jury returns a verdict for Potter. Milne believes that the jury's verdict is completely unsupported by the evidence.
   a. May Milne now move for judgment as a matter of law (j.n.o.v.)?
   b. May he move for a new trial?

3. Assume, as in example 1, that Potter (the defendant) moved for judgment as a matter of law (d.v.) at the close of Milne's evidence but did not renew her motion at the close of all the evidence. The verdict went for Milne, and Potter now moves again for judgment as a matter of law (j.n.o.v.). Is the motion proper under the Rule?

4. Potter moves for judgment as a matter of law (d.v.) at the close of the evidence. The motion is denied, and the jury returns a verdict for Milne. Judgment is entered on the verdict. Potter believes that the verdict is completely unsupported by the evidence. Three days after judgment is

entered, she renews her motion for judgment as a matter of law, under Rule 50(b). The judge denies the motion five weeks later. Potter now moves for a new trial, on the ground that the judge improperly excluded important evidence at trial and that the verdict is against the weight of the evidence. The judge, after research, agrees on the exclusion-of-evidence point but not on the weight-of-the-evidence point. What should the judge do?

## Contingency Planning

5. Assume the same basic facts as example 4, except that both parties have some complaints about the trial. The jury rendered a verdict for the plaintiff, Milne, but Potter believes that the judge should have granted her motion for judgment as a matter of law (d.v.). She also objects to the judge's instruction on the standard for liability. Milne is satisfied with the verdict but is also convinced that his case would have been stronger if the judge had not excluded important evidence that he offered at trial.
   a. How should Potter present her objections?
   b. What should Milne do about his objection to the exclusion of the evidence? See Fed. R. Civ. P. 50(d).

6. Assume that Milne's case is tried to a jury, which returns a verdict for Potter. Milne moves for a new trial on the ground that the judge improperly instructed the jury on the standard for recovery under the copyright statute. Potter argues strenuously that the instructions were proper. The judge concludes that Milne is right and orders a new trial. What happens next?

7. Assume that Potter moves for judgment as a matter of law at the close of the evidence on the ground that Milne's evidence is too weak to support a verdict. The motion is denied, and the jury returns a verdict for Milne. In frustration, Potter reviews her trial notes and recalls that the judge allowed Milne to introduce hearsay evidence that probably should have been excluded. Although she did not object at the time, Potter researches the evidentiary issue and concludes that the evidence was indeed improperly admitted. Within the ten-day period, she makes two motions, one for a new trial on the ground that the evidence should have been excluded, and a second motion for judgment as a matter of law (j.n.o.v.) on the ground that without the inadmissible evidence, Milne's case was too weak to go to the jury.
   a. Should the judge grant the motion for a new trial?
   b. Should he grant the motion for judgment as a matter of law?

8. Assume that Milne v. Potter was tried before the judge, instead of a jury. After a full hearing, the judge finds for Milne and enters judgment

accordingly. Potter believes that the judge improperly excluded important evidence she had offered on the liability issue.

a.  How should Potter present her objection before the trial court?

b.  What will the judge do if he agrees with Potter?

---

# COMBINED MOTIONS AND APPELLATE REVIEW

As the examples above suggest, counsel for both parties may have multiple objections to the course of the trial, which they will seek to raise after trial by combined post-trial motions. Subsections (c) and (d) of Rule 50 set forth the procedure for presenting such objections in motions for judgment as a matter of law (j.n.o.v.) and new trial, and for appellate review of such combined motions.

Under Rule 50(c)(1), the trial judge confronted with a combined motion for judgment as a matter of law (j.n.o.v.) and for a new trial must not only rule on the j.n.o.v. motion, but also make a conditional ruling on the alternative motion for a new trial. That way, the court of appeals can address both issues at once if the case is appealed.

Rule 50(d) addresses the scenario in which a party wins a verdict, and then has it taken away by the trial judge, who grants j.n.o.v. for the other party. If the winning party (now the loser on j.n.o.v.) has objections to the trial that might support a grant of a new trial, Rule 50(d) authorizes her, after her verdict is nullified by the grant of j.n.o.v., to move for a new trial on the basis of those objections within ten days of the entry of the judgment for the opposing party.

Similarly, Rule 50(e) addresses the case in which a party wins the verdict, but has it taken away on appeal, because the court of appeals concludes that j.n.o.v. should have been granted for the other party. The party who won at trial (but now faces judgment against her as a matter of law) may have arguments that the first trial was unfair, for one reason or another. Rule 50(e) allows her to advance those arguments for a new trial in the court of appeals. If that court concludes that j.n.o.v. should be granted for the verdict loser, it will then consider the verdict winner's arguments for a new trial.

The examples that follow should help you to see how the use of combined motions under these two intimidating provisions facilitates the disposition of cases on appeal. For some very helpful background you may want to read *Montgomery Ward & Co. v. Duncan*, 311 U.S. 243 (1940), in which the Supreme Court established the broad outlines of the procedure later embodied in Rule 50(c), (d), and (e). However, you should be able to analyze the examples from a careful reading of these parts of the rule alone.

## Examples

### No Stone Unturned

9. Carroll sues Alcott for breach of contract. Alcott moves for judgment as matter of law (d.v.) at the close of all the evidence. After the motion is denied, the jury returns a verdict for Carroll and judgment is entered on the verdict. Alcott moves for judgment as a matter of law (j.n.o.v.) and, in the alternative, for a new trial on the ground that the verdict was against the weight of the evidence. The judge grants the j.n.o.v. motion and "conditionally" grants the new trial motion as well.

   a. May Carroll appeal at this point?

   b. Assume that the court of appeals holds that the evidence was sufficient to go to the jury, so that judgment as a matter of law (j.n.o. v.) should not have been granted. What will that court do next?

10. Alcott, the defendant, loses at trial and moves for judgment as a matter of law (j.n.o.v.) and for a new trial on the grounds that the verdict was against the weight of the evidence and that the judge's instructions to the jury were improper. The judge denies both motions. Alcott appeals. What will the court of appeals do if

    a. it concludes that judgment as a matter of law (j.n.o.v.) should have been granted?

    b. it concludes that j.n.o.v. was properly denied and that the verdict was not against the weight of the evidence but that the instructions were improper?

### Delayed Reaction

11. Assume that both Alcott and Carroll are unhappy with the trial. The jury returned a verdict for Carroll, the plaintiff, but Alcott believes that the evidence was too weak to support the verdict. Carroll believes the verdict is proper but also believes that the judge improperly excluded evidence that would have strengthened his case. Alcott moves for judgment as a matter of law (j.n.o.v.); Carroll opposes the motion but makes none of his own. The j.n.o.v. motion is denied. Alcott appeals on the ground that j.n.o.v. should have been granted, and the court of appeals agrees. Where does the case go from here? How should Carroll assert his objection about the excluded evidence?

### Practice Makes Perfect

12. Consider the following possible outcomes at the trial and appellate level. Assume in each case that the plaintiff won the verdict, and that the defendant seeks judgment as a matter of law (j.n.o.v.) on the basis that the evidence was too weak to support a plaintiff's verdict, and, in

the alternative, a new trial on the ground that the judge mistakenly excluded important evidence offered by the defendant.

Assume, in each scenario, that the losing party appeals. What should the appellate court do in each case?

| Trial court | Appellate court |
| --- | --- |
| a. grants *D*'s motion for j.n.o.v., and his conditional motion for new trial | agrees that j.n.o.v. proper, but not new trial |
| b. grants *D*'s motion for j.n.o.v. and grants his conditional motion for new trial | agrees with both decisions |
| c. denies *D*'s motion for j.n.o.v. and grants his conditional motion for new trial | agrees on j.n.o.v., disagrees on new trial |
| d. grants j.n.o.v. for *D*, denies *D*'s conditional motion for new trial | disagrees on both |

## Explanations

### Never Say Die

1. In this case Potter has already twice asked the judge to rule that Milne's evidence is too weak to go to the jury. Each time the judge has allowed the case to proceed. However, this does not bar Potter from renewing her challenge to the sufficiency of the evidence by seeking judgment as a matter of law (j.n.o.v.) after the verdict for Milne. As the Introduction indicates, the rule *requires* that the motion be made before verdict (d.v.) in order to preserve the right to make the motion after verdict (j.n.o.v.). Thus, every party who seeks judgment as a matter of law after the verdict will be renewing a similar motion made before the jury retires. The judge's denial of the pre-verdict motions does not necessarily indicate that he believes the evidence poses a jury issue; he may simply wish to reserve judgment on the issue, so as to get the jury's verdict and save a complete retrial if the decision to grant judgment as a matter of law after verdict (j.n.o.v.) is reversed on appeal.

2. a. Rule 50(b) only authorizes a party who has moved for judgment as a matter of law before the verdict (d.v.) to renew the motion after the verdict (j.n.o.v.), for the reasons discussed in the Introduction. Although Potter sought judgment as a matter of law (d.v.) at the close of the case, Milne did not. Thus, Milne's failure to make a

similar motion will bar him from seeking judgment notwithstanding the verdict after the jury finds for Potter.

Milne may not argue that his motion is proper because *Potter* sought judgment as a matter of law (d.v.) before the case went to the jury. As discussed in the Introduction, the motion must be made before the verdict in order to alert the opposing party to weaknesses in that party's case. Potter's motion was obviously directed to the weaknesses in Milne's case, not her own.

b. Milne is barred from seeking entry of judgment in his favor under Rule 50(b), but Rule 59 contains no analogous requirement of a prior motion for judgment as a matter of law (d.v.) (or for a new trial) in order to move for a new trial on the ground that the verdict is against the weight of the evidence. Since Milne believes the evidence was too weak to support a rational verdict for Potter, he presumably also believes that the verdict is against the great weight of the evidence. Thus, Milne can at least ask the judge to vacate the verdict and grant a new trial on this ground. That will not get him the judgment but will at least give him the opportunity to convince another jury of the strength of his case.

3. In this case, Potter moved for judgment as a matter of law at the close of the plaintiff's case, but she did not renew the motion after presenting her own evidence. For many years, Rule 50(b) provided that only a Rule 50(a) motion made "at the close of all the evidence" could be renewed after the jury's verdict. However, this was changed by a 2006 amendment to Rule 50(b). Under the current Rule, a party may move for judgment as a matter of law (j.n.o.v.) after the verdict as long as she made a proper motion for judgment as a matter of law (d.v.) before the verdict. Under Rule 50(a), a motion for judgment is only proper "if a party has been fully heard" on the issue as to which the adequacy of proof is challenged. At the close of Milne's case, Milne has had her full opportunity to produce her proof, so it is appropriate to argue that her proof is insufficient at that point. And the motion apprises Milne of the weakness at a time when she can reopen her case if she has additional evidence. Thus, even though Potter did not renew the motion at the close of his own case, the purposes of Rule 50(b) are served. Potter's renewed motion is proper.

4. The judge must deny the motion despite his conclusion that Potter has a valid claim that the trial was unfair. Under Rule 59, as under Rule 50(b), the motion must be filed within ten days of the entry of judgment. Potter's Rule 50(b) motion (j.n.o.v.) was timely, but her subsequent new trial motion was not, and the making of one post-trial motion does not suspend the time for making the other. Potter should have made both motions together within ten days of entry of judgment in order to assert all her objections in a timely fashion. See Rule 50(b),

second sentence, which authorizes combined motions for new trial and judgment as a matter of law (j.n.o.v.).

Nor may the judge relieve Potter of her procedural mistake by granting the motion for a new trial "sua sponte" (on his own initiative). Rule 59(d) authorizes the trial judge to grant a new trial sua sponte but requires him to do so within ten days of the entry of judgment. The implication is that he may not correct an error brought to his attention after this period has lapsed. This limitation seems unfortunate, at least where the judge becomes convinced of the error within the 30-day appeal period in Fed. R. App. P. 4(a)(1). If the judge is really convinced that he improperly excluded evidence that would have affected the result, it makes sense to allow him to grant the new trial. Otherwise, Potter will be forced to appeal, and the court of appeals will be forced to hear and decide an appeal that could have been avoided by the grant of a new trial as soon as the error became apparent.[8]

The strict limit on the time for granting a new trial reflects a strong policy in favor of finality of judgments. Parties must know at some point that the decision rendered in an action will not be revised, so they can order their affairs accordingly. If the judge could reconsider at any time, the outcome would still remain uncertain despite the entry of a "final" judgment.

## Contingency Planning

5. a. It is not unusual for both parties to have complaints about the conduct of a trial. Here, Potter believes that the outcome was unwarranted by the evidence, and, in addition, that the process was tainted due to improper instructions. Milne is content with the outcome but believes that he could have made an even stronger case if all his evidence had been placed before the jury.

   Potter, of course, should renew her motion for judgment as a matter of law (seek j.n.o.v.), since she believes that the evidence was too weak to support a rational verdict for Milne. In addition, since she believes the evidence was too weak to go to the jury, she must also believe it was against the great weight of the evidence. Consequently, she should join a motion under Rule 59 for a new trial on this ground with her Rule 50(b) motion. Finally, she should assert the improper jury instruction as an alternate ground for a new trial. She may assert all three grounds in a combined motion, but must do so within ten days of entry of judgment.

---

8. The judge might achieve the same result by granting relief from the judgment under Fed. R. Civ. P. 60(b), at least before the period for appeal of the judgment has run.

b. Milne is in a slightly different position. Because he won the verdict, he has no cause to press his objection to the exclusion of evidence (unless, of course, the evidence went to the size of the verdict and he is unhappy with that). He prevailed without the evidence and presumably has no interest in trying the suit again just to have a perfect process. However, Milne is still somewhat at risk since Potter has asked the judge to displace the jury's verdict. If the judge grants judgment for Potter (j.n.o.v.) on the ground that Milne did not produce sufficient evidence to pose a jury issue, Milne will surely wish to argue that he *could* have made a submissible case if the judge had not excluded important evidence.

Of course, the rulemakers have provided for this contingency. If the judge deprives Milne of his victory by entering judgment as a matter of law (j.n.o.v.) for Potter, Rule 50(d) allows Milne to move for a new trial within ten days after entry of *that* judgment, on the ground that the evidence was improperly excluded. Thus, he need not raise the objection until the verdict in his favor is taken away. At that point, it becomes apparent that the judge's evidentiary ruling has harmed Milne's case, and he may ask the court to grant a new trial on that ground.

6. If Potter believes that the instruction was proper, she would like to appeal immediately, in hopes that the court of appeals will agree with her, reverse the new trial grant, and enter judgment on the jury's verdict. However, when a new trial motion is granted, the judge will enter an order for the case to be retried. As the Introduction states, in federal court parties in Potter's position may not appeal the grant of a new trial until after the new trial is held because a new trial grant is not considered a final judgment under federal practice. See 28 U.S.C. §1291 (authorizing appeal from "final decisions" of the district courts).

Thus, Potter will have to go through the second trial before appealing. If she wins at the second trial, she will presumably be satisfied with the result (though not the elongated process to reach it) and have no incentive to appeal the grant of the new trial. However, if she loses at the second trial, Potter will be entitled to appeal the judge's earlier decision to grant the new trial since the court will render a final judgment for Milne on the second verdict (assuming no further motions for new trial are granted after the *second* trial). The court of appeals will then review the disputed instruction from the first trial. If it agrees with Potter that the original instruction was proper, it will enter judgment on the *original* verdict for her. If it concludes that the trial judge's initial instruction was wrong, it will uphold the grant of the new trial and (assuming no reversible error in the second trial) affirm the judgment for Milne.

Although there is logic to delaying review of the new trial grant in these cases, there is also much to be said for immediate appeal. If the case is reviewed before the new trial and the new trial order is reversed, it will save the considerable effort of trying the case a second time, perhaps to no purpose.[9] For this reason some state systems allow interlocutory review of new trial grants. See Friedenthal, Kane, and Miller at p. 598.

7. a. The example here indicates that Potter did not object to the judge's error in admitting the evidence at the time that the error was made. In most cases, a party who fails to object to a ruling during trial will not be allowed to challenge that ruling by a motion for new trial afterwards. See Wright & Miller at §2805 pp.57-59 (in absence of a timely objection, new trial will not be granted "unless the error was so fundamental that gross injustice would result"). Although this rule seems draconian, especially given the pressures of trial, it makes good sense. If the error is brought to the judge's attention immediately, he may exclude the evidence and avoid a reversible error. If it is only raised after trial on a new trial motion, it is too late to save the trial.

If Potter could raise such objections without having objected during trial, it would open the door to manipulation of the trial process. She might deliberately withhold objection to one or more arguably prejudicial decisions of the trial judge. Then if she lost the verdict, she could undermine the unfavorable verdict by pulling these objections out of her hat as grounds for a new trial.

   b. The judge will also deny Potter's motion for judgment as a matter of law (j.n.o.v.). Her argument here is that the evidence would have been too weak to go to the jury if the disputed evidence had not been admitted. Here again Potter should have avoided the error by a timely objection, rather than invoking it later to overturn the jury's verdict. Note that, while Potter did make a motion for judgment as a matter of law (d.v.) before the case went to the jury, it *was not on the ground of admission of the improper evidence.* Thus, neither the court nor Milne was given a chance to cure that problem.

A Rule 50(a) motion at the close of all the evidence on one ground will not preserve the right to seek judgment as a matter of law (j.n.o.v.) on a different ground. The purpose for the prior motion is to point out the problem at a time when it can be cured.

---

9. In *Roy v. Volkswagen of America, Inc.,* 896 F.2d 1174 (1990), for example, the plaintiffs won a verdict of $3 million in a negligence action after a 21-day trial. The judge ordered a new trial. The Roys attempted an appeal, which was dismissed because the new trial order prevented a final judgment. At the new trial, the jury found for the defendant. On appeal by the Roys from this judgment, the court held that the evidence was "substantially balanced" (896 F.2d at 1179) so that the new trial should not have been granted in the first place. Consequently, the court ordered judgment entered on the original jury verdict for the Roys — some six years after that verdict was rendered.

Here Potter raised the objection that the evidence before the jury was too weak to support a verdict but did not raise the hearsay problem. Thus, her motion did not alert the court or Milne to the other evidentiary problem at a time when it could have been cured. See *Lifshitz v. Walter Drake & Sons, Inc.*, 806 F.2d 1426, 1428-1429 (9th Cir. 1986) (directed verdict motion only preserves right to seek j.n.o.v. on the specific grounds raised in the motion).

8. a. Parties have the same right to seek a new trial in cases tried to the judge as they do in jury cases. See Fed R. Civ. P. 59(a)(2). Potter should make her motion for a new trial (often called a "rehearing" in nonjury cases) within ten days of entry of judgment, stating as her ground the exclusion of the disputed evidence.

   b. Although the procedure for presenting the motion is similar, a rehearing after a nonjury trial differs significantly from a new trial in a jury case. In a jury case, the jury is discharged after a verdict is reached. They cannot be called back after the new trial is granted to hear the additional evidence that had been wrongly excluded. Thus, the only way to provide both parties with a full opportunity to be heard is to start over and present all the evidence to a new jury in a complete new trial.

   In a nonjury case the judge need not go back and start from square one. He has already heard all the evidence and decided the relevant legal rules to apply in reaching a decision. If Potter's only objection is that the judge failed to consider certain evidence (and if the judge concludes that she is right), the judge can reopen the hearing, hear that evidence, and reconsider the case, taking the additional evidence into account. Thus, the rehearing in such cases can be a relatively brief proceeding to simply augment the record with the additional evidence. Fed. R. Civ. P. 59(a)(2).

   If Potter's objection had been that the judge *admitted* evidence that should have been excluded, the "rehearing" might be even simpler. The judge could simply sustain the motion and reconsider the case without taking the inadmissible evidence into account. At least that's the theory. In practice it is obviously questionable whether the judge can really disregard persuasive evidence that he has already heard simply on the technical ground that it is inadmissible under the rules of evidence.[10]

---

10. If one party in a case has evidence that is extremely persuasive but probably inadmissible under the rules of evidence, this may be a strong tactical reason for the other party to seek a jury trial. The judge must often see the evidence that is offered in order to pass on its admissibility. If he is also the factfinder, it will be difficult for him to disregard what he has seen. If the case is tried to a jury, however, the judge will see such evidence, but the factfinder (the jury) will not.

## No Stone Unturned

9. a. Carroll may appeal the judge's combined ruling, even though the new trial was "conditionally" (Fed. R. Civ. P. 50(c)(1)) granted. The judge has ordered judgment as a matter of law (j.n.o.v.) for Alcott. Rule 50(c)(2) clearly states that the decision on the new trial motion does not prevent this from being a final judgment. Alcott is the winner and if no one appeals the case is over. What the judge is saying by the conditional grant of the new trial is this: "I find that Carroll's case was too weak to support a rational verdict for him. So I order judgment for Alcott. However, if I were not granting j.n.o.v. for Alcott, [or if my j.n.o.v. ruling is overturned] I would grant a new trial for him, because I think the jury's verdict for Carroll is against the great weight of the evidence."

   The purpose for requiring the judge to rule conditionally on the new trial motion, even though he has granted judgment for Carroll and the case is over, is to help the court of appeals to decide how to dispose of the case if it reverses the decision to enter judgment as a matter of law for Alcott. If the j.n.o.v. stands, the conditional grant of the new trial has no effect; Alcott won't have any interest in a new trial if the court upholds j.n.o.v. in his favor.

   b. If Carroll appeals and the court reverses the entry of judgment as a matter of law for Alcott, the judge's conditional ruling on the new trial motion assists the appellate court in deciding what should happen next in the case. The court of appeals can now review the judge's conditional decision that a new trial should be granted. If it concludes that the judge did not abuse his discretion in concluding that the verdict went against the clear weight of the evidence, the court can uphold the grant of the new trial and remand the case to the trial court for retrial. See Fed. R. Civ. P. 50(c)(2). If, on the other hand, the court concludes that even the new trial motion should not have been granted (an unlikely decision, given the broad discretion accorded the trial court in making the new trial decision), it may reverse both decisions and order entry of judgment for Carroll on the jury's verdict.

   The good sense of this procedure is highlighted by considering the alternative. If the trial judge decided only the Rule 50(b) motion, and that was reversed, the court of appeals would have to remand for the judge to consider whether a new trial should be granted. If he granted it on remand, the new trial would proceed, since the grant of a new trial is an interlocutory decision. Only after a second trial would Carroll be able to challenge the new trial grant, on a second appeal.

On the other hand, if the judge denied the motion for a new trial on remand after reversal of the judgment as a matter of law (j.n.o.v.), Alcott could appeal that denial. Here, too, a second trip to the court of appeals would be needed to fully dispose of the case. The Rule 50(c) procedure for conditional rulings on both motions allows the appellate court to fully dispose of these rulings in a single appeal.

10. a. If the court concludes that judgment should have been granted for Alcott because Carroll's evidence was too weak to go to the jury, it will enter judgment as a matter of law (j.n.o.v.) for Alcott. Unlike the discretionary Rule 59 decision as to whether the verdict was contrary to the clear weight of the evidence, which involves consideration of the credibility of witnesses, the j.n.o.v. decision is a question of law that the appellate court reviews de novo. The court must review all the evidence, consider it in the light most favorable to the nonmoving party, and make its own judgment as to whether Carroll's case was legally sufficient to submit to the jury.

   b. If the court of appeals concludes that judgment as a matter of law (j.n.o.v.) was properly denied and that the verdict is not against the weight of the evidence, it will then consider whether the new trial should have been granted due to legal error in the instructions. The issue of the proper rules for the jury to apply in deciding the case is a question of law, which the court of appeals decides de novo. If the court concludes that the jury was not properly instructed, it can remand for a new trial. If the instructions were correct, it can affirm the denial of the new trial and (since it had already ruled that j.n.o.v. was properly denied) affirm the entry of judgment for Carroll. Either way, the use of combined motions again allows the appellate court to consider all of the losing party's objections without remand for decision of further post-trial motions.

## Delayed Reaction

11. The situation here is similar to that in example 5b, in which the plaintiff won the verdict but had the victory snatched away when the trial judge granted j.n.o.v. for the defendant. Here, the same thing happened, except that it was the court of appeals rather than the trial judge that displaced the verdict. Until judgment was granted for Alcott on appeal, Carroll was content with the result of the original trial. Although he believed his case would have been stronger if the excluded evidence had been admitted, it was already strong enough to win. Thus, Carroll had no reason to seek a new trial due to the exclusion of the evidence.

It is only after the court of appeals deprives him of his judgment by granting judgment as a matter of law (j.n.o.v.) for Alcott that Carroll will wish to raise his objection to the evidentiary ruling. At that point, he will want to argue that the original trial was flawed and that he is entitled to a new trial at which the excluded evidence is placed before the jury. After all, it may be that his case was too weak to reach the jury precisely because that evidence was excluded.

Under Rule 50(e) Carroll may raise this argument at the appeal stage even if he did not seek a new trial in the district court. (Of course, he would have had to object at the time the evidence was excluded. See the answer to example 7.) If Carroll raises the issue on appeal, and the court of appeals reverses the denial of j.n.o.v., that court will consider the evidentiary point as well. It may order a new trial on this ground or remand to allow the trial judge to address the motion. Fed R. Civ. P. 50(e). Or, of course, it may deny the new trial if the evidence was properly excluded and enter judgment for Alcott based on its conclusion that j.n.o.v. should have been granted for her.

## Practice Makes Perfect

12. a. The appellate court affirms the judgment for the defendant, since it agrees that the plaintiff's case was too weak to support a verdict. Although the decision that the defendant is entitled to a new trial due to the exclusion of the evidence was erroneous, the error is harmless. The defendant has now prevailed without the evidence; the last thing he wants is a new trial.
    b. Judgment is entered for the defendant, since both trial and appelate courts agree that the plaintiff's case was too weak to support a verdict. Once again, the defendant has no further interest in a new trial, though both courts agree that he would be entitled to one if the plaintiff's case were strong enough to go to the jury.
    c. Initially, the appellate court won't do anything at all. Since the trial judge denied the j.n.o.v. motion, but granted the new trial motion, the case will be scheduled for a new trial. (Remember that in the federal courts, the grant of a new trial motion is an "interlocutory" decision, since the case is not over in the trial court.) If the plaintiff wins at the second trial, she will presumably not appeal. However, if she loses at the second trial, she may then appeal the decision to grant a new trial. If, as the example suggests, the appeals court concludes that there was no ground for granting the new trial, it will reverse the entry of the order for a new trial and (since it agrees with the trial judge's decision to deny j.n.o.v.) order entry of judgment on the first jury's verdict.

d. Here, the case is immediately appealable, because the court has entered judgment as a matter of law for the defendant on the basis that the case was too weak to go to the jury. Because the appellate court disagrees with this conclusion, it should reverse the entry of judgment for the defendant. However, since it concludes that a new trial was warranted due to the exclusion of the evidence, it should remand the case to the trial court for a retrial at which the evidence will be admitted.

# The Effect of
# the Judgment

# Res Judicata

## The Limits of Procedural Liberality

---

## INTRODUCTION

Perhaps you are thoroughly tired of hearing how *reasonable* the Federal Rules of Civil Procedure are. Certainly, one of the recurrent themes of the Rules is to create a flexible procedural system in order to prevent procedure from dominating substance, to assure that the merits of the parties' claims, not procedural missteps, determine the outcome of lawsuits.

For example, parties are given broad power to join claims and parties in a single suit. Fed. R. Civ. P. 13, 14, 18, 20, 24. They are given the latitude to plead all their possible claims against opposing parties, within the limits of proper pleading. Fed. R. Civ. P. 8(a), 8(d)(2), 11. Pleadings are liberally construed, Fed. R. Civ. P. 8(e); and amendments freely allowed. Fed. R. Civ. P. 15(a). Even if amendments are not offered, the court can treat the pleadings *as though* they had been amended, when justice so requires, Fed. R. Civ. P. 15(b), and may grant parties the relief to which they are entitled even though they never asked for it. Fed. R. Civ. P. 54(c). If the process still goes awry, despite all these opportunities to correct procedural errors, the court may grant a new trial under Fed. R. Civ. P. 59, or relief from judgment under Fed. R. Civ. P. 60(b).

Given all this procedural liberality, you might expect that the rules governing relitigation of claims would be correspondingly indulgent. However, the exact opposite is true. Once the parties have had a full and fair opportunity to be heard under the flexible rules reviewed above, all this paternalistic indulgence comes to an abrupt halt. Regardless of a party's reason for wishing to relitigate a dispute, the doctrine of res judicata stands like a brutish, unreflecting myrmidon, guarding the doors of the courthouse.[1] While the Rules are liberal, res judicata is strict and uncharitable. No matter how unfair the result in the first suit may seem or indeed, no matter how unfair it may actually have been, the myrmidon will not step aside.

For example, suppose that the plaintiff in the *Schulansky* case recovers $7,000 from Ronan for breach of contract. If Schulansky believes that the verdict was too low, she cannot bring a second action against Ronan for more. Or, if she discovers a statute that allows a more generous measure of damages, she cannot bring a new action based on that statute. If Schulansky loses but believes that her lawyer did not litigate the case energetically, she will be barred by res judicata from trying again with a new lawyer.

In the traditional terminology, Schulansky's claim was said to be "merged" into the judgment she had won. That is, the claim was extinguished and replaced by the judgment. Restatement (Second) of Judgments §§17, 18 (1982). Once the judgment was entered, a suit could be brought to enforce that judgment if necessary (see Chapter 3, pp. 50-51), but no further suit could be brought on the extinguished claim. Conversely, if Schulansky lost, her claim was said to be "barred" by the adverse judgment so that no further suit could be brought on the claim.

The rationale for the doctrine is ancient and fundamental. Litigation is burdensome enough the first time without redoing it again whenever one of the parties is unhappy with the result — as at least one will be in every case. Parties must also get on with their affairs; without the certainty provided by res judicata, parties would not be able to rely on court decisions in planning their future conduct. Finally, from the point of view of the system, there is no justification for multiplying the costs and delay of litigation by allowing parties to go at it again once they have had a full and fair opportunity to litigate a claim.

Of course, the efficiency of res judicata would not be justified if it were achieved at the expense of fairness to the parties in presenting meritorious claims. For example, it would be a hard system indeed that barred the plaintiff from amending her complaint in the first action to assert new theories for relief unearthed during discovery and also barred her from bringing a separate action based on those theories. But, if amendments are liberally allowed in the first suit, it is fair to bar a second action on theories left out of the first suit. Thus, it is precisely because the Rules of Civil Procedure are so liberal in facilitating presentation of claims

---

1. A myrmidon is a servant who mindlessly but doggedly obeys his master's every command. The first myrmidons were ants, who were changed into men by Zeus to repopulate the island kingdom of Aegina. They were known for their loyalty and courage in following their leader, Achilles, in the Trojan War. See E. Hamilton, Mythology 296 (1969).

in the first action that the res judicata myrmidon can so stubbornly bar a second try. Indeed, the specter of res judicata encourages parties to take full advantage of the Rules to present their claims initially, since they know that they will not get a second chance to try the suit, that there will be no "second bite at the apple."

In most jurisdictions, there are four prerequisites for res judicata: (1) there must be a final judgment; (2) the judgment must be "on the merits"; (3) the claims must be the same in the first and second suits; and (4) the parties in the second action must be the same as those in the first (or have been represented by a party to the prior action). Most of the interpretive issues in applying the doctrine concern the requirements that the claims be the same in both suits and that the original judgment be on the merits.

# THE "SAME CLAIM" REQUIREMENT

The definition of a single "claim" for res judicata purposes varies from one jurisdiction to another. See generally Friedenthal, Kane, and Miller at §14.4. The federal courts and an increasing number of states have adopted the standard in the Restatement (Second) of Judgments §24 (1982), which essentially equates a party's claim for res judicata purposes with the "transaction or occurrence" test of the federal joinder rules. See 18 Wright & Miller at §4407 at n.22. Under this approach, a party who has asserted a right to relief arising out of a particular transaction or occurrence must join all claims she has arising from it, or the omitted claims will be barred by res judicata.

There is good sense to a theory that makes the scope of preclusion mirror the test for allowing initial joinder under the Rules. If a party had the right to join two claims for relief arising from the same transaction in the first suit, it is reasonable to require her to do so, instead of bringing two suits that will rehash the same facts. Conversely, if the scope of preclusion is to mirror the scope of permissible joinder, res judicata should not bar claims that could not have been joined in the first action. For example, before the development of the unified civil action under the Rules, parties could not always seek legal and equitable relief in the same proceeding. They were often forced to split their claims between the law courts (for damage claims) and the equity courts (for claims to equitable relief, such as specific performance or injunctions). See generally Wright & Miller §4410. In such cases, a party who had sought damages in an action at law was not precluded from seeking injunctive relief based on the same transaction or occurrence from a court of equity because she could not have obtained an injunction in the prior action at law. Under the Federal

Rules, however, parties may almost always assert all their claims in a single suit, and res judicata is correspondingly broad.[2]

Under the transaction or occurrence test, preclusion turns on the *right* to join the claim in the original action, not on whether the claim actually was asserted. Consequently, claims need not have actually been litigated to be barred in a later action; they need only have been *available* to the plaintiff in the first suit. For example, it is clear that Schulansky, after recovering $7,000 from Ronan in the contract action described in Part VI, could not sue Ronan again for this claim on a breach of contract theory. However, res judicata will also bar Schulansky from suing Ronan for fraud connected with the addition work, even though she had never pleaded fraud in her first suit, never tried the case on a fraud theory, and in fact never thought of it. Indeed, the message of res judicata is that Schulansky (or, more particularly, Schulansky's lawyer) had *better* think of it, sooner rather than later.

The Second Restatement of Judgments approach, which equates the scope of a "claim" with the scope of the underlying transaction or occurrence that gave rise to the suit, is followed in the federal courts and in many state courts. However, there are other approaches. Some courts bar a second action if allowing it might impair or contradict the judgment in the first, if the same evidence would support the claims in both actions, or if the same "primary right" is at issue in both suits. For a good discussion of these alternative — generally older — approaches to the definition of a single claim, see Friedenthal, Kane, and Miller, s. 14.4. These earlier approaches have often proved frustratingly ambiguous. The same-underlying-transaction approach involves ambiguities of its own, but has the distinct advantage that it focuses the analysis on a single set of historical facts, regardless of what legal theories are asserted in the two actions or how much overlap there is in the evidence supporting the first and second actions.

# JUDGMENT "ON THE MERITS"

Another res judicata prerequisite that has raised interpretive problems is the requirement of a decision "on the merits" in the first action. Clearly, a full trial followed by a verdict and judgment is the paradigm of a decision on the merits. At the other extreme, some dismissals, such as dismissals for improper venue or lack of personal jurisdiction, do not bar a second action, on the rationale that the court never reached the merits in the first

---

2. However, the right to join claims under the Rules does not automatically lead to the conclusion that res judicata will bar a separate suit on those claims. See Chapter 27.

action, much less decided it after a full opportunity to be heard. The very basis of such dismissals is that the court does not have the power to reach the merits because the plaintiff has chosen an improper court under the "three ring" analysis.

The toughest cases fall between these extremes. For example, jurisdictions differ as to whether a dismissal for failure to state a claim (see Fed. R. Civ. P. 12(b)(6)) should bar a second action. The Second Restatement of Judgments concludes that such dismissals should bar relitigation, on the theory that a plaintiff whose complaint is dismissed for failure to state a claim is allowed liberal opportunities to amend. Restatement (Second) of Judgments §19, comment d (1982). If she cannot amend to state a compensable claim on a second or third try, it is presumably because she has no right to relief under the law. If that is true, there is no reason to allow her to harass the defendant with a new action. This is the rule applied in the federal courts. *Federated Department Stores v. Moitie*, 452 U.S. 394, 399 n.3 (1981); Moore's §131.30[3][e]. However, some state courts allow a second action under these circumstances because comparatively little litigation effort goes into these preliminary dismissals, and hence a basic value underlying res judicata, preservation of scarce judicial resources, is not compromised by allowing a new action.

Actually, it is a bit of a misnomer to say that judgment must be "on the merits" to bar a second action. In fact, the court need not decide the facts or conduct a trial at all for its judgment to have full res judicata effect. For example, if the plaintiff files suit, but does not pursue the case, it will eventually be dismissed for failure to prosecute. Clearly the parties have not litigated the merits in such cases; they haven't litigated anything at all. But such a dismissal is deemed "on the merits" in the sense that it will bar a subsequent action because the plaintiff had a full opportunity to litigate the merits in the first action. If she doesn't choose to take the opportunity, she must accept the res judicata consequences. Similarly, a defendant who defaults (that is, never answers to the merits and therefore loses by default), is also barred by res judicata on the same reasoning.

# FINAL JUDGMENT

A judgment must also be "final" before res judicata attaches. There is obviously little point in barring a second action on a claim that has not yet been fully resolved in the first. Suppose, for example, that Schulansky sues Ronan in federal court on breach of contract and fraud theories, and the court dismisses the fraud claim under Fed. R. Civ. P. 12(b)(6) but allows the contract claim to proceed. Generally, courts remain free to reexamine interlocutory rulings made in the course of suit, including a ruling dismissing one of the plaintiff's claims. See 18 Wright & Miller at §4478 p. 667. Thus the dismissal of the fraud claim might be reconsidered and vacated by the judge in the first action before the case is finally determined in the trial court. Thus, until final judgment is entered in the trial court, it remains too uncertain to support a res judicata plea in a separate action between the parties.

However, many courts give res judicata effect to a judgment once it has become final in the trial court, even if an appeal is pending. This is the Restatement view. Restatement (Second) of Judgments §13, comment f (1982). Under this approach, a judgment may bar relitigation even though the original case is still being litigated and is not yet enforceable by execution or otherwise. Some courts, however, only give res judicata effect to judgments if the time for appeal has passed or the case has been finally resolved by the appellate court. See H. Erickson, Interjurisdictional Preclusion, 96 Mich. L. Rev. 945, 972-973 (1998).

In working through the examples that follow assume that all suits are brought in federal court and that the Restatement principles discussed above apply. If you want further background, try Friedenthal, Kane, and Miller, §14.4-14.5, pp. 658-674. I also recommend the Second Restatement itself, which is replete with helpful examples and comments. Restatement (Second) of Judgments §§13-26 (1982). But keep in mind (not for the examples below but for those long lawyering years ahead) that the doctrine varies from one jurisdiction to another. Even if the Restatement principles are generally followed, each jurisdiction is likely to have its own quirks and quiddities that can only be learned from studying local practice.

## Examples

### Fielder's Choices

1. Rizzuto's eye is injured when his baseball glove breaks while he is fielding a vicious grounder. He sues Allston Leather Company for negligent manufacture of the glove. The case is tried and judgment is entered for Allston. Later, Rizzuto sues again. He argues that the judge in the first suit erroneously excluded important evidence from Rizzuto's expert on baseball glove manufacturing standards and that he should have a chance to have a trial with all the admissible evidence properly before the jury. Allston pleads res judicata. Will the defense bar Rizzuto's second action?

2. After the judgment for Allston in Rizzuto's case, Boyer tells Rizzuto that he was also injured using the same type of Allston glove and recovered judgment against Allston on a strict liability theory, which did not require proof that Allston was negligent. Rizzuto files a new action

against Allston based on the original accident but asserting a right to recover only on the basis of strict liability. Will the claim be barred?

3. Assume that Rizzuto won his first suit against Allston and recovered $3,000 in compensatory damages. Boyer subsequently tells him that he had claimed gross negligence by Allston in a prior suit based on the same defective glove and recovered punitive damages. Rizzuto brings a second action against Allston for punitive damages based on gross negligence. Can Allston successfully plead res judicata?

4. Assume that Rizzuto recovered $15,000 in an action against Allston, but Allston was in shaky financial condition and never paid. Rizzuto later brings a new action against Allston after learning that its financial condition has improved. Does res judicata bar the second suit?

5. Assume that Rizzuto presented evidence in the original action against Allston that he suffered impaired vision in his eye for several weeks as a result of the accident, missed two weeks of the baseball season, and had some pain from the injury. This is the only evidence he presented on damages. The jury finds for Rizzuto and awards him $10,000 damages. Three years later, after the judgment has been entered and paid, Rizzuto develops migraine headaches. His doctor tells him that these often result from an eye injury and are likely to continue indefinitely. Can Rizzuto sue Allston for damages for these headaches?

## An Absurd Hypothetical

6. Imagine that Rizzuto's vicious grounder breaks through his glove, whacks him in the eye, and bounces off Kubek, injuring him as well. Kubek sues Allston and recovers. Rizzuto testifies in Kubek's suit. Rizzuto now takes the cue and brings an action to recover for his injuries in the same accident. Allston pleads the inevitable res judicata. Is the suit barred?

7. At the time Rizzuto was injured using Allston's glove, he had an endorsement contract with them to promote the glove in television commercials. He had made the ads but had not been paid by Allston.

    Acting on the advice of his lawyers that asserting the contract claim in the negligence suit would confuse matters, Rizzuto did not assert his contract claim in the negligence suit against Allston. Instead, he sues separately on the contract claim after judgment in the negligence action. Allston pleads res judicata. Was the lawyers' advice sound?

8. Assume that Rizzuto's contract calls for royalties (or "residuals" in the language of the trade) to be paid to Rizzuto for each year that the commercials are used. Allston pays the residuals in the first year at 5 percent, while Rizzuto claims it should be 10 percent. Rizzuto sues

and wins. At the end of the next year, Allston pays Rizzuto again at the 5 percent rate. Rizzuto sues again, for the second year's residuals. Allston pleads res judicata. Is the second action barred?

9. Rizzuto sues Allston to collect under the endorsement contract. Allston defends the action and wins on the ground that Rizzuto had not performed his obligations under the contract because he abandoned filming after making several commercials. Allston subsequently brings a separate suit against Rizzuto for damages for his breach of the contract. Is Allston's suit precluded by res judicata?

## Judgment on the Merits

10. Rizzuto sues Allston on the negligence claim in federal court. Allston moves to dismiss under Fed. R. Civ. P. 12(b)(1) for lack of subject matter jurisdiction on the ground that complete diversity does not exist because its principal place of business is in New York (Rizzuto's home state). The court holds a full evidentiary hearing on the motion, including extensive testimony from officials of Allston as to the extent of Allston's business activities in New York and other states. After presentation of the evidence and briefs and argument by the parties, the court concludes that Allston's principal place of business is New York and therefore dismisses the suit. Rizzuto now sues in a New York state court, and Allston pleads res judicata. Will the defense prevail?

11. Assume that the court in the case described in example 10 concludes that it has subject matter jurisdiction. Allston therefore answers Rizzuto's negligence complaint and subsequently moves for summary judgment on the ground that Rizzuto cannot prove any negligence of Allston. It submits supporting affidavits of its employees, stating under oath that they had examined the glove after the accident and it was not damaged or defective in any way. Rizzuto submits no opposing affidavit, and summary judgment is entered for Allston. Subsequently, Rizzuto sues again. Is the second suit barred?

## Pendent or Independent?

12. Koufax sues Throneberry in state court under a state unfair competition statute. He claims that Throneberry wrote a book about great baseball heroes of the 1950s, which plagiarized a similar book by Koufax. The court dismisses Koufax's claim on the ground that he cannot establish the elements of an unfair competition claim. Subsequently, he sues in federal court under the federal copyright laws, based on the same acts. Is the second action barred by res judicata? Look at 28 U.S.C. §1338(a) before answering this example.

13. Suppose that Koufax sued first in federal court on the federal copyright claim, and the court held that Throneberry's book was sufficiently distinct that it did not violate Koufax's copyright. Koufax loses. Subsequently, Koufax sues Throneberry in state court under a state unfair competition statute, based on the same acts. Will the second action be barred?

## "The Game Ain't Over 'til It's Over"

14. Berra sues Durocher in a New York state court for intentional infliction of emotional distress, arising out of an altercation behind home plate at Yankee Stadium. The court dismisses the suit on the ground that New York case law bars recovery for infliction of emotional distress unless the plaintiff also suffered physical injury. Judgment is entered for Durocher. Sixteen months later, the New York Court of Appeals (New York's highest court) overrules this approach in another case, holding that a plaintiff may recover for intentional infliction of emotional distress without proof of physical injury. Berra brings a new action to recover for the same incident. Is the suit barred?

15. Assume that Berra sued Durocher for intentional infliction of emotional distress in a New York state court. The court dismissed the suit on the ground that the applicable law did not allow recovery for infliction of emotional distress unless the plaintiff also suffered physical injury. Berra appealed. While the appeal was pending, the New York Court of Appeals held in a separate case that plaintiffs may recover for infliction of emotional distress without accompanying physical injury. Which rule should apply to Berra's case?

16. Assume that Berra learns of the change in the law six months after the judgment in his original suit became final. Rather than bring a new action on the claim, Berra takes a different tack: He brings a motion for relief from the *original* judgment, under Fed. R. Civ. P. 60(b), asking the trial court to reopen the first case in light of the change in the applicable law. Should the court grant the motion?

17. Fred and Martha get a divorce. Fred gets custody of the children. As part of the decree the court orders Martha to pay $400 a week in child support. Three years later, after two years of high inflation, Fred moves to reopen the judgment and for an increase in the weekly support. Should the court deny the motion on the basis of res judicata?

## Double Plays

18. Schulansky sues Ronan for negligence in constructing an addition to her antique home in New Hampshire. She claims that his negligence in

doing the work caused the foundation of the main house to subside, resulting in damage to the older part of the house. The jury concludes that the damage was caused by natural subsidence, not by Ronan's negligence. Judgment is entered for Ronan.

Which of the following later suits would be precluded by the judgment in *Schulansky v. Ronan?*

    a. Schulansky sues Ronan for breach of contract, claiming that he agreed in his contract to conduct the work carefully and without causing damage to the main structure, and that he failed to do so.

    b. Schulansky sues Ronan for damages, claiming that he constructed the addition one hundred square feet smaller than the contract required.

    c. Schulansky sues Ronan for damage to plantings at her house in Massachusetts, caused when Ronan constructed an addition on her Massachusetts house before the New Hampshire job.

    d. Schulansky sues Ronan for the negligence of Jones, the backhoe contractor he hired to dig the foundation for the addition to the New Hampshire house. She claims that Jones's digging undermined the foundation of the main house, causing the damage, and that Ronan is liable for Jones's negligence under respondeat superior.

    e. Schulansky sues Ronan for fraud, claiming that in negotiating the contract for the construction of the addition to her New Hampshire house, Ronan misrepresented his experience with older houses, and that the damage resulted from his lack of expertise in working on historic structures.

    f. Schulansky sues Jones, claiming that his backhoe work undermined the foundation, causing the damage to her New Hamsphire house.

## Explanations

### Fielder's Choices

1. Res judicata will bar Rizzuto's second action. A judgment need not be right to preclude further litigation; it need only be final and on the merits. "Decisions that plainly are wrong and that would be reversed on appeal, were that route available, are valid final judgments for res judicata purposes. After all, the policies of res judicata — finality of decision and protection from harassment — would be frustrated completely if a plaintiff could evade the doctrine simply by arguing that the original decision was wrong. Res judicata reflects the policy that sometimes it is more important that a judgment be stable than that it be correct." Friedenthal, Kane, and Miller at 655. Here, Rizzuto tried his case and lost, and final judgment was entered for Allston "on the

merits," that is, based on a verdict by the jury finding that Allston was not negligent. That judgment bars a second suit by Rizzuto on the same claim even if evidence was wrongly excluded. If that exclusion was improper, Rizzuto should have appealed on that ground in the first suit, not attempted to relitigate it in a second. See *Federated Department Stores, Inc. v. Moitie*, 452 U.S. 394, 398 (1981).

If Rizzuto could avoid the effect of the first judgment by claiming it was wrong, the res judicata doctrine would lose much of its value. A major purpose of the doctrine is to preserve judicial resources by barring rehearing of cases already litigated and decided. This purpose would be undermined if the evidence would have to be reheard in order to ascertain whether the first case was rightly decided. It would also place the judge in the second suit in the inappropriate position of reviewing the first trial to determine whether it was error-free in order to determine whether it should have res judicata effect.

2. Res judicata bars not only those claims that were asserted in the first suit, but also any others arising out of that transaction that could have been asserted but were not. Here, Rizzuto has simply switched theories of relief and sued again based on the same vicious grounder he complained of in the earlier suit. Since his suit arises out of the same occurrence as the first, it will be barred.

The rigidity of this rule forces parties to litigate their claims fully in their first suit. Lawyers, knowing they will get only one bite at the apple, must consider all possible grounds for relief raised by the underlying facts and plead them in the first action. This is one reason why complaints often contain numerous counts based on different legal theories. It is better to be comprehensive in the original action (subject, of course, to the ethical constraints of Rule 11) than to try to battle the res judicata myrmidon in a subsequent action.

3. Allston will also prevail on his res judicata defense here. In example 2, Rizzuto tried to "split his claim" by asserting one theory of relief in the first action and another in the second. Here he has tried a different type of claim-splitting, seeking different types of damages in different actions. Here too, the myrmidon says no. The claim for punitive damages is based on the same incident as the prior suit. It could have been, and therefore should have been, asserted in the first action. No matter how clear Rizzuto's right to punitive damages, the court will not hear this claim.

In an earlier day many states allowed "claim-splitting" based on distinct types of damages. For example, plaintiffs in auto negligence cases were frequently allowed to seek recovery for their personal injuries and damage to their vehicles in separate actions, on the theory that these involved discrete rights protected by distinct causes of action. See, e.g., *Vasu v. Koblers, Inc.*, 61 N.E.2d 707 (Ohio 1945). This rule has given way in many jurisdictions to the view that all damages from a single incident must be sought in a single suit. See *Rush v. City of Maple Heights*, 147 N.E.2d 599 (Ohio), *cert. denied*, 358 U.S. 814 (1958) (effectively overruling *Vasu*).

4. Rizzuto's problem here is not dissatisfaction with the relief he obtained in the first action but difficulty in collecting it from the defendant. The fact that the defendant has not satisfied the judgment does not give the plaintiff the right to bring a second action on the original claim. Under res judicata theory, his claim is "merged into the judgment"; once he obtains the judgment, his right to sue on the original claim is replaced by a right to enforce the judgment. In most jurisdictions a judgment remains enforceable for many years, as long as an execution is issued promptly after judgment. See, e.g., Wis. Stat. Ann. §815.04 (20 years); S.D. Codified Laws Ann. §15-18-1 (20 years). There is no need for Rizzuto to bring a new suit and relitigate matters already settled in his favor. When Rizzuto learns that Allston is in a position to pay, he should seek execution on the original judgment or bring an action on the judgment in another state where Allston has assets that can be taken on execution. See Chapter 3, pp. 49-51.

5. This is a hard case indeed. Here Rizzuto sought all his known damages in his original suit but did not seek recovery for a potential future consequence of the injury. Naturally when that consequence arises he feels entitled to compensation for it as well. And since res judicata only bars claims that could have been joined in the original action, he has a good argument for a new action.

Rizzuto's position is certainly sympathetic, but it has generally been rejected by the courts. Imagine the havoc that would result if plaintiffs could relitigate claims whenever their disabilities or medical expenses turned out to be greater than expected at the time of trial. Judgments would never be final because they would be subject to revision in the light of future events. Defendants would be unable to rely on the finality of judgments in planning their future conduct and estimating their liabilities. In most cases the benefit of providing full relief based on subsequent evidence would be far outweighed by the burden of renewed litigation and the uncertainty that would result.

Consequently, the usual rule is that a plaintiff must recover for all her damages in the original action, including those suffered prior to trial and all future damages that are reasonably likely to ensue. Restatement (Second) of Judgments §25, comment c. Here, for example, Rizzuto should have presented evidence in his original suit that victims of this type of eye injury are likely to develop headaches. The jury could then have assessed additional damages based on this probable consequence of the injury. Admittedly, this is a very rough measure of Rizzuto's actual damages, but it is the best that the system can do without retrying Rizzuto's case repeatedly in future years.[3]

A related problem arises in many asbestos personal injury cases. Frequently, the plaintiff sues and recovers for asbestosis caused by exposure to asbestos, and later — often many years later — develops cancer. Under strict res judicata doctrine, a second suit for the cancer is barred. This is a hard result, in view of the long latency period for the cancer (often 30 to 35 years from date of exposure) and the uncertainty as to whether it will develop at all. Some courts have allowed the plaintiff to bring a second action in such circumstances, but there is no doubt that in doing so they are bending the traditional rules of claim preclusion. See, e.g., *Mauro v. Raymark Industries, Inc.*, 561 A.2d 257, 264-267 (N.J. 1989) (recognizing the right to bring a second action for cancer after prior recovery for asbestosis caused by the same exposure to asbestos); compare *Gideon v. Johns-Mansville Sales Corp.*, 761 F.2d 1129, 1136-1137 (5th Cir. 1985) (under Texas law asbestos victim must recover all resulting damages in a single action; see now *Pustejovsky v. Rapid-America Corp.*, 35 S.W. 3d 643 (Tex. 2000) (adopting "two disease" approach).

This so-called "two-disease" rule, which allows an asbestos plaintiff to sue for later-developing cancer even if she was previously aware of a separate injury from exposure (such as asbestosis), is now clearly the majority approach. See, e.g., *Sopha v. Owens-Corning Fiberglas Corp.*, 601 N.W.2d 627 (Wis. 1999); *Wilber v. Owens-Corning Fiberglass Corp.*, 476 N.W.2d 74 (Iowa 1991). It will be interesting to see whether this inroad on the traditional res judicata rules spreads to cases like Rizzuto's, where the later "injury" is not a separate disease, but simply an unexpected consequence of the first. Perhaps the myrmidon will turn out to be a cream puff after all.[4]

---

3. Rizzuto would have an alternative remedy if his headaches appeared within a year. See Fed. R. Civ. P. 60(b)(2), which allows a party to seek relief from the *original* judgment within one year on the ground that newly discovered evidence should be considered.

4. In *Faulkner v. Caledonia County Fair Assoc.*, 869 A.2d 103 (Vt. 2004), the plaintiff invoked these "two disease" decisions to avoid res judicata in a traditional personal injury case. Faulkner was hit on the head by a metal panel at the county fair and recovered $5,000 for her injuries. Eight years later she was diagnosed with epilepsy, evidently caused by the blow at the fair. Faulkner sued again and argued that this was a different injury, relying on *Pustejovsky* and other "two-disease" cases. In a myrmidon-ish decision, the Vermont Supreme Court distinguished these cases:

> the instant case involves a traumatic injury the consequences of which turned out to be more severe than they appeared at the time of plaintiff's first lawsuit, not two separate and distinct diseases or injuries. Therefore, the asbestos and similar workplace exposure cases are inapposite. . . . The instant case fits the "traumatic event/latent manifestation" profile — plaintiff's claim accrued when she suffered the blow to her head in 1991, and it is "immaterial" for claim preclusion purposes that her injuries turned out to be more severe than those for which she sought damages in her 1994 lawsuit. Restatement (Second) §25, comment c.

No cream puff yet.

## An Absurd Hypothetical

6. The four prerequisites for application of res judicata are not met here since the parties are not the same in the second action. Rizzuto was not a party in the first suit; though Allston was, both parties must be the same (or represented by the prior parties) for res judicata to apply. In addition, the "claim" is not the same in the second action. The rights of different plaintiffs to relief arising out of a single incident are not considered one "claim" simply because they arise out of one transaction or occurrence. Every potential plaintiff who suffers injury from a transaction or occurrence has a distinct claim for res judicata purposes. Here, for example, although Kubek's and Rizzuto's claims both arise out of the same incident, the two claims are distinct. The fact that Kubek has sued for his injuries does not bar Rizzuto from suing separately for his.

   If res judicata barred a second suit in a situation like this, all plaintiffs with claims arising out of a single incident would be forced to sue together. The usual rule in American courts is to the contrary: The "plaintiff is master of her claim" and may sue jointly with other plaintiffs (see Fed. R. Civ. P. 20(a)(1)) but need not. Even though he knew of Kubek's suit and appeared as a witness, Rizzuto still has the right to sue separately.

7. The advice that Rizzuto may sue separately on the contract claim without fear of the myrmidon is sound. Even though the contract claim had accrued at the time of the negligence suit (that is, the breach had occurred and Rizzuto had a right to sue on it), Rizzuto is not required to assert this claim in the negligence action. Under the Restatement definition of a single "claim," these are separate claims because they arise out of separate transactions. Restatement (Second) of Judgments §24. Rizzuto's first action was based on an accident on the playing field. His second is based on a separate transaction, the contract to promote Allston gloves on television.

   This example highlights several important points. First, it is important to understand that Rizzuto's right to sue separately on these claims is not based on the fact that one action is for tort and the other for contract. In many cases a plaintiff has a right to recover under both tort and contract theories, based on a single incident. In the Schulansky case, for example, Schulansky asserts contract and tort claims against the defendants, which both arise out of the construction of the addition on her house. See the Schulansky complaint infra p. 636. If either of these were left out, res judicata would bar Schulansky from suing on it separately. By contrast, Rizzuto may sue separately here because his contract claim arises from a different set of historical facts.

   Second, note that Rizzuto could have joined both of these unrelated claims in a single action under Fed. R. Civ. P. 18(a). It does not always follow that you must join claims in a single action simply because the Rules allow you to do so. See Chapter 27, which explores in more detail the relationship between res judicata and the joinder rules.

8. On these facts Rizzuto's second action will not be barred. At the time of his first suit Rizzuto did not have a claim for the second year's royalties. He can hardly be expected to predict future defaults and sue for them before they occur. Even though the two suits arise out of a single contract, the separate breaches in successive years are different occurrences that may be sued on separately.

That would not be true, however, if Rizzuto had waited until the end of the second year to sue. At that point, the royalties for both years had accrued, and the usual rule is that Rizzuto must sue for them all as a single debt due on an account. Friedenthal, Kane, and Miller at 669; Restatement (Second) of Judgments §24, comment d. Similarly, a landlord who sues a tenant for back rent must seek recovery for all months' rent due but not future defaults. This reflects the basic premise that res judicata bars all claims arising out of a single transaction or occurrence that could have been raised in the original action. But here, the claims for future nonpayment could not have been raised since the plaintiff has no right to sue for these claims until they accrue.

Although res judicata will not bar Rizzuto's second suit here, collateral estoppel will bar relitigation of issues that were litigated and decided in the first suit. For example, if the court held that the contract called for payment of all royalties at the 10 percent rate, Allston will be estopped from claiming that the rate should be 5 percent in the second action. See Chapter 28, p. 578.

9. If you focused carefully on the prerequisites for res judicata discussed in the Introduction, you should have concluded that the myrmidon will not bar Allston's suit against Rizzuto. As example 6 suggests, every separate party has a separate claim for res judicata purposes even though their claims arise out of the same incident. Thus, Allston's claim against Rizzuto is not the "same claim" as Rizzuto's claim against Allston, even though it arises out of the same transaction.

However, while traditional res judicata doctrine does not bar Allston's claim, many jurisdictions provide by court rule that counterclaims arising out of the same transaction or occurrence must be brought in the original action. See, e.g., Fed. R. Civ. P. 13(a)(1) (counterclaim is compulsory if it arises out of same transaction or occurrence as the opposing party's claim). If the defendant fails to join a compulsory counterclaim, she will then be barred from bringing it later, not because the common law res judicata doctrine applies, but in order to enforce the compulsory counterclaim rule. See Moore's §131.21[3][c][ii]. Under this approach, Allston's suit would be barred.

In a jurisdiction that does not have a compulsory counterclaim rule, Allston would remain free to assert its claim in a separate action. However, the crucial issues underlying its claim may have been decided in the original suit anyway. In this case, for example, the earlier action determined that Rizzuto had breached his contract. In Allston's separate action, collateral estoppel would bar Rizzuto from relitigating that issue.

## Judgment on the Merits

10. Res judicata does not apply here because the claim has never been decided on the merits. Although an actual hearing was held and testimony and argument heard, the issue under consideration was the power of the court to hear the action, not the substance of Rizzuto's claim. Since the court held that it lacked subject matter jurisdiction over the suit, it never reached the merits. Consequently, one of the prerequisites for res judicata is not met.

It would certainly be a hard rule if litigants in Rizzuto's position were barred from going to a second court after dismissal for lack of jurisdiction in the first. Under that approach, the second suit would be barred even though the first court never considered the merits of plaintiff's case and, in fact, never had the power to do so. To avoid this risk, the plaintiff would be forced to choose a court that definitely has jurisdiction, even though she would prefer to sue in another that may have it. The res judicata doctrine does not put the parties to such risks. The "on the merits" requirement assures that preliminary dismissals due to lack of jurisdiction or venue will not bar suit in another court that has the power to proceed.

11. In this case, although Rizzuto's claim has been resolved without trial, it has been decided on the merits. Summary judgment in Allston's favor was based on the court's conclusion that Rizzuto has no evidence to support his contention that his accident resulted from Allston's negligence, and therefore no jury could find for Rizzuto on the negligence issue. Because Rizzuto cannot prove an essential element of his claim, judgment for Allston is proper. This is "on the merits" because it represents an adjudication of Rizzuto's substantive claim for relief, not a preliminary issue. Similarly, a judgment as a matter of law under Rule 50 is given res judicata effect because it determines that the plaintiff's claim has so little "merit" that no reasonable jury could uphold it. Restatement (Second) of Judgments §19, comments g, h.

## Pendent or Independent?

12. Under the usual four prerequisites, Koufax's second action should be barred since he is suing the same defendant again on a claim arising out of the same events as the suit. The procedural quirk here, however, is that Koufax could not have included the federal copyright claim in the state law action: The federal courts have exclusive jurisdiction over federal copyright claims under 28 U.S.C. §1338 (a).

    There is another twist in this example as well, which wasn't discussed in the Introduction. That is the question of which court's res judicata rules should apply: those of the federal court, where the second action is brought, or those of the state court, which rendered the original decision? This is a complex matter, but the basic answer is that the court hearing the second suit will ask whether a second suit would have been barred in the court system that rendered the original judgment. See generally Friedenthal, Kane, and Miller, §14.15. The second court will give "full faith and credit" to the first court's judgment by giving it the same res judicata effect it would have in the first court. So, in this case, the federal court would have to look to the preclusion law of the rendering state to decide whether the second action was barred.

    Most courts would hold that the second suit is not barred, where the claim asserted in that action could not have been asserted in the first. If the federal suit were barred here, Koufax would be forced to sue in federal court, to avoid losing his federal copyright claim by operation of res judicata. Consequently he would lose the chance to have the state court decide his state unfair competition claim. Most courts have concluded that it is better to allow the second action in such cases so as to avoid interfering with the authority of state courts to hear claims created by their own law. See Restatement (Second) of Judgments §26 (1)(c) and illustration 2.

13. When the first suit is brought in federal court, the situation is somewhat different. The state unfair competition claim is a state law claim that would be within the court's supplemental jurisdiction in the federal copyright suit. See 28 U.S.C. §1367(a); Chapter 16, example 1. However, under §1367(c) the court has discretion to hear or dismiss the supplemental claims. It might not have heard Koufax's state law claim even if he had asserted it in his federal suit.

    The general rule is that plaintiffs like Koufax who are in federal court must assert their supplemental claims or lose them by operation of res judicata. If the federal court entertains the state unfair competition claim, it will contribute to judicial efficiency and consistency of decisionmaking, two goals of the res judicata doctrine. If the court refuses to hear it, then Koufax will not be barred from suing separately on the claim in state court, since it could not be heard in the first action, and the plaintiff has therefore not had an opportunity to litigate that claim. All that Koufax can do is ask; if he does and the court refuses, he is protected. If he doesn't ask, the potential benefits of joint litigation are lost through his own neglect, and the myrmidon will be characteristically unsympathetic.

By the way, it is worth noting that res judicata is an affirmative defense that must be pleaded by the party asserting that the second action is barred. Fed. R. Civ. P. 8(c). If it is not pleaded, the case may go forward. Given the fact that claim preclusion protects not only the parties but the courts themselves, it seems appropriate that the court itself should have the authority to bar relitigation by raising the defense *sua sponte*. I haven't researched the point, but wouldn't be surprised to find cases supporting that view. Even if the court cannot dismiss *sua sponte* on res judicata grounds, judges are practical people who should have little trouble throwing a hint to the party with an incentive to assert the defense that she should do so.

## "The Game Ain't Over 'til It's Over"

14. Assuming that the New York courts, like federal courts, give res judicata effect to dismissals for failure to state a claim, Berra's second action will be barred, unless the subsequent change in the substantive law provides a basis to avoid the usual effect of res judicata.

This subsequent change in the law will not allow Berra to start a new action. Parties are not entitled to have their cases decided under the law as it will be at some future time; each case must be decided under the law at the time it is considered. See Moore's at §131.21 [2]. Imagine the confusion that would ensue if parties could bring new suits if the law changed after they lost a case. Finality of judgments would be meaningless since cases might be reopened (or nullified by the results in a later suit) at some indeterminate time in the future. How long would parties have to reopen the judgment? How much later could the law change and still be applied to a previously decided case?

Clearly, such a principle, even if circumscribed by some form of statute of limitations, would undermine two goals of the res judicata doctrine: judicial economy and certainty of judgments. Besides, rules may be fair at the time they are applied even though they change later, when conditions have changed. See Chapter 10, p. 182 (suggesting that Athenians of one generation may choose to live under different laws than those of their predecessors). Better to leave it at that than to undermine the finality of judgments by reconsidering them every time the underlying substantive law is reconsidered.

If Berra believed that the physical injury rule should be overruled, he should have appealed on that ground instead of waiting for a future plaintiff to carry the laboring oar. Perhaps the New York Court of Appeals would have changed the rule in his case instead of the next one sixteen months down the line. See, for a similar holding, *Federated Department Stores, Inc. v. Moitie*, 452 U.S. 394 (1981).

15. There is a crucial difference between this case and the last. Here, Berra's first action is still going on. Although he lost in the trial court under the old approach to intentional infliction, he has taken his appeal and asked the higher court to change the rule. If the court had not adopted the new rule in the other case raising the issue, it presumably would have done so in his. He should not be disadvantaged by the fact that the appeal in the other case was heard first. Consequently, the general rule is that the court will apply the law as it stands when the pending appeal is decided, not the law as it stood at the time of trial. The dismissal of Berra's case will be reversed, and it will be sent back for trial on the merits.

16. If Berra could get the trial judge to reopen the original action, it would undermine the finality of the judgment just as clearly as allowing a new action would in example 14. Instead of starting a new suit, he could simply revive the old one and ask the court to retry the case under the new state of the law. The majority rule in the federal courts, therefore, appears to be that the court may not grant relief from judgment due to a change in the substantive law once the period for appeal has passed. See, e.g., *Morris v. Adams-Millis Corp.*, 758 F.2d 1352, 1358-1359 (10th Cir. 1985); cf. *De Weerth v. Baldinger*, 38 F.3d 1266 (2d Cir. 1994) (reaching same result in diversity case after clarification of applicable state law). But see *Adams v. Merrill, Lynch, Pierce, Fenner & Smith*, 888 F.2d 696, 702 (10th Cir. 1989) (in Tenth Circuit, Supreme Court change in law warrants relief from judgment); *Sprou v. Union Texas Products Corp.*, 944 F.2d 911 (10th Cir. 1991).

17. Strictly speaking, res judicata doesn't apply here at all: Fred has not brought a new action based on the same claim as before. Instead, he has moved to reopen the judgment in the first action and get the decree in that action changed. However, the motion does compromise several of the values protected by res judicata. It requires the court to revisit a case previously settled by the judgment, and it unsettles the expectations of the parties.

    As an equitable doctrine, however, res judicata must sometimes step aside in deference to other values. Where a judgment has prospective application (that is, it doesn't simply order payment of a dollar judgment but governs the ongoing future conduct of the parties), the court must retain authority to modify its orders in light of changed conditions. Here, for example, it may be entirely appropriate to adjust the child support payments in light of high inflation and increases in Martha's income. The power to do so is quite generally recognized. See Restatement (Second) of Judgments §73 (power to modify judgment in light of "substantial change in the circumstances" that would make it unjust to continue the prior judgment in effect).

## Double Plays

18. a. This action is barred. It arises from the same transaction as the first—the construction of the addition. Schulansky has simply switched legal theories.

   b. This one is barred too; again, it arises from the same construction work, but simply asserts a different type of damage caused by that work.

   c. This one arises from a separate transaction, the work on her house in Massachusetts. Even though it had accrued at the time she brought her first action against Ronan, she was not required to assert it in that action, since it is not the "same claim" as her claim for damages for the New Hampshire job.

   d. This claim is also barred by res judicata. It is a claim against Ronan for damages for the New Hampshire job. Schulansky has switched theories, but the underlying transaction for which she seeks a remedy is the same as in her first suit.

   e. This one would be barred too. Schulansky will presumably argue that she bases her claim on Ronan's prior misrepresentations, not the addition work. But Schulansky's complaint is still based on the construction work on her New Hampshire house. Even though the transaction may have arisen because of earlier misrepresentations, the basic focus is the same set of events as the earlier claim. Res judicata forces Schulansky's lawyers to assert all claims arising from that work at the same time, to avoid multiple suits over the same events. The effect of the doctrine would be undermined (excuse the pun) if she could argue that this action was based on earlier acts of Ronan which led to the defective work on the house.

     Consider the problem if this were not barred. A plaintiff could sue a defendant for injuries suffered in an auto accident, claiming that the defendant had failed to signal a turn. If she lost, she could sue her again for negligence in fixing her brakes a month before the accident. There would be as many "claims" as there were earlier acts which arguably contributed to the ultimate injury. Better to take a broader view of the meaning of a "transaction" to include prior acts that lead up to the accident than to open that can of worms.

f. Here the myrmidon steps aside. Jones is a different party whom Schulansky has not sued before; she is free to sue him in a separate action. However, collateral estoppel may bar her from proving that his backhoe work caused the subsidence since she litigated and lost on the issue before.

# Res Judicata and the Rules of Joinder

## When Does *May* Mean *Must?*

---

## INTRODUCTION

In any reasonable civil procedure world, there ought to be a close relationship between the parties' right to join claims in their first lawsuit and the scope of res judicata in subsequent suits between them. If, for example, the rules of joinder did not allow plaintiffs to join counts for property damage and personal injury in a single lawsuit, it would be a rigid system indeed that barred an accident plaintiff who had sued for damage to his car in one suit from bringing a separate action to recover for his personal injuries in the accident. Similarly, if the joinder rules limited a plaintiff to proceeding on a single theory, such as negligence, in his first suit, it would be unfair to bar him from starting a second action on a strict liability theory. One way or another, the system ought to offer parties a chance to have all of their claims heard, either through limited claims in multiple suits or multiple claims in a single suit.

The early English common law followed the first course, allowing multiple actions on different theories or seeking different relief. Under the common law system, the rigid limitations on joinder of claims frequently prevented plaintiffs from seeking full relief in a single action. For example, a plaintiff who sued at law for damages for trespass could not get an injunction against further trespasses in the same suit; he had to go to an equity court for that. Because the plaintiff was forced by these limitations to split his cause of action, the preclusion rules did not bar him from bringing the second action even though it arose out of the same occurrence as the first.

The federal courts (and many state systems as well) have chosen the second course, allowing many claims to be heard in a single action. This approach is implemented by extremely broad rules governing pleading and joinder. See Rules 8(a)(3), 8(d)(3), 13, 14, 18, 20. Under these liberal joinder rules, plaintiffs have broad power to join all their theories of recovery in their initial suit. Consequently, they will seldom be able to argue that they should be allowed to start a new action based on the same occurrence because they were unable to assert an omitted claim in the first suit.

For example, Fed. R. Civ. P. 18(a) allows the plaintiff to join virtually all possible theories of recovery in a single action. It is hardly unreasonable therefore to hold that res judicata bars him from suing later on any theory that is omitted from the first suit. In this situation the *may* of the rules clearly means *must* when the effects of res judicata are considered. If Elbers sues Doe Chemical Company for negligently manufacturing a drug, Rule 18(a) allows but does not require him to assert a separate strict liability claim against Doe based on the same events. See also Fed. R. Civ. P. 8(d)(3) (authorizing alternative or inconsistent pleading). However, if Elbers leaves out the strict liability claim, res judicata will bar him from asserting it in a later action. This is simply another theory of recovery for the same injuries already sued upon, and any claims arising from that occurrence that are not joined in Elber's first action will be barred by res judicata. See Chapter 26, example 2.

There are a few instances, despite Rule 18(a), when initial joinder of a particular claim is not available. In such cases the res judicata myrmidon[1] grudgingly steps aside to allow the plaintiff to reenter the courthouse door. Suppose, for example, that Allen sues Moser in state court under a state unfair competition statute. Suppose further that Allen might also recover against Moser for patent infringement, a federal claim over which the federal courts have exclusive jurisdiction. Here, Allen could not have included his federal theory in the first state court action because the federal courts have exclusive jurisdiction over patent claims. Consequently, he will usually not be barred from asserting the patent claim in a later suit. See generally Restatement (Second) of Judgments §26(1)(c).

It would make life a lot easier for civil procedure students, as well as for practicing lawyers, if it were invariably true that every claim that could have been joined in the initial action will be barred in a later action. Alas, though this would be neat and symmetrical, it just isn't so. Although *theories* that could have been joined are generally barred, the scope of permissible

---

1. For a natural history of this creature, see Chapter 26, n.1.

joinder of *parties* is much broader than the dimensions of a single "claim" for res judicata purposes. Thus, in many cases, claims against additional parties could be joined under the Rules but will not be barred by res judicata if they are not.

For example, if Fellows is involved in a three-car collision with Rich and Rontowski, he could sue them as codefendants in a single lawsuit. Fed. R. Civ. P. 20(a)(1). However, he doesn't *have* to: If he sues Rich alone, he is not precluded from suing Rontowski later in a separate action. A plaintiff's rights to recover from separate defendants are considered distinct "claims" under res judicata analysis, even though they arise out of the same occurrence. In addition, the "same parties" requirement of res judicata is not met in such cases since the defendants differ in the two actions.

This is puzzling at first, but if it were not true, the res judicata rules would convert permissive joinder under the Rules into compulsory joinder. Rule 20(a)(1) says that Fellows *may* choose to sue Rich and Rontowski together. Clearly, the rulemakers have chosen to allow him to sue them jointly but also have given him the option not to. This reflects the traditional precept that the "plaintiff is master of his claim," free to choose when and where to sue each potential defendant. But, if res judicata barred Fellows from suing Rontowski because he had previously sued Rich without joining Rontowski, the *may* of Rule 20(a) would be converted to *must* by the preclusion rules: Fellows would be forced to sue them both in the first action. Although such a compulsory joinder of parties rule might make sense from an efficiency point of view, the rulemakers have favored freedom of choice over efficiency.[2] And the res judicata rules should be crafted to protect that policy decision.

This principle, that claims against different parties need not be joined even if the rules would allow it, does not prevent the first action from having some preclusive effect, however. If Fellows loses his suit against Rich on the ground that he was contributorily negligent, Rontowski may be able to invoke collateral estoppel to establish Fellows's negligence if Fellows subsequently sues him. See *Blonder-Tongue Laboratories, Inc. v. University of Illinois Foundation*, 402 U.S. 313 (1971); Chapter 29, pp. 598-599. Certainly, this inhibits Fellows's freedom of choice to some extent, since he cannot start his action against Rontowski with a completely clean slate.

The following examples will help you sort out the relationship between the joinder and res judicata rules. Assume that all actions are brought in federal court, that subject matter jurisdiction is proper in each case, and that the broad "transactional" test of the Second Restatement of Judgments applies. Consider in each case whether the omitted claim could

---

2. Some of the reasons for that choice are discussed in Chapter 13, example 1.

have been joined under the rules and, if so, whether res judicata will bar the second action.

## Examples

### A Few Warm-Ups

1. Roosevelt is hit by a car while walking across Park Avenue in New York City. The only occupants of the car were Kefauver and Warren, but each denies that he was driving. Roosevelt sues Kefauver, a Tennessee citizen, in the federal court for the Middle District of Tennessee. She loses. Now Roosevelt sues Warren, a New Yorker, in the Southern District of New York.
   a. Could Roosevelt have joined Kefauver and Warren in the first action?
   b. Is Roosevelt's second suit barred?

2. Roosevelt sues Kefauver in the Tennessee federal court for battery, based on the collision on Park Avenue. The jury finds that Kefauver did not hit Roosevelt intentionally, and judgment is entered for Kefauver. Subsequently, Roosevelt sues Kefauver in the Southern District of New York for negligently injuring her in the collision.
   a. Could Roosevelt have joined the negligence claim in the first suit?
   b. Is the second suit barred by res judicata?

3. Roosevelt sues Kefauver for battery and for negligence based on the accident. She later sues Kefauver again in the same court for a breach of contract that took place before the accident.
   a. Could Roosevelt have joined the contract claim in the first action?
   b. Is the second suit precluded by res judicata?

4. Stanton sues Anthony for her injuries in a two-car collision and recovers $17,000. Now, Blatch, a passenger in Stanton's car, sues Anthony for her injuries in the collision.
   a. Could Stanton and Blatch have joined as coplaintiffs in the first action?
   b. Could Blatch have intervened in Stanton's suit against Anthony? See Fed. R. Civ. P. 24.
   c. Is Blatch barred by res judicata from bringing her suit?

### A Hybrid Case

5. Grasso sues Adams for breach of contract, arising out of a contract for the delivery of livestock to Grasso. Grasso loses. Subsequently, Adams sues Grasso for breach of the contract, seeking to collect the balance due under the contract.
   a. Could Adams have joined his contract claim in the original action?
   b. Is Adams's action against Grasso barred by res judicata?

6. After Grasso sues Adams for breach of the livestock contract, could Adams start a separate action against Grasso on an unrelated fraud claim that accrued before the contract dispute?

7. Grasso sues Adams Pharmacy and Johnson Drug Co. for personal injuries suffered as a result of using a drug made by Johnson and sold to her by Adams. She recovers judgment for $35,000 against each defendant. Adams pays the judgment and then sues Johnson for indemnification, claiming that since the negligent manufacture of the drug caused Grasso's injuries, Adams should be indemnified by Johnson for the damages it paid to Grasso.
   a. Could the claim have been asserted in the first action?
   b. Is Adams barred from bringing the second suit?

## A Myrmidon in the Labyrinth

8. Assume that Grasso sued Adams Pharmacy alone on the drug claim and recovered. Now Adams sues Johnson for indemnification.
   a. Could Adams have asserted this claim in the original action?
   b. Is its action against Johnson precluded?

9. Smith, from South Dakota, sues Bryan, from Minnesota, for breach of a contract to construct a home for him. Smith claims that the foundation of the house was improperly poured. Bryan impleads Coolidge, a South Dakota subcontractor who poured the foundation, for indemnification. The court holds that the foundation meets the specifications, and therefore judgment is entered for Bryan on the main claim and for Coolidge on the third-party claim. Subsequently, Bryan sues Coolidge to collect the wages of five laborers Bryan had lent to Coolidge to help him perform the foundation work.
   a. Could Bryan have asserted the wage claim in the first action?
   b. Is the second suit barred by res judicata?

10. Assume the same facts as example 9, but that the claim Bryan asserted in the second action was for a previous breach of another contract between him and Coolidge.
    a. Could Bryan have asserted the second contract claim in the first action?
    b. Is he barred from bringing it in the second suit?

11. On the same facts as example 9, assume that Smith sues Bryan on the foundation claim, and that Bryan impleads Coolidge. The case is tried and Smith loses, since the jury finds that the work was properly done. Now, Coolidge sues Smith, the owner, seeking the price of his foundation work on a quantum meruit theory.
    a. Could Coolidge have asserted this claim in the first suit?

b. Would the court have had subject matter jurisdiction over this claim in the first action?

c. Is Coolidge's suit against Smith barred by res judicata?

## When Does *May Not* Mean *Must?*

12. Suppose that Smith sued Bryan for breach of the contract, as a result of defects in the foundation. Three years into the suit, when the parties have completed discovery and trial is imminent, Smith moves to amend the complaint to assert a second claim against Bryan for negligence, on the ground that the foundation was inadequately poured. The court denies the motion to amend on the ground that it is untimely, since it could have been asserted earlier in the suit, and allowance of the motion would delay the trial and prejudice Bryan's ability to prepare his defense. See *Foman v. Davis*, 371 U.S. 178, 181-182 (1962) (delay in seeking amendment and prejudice to opponent may justify denial of leave to amend).

The breach of contract claim is tried and Smith loses. He then brings a second action against Bryan, asserting only the negligence claim. (Assume that the applicable statute of limitations is six years, so that the action is not yet barred on this ground.) Bryan pleads res judicata.

a. If you represented Smith, how would you argue that the second action is not barred by res judicata?

b. How will the judge rule on the res judicata defense?

## Explanations

### A Few Warm-Ups

1. Joinder:   Yes      Res judicata:   No

a. This is a simple case of one plaintiff who has claims against two defendants. Rule 20(a)(2) allows Roosevelt to sue them together because the claims arise from the same accident and will involve the common issue of who was driving the car. However, Rule 20(a)(2) does not require Roosevelt to sue the defendants together; the rule says *may* and means it. In this case Roosevelt might have been well advised to sue them jointly. As it is, the first jury may conclude that Warren was driving, and the second that Kefauver was, leaving Roosevelt a double loser. For one reason or another, Roosevelt has chosen to take that risk, as the joinder rules allow her to do.

b. Roosevelt's second action is not barred because her claim against Warren is distinct from her claim against Kefauver, and they are not the same parties. If res judicata did bar the second action, it would force Roosevelt to sue the two defendants together, thus undermining the choice given to Roosevelt by the rules. Consider the consequences that such a result would have for Roosevelt's case. It is unlikely that she could get personal jurisdiction over Warren in Tennessee for this New York accident. Consequently, if the res judicata rules forced her to sue the two together, Roosevelt would lose her choice of forum against Kefauver. She would be forced to sue in New York, where she could obtain personal jurisdiction over both defendants because the claim arose there.

This is another example of the intricate interrelations of various civil procedure doctrines. A change in this aspect of the res judicata rules would directly affect the joinder rules and the choice of forum rules. The rulemakers have chosen to preserve one value — the plaintiff's right to choose his forum against each defendant — and have had to mold the related joinder and preclusion rules accordingly.

As indicated in the Introduction, however, it is still possible that the first suit will affect the second if the court in the second action allows Warren to invoke nonmutual collateral estoppel to bar relitigation of any issues decided against Roosevelt in the first.

2. Joinder:    Yes    Res judicata:    Yes
   a. The issue here is joinder of "claims" (in the sense of theories of recovery) rather than joinder of parties. Rule 18(a), the epitome of liberality, allows a plaintiff to join any claims he has against a defending party. But again, the rule is permissive; under Rule 18(a) Roosevelt has the option but is not required to join the negligence claim in the first action.
   b. The myrmidon[3] will stubbornly resist Roosevelt's efforts to bring this second action. Joinder of these "claims" may be permissive under the rules but is made mandatory by the res judicata principles applied in the federal courts. Under those principles, all theories for recovery arising out of a single transaction constitute a single "claim" for preclusion purposes. See Chapter 26, pp. 543-544. A party who seeks relief based on a particular set of historical facts must join all his grounds for recovery on those facts in the first action or face the res judicata defense if he tries to sue later on one of these grounds. Thus, Roosevelt's second suit for negligence will be barred even though Rule 18(a) appears to give her the option to join or withhold it in the first action. Here, unlike the joinder-of-parties situation in example 1, the preclusion doctrine demands what the rule merely permits.

---

3. I will drop this metaphor eventually. There's no point in beating a dead myrmidon.

It makes no difference that Roosevelt's second action is brought in a different court. Under full faith and credit principles, each court within the system will honor the judgments of its sister courts by giving them full res judicata effect. See Friedenthal, Kane, and Miller, 4th. ed. §14.15.

3. Joinder:   Yes      Res judicata:   No

a. Rule 18(a) authorizes joinder of "claims," both in the sense of different theories arising out of the same events and also completely unrelated claims arising out of completely separate events. Thus, Roosevelt could have joined her contract claim with her other claims in the first action even though it arises from a separate transaction.

b. Roosevelt's second action is not barred. Unlike example 2, in which the omitted "claim" simply asserted a different theory of recovery for the same incident litigated in the first suit, the contract claim here arose out of a separate incident from the negligence and battery claims. Roosevelt's prior suit based on the accident will bar all future suits against Kefauver based on that accident but not other suits based on separate events.

Thus Roosevelt is free to bring a separate action on the contract claim even though she could have joined it in the first suit. Here, the *may* of the rule does not mean *must* under res judicata because the claim does not satisfy the res judicata definition of a single "claim." See Restatement (Second) of Judgments §24 (single claim under res judicata analysis includes all grounds for relief arising out of a single transaction).

4. Joinder:   Yes      Intervention:   Maybe      Res judicata:   No

a. Rule 20(a)(1) authorizes, but does not require, Stanton and Blatch to sue jointly since they seek relief arising from the same occurrence, and their claims will involve a number of common questions of law or fact, including the central question of the cause of the accident.

b. Blatch could at least have tried to intervene under Rule 24(b) since her claim and Stanton's will involve a common question of fact — whether Anthony's negligence caused the accident. But intervention under Rule 24(b) is permissive; the court might have declined to allow Blatch into the suit for a variety of reasons.

It is unlikely that Blatch could have intervened in Stanton's suit as a matter of right under Rule 24(a). She will not be prejudiced by the Stanton/Anthony litigation unless she will be barred from bringing her own action against Anthony. As explained immediately below, she will not be barred from doing so. In addition, even if Blatch meets the criteria for intervention as of right, she is still under no duty to intervene. Rule 24(a) authorizes intervention as of right but does not force parties to intervene even when they would have a right to do so. Last, there may be jurisdictional problems if there is not complete diversity among the parties. See 28 U.S.C. §1367(b) (barring supplemental jurisdiction over claims by intervening plaintiffs in diversity cases if inconsistent with requirements of §1332).

c. Blatch's suit against Anthony is not precluded by Stanton's because she is a different party from the original parties and because her claim against Anthony is not the same as Stanton's claim against Anthony. Thus, two of the prerequisites to res judicata are not met. While Blatch had several avenues for getting into the first action, they are both permissive, and *may* is not converted to *must* here because the separate requirements for preclusion are not met. See *Martin v. Wilkes*, 490 U.S. 755, 761-762 (1989) (non-party not bound by judgment in suit involving others).

Blatch may obtain some benefit from Stanton's action, however: Because Stanton has proved Anthony's negligence, Blatch may be able to invoke offensive nonmutual collateral estoppel to bar Anthony from relitigating the issue. See Chapter 29, pp. 599-601.

## A Hybrid Case

5. Joinder: Yes    Res judicata: In a way

   a. Adams's claim for the payments due under the contract was a compulsory counterclaim in the first action since it arose out of the same events as Grasso's original claim. Under Fed. R. Civ. P. 13(a), Adams was *required* to assert this claim in the original action. The drafters of Rule 13(a) decided that the gain in litigation efficiency from hearing a defendant's related claims in the original action outweighed the defendant's usual right to choose his own forum. Consequently, they required such related claims to be asserted in the original action.

   b. The rulemakers' goal will only be achieved if Adams is barred from suing separately on the omitted counterclaim. Under traditional res judicata doctrine, however, Adams would not be precluded from suing separately on this claim because Adams's claim against Grasso is not the "same claim" as Grasso's claim against him. However, the courts have barred parties in Adams's position from suing separately on the omitted counterclaim, simply to enforce the policy underlying the compulsory counterclaim rule. This form of "rule-based res judicata" applies even though the same claim requirement of res judicata is not met. See Friedenthal, Kane, and Miller 4th ed. §14.6.

   In some state systems counterclaims are not compulsory, even if they arise out of the same transaction as the main claim. In those systems Adams would not be barred from starting a second action on the counterclaim. However, such jurisdictions sometimes hold that a party waives his right to sue separately on an omitted counterclaim if the same issues were raised defensively in the prior action. Id.

6. In this example, Adams's claim was available at the time of the original action and could have been joined as a permissive counterclaim under Rule 13(b). However, Adams was not required to join it in the first suit, and it will not be barred by res judicata if he omits it. By definition, a permissive counterclaim arises out of a separate transaction from the main claim. See Fed. R. Civ. P. 13(b). Thus, it is not part of the "same claim" as the plaintiff's claim, nor is it barred by rule-based preclusion, as a compulsory counterclaim would be. Here, *may* really means *may*; Adams's fraud claim will not be barred.

   If the claim were barred by res judicata if omitted from the first action, the preclusion rules would make permissive counterclaims compulsory, undermining the rulemakers' choice and raising serious jurisdictional problems in many federal cases.

7. Joinder: Yes    Res judicata: No
   a. Adams could have joined this indemnification claim as a cross-claim in the original action, under Rule 13(g). That authorizes but does not require a defendant to assert any related claim he has against a codefendant in the original action.
   b. Res judicata will not bar Adams from seeking indemnification from Johnson in a second suit. Under the res judicata analysis, Adams's claim against Johnson is not the same as Grasso's claim against Adams, so that Grasso's suit does not bar Adams from suing Johnson separately. Again, this result is consistent with the policy of the Rules. The rulemakers have chosen to make cross-claims permissive. See Fed. R. Civ. P. 13(g). If res judicata barred subsequent assertion of omitted cross-claims they would effectively be compulsory.

      Compulsory cross-claims actually might not be a bad idea. As long as all the parties are already in the case, why not force them to litigate all claims among them arising out of the same transaction? The Rules make defendants do so under Rule 13(a) but draw the line at forcing the assertion of other related claims such as cross-claims and third-party claims.

## A Myrmidon in the Labyrinth

8. Joinder: Yes    Res judicata: No
   a. Adams could have impleaded Johnson for indemnification under Rule 14(a)(1) since Adams seeks recovery from Johnson for the damages Grasso seeks from it.

b. If Adams is free to refrain from asserting this claim against Johnson in the last example, in which they are both already in the suit, it should similarly be free not to implead Johnson when sued by Grasso. Impleader is permissive, and Adams is free to sue Johnson separately for indemnification instead if it prefers. Res judicata will not bar the suit.

Tactically, it may be preferable to implead Johnson to prevent the risk of inconsistent judgments, but Adams may have reasons for failing to do so, such as lack of personal jurisdiction over Johnson. It would certainly be inappropriate to force Adams to join Johnson if it couldn't obtain personal jurisdiction over Johnson. Such problems were undoubtedly in the minds of the rulemakers when they decided not to make Rule 14 impleader claims compulsory.

However, if Adams did implead Johnson, res judicata obviously would bar it from bringing a separate action against Johnson on the same claim. Further, Johnson may be able to invoke collateral estoppel in the second action on issues decided against Adams in the first.

9. Joinder: Yes    Res judicata: Yes
    a. Bryan could have asserted this claim against Coolidge under Rule 18(a), which provides that a party seeking relief from an opposing party may assert as many claims as he has against that opposing party. Granted, Bryan could not have impleaded Coolidge on the basis of this claim alone because it does not satisfy the Rule 14(a)(1) requirement that Coolidge may be liable to Bryan for all or part of the plaintiff's claim. See Chapter 14, pp. 271-272. Once Bryan has properly impleaded Coolidge on the indemnification claim, however, he may assert whatever claims he has against Coolidge, related or unrelated.

    Of course, there would also have to be a basis for subject matter jurisdiction over Bryan's additional claim for it to be asserted in the original action. The supplemental jurisdiction statute, 28 U.S.C. §1367, provides a basis for jurisdiction, since Bryan's wage claim arises from the same foundation work as the main claim brought by Smith. (There may not even be a need to invoke §1367, since the parties to the wage claim are diverse and Bryan may aggregate his claims against Coolidge. If Bryan sought more than $75,000 in damages on the combined claims the amount-in-controversy requirement would be met, and the court would have jurisdiction based on diversity.)

    b. Assuming that there was subject matter jurisdiction over the wage claim in the original suit, res judicata will bar Bryan from suing on the claim later. Res judicata applies not only to a plaintiff who has asserted claims against a defendant, but to other parties in the suit who have asserted claims. Here, Bryan has asserted a claim against Coolidge by impleading him on the foundation claim. Having done so, the res judicata rules require him to assert all claims he has against Coolidge arising out of that transaction. Bryan omitted the wage claim, which also arose from the construction of the foundation, and he is therefore barred from asserting it in a new action.

Bryan had the option not to implead Coolidge at all, in which case he could have asserted the indemnification and wage claims in a separate suit (but not in two separate suits). However, once he has joined issue with Coolidge on claims arising out of the foundation work, he must assert all his claims arising from it in that suit. Although Rule 18(a) says he *may* assert his related wage claim, the res judicata rules convert that to *must* in this situation.[4]

10. Joinder: Maybe     Res judicata: No
   a. As in example 9, Rule 18(a) authorizes Bryan to assert this claim along with his third-party indemnification claim. Here, of course, the claim is completely unrelated to the impleader claim, but Rule 18 doesn't seem to care. However, there would not be supplemental jurisdiction over this claim since it arises from an unrelated contract breach. Bryan would have to establish independent jurisdiction over the added claim based on diversity. He might have been able to do so, if the impleader claim and the unrelated claim together sought more than $75,000 in damages.[5]
   b. Bryan is not barred from suing separately on this claim, since the claim asserted in the second action does not arise out of the same transaction as the impleader claim against Coolidge in the first suit. Therefore, it does not satisfy the "same claim" requirement of res judicata, and Bryan was not required to assert it in the prior action.

   If Bryan were forced to join this unrelated claim, the symmetry of the res judicata and jurisdiction rules would be lost. The court would not have supplemental jurisdiction over the unrelated claim, since it is not part of the same "case or controversy" under §1367(a). If there were no independent basis for subject matter jurisdiction, Bryan would be forced by the preclusion rules to join this claim but prevented by the jurisdiction rules from doing so.

---

4. Of course, if jurisdiction were based on 28 U.S.C. §1367, the court might have declined to exercise jurisdiction, in its discretion, under §1367(c). If the first court had refused to hear the wage claim, then it would not be barred in a later suit. See Chapter 26, pp. 557-558.
5. Remember, a single claimant can aggregate amounts on separate claims against a single defendant to meet the amount-in-controversy requirement. See Chapter 5, example 12b.

11. a. Yes. Rule 14(a)(2)(D) authorizes (but does not require) a third-party defendant to assert claims against the plaintiff if they arise out of the same transaction or occurrence as the main claim. Since Coolidge's claim arises from the foundation work this test is satisfied. Visually, the case would look like the diagram in Figure 27-1.

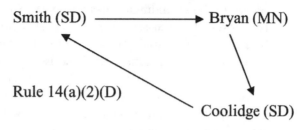

**Figure 27-1.**

   b. Yes. Although there is no diversity, §1367(a) would authorize supplemental jurisdiction over this claim, since it arises from the same dispute as the main claim. And §1367(b) does not bar the claim, since it is not a claim by a plaintiff. See Chapter 16, example 9.

   c. Coolidge's suit is not barred. Because he never asserted any claim against Smith in suit one, and assertion of the claim was permissive under Rule 14, he is free to save this claim and sue on it separately. Note that this claim was not a counterclaim in suit one, because he and Smith, while both parties in the first action, were not "opposing parties" in that action. So, Rule 13(a) did not require Coolidge to assert this claim against Smith in that suit. It might make sense to amend the Rules to force Coolidge to assert this claim in the initial action, but currently they don't. Consequently, it would be anomalous for the res judicata rules to bar the second action.

## When Does *May Not* Mean *Must*?

12. a. Ordinarily, Smith's negligence claim would be barred because it arose out of the same transaction as the breach of contract claim. However, Smith may argue that he should be allowed to bring a second action on the negligence claim because he tried to join it in the first action, but the court refused to hear it. The situation is roughly analogous to the case of supplemental claims, which must be asserted in the original action but will not be barred if the court refuses in its discretion to entertain them. See Chapter 26, example 13. Similarly, in this case Smith will argue that he sought but was

denied the right to assert the claim in the original suit and should therefore be allowed to resurrect it here.

b. Smith's argument is clever, but the analogy is a bit too rough to carry the day. Here, the negligence claim was disallowed because it was asserted in an untimely manner. Once Smith brought suit against Bryan, Smith had to assert all his claims properly in that action. Although the amendment rules are liberal, Smith has no right to hold back some claims arising from the construction and spring them on Bryan just before trial. At some point the defendant has a right to focus his trial preparation on those issues that have been properly placed in dispute and let the others go. See *Professional Management Assocs., Inc. v. KPMG-LLP*, 345 F.3d 1030 (8th Cir. 2003); 18 Wright & Miller §4412, text at n.44 ff. This claim will be barred because it arose from the same transaction as the original claim and was available to Smith if timely asserted in the first suit.

The irony here, of course, is that if Smith had waited for three years to bring the entire suit, he could have asserted all of his claims, since the limitations period had not expired. But, once the suit has been commenced and the case approaches trial, fairness to the defendant and the need to expedite litigation may prevent the assertion of additional claims even though they would not be barred by the statute of limitations. In this case, the court's refusal to allow Smith to amend means that the omitted claim is lost.

# Collateral Estoppel

## Fine-Tuning the Preclusion Doctrine

---

# INTRODUCTION

If law is a mysterious profession, it is partly because lawyers have such a knack for attaching intimidating names to relatively commonsense principles. Names such as "res judicata" and "collateral estoppel," for example; handles like these are enough to intimidate any client and most lawyers. But once you rub elbows with these related doctrines for a while, they will lose their power to intimidate, and you will recognize them for what they are, essential and sensible tools of the trade.

Although they serve related functions, these two tools are different in character. Res judicata acts like a bludgeon, indiscriminately smashing all efforts of a party to relitigate events that have already been litigated and decided in a prior suit. Collateral estoppel, by contrast, operates like a scalpel, dissecting a lawsuit into its various issues and surgically removing from reconsideration any that have been properly decided in a prior action.

Speaking less metaphorically, res judicata bars Smith from suing Jones for any kind of relief arising from a particular transaction or occurrence if Smith had previously brought an action against Jones based on that transaction or occurrence, and the prior action was decided on the merits. Restatement (Second) of Judgments §24 (1982).[1] Res judicata bars any

---

1. The discussion in this chapter is based on the principles of the Second Restatement of Judgments. These principles have been widely applied in the federal courts. See, e.g., *Montana v. United States*, 440 U.S. 147, 153, 162 (1979); *United States v. Stauffer Chemical Co.*, 464 U.S. 165, 171 (1984). They have been increasingly adopted by state courts as well.

relitigation of Smith's rights against Jones based on those events, including not only the claims that Smith did raise the first time around but also any other claims arising out of the same set of facts that Smith could have raised (but did not) in the first action.

Collateral estoppel is more narrowly focused. It only precludes Smith from relitigating issues that were actually litigated and decided in a prior action with Jones. If an issue could have been raised in the first case but was not explicitly raised and decided, collateral estoppel will not bar Smith from litigating that issue in a subsequent action against Jones.

An example will help to distinguish the two. Smith sues Jones for trespass on her property. Jones defends on the ground that she holds an easement to enter on the land to cut firewood. The court concludes that the easement is valid and enters judgment for Jones. Res judicata would bar Smith from suing Jones again based on the same wood-cutting incident. For example, Smith could not bring a new action on the theory that an implied condition of the easement was that Jones pay fair value for the timber cut. Nor could she seek damages for property damage done to her land during the cutting. When Smith sues Jones for that occurrence, res judicata forces her to bring forth all claims she has arising from it in the original action, rather than plaguing Jones with successive suits based on the same incident but asserting new theories for recovery or seeking different types of relief.

Collateral estoppel, by contrast, would bar Smith from relitigating specific issues decided in the first action, such as the validity of Jones's easement. If Jones returns to cut wood again on Smith's land and Smith sues, this second suit will not be barred by res judicata because she is not suing for the same incident as the original action. However, Smith will be collaterally estopped from trying again to prove that Jones's easement is invalid because that issue was litigated and decided in the original action. But Smith would be free to litigate other issues not resolved in the earlier action. For example, Smith could still claim in the later suit based on the second incident that an implied condition of the easement required payment for the timber. This issue would not be barred by collateral estoppel because it was not raised and decided in the first action.

At this point you may be asking, "Well, who needs collateral estoppel?" If res judicata so broadly precludes relitigation, whether or not an issue was previously raised, what is the need for a separate doctrine with another mysterious name?[2] The answer is that collateral estoppel is needed because issues already litigated may come up again in later litigation based on separate events. Smith's second action against Jones for the later woodcutting incident would not be barred by res judicata since this is a

---

2. With two mysterious names, actually. Collateral estoppel is also frequently referred to as "issue preclusion," and res judicata as "claim preclusion."

new "claim" that has not been litigated before. See Restatement (Second) of Judgments §24 (1982) (defining "claim" to include all rights arising out of a single transaction). But the issue of whether Smith has an easement to cut timber will arise again in the new action. Collateral estoppel will preclude litigation of that issue even though res judicata is inapplicable.

This example shows that collateral estoppel is both broader and narrower than res judicata. It is narrower in that it does not preclude all possible issues that might have been raised in a prior action but only those actually decided in that action. But it is also broader in that it can foreclose litigation of a particular issue in an entirely new context. Once the validity of Jones's easement has been determined between the parties, estoppel may preclude either party from relitigating that issue in suits arising out of completely different underlying facts. Suppose, for example, that Jones went to cut wood again on Smith's property and was injured when she fell in an abandoned well. Under common law negligence principles, the duty of care Smith owed to her might depend on whether she was a trespasser. In her negligence action Jones could estop Smith from defending on the ground that Jones was a trespasser, since the prior suit determined that the easement allowed her to enter the property. Although the context is different in the second action (in fact, the original plaintiff is now the defendant), Jones's right to be on the land is at issue in both suits and there is no reason to allow Smith to relitigate it.

## PREREQUISITES FOR ESTOPPEL

Collateral estoppel is a flexible doctrine, which varies in its application from one jurisdiction to another. However, the basic prerequisites are fairly uniform. First, the issue in the second case must be the same as the issue in the first. In the example above, the issue in both suits is whether Jones has a legal right to enter upon Smith's property to cut wood. But if Smith sues Jones for breach of a contract made in June of 2002, and Jones is held to have been incompetent to make the contract because she was a minor, it does not follow that Jones was incompetent to make another contract in October of 2004. Here, the issues are not the same, and the resolution of one should not preclude litigation on the other.

Second, the issue must have been actually litigated. Restatement (Second) of Judgments §27 (1982). This requirement will obviously not be satisfied when a party failed to raise an issue in a previous action, such as Smith failing to assert a right to be paid for the wood Jones cut in the first suit. But an issue may not have been "actually litigated" even though it *was* raised in a prior action. Suppose, for example, that Smith sues Jones for breach of contract and Jones admits in her answer that she made the contract but defends the action on another ground. Under the Restatement view, Jones may defend a second suit for a later breach of the same contract on the ground that she never made the contract, since she never actually litigated that issue in the original suit.

> There are many reasons why a party may choose not to raise an issue, or to contest an assertion, in a particular action. The action may involve so small an amount that litigation of the issue may cost more than the value of the lawsuit. Or the forum may be an inconvenient one in which to produce the necessary evidence or in which to litigate at all. The interests of conserving judicial resources, of maintaining consistency, and of avoiding oppression or harassment of the adverse party are less compelling when the issue on which preclusion is sought has not actually been litigated before. And if preclusive effect were given to issues not litigated, the result might serve to discourage compromise, to decrease the likelihood that the issues in an action would be narrowed by stipulation, and thus to intensify litigation.

Restatement (Second) of Judgments §27, comment e (1982).

Third, even if an issue was litigated in a prior action, collateral estoppel will not bar relitigation unless the issue was actually decided in that action. Restatement (Second) of Judgments §27 (1982). Suppose, for example, that Jones publishes a book that Smith claims to hold all rights to publish, and Smith sues Jones on copyright infringement and breach of contract theories. The case goes to trial on both issues. If the court finds for Smith on the ground that Jones breached the contract (and therefore does not decide the copyright issue), collateral estoppel will not bar relitigation of the copyright infringement issue in another context, even though both sides fully presented their evidence on the copyright issue in the first case. The parties have fully litigated the issue, and it seems wasteful to have them relitigate it in another suit. However, it is a little hard to apply collateral estoppel without knowing which party to estop. Without a winner or loser on the copyright issue, the court in the later action has no choice but to rehear it.

Fourth, it is usually said that collateral estoppel will not apply unless the decision on the issue in the prior action was necessary to the court's judgment. Restatement (Second) of Judgments §27 (1982). In the course of a suit, the judge may decide a number of issues that do not ultimately determine the outcome of the case. Here's a nice example: In *Balcom v. Lynn Ladder and Scaffolding Co. Inc.*, 806 F.2d 1127 (1st Cir. 1986), the plaintiff sued a scaffolding company for injuries suffered on a ladder. The defendant impleaded a ladder manufacturer, claiming that it had made the defective ladder and should indemnify the defendant for any damages awarded. The jury found that the manufacturer had built the ladder, and that the ladder was defective, but that the defect had not caused the plaintiff's injury. The First Circuit held that collateral estoppel would not bar the manufacturer from relitigating the issue of who made the ladder, since that finding was not "necessary to the judgment." The finding that had led to the verdict in the manufacturer's favor was the finding that the ladder did not cause the injury, not the finding that the manufacturer made the ladder. Because this latter finding did not affect the outcome of the suit, the manufacturer could not appeal it. Consequently, it should not be barred from relitigating the issue in a later action.

In other cases, a court may find for a litigant on two independent, sufficient grounds. For example, suppose that the court in Smith's copyright and contract action finds that Jones breached her contract with Smith *and* that she infringed Smith's copyright. Each issue has been actually litigated and actually decided, but the Restatement would deny collateral estoppel effect to either decision since it is impossible to tell which decision was necessary to the judgment:

> First a determination in the alternative may not have been as carefully or rigorously considered as it would have been if it had been necessary to the result, and in that sense it has some of the characteristics of dicta. Second, and of critical importance, the losing party, although entitled to appeal from both determinations, might be dissuaded from doing so because of the likelihood that at least one of them would be upheld and the other not even reached. If he were to appeal solely for the purpose of avoiding the application of the rule of issue preclusion, then the rule might be responsible for increasing the burdens of litigation on the parties and the courts rather than lightening those burdens.

Restatement (Second) of Judgments §27, comment i (1982). See *Halpern v. Schwartz*, 426 F.2d 102, 105-106 (2d Cir. 1970). However, this rationale has not been universally accepted; some courts have given collateral estoppel effect to *both* alternative determinations in these circumstances. See, e.g., *Winters v. Levine*, 574 F.2d 46, 67 (2d Cir. 1978), in which the Second Circuit appeared to limit *Halpern* to bankruptcy cases. Other cases and commentators have suggested a flexible middle ground between these extremes, which would apply estoppel if the second court can determine from the record of the first that both holdings were given full consideration. See *Malloy v. Trombley*, 427 N.Y.S.2d 969 (1980); see generally 18 Wright & Miller at §4421, pp. 564-582.[3]

There are further wrinkles to the collateral estoppel doctrine. In particular, the issue of nonmutual estoppel, considered in *Parklane Hosiery Co., Inc. v. Shore*, 439 U.S. 322 (1979), adds an additional level of complexity to the analysis, which is explored in the following chapter. For the moment,

---

3. This issue continues to divide the courts. Compare *In re Carozza*, 167 B.R. 331, 338-340 (Bankr. E.D.N.Y. 1994) (following *Winters v. Levine*) with *York Ford, Inc. v. Building Inspector and Zoning Administrator of Saugus*, 38 Mass. App. Ct. 938, 940-942 (1995) (adopting Second Restatement view and characterizing it as "the trend" ).

however, we will focus on the basics. In analyzing the following examples, assume that all actions are brought in federal court and that the "modern" Second Restatement principles of collateral estoppel apply.

## Examples

### First Principles

1. Vanderbilt enters into a contract with Fisk for the delivery of 50 tons of coal per week to Vanderbilt's power plant, for the period from January 2001 to December 2005. In 2002 Vanderbilt sues Fisk for breach of contract. He claims that the coal delivered from March to August 2001 was "grade AB" rather than "first quality" coal, as required by the contract. Fisk denies the allegation that he delivered grade AB coal instead of first quality coal and prevails in a jury trial.

   Subsequently, Vanderbilt sues Fisk again for breach of contract on the ground that the coal delivered between February and June 2003 was grade AB. Fisk again denies that he delivered AB coal.
   a. Why is Vanderbilt's second suit not barred by res judicata?
   b. Does collateral estoppel bar relitigation of any issue decided in the first suit?

2. Assume that Vanderbilt claims in the first suit that Fisk delivered grade AB coal from March to August of 2001, which did not comply with the contract specification for "first quality" coal. Fisk admits that he delivered grade AB coal during that period but defends on the ground that AB coal satisfies the contract specification. The case is tried to a jury, which finds for Vanderbilt and awards him damages.
   a. Vanderbilt sues Fisk again for delivering grade AB coal from February to June 2003. Will collateral estoppel apply to any issue?
   b. If Vanderbilt sues for the second (2003) breach, could Fisk defend on the ground that the contract is void because the parties entered into it on the basis of a mutual mistake as to the type of coal to be delivered?
   c. Assume that in Vanderbilt's second action Fisk defends on the ground that AB coal satisfies the contract specifications. He offers expert testimony, not offered in the original action, that AB coal is universally accepted in the industry as "first quality" coal. Will the court bar him from relitigating the issue?
   d. Assume that Vanderbilt's second suit against Fisk is for delivering grade AB coal from September to December 2005. Fisk defends on the ground that Vanderbilt had agreed to an oral modification of the contract allowing delivery of grade AB coal due to a national shortage of "first quality" coal during those months. Will collateral estoppel bar Fisk from relying on this defense?

## Decisions, Decisions

3. Vanderbilt sues Fisk for breach of the coal delivery contract, claiming that Fisk delivered AB coal from March to August 2001. Fisk defends on the ground that the contract was invalid due to mutual mistake and, in the alternative, that AB coal complies with the contract specifications. The jury renders a general verdict[4] for Fisk.

    a. Later, Vanderbilt sues Fisk for a subsequent breach of the contract by delivering AB coal from February to June 2003. Fisk again defends on the ground that AB coal satisfies the contract specifications. Does collateral estoppel bar relitigation of this issue?

    b. Assume that in the original suit described in this example Vanderbilt moved for judgment as a matter of law on Fisk's mutual mistake defense, and the court granted the motion, finding, as a matter of law, that there was no mutual mistake. The case went to the jury on the defense that AB coal was adequate under the contract, and the jury rendered a verdict for Fisk. Subsequently, Vanderbilt sues Fisk for the 2003 breach. Fisk raises the same defenses. May Fisk estop Vanderbilt from claiming that AB coal does not meet the contract specifications?

    c. On the preceding facts, may Vanderbilt bar Fisk from relitigating the mutual mistake defense?

    d. Assume that the first case went to the jury on both defenses, and the jury rendered a verdict for Vanderbilt in the first suit. Now Vanderbilt sues for the second breach during 2003, and Fisk defends on the ground that the parties entered into the contract under a mutual mistake. May Vanderbilt estop Fisk from relitigating the issue of mutual mistake?

4. Consider again the facts of example 3d. In the first case Vanderbilt sued for delivering AB coal in 2001, and Fisk raised two defenses: that the contract had been based on a mutual mistake and that AB coal satisfies the contract specifications. Vanderbilt wins the case and recovers damages. Later, he sues Fisk for a 2003 breach of the contract, and Fisk again raises the defense that AB coal satisfies the specifications. Vanderbilt's counsel recognizes that collateral estoppel should bar Fisk from relitigating the defense (see the explanation to example 3d).

    a. What procedural motion should Vanderbilt make to present his collateral estoppel objection to the court?

    b. What evidence should Vanderbilt use to support his motion?

---

4. A general verdict is a simple verdict for the plaintiff or defendant without specifying the ground upon which the decision is based.

## Isn't This Example in the Wrong Chapter?

5. Morgan sues Gould for violation of his federal civil rights, in the federal district court for the Southern District of New York. Gould moves to dismiss for lack of personal jurisdiction. The court allows discovery on the jurisdictional issue, takes evidence on the issue at a hearing, hears oral argument, and subsequently denies the motion. Gould defaults on the merits, and Morgan gets judgment. Morgan then brings an action to enforce the judgment in Florida. Gould opposes enforcement of the judgment on the ground that the New York court lacked personal jurisdiction over him.
   a. Will collateral estoppel bar relitigation of the personal jurisdiction issue?
   b. Will collateral estoppel bar relitigation of the merits of the civil rights claim?

6. Carnegie sues Astor in California for manufacturing a type of railroad engine in that state. Carnegie bases his suit on two claims. First, he alleges that he has a patent on the engine under the federal patent laws and that Astor is infringing his patent by building the engine without his permission. Second, he claims that Astor is violating California's unfair competition statute by using Carnegie's engine design. The case is tried to a jury, which renders a general verdict for Carnegie and awards him damages.

   Subsequently, Astor resumes making the same engines in Nevada, which (we will assume) has no unfair competition statute. Carnegie sues him for patent infringement. Does collateral estoppel bar relitigation of the infringement issue?

## A Brainteaser with a Commonsense Answer

7. Assume the same facts as example 6, except that Astor resumed making the engines in California. Carnegie sues him there again. He seeks to enjoin Astor from making the engines and argues that the decision in the prior suit establishes his right to the injunction. Will collateral estoppel bar Astor from relitigating the legality of his conduct?

8. Assume that Carnegie's first suit against Astor was tried to the court rather than the jury and that the judge's written decision expressly finds that Astor is liable on both theories. Astor then begins production of the engines in Nevada, and Carnegie brings a second action against him there. Will collateral estoppel bar Astor from claiming that he has not infringed Carnegie's patent?

## Mega-Hypo: Exercise for the Enthusiast

9. The examples above illustrate particular issues in the application of collateral estoppel. Often, though, cases are not so conceptually clean; it is necessary to cull through a long procedural history and voluminous record to prove that the requirements of collateral estoppel are met. Indeed, it may take as much litigation to prove that the issue is precluded as it would to relitigate it, thus undermining one of the policy reasons for allowing issue preclusion. For a taste of these complexities, try the following example.

Hill buys two identical blast furnaces from Villard. One of them explodes, and Hill sues Villard for his injuries. He asserts claims for negligent design, breach of warranty, and strict liability. He seeks compensatory damages on all three counts and punitive damages, which are only available on the negligence claim. Villard admits that he made the furnace but denies that the design was negligent. He admits that a warranty of fitness for its intended use arose upon the sale but denies that he breached the warranty. He also denies that he is strictly liable for injuries resulting from the explosion. In addition, he raises contributory negligence as a defense on the negligence claim (a complete defense under applicable law) and claims that Hill's negligence claim is barred by the statute of limitations. The judge dismisses the strict liability claim under Rule 12(b)(6), on the ground that the applicable law does not allow recovery on a strict liability theory. Villard moves for summary judgment on the statute of limitations defense, but the judge denies the motion. At trial Hill moves for judgment as a matter of law on the negligent design issue. The judge denies it. The jury returns a verdict for the plaintiff and awards compensatory and punitive damages.

Two weeks after the judgment in the original suit, the second furnace explodes, and Hill sues Villard on the same theories. What issues will be precluded in the second action?

## Explanations

### First Principles

1. a. It is important at the outset to distinguish the relitigation of claims from the relitigation of issues. Res judicata only bars relitigation of the same claim, that is, the same transaction or occurrence that was the subject of the first suit. See Chapter 26, pp. 543-544. Vanderbilt is not seeking to relitigate his original claim for the breach of contract that took place in 2001. Rather, he is litigating a new claim for a later breach of the same contract. This second breach is not the same transaction or occurrence as the first, even though it involves the same contract. Indeed, since it had not occurred when Vanderbilt

first sued Fisk, it obviously could not have been joined in the first action.

b. Collateral estoppel, in contrast to res judicata, precludes relitigation of issues in a second suit that have previously been litigated and decided in a prior action. Even though the second suit is for a separate claim, so that res judicata does not apply, a subsequent suit may involve issues already settled in an earlier suit between the same parties. If so, it makes no sense to allow the parties to relitigate those issues.

However, the first prerequisite for collateral estoppel is that the issues in the two suits must be the same. Therefore, analysis of collateral estoppel issues should always begin with a determination of what was decided in the first action. In this case the issue in the first suit was whether Fisk had delivered first-quality coal from March to August 2001. The issue in the second suit was whether Fisk delivered first-quality coal during a subsequent period. This is a different factual issue, which was not raised in the prior suit and must be litigated in the new one.

2. a. In this example, the issue in the first suit was not whether Fisk actually delivered AB coal (he admits that he did), but whether AB coal was insufficient under the contract specifications. Since this was the basis for Vanderbilt's claim that Fisk breached the contract, and the jury found for Vanderbilt, they must have concluded that AB coal did not satisfy the specifications. Since that issue was litigated and decided in the first suit, the court in Vanderbilt's second action for a later breach will estop Fisk from defending the second suit on the ground that AB coal satisfies the specifications. Here, although the issue in the second suit arises from a later transaction (and thus would not be barred by res judicata), it will be barred by collateral estoppel since the issue was previously litigated and decided between the parties.

b. As indicated above, the issue that was raised and decided in the first suit was whether AB coal satisfied the contract specifications. Although the separate defense of mutual mistake at the time of entering into the contract was available to Fisk in the prior action, he failed to raise it. However, collateral estoppel does not bar him from doing so later in a second suit for a new breach of the contract. Collateral estoppel only bars issues that were litigated and decided in the prior action; it does not affect claims or defenses that *could have been* raised but were not.

Compare res judicata doctrine, which bars litigation of any issues that could have been raised in a prior suit on the same claim.

Res judicata does not apply in this hypothetical because Vanderbilt's second suit is for a separate claim, the 2003 breach.

c. Essentially, Fisk's position here is that he should be able to relitigate the AB coal issue because, while he failed to prove his defense the first time, he can prove it now. As long as Fisk had a full chance to present his case in the first suit, this argument will fall on deaf ears. This testimony could presumably have been offered in the original suit and should have been. There is no reason why preclusion should operate against parties who litigated carefully the first time around but not against those who did not. Nor is there a requirement that the original finding has to be "right" to preclude relitigation. If that were true, the second court would have to rehear the issue to determine whether it was correctly decided the first time, thus completely undermining the purpose of the doctrine itself.

In limited situations, a party who discovers new evidence on an issue may move for relief from judgment under Fed. R. Civ. P. 60(b)(2). Under this rule, Fisk could seek to reopen the original action and overturn the finding that AB coal was insufficient. If he succeeded, of course, that original finding would no longer be entitled to collateral estoppel effect in subsequent suits.[5]

d. In this case the original finding that AB coal did not comply with the specifications could not be relitigated. However, Fisk's defense is not that AB coal is sufficient under the original contract but that a subsequent modification of the contract allows him to deliver AB coal. This is a new issue, which was not raised in the original action, has never been litigated or decided, and is available to Fisk as a defense to the new action.

## Decisions, Decisions

3. a. Collateral estoppel does not apply unless the issue was decided in the prior suit. In this case Fisk raised two defenses to Vanderbilt's first claim. If the jury accepted either defense, they would have had to find for Fisk. Obviously, they did accept one of those defenses, but it is impossible to tell from the jury's general verdict for Fisk which one it was. When a case is submitted to a jury with a general verdict

---

5. Fisk would have an uphill fight in obtaining relief from judgment here. First, Rule 60(b)(2) only allows the court to reopen the suit due to newly discovered evidence within one year after judgment. In addition, the moving party on such a motion must show that the new evidence could not have been discovered in the exercise of due diligence in time for presentation at the original trial.

In a few cases, courts have refused to apply collateral estoppel because new scientific evidence on a complex issue has been developed since the prior action. See S. Madden, Issue Preclusion in Products Liability, 11 Pace L. Rev. 87, 117 (1990) (describing several complex medical causation cases which refused estoppel on this ground).

form, the jury is simply asked to find for the plaintiff or for the defendant (and if it finds for the plaintiff, to find the amount of the plaintiff's damages). In this case, the jury's general finding "for the defendant" does not indicate whether it found the contract void or, alternatively, that AB coal complied with the specifications. Because it is impossible to tell which issue was decided, Fisk will not be able to demonstrate that the issue of whether the coal was sufficient was actually decided or necessary to the judgment. Consequently, collateral estoppel will not bar relitigation of that issue.

b. The result here is different because the procedural history of the suit clearly indicates what issues were decided. The judge's entry of judgment as a matter of law for Vanderbilt on the mutual mistake defense is a decision on that issue; it constitutes a finding that on the evidence produced by the parties no reasonable jury could find for Fisk on that issue. Thus, that issue was actually litigated and decided in Vanderbilt's favor. That left only one defense, that the AB coal complied with the contract specifications. The jury's verdict for Fisk must have been based on this defense.

In this case, therefore, unlike example 3a, it is clear that the AB coal issue was decided in Fisk's favor in the previous action and that it was the basis for the jury's verdict for Fisk. Consequently, Vanderbilt will be estopped from relitigating that issue; the court will grant judgment for Fisk if Vanderbilt sues him for damages on the ground that AB coal was inadequate under the contract.

As this example indicates, collateral estoppel can work for either party. In example 2a, Vanderbilt used it to establish an issue crucial to obtaining relief. In this case Fisk uses it to establish a defense that had been previously litigated and decided in his favor.

c. If Fisk raises the defense of mutual mistake again, Vanderbilt will argue that Fisk should be estopped from relitigating the issue since it was litigated and decided adversely to Fisk in the first suit. Unfortunately for Vanderbilt, this will not work, since the finding for Vanderbilt that there was no mutual mistake was not necessary to support the original judgment. That judgment was for Fisk and was based on the jury's finding that Fisk had proved his defense that AB coal was adequate under the contract. Vanderbilt lost *even though* the contract was valid, because the AB coal complied with it; the finding that there was no mutual mistake did not lead to the judgment. Thus, although the mistake issue was litigated and decided, the court will deny collateral estoppel effect on that issue since it was not essential to the decision of the case.

Although this seems artificial, consider Fisk's point of view. Even if he believes that the court wrongly decided the mistake issue, he has no incentive to appeal since he won the verdict. If he did appeal for fear that some future court might apply collateral estoppel on the mutual mistake issue, the appellate court would probably refuse to hear the appeal, since Fisk won below and review of the mutual mistake issue would therefore serve no purpose. In a sense, then, there has been no final decision on the issue; Fisk should not be estopped by a potentially erroneous decision that he has no opportunity or incentive to correct.

d. Here, Vanderbilt may invoke collateral estoppel to bar Fisk from relitigating the mutual mistake issue. In this example Fisk raised two defenses in the first suit. If the jury accepted either one they would have found for Fisk. Because they found for Vanderbilt, they must have considered each of the defenses and concluded that Fisk had not proved either one. In addition, the decision on each defense was necessary to the judgment since they had to consider and reject each defense raised by Fisk in order to find for Vanderbilt: If the jury had found either a mutual mistake in making the contract or that AB coal was sufficient, Fisk would have won.

4. a. Vanderbilt should move for partial summary judgment under Fed. R. Civ. P. 56 on Fisk's defense that AB coal satisfies the contract specifications. His position is that Fisk is barred from asserting this defense, because he litigated and lost on the defense in the earlier lawsuit. If he can show that collateral estoppel applies, there is "no genuine issue as to any material fact" (Fed. R. Civ. P. 56(c)) on that defense, and he, Vanderbilt, is "entitled to judgment as a matter of law." Id. His position is that as a matter of law Fisk cannot prove the AB-coal-suffices defense, because he failed to prove it earlier and is not allowed (under collateral estoppel) to try to prove it again.

b. To prevail on his motion, Vanderbilt would have to establish that the issue was tried in the earlier suit, was decided in his favor, and led to the judgment in the prior suit. To show that it was raised, he could submit the pleadings from the prior suit, which would show that Fisk raised the AB-coal-suffices defense. He could also submit the judge's instructions to the jury, which would show that the issue had been litigated at trial and submitted to the jury for decision. Last, the jury's verdict slip finding in favor of Vanderbilt and the court's judgment on the verdict would demonstrate that the jury had rejected the defense (since they could not have found for Vanderbilt unless they did) and that rejection of the defense had led to the judgment for Vanderbilt.

Of course, if Vanderbilt moves for summary judgment on this issue, and prevails, the case will not be over. Vanderbilt will get partial summary judgment on the AB coal defense; that defense will be stricken, but he will still have to establish the basic elements of his breach of contract claim and prove his damages. However, he can at least use estoppel to avoid relitigating a major issue that was already decided in the earlier action.

## Isn't This Example in the Wrong Chapter?

5. a. This situation should sound familiar: It echoes example 5 from Chapter 3. If you look at that example, you will see that the defendant was barred from relitigating whether the rendering court had personal jurisdiction over him because he had already raised and litigated that issue in the rendering court. Now it should be clear to you that this result is a straightforward application of collateral estoppel principles: The personal jurisdiction issue[6] was raised, litigated, and decided in the original action and was necessary to the judgment as well, since the court would not have taken jurisdiction and entered a default judgment for Morgan if it had concluded that it lacked jurisdiction over Gould. Thus, all the requirements for collateral estoppel are met, and Gould will be barred from relitigating the issue.

Note that in this case Morgan invokes collateral estoppel on an issue that has nothing to do with the merits of the lawsuit, indeed, in a situation where the merits were never litigated at all. So long as the particular issue, be it procedural or substantive, was litigated and decided and necessary to the judgment, issue preclusion will bar relitigation of the issue. This result makes good sense. Gould should not be allowed to relitigate the personal jurisdiction question if it has been fully and fairly decided in another court.

Distinguish res judicata, however. That doctrine only bars relitigation of *claims* once they have been decided on the merits or, at least, the parties have had the chance to reach the merits. When a case is dismissed on procedural grounds, the merits have never been litigated, and the plaintiff may sue again in a court that can properly reach the merits.

b. Collateral estoppel will not bar relitigation of the underlying claim. None of the substantive issues in the case were litigated on the merits in the New York court, so none were "actually litigated" or "actually decided" there. However, res judicata will bar Gould from litigating the merits in Florida. Under res judicata principles, the New York default judgment is a decision "on the merits" in favor of Morgan which bars relitigating any claims arising out of the underlying events giving rise to the case. (Note that, for res judicata to apply,

---

6. Note that the relevant issue, in both courts, is whether the *New York* court (the court that rendered the judgment) had jurisdiction over Gould. So the "same issue" requirement is met here as well.

there is no requirement that the substantive issues have been "actually litigated," as there is for collateral estoppel.) Under full faith and credit principles, the Florida court will give the New York default judgment the same res judicata effect it would have in New York.

6. Carnegie will have to relitigate the patent infringement issue. Although he won the first suit, it is impossible to tell from the general verdict which claim prevailed before the jury. They may have decided that Astor infringed Carnegie's patent, or that he violated the state unfair competition statute (or both). Thus, it is not possible to tell whether the "actually decided" and "necessary to the judgment" requirements are met.

Because a general verdict obscures the basis of the jury's decision, one or both of the parties may want to request use of a special verdict form, under Fed. R. Civ. P. 49, if they foresee the possibility of future litigation involving the same issues. A special verdict asks the jury to make findings on particular issues, rather than finding generally for the plaintiff or defendant. See Friedenthal, Kane, and Miller §12.1. In this case, for example, the jury could be asked specifically whether they find that Astor infringed Carnegie's patent and whether they find that he violated California's unfair competition laws. If they answered "yes" on the patent infringement issue but "no" on the unfair competition issue, then it would be possible to prove in subsequent actions that the patent question was actually decided and necessary to the decision of the original suit.

The situation would be different if Carnegie had lost the first case. Then it would be clear — even with a general verdict — that the jury had rejected both Carnegie's theories, and collateral estoppel could prevent relitigation of either.

## A Brainteaser with a Commonsense Answer

7. At first glance, it seems that the answer here ought to be "no" in light of the answer to example 6. It is unclear whether the jury in the first suit found for Carnegie on the patent claim or the unfair competition claim. However, it is clear that they found that Astor's conduct infringed on Carnegie's rights on one ground or the other. This should be sufficient to preclude relitigation in some contexts, at least. Carnegie may invoke collateral estoppel to bar relitigation of Astor's right to make the engines, on the ground that the original judgment necessarily decided that he had no right to do so. The court may not need to decide which of Carnegie's theories the jury accepted in the first action; it may be enough to support the injunction that they accepted one.

However, if Carnegie seeks damages from Astor in the second suit, it might not be possible for him to rely on the previous judgment. If the measure of damages under the two claims differed, it would be necessary to determine which theory of liability applied in order to assess the damages. Because Carnegie can only show that the first suit determined that Astor was barred from making the engines, but not which theory that determination was based on, the jury in a second damage action would have to decide anew whether Astor is liable and, if so, on which ground.

8. This example raises the "alternative holdings" problem discussed in the Introduction. The judge's opinion leaves no doubt that both the patent and unfair competition issues were actually litigated and decided. However, there is a problem as to whether either is "necessary to the judgment" when each is sufficient to support the judgment: Presumably, if either of the alternative holdings had been left out, the outcome would have been the same anyway, based on the other ground.

The Second Restatement of Judgments takes the position that neither holding is entitled to preclusive effect because it is impossible to tell whether each received full consideration and because the losing party has no incentive to appeal on one arguably incorrect ground if the other would support the judgment. As indicated in the Introduction, however some courts take the opposite view, that both holdings are entitled to collateral estoppel effect.

## Mega-Hypo: Exercise for the Enthusiast

9. This is not a particularly unusual scenario for a products liability action, yet it takes some doing to unravel the procedural history and ascertain whether any issues will be barred in the second suit.

A good place to start is to determine what issues were decided in the original action. Villard admitted that he made the furnace and that a warranty of fitness for its intended use arose upon the sale. However, as the Introduction points out, these admissions do not satisfy the "actually litigated" requirement for collateral estoppel purposes.

The denial of the motion for summary judgment on the limitations issue does not "actually decide" that issue; it simply indicates that both parties have some evidence on that issue and therefore ought to have the opportunity to go to trial on it. See Chapter 23, p. 478. Similarly, the denial of the motion for judgment as a matter of law on negligent design does not satisfy the requirement that the issue be "actually decided." That denial simply indicates that there is enough evidence to support a rational verdict for Villard, the nonmoving party, on that issue.

By contrast, the judge's dismissal of the strict liability claim clearly indicates that he decided as a matter of law that there is no strict liability claim arising out of the sale. A dismissal under Rule 12(b)(6) does "actually decide" the issue of whether strict liability applies, so this might give rise to issue preclusion later.

How about the verdict; can we discern what the jury actually decided in reaching their verdict for Hill? The case went to trial on breach of warranty and negligence (but not on strict liability since the judge dismissed that claim), and the jury's general verdict does not expressly indicate whether the jury found for Hill on one or both theories. However, the jury awarded punitive damages, which were only available on the negligent design claim. Thus, the jury must have found for Hill on that claim. And in order to do so it must have rejected the defense that the negligence claim is barred by the statute of limitations. It must also have found that Hill was not contributorily negligent; if he were, they would have had to find for Villard on the negligence claim.

The jury may have also found for Hill on the breach of warranty claim, but we can't tell, since compensatory damages are available on both theories. Even if the jury found for Hill on both theories, it would only award him his actual losses as compensatory damages: Thus, the amount of the compensatory damages does not reveal whether the jury accepted both theories or only one.

We have identified four issues as actually litigated and decided: whether the statute of limitations barred the negligence claim, whether Hill's contributory negligence barred the negligence claim, whether the furnace was negligently designed, and whether Villard is strictly liable for the injuries resulting from the explosion. The first three were necessary to the judgment since the jury could not have found for Hill on the negligence claim without rejecting the statute of limitations and contributory negligence defenses and finding that the design was negligent. The dismissal of the strict liability claim is not necessary to the judgment, however. Clearly, Hill did not win because strict liability is not recognized under the applicable law — this holding tends to defeat rather than establish liability. He won the verdict despite this finding, not because of it. Nor would he have any incentive to appeal this adverse decision, since he won the case anyway on other grounds. So Hill should be free to relitigate whether strict liability is a viable claim in the second suit.

Only three issues, then, satisfy the prerequisites. But two of those, the statute of limitations and contributory negligence issues, are not likely to be the same in the two suits since the two explosions took place at different times and perhaps under different circumstances.[7] Only the negligent design issue remains. That issue will presumably be the same since the two furnaces are identical.

Even though Hill will have to go through all of that to show that collateral estoppel applies, he will still have a strong incentive to do so. If he can get the judge to travel this long road, at the end of it he will have established an issue crucial to his right to relief, without relitigating the merits of that issue and without the risk of losing on it before the second jury. For Hill, the value of invoking collateral estoppel is not merely to save litigation time, but to assure the same favorable result he obtained in the first suit and avoid the risk that a second jury would reach an opposite verdict. Ironically, he may be willing to spend as much litigation time to obtain that result as it would take to try the issue again.

---

7. In some circumstances, the contributory negligence issue might be the same, so that the rejection of the defense in the first action would bar Villard from asserting it in the second. Suppose, for example, that Hill installed the two furnaces in the same way at the same time, and Villard claimed in the first suit that inadequate installation contributed to the explosion. On those facts the issue would be the same in the second suit, and Villard would be barred by collateral estoppel from raising the defense again. But Hill would still have to prove that the furnaces *were* installed in the same way in order to support estoppel.

# The Obscure Kingdom

## Nonmutual Collateral Estoppel

## INTRODUCTION

We began this journey at the beginning (see p. 3), and we should end at the end . . . but nothing is quite that simple in civil procedure. A lawsuit "ends" when a final judgment is entered or an appeal of the trial court judgment is decided. But the suit may send out waves that break on very distant shores. Under collateral estoppel doctrine, issues decided in one lawsuit may have effects in another suit between the parties at a later time or in a different court. And, beyond this fairly well-mapped terrain lies the more obscure kingdom of nonmutual collateral estoppel.

Under traditional issue preclusion principles, a party may be estopped from relitigating an issue that he had litigated in a prior suit and lost. Restatement (Second) of Judgments §27 (1982); Chapter 28, pp. 578-579. Assume, for example, that Cartier sues La Salle, a tenant in his shopping center, for breach of a provision in the standard lease signed by all Cartier's tenants. If the court finds that the lease provision is invalid, La Salle may estop Cartier in a future suit involving the same lease from claiming that the disputed provision is enforceable. Conversely, if the provision had been held valid, Cartier could estop La Salle from defending a future action based on the same lease on the ground that the provision was invalid.

Nonmutual collateral estoppel goes a step beyond this basic doctrine by allowing a new party to invoke collateral estoppel against a party who litigated and lost on an issue in a prior action. Suppose, for example, that

Cartier, after losing his suit against La Salle on the ground that the lease provision was unenforceable, sues Cortez, another tenant who had signed the same standard lease. Under nonmutual preclusion principles, Cortez, the new defendant, could estop Cartier from claiming that the disputed provision was enforceable, since Cartier had previously litigated that issue against La Salle and lost.

For many years, this frontier concept remained, if not undiscovered, at least unexplored by most courts. The general rule was that "estoppels must be mutual" that is, the only parties who could invoke collateral estoppel were those who were involved in the suit in which the issue was initially decided. This "doctrine of mutuality" allowed La Salle to estop Cartier on the issue of the validity of the lease provision but would not allow Cortez, a stranger to the first suit, to do so. The courts reasoned that La Salle had litigated in the first action; he took the risk that, if he lost on the issue, he would be bound by that finding in subsequent suits, under basic collateral estoppel doctrine, and therefore he — and only he — had earned the right to assert estoppel if he won. But Cortez was not a party to the first action; he took no risk of being bound by an adverse judgment if Cartier proved that the lease provision *was* valid. Consequently, since he would not be bound by an unfavorable finding, the mutuality doctrine barred Cortez from taking advantage of a favorable finding in the La Salle/Cartier suit.

## A Fundamental Question

1. Why is it true, whether or not the mutuality rule applies, that Cortez could not be bound by a finding in the original suit that the lease provision was valid?

Courts that applied the mutuality rule were also influenced by an additional reason in confining estoppel to the original parties. If the litigants know that findings will only affect other suits with the same adversaries, they can usually anticipate the future implications of an adverse decision in the original suit. However, if estoppel is available to new parties, the litigants may be forced to over-litigate issues in the original action for fear of unknown risks of estoppel in future actions involving new parties.

While the mutuality rule has had a respectable history and widespread acceptance, it has been abandoned in many jurisdictions since the landmark case of *Bernhard v. Bank of America National Trust & Savings Assn.*, 122 P.2d 892 (Cal. 1942). In *Bernhard*, Mrs. Bernhard claimed that certain funds held by Cook, the executor of an estate, belonged to the estate. Cook claimed they were a gift to him from the decedent, which he need not include in the assets of the estate. Bernhard challenged Cook's claim in a probate proceeding during the course of the settlement of the estate, and the court held that the funds were a gift to Cook. Bernhard then sued the bank that had been holding the funds and paid them to Cook, alleging again that the funds were assets of the estate that should have been paid to the estate rather than to Cook.

The bank pleaded collateral estoppel, arguing that Bernhard had already adjudicated the right to the funds in the probate proceeding, had lost, and should be precluded from relitigating the issue against the bank.

## Who's Who?

2. Why was the bank's invocation of collateral estoppel in *Bernhard* "non-mutual"?

In *Bernhard*, Justice Traynor concluded that it was not categorically improper to allow a new party to take advantage of findings in an earlier suit to estop a party who had litigated the issue in the prior action. Instead of focusing on the "free ride" that the bank received by borrowing the favorable result achieved by Cook in the earlier case, Justice Traynor emphasized the fact that Bernhard, the party *against* whom the estoppel was asserted, had been a party to the first action and had had a full and fair opportunity to litigate the issue there. *Bernhard* at 895. In such circumstances, the court saw no reason to allow her to relitigate the decided issue by simply switching adversaries.

The United States Supreme Court first endorsed the use of nonmutual estoppel in the federal courts in *Blonder-Tongue Laboratories, Inc. v. University of Illinois Foundation*, 402 U.S. 313 (1971). The situation in *Blonder-Tongue* was analogous to *Bernhard*. The University of Illinois Foundation sued one defendant for infringing a patent but lost on the ground that its patent was invalid. It then "switched adversaries," bringing suit against another defendant for infringement of the same patent. The Supreme Court reversed its long-standing rule allowing such relitigation and approved use of nonmutual collateral estoppel against the foundation on the issue of the validity of the patent. The Court noted the unfairness and waste of judicial resources that flows from allowing "repeated litigation of the same issue as long as the supply of unrelated defendants holds out." *Blonder-Tongue* at 329.

Like the *Bernhard* court, the Court in *Blonder-Tongue* emphasized that preclusion was only appropriate if the precluded party had had a full and fair opportunity to litigate the issue in the first action. *Blonder-Tongue* at 332-334. In addition, the Court emphasized the unique burdens that patent infringement actions impose on the courts. However, the lower federal courts have not construed the Court's holding as limited to patent cases. Subsequent cases have applied nonmutual collateral estoppel in a wide variety of cases, at least when the posture of the parties in the successive actions is similar to that of the parties in *Blonder-Tongue* and *Bernhard*. See generally 18 Wright & Miller at §4464.

# DEFENSIVE NONMUTUAL ESTOPPEL

This matter of the posture of the parties introduces a further wrinkle to the nonmutual preclusion problem. In both *Blonder-Tongue* and *Bernhard*, the new party in the second action was a defendant who invoked estoppel to prevent the plaintiff from establishing a fact that the plaintiff had been unable to establish in the first suit. *Bernhard*, for example, had essentially been a plaintiff in the first probate proceeding, trying to establish the estate's right to the funds held by Cook. In the second action, she was again the plaintiff, attempting to prove the same issue in order to recover from the bank. The bank asserted estoppel "defensively," to prevent her from proving an essential element of her claim. Similarly, in *Blonder-Tongue*, the university foundation had brought the first suit and lost and was also the plaintiff in the second suit. The new defendant asserted defensive nonmutual estoppel to prevent the foundation from establishing the validity of a patent previously held invalid. See *Parklane Hosiery v. Shore*, 439 U.S. 322, 326 n.4 (1979) ("[d]efensive use occurs when a defendant seeks to prevent a plaintiff from asserting a claim the plaintiff has previously litigated and lost against another defendant"). This use of estoppel is "nonmutual" because the party asserting the estoppel on the issue was not a party to the action in which the issue was first litigated. Visually the sequence looks like this:

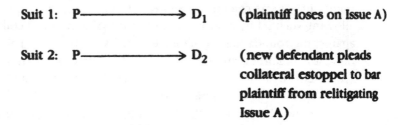

This defensive assertion of nonmutual estoppel is more easily justified than the offensive use of estoppel discussed in *Parklane*. In defensive estoppel cases, the party being estopped was usually the plaintiff in the original suit and chose the forum and the defendant against whom to litigate the issue. When that is true, it hardly seems unfair to bind the plaintiff to the first resolution of the recurring issue.

# OFFENSIVE NONMUTUAL ESTOPPEL

By contrast, offensive use of collateral estoppel usually involves a new plaintiff who seeks to borrow a finding from a prior action to impose liability on a party who was a defendant in the prior action. See *Parklane* at 326 n.4 ("offensive use of collateral estoppel occurs when the plaintiff seeks to foreclose the defendant from litigating an issue the defendant has previously litigated unsuccessfully in an action with another party"). For example, suppose that La Salle had brought suit against Cartier to enjoin him from enforcing the disputed provision of the standard lease, and the provision was held invalid. If Cortez now sued Cartier for damages resulting from the invalid provision and invoked collateral estoppel to prevent Cartier from relitigating the validity of the provision, that would be offensive, nonmutual estoppel. The new plaintiff, Cortez, would be taking advantage of the finding against Cartier, a defendant in the prior action, to help establish a claim against Cartier in a new suit.

This is exactly what the plaintiff did in *Parklane*. In the first case to go to judgment, the Securities and Exchange Commission had claimed — and the court had held — that Parklane Hosiery had issued a false and misleading proxy statement. Subsequently, the plaintiffs in a class action suit against Parklane, based on the same proxy statement, invoked collateral estoppel against Parklane on the question of whether the statement was false and misleading. Since Parklane had litigated and lost that issue in the S.E.C. suit, the class plaintiffs argued that it had had its day in court on the issue and should be barred from relitigating it. The plaintiffs' use of estoppel was "offensive," since they sought to use it to establish the defendant's liability in a new action. It was nonmutual, because they were not parties to the action in which the issue was first litigated. The sequence of suits looks like this:

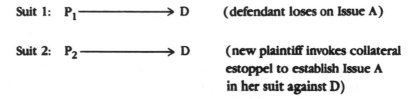

Suit 1: $P_1 \longrightarrow D$    (defendant loses on Issue A)

Suit 2: $P_2 \longrightarrow D$    (new plaintiff invokes collateral estoppel to establish Issue A in her suit against D)

In these offensive nonmutual estoppel situations, there are a number of reasons for the courts to exercise particular caution in deciding whether to apply nonmutual collateral estoppel. For one thing, the party against whom estoppel is asserted in the second action (i.e., Parklane in the *Parklane* case and Cartier in the preceding example) was usually a defendant in the first suit and did not choose the forum in which the issue was initially decided. While it is possible to say that the losing party in a defensive-use situation gave it his best shot in the original action, this is not so clear in the offensive-use situation, in which the estopped party did not choose the time and place of the first suit or the adversary against whom to try the issue.

The Supreme Court in *Parklane* noted several other risks posed by offensive use of estoppel. First, the prospect of taking advantage of another plaintiff's victory to establish crucial issues without trial may lead plaintiffs to "wait and see," that is, to hold back from joining in the first plaintiff's suit. After all, if La Salle lost the first action against Cartier because the lease provision was held valid, Cortez would not be barred from relitigating the issue because he has never litigated it, and no party can be estopped until he (or someone in privity with him) has had his day in court on the issue. But if La Salle wins and the court recognizes nonmutual collateral estoppel, Cortez may be able to establish this crucial issue without trial and the resulting risk of losing on the issue altogether.

Second, the *Parklane* Court recognized that a party might not have litigated the issue aggressively in the first action if the stakes were small or the forum inconvenient. It may be inappropriate to apply estoppel in a second suit if the estopped party did not have the incentive to litigate the issue fully in the first. Third, the Court noted that it may not have been possible for the losing party to litigate effectively in the first action if the procedural rules of the court that decided the first case were more restrictive than those of the court hearing the second.[1] Last, one or more prior inconsistent judgments on the issue may suggest that it would be unfair to give conclusive effect to any one of them.

In *Parklane* the Supreme Court did not categorically endorse or reject offensive nonmutual collateral estoppel. As modern courts are wont to do, the Court held that lower courts should exercise discretion in deciding whether to allow such offensive assertions of estoppel. The court should consider, on the facts of each case, all the factors described above and any other factors that may indicate that the issue was not fully and fairly decided in the first suit. If, considering all the circumstances, the court is convinced that the issue was fully adjudicated in the first action, then it may allow preclusion, including offensive nonmutual estoppel. If, on the other hand, the court is doubtful, for whatever reason, that the party being estopped had a full "bite at the apple" in the first action, it should deny

---

1. This could be true in a number of ways. For example, the second court's civil procedure rules might allow broader discovery. The rules of evidence might allow crucial evidence that was excluded in the first case. The long-arm statute might authorize personal jurisdiction over defendants who could not be brought into the first case. Or the rules governing the subpoena power might authorize the court to order the appearance of witnesses in the second action who could not be subpoenaed in the first.

estoppel.[2] See generally Restatement (Second) of Judgments §29 (detailing factors to consider in analyzing nonmutual estoppel).

Although the *Parklane* case goes into more detail than *Blonder-Tongue* concerning the risks of nonmutual collateral estoppel, the two cases are entirely consistent. The Court in *Blonder-Tongue* emphasized that the court in the second action must be convinced that the estopped party had a full opportunity to litigate the issue in the first case. *Parklane* emphasizes the same fundamental prerequisite but spells out in more detail the factors to be considered in making that determination. In fact, most of the cautionary factors discussed in *Parklane* are equally applicable to defensive use situations, such as whether the estopped party had a strong incentive to litigate in the first suit, whether the procedural opportunities to do so were as broad in that action, and whether there are any prior inconsistent judgments. Other factors, however, such as whether the plaintiff should have joined in an earlier action, are unique to offensive estoppel.

Not all commentators applaud the trend toward recognition of non-mutual estoppel. Professor Clermont questions the wisdom of treating a finding in a suit "as a determinate truth that free-floats to conclusiveness in other contexts." K. Clermont, Principles of Civil Procedure 339. He argues that this may discourage plaintiffs from joining in the first action, lead opponents to overlitigate issues for fear of estoppel in later actions, and generate additional litigation about the preclusion issue itself.

> Most fundamentally, nonmutuality destroys the equivalence of litigating risk by weighting the scale against the common party, and so changes the most basic of the procedural system's rules, namely, procedure must provide a level playing field. Take the mass tort as an example: the first plaintiff risks losing only the one case, which is all the defendant can win; meanwhile the defendant risks losing all the cases at once; the first plaintiff thereby acquires tremendous settlement leverage, while in the absence of settlement he will face an opponent willing to litigate down to the scorched earth; and over the series of cases, the odds overwhelmingly disfavor the defendant.

*Id.* Keep in mind that a good many state courts still share Professor Clermont's reluctance to embrace nonmutual estoppel.

---

2. When the Supreme Court takes cases in which to adopt a new principle, they often take ones that present good facts for application of the new principle. *Parklane* is an example. On the facts of the case, all of the factors the court discussed argued for estoppel: There were no prior inconsistent judgments; the procedural opportunities available in the two cases were the same, since both were filed in federal court; and the plaintiffs in the second action could not have joined in the first, since private litigants are not permitted to join in securities actions brought by the government. See *Parklane* at 332 n.17. Finally, Parklane had every incentive to litigate aggressively in the first suit: Corporations can expect shareholder suits in the wake of a government action for securities violations, and in this case the class action against Parklane was filed *before* the government's suit, though the latter went to judgment first.

Let me end this introduction with a truism. Nonmutual collateral estoppel, whether of the offensive or defensive persuasion, is a form of collateral estoppel. As such, it must meet all of the basic prerequisites for application of estoppel discussed in the previous chapter. In every case, mutual or nonmutual, the court must find that the issue is the same, that it was actually litigated and decided in the prior action, and that it was necessary to the judgment in the first action before it can apply estoppel in a second action. However, in nonmutual preclusion situations, the court must consider not only these basic requirements for estoppel but also the additional factors discussed above in order to determine whether it would be fair to preclude relitigation of findings from the prior action in a new suit involving a new party.

In analyzing the following examples, assume that contributory negligence constitutes a complete defense if it is proved. Also, assume that all actions are brought in state court unless otherwise specified.

## Examples

### Charting the Terrain

3. Lewis sues Clark for trespassing on his property. Clark denies that Lewis owns the land. The court determines that Lewis owns the land and awards him damages for the trespass.

    Subsequently, Lewis sues Fremont for trespass on the same piece of land.
    a. Who would be likely to invoke collateral estoppel in the second action?
    b. Would estoppel be allowed in a mutuality jurisdiction?
    c. Would estoppel be allowed in a jurisdiction that allows nonmutual estoppel?

4. Suppose that Lewis sued Clark for the trespass, and the court found for Clark on the ground that Lewis does not own the land. Subsequently, Lewis sues Fremont for trespassing on the same property.
    a. Who would be likely to invoke collateral estoppel?
    b. Would this be mutual or nonmutual use of collateral estoppel?
    c. Would it be defensive or offensive use of estoppel?
    d. Could the court apply collateral estoppel in the second suit if the suits were brought in a jurisdiction that has abandoned the mutuality doctrine?

5. Earhart, a passenger, brings a negligence action against Lindbergh for serious injuries suffered when a plane Lindbergh was piloting crashed. The jury finds for Earhart and awards her damages. Subsequently, Wright, another passenger in Lindbergh's plane, brings a separate action

against Lindbergh for his injuries in the same accident. Wright invokes collateral estoppel to prevent Lindbergh from relitigating the issue of his negligence.

   a. Is this offensive or defensive collateral estoppel?

   b. Is it mutual or nonmutual?

   c. Could the court apply collateral estoppel in the second action if both suits were brought in federal court?

## New Frontiers

6. Mr. and Mrs. Byrd sue Da Gama for serious injuries suffered in a collision involving three cars: the Byrds', Da Gama's, and Vespucci's. Da Gama pleads contributory negligence as a defense against Mr. Byrd, who was driving the Byrd car, but not against Mrs. Byrd. (Assume that any contributory negligence by Mr. Byrd would bar his recovery.) The jury returns a verdict for Da Gama, the defendant, on Mr. Byrd's claim but for Mrs. Byrd on her claim for her own injuries.

     Mr. Byrd now sues Vespucci, the third driver involved in the collision, to recover for his injuries. Vespucci pleads contributory negligence.

   a. Who would seek to invoke collateral estoppel in the second action? On what issue?

   b. Would this be offensive or defensive use?

   c. Would it be permissible in a jurisdiction that requires mutuality?

   d. Would it be permissible in a jurisdiction that has abandoned the mutuality doctrine?

7. In 1981 Carol Burnett brought a libel suit in California against the *National Enquirer*, arising out of a story in the *Enquirer* about her behavior in a Washington restaurant. One of the *Enquirer*'s defenses was that it had printed a retraction of the story; under a California statute a newspaper can avoid substantial liability by printing a timely retraction. See Cal. Civ. Code §48a. A major issue in the case was whether the *Enquirer* was a newspaper, which enjoys the protection of the statute, or a magazine, which would not. The court held that the *Enquirer* was a magazine and thus not entitled to the protection of the retraction statute. Burnett recovered a very substantial verdict.

     A *Boston Globe* story about the verdict went on to state

> Burnett's case has been watched closely by other celebrities who have sued, or want to sue, the tabloid and other gossip publications over items they consider fiction and harmful to their careers.

> Singer Helen Reddy and her manager-husband Jeff Wald were the most recent to sue the *National Enquirer*, asking $30 million this week for a March 3 article about them.

*Boston Globe*, March 27, 1981, p. 4.

Assume that the *Enquirer* printed a similar retraction of the Reddy/ Wald article. After the decision in the Burnett case, Reddy and Wald bring suit against the *Enquirer*, it raises the retraction defense, and the plaintiffs assert collateral estoppel on the issue of whether the *Enquirer* is a magazine or a newspaper.

a. Would this be offensive or defensive use of estoppel?

b. Would this be allowed if both actions were brought in courts that applied the mutuality doctrine?

c. Would it be allowed if both suits were brought in courts that have abandoned the mutuality approach?

## Outer Space

8. Armstrong sues Ride and Gagarin in federal court for injuries arising out of a three-car auto accident. Each defendant denies negligence and claims that Armstrong was negligent, a complete defense under applicable negligence law. After trial, the jury finds for Armstrong against Ride but finds Gagarin not liable.

Subsequently, Gagarin sues Ride for his injuries in the accident. Ride pleads contributory negligence (a complete defense). Visually, the two cases look like this:

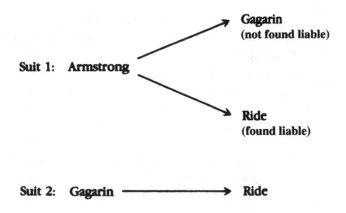

a. Could Gagarin have joined his claim against Ride in the first suit?

b. Who would seek to invoke collateral estoppel in the second action? On what issues?

c. Is this mutual or nonmutual estoppel?

     d. Which party would invoke defensive estoppel and which would invoke offensive estoppel?

     e. Will the court allow use of estoppel on any issues?

# Explanations

## A Fundamental Question

1. We began this voyage by emphasizing that every litigant is entitled to due process of law before a court adjudicates his rights. See Chapter 1, p. 3. The very essence of due process is an opportunity for the parties to be heard, to litigate the issues before those issues are resolved for or against them. If Cartier won his suit against La Salle and then sued Cortez for violating the same lease provision, Cortez would be a new party who has never had an opportunity to litigate the validity of the provision. It would come as quite a surprise to Cortez to learn that he had effectively lost his action (because the crucial issue was already decided in Cartier's favor) before he had even reached the courthouse, simply because La Salle had previously lost his suit. Cortez may well believe that he can litigate the lease question more effectively than La Salle, who may not have had the resources to litigate the issue aggressively or may have made a tactical decision to focus his defense on other grounds. Maybe Cortez won't do better but under the due process clause every party gets one chance to try, and Cortez has not yet had his "bite at the apple."

    Although it would promote efficiency to estop Cortez from relitigating decided issues (just as it promotes efficiency to bar La Salle from doing so under traditional estoppel doctrine), efficiency is only one goal of the procedural system. In this case it is outweighed by the countervailing value of fairness to new parties.

## Who's Who?

2. The *Bernhard* case is an example of nonmutual collateral estoppel because the party seeking to invoke estoppel was not a party to the suit in which the issue was initially decided. That action was between the heirs (including Bernhard) and Cook. Under mutuality doctrine, only these original parties could use or be barred by estoppel in subsequent cases. The bank, a new party, would not be entitled to assert estoppel because it was not a party to the original suit and hence took no risk of being estopped on the issue if it were decided in Bernhard's favor. Since the bank could not be burdened by the result in the original case (see the explanation above for example 1), courts that adhered to the mutuality

rule concluded that it should not be able to benefit from the prior decision if Bernhard lost.

## Charting the Terrain

3. a. The issue that is common to both actions is whether Lewis owns the land. Lewis won on this issue in the first suit and is therefore the party likely to assert estoppel in the second to establish his ownership of the property.

   b. Lewis will not be allowed to estop Fremont on the ownership issue because Fremont, like Cortez in the earlier example, has never had his day in court on the question of Lewis's title, and no court will estop him from litigating that issue until he has had a full and fair opportunity to do so. Besides, Fremont was not a party to the original action, and the mutuality doctrine confines estoppel to the parties to the original suit or those in privity with the original parties.

   c. It is crucial to understand that estoppel would also be denied on these facts in a nonmutuality jurisdiction. As indicated above, Fremont has never had an opportunity to litigate the issue of Lewis's title to the land; due process entitles Fremont to an opportunity to do so. The abandonment of mutuality has *not* changed this basic tenet of the system. In every nonmutual estoppel situation, the estopped party must have been a party in the first suit and therefore had his chance to litigate the issue. Thus, the crucial question in such cases is the one emphasized in *Bernhard*: whether the party being estopped litigated the issue in the prior action. Because Fremont was not a party in the first suit and did not litigate and lose on the issue, estoppel would not bar him from litigating the issue in the second action.

4. a. In this case, Fremont would seek to take advantage of the finding in the prior action that Lewis did not own the land. If Fremont can estop Lewis from trying to prove that he owns the land, Fremont will defeat Lewis's claim, since a plaintiff must prove that he has an interest in the property to recover for trespass.

   b. Fremont would be invoking nonmutual collateral estoppel since he was not a party to the prior action. The only parties who could use mutual collateral estoppel are Lewis and Clark, the parties to the first suit. Here estoppel is invoked against a prior party by a stranger to the original action

   c. This would be defensive collateral estoppel since Fremont, the defendant, would invoke estoppel to prevent Lewis, the plaintiff in the first suit, from relitigating the ownership issue that he had previously litigated and lost. Lewis is analogous to the university foundation in

*Blonder-Tongue*, which was barred from relitigating the validity of its patent against a second defendant after failing to prove it in a prior action. See the diagram on p. 598.

d. In a jurisdiction that has abandoned mutuality, the court would have the authority to apply defensive nonmutual collateral estoppel to bar Lewis from relitigating the ownership issue. Under *Bernhard* and *Blonder-Tongue*, a court may allow the use of defensive estoppel by a new party, so long as the party being estopped was a party to the prior action and litigated the issue there. Those criteria are met here because Lewis was a party to the prior suit against Clark and litigated and lost on the ownership issue in that action.

However, the court would not automatically apply defensive estoppel to bar Lewis from relitigating. As the *Bernhard* court pointed out, and the Supreme Court reiterated in *Blonder-Tongue*, a party who has already litigated an issue should not be estopped from relitigating it unless he had a full and fair opportunity to contest the issue in the first action. Thus, the court will only apply estoppel if it is convinced, after review of the proceedings in the first suit, that Lewis had the incentive and opportunity to litigate the ownership issue tenaciously against Clark.

The burden to establish that the issue was fully litigated falls on Fremont, the party invoking estoppel. Friedenthal, Kane, and Miller at §14.11. Thus, the abandonment of mutuality opens the door to preclusion in situations like this, but the court must exercise caution in deciding who to let in.

5. a. This is an example of offensive estoppel. Here, Wright invokes the negligence finding from the first action to *establish* an issue necessary for recovery against Lindbergh, the defendant in both the first and second suits. Wright seeks to use estoppel "as a sword," to establish a fact necessary to recovery, rather than as a "shield" against liability, as in example 4. See the diagram on p. 599 supra.

b. Because estoppel is invoked by Wright, a new party who did not litigate the negligence issue in the first action, this is nonmutual estoppel. Of course, Lindbergh *was* a party to the first suit; in every nonmutual estoppel case *one* of the parties in the second suit will have been a party (or in privity with a party) to the first, since estoppel may only be invoked against a party who litigated and lost on the issue before.

c. The Supreme Court held in *Parklane* that the federal courts may apply offensive nonmutual collateral estoppel in situations such as this in which a new plaintiff invokes estoppel to establish an issue that was decided against the defendant in a prior suit. Although Wright, the new party invoking estoppel, was not a party to the original action, the party against whom it was invoked (in this case Lindbergh) was there and litigated the issue in the first suit. Lindbergh has had an opportunity to be heard on the issue, the fundamental prerequisite to barring relitigation.

However, as in the defensive estoppel cases, the court will not automatically bar Lindbergh from relitigating. The court must examine the circumstances of the first case to determine whether Lindbergh had an adequate opportunity to litigate and whether other cautionary factors (such as whether Wright sat out the first suit to see how Earhart would fare) counsel against application of estoppel.

In this case, several of these factors favor application of estoppel. First, since Earhart's injuries were serious, Lindbergh presumably had a strong incentive to defend her action vigorously to avoid paying substantial damages. Second, Wright was a passenger in the same plane; surely Lindbergh would foresee that he would sue as well. Third, the example indicates that both suits were brought in federal court. Thus, there are not likely to be procedural advantages available to Lindbergh in the second suit that were not available in the first; both will governed by the Federal Rules of Civil Procedure. Absent other factors suggesting unfairness to Lindbergh, this case looks like a good candidate for application of nonmutual offensive collateral estoppel.[3]

## New Frontiers

6. a. The first step in analyzing this case, as in every collateral estoppel case, mutual or otherwise, is to determine what issues were decided in the first action that may recur in the second. In this case the verdict for Mrs. Byrd indicates that the jury found Da Gama negligent. However, their verdict for Da Gama against Mr. Byrd indicates that they also found Mr. Byrd contributorily negligent.[4] It is this finding that is relevant to the second action: If Vespucci pleads contributory negligence as a defense to Mr. Byrd's suit and is able to invoke collateral estoppel to establish it, he will escape liability regardless of his own negligence.

   b. This example looks partly like offensive estoppel and partly like defensive estoppel. It is like defensive use because the defendant in the second action invokes estoppel to preclude Byrd, a plaintiff in

---

3. The four factors discussed in *Parklane* are not exclusive. Other factors may also counsel against giving the prior determination preclusive effect. See Restatement (Second) of Judgments §29.

4. This assumes that the evidence of Mr. Byrd's injuries eliminates the possibility that the jury found that he had suffered no damages. Compare *Illinois Central Gulf R.R. Co. v. Parks*, 390 N.E.2d 1078 (Ind. App. 1979)

both the first and second suits, from relitigating an issue that he litigated and lost upon in the prior suit.

However, the case is like offensive use in that Vespucci uses estoppel to establish a fact — in this case, the *affirmative defense* of Byrd's negligence — that Byrd lost on in the first case. In cases such as *Blonder-Tongue*, the plaintiff lost on an issue that was an element of his prima facie case and was precluded in a later action from proving that element. In this case, Vespucci is not trying to use estoppel to prevent Byrd from proving an element of his case; he is using it to establish a defense against the claim based on Byrd's contributory negligence. In one sense he uses it as a "sword" to establish a fact, Byrd's negligence. In another, he uses it as a "shield," to prevent Byrd from proving that he is liable by borrowing the finding from an earlier suit in which Byrd lost on the same issue. Thus, it is a hybrid case, not quite like the classic defensive or offensive situation. Most courts would probably call this defensive estoppel, based on the fact that the party invoking estoppel is a defendant, as in *Bernhard* and *Blonder-Tongue*, and that the defendant invokes estoppel to avoid liability.[5]

c. Vespucci would not be able to assert collateral estoppel in a mutuality jurisdiction since he was not a party to the first suit and therefore is not allowed to take advantage of favorable findings in that action.

d. A court in a nonmutuality jurisdiction could allow Vespucci to invoke collateral estoppel even though he was not a party to the Byrd/Da Gama suit in which Byrd's negligence was initially established. As in all nonmutual estoppel cases, however, estoppel would be discretionary. The court will only apply estoppel if it is convinced that Byrd had a full opportunity and incentive to litigate the issue of his negligence in the first action.

7. a. The *Enquirer* was the defendant in the first action, and lost on the issue of whether it is a newspaper within the meaning of the California statute. In the second action, two new plaintiffs try to use the finding from the first case to help establish their case against the *Enquirer*, a defendant in each suit. Based on the configuration of the parties, this would likely be classified as offensive collateral estoppel.

Just as example 6 represents a twist on the typical defensive estoppel case, this is not quite the classic example of offensive nonmutual estoppel. Here the new plaintiff asserts estoppel to preclude the

---

5. This is not entirely a matter of semantics. The characterization can make a difference, since some courts are more receptive to defensive nonmutual estoppel than to offensive nonmutual estoppel.

defendant from proving a defense that failed in the first action. In the more typical offensive use situation, the plaintiff asserts collateral estoppel to establish an element of his prima facie case (such as the defendant's negligence) after another plaintiff proved that element against the same defendant in a prior action. In *Parklane*, for example, the plaintiffs in the second suit had to prove that the proxy statement was false and misleading in order to recover. They sought to do so by borrowing the court's finding to that effect in the earlier action.

b. Estoppel would be denied in a mutuality jurisdiction since Reddy and Wald were not parties to the prior action or in privity with the plaintiff in that action.

c. The answer to this example is a cautious "maybe." The analysis must start with the truism at the end of the Introduction. Nonmutual estoppel is a species of collateral estoppel; as such, it is only applicable if the basic prerequisites for estoppel are satisfied. Before collateral estoppel can ever be applied, the court must determine that the issue in the first and second actions is the same. Here, it is clear that the issue of the *Enquirer*'s status as a magazine or newspaper under the California statute was litigated and decided in the first action. But obviously, estoppel will only apply if the issue in the Reddy/Wald suit is the same, that is, if the California statute applies. If Reddy and Wald reside in Virginia and suffered most of their damages there, a court might not apply the California statute to their suit at all; it might apply Virginia law, which might authorize magazines as well as newspapers to escape liability by printing a retraction or not allow the retraction defense at all. Thus, the issue may be different in the second suit or irrelevant to it.

Assuming that the California statute would apply in the Reddy/Wald suit, the court would still have to consider the various factors that may make offensive nonmutual estoppel inappropriate. Although it certainly appears that the *Enquirer* had a strong incentive to litigate the issue in the Burnett case, it might not be fair to apply estoppel if the procedural system in which the second suit was brought was more flexible, or if important witnesses were unavailable to the *Enquirer* in the first case but can be produced in the second. Or the court could deny preclusion if it determined that Reddy and Wald had deliberately decided *not* to join in the Burnett case in order to get the advantage of nonmutual estoppel without taking the risk of losing on the issue in the first action. (This would not be a problem on the facts here because the incident involving Reddy and Wald took place long after the Burnett case was filed.) Once again, the point is that the abandonment of mutuality opens the door to case-by-case consideration of whether estoppel should be available to the new party; it does not automatically lead to preclusion.

## Outer Space

8. a. Gagarin could have cross-claimed against Ride for his injuries in the first action, under Fed. R. Civ. P. 13(g), but was not required to do so, since Rule 13(g) is permissive. Thus, he may bring the claim separately. Res judicata does not bar the separate suit because Gagarin's claim against Ride was never adjudicated in the first suit: he never asserted a right to relief against her. See Chapter 27, example 7.

   b. The verdicts in the first action indicate that the jury found Ride negligent, but not Gagarin or Armstrong. If Armstrong was negligent, he would have lost against Ride. If Gagarin was negligent, he would have been held liable along with Ride. In the second action, Gagarin would assert collateral estoppel to estop Ride from relitigating both her own negligence and Gagarin's.

   c. This could be either mutual or nonmutual estoppel, depending on what Ride and Gagarin actually attempted to prove in the first action. Although they were both parties to the prior suit, they were not adversaries, and neither had to try to prove the other's negligence. Ride, for example, may have defended by trying to show that she acted with due care and that Armstrong's negligence caused the accident. If that is true, then she has not litigated the issue of Gagarin's negligence. Similarly, Gagarin may have simply tried to show that he was careful and Armstrong was not. If that is true, then he has not litigated the question of Ride's negligence. On these assumptions, use of estoppel in the second action would be nonmutual, since (while Ride and Gagarin were both parties to the first suit) neither has litigated the other's negligence. Consequently, they would not be able to assert preclusion against each other in a mutuality jurisdiction. The key to "mutuality" is not just having been a party to a prior suit but actually having litigated issues against one another.

   Suppose, however, that Ride and Gagarin had each defended against Armstrong by trying to show that the other was negligent. Then they *would* have litigated each other's negligence in the prior suit, even though they did not assert claims for relief against each other. On this assumption, they would each be bound by the decision on those issues, even in a mutuality jurisdiction.

   d. Gagarin's assertion of estoppel on the issue of Ride's negligence is an offensive use of estoppel: He invokes estoppel as a "sword" to establish Ride's negligence, a fact necessary to impose liability on Ride, which was established in the prior action. Assuming that Gagarin had not tried to prove Ride's negligence in the prior action, this would be nonmutual offensive collateral estoppel since he would be seeking to establish Ride's negligence on the basis of the fact that Armstrong had proved it in the first case.

Gagarin might also invoke defensive estoppel to defeat Ride's contributory negligence defense. That is, he would claim that since he was found free of negligence in the first action, estoppel should bar relitigation of the issue. Assuming again that Gagarin and Ride did not try to prove each other negligent in the first suit, this would be nonmutual estoppel. Gagarin would be trying to estop Ride from proving his negligence because Armstrong (the plaintiff in the prior action) had failed to prove it.

e. First, let's consider Gagarin's use of defensive estoppel against Ride. If Ride and Gagarin did not attempt to prove each other's negligence in the prior action, the court will not allow Gagarin to estop Ride from relitigating Gagarin's negligence. Ride was under no duty to litigate Gagarin's negligence to defend the first suit, and she chose not to do so. Although they were both parties to the suit, they were not adversaries and were not required under the procedural rules to assert claims against each other. Although Armstrong was unable to prove Gagarin's negligence, Ride will be entitled to her opportunity to do so unless it is clear from the record of the first action that she tried to in that suit.

The situation is different as to Gagarin's use of offensive estoppel on the issue of Ride's negligence. Ride did fully litigate that question in the prior action and lost. Gagarin now seeks to use offensive estoppel to establish Ride's negligence in his own action for damages. The court will have to review the proceedings in the first action to determine whether it would be appropriate, under the *Parklane* analysis, to apply collateral estoppel based on it.

Ride will no doubt argue that Gagarin decided to "wait and see" whether Ride was found negligent in the first action, in hopes of using offensive collateral estoppel in the second. See *Parklane* at 330. Gagarin could have asserted his claim for damages as a cross-claim in the prior action and the court would have had supplemental jurisdiction over it. See Chapter 16, example 3. Although he had the right to withhold the claim in the first action, since cross-claims under Fed. R. Civ. P. 13(g) are permissive, the court (Ride will argue) should deny him the further benefit of offensive collateral estoppel since he chose this less efficient course.

Few cases address whether a party will be barred from using offensive collateral estoppel because he failed to assert a claim in a prior action. This seems like a particularly strong case for denying estoppel, since Gagarin was already in the suit and the negligence issues were already being litigated against another party. See Restatement (Second) of Judgments, §29(3) (ability to join claim in prior suit supports denial of nonmutual estoppel). However, refusing to apply estoppel in this case, in order to deprive Gagarin of the benefit of holding back his claim, also burdens the court system with additional litigation on an issue already resolved. If all the other prudential factors favor preclusion, it seems doubtful that the court will refuse to apply it simply because Gagarin exercised his right under the rules to bring his own action against Ride. See, however, *Nanninga v. Three Rivers Electric Co-op.*, 203 F.3d 529 (8th Cir. 2000) (relying on *Parklane* in refusing to allow party who could have joined prior action to assert offensive nonmutual collateral estoppel).

# Thinking Procedurally: The Rules in Action

# An Introduction to the Pretrial Litigation Process

Setting the Stage for the *Schulansky* Case

The first five parts of this book have dealt with the "substance" of civil procedure, that is, the various judicial rules and doctrines that govern the litigation process. The chapters that follow are intended to give you a sense of how the process actually works by chronicling the early stages of a typical (though hypothetical) civil case, *Schulansky v. Ronan*. Each chapter includes the court papers filed at one stage of the *Schulansky* suit, including typical pleadings, motions, and supporting documents. In addition, the materials provide a look at the legal and tactical questions that the attorneys considered in drafting those documents. This chapter is intended to help you to place the ones that follow in context, by providing a brief description of the process of litigating a civil suit from the beginning up until trial.

## PREPARATION FOR FILING SUIT

In most cases the litigation process begins well before the parties get to court. Obviously, the first step is for the client to bring a dispute to a lawyer. The plaintiff's lawyer will obtain as much information as possible from the client. On the basis of this information, some investigation, and her assessment of the client, the lawyer must make a judgment as to whether to take the case. If she does agree to take it, she will propose a fee arrangement, and if the client accepts, a contract for services will be signed. In personal injury actions the agreement will frequently provide for a contingent fee, that is, an attorney's fee based on a percentage of any

**617**

eventual recovery, frequently set at one-third of the amount recovered. The expenses of the action, such as filing fees, deposition costs, expert witness fees, and other out-of-pocket expenditures, will also be paid out of the recovery.

Once the plaintiff's lawyer has agreed to handle the case, she will conduct a preliminary investigation of the events giving rise to the claim. She will obtain as much information as possible from her client and from other witnesses who are willing to discuss the case. She will gather and review documentary evidence, such as accident reports, correspondence, business records, government reports, or other available materials. She will also do preliminary legal research if the case involves novel theories of recovery or other critical issues of law, in order to ascertain whether her client's injuries give rise to a right to relief.

On the basis of this preliminary development of the case, the plaintiff's attorney will usually send a claim letter to the defendant or her insurer, or discuss the claim with the defendant's counsel in order to explore the possibility of settling the claim without bringing suit. Many claims can be settled without the expense of litigation, particularly if there is little question as to liability and the only issue is the extent of the plaintiff's damages. However, in other cases the settlement value of a claim will depend on facts that have not yet been fully explored at this early stage. In the *Schulansky* case, for example, the defendant's judgment of the settlement value of the claim will turn in part on the parties' testimony as to their negotiations before the construction work began. The plaintiff's testimony as to those negotiations will only be available to the defendant through court-supervised "discovery" in the course of litigation. In such cases the parties will be less likely to reach an agreement until suit is brought and the facts are more fully developed.

The plaintiff's attorney must also consider a number of tactical issues in deciding whether to file suit. She must consider whether the case is strong enough and the value of a potential judgment high enough to justify the considerable expense of litigation. She must assess whether the client is patient enough and financially solvent enough to await a judgment several years down the road. She must consider possible alternative means of obtaining a remedy, such as invoking the assistance of a public agency, seeking an administrative remedy, or agreeing to mediation or arbitration.

## DRAFTING THE COMPLAINT

Assuming that informal settlement efforts fail, and the plaintiff's attorney concludes that it makes sense to file suit on the claim, she will begin the lawsuit by filing a complaint, the first "pleading" required under the Federal

Rules (and many similar state rules). Pleadings are the papers filed by the parties at the beginning of the action, in which they set forth their positions as to the facts in issue. Pleadings are not evidence; they are not even sworn testimony by the parties or their attorneys. They are simply statements of the parties' positions on the factual and legal issues in dispute.

In the simplest two-party suit the only pleadings required will be a complaint, in which the plaintiff sets forth her claim, and an answer, in which the defendant responds by stating her position as to each of the allegations in the complaint and asserting any other defenses she may have to the plaintiff's claim. See the plaintiff's complaint in the *Schulansky* case, infra p. 634, and Ronan's answer, infra p. 663. But further pleadings may be necessary if additional parties are brought into the suit or if counter-claims are asserted. See, e.g., Chapter 34, which includes a third-party complaint; see also Fed. R. Civ. P. 7(a), which describes the various pleadings that may be filed in appropriate circumstances.

Both the form and the content of the complaint are governed by the rules of procedure applicable in the court where the suit is filed. Because the *Schulansky* case was filed in the Massachusetts Superior Court, it must comply with the Massachusetts Rules of Civil Procedure, which are quite similar to the Federal Rules. Chapter 31 illustrates in detail how the complaint was drafted to comply with those rules. In addition, most courts have local rules of procedure that supplement the general civil rules. For example, the Massachusetts Superior Court has its own supplementary rules that cover numerous details of practice before that court. Thus, all applicable local rules must be checked in order to comply with any additional requirements.

In drafting the complaint, counsel must also consider whether the procedural rules allow joinder of all the desired parties as plaintiffs or defendants. (The joinder rules are analyzed in Chapters 13-17). The substantive law governing the plaintiff's claims must also be analyzed to ascertain whether there is good ground to file suit on the claims asserted in the complaint. A large part of the attorneys' memos in the following chapters is devoted to considering whether the law of contracts and negligence will support the claims for relief in the *Schulansky* case, and, if so, how those claims should be asserted in the pleadings.

# TACTICAL CONSIDERATIONS IN CHOOSING THE FORUM

The plaintiff's counsel faces a number of "real world" tactical issues in deciding where to bring a lawsuit. To begin with, she must choose a court that has subject matter jurisdiction, personal jurisdiction over the defendant, and satisfies the applicable rules of venue. See Part I for a detailed analysis of those requirements. It may not always be clear from the facts whether jurisdiction and venue are proper in a particular court. (In *Schulansky*, for example, there is some doubt as to whether the Massachusetts court has personal jurisdiction over the defendants.) If so, the attorney will have to make a judgment as to whether the advantages of litigating in her chosen forum are outweighed by the risk that the suit will be dismissed on one of these grounds, causing additional expense to the client and possible statute of limitations problems.

The plaintiff's counsel must also decide whether to file suit in federal or state court, assuming, as will frequently be the case, that jurisdiction and venue are satisfied in both. Numerous factors may be important in making that choice. For example, the scope of pretrial discovery may be broader in federal court. Federal courts also have broader power to transfer cases than do state courts. On the other hand, the scope of interlocutory review may be broader in state court than federal court. (See Chapter 3, example 9, concerning interlocutory appeal of decisions on motions to dismiss for lack of personal jurisdiction.) The right to join additional parties may differ, as may the court's power to exercise personal jurisdiction over them.

Differences involving the trial process itself may also be important in a case. For example, the rules of evidence in the state and federal courts may differ in crucial respects. The power of the court to subpoena witnesses will differ. The ethnic and economic characteristics of the jury will differ because a federal court jury will be drawn from a broader geographical area. The judges in one system may be more familiar with the type of case in suit. It may be possible to get to trial a good deal more quickly in one system than another (or in one state than another).

Convenience may also play an important role in the decision. The plaintiff's lawyer may be more familiar with practice in one system. One court may be more conveniently located for the plaintiff (or her attorney) or more inconvenient for the defendant (or her attorney). Attorney Slater's initial memo in the *Schulansky* case does not reveal all of the factors she considered in deciding to go to state court, but proximity to her client's home and her own office was undoubtedly an important one in such a relatively small case. Innumerable other such factors may also be significant in a particular case.[1]

---

1. For a more detailed discussion of the tactical reasons for choosing state or federal court, see S. Steinglass, The Emerging State Court §1983 Action: A Procedural Review, 38 U. Miami L. Rev. 381, 412-424 (1984).

# FILING THE COMPLAINT

In view of all these considerations, the attorney will draft the complaint, file it with the clerk of the appropriate court, and serve it on the defendant. (As to the proper methods of service, see Chapter 18.) If the defendant is already represented by counsel, the plaintiff's lawyer may as a matter of courtesy call the defendant's lawyer to let her know that suit is being filed. In turn, the defendant's counsel may agree to accept service of the complaint and summons without compliance with the formal service rules.

It is only upon the filing of the complaint that the court gets involved in the case. At least initially, its involvement will be minimal. The clerk will assign a docket number to the case and establish a case file. All subsequent pleadings and other papers filed in the case will be "docketed," that is, entered on a docket sheet kept with the case file, and added to the file. Not surprisingly, case dockets are increasingly computerized, and many courts now allow electronic access to court records and electronic filing of pleadings and other papers. In federal courts, the case will usually be assigned to a judge when the complaint is filed; that judge will then preside over the case for the duration.

In some state courts, however, the case is not permanently assigned; different proceedings will be heard by different judges depending on which judge is "sitting" at the time a motion comes up for hearing or when the case is reached on the trial list. For example, if the Schulansky case had remained in Massachusetts state court, the motion to dismiss might have been heard by Judge A, but a motion for summary judgment by Judge B. Judge B would have no previous knowledge of the case but would have to review the pleadings and other papers before or during the hearing to familiarize herself with the suit. When the case reached trial, it might be tried before Judge C, who was assigned to the civil jury session at the time the case was reached on the trial list. By contrast, in federal court the same judge would preside over the suit from the outset and would develop a "feel" for the case through hearings on motions, discovery conferences, and other pretrial proceedings. Knowing which judge will preside over the case can have an important effect on the attorneys' tactical decisions.

# RESPONDING TO THE COMPLAINT

Once the defendant or her counsel receives the complaint, she must respond. In most cases, the defendant will answer the complaint. If the defendant has certain preliminary objections to the suit, however, she may move to dismiss instead. See the motion to dismiss for lack of personal jurisdiction filed by Jones, the third-party defendant in the *Schulansky* case, infra p. 693. Chapter 19 reviews in detail the circumstances in which a motion to dismiss may be filed instead of an answer.

It is important to understand the difference between a pleading and a motion. A motion is not a pleading. See Fed. R. Civ. P. 7(a) and (b), which provide separately for pleadings and motions. The pleadings set forth the positions of the parties on the claim. A motion, by contrast, is a direct application to the court for an order. Whenever a party seeks action from the court, a motion is the appropriate way to do so. For example, a defendant's motion to dismiss for lack of personal jurisdiction is a direct request to the court to dismiss the case.

Although many types of motions are specifically provided for in the Rules (see, e.g., Fed. R. Civ. P. 12(b), (e); 56), the motion is a flexible device for seeking any type of action from the court. Other common examples are motions for further discovery, motions to place a case on the trial list, to convene a discovery conference, to implead a third party, to amend the complaint or answer, to extend the time to answer, or for any other assistance in the litigation process. (One well-known pro se litigant in Massachusetts is rumored to have filed a "Motion for a Landmark Decision"!)

If the defendant answers the complaint instead of moving to dismiss, her answer must set forth her position on the allegations in the complaint. As Chapter 31 demonstrates, the Federal Rules of Civil Procedure require the plaintiff in federal suits to set forth her allegations in numbered paragraphs. The defendant's answer must respond to each allegation, paragraph by paragraph. The defendant may also assert affirmative defenses or counterclaims in the answer, as Ronan has done. The answer usually must be filed with the court and served on the plaintiff. The rules require the answer or motion to dismiss to be filed within 20 days, but extensions of time to answer are frequently granted, often with the consent of the opposing party.

# DISCOVERY

Once the pleadings are complete, the case will move into the *discovery phase*. Discovery is the process by which the parties obtain information from each other and outside witnesses through several commonsense devices authorized by the rules of procedure. In the federal courts, four primary discovery devices are used to develop factual evidence in preparation for trial. *Interrogatories*, authorized by Fed. R. Civ. P. 33, are written questions sent by one party to another, which must be answered under oath. *Requests for production of documents*, under Fed. R. Civ. P. 34, are requests from a party for an opposing party to produce documents that may be relevant to the issues in suit, for inspection or copying by the requesting party. The third basic discovery tool is the *oral deposition*, authorized by Fed. R. Civ. P. 30. A deposition is a procedure for taking oral testimony from a witness. Fourth, the federal discovery rules require parties to make automatic disclosure of certain information regarding the case. In most federal court cases, the parties are now required to confer and plan for disclosures and discovery before they begin the discovery process. Fed. R. Civ. P. 26(d), (f).

Usually counsel will take the depositions of crucial witnesses for the other party, in order to prepare for trial and to get the witness's testimony "on the record." The deposition is taken before a licensed court reporter, usually at the office of one of the parties' attorneys. The witness testifies under oath and may be represented by counsel. Counsel for opposing parties are entitled to cross-examine but usually do not do so extensively unless the deposition will be used at trial in place of live testimony.

Many cases involve complex technical issues, sophisticated reconstruction of accidents, complex statistical or economic projections, or specialized knowledge of medical procedures. In such cases, a crucial aspect of trial preparation is the hiring and preparation of expert witnesses. Both sides will retain, often at considerable expense, recognized experts in the relevant discipline to testify on issues like causation, proper technique for industrial or medical procedures, accident reconstruction, or probable future damages. Both sides will seek discovery of the other side's experts. Much time will also be spent educating their own experts about the case, conducting experiments or calculations, and preparing them for direct and cross-examination.

As with other aspects of life, the computer has changed the process of litigation. Lawyers now need a good deal of technical savvy and support to litigate effectively. Increasingly, parties employ sophisticated computer programs to store, organize, and retrieve litigation data, and to develop effective courtroom presentations. An even greater impact of technology has been the change in the form of discoverable information. Some 90 percent of business documents now exist only in cyberspace; they are never printed out. R. Marcus, M. Redish, E. Sherman, Civil Procedure: A Modern Approach 377. Critical information may lurk on back-up disks, servers, hard drives, in "metadata" files, and other newfangled and mysterious places. There is exponentially more information and more complexity in retrieving and protecting it. "E-discovery" is upon us, whether we are ready for it or not.

Despite the emphasis in this book on procedural rules and doctrines, the most crucial phase of a lawsuit is the development of the evidence through the discovery process and investigation by the attorneys. Most cases are won, lost, or settled on the basis of the strength of the facts, and it is through discovery that the facts and the credibility of the crucial witnesses can be evaluated. Typically, the discovery phase will take at least a year in a substantial case, but it may take considerably longer.

## ATTORNEY COOPERATION IN THE DISCOVERY PROCESS

Throughout this period, it is the attorneys who conduct the litigation by using the discovery tools provided in the rules, reponding to discovery requests from the other side, and developing the evidence to support their cases at trial. In many cases judicial involvement may be minimal right down to the time of trial. The attorneys carry the laboring oar by filing their pleadings, sending and responding to requests for discovery, scheduling and conducting depositions, meeting to discuss settlement, and, where possible, agreeing to stipulations of the undisputed facts to shorten the trial.

Because discovery is conducted primarily by the attorneys, it is important for opposing counsel to cooperate in the discovery process. The formality of the civil procedure rules and the adversary nature of litigation practice frequently lead beginning attorneys to conclude that they are not serving their clients unless they resist every request of opposing counsel. In the long run, however, unrestrained belligerence is counter-productive. It is entirely feasible for counsel to work together to facilitate moving a case to trial without in any way compromising their clients' substantive rights.

For example, many questions will arise during the pleading and discovery phases of the suit that can be resolved by agreements of counsel. Extensions of time to file pleadings can be agreed to, saving the need to argue a contested motion for an extension. Stipulations of agreed facts can be drawn up to obviate the need to prove those facts at trial. Disagreements as to the scope or timing of discovery, claims of attorney-client privilege, or limits imposed by a preliminary injunction may often be worked out by counsel instead of taking court time. In addition, scheduling of depositions and hearings on pretrial motions can be arranged with opposing counsel. In these and other ways, the process will run much more smoothly (and inexpensively) for all concerned if the attorneys cooperate.

## THE CHANGING JUDICIAL ROLE IN LITIGATION

Under the traditional model (still followed to a degree in many state courts) the court itself plays a largely passive role in litigation. The parties file the pleadings, conduct discovery, initiate settlement discussions, and seek a trial when ready. Under this system, there is no active, periodic judicial review of pending cases. For example, a judge will not review complaints as they are filed to determine whether the court has personal jurisdiction over the defendant or the complaint states a claim upon which relief can be granted. It is up to the attorneys to raise such questions by filing an appropriate motion. The court is simply there as a referee to respond to motions by the parties if the pleading or discovery process goes awry and to supply a judge to preside over the trial when and if a trial is necessary. If the attorneys choose to litigate at a leisurely pace, the court under this model does little to force them to trial.

However, the litigation process is moving away from this "hands off" model as the volume of litigation increasingly strains court resources. Particularly in the federal courts, judges are taking an activist role in managing cases by monitoring the discovery and disclosure process, limiting the issues in pretrial conferences, and setting deadlines for discovery and trial. For example, the court in federal cases is now required to enter a scheduling order in many cases, setting deadlines for the joinder of additional parties, amendment of pleadings, and completion of discovery. See Fed. R. Civ. P. 16 (b). The court may also schedule discovery conferences with the attorneys to monitor the progress of discovery, to narrow the issues, and to encourage settlement discussions. See Fed. R. Civ. P. 16(a), (c).

---

# MOVING TOWARDS TRIAL

As discussed in Chapter 23, lawsuits may be cut short by pretrial dismissal or summary judgment. However, most cases survive these hurdles and, if not settled during the discovery phase, continue on track toward the culmination of the litigation process: a trial on the merits. As the discovery process nears completion, the court will usually hold a pretrial conference to resolve pending motions, address evidentiary issues, encourage stipulations as to undisputed facts, determine the issues and witnesses for trial, explore the possibility of settlement, and set a final schedule for trial. See Fed. R. Civ. P. 16. In some systems, trials may be fairly prompt, but in others the court's caseload forces long delays before the case is reached on the trial list. Such delays may lead counsel to agree to various alternative dispute resolution mechanisms — such as mediation, arbitration, or a summary trial — to try to resolve the case without waiting for a formal trial. If the parties persevere, they will eventually get a trial, but it is almost impossible in many systems to predict or control exactly when that will be.

Most cases, even if they are actively litigated through the discovery phase and are set down for trial, are never tried. More than 90 percent of all civil actions are ultimately settled, many on the eve of trial. However, the considerable effort that goes into discovery and pretrial preparation in such cases is not wasted. It is the intensive development of the facts and the parties' increasingly sophisticated understanding of the strengths and weaknesses of their positions that make an equitable settlement possible. As trial approaches, settlement discussions become more focused, and the parties usually begin to move toward an acceptable middle ground. In addition, the incentive to settle increases markedly as trial becomes an impending reality rather than a distant possibility.

# THE ATTORNEY'S EXPERIENCE OF LITIGATION

All of this is very well, but it still gives little impression of what the experience of litigation is like for the lawyers who conduct it. In practice, litigation is episodic. A lawyer may have anywhere from 20 to 50 or more active cases at a time, at various stages from pre-filing investigation to post-trial motions. At any given time, there will not be much happening in many of those cases: The lawyer might be awaiting responses to discovery requests in one, awaiting judicial action on a motion to dismiss in another, discussing responses to interrogatories with her client in another, drafting an answer in another, awaiting a trial date in another, conducting settlement negotiations, and so on.

Much of the average litigator's time is spent in detailed factual investigation: reviewing depositions and documents produced under discovery requests, interviewing witnesses, meeting with clients or experts, tracking down other sources of proof, and preparing and organizing testimony for trial. The work requires a painstaking attention to detail; a good memory and a methodical approach to trial preparation helps. In addition, a good deal of time is spent drafting pleadings, motions, supporting affidavits, and other materials. There is frequently legal research to be done (especially by junior attorneys in the office) and memoranda to be written in support of or in opposition to pending motions.

A litigator's cases have a way of "acting up" unexpectedly. The morning mail (or e-mail) may bring a motion for summary judgment in a case that has been sitting on the back burner, a motion to compel in a case based on an allegedly inadequate response to a request for production of documents, notice of a deposition of an important witness, or an order from the court to appear for a pretrial conference. The phone rings a lot, often with calls from opposing counsel or a frantic client. Often these litigation events require a prompt response—a memorandum in opposition to a motion, an appearance in court to argue a motion, a conference with a client to draw up answers to interrogatories or plan for a settlement conference, or preparation for and attendance at a deposition.

Often during this process, the litigator must deal with others who are unhappy with her: opposing counsel who doesn't want to produce documents or schedule a deposition, a court clerk who refuses to change a hearing date, a client who can't understand why everything takes so long, a colleague who needs a motion and memo "right away." Stress levels can rise. Diplomacy and patience — two courses not taught in law school — are much-needed survival skills.

Thus, a litigator is constantly juggling a number of cases, trying to keep all the balls in the air at once. The unexpected happens frequently, and a constant procession of deadlines beckons. Occasionally, the process is punctuated by trials, which usually involve an intensive period of long hours and single-minded attention to one case (with consequent reshuffling of commitments in other cases). However, for most litigators, trials are infrequent; litigation practice resembles continuously preparing for exams, most of which are then called off at the last minute. Some lawyers find it exhilarating; others, simply nerve-wracking. Few find it dull.

# First Moves

## Schulansky Goes to Court

## THE DRAFTING REQUEST

### MEMORANDUM

**TO:** David E. Howard
Associate

**FROM:** Phyllis Slater

**RE:** Schulansky construction dispute
Our file No. 06-1248

**DATE:** November 20, 2006

---

Deborah Schulansky, a client of ours, has consulted me concerning a dispute that has arisen between her and a contractor who recently built an addition to her vacation home. It appears that this problem cannot be resolved without filing suit. I would like you to help me with the case.

Although Schulansky lives here in Plymouth, Massachusetts, she also owns an antique colonial home in Alton, New Hampshire, which she uses as a vacation home. The house dates from 1782 and is listed in the National Register of Historic Places. Last spring, Ms. Schulansky met Richard Ronan, a New Hampshire contractor, while he was restoring a house in Plymouth. After some negotiations at her home in Plymouth, the parties agreed that Ronan would build an addition on the back of the Alton house. Ronan mailed a "Proposal and Estimate" to Schulansky in Plymouth, and she signed and returned it. I have attached a copy of the Proposal and Estimate for the job, signed by both parties. [See p. 638 — ED.]

The work involved taking out part of the back wall of the house and building an $18' \times 25'$ addition behind the living room, with a full cellar under the addition. The contractor was to excavate the earth from the original foundation, excavate the adjacent area to be occupied by the addition, lay a cellar floor and foundation walls in the excavated area to support the addition, and build the addition above the new cellar area. In order to provide access to the new cellar, the contractor was to break a doorway through the original foundation of the main house adjacent to the addition.

There were problems from the beginning of the construction work. Ronan hired a backhoe operator named Jones to do the excavation work, as he had told Schulansky he would. When Jones excavated the earth from the original foundation with his backhoe, he discovered that the lower part of the foundation was simply loose rubble. Evidently, in colonial days it was fairly common to simply pile large rocks around the perimeter of the house site and build brick and mortar foundations on top of the rocks. These rubble foundations apparently last remarkably well as long as they are undisturbed, but are less stable if exposed, as was necessary here to construct the cellar for the new addition.

Apparently, there was some discussion during the negotiations about possible problems with the old foundation. Schulansky asked Ronan if he anticipated any problems due to disturbance of the foundation. He responded that he doubted that it would be a problem, but if anything was loose he would do whatever was needed to provide adequate support for the addition. When Schulansky visited the site during construction and observed the excavation, she became concerned about the stability of the original foundation. For one thing, she could see that the foundation was just loose rubble, with no mortar or other support except the surrounding earth. For another, the backhoe had repeatedly ploughed into the old foundation in the course of excavating the new cellar, and loose rocks from the foundation were lying in the ditch next to the foundation. Schulansky asked Ronan several times if the old foundation was adequate and asked him to reinforce or rebuild it. Ronan refused to do any major reconstruction, on the ground that he had not agreed to do so and that it was unnecessary. Instead, he simply poured some cement in between the rocks and left it at that.

In May, when the job was virtually complete, Schulansky began to notice cracks in the plaster walls of the living room, in the bedroom above it, and in the addition itself. She also observed some sagging in the floor at the joint between the main house and the addition. She had a friend who is a structural engineer come and look at the house. He concluded that the cracks resulted from settling of the old foundation, evidently due to shifting of the rubble after exposure during the excavation. He is unsure whether the settling resulted from negligent excavation (that is, the rubble being disturbed by the backhoe), or from the removal of the supporting earth on the outside of the old foundation.

In either case, his opinion is that the settling will continue, causing major structural damage, unless the foundation is rebuilt. Because the addition is now completed, that reconstruction will be substantially more expensive than it would have been if it had been done during construction of the addition. He estimates that it could cost as much as $25,000 to jack up the house and reconstruct the foundation, and another $80,000 to repair the damage to the house due to the settlement of the foundation.

Schulansky has tried to work this out with Ronan, but he denies any responsibility. Consequently, she refused to make the final payment under the contract. I have talked to Ronan myself, and written him a demand letter, but it is clear that he will refuse to provide any satisfaction to our client. Instead, he has threatened to file suit himself if Schulansky does not pay him the last progress payment under the contract.

I intend to initiate suit against Ronan personally and against Ronan Construction Company for breach of contract and negligence. Although we could probably bring suit in federal court on the basis of diversity (Ronan lives in Nashua, Ronan Construction is incorporated in New Hampshire, and its principal place of business is probably in New Hampshire), I would prefer to litigate here in Plymouth Superior Court.

I realize that we may have a claim against Jones as well. At the moment, however, I am not even sure of Jones's full name, much less where he lives, whether he is insured, and whether he is subject to personal jurisdiction here. We will have to learn more about Jones through discovery and amend to add him if necessary. But I have some hope that this can be settled quickly without the expense of lengthy, multi-party litigation.

Please draft a complaint and summons to initiate this suit in the Superior Court for Plymouth County. If you need further information, talk to me or call Ms. Schulansky directly. As you know, Rules 8-11 of the Massachusetts Rules of Civil Procedure are similar to Rules 8-11 of the Federal Rules of Civil Procedure. One important distinction for our purposes is that it is unnecessary under the Massachusetts version of Rule 8 to allege the basis for subject matter jurisdiction. Compare Fed. R. Civ. P. 8(a)(1).

We will also want to assert our right to a jury trial. See Mass. R. Civ. P. 38(b) (identical in relevant part to Fed. R. Civ. P. 38(b)).

# THE ASSOCIATE'S RESPONSE

## MEMORANDUM

**TO:**  Phyllis Slater

**FROM:**  David E. Howard

**RE:**  Complaint in *Schulansky v. Ronan*
Our file No. 06-1248

**DATE:**  December 1, 2006

------------------------------------------------------------------------

I have attached a draft complaint and summons in the Schulansky matter. Please note that I have made both Richard Ronan and Ronan Construction Company defendants in the suit. (I refer to them collectively as "Ronan" in this memo.) The contract is signed by Richard Ronan, but on the stationery of Ronan Construction Company. At this stage, it is not clear whether Ronan signed on behalf of the corporation or individually, or both. Since either or both may be liable, I have named both as defendants.

As my draft complaint indicates, Schulansky may be entitled to relief on two separate theories, breach of contract and negligence. Ronan may have breached the contract in several ways. First, Ronan may have agreed to reconstruct the foundation if necessary, but failed to do so. The Proposal and Estimate is hardly clear on this; the only relevant provision is paragraph two, which requires construction of " . . . foundation walls to support 18' × 25' addition." However, an argument can be made that the old foundation wall at the juncture of the house and the addition is part of the foundation of the addition, and therefore the contractor had a duty to make sure that that part of the foundation was solid as well. Paragraphs 23 and 24 of the draft complaint assert this basis for recovery for breach of contract.

Our argument that paragraph two required Ronan to reconstruct the foundation is bolstered by the negotiations between Ronan and Schulansky concerning possible reconstruction of the foundation if it turned out to be inadequate. The potential problem here is that these discussions took place before the Proposal and Estimate was signed. The defendants will no doubt argue that the written contract embodies the entire agreement between the parties, that on its face it does not include any obligation to reconstruct the old foundation, and that the parol evidence rule bars evidence of prior negotiations to vary the terms of the contract. See generally, Farnsworth on Contracts §7.12 (1998). We will have to argue that paragraph two is ambiguous, so that evidence of the prior negotiations is proper to demonstrate the intent of the parties.

Alternatively, it may turn out that the settling resulted from damage done to the foundation by Jones in the course of excavating the cellar. If this is true, Ronan would still be liable on a breach of contract theory. Certainly, an implied term of the contract between Ronan and Schulansky is that the work will be carried out in a careful manner, including the work that Ronan chooses to delegate to his employees or agents. See Restatement (Second) of Contracts §318(3) (delegation of duties under contract does not discharge delegating party from its duty to perform those duties). Even if it was Jones who damaged the foundation with the backhoe, this would constitute a breach of Ronan's duty to perform the contract work carefully. Thus, even if we cannot prove that Ronan had agreed to rebuild the foundation, this would constitute a separate breach of the contract, which gives rise to a claim for whatever subsidence resulted from the damage. I have included this allegation in paragraph 25 of the draft.

The second claim for relief in my draft complaint asserts a tort claim for negligence, based on the allegation that the negligent excavation by Jones led to the subsidence. If Jones acted as Ronan's employee in performing the excavation work, Ronan will be liable for Jones's negligent acts, since employers are liable for the torts of their employees in the scope of employment. Restatement (Third) of Agency §7.07(1). It is not clear at this stage whether Jones operated as an employee or independent subcontractor in performing the excavation work. The legal distinction between an employee and independent contractor turns on the employer's right to control the details of the work. *Cowan v. Eastern Racing Assn.*, 330 Mass. 135, 141-142 (1953); see generally J. Glannon, The Law of Torts: Examples and Explanations, 3rd ed. 479-481; Restatement (Third) of Agency §7.07, comment f. If Ronan exercised detailed control over Jones in the manner of digging the new cellar, Jones acted as Ronan's employee, and Ronan would be liable for Jones's negligence. However, if Ronan simply hired Jones to complete the excavation work in his own manner for an agreed price, Jones may have acted as an independent subcontractor.

There is some reason to believe that Jones acted as Ronan's employee, since (according to Schulansky) Ronan appeared to direct him in the course of the excavation work. Thus, I have drafted the second claim for relief on this theory. An important goal of discovery on our second claim for relief will be to ascertain the exact course of dealing between Ronan and Jones, to determine whether Jones acted as Ronan's employee or as an independent contractor.

Once you have reviewed the draft and made any changes, I will arrange for filing of the complaint and service on the defendants in New Hampshire.

# THE RESULTING DOCUMENTS

COMMONWEALTH OF MASSACHUSETTS

PLYMOUTH COUNTY                     SUPERIOR COURT
                                    CIVIL ACTION NO.

DEBORAH SCHULANSKY

      Plaintiff

      v.                           COMPLAINT AND
                                   DEMAND FOR
RICHARD L. RONAN                   JURY TRIAL
RONAN CONSTRUCTION CO.

      Defendants

**2.** → <u>PARTIES</u>

3.

1. The plaintiff, Deborah Schulansky, is an individual residing at 219 Parker Street, Plymouth, Plymouth County, Massachusetts.

2. The defendant Ronan Construction Company is a corporation incorporated in New Hampshire with offices at 1124 Newark Road, Nashua, New Hampshire.

3. The defendant Richard L. Ronan is an individual residing at 3 Carleton Drive, Nashua, New Hampshire, and the president of Ronan Construction Company.

4. At all relevant times, the defendant Richard L. Ronan acted as the authorized agent of Ronan Construction Company.

**4.** → <u>FACTS</u>

5.

5. The plaintiff owns an antique colonial house located at 53 School Street, Alton, New Hampshire. The house was built in 1782, and is listed in the National Register of Historic Places.

6. In February, 2006, the plaintiff met the defendant, Richard L. Ronan, while Ronan was working on a restoration project in Plymouth, Massachusetts.

7. At this first meeting, Ronan represented to the plaintiff that he was experienced at restoration of historic houses in New Hampshire and Massachusetts.

8. In early March, 2006, the plaintiff met with Ronan at her home in Plymouth, Massachusetts, to discuss the possibility of hiring him to build an addition on her house in Alton, New Hampshire.

9. During that meeting, the parties discussed the need for extensive rebuilding of the foundation of the main house adjacent to the planned addition.

10. During that meeting, the defendant Richard L. Ronan agreed that any necessary reconstruction of the old foundation would be included as part of the construction of an adequate foundation for the addition.

11. After the March meeting, Richard L, Ronan sent a Proposal and Estimate to the plaintiff in Plymouth, Massachusetts, describing the work to be done and offering to perform the work for $50,000. A copy of the Proposal and Estimate is attached to this complaint as Exhibit A.

**6.**

12. The plaintiff accepted the defendants' offer by signing the Proposal and Estimate and mailing it to the defendants, at their office in Nashua, New Hampshire, on April 3, 2006.

13. The defendants commenced work on the addition on April 15, 2006, and continued until June 3, 2006.

14. In the course of the work, the defendants or their agents excavated the earth from the outside of the foundation of the main house to a depth of approximately seven feet.

15. This excavation revealed that the base of the foundation consisted of loose rocks piled on top of each other and held in place by the surrounding earth.

16. In the process of excavation, the defendants or their agents damaged the foundation of the main house by digging up and displacing large boulders, which formed part of that foundation.

17. As a result of the removal of the supporting earth outside the foundation, or the damage done to it during the excavation, or both, it became necessary to reconstruct this part of the foundation to adequately support the main house and the addition.

18. Despite their agreement to do so, the defendants failed to reconstruct the original foundation to provide adequate support for the house and the addition.

19. Even after the plaintiff brought the problem to the defendants' attention during construction, and demanded that they reconstruct the foundation in accordance with their agreement, the defendants refused to do so.

20. As a result of the inadequate foundation work, the main house and the addition have sustained major

structural damage, including cracks in the walls and sagging of the first floor immediately above the affected area.

**7.** ⟶

FIRST CLAIM FOR RELIEF:

BREACH OF CONTRACT

**8.** ⟶ 21. The plaintiff repeats and realleges the allegations in paragraphs 1-20 of the complaint.

22. The Proposal and Estimate signed by the defendant Richard L. Ronan and the plaintiff constitutes a written contract for a valuable consideration between the defendants and the plaintiff.

23. Under paragraph two of the contract, the defendants agreed to construct an adequate foundation to support the addition and adjacent portion of the main house.

24. The defendants breached the contract by failing to perform their obligation to construct an adequate foundation for the addition.

25. The defendants also breached the contract by failing to perform the excavation work required by the contract in a careful manner, which resulted in damage to the existing foundation of the house.

26. The plaintiff made all progress payments under the contract in a timely manner, until she became aware of the defendants' breach.

27. As a result of the defendants' breach, both the main house and the addition have sustained severe structural damage, which will require extensive repair and reconstruction.

SECOND CLAIM FOR RELIEF:

NEGLIGENCE

28. The plaintiff repeats and realleges the allegations in paragraphs 1-20 of the complaint.

29. In the course of the construction of the addition, the defendants or their employees negligently excavated the area adjacent to the foundation of the main house.

30. As a result of this negligent excavation, the foundation of the main house was displaced and damaged, causing subsidence of the foundation and structural damage to the main house and the addition.

9. ⟶ <u>DEMAND</u> <u>FOR</u> <u>RELIEF</u>

WHEREFORE, the plaintiff demands judgment in the amount of her actual damages plus interest and costs, and such other relief as the court finds just and equitable.

10. ⟶ <u>DEMAND</u> <u>FOR</u> <u>JURY</u> <u>TRIAL</u>

Pursuant to Mass. R. Civ. P. 38(b), the plaintiff demands jury trial of all issues triable of right by a jury.

11. ⟶ *Phyllis Slater*

Phyllis Slater
Gomez, Robbins and Slater
Attorney for Plaintiff
322 Puritan Road
Plymouth, MA 02360
(508) 293-7024

RONAN CONSTRUCTION CO.
1124 Newark Road
Nashua, New Hampshire 03061


TO:    Deborah Schulansky
       219 Parker Street
       Plymouth, MA 02360

RE:    Addition to premises at 53 School Street,
       Alton, New Hampshire

DATE:    March 18, 2006

### PROPOSAL AND ESTIMATE

1. Excavate $18' \times 25' \times 7'$ deep area at right rear of house; remove fill.

2. Construct footings, cellar floor, and foundation walls to support $18' \times 25'$ addition.

3. Cut doorway through present foundation into new cellar area.

4. Construct one-story addition with peaked roof and unfinished attic crawl space — standard frame construction, including cedar clapboard siding and asphalt shingle roof.

5. Two standard double-hung windows each side (west and east), and two $6'$ bay windows (double glazed) on main south wall.

6. Interior walls standard drywall construction; clear maple finish floor and baseboards.

7. Remove wall where addition abuts house; support upper floors with steel beam spanning opening.

8. Clean-up of site; broom clean, no seeding or planting.

9. Electrical work to be done by separate contractor hired by owner.

10. Contractor reserves the right to sub-contract excavating and concrete work.

11. Work to be completed by June 20, 2006.

Estimated Cost:        $50,000

Payment schedule:      $6,000 on completion of excavation
$6,000 on completion of foundation
$10,000 on completion of framing
$10,000 on completion of exterior
Finish work
Balance upon completion of job.

*Richard L. Ronan*

Richard L. Ronan

Bid accepted:        *Deborah Schulansky*

Deborah Schulansky

COMMONWEALTH OF MASSACHUSETTS

PLYMOUTH, ss.

SUPERIOR COURT DEPARTMENT OF THE TRIAL COURT OF THE COMMONWEALTH
CIVIL ACTION NO.

Deborah Schulansky............................., Plaintiff(s)

vs.

Richard L. Ronan
Ronan Construction Company......, Defendant(s)

### SUMMONS

To the above-named defendant:

Phyllis Slater,
You are hereby summoned and required to serve upon ........................ Gomez, Robbins & Slater,........ plaintiff
attorney, whose address is 322 Puritan Rd., Plymouth, MA 02360, an answer to the complaint
which is herewith served upon you, within 20 days after service of this summons upon you, exclusive of the
day of service. If you fail to do so, judgment by default will be taken against you for the relief demanded in
the complaint. You are also required to file your answer to the complaint in the office of the Clerk of this
court at Plymouth either before service upon plaintiff     attorney or within a reasonable time thereafter.

Unless otherwise provided by Rule 13(a), your answer must state as a counterclaim any claim which
you may have against the plaintiff     which arises out of the transaction or occurrence that is the subject
matter of the plaintiff     claim or you will thereafter be barred from making such claim in any other action.

Witness, Barbara J. Rouse Esquire, at Plymouth the ......Eighth..........................day of

...December............................, in the year of our Lord Two thousand and ...four............ .

*Frank R. Forras*

CLERK.

### NOTES
1.   This summons is issued pursuant to Rule 4 of the Massachusetts Rules of Civil Procedure.
2.   When more than one defendant is involved, the names of all defendants should appear in the caption.
     If a separate summons is used for each defendant, each should be addressed to the particular
     defendant.
3.   To the plaintiff's attorney: please circle type of action involved-Tort-Motor Vehicle Tort-Contract-
     Equitable Relief-Other.

### PROOF OF SERVICE OF PROCESS
I hereby certify and return that on ......................................., 200 , I served a copy of the within summons
together with a copy with a copy of the complaint in this action, upon the within-named defendant     , in the
following manner(See Mass. R. Civ. P. 4(d)(1-5):..................................................................................

......................................................................................................................................................

......................................................................................................................................................

Dated:                    , 200 ...........................................................................................................

N.B.     TO PROCESS SERVER:-
         PLEASE PLACE DATE YOU MAKE SERVICE ON DEFENDANT IN THIS BOX ON THE
ORIGINAL AND ON COPY SERVED ON DEFENDANT.

|  | 200 |
|---|---|

# COMMENTS ON THE SCHULANSKY COMPLAINT

Although Schulansky's complaint has been drafted to comply with the pleading requirements of the Massachusetts Rules of Civil Procedure (Mass. R. Civ. P. 8-11), those rules are very similar to Rules 8-11 of the Federal Rules of Civil Procedure. The following comments (keyed to the numbers to the left of the complaint) therefore refer to the rules generically unless the federal and state versions differ on the particular point under discussion.

1. While some of the contents of pleadings are a matter of custom in a particular court or personal preference of the drafting attorney, the Rules specifically govern many aspects of pleading. For example, Rule 10(a) requires every pleading to have a caption such as that in Schulansky's complaint. Under Rule 10(a), the caption must include the name of the court (*Commonwealth of Massachusetts, Plymouth County, Superior Court Department*), the docket number of the action (*Civil Action No.*), the names of the parties, and a designation of the pleading (*Complaint and Demand for Jury Trial*).

   The docket number is a number assigned to each case by the court clerk, for administrative purposes. On Schulansky's complaint, the docket number is left blank because the case will not be assigned a docket number until the complaint is filed with the clerk.

2. Note that Howard has included a number of subheadings in the complaint. While these are not required by the Rules, such subheadings are frequently included for the sake of clarity. Particularly in a lengthy complaint that asserts a number of claims, or where the factual allegations are complex, separate sections for *Parties, Facts,* and *Claims for Relief* make it easy for the court and the parties to quickly find and review parts of the complaint during motion arguments and other proceedings.

   In federal actions, a *Jurisdiction* subheading is frequently added because Fed. R. Civ. P. 8(a)(1) specifically requires the plaintiff to allege the basis for subject matter jurisdiction over the action. Such an allegation is not required under Massachusetts Rule 8 because, unlike the federal district courts, the Superior Court is a court of general jurisdiction.

   For many simple cases, such as an action on a note or a straightforward motor vehicle tort case, the complaint may be so brief that subheadings are unnecessary. See the Appendix of Forms accompanying the Federal Rules of Civil Procedure, Forms 10-15 for examples of such complaints.

3. The Federal Rules do not explicitly require separate paragraphs identifying the parties to the action.[1] However, it is customary to begin the complaint with descriptions of the plaintiff(s) and the defendant(s). This information is important to various issues, including personal jurisdiction, venue, capacity to sue and be sued, and (particularly in federal diversity actions) subject matter jurisdiction. In Schulansky's complaint, for example, the allegation that Schulansky resides in Plymouth County indicates the plaintiff's basis under state law for filing suit there. See Mass. Gen. L. ch. 223, §1 (venue proper in county where plaintiff lives).

4. Many complaints will include a subheading entitled *Facts*, or *Factual Allegations*, setting forth a brief description of the events that gave rise to the plaintiff's claim for relief. This type of breakdown is useful, particularly in complex cases, to distinguish the underlying facts giving rise to the claim from the plaintiff's asserted claims arising out of those facts.

   In Schulansky's case, for example, there is enough factual background that a separate facts section facilitates a clear understanding of her claims. It is true that Rule 8(a)(2) only requires a "short and plain statement of the claim," and that very brief, general allegations will usually suffice to avoid dismissal. But a little more detail than the minimum required by the pleading rules will give the court a clearer picture of the case, from the plaintiff's point of view. And since Rule 8(b) requires the defendant to respond paragraph by paragraph to the allegations in the complaint, a more detailed complaint will elicit more specific denials or admissions in the defendant's answer.

5. The Rules require all allegations in the body of the complaint to be set forth in numbered paragraphs. Rule 10(b). This facilitates quick reference to the allegations in the complaint. It also allows defendants to respond to each of the plaintiff's allegations by number and allows the plaintiff to incorporate allegations by number in later parts of the complaint, as Howard has done in paragraphs 21 and 28 of the Schulansky complaint.

   Rule 10(b) also provides that the allegations in each paragraph of the complaint shall be "limited as far as practicable to a single set of circumstances. . . ." However, reducing specificity to the atomic level (for example, by breaking Schulansky's paragraph five into three paragraphs), would make the complaint unduly tedious. The allegations in paragraph five all relate closely to the issue of the age and value of the house and form a logical grouping for a single

---

1. The Massachusetts rules do, however, require that the residence or place of business of the parties be specified. Mass. R. Civ. P. 10(d).

paragraph. The Rule does not limit each paragraph to a single fact, but to a single "set of circumstances," and calls for a commonsense breakdown of allegations "as far as practicable."

6. The Rules authorize parties to attach exhibits to their pleadings, as Schulansky has done here. Rule 10(c). Parties should exercise care in incorporating documents in the complaint, however, since doing so may constitute an admission at least of the authenticity of the documents, if not their accuracy. Here, for example, Schulansky's inclusion of the Proposal and Estimate, together with her allegation that it constitutes the contract between her and Ronan, may weaken her argument that Ronan had an additional duty, arising from their prior discussions, to repair the old foundation. See the Third Defense in Ronan's answer p. 666.

7. In paragraphs 21-27 and 28-30, Howard has recast the factual allegations in terms of claims for relief for breach of contract and negligence. These sections of the complaint are intended to show the court that the facts alleged satisfy the elements of legally recognized claims that, if proved, entitle Schulansky to relief.[2] The subheading *Claim for Relief* tracks the language of Rule 8(a)(2), which requires the complaint to include a "short and plain statement of the claim showing that the pleader is entitled to relief." Here, Schulansky has asserted a right to relief under two distinct theories. If the court concludes that she has proved a right to recovery on either her contract theory or her tort theory, it will grant her whatever relief is proper under that claim. This "pleading in the alternative" is expressly authorized by Rule 8(d)(2).

The rules do not require the pleader to state the legal theory on which he claims a right to relief. A brief description of the "claim," that is, the events giving rise to the action, is sufficient. See Friedenthal, Kane and Miller, §5.7. However, it is certainly appropriate and helpful to allege the elements of each claim clearly, especially in cases involving multiple theories of relief based on the same underlying facts. See *O'Donnell v. Elgin, J & E. Ry. Co.*, 338 U.S. 384, 392 (1949) ("We no longer insist upon technical rules of pleading, but it will ever be difficult in a jury trial to segregate issues which counsel do not separate in their pleading, preparation or thinking.").

Separate pleading theories are often labeled as different "counts" instead of Claims for Relief. In simple complaints, such

---

2. Schulansky might have other claims for relief in addition to the two asserted in the complaint. For example, other claims might be based on the failure of Ronan to properly supervise Jones or negligent selection of Jones as the subcontractor. For illustration purposes, however, I have tried to keep the complaint to a manageable length.

subdivisions are unnecessary. See, e.g., Appendix of Forms accompanying Federal Rules of Civil Procedure, Form 19, which asserts two theories of relief quite clearly without separate counts or subheadings.

Students sometimes ask why Schulansky's counsel assert two theories of relief. If they have a viable claim for breach of contract, why take on the extra burden of alleging and proving the negligence claim as well? Well, Schulansky's lawyers would do their client a serious disservice by omitting the negligence claim from their complaint. After all, they may not recover on the breach of contract claim. Perhaps they missed the limitations period, or the jury will find that Schulansky had waived the rebuilding of the foundation, or for some other reason the contract theory may fall by the wayside. If so, Schulansky's counsel will clearly want to preserve their options, by asserting any other viable theories of relief based on the defendants' conduct. Indeed, they would likely be liable for malpractice if they put all their eggs in one basket, by leaving out a viable negligence claim, only later to lose on the contract claim. Clients expect their lawyers to assert all supportable rights they may have, not pick and choose among them based on which they think has the best chance of success.

Thus, lawyers feel considerable pressure to include any supportable theory of recovery in their complaints. Better to assert it and lose on it rather than leave it out and explain to the client later why they abandoned a claim that might have provided her some relief. At the same time, lawyers are under considerable pressure under Rule 11 of the Rules of Civil Procedure not to assert theories for which they lack support. See note 11 below. Such conflicting pressures, among other things, make a litigator's life interesting.

8. Rule 10(c) authorizes a pleader to incorporate prior allegations by reference in later parts of his pleading. Here Howard has done so in order to make clear that the breach of contract claim is based on the facts alleged in the cited paragraphs.

9. At the end of the complaint, Howard includes a demand for the relief Schulansky seeks on both claims, as required by Rule 8(a)(3). In this case, the relief sought is damages, but in other actions different types of relief are also commonly sought, such as specific performance, an injunction, a divorce, or a declaration of the rights of the parties.

Attorneys differ as to whether to put a demand for relief after each claim for relief, or to place a single demand at the end of the complaint. Clearly, if the relief requested differs on the different claims, separate demands for relief are appropriate. For example, if Schulansky were seeking specific performance of the contract with

Ronan, inserting separate demands for relief after each claim for relief would help to make it clear that specific performance is sought under the contract claim rather than the negligence claim (which would not support a demand for specific performance). Because she seeks only damages on each claim, however, and the measure of damages on each theory is apparently the same, either a single demand at the end of the complaint or demands after each claim would be appropriate. Compare the separate demands for relief in Ronan's third-party complaint, infra pp. 681-683.

Note that the demand for relief in the Schulansky complaint does not state a specific dollar amount requested. This is because a Massachusetts statute bars plaintiffs from stating a specific dollar demand. Mass. Gen. L. ch. 231, §13B. Several states have enacted such statutes, to avoid adverse publicity and possible jury prejudice from inflated damage figures in pleadings.

10. Rule 38(b) provides that a demand for jury trial may be asserted in the complaint (or answer). Because the right to trial by jury is waived if not demanded within ten days of the close of the pleadings (see Rule 38(b)), it is wise to insert the demand for jury trial in the complaint. Otherwise, plaintiff's counsel may forget about it, and the period for seeking jury trial may slip by unnoticed.

11. Rule 11 governs signature of the complaint and other pleadings.[3] It requires the attorney to sign the complaint and state his address. The rule also imposes important ethical duties on attorneys who sign complaints and other court papers. Under Federal Rule 11, an attorney's signature on a complaint certifies to the court that the attorney believes, after reasonable inquiry, that the factual allegations in the complaint "have evidentiary support," or (for specifically identified allegations) "will likely have evidentiary support after a reasonable opportunity for further investigation or discovery." The attorney's signature also certifies that the legal positions taken in the complaint (in the Schulansky case, for example, that the plaintiff has the right to sue for breach of contract, or that Ronan is liable for the acts of Jones) "are warranted by existing law or by a nonfrivolous argument for extending, modifying, or reversing existing law or for establishing new law." Rule 11(b)(2). Last, the signing attorney certifies that the pleading or motion is not filed for any improper purpose. Rule 11(b)(1).

---

3. The complaint is shown here with the attorney's signature affixed. Subsequent pleadings and motions have not been signed because they are suggested pleadings for the partner's review and have not yet been filed in court.

The "reasonable inquiry" requirement was added to Federal Rule 11 in 1983 to strengthen the attorney's obligation to the court to avoid frivolous or unethical pleadings. This language does not require Slater and Howard to complete their research or investigation before filing suit against Ronan, but it does require them to have a factual basis beyond mere opinion or speculation to support the pleaded facts, as well as a colorable argument for the legal positions asserted in the complaint.

The factual standard in Rule 11 would be met by the information Schulansky gave her attorneys about the construction problem before they drafted the complaint. They knew that the damage appeared shortly after the construction work began, in the area where the work was being done. They also knew that an engineer had viewed the damage and concluded that it resulted from the inadequate construction work. This provides "evidentiary support" for the factual allegations in the *Schulansky* complaint. The rule does not require certainty or admissible evidence at this early stage of the suit, only a reasonable pre-filing inquiry.

The legal standard in Rule 11 would also be satisfied in the *Schulansky* case. Howard and Slater had a copy of the contract, which required Ronan to construct walls to support the addition. If the damage to the house resulted from inadequate support, that would arguably constitute a breach of the contract. In addition, the discussions between Ronan and Schulansky during the negotiations may well support a claim that Ronan had agreed to reinforce or rebuild the foundation. Similarly, if the engineer's alternative conclusion that the backhoe damaged the foundation is accurate, that would certainly constitute actionable negligence.

Interestingly, the pleading requirements in Massachusetts Rule 11 are less stringent than those in Federal Rule 11. Under Massachusetts Rule 11, the attorney's signature certifies that "to the best of his knowledge, information and belief there is good ground to support" the pleading, and that it is not interposed for delay. It does not impose a requirement of pre-filing inquiry and does not make reference to improper purposes other than delay (as, for example, escalating the expense of litigation to the point where the opponent cannot sustain it). In addition, the Massachusetts version only authorizes sanctions for "wilful violations." The Massachusetts rulemakers have been unwilling to impose the stricter requirements of Federal Rule 11. Consequently, sanctions for improper pleading are invoked less frequently in the Massachusetts state courts than in the federal courts.

# COMMENTS ON THE SUMMONS

Rule 4 requires both a summons and complaint to be served on the defendant. The complaint is written by the plaintiff or his attorney, setting out the allegations against the defendant. The summons, by contrast, is an official order from the court requiring the defendant to respond to the complaint. Hence, Rule 4 requires that the summons bear the seal of the court and be signed by the clerk.

In many courts printed summonses like the one used here, already signed and sealed, may be obtained in blank from the clerk's office. The plaintiff's attorney fills in the blanks and arranges for service of the summons with the complaint. Compare the printed summons with the detailed requirements of Federal Rule 4(a). (Mass. R. Civ. P. 4(b) closely parallels Federal Rule 4(a).) The summons includes the seal of the court,[4] the name of the court, space for the names of the parties, and the name and address of the plaintiff's attorney. It also warns the defendant, as required by Massachusetts Rule 4(b), that he must answer within 20 days or default judgment will be entered against him. See Rule 55, which authorizes entry of a default judgment if the defendant fails to respond to the complaint.

The first paragraph of the summons quite properly distinguishes between service and filing of the defendant's answer. Rule 12(a) requires the defendant to *serve* his answer on the plaintiff within 20 days of service of the complaint. See Chapter 18 for a discussion of methods of service of process. As the summons states, the answer must also be filed with the court before it is served or within a reasonable time thereafter.

Nothing in Rule 4(b) requires inclusion of the second paragraph of the summons, warning defendants that they must assert compulsory counterclaims under Rule 13(a). The purpose of the warning is obviously to remind defendants, who must respond within a short time, that they must assert any compulsory counterclaims in their answer or risk loss of those claims.

The printed summons usually includes space (here, at the bottom of the page) for the sheriff, constable, or other process server to provide proof of service. See Federal Rule 4(l). The server fills out the form, indicating the date and manner in which service was made, and files it with the court.

If service is made directly by the plaintiff's attorney (for example, in a case such as this one, where service on the out-of-state defendants will likely be made by mail), a separate sworn affidavit must be filed setting forth the time and manner in which service was made. Federal Rule 4(l).

---

4. The court seal is embossed on the *Schulansky* summons, but does not show up in the reproduction.

# A Change of Forum

## Ronan Removes to Federal Court

---

## THE DRAFTING REQUEST

### MEMORANDUM

**TO:**   Marcia Losordo
          Associate

**FROM:** Arthur Ackerman

**RE:**   *Schulansky v. Ronan*
          Plymouth Superior Court No. 2006-2982

**DATE:** December 19, 2006

-------------------------------------------------------------------------------

As you know, this office frequently handles litigation for Federal Security Insurance Company, a large insurer specializing in construction accounts. Federal Security has just asked us to represent one of their insureds, a New Hampshire contractor named Richard Ronan. On December 10 Ronan was served with process in a suit commenced against him and Ronan Construction Company in the Plymouth Superior Court. Copies of the complaint and summons are attached.

Ronan was in this morning for an initial interview on the case (I would have asked you to sit in, but you were in court.) Although I didn't have much time, I did get the relevant background information on the case. The suit arises out of some work Ronan did for the plaintiff, Deborah Schulansky, on her second home in Alton, New Hampshire. Schulansky claims that Ronan agreed to build an addition to the house but failed to reinforce the foundation adequately, causing the main part of the house to settle. Ronan denies that the house has settled or, if it has, that it resulted from his work.

My initial reaction was that it seems doubtful that Ronan is subject to personal jurisdiction in Massachusetts for this claim, since the work was done out of state and Ronan is from New Hampshire. However, he did negotiate the contract with the plaintiff in Massachusetts, so he does at least have some relevant contacts here.

If Ronan is subject to jurisdiction in Massachusetts, I would prefer to litigate in federal district court here in Boston rather than down in Plymouth. Ronan lives in Nashua, New Hampshire, and Ronan Construction Company is incorporated in New Hampshire with its principal place of business in Nashua, so the case is removable on diversity grounds.

I need some quick information on removal of this case. Could you please write me a short memo answering the following questions:

1. Should the notice of removal be filed in the state or federal court?
2. What documents must be filed with the notice of removal?
3. Can we file our motion to dismiss for lack of personal jurisdiction in the state court and wait for a decision on that motion before removing the suit?
4. Do we have to answer or move to dismiss before removing? If not, when is our response due in federal court?
5. The plaintiff has demanded trial by jury in her state court complaint. If we also want a jury, do we have to request it again in the federal court after removal?

If we have to remove right away, rather than waiting for the state court to resolve the personal jurisdiction issue, please draft a notice of removal as well. Even though the holidays are imminent, please get to this during the next week; I believe there is a 30-day limit on removal, and we've already lost nine of them.

---

# THE ASSOCIATE'S RESPONSE

## MEMORANDUM

**TO:**     Arthur Ackerman

**FROM:**   Marcia Losordo

**RE:**     Removal of *Schulansky v. Ronan*
            Plymouth Superior Court No. 2006-2982

**DATE:**   December 23, 2006

-----------------------------------------------------------------------------

I have researched your questions on removal of the *Schulansky* case. In addition, since I conclude that we must remove the case within 30 days even if the state court lacks personal jurisdiction, I have also drafted a notice of removal and other required documents, which I attach for your review.

The answers to your questions are as follows:

1. Should the notice be filed in the state or federal court?

The notice of removal must be filed in the federal district court "for the district and division within which such action is pending." 28 U.S.C. §1446(a). A copy of the notice must then be filed in the state court. 28 U.S.C. §1446(d). The case is only properly removed when the state court and the other parties to the action have been notified. Id.

2. What must be filed with the notice of removal?

Under 28 U.S.C. §1446(a), copies of "all process, pleadings, and orders" served upon the defendants must be filed with the notice of removal. In this case that includes only the summons and complaint served on each defendant.

A party who removes to federal court must give written notice of the filing to all other parties to the action "promptly after the filing of such notice." 28 U.S.C. §1446(d). I have prepared a notification form, as well as copies of the notice of removal for service on the plaintiff and filing in the state court.

3. Can I file my motion to dismiss for lack of personal jurisdiction in the state court and wait for a decision on that motion before removing the suit?

It is certainly permissible to file the motion to dismiss before removing. Until it is removed, the case is governed by the state court rules, which require a response to the complaint within 20 days. Mass. R. Civ. P. 12(a)(1).

However, §1446(b) provides that the notice of removal must be filed within 30 days after the defendant is served with the complaint. Nothing in the statute suggests that the 30-day period is suspended by any pending motions, and it is very unlikely that the motion to dismiss would be acted on by the state court before the 30 days elapse. Therefore, we cannot await decision on the motion before removing the case. We should remove the case now; the federal court will then decide whether to grant the motion to dismiss.

4. Do I have to answer or move to dismiss before removing? If not, when is my response due in federal court?

As indicated in the previous answer, the Massachusetts rules require a response within 20 days after service of the complaint and summons. If we do not remove within the first 20 days, a response to the complaint will be due, and we will have to file one or be in default. We should either remove before the response is due or file an answer or motion to dismiss in the state court. If we do answer before removing, the answer will stand as the answer in federal court, unless that court orders a further answer. Fed R. Civ. P. 81(c)(2).

One reason why we might wish to remove before answering is that some authorities suggest that a defendant may waive the right to remove by taking some actions in state court, such as filing a counterclaim. See Friedenthal, Kane, and Miller, Civil Procedure, 4th ed., p. 67. The rationale for this view is that the defendant has demonstrated her willingness to have the state court adjudicate the case by taking affirmative steps in the state court. Removing and then answering in federal court will avoid any risk of raising the waiver issue.

If we remove before responding to the complaint, Fed. R. Civ. P. 81(c)(2) provides that we must answer within 20 days of service of the complaint or 5 days after the notice of removal is filed, whichever is longer. Thus, we had better begin preparing an answer immediately or move for an extension of time in which to answer, under Fed. R. Civ. P. 6(b).

5. The plaintiff has demanded trial by jury in her state court complaint. If we also want a jury, do we have to request it again in the federal court after removal?

Rule 81(c)(3)(A) provides that a party who has properly requested jury trial prior to removal need not renew the request in the federal court. Once the case is removed, the federal rules will govern the action (Fed. R. Civ. P. 81(c)(1)), including Fed. R. Civ. P. 38(d), which provides that a jury trial demand cannot be withdrawn without the consent of the parties. Therefore, this action will be tried to a jury unless both sides later consent to trial before the judge.

However, I am not sure whether the plaintiff's general demand for jury trial would apply to any counterclaim we may assert in our answer. If the case reaches the point of filing an answer, and we decide to assert any counterclaims, a separate demand for jury trial should be made as to them.

# THE RESULTING DOCUMENTS

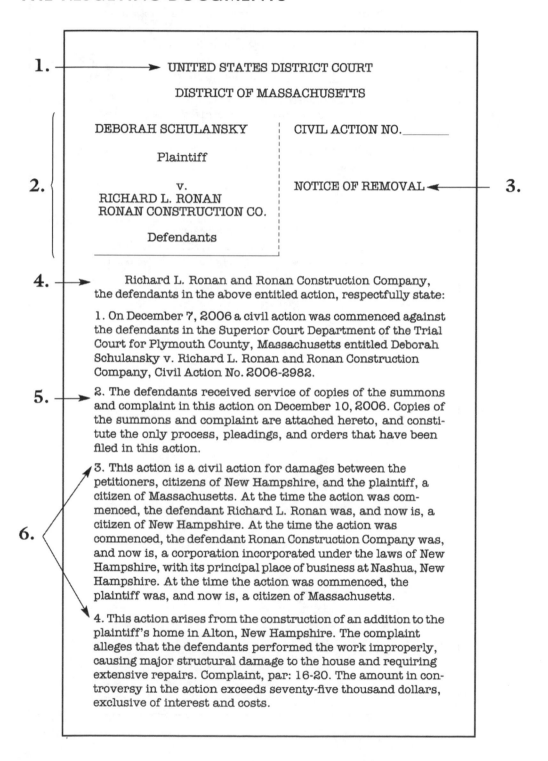

**1.**

UNITED STATES DISTRICT COURT

DISTRICT OF MASSACHUSETTS

**2.**

DEBORAH SCHULANSKY

Plaintiff

v.

RICHARD L. RONAN
RONAN CONSTRUCTION CO.

Defendants

CIVIL ACTION NO._____

**3.**

NOTICE OF REMOVAL

**4.**

Richard L. Ronan and Ronan Construction Company, the defendants in the above entitled action, respectfully state:

1. On December 7, 2006 a civil action was commenced against the defendants in the Superior Court Department of the Trial Court for Plymouth County, Massachusetts entitled Deborah Schulansky v. Richard L. Ronan and Ronan Construction Company, Civil Action No. 2006-2982.

**5.**

2. The defendants received service of copies of the summons and complaint in this action on December 10, 2006. Copies of the summons and complaint are attached hereto, and constitute the only process, pleadings, and orders that have been filed in this action.

**6.**

3. This action is a civil action for damages between the petitioners, citizens of New Hampshire, and the plaintiff, a citizen of Massachusetts. At the time the action was commenced, the defendant Richard L. Ronan was, and now is, a citizen of New Hampshire. At the time the action was commenced, the defendant Ronan Construction Company was, and now is, a corporation incorporated under the laws of New Hampshire, with its principal place of business at Nashua, New Hampshire. At the time the action was commenced, the plaintiff was, and now is, a citizen of Massachusetts.

4. This action arises from the construction of an addition to the plaintiff's home in Alton, New Hampshire. The complaint alleges that the defendants performed the work improperly, causing major structural damage to the house and requiring extensive repairs. Complaint, par: 16-20. The amount in controversy in the action exceeds seventy-five thousand dollars, exclusive of interest and costs.

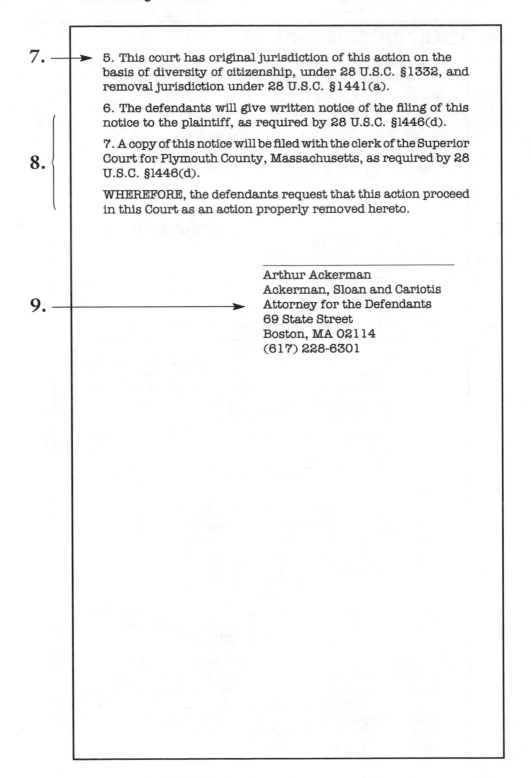

7. ——▶ 5. This court has original jurisdiction of this action on the basis of diversity of citizenship, under 28 U.S.C. §1332, and removal jurisdiction under 28 U.S.C. §1441(a).

6. The defendants will give written notice of the filing of this notice to the plaintiff, as required by 28 U.S.C. §1446(d).

8. { 7. A copy of this notice will be filed with the clerk of the Superior Court for Plymouth County, Massachusetts, as required by 28 U.S.C. §1446(d).

WHEREFORE, the defendants request that this action proceed in this Court as an action properly removed hereto.

9. ——————————▶ Arthur Ackerman
Ackerman, Sloan and Cariotis
Attorney for the Defendants
69 State Street
Boston, MA 02114
(617) 228-6301

UNITED STATES DISTRICT COURT

DISTRICT OF MASSACHUSETTS

| | |
|---|---|
| DEBORAH SCHULANSKY | CIVIL ACTION NO._____ |
| Plaintiff | |
| v. | NOTIFICATION OF FILING OF NOTICE OF REMOVAL ◄── **10.** |
| RICHARD L. RONAN RONAN CONSTRUCTION CO. | |
| Defendants | |

TO:  Phyllis Slater
     Gomez, Robbins and Slater
     Attorney for Plaintiff
     322 Puritan Road
     Plymouth, MA 02360

Please take notice that the defendants in the above-entitled action have this date filed their notice of removal of this action in the Office of the Clerk of the United States District Court for the District of Massachusetts. A copy of the notice is attached hereto.

You are further advised that the defendants, upon filing of the notice of removal, also filed a copy of the notice with the Clerk of the Superior Court for Plymouth County, thus effecting removal under 28 U.S.C. §1446(d).

Date:_____

                                    _____
                                    Arthur Ackerman
                                    Ackerman, Sloan and Cariotis
                                    Attorney for the Defendants
                                    69 State Street
                                    Boston, MA 02114
                                    (617) 228-6301

# COMMENTS ON THE NOTICE OF REMOVAL

1. The caption on the notice of removal reflects the fact that the notice is filed in the federal district court, not in the state court in which Schulansky filed suit.

2. Although Fed. R. Civ. P. 10(a) only governs the caption for pleadings, and a notice of removal is not a pleading (see Fed. R. Civ. P. 7(a)), it is customary to use the same caption in all papers filed in the suit. (Indeed, this may be required by local rules of the federal district, as it is in Massachusetts. See United States District Court, District of Massachusetts, Local Rule 5.1(a).) Of course, the title of the paper will change, but the court, names of the parties, and docket number will appear on all filed papers. Note again that the docket number has not been filled in since the case will receive a new federal court docket number when the notice of removal is filed.

3. Until 1988, a defendant filed a "petition to remove" a case to federal court rather than a notice of removal. The "petition" terminology suggested that the defendant was requesting the federal court to hear the case, and that it might choose to grant or refuse that request. The substituted term, "notice," reflects the fact that the defendant has a right to remove if the case falls within the federal court's removal jurisdiction and is "notifying" the court that she is exercising that option. If the federal court has jurisdiction over the action, it must hear it upon removal.

4. Although the removal statutes are not entirely clear on the point, the courts have held that all defendants must agree to the removal. See Chapter 7, example 7. This requirement is met here since both Ronan and Ronan Construction Company file the notice of removal.

5. The allegation as to the date of service of the complaint indicates to the court that removal is timely, since the 30-day removal period begins to run on the date of service of the summons and complaint on the defendants. 28 U.S.C. §1446(b). This paragraph of the notice also indicates that the defendants have complied with the requirement of 28 U.S.C. §1446(a), that "a copy of all process, pleadings, and orders served upon such defendant or defendants" be filed with the notice.

6. It will not always be clear from the plaintiff's complaint that a case meets the requirements for original or removal jurisdiction of the federal court. For example, Schulansky's state court complaint did not allege where Ronan Construction Company's principal place of business was, since it was not necessary to do so to invoke the state court's jurisdiction over the action.

Section 1446(a) authorizes the removing defendant to state facts in the notice of removal that are necessary to demonstrate that the federal court has jurisdiction. The information in paragraphs three and four of the notice of removal is intended to show the court that this is a proper diversity case, which could have been brought originally in federal court. These paragraphs also demonstrate that none of the defendants is a citizen of the forum state, a separate requirement in 28 U.S.C, §1441(b) for removal of diversity cases.

As was noted in Chapter 31, the Demand for Relief in Schulansky's complaint does not state a specific dollar demand — in fact, a statute barred her from including a dollar figure in the demand. This poses an awkward situation for the defendants. First, how is Ronan to know if the amount in controversy exceeds $75,000, as required by 28 U.S.C. §1332(a), when he contends that Schulansky hasn't suffered any damages at all from his work? Ronan is an experienced construction contractor, and he is familiar with the house and the work he did on it. In addition, he has the factual allegations as to the nature of damages and the type of repair needed, so he should have a factual basis for roughly estimating the possible damages. Naturally, he can't be very accurate about it, but the *St. Paul Mercury* rule doesn't require him to be. So long as there is a possible basis for damages in excess of $75,000, the requirement is met. Section 1446(a) requires Ronan to put in the notice of removal a statement of the grounds for believing that the amount-in-controversy requirement has been met, as he has done in paragraph four.

Including this statement is also awkward for Ronan for another reason. By alleging that the amount requirement is satisfied, he in some sense lends credibility to the argument that the plaintiff has suffered extensive damages, an allegation he will presumably deny in his answer. But again, remember that the amount-in-controversy requirement refers to the amount that is in dispute between the parties, not to the actual damages the plaintiff has suffered. See Chapter 5, p. 96. Ronan does not concede, by asserting in the notice of removal that the dispute concerns more than $75,000, that the plaintiff has actually suffered that great a loss, or any loss at all. Nor will the jury likely be aware of the amount-in-controversy requirement or that Ronan has invoked federal jurisdiction on the basis that a particular amount is disputed.

7. The fundamental requirement for removal is that the case could have been brought initially in federal court. 28 U.S.C. §1441(a). In paragraph five, the defendants state that original jurisdiction existed and that removal is therefore proper under §1441(a).

8. Paragraphs six and seven indicate that the removing defendants will comply with the requirements of 28 U.S.C. §1446(d), that the plaintiff be notified of the removal, and that a copy of the notice be filed in the state court.

9. Section 1446(a) now explicitly states that the representations made in the notice of removal are subject to the ethical requirements of Rule 11. Thus, as with Slater's signature on the complaint, Ackerman's signature certifies to the court that he has made a preliminary inquiry both as to the supporting facts and legal right to remove and concluded that he has support for the positions taken in the notice of removal.

10. The Notification of Filing of Notice of Removal is a fairly commonsensical document drawn up to comply with the requirement of 28 U.S.C. §1446(d), that the defendant give notice to the adverse parties of the filing of the notice. As with the notice itself, it is intended to demonstrate to the court and the plaintiff that the defendants have complied with the removal requirements.

The third question Ackerman asks in his memo is interesting. It seems like an unnecessary hassle to go through the formalities of removal if the action is likely to be dismissed for lack of personal jurisdiction anyway. However, as Losordo's response indicates, the removal statute does not allow the defendants to litigate preliminary objections in the state court before exercising their right to remove; removal must take place within 30 days, regardless of objections the defendant may have to jurisdiction, venue, or other matters relating to the state court's competence to entertain the action.

Thus, even if Ackerman believes that he might fare better on some issues in the case in state court, he does not have the choice to litigate some issues there and then remove to federal court. Removal must be done immediately and brings the entire action into the federal court. Thus, he must make a quick decision as to whether the overall advantages of litigating in federal court outweigh those of staying in state court, (Some of the many considerations that may influence that decision are discussed in Chapter 30, pp. 619-620.) This is a difficult position to be in, particularly if the suit was not expected. When the case came into Ackerman's office nine days of the removal period had already elapsed, leaving little time to research all of the strategic ramifications of removal. Thus, the decision will be based on a preliminary understanding of the case, and may be regretted later on as counsel develop a fuller appreciation of these strategic considerations.

# CHAPTER 33

# The Defendants' Perspective

## Ronan's Answer and Counterclaim

---

# THE DRAFTING REQUEST

### MEMORANDUM

**TO:** Marcia Losordo
Associate

**FROM:** Arthur Ackerman

**RE:** Answer and counterclaim in *Schulansky v. Ronan*
U.S. District Court No. 2006-6719

**DATE:** December 28, 2006

--------------------------------------------------------------------

Thank you for your informative memo and removal documents in this case. I have filed the notice of removal today and notified the plaintiff and the state court, so we are officially in federal court.

I have decided to file an answer to the complaint (instead of a Rule 12(b) motion) and would appreciate your assistance in drafting it. I realize that you have not yet had any Christmas vacation, but as your memo indicates, we are under the gun because Fed. R. Civ. P. 81(c)(2) requires us to respond to the complaint within five days of removing the case.

Not surprisingly, Dick Ronan's version of the facts in this case differs significantly from the allegations in Schulansky's complaint. First of all, although there was some discussion about the old foundation during their negotiations, Ronan's position is that he never assumed responsibility for any extensive reconstruction work. He never said anything about rebuilding the

**659**

foundation, except that he doubted it would be necessary. He did say he would pour cement into any gaps in the exposed boulders but definitely did not agree to anything more than that. He points out that reconstructing the foundation on a house that old is a very substantial job; he could never have quoted her the price he did if such reconstruction were included in the work.

Second, according to Ronan, he and Schulansky discussed the problem again after the old foundation had been exposed. She asked him whether it ought to be rebuilt, and Ronan said that he did not think it was necessary and that it was beyond the scope of the contract. He specifically recalls telling her at that time that he thought the foundation would be sufficient if he filled in the gaps with concrete, but "you can never be 100 percent sure — old houses are unpredictable." She agreed to his suggestion, and that is what he did.

Ronan also denies any negligence in excavating the foundation. There were some loose boulders in the excavated area near the foundation, which Schulansky assumed had been knocked out by the backhoe. Ronan admits that the backhoe hit the foundation a number of times, but he thinks those rocks were probably excavated from the new cellar area instead. He also states that digging the earth away from the foundation did not weaken it. According to him, it is the direct downward pressure of the structure on top of the rocks in the foundation, not the surrounding earth, that keeps the foundation — and the house itself — in place.

Last, Ronan denies that Schulansky's house has settled as a result of his construction work or any defect in the old foundation. He claims that most of the cracks she refers to were already there when he inspected the house before he bid on the job; after all, the house is over 200 years old, and there is evidence of settling in every room of the house. While he does not doubt the good faith of the plaintiff, he thinks she simply had not noticed these problems until the construction work caused her to take a close look at the structure of the house.

Please draft an answer to the Schulansky complaint, based on Ronan's understanding of the facts outlined above. Please contact Ronan directly for any further information you need.

Our answer should not only respond to the individual allegations in Schulansky's complaint, but also raise several additional defenses. First, I think we should take the position that the Proposal and Estimate constitutes the entire agreement between the parties and that Ronan is under no duty to rebuild the foundation if the Proposal and Estimate does not require it. Even if there was some prior discussion in which Ronan arguably agreed to rebuild the foundation, it is the contract itself, not the discussions leading up to it, that defines the parties' obligations. As you know, where a contract is clear and complete on its face, the parol evidence rule bars either party from varying or contradicting the terms of the contract by evidence of prior inconsistent negotiations. Here, the contract is clear: Paragraph two requires Ronan to build a foundation for the addition, not to rebuild the preexisting foundation.

Second, Ronan states (and the plaintiff's complaint admits) that Schulansky was present when the foundation was exposed. Ronan told her what he planned to do, and she evidently accepted his proposal to reinforce it rather than rebuild it. Thus, I think we can make a strong argument that Schulansky has waived any right to reconstruction of the old foundation.

Our answer should also raise the objection that the court lacks personal jurisdiction over both defendants. I realize that we could postpone answering by filing a motion to dismiss on this ground, but I have decided to answer instead. I am somewhat doubtful that the court will dismiss on this ground. If the court postpones decision on the motion (as it may under Fed. R. Civ. P. 12(i)), I would rather have our answer to the complaint, setting forth our position on the merits, before the court from the beginning of the litigation.

Please also include a counterclaim for the final payment under the contract, which Schulansky has never made. In addition, it is our position that Richard Ronan signed the contract as an agent of Ronan Construction Company, not on his own behalf. Consequently, he was not a party to the contract and is not personally liable for any breach of that contract. Please be careful in drafting the answer to observe this distinction in responding to the allegations in the complaint and in drafting the counterclaim.

We may also wish to file a third-party complaint against the excavation subcontractor, Arlen Jones. Please let me know whether this must be filed with the answer. I certainly would prefer to have more time to decide whether to file a third-party claim and, if so, whether there will be any jurisdictional problems involved. (Jones is apparently from New Hampshire, but I am not sure whether he may be subject to personal jurisdiction here on some ground.)

# THE ASSOCIATE'S RESPONSE

## MEMORANDUM

**TO:** Arthur Ackerman

**FROM:** Marcia Losordo

**RE:** Answer and Counterclaim in *Schulansky v. Ronan*
U.S. District Court No. 2006-6719

**DATE:** December 30, 2006

--------------------------------------------------------------------------------

I have attached a proposed answer and counterclaim in the Schulansky case.

I have based my responses to the plaintiff's allegations on the facts as you set them out in your memo and on direct conversations with Dick Ronan. In responding to the plaintiff's first claim for relief, for breach of contract, I have

**661**

consistently taken the position that Ronan's only obligation was to construct foundation walls for the addition, not for any part of the main house.

The plaintiff's second claim for relief on a negligence theory is evidently premised on the assumption that Jones was an employee of either Ronan personally or Ronan Construction Company, so that one or the other would be liable for his negligence. However, it is not at all clear that Jones was an employee, as opposed to an independent contractor with Ronan. The decision turns on whether Ronan had the right of control over Jones in the detailed performance of the work. Restatement (Third) of Agency §7.07(2). If he did, Jones was an employee; if not, he acted as an independent contractor.

From what Ronan tells me, it is unclear whether the court would characterize Jones as an employee of Ronan or as an independent contractor. On the one hand, Jones was paid a flat fee for the job pursuant to a letter agreement and used his own backhoe, factors that suggest that he was independent. Restatement (Third) of Agency §7.07, comment f. On the other, Jones worked for Ronan on a regular basis, and generally did whatever Ronan told him to do. These facts might support a finding that Jones was an employee. Where the facts could reasonably support the conclusion that Jones was independent, I conclude that it is proper under Fed. R. Civ. P. 11 to deny that he was Ronan's employee, and I have done so. See paragraph 29 of the First Defense and the Sixth Defense.

If you decide to file a third-party complaint against Jones, it need not be filed with the answer. You may serve a third-party complaint without leave of court within ten days of serving the answer in the original action. Fed. R. Civ. P. 14(a)(1). After that you will need leave of court, after notice to the plaintiff, to assert any third-party claims. Id. However, even if we file within the ten-day period for filing as of right, the court does not have to entertain the third-party claim. The decision to allow or dismiss a third-party claim is a discretionary one in each case. Moore's Federal Practice §14.20. If the court concludes that entertaining the additional claim would not advance the efficient and fair resolution of the entire dispute, it may dismiss it at any time.

As I read the technicalities of Fed. R. Civ. P. 6(a), our answer is due on January 5. Our answer is due five days after removal. Fed. R. Civ. P. 81(c)(2)(C). In calculating the time period, the day of removal doesn't count. See Fed. R. Civ. P. 6(a)(1). So Thursday, December 28, doesn't count, but Friday the 29th does. Saturday the 30th, Sunday the 31st, and Monday, January 1, don't count, under Rule 6(a)(2). Tuesday, January 2, Wednesday, January 3, and Thursday, January 4, count, so the answer is due on Friday, January 5. Even though the New Year's holiday is coming up, please be sure to save time to review the documents before that date.

One last point you may wish to consider. Is it possible that, by seeking affirmative relief from Schulansky in our counterclaim, we will waive our objection to personal jurisdiction? I have not researched this point but will do so if you think this is a possible problem.

# THE RESULTING DOCUMENTS

**1.**

UNITED STATES DISTRICT COURT

DISTRICT OF MASSACHUSETTS

CIVIL ACTION NO. 2006-6719

DEBORAH SCHULANSKY

Plaintiff

v.

RICHARD L. RONAN, et al.

Defendants

ANSWER AND

COUNTERCLAIM

**2.** → <u>FIRST DEFENSE</u>

1. The defendants admit the allegations in paragraph one of the complaint.

2. The defendants admit the allegations in paragraph two of the complaint.

3. The defendants admit the allegations in paragraph three of the complaint.

4. The defendants admit the allegations in paragraph four of the complaint.

**3.** →
5. The defendants admit the allegations in paragraph five that the plaintiff owns a colonial home in Alton, New Hampshire, but are without sufficient knowledge or information to form a belief as to the truth of the remaining allegations in paragraph five of the complaint.

6. The defendants admit the allegations in paragraph six of the complaint.

**4.** →
7. The defendants admit the allegation in paragraph seven that Richard Ronan told the plaintiff that he had worked on older houses in both states. The defendants deny the remaining allegations in paragraph seven of the complaint.

8. The attendants admit the allegations in paragraph eight of the complaint.

9. The defendants admit the allegation in paragraph nine that the parties discussed the condition of the old foundation at the March meeting. The defendants deny the remaining allegations in paragraph nine of the complaint.

10. The defendants deny the allegation in paragraph ten that they, or either one of them, agreed to reconstruct the foundation, or that such reconstruction was part of the construction of the foundation for the addition agreed to in the contract between the plaintiff and Ronan Construction Company.

11. The defendants admit the allegation in paragraph eleven that the defendant Richard Ronan sent a Proposal and Estimate to the plaintiff. The defendants further state that the Proposal and Estimate constituted an offer by the Ronan Construction Company, not by the defendant Richard Ronan individually.

12. The defendants admit the allegation in paragraph twelve that the plaintiff signed and returned the Proposal and Estimate on or around April 3, 2006, but further state that the Proposal and Estimate constituted an offer solely by Ronan Construction Company.

13. The defendants admit the allegations in paragraph thirteen of the complaint.

14. The defendants admit the allegations in paragraph fourteen of the complaint.

15. The defendants admit the allegation in paragraph fifteen that the foundation consisted of loose boulders without mortar. The defendants deny the remaining allegations in paragraph fifteen of the complaint.

16. The defendants deny the allegations in paragraph sixteen of the complaint.

17. The defendants deny the allegations in paragraph seventeen of the complaint.

18. The defendants admit the allegation in paragraph eighteen that they did not completely reconstruct the preexisting foundation, but deny that they had agreed to do so, or that such reconstruction was necessary to provide adequate support for the house or the addition. The defendants did heavily reinforce the preexisting foundation with concrete in the course of constructing the addition.

19. The defendants deny the allegations in paragraph nineteen of the complaint.

20. The defendants deny the allegations of paragraph twenty of the complaint.

**5.** → 21. The defendants repeat and reallege their responses to the allegations in paragraphs one to twenty of the complaint.

22. The defendants admit the allegation in paragraph twenty-two that the Proposal and Estimate constitutes a contract between Ronan Construction Company and the plaintiff. The defendants deny that Richard L. Ronan is a party to the contract.

23. The defendants admit the allegation in paragraph twenty-three that, under the contract, the defendant Ronan Construction Company agreed to construct an adequate foundation for the addition. They deny that the contract imposed any obligation upon Ronan Construction Company to reconstruct the foundation of the main house. They deny that Richard L. Ronan personally undertook any obligations under the contract.

24. The defendants deny the allegations in paragraph twenty-four of the complaint.

25. The defendants deny the allegations in paragraph twenty-five of the complaint.

26. The defendants admit the allegation in paragraph twenty-six that the plaintiff made the first four progress payments under the contract, but deny that they breached the contract. The defendants further state that the plaintiff has refused to make the final payment due under the contract, in the amount of $18,000, although the defendant Ronan Construction Company has performed all of its obligations under the contract in a timely and satisfactory manner and has demanded payment of the balance due under the contract.

27. The defendants deny the allegations in paragraph twenty-seven of the complaint.

28. The defendants repeat and reallege their responses to paragraphs one to twenty of the complaint.

29. The defendants deny the allegations in paragraph twenty-nine of the complaint.

30. The defendants deny the allegations in paragraph thirty of the complaint.

**6.** →                    SECOND DEFENSE

This action must be dismissed because the court lacks personal jurisdiction over the defendants under the Fourteenth Amendment and the Massachusetts Long-Arm Statute, Mass. G.L. c. 223A, §3.

<u>THIRD</u> <u>DEFENSE</u>

The plaintiff's first claim for relief fails to state a claim upon which relief can be granted, because the Proposal and Estimate constitutes the entire agreement between the parties, and does not require any reconstruction of the original foundation.

**7.** ⟶ <u>FOURTH</u> <u>DEFENSE</u>

If the defendants had any obligation under the contract to reconstruct the preexisting foundation, the plaintiff waived performance of that obligation on or about April 17, 2006, when she agreed that the defendants could fulfill their obligations under the contract by reinforcing the preexisting foundation with cement.

<u>FIFTH</u> <u>DEFENSE</u>

The plaintiff's first claim for relief fails to state a claim upon which relief can be granted against the defendant Richard L. Ronan, because he was not a party to the contract.

<u>SIXTH</u> <u>DEFENSE</u>

If there was any negligence in the excavation of the foundation, that negligence was solely the act of Arlen Jones, an independent contractor for whose negligence the defendants cannot be held liable.

**8.** ⟶ WHEREFORE, the defendants request that the court dismiss the plaintiff's complaint and award the defendants their costs, together with such other relief as the court finds just and equitable.

**9.** ⟶ <u>COUNTERCLAIM</u> <u>OF</u> <u>RONAN</u> <u>CONSTRUCTION</u> <u>COMPANY</u> — <u>BREACH</u> <u>OF</u> <u>CONTRACT</u>

The defendant Ronan Construction Company counterclaims against the plaintiff as follows:

**10.** ⟶ 1. This court has subject matter jurisdiction of this action under Article III, §2 of the United States Constitution and 28 U.S.C. §1332. This counterclaim is a compulsory counterclaim under Fed. R. Civ. P. 13(a). This court has supplemental jurisdiction over the counterclaim under 28 U.S.C. §1367(a).

**11.**

2. The signed Proposal and Estimate attached to the plaintiff's complaint constitutes a valid contract between the plaintiff and the defendant Ronan Construction Company.

3. Under that contract, the plaintiff agreed to pay Ronan Construction Company $50,000 for the construction of an addition to her home at 53 School Street, Alton, New Hampshire.

4. The defendant Ronan Construction Company has fully performed all of its obligations under the contract.

6. Although the defendant Ronan Construction Company has demanded payment of the final balance due under the contract, the plaintiff has failed to pay Ronan Construction Company the final progress payment of $20,000.

WHEREFORE, the defendant Ronan Construction Company demands judgment from the plaintiff in the amount of $18,000 and interest and costs and such other relief as the court finds just and equitable.

<u>DEMAND</u> <u>FOR</u> <u>JURY</u> <u>TRIAL</u>

**12.** Under Fed. R. Civ. P. 38(b), the defendants demand jury trial of all issues raised by the plaintiff's complaint and the defendant Ronan Construction Company's counterclaim.

**13.**
_____
Arthur Ackerman
Ackerman, Sloan and Cariotis
Attorney for the Defendants
59 State Street
Boston, MA 02114
(617) 228-6301

**14.** <u>CERTIFICATE</u> <u>OF</u> <u>SERVICE</u>

I hereby certify that on this date I served a true copy of the above answer and counterclaim upon Phyllis Slater, Gomez, Robbins and Slater, 322 Puritan Road, Plymouth, MA 02360, by First Class mail, postage prepaid.

Date:_____

_____
Arthur Ackerman
Ackerman, Sloan and Cariotis
59 State Street
Boston, MA 02114
(617) 228-6301

# COMMENTS ON THE ANSWER AND COUNTERCLAIM

1. Rule 10(a) governs the caption of the answer as well as the complaint and all other pleadings. Note that the federal docket number is now known and will be used in all subsequent pleadings and other papers.

2. Rule 8(b) specifically requires the defendant to respond to each allegation in the complaint by admitting or denying the allegations, stating the parts that are true and denying the remainder, or stating that the defendant does not have enough information to assess the truth of the allegation. In his First Defense, Ronan complies with this requirement by responding, paragraph by paragraph, to the allegations in the plaintiff's complaint. Rule 10(b) requires these responses to be set forth in numbered paragraphs, and the drafting attorney here has numbered her admissions and denials to correspond to the appropriate paragraphs in the complaint. This will make it easy for the parties and the court to compare the pleadings during the course of the suit, in order to quickly ascertain the positions of the parties on the various issues.

   In some cases, the defendant may group his responses to parts of the complaint in a single sentence. For example, the answer might state that "the defendant admits the allegations in paragraphs one to eleven and sixteen to twenty-one of the complaint." This saves space and time, but in cases with a large number of paragraphs and varied responses it is less helpful for quick reference in comparing the complaint and the answer.

3. It is permissible for a party to respond by stating that he lacks sufficient information to admit or deny an allegation. Fed. R. Civ. P. 8(b)(5). The defendants here probably have no particular knowledge of the National Register of Historic Places and are under no duty to scurry around and verify this allegation in order to answer the complaint.

4. Under Rule 8, the defendant must respond clearly and forthrightly to the allegations in the complaint. "A denial must fairly respond to the substance of the allegation." Fed. R. Civ. P. 8(b)(2). If the pleader denies only a part of an allegation in the complaint, the pleader should deny the part she disputes and admit the rest. See Fed. R. Civ. P. 8(b)(4). It would not be proper for the defendants here to simply deny the entire allegation in paragraph seven, because Ronan had told the plaintiff that he had worked on old houses. However, the defendants do not accept the plaintiff's characterization of Ronan's

statements and have therefore crafted their response to paragraph seven to negate any inference that Ronan represented himself as an expert in this area. A number of the defendants' other responses also admit some parts of the allegations but deny other parts or recharacterize allegations in the complaint. See, e.g., paragraphs 11, 15, 18, and 26.

5. Rule 10(c) authorizes adoption by reference of parts of a pleading in another part of the pleading. The language of the rule is general, so it is clear that a defendant — or any other pleader — may do so as well as a plaintiff. Because Schulansky incorporated all of her factual allegations by reference into her First Claim for Relief, Ronan has similarly incorporated his answers to the earlier paragraphs in his answer to her First Claim for Relief.

6. As you are probably aware, defending parties will frequently have further defenses to the plaintiff's claims, in addition to denials of the allegations in the complaint. After responding in the First Defense to each of the allegations of the complaint, the answer goes on to set forth several further defenses. This breakdown is proper under Rule 10(b), which provides in part that "each defense other than a denial — shall be stated in a separate count or defense."

The defendants' Second Defense here is an objection to the court's power to adjudicate, on the ground that it lacks personal jurisdiction over the defendants. This objection could be raised by pre-answer motion under Rule 12(b), but it does not have to be. It is always proper to include this objection in the answer instead of raising it by pre-answer motion, so long as no pre-answer motion is made. See Chapter 19, p. 367. As Ackerman's memo indicates, the decision to answer rather than move to dismiss is a tactical one.

Careful counsel should be aware, however, that inserting an objection to personal jurisdiction in the answer, as the defendants have done here, may not be enough to preserve the defense. Some courts have held that defendants who assert the personal jurisdiction defense in the answer must subsequently take the initiative to seek a ruling on the issue, by moving to dismiss the case or asking for a hearing on the defense, or else forfeit the defense for failure to pursue it. See, e.g., *Hamilton v. Atlas Turner, Inc.*, 197 F.3d 58, 61-62 (2d Cir. 1999). This is a serious trap for the unwary lawyer who raises the defense in the answer and assumes that the court will eventually get around to doing something about it.

7. The defendants' Fourth Defense raises an affirmative defense of waiver. The defendants take the position that, even if the contract required reconstruction of the foundation and the defendants failed to do so, the plaintiff waived performance of this obligation by her

assent to Ronan's alternative suggestion. An affirmative defense asserts new facts that avoid liability even if the plaintiff proves her basic allegations. It is akin to the old common law "confession and avoidance" device, except that the defendant need not admit the plaintiff's allegations ("confess") in order to allege additional facts that avoid liability.

Unfortunately, many litigators tend to throw boilerplate affirmative defenses into every answer even though most of them are irrelevant to the particular case. Thus, many answers promiscuously assert passage of the statute of limitations, failure to mitigate damages, comparative fault, unclean hands, the failure to fulfill conditions precedent, res judicata, and other affirmative defenses, although there is no support for them in the case. This is surely contrary to the spirit of the pleading rules, and often a clear violation of Fed. R. Civ. P. 11. The practice persists, however, because of human nature. Litigators are more worried about a suit for malpractice based on leaving out an affirmative defense than they are about the court sanctioning them for throwing one in. A colleague, fed up with reading these misleading allegations, once moved to strike the most egregious ones from the defendant's answer. Although his motion was on solid legal footing, the judge was simply annoyed that he had taken up the court's time with the motion.

Under Rule 8(e)(3), a defendant may plead inconsistently, and the *Schulansky* defendants have done so in their answer. In their First Defense, they deny that they agreed to reconstruct the foundation. In their Fourth Defense, they assert that, even if they did agree to do so, the plaintiff waived performance of that obligation.

The order of the various defenses is not prescribed by the rules. On occasion, you will see an answer that begins with objections and affirmative defenses and leaves the admissions and denials until later. Of paramount importance, of course, is that all defenses be raised in the answer, to avoid waiving any by omission.

8. Defendants frequently include a paragraph like this at the end of the answer, asking the court, on the basis of the defenses and denials in the answer, to dismiss the complaint. In the federal courts (and state systems as well) a prevailing party is entitled to recover certain costs of suit, such as witness fees and the cost of transcripts. See 28 U.S.C §1920. It is customary to ask for these in the answer and, in a lawyerly excess of caution, to append a request for any other relief the court finds "just and equitable" as well.

9. It is entirely proper to include a counterclaim within the answer. It should be set apart from the rest of the answer, however, and clearly labeled as a counterclaim. If a counterclaim is not clearly

labeled as such, it may look a good deal like an affirmative defense. (Compare, for example, paragraph 26 of the answer, which could be construed to seek relief from Schulansky for the unpaid balance under the contract.) Unless it is clearly labeled as a counterclaim and set apart from the various defenses, it may be unclear whether Ronan is defending on the basis of Schulansky's failure to fulfill her obligations under the contract or seeking independent, affirmative relief by way of counterclaim.

Note that Losordo has consistently taken the position in drafting the answer that the contract is between Ronan Construction Company and Schulansky. See paragraphs 10, 11, 12, 22, 23, and 26 of the First Defense. Thus, the company is the proper party to assert the counterclaim for breach of the contract. Indeed, Losordo might have chosen to emphasize the difference in the positions of Ronan and Ronan Construction Company by filing completely separate answers for them. The rules do not require the defendants to file a joint answer, and in cases where their interests are clearly divergent, they will not do so.

10. Federal Rule 8(a) requires "a pleading that states a claim for relief" to include a statement of the grounds for the court's jurisdiction. A counterclaim is such a pleading, and Losordo has accordingly asserted here that the court has supplemental jurisdiction over it. Supplemental jurisdiction is proper for this claim because it is a compulsory counterclaim. See Chapter 16, example 4.

Strictly speaking, this is probably overpleading. Rule 8(a)(1) does not require a jurisdiction allegation if the court already has jurisdiction (i.e., if an earlier pleading has already provided a basis for jurisdiction over the action), and the new pleading does not require "new grounds" for jurisdiction. In this case, the court has jurisdiction over the main claim based on diversity, and supplemental jurisdiction over the related counterclaim is arguably not a "new ground." However, since Schulansky's complaint was originally filed in state court, it contained no explicit allegation as to the basis of jurisdiction, and it is certainly appropriate, even if not required, to assert the ground of jurisdiction in the counterclaim.

The Rule 8(a)(1) requirement to state the ground of the court's jurisdiction refers to subject matter jurisdiction, not personal jurisdiction. *Sterling Homex Corp. v. Homasote Co.*, 437 F.2d 87, 88 (2d Cir. 1971). It is not necessary to assert in a pleading that the court has personal jurisdiction over the defendant, but, of course, the court must have it in order to proceed.

11. The general rules of pleading govern the allegations in a counterclaim, including the use of numbered paragraphs and inclusion of a

demand for relief.[1] Like an original complaint, a counterclaim may include a number of claims for relief based on different theories. It is even permissible to assert completely unrelated counterclaims (see Fed R. Civ. P. 13(b)), although there will not be supplemental jurisdiction over such claims.

Unlike the common law, where the parties might plead back and forth a number of times before a single issue was reached, the answer usually ends the pleadings under the Federal Rules. However, Fed. R. Civ. P. 7(a)(3) does require the plaintiff to file an answer to a counterclaim if it is "designated as a counterclaim." If the defendant does not clearly label the counterclaim in the answer, the plaintiff need not file an answer to it. Thus, he need not guess whether vague allegations in an answer are affirmative defenses, denials, or counterclaims. Schulansky would be required to answer this counterclaim, since Ronan's counsel has clearly labeled it as such, putting Schulansky on notice that Ronan is claiming affirmative relief from her.

The plaintiff's answer to a counterclaim is governed by the same pleading requirements as Ronan's answer and should include responses to each of the paragraphs in the counterclaim as well as affirmative defenses. Of course, the answer will only address the allegations in the counterclaim itself, since the parties' positions on the main claim are already established by the complaint and the original answer. The answer to a counterclaim must be served within 20 days after service of the pleading that asserts the counterclaim. Fed. R. Civ. P. 12(a)(1)(B).

12. Losordo has followed her own suggestion in her memo on removal (see infra p. 652) and included a demand for jury trial on the counterclaim. It may be that the jury demand is unnecessary, but at most it is redundant. Rather than invest substantial research time (and the client's money) in finding a definitive answer to this question, Losordo has simply erred on the side of caution by including it in the answer. Just to cover all the bases, she has also demanded jury trial on the main claim as well.

13. The answer, like the complaint and all other pleadings and motions, must be signed by the attorney and is subject to the ethical constraints and sanctions set forth in Fed. R. Civ. P. 11.

---

1. In putting a dollar demand in his counterclaim, Ronan has not ignored Mass. Gen. L. ch. 231, §13B, the statute that bars putting a dollar demand in some complaints. That statute only bars a dollar demand in cases of unliquidated damages, that is, damages that cannot easily be calculated. In cases where the damages can be easily ascertained by calculation, a specific demand is proper. Here, all Ronan has to do to ascertain the damages is to subtract the earlier progress payments from the contract price.

14. The elaborate service provisions of Fed. R. Civ. P. 4 only govern service of the complaint. Subsequent papers may be served under the simpler provisions of Fed. R. Civ. P. 5(b), which authorizes service by personal delivery or regular mail to the attorney for the opposing party. Once properly notified that the suit has been commenced, the parties should be in contact and should watch the docket for subsequent filings. But a party who never receives initial notice of a suit cannot take such precautions.

The certificate of service constitutes a representation by the serving attorney that he has complied with the service requirements of Rule 5(b). It is often drafted as a separate document, but the local rules for the District of Massachusetts provide that the certificate of service must appear on the pleading or motion itself, rather than on a separate sheet. Local Rule 5.2(b)(2).[2]

Losordo raises an interesting question at the end of her memo, concerning the possibility that asserting the counterclaim might waive the defendant's objection to personal jurisdiction. In fact, if Ronan's attorneys look into this issue, they will find that the courts are split on this question. Some cases have held that a defendant waives his objection to personal jurisdiction by asking the court to adjudicate a counterclaim. Others, however, have recognized that this puts the defendant in an awkward position, because Fed. R. Civ. P. 13(a) *requires* him to assert any counterclaim that arises out of the same events as the plaintiff's claim. (Of course, the defendant could present the personal jurisdiction issue by pre-answer motion, thus obtaining resolution of that issue before answering.) Cf. *Rates Technology Inc. v. Nortel Networks Corp.*, 399 F.3d 1302 (Fed. Cir. 2005) (assertion of permissive counterclaim did not waive properly asserted objection to personal jurisdiction); see generally 5A Wright & Miller at §1397, which reviews this issue and suggests that assertion of a compulsory counterclaim should not waive the personal jurisdiction defense.

One of the things that makes a litigation practice unnerving is the number of uncertainties that arise in the course of a case, in circumstances that make it impossible to give those issues the full attention they deserve. Here, the attorneys are under the gun to get their responsive pleading in and are doubtless handling many other matters as well. Many lawyers would never even have thought of this rather subtle ramification of the counterclaim. Even if their client could afford to have exhaustive research

---

2. Some district courts — including the District of Massachusetts — allow electronic filing of pleadings and other documents. See Fed. R. Civ. P. 5(b)(2)(E). When documents are filed electronically, the court can "serve" them on all parties by electronically forwarding them to the e-mail addresses for all counsel of record. Thus, no certificate of service would be required.

done on this point, it would have been hard for Ronan's lawyers to find the time to do it before answering. They probably would not have found a definitive answer even if they had researched the point.

It is also interesting to compare the facts as stated in the Slater memo (pp. 629-630) and Ackerman's memo in this chapter. The dispute looks quite different from the two parties' points of view. It is unlikely that either is lying or deliberately distorting the facts; they just see things from different perspectives, like Republicans and Democrats, or Mainers and Californians. The truth, if there is such a thing in a case like this, is likely to be ambiguous and elusive. If there is a trial, the system will resolve the dispute one way or the other, but it is unlikely that it will definitely determine who is "right" or leave either party feeling fully satisfied for the effort and emotional stress it engenders.

Naturally, the attorneys' job in drafting the pleadings, and in representing the parties generally, is to state the case most strongly from their clients' viewpoints. Hopefully, providing vigorous advocacy will not prevent them from seeing the facts as they are likely to play out at trial and advising their clients accordingly. But even if they keep some perspective on the case, there is little doubt that the lawyer's duty in an adversary system tends to accentuate the differences in the parties' views rather than the search for common ground. This has spawned an increasing emphasis on alternatives to litigation, such as mediation, which try to educate the parties about each other's views and bring the parties together rather than focus, as the litigation system tends to, on the differences in their points of view.

# Chain Reaction

## Ronan Brings In Jones

---

## THE DRAFTING REQUEST

### MEMORANDUM

**TO:**    Marcia Losordo
Associate

**FROM:**    Arthur Ackerman

**RE:**    Third-party complaint in *Schulansky v. Ronan*
U.S. District Court No. 2006-6719

**DATE:**    January 4, 2007

---------------------------------------------------------------------------------

I have reviewed and filed your answer and counterclaim in the Schulansky case. I have also discussed with Dick Ronan the possibility of filing a third-party complaint against Arlen Jones, the backhoe operator who did the excavation work on the job. On the basis of that discussion, I have decided to proceed with the third-party complaint.

As you are no doubt aware, Fed. R. Civ. P. 14(a)(1) allows us to implead Jones if he "is or may be liable to [our clients] for all or part of the plaintiff's claim" against them. In other words, we can implead Jones if we have a right to reimbursement from him for any damages Schulansky recovers from us. In my judgment, we may be able to obtain indemnification from Jones if Schulansky recovers on either her breach of contract claim or her negligence claim. Please let me know if you agree with the following line of reasoning, which leads me to that conclusion.

As you suggested in your earlier memo, it is not clear whether Jones acted as a subcontractor to Ronan or as Ronan's employee in doing the excavation work. The accepted test is the extent of control Ronan could exercise over Jones in the course of the work, and the facts on this are ambiguous. On the one hand, Ronan apparently did have an informal letter agreement with Jones for the excavation work. This, and the facts that Jones worked for a flat price and used his own equipment support the argument that he acted as an independent contractor. On the other hand, according to Ronan, he consistently directed Jones in the course of the work and considered Jones (who worked quite regularly for Ronan) an employee, even though he usually paid him by the job. In addition, the informality of their arrangement suggests an employment relationship more than a contract. Given the ambiguity in the evidence, it will likely be a jury question whether Jones should be characterized as an employee or independent contractor.

If the jury were to find that Jones was Ronan's employee, Ronan would be liable for his negligence, under respondent superior principles (Restatement (Third) of Agency §7.07(1)), but would have a right to indemnification from Jones. Thus, if Schulansky proves that Jones negligently disturbed the existing foundation during the excavation, and the jury concludes that Jones acted as an employee in doing the work, Schulansky will recover judgment from us, but Jones will be liable to indemnify us for the entire judgment.

Alternatively, if the jury finds that Jones was not directly under Ronan's control and therefore acted as a subcontractor to Ronan, Ronan should still have a right of indemnification from him under contract principles. If Jones's negligent excavation caused a breach of the main contract between Ronan and Schulansky, Ronan would be liable directly to Schulansky for the breach by his subcontractor. However, Jones would have breached his subcontract with Ronan by failing to perform the work properly, so Ronan would have a cause of action against him for breach of the subcontract. The damages for this breach would include the judgment Ronan incurred to Schulansky, as well as any attorneys' fees Ronan pays us for defending the claim. Thus, if Schulansky recovers on her breach of contract claim, we should be entitled to recover from Jones both the damages we pay to Schulansky and our fees for defending the main action.

If you agree with my reasoning, please draft a third-party complaint against Jones for indemnification on both of the plaintiff's claims. I realize that our theories for indemnification are based on inconsistent allegations, since we will allege on the negligence claim that Jones was an employee, but on the contract claim that he was a subcontractor. However, Rule 8(e)(3) expressly allows us to plead inconsistent versions of our claim. Nor do I view this as inappropriate under the ethical pleading requirements in Rule 11, since there is factual support for characterizing Jones either as an employee or an independent contractor. Where the jury could properly reach either conclusion, it is appropriate to assert whatever rights we may have against Jones based on either theory.

As you pointed out in our discussions, it is a little awkward to deny that the foundation was damaged at all during the excavation (as we did in our answer) but to turn around and implead Jones for causing that damage. Ronan tells me that he is not convinced that Jones's excavation work destabilized the foundation, or that anything did. But there is some evidence to support a finding that Jones was negligent. Apparently Jones did hit the foundation a number of times with his backhoe, and the excavation turned up some loose rocks along the edge of the foundation. Schulansky was present at the time, and this is probably what is behind her negligence claim.

I do not think the Rules require us to disregard our possible rights against Jones just because we denied in our answer that any negligence took place. As indicated above, the Rules specifically authorize inconsistent pleading. Of course, we must have evidentiary support for the allegations under Rule 11, but I believe Ronan's observations about Jones's encounters with the foundation during the excavation meet this test, since they suggest that Jones may have damaged the foundation in the course of the excavation. We shouldn't have to abandon a possible right to indemnification against Jones just because we think the stronger argument is that there was no negligence in the first place.

We may have a serious problem obtaining personal jurisdiction over Jones in Massachusetts. Jones lives in New Hampshire, agreed to do the work in a telephone conversation with Ronan, and performed all the work in New Hampshire. According to Ronan, Jones does work occasionally in Massachusetts, but I doubt that this occasional work in the state is sufficient to support personal jurisdiction over Jones for a claim unrelated to his work here in the state. On the other hand, since Jones occasionally works for contractors here in Massachusetts perhaps we can serve process on him while he is working here and obtain jurisdiction based on in-state service. Please do a little research to determine whether this would establish personal jurisdiction over Jones here.

I realize you have not yet had a chance to open your Christmas presents, but please get on this right away. I would like to file this within the ten-day limit for filing the third-party complaint without leave of court.

# THE ASSOCIATE'S RESPONSE

## MEMORANDUM

**TO:** Arthur Ackerman

**FROM:** Marcia Losordo

**RE:** Third-party complaint in *Schulansky v. Ronan*
U.S. District Court No. 2006-6719

**DATE:** January 7, 2007

---

I have attached a draft third-party complaint against Jones in the Schulansky case. I agree with your analysis of Jones's potential liability to us, but I have several additional observations. First, it is conceivable that Schulansky would recover from us for breach of contract on both grounds alleged in her complaint. It may turn out that the structural damage resulted in part from Ronan's failure to rebuild the foundation, and in part from damage caused by Jones's backhoe. If the jury finds that both causes contributed to the settling, we would have a right to partial indemnification from Jones: Presumably the court would apportion the damages between the two causes, and Jones only contributed to one of them.

It is proper to implead a third party for partial as well as full indemnification; Rule 14(a)(1) authorizes impleader of a party who "is or may be liable to [the third-party plaintiff] for all *or part* of the claim against it . . ." (emphasis supplied). Thus, I have asserted two claims for relief based on the theory that Jones breached his subcontract with Ronan, one for full indemnification and a separate claim for partial indemnification.

Second, note that our claim against Jones for any attorneys' fees Ronan pays us to defend Schulansky's claim against him does not satisfy the Rule 14 requirement, since this is not reimbursement for damages Ronan must pay Schulansky. These fees represent separate consequential damages Ronan has suffered as a result of Jones's breach of the subcontract, and the resulting need to defend Schulansky's lawsuit. However, it is proper to assert this additional claim in the third-party complaint. Once a defendant has asserted a proper impleader claim under Rule 14(a), she may also assert independent claims against the third-party defendant under Fed. R. Civ. P. 18(a). Since the claim arises from the same events as the main claim, the court will have supplemental jurisdiction over it under 28 U.S.C. §1367(a).

As you suggest, the fact that Jones does occasional business in Massachusetts is not sufficient under the *International Shoe* minimum contacts test to support personal jurisdiction over him for a claim unrelated to the in-state business. See *Helicopteros Nacionales de Columbia, S.A. v. Hall*, 466 U.S.

408, 414-415 (1984) (where claim does not arise out of contacts with forum state, the defendant must have continuous and systematic contacts there to support jurisdiction). Since Jones only works in Massachusetts occasionally, it is doubtful that he would be subject to general in personam jurisdiction here. However, personal jurisdiction can be obtained over Jones by serving process on him here in Massachusetts, under the hoary doctrine of *Pennoyer v. Neff*. The Supreme Court appears to have reaffirmed the sufficiency of such "transient personal service" in *Burnham v. Superior Court of California*, 495 U.S. 604 (1990). Of course, this requires us to keep track of Jones's movements, locate him on the job site in Massachusetts, and actually serve him in person in the state.

Alternatively, we may be able to serve Jones in New Hampshire under Fed. R. Civ. P. 4(k)(1)(B), the "100-mile bulge" provision for service on certain additional parties to actions in federal court. Under Rule 4(k)(1)(B), a third-party defendant may be served with process outside the forum state but within 100 miles of the courthouse. This provision authorizes service on Jones in New Hampshire, as long as he is served within 100 miles of the courthouse in Boston. Evidently, Rule 4(k)(1)(B) not only authorizes service of process on Jones within the bulge area, but also *makes him subject to personal jurisdiction in Massachusetts*, even if he would not be subject to jurisdiction under Fourteenth Amendment due process analysis. In other words, even if a Massachusetts state court could not subject Jones to personal jurisdiction, because he lacks minimum contacts with Massachusetts, the federal court here could apparently require Jones to defend in Massachusetts under Rule 4(k)(1)(B). See the title of Rule 4(k) ("Territorial Limits of Effective Service").

However, Rule 4 clearly cannot confer jurisdiction if it would be unconstitutional to exercise it: Neither the rulemakers nor Congress can repeal the restrictions of the due process clause. (I am not even clear as to what due process restrictions actually apply here — state standards under the Fourteenth Amendment or federal standards under the Fifth?) Thus, there is some question as to whether serving Jones under Rule 4(k)(1)(B) will force him to defend in Massachusetts.

This is a very sophisticated personal jurisdiction issue, which could require extensive research and briefing if it is contested. But the issue won't arise if we serve Jones in Massachusetts, or if we serve him in New Hampshire under Rule 4(k)(1)(B), and he does not raise an objection to personal jurisdiction. I suggest that we serve him on the job in Massachusetts if possible, and if not, within the 100-mile bulge. (Please note that the third-party complaint and summons must be served on Jones under the provisions of Fed. R. Civ. P. 4, not under Rule 5.) If he does not object to jurisdiction, we will save our clients a good deal of expense in a relatively small-stakes case.

1.

UNITED STATES DISTRICT COURT

DISTRICT OF MASSACHUSETTS

CIVIL ACTION NO. 2006-6719  ◄── 2.

DEBORAH SCHULANSKY

    Plaintiff

      v.

RICHARD L. RONAN
RONAN CONSTRUCTION CO.

    Defendants
    and Third-Party      THIRD-PARTY COMPLAINT
    Plaintiffs

      v.

ARLEN JONES

    Third-Party
    Defendant

3. ──────────►   — FIRST CLAIM FOR RELIEF —

INDEMNIFICATION FOR BREACH OF SUBCONTRACT

4.

1. The plaintiff Deborah Schulansky has filed a complaint against the defendants/third-party plaintiffs Richard L. Ronan and Ronan Construction Company (hereinafter referred to as the defendants) for damages arising out of the construction of an addition to her property at 53 School Street, Alton, New Hampshire. A copy of the complaint is attached as Exhibit A.

2. This action was removed to this court by the defendants, and is currently pending in that court as Civil Action No. 2006-6719.

3. The third-party defendant Arlen Jones is an individual residing at 88 Warren Avenue, Littleton, New Hampshire.

4. This court has jurisdiction over this third-party action under 28 U.S.C. s. 1367(a), because the third-party claim arises out of the same transaction as the claim between the plaintiff and the third-party plaintiffs, and is therefore part of the same case or controversy as that claim.

5. On or about April 10, 2006, the defendant Ronan Construction Company entered into an oral subcontract with the

third-party defendant, Arlen Jones, for performance of the excavation work on the addition.

6. Under the contract, the third-party defendant agreed to perform all the excavation work required by the main contract, using his own labor and equipment, and the defendants agreed to pay the third-party defendant the sum of $3,000 upon completion of the work.

7. The excavation work was performed entirely by the third-party defendant, on or about April 15-18, 2006.

8. The First Claim for Relief in the plaintiff's complaint alleges a right to relief for breach of contract, on the ground that the defendants breached their contract with her by failing to perform the excavation work in a careful manner, resulting in damage to the existing foundation of the house.

9. If defendants breached their contract with the plaintiff by failing to perform the excavation work in a careful manner, that breach and any resulting damage was caused solely by the acts of the third-party defendant.

10. If the third-party defendant failed to perform the excavation work in a careful manner, that failure constituted a breach of the contract between the defendants and the third-party defendant.

**5.** ➤ 11. If the plaintiff recovers against the defendants on the ground that the damage to the foundation in the course of excavation constituted a breach of their contract, the third-party defendant is liable to the defendants for any damages adjudged against them in the main action described in paragraph one.

**6.** ➤ WHEREFORE, the defendants demand judgment against the third-party defendant as follows:

    a. For any and all sums that may be adjudged against them in the plaintiff's main action against them.

**7.** ➤     b. For all costs, including attorneys' fees, incurred in defense of this action.

    c. For such other relief as the court deems just and proper.

SECOND CLAIM FOR RELIEF —

PARTIAL INDEMNIFICATION FOR BREACH
OF SUBCONTRACT

12. The defendants repeat and reallege the allegations in paragraphs one to ten of the third-party complaint.

13. If the plaintiff recovers damages for breach of contract from the defendants based partly on the faulty excavation of the foundation by third-party defendant Jones, and partly on other grounds, the third party defendant is liable to the defendants under the subcontract for that part of the damages resulting from the faulty excavation.

WHEREFORE, the defendants demand judgment from the third-party defendant as follows:

a. For any and all sums that may be adjudged against them for breach of contract resulting from the third-party defendant's negligent excavation.
b. For that part of the defendants' attorneys' fees and costs in defending this action attributable to the plaintiff's claim for negligent excavation.
c. For such other relief as the court deems just and proper.

THIRD CLAIM FOR RELIEF —

INDEMNIFICATION FOR NEGLIGENCE

14. The defendants repeat and reallege the allegations in paragraph one of the third-party complaint.

15. The Second Claim for Relief in the plaintiff's complaint alleges a right to recover from the defendants on the ground that the defendants were negligent in excavating the area in which the addition was to be constructed.

8.

16. On or about April 10, 2006, the defendants employed the third-party defendant Jones to perform the excavation work for the addition.

17. The excavation work was done entirely by the third-party defendant in the course of his employment for the defendants.

18. If the excavation work was negligently performed, any negligence in the work was due solely to acts of the third-party defendant.

19. If the plaintiff recovers from the defendant on her Second Claim for Relief, the defendants are entitled to indemnification from the third-party defendant for any and all damages that they are ordered to pay to the plaintiff on that claim.

WHEREFORE, the defendants demand judgment from the third-party defendant as follows:

a. For all damages that the defendants are ordered to pay to the plaintiff on her second claim for relief.

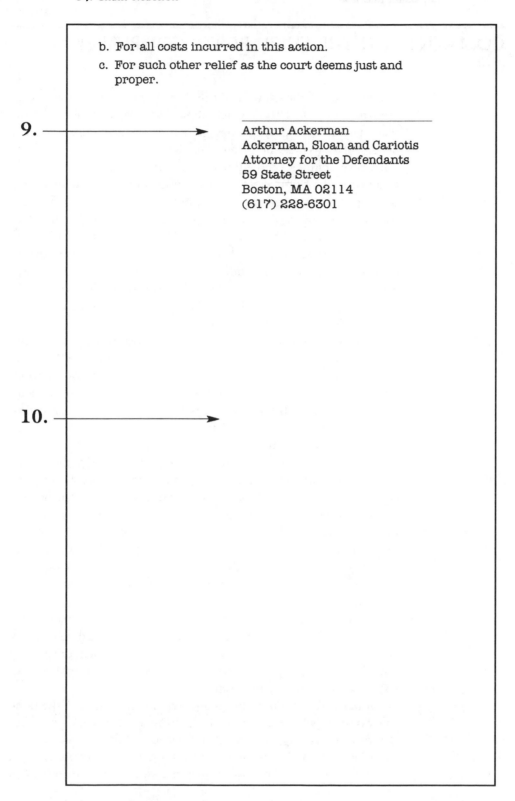

b. For all costs incurred in this action.

c. For such other relief as the court deems just and proper.

9. ───────────────────────▶

Arthur Ackerman
Ackerman, Sloan and Cariotis
Attorney for the Defendants
59 State Street
Boston, MA 02114
(617) 228-6301

10. ──────────────────▶

# COMMENTS ON THE THIRD-PARTY COMPLAINT

1. The contents of the caption of the third-party complaint are again governed by Rule 10(a), which applies to "every pleading." Note that the title of the action has grown to include the third-party defendant as well as the original parties.

2. The docket number on the third-party complaint is the same as that assigned to the original action. This reflects the fact that the third-party action is *not* a separate action, but an additional claim asserted by the defendant against a new party in the original action. This new claim will be litigated along with the main claim unless the court orders separate trials. Thus, all three parties will be entitled to seek discovery from each other (see, e.g., Fed. R. Civ. P. 33, 34, 36), all motions and other papers will be served on all other parties, all parties will participate in any hearings or pretrial proceedings, and all claims will be tried at the same time.

3. A third-party complaint is a pleading that asserts a right to relief against a new defendant. Thus, its contents are governed by Rule 8(a), which applies to any pleading that sets forth a claim for relief. Like an original complaint, the third-party complaint must contain an allegation as to the court's basis for subject matter jurisdiction (see paragraph 4 in the third-party complaint), a short and plain statement of the plaintiff's claim, and a demand for relief.

   Because it is subject to the regular pleading rules, the defendants' third-party complaint is organized much like an original complaint, with separate claims for relief asserting the defendants' various theories for holding Jones liable to them, and demands for relief following each claim. The defendants have not included a separate Facts section as in Schulansky's complaint because most of the relevant facts are already in the original complaint, and the additional facts can be set forth clearly within the *Claim for Relief* sections.

4. The underlying premise of the defendants' impleader claims is a right to recover from Jones for damages they are ordered to pay Schulansky in this lawsuit. They therefore begin their third-party complaint by alleging the existence of the primary suit, which gives rise to their claims for indemnification.

   A third-party claim requires an answer conforming to the same rules as the original answer. See Fed. R. Civ. P. 7(a), which specifies that proper pleadings include an answer to a third-party complaint. In order to properly respond to Ronan's claim against him, Jones will need to have Schulansky's original complaint before him as well as the third-party complaint. For example, Rule 14(a)(2)(C) allows Jones to raise defenses that *Ronan* may have to Schulansky's primary complaint, on the theory that, if Ronan is not held liable to her, then Jones cannot be held liable to Ronan. Jones can only do this if he has the original complaint to work with in formulating an answer. The defendants should therefore append a copy of the original complaint to the third-party complaint.

5. The defendants may bring in Jones if he is or may be liable to them for all or part of Schulansky's claim against them. The third-party complaint properly seeks recovery from Jones for those damages that the defendants are ordered to pay Schulansky.

6. Since the third-party complaint is governed by the pleading requirements of Rule 8(a), it must include a demand for relief. Again, since Ronan seeks recovery over against Jones, their main demand for relief (subparagraph 11a) is for the damages they must pay Schulansky. Here the defendants have included separate demands for damages after each claim for relief. Since the potential damages differ under at least the first two claims, including separate demands after each claim makes it easier to understand each claim. Compare the original complaint, supra p. 637, which includes a single demand at the end of the entire complaint, and comment 10 following it.

7. The associate's point about the right to attorneys' fees is a perceptive one. While Ronan's claim to recover from Jones any damages he pays to Schulansky is derivative under Rule 14, his claim for fees is for a separate loss he suffered as a result of Jones's acts. Essentially, Ronan's fees claim is based on the theory that he would not have had to defend Schulansky's suit if Jones had done his job properly. Thus, the fees expended in the defense are a consequential loss resulting from Jones's breach, although they are paid to Ronan's lawyer, not to Schulansky. They constitute a distinct claim that does not satisfy Rule 14 but may be asserted along with the idemnnification claim under Fed. R. Civ. P. 18(a). Compare Chapter 15, example 6. It is quite likely that the court would have jurisdiction over this related claim under the supplemental jurisdiction statute. 28 U.S.C. §1367(a).

Actually, it is unlikely that Ronan would directly incur attorneys' fees for the defense of this action. His liability insurance coverage almost certainly would include the costs of defense as well as coverage for any liability that results from the action. However, his coverage might not cover claims for breach of contract; if that is true, the insurer might disavow the duty to defend on this claim, or make some arrangement for Ronan Construction to cover part of the costs of defense. If so, then Ronan could seek those from Jones on an indemnification theory.

8. In paragraphs 16 and 17 of the third claim for relief, Ronan alleges that Jones acted in the scope of his employment for Ronan. Compare paragraphs five and six of his first claim for relief against Jones, which allege a contractual relationship. As Ackerman's memo indicates, the two theories of relief are premised on differing underlying factual conclusions that the jury might reach. Consequently, the factual allegations in the two claims for relief reflect these inconsistent positions.

9. The attorney's signature on the third-party complaint, as on any other pleading or motion, is subject to the ethical requirements of Rule 11. As Ackerman's memo indicates, he gave considerable thought to those requirements before including inconsistent allegations concerning Jones's status in the third-party complaint.

10. Note that there is no attorney's certificate of service at the end of the third-party complaint. The reason is that the third-party complaint must be served on Jones, a new party who has no prior notice of the action, under the more exacting provisions of Rule 4, not Rule 5. Consequently, proof of service will be made in the manner provided by Rule 4(1), not by a simple attorney's certificate. (However, the third-party complaint would be served on *Schulansky* under the provisions of Rule 5.)

Losordo's suggestion in her memo that they postpone research on the issue of personal jurisdiction over Jones is a good one. Any practicing lawyer will attest that innumerable complex issues arise in the practice of law. Sometimes it is evident from the outset that a case will turn on such an issue. Often, however, issues arise that may turn out to be important or may not, depending on the course of the suit, the evidence turned up in discovery, whether the opposing party raises the issue, and whether the case goes to trial. Attorneys constantly make pragmatic judgments about which issues to spend their time and their clients' money researching. Frequently, those complex issues just go away for one reason or another.

In this case, for example, the issue of Jones's amenability to jurisdiction under Fed. R. Civ. P. 4(k)(1)(B) could be a complicated one. But it may never need to be decided, if Jones is served in Massachusetts, or if he does not object to jurisdiction, or if he does but the case settles before the issue is litigated. Here, Losordo has noted the potential problem but quite sensibly delayed extensive research on the issue until it becomes clear that it will have to be resolved.

# Preliminary Objections

## Jones Seeks a Way Out

---

## THE DRAFTING REQUEST

### MEMORANDUM

**TO:** Phillip Torres

**FROM:** Don Philbrook

**RE:** Arlen Jones Construction Case

**DATE:** January 21, 2007

-------------------------------------------------------------------------------

I represent Arlen Jones, a neighbor of mine who is in the excavation business. He has just been served with process in a federal court suit down in Boston, arising out of some work he did on a house over in Alton. I have attached the original complaint in the action and the third-party complaint against Jones. He is surprised and puzzled by the suit, since he thought the job went fine and the owner was happy. He is also concerned about defending an action down in Boston. Arlen is a local guy with a small business; he is hardly in a position to pay big city legal fees. (I'm not even sure he'll be able to manage mine . . . I'll probably have to put in a pool so he can pay me off by doing the excavation!)

Naturally, Jones would rather litigate up here than down in Boston, or, better still, get out of this suit entirely. It seems to me that we may have several grounds for dismissal of this action by motion. First, it seems dubious to me that Jones should be subject to personal jurisdiction in

Massachusetts on this claim. He negotiated with the general contractor, Ronan Construction Company, here in New Hampshire. He did the work in New Hampshire. The job was a small one at that, only a few days' work for something like $3,000. Whatever damages the owner suffered were suffered here. Thus, this claim does not arise out of any "minimum contacts" Jones has with Massachusetts. Nor is he subject to general in personam jurisdiction there; he lives next door to me here in Littleton, and though he works in Massachusetts once in a while, he does not do business there regularly.

Jones wasn't even served with process in the suit in Massachusetts; Ronan had the summons and complaint served on Jones while he was working on a job down in Dover. Now, I'm just an old country lawyer, and you young fellas may know more about these things than I do, but it seems dubious to me that Jones could be served with process here in New Hampshire, and dragged down to defend a federal court case in Massachusetts, if he lacks minimum contacts with that state. Please do a little research on this issue. Don't go overboard on it — we're not talking million dollar damages here, and Jones can't afford to pay for overkill — but give it a few hours to see if we may have grounds for filing a Rule 12(b) motion to dismiss based on lack of personal jurisdiction and draft an appropriate motion for my signature if there is reasonable support for it.

We may also be able to move to dismiss for lack of subject matter jurisdiction, since we are from the same state as Ronan, the third-party plaintiff, and this is a state law claim. I believe there is a statute now that governs such ancillary claims in federal court. I haven't looked at it for a while, but I thought it barred claims brought under Rule 14. Please research and advise me on this as well.

If we can't get the claim against Jones dismissed under Fed. R. Civ. P. 12(b)(1) or (2), perhaps we can convince the court to transfer this action to the District of New Hampshire under 28 U.S.C. §1404(a). It seems to me that it makes much more sense to litigate this case here than in Boston. The work was done here, both of the defendants and the third-party defendant live and do business here, and any damages resulting from the job were suffered here. I assume that most of the witnesses other than Schulansky will be from New Hampshire, since Jones tells me that all of Ronan's employees are also local.

Please take a quick look at the case law on the grounds for transfer of venue. If the cases support our argument for transfer, please draft a separate motion to transfer this action to the District of New Hampshire and advise me as to whether you think we should file it along with our motion to dismiss or hold off until decision of that motion. Be sure to check the local rules of the District of Massachusetts for any special requirements pertaining to motions filed in that court. Feel free to call Jones directly if you need further information from him.

Our response is due within 10 days (the 20-day period under the rule minus the 10 days it took Jones to come to me), so please take care of this right away.

---

# THE ASSOCIATE'S RESPONSE

## MEMORANDUM

**TO:** Donald Philbrook

**FROM:** Phillip Torres

**RE:** Preliminary Motions in *Ronan v. Jones*
Ma. Federal Dist. Ct. Civil Action No. 2006-6719

**DATE:** January 24, 2007

--------------------------------------------------------------------------------

I have done preliminary research on the three issues you raised in your memo. I conclude that we do not have grounds to move to dismiss for lack of subject matter jurisdiction. On the personal jurisdiction issue, I conclude that there is a slim argument for dismissal but that we are very unlikely to prevail. The strongest argument is for transfer under 28 U.S.C. §1404(a). I recommend making a motion to transfer only.

## I. Subject Matter Jurisdiction

It appears that we do not have a valid objection to subject matter jurisdiction over Ronan's claim against Jones. Under 28 U.S.C. §1367, state law claims that are related to a case properly before the federal court may also be heard by the court. See 28 U.S.C. §1367(a), which provides that claims that are part of the same "case or controversy" as the main claim may be brought in federal court along with it. There is little question that the statute authorizes "supplemental jurisdiction" over third-party claims where there is no independent basis for subject matter jurisdiction. See J. Glannon, Civil Procedure: Examples and Explanations, Chapter 16, ex. 7 (5th ed. 2006). Consequently, I have not included this defense in the motion to dismiss.

Your memory is correct that the statute contains a special provision governing certain Rule 14 claims. See §1367(b). This provision bars supplemental jurisdiction over claims by *plaintiffs* against persons made parties under Rule 14 (and other rules), but it does not apply to claims by a defendant against an impleaded party.

## 2. Personal Jurisdiction

I spent several hours researching whether Jones is subject to personal jurisdiction in the Massachusetts federal court on the basis of personal service in New Hampshire. My preliminary analysis is as follows:

In *Burnham v. Superior Court of California*, 495 U.S. 604 (1990), the Supreme Court held that personal jurisdiction may frequently be based on service of process within the forum state, but *Burnham* does not authorize personal jurisdiction in Massachusetts based on service in New Hampshire. However, service in this case may be proper under Fed. R. Civ. P. 4(k)(1)(b), the "100-mile bulge" provision of Rule 4. Frankly, I had never heard of Rule 4(k)(1)(b) until I started to research this issue. It provides that certain parties (including parties like Jones who are brought in under Rule 14) may be served anywhere within 100 miles of the courthouse. Dover, where Jones was served, is well within that limit. So it is clear that Ronan was authorized to *serve* Jones in this manner.

It is not absolutely clear, however, that Jones can be forced to defend in Massachusetts just because he is served in New Hampshire under the 100-mile bulge provision, since he has no minimum contacts with the state where he is being forced to appear. Rule 4(k) is clearly intended to be a federal long-arm provision as well as a service-of-process provision; that is, it is intended not only to authorize service of process within the bulge area but also to authorize the exercise of personal jurisdiction over parties served there. See Fed. R. Civ. P. 4(k)(1) ("[s]erving a summons . . . establishes jurisdiction over a defendant [who fits into one of the categories in the rule]"); see also Advisory Committee note to 1993 revisions of Rule 4, subdivision k.

Even though the rulemakers explicitly sought to extend personal jurisdiction to parties served under Rule 4(k), the rule still must not exceed the bounds of due process. Under the old rule, there was some authority that suggested that it would exceed due process limits to exercise personal jurisdiction over a bulge defendant if he had no contacts with the forum state. See *Karlsen v. Hauff*, 278 F. Supp. 864 (S.D.N.Y. 1967) (overruled by *Coleman v. American Export Isbrandtsen Lines, Inc.*, 405 F.2d 250, 251-253 (2d Cir. 1968). Most of the cases under earlier versions of this rule, however, allowed personal jurisdiction if the bulge defendant had relevant minimum contacts with the bulge area itself, which Jones clearly does — he did the work in Alton, which is within 100 miles of Boston. Even though this is a diversity case, the federal courts' power to exercise personal jurisdiction is limited by the Fifth Amendment due process clause, not the Fourteenth. *Peay v. Bell South Medical Assistance Plan*, 205 F.3d 1206, 1212 (10th Cir. 2000). Thus, the weight of authority — plus the clear view of the rulemakers that federal courts may assert jurisdiction over bulge defendants — suggests that the court is not likely to grant the motion to dismiss on this ground. See L. Teply and R. Whitten, Civil Procedure (3d ed.) 329-331. I think we are very unlikely to get out on this basis, and it is not worth the expense to the client of pursuing it.[1]

I have drafted a motion to dismiss for lack of personal jurisdiction for your consideration. If you want to pursue this objection, I will research it more fully.

## 3. Transfer under 28 U.S.C. §1404(a)

Our strongest argument is for transfer of the case under 28 U.S.C. §1404(a). Under §1404(a), the court may transfer cases "for the convenience of parties and witnesses, in the interest of justice." The primary factors to be considered are those established in *Gulf Oil Corp. v. Gilbert*, 330 U.S. 501 (1947) (decided under the related doctrine of forum non conveniens), including the plaintiff's choice of a forum, relative ease of access to sources of proof, availability of compulsory process, convenience of the parties and witnesses, possibility of a view, and advantages of enforceability of a judgment. See generally Moore's Federal Practice, §111.13[1][b].

Many of these factors support an argument for transfer of this action. As you indicate, the events that gave rise to the suit took place in New Hampshire, and all witnesses and parties except for Schulansky live here. In fact, it will not be possible to compel all of Ronan's employees to testify in Massachusetts because several of them are not subject to the subpoena power of the Massachusetts court and Jones tells me that they no longer work for Ronan. It may also be necessary for the court and the jury to view the house, which would obviously make trial here more appropriate.

In addition, while I have not yet had the time to research the issue, it seems likely that the Massachusetts federal court, applying Massachusetts

---

1. There is another argument we could make here. Even if jurisdiction is proper if the defendant has minimum contacts with the "bulge" area, Jones's contacts, which gave rise to this claim, are with Alton, New Hampshire. A quick look at the atlas indicates that Alton is about 75-80 *air miles* from Boston, but probably over 100 by road. We could argue that the miles should be measured by road, since this is how people usually get from place to place.

Believe it or not, this esoteric issue has also been litigated, See, e.g., *Sprow v. Hartford Ins. Co.*, 594 F.2d 412, 417-418 (5th Cir. 1979), which concluded that the better approach is to measure the 100 miles "as the crow flies." Wright and Miller also advocate this approach. 4A Wright & Miller §1127 n.1. So I think this argument is also likely to be a loser.

conflicts of law doctrine (see *Klaxon Co. v. Stentor Electric Mfg. Co.*, 313 U.S. 487 (1941)) would apply the contract and tort law of New Hampshire to this case, since most of the events giving rise to the action took place here, the property is located here, and the damage was suffered here. A number of cases have concluded that the need to apply the law of another state is a factor in favor of transfer. See, e.g., *Laumann Mfg. Corp. v. Castings U.S.A, Inc.*, 913 F. Supp. 712, 721-722 (E.D.N.Y. 1996); *Gundle Lining Constr. Corp. v. Fireman's Fund Ins. Co.*, 844 F. Supp. 1163, 1166 (S.D. Tex. 1994); but cf. *Houk v. Kimberley-Clark Corp.*, 613 F. Supp. 923, 932 (W.D. Mo. 1985) (applicable law not given great weight unless it is complex or unsettled).

Because a major reason for transfer under §1404(a) is for the convenience of the parties, it would certainly bolster our position if the defendants were willing to join in the motion to transfer. You may wish to call Ronan's counsel to see if he is willing to do so. Ironically, while it would be more convenient for Ronan personally to litigate up here, it would be less so for his lawyers because Ackerman, Sloan and Cariotis only have offices in Boston. You might get a more enthusiastic reception if you could suggest this directly to Ronan. However, I realize this would be improper under the rules of professional conduct.

I have attached draft motions to dismiss and to transfer, along with supporting affidavits from Jones. Tactically, we could file the motion to dismiss under Fed. R. Civ. P. 12(b)(2) and hold our motion to transfer, as there is no requirement that the transfer motion be filed before answering the complaint. However, since the argument based on lack of personal jurisdiction looks doubtful, we may want to file both motions together. Perhaps the judge will latch on to the transfer motion as a means of avoiding the more complicated personal jurisdiction question. Last, since we will have to participate in discovery while the motions are pending, we should present both motions in hopes of getting out of the Massachusetts court as soon as possible.

Thank you for reminding me to check the local district court rules. Rule 7.1(B)(1) of the Local Rules of the District of Massachusetts provides that affidavits and other supporting materials, including supporting memoranda, must be filed with the motion. Otherwise, they may only be filed with leave of court. In view of this rule, I suggest that we file a motion for an extension of time to file a responsive pleading under Fed. R. Civ. P. 6(b) or ask Ronan's counsel to assent to an extension, to give us adequate time to prepare a supporting memorandum of law to file with these motions. Alternatively, I have included a request in each motion for leave to file supporting memos at a time specified by the court.

# THE RESULTING DOCUMENTS

UNITED STATES DISTRICT COURT

DISTRICT OF MASSACHUSETTS

CIVIL ACTION NO. 2006-6719

| | |
|---|---|
| DEBORAH SCHULANSKY | |
| Plaintiff | |
| v. | THIRD-PARTY DEFENDANT'S |
| RICHARD L. RONAN | |
| RONAN CONSTRUCTION CO. | MOTION TO DISMISS THE |
| Defendants | THIRD-PARTY COMPLAINT |
| v. | FOR LACK OF PERSONAL |
| ARLEN JONES | JURISDICTION |
| Third-Party Defendant | |

The third-party defendant, Arlen Jones, moves to dismiss the third-party complaint under Fed. R. Civ. P. 12(b)(2) on the ground that the court lacks personal jurisdiction over him on this claim. In support of the motion the third-party defendant states as follows:

1. The third-party defendant is not domiciled in Massachusetts or doing business in Massachusetts on a regular basis, as more fully appears from the Affidavit of Arlen Jones, paragraphs one and three, attached as Exhibit A to this motion.

2. This claim arises out of construction work performed by the third-party defendant in Alton, New Hampshire, as more fully appears from paragraphs one to four of the Third-Party Complaint, and paragraphs four and five of the attached Affidavit of Arlen Jones.

3. The third-party defendant has no contacts with Massachusetts that are related to this claim, as further appears from the Affidavit of Arlen Jones.

4. The exercise of personal jurisdiction over the third-party defendant in these circumstances exceeds the limits of due process under the United States Constitution.

### REQUEST FOR ORAL ARGUMENT

The third-party defendant requests twenty minutes for oral argument on this motion, pursuant to Local Rule 7.1(D), and leave to file a supporting memorandum at a time specified by the court.

_____
Donald R. Philbrook
Attorney for Third-Party Defendant
11A Grove Street
Littleton, New Hampshire 03561
(603) 471-8200

UNITED STATES DISTRICT COURT

DISTRICT OF MASSACHUSETTS

CIVIL ACTION NO. 2006-6719

DEBORAH SCHULANSKY

Plaintiff

v.

RICHARD L. RONAN
RONAN CONSTRUCTION CO.

Defendants

v.

ARLEN JONES

Third-Party
Defendant

AFFIDAVIT OF ARLEN JONES

IN SUPPORT OF MOTION TO

DISMISS THIRD-PARTY

COMPLAINT

State of New Hampshire

County of Littleton

} ss.:

Arlen Jones, being first duly sworn, states as follows:

1. On January 11, 2007, I was personally served with a summons and Third-Party Complaint in the above-captioned action. Service was made at Dover, New Hampshire, while I was engaged in a small excavating project for a condominium complex there.

2. At the time of service and at all other times relevant to this action I resided at 88 Warner Avenue, Littleton, New Hampshire, and conducted a small excavating business from that address as a sole proprietor.

3. Although I occasionally (approximately once per year) do small excavation jobs in Massachusetts, I am not licensed to do business in Massachusetts, do not conduct business there on a regular basis, and receive less than 5% of my income from Massachusetts business.

4. This action arises out of renovation work performed by Richard Ronan on the plaintiff's house in Alton, New Hampshire. The third-party complaint alleges a right to relief for faulty excavation work performed as part of the renovation work at the Alton site.

5. All negotiations, agreements, preparation, and performance of the work giving rise to this claim took place in New Hampshire. I did not solicit this job in Massachusetts nor perform any act related to the events in suit in Massachusetts, nor was I aware until I received process in this action that the plaintiff resided there.

6. I have never consented to suit in Massachusetts on this claim.

_____
Arlen Jones

    Subscribed and sworn to before me this __ day of _____, 2007.

_____
Notary Public

My commission expires:

_____

UNITED STATES DISTRICT COURT

DISTRICT OF MASSACHUSETTS

CIVIL ACTION NO. 2006-6719

DEBORAH SCHULANSKY

Plaintiff

v.

RICHARD L. RONAN
RONAN CONSTRUCTION CO.

Defendants

v.

ARLEN JONES

Third-Party
Defendant

THIRD-PARTY DEFENDANT'S

MOTION TO TRANSFER

UNDER 28 U.S.C. § 1404(a)

The third-party defendant, Arlen Jones, moves to transfer this action to the federal district court for the District of New Hampshire, under 28 U.S.C. § 1404(a), for the convenience of the parties and in the interest of justice. In support of the motion, the third-party defendant states as follows:

1. This action arises out of construction work performed on the plaintiff's home in Alton, New Hampshire, as more fully appears from paragraphs 5 and 14-20 of the plaintiff's complaint and paragraphs 7-9 of the Affidavit of Arlen Jones, attached hereto as Exhibit A.

2. The defendants on the main claim are a New Hampshire resident and a New Hampshire corporation, as more fully appears from paragraphs 2-3 of the plaintiff's complaint.

3. All negotiations between the defendant and the third-party defendant concerning the excavation work took place in New Hampshire, as more fully appears from the Affidavit of Arlen Jones, paragraph 8.

4. All of the construction work giving rise to both the plaintiff's claims against the defendants and the defendants' claims against the third-party defendant took place in Alton, New Hampshire, as more fully appears from the Affidavit of Arlen Jones, paragraph 9.

5. Any damages suffered by the plaintiff or the defendants were suffered in New Hampshire, where the premises involved in this action are located and the defendants are located.

6. All potential witnesses who worked on the construction of the addition reside in New Hampshire, as more fully appears from the Affidavit of Arlen Jones, paragraph 10.

7. At least some of the potential witnesses in this action are beyond the subpoena power of this court, as more fully appears from the Affidavit of Arlen Jones, paragraph 10.

8. This claim could have been brought in the District of New Hampshire because the events giving rise to the claim took place there and all defendants are subject to service of process in that district.

REQUEST FOR ORAL ARGUMENT

The third-party defendant requests one half hour for oral argument of this motion, and leave to file a supporting memorandum at a time specified by the court.

Donald R. Philbrook
Attorney for Third-Party Defendant
11A Grove Street
Littleton, New Hampshire 03561
(603) 471-8200

UNITED STATES DISTRICT COURT

DISTRICT OF MASSACHUSETTS

CIVIL ACTION NO. 2006-6719

DEBORAH SCHULANSKY

Plaintiff

v.

RICHARD L. RONAN
RONAN CONSTRUCTION CO.

Defendants

v.

ARLEN JONES

Third-Party
Defendant

AFFIDAVIT OF ARLEN JONES

IN SUPPORT OF MOTION TO

TRANSFER UNDER

28 U.S.C. §1404(a)

State of New Hampshire }
County of Littleton } ss.:

Arlen Jones, being first duly sworn, states as follows:

1. I reside at 88 Warner Avenue, Littleton, New Hampshire, approximately 126 miles from Boston, and have resided there at all times relevant to the events involved in this action.

2. I operate a small excavation business, as a sole proprietor. The business is operated out of my home and grosses about $80,000 per year.

3. Over 90% of my business is done in New Hampshire, most of it in the Littleton area of northern New Hampshire. While I occasionally do small jobs in Massachusetts, I do not work there more than approximately once a year. I do not currently have any orders for future jobs in Massachusetts.

4. I am currently booked solid for the new construction season with jobs all over New Hampshire. Since I am a small proprietor, and must attend to my business every day, it would seriously inconvenience me to litigate this action, which arises out of one of the smallest jobs I did last year, in Massachusetts.

5. At no time did I have any direct negotiations with the plaintiff in this action, nor was I apprised of the fact that she lives in Massachusetts or of any other facts that would have led me to expect to have to defend this claim in a Massachusetts court.

6. On information and belief, the defendants Richard Ronan and Ronan Construction Company are primarily engaged in residential construction in New Hampshire.

7. Sometime during the first week of April 2006, Richard Ronan called me in Littleton concerning an excavation job on the Schulansky house in Alton, New Hampshire.

8. After several phone calls between Ronan and me, all of which took place in New Hampshire, I agreed to do the excavation work on the Alton job, for $3,000.

9. I commenced work on the Schulansky job on April 15, 2006, and completed the work on April 17. All preparation and performance of the work took place in either Littleton, New Hampshire or Alton, New Hampshire.

10. I have done at least twenty excavation jobs for Ronan and/or Ronan Construction Company during the past three years. I am acquainted with all of Ronan's employees who worked on the Schulansky job. All of those employees live in New Hampshire, and at least four of them in the Littleton area, more than 100 miles from Boston.

11. Since the Schulansky job in April 2006, several of the carpenters who worked on the job have left Ronan's employ.

_____
Arlen Jones

Subscribed and sworn to before me this ___ day of _____, 2007.

_____
Notary Public

My commission expires:

_____

# COMMENTS ON THE THIRD-PARTY MOTIONS

1. The same formal rules that govern captions for pleadings also apply to motions and to affidavits as well. See Fed. R. Civ. P. 7(b)(2). In addition, the ethical constraints on pleadings in Rule 11 also apply to motions. Fed. R. Civ. P. 11(a), (b). Under Rule 11, attorneys must investigate both the factual and legal bases for filing motions before doing so. Under earlier practice, defense counsel would frequently respond to a complaint with a motion to dismiss, including a long laundry list of dubious objections. Such habits, while they die slowly, are clearly inconsistent with the Rule 11 requirements for reasonable inquiry and evidentiary support for such objections.

2. Rule 7(b)(1) provides that a motion shall "state with particularity the grounds for seeking the order." In both the motion to dismiss and the motion to transfer, Jones's counsel has set forth briefly the reasons that support the particular order sought in the motion. This satisfies the requirement of "particularity" and assists the court in understanding the basis of the motions. A motion must also "set forth the relief or order sought." Id. Torres's draft motions do this as well: The first seeks dismissal and the second, transfer. See the first paragraph of each motion.

   However, the motion itself is not the right place to *argue* the merits of the motion, or to set forth in detail the facts that support the motion. The supporting arguments and discussion of authority should be set forth in an accompanying memorandum of law. The local rules of some federal districts provide that the memorandum in support of a motion should be consolidated with the motion in a single document. See, e.g., Rules of the United States District Court for the District of Maine, Rule 7(a) ("every motion shall incorporate a memorandum of law, including citations and supporting authorities"). Other districts, however, including the District of Massachusetts, provide for a separate legal memorandum in support of motions. Rules for the United States District Court for the District of Massachusetts, Rule 7(B)(1). Any facts necessary to support the motion should be provided in accompanying affidavits, deposition transcripts, interrogatories, business records, or other evidentiary documents.

3. An affidavit is a sworn statement by a witness. It is usually notarized and is signed subject to the penalties of perjury. The "ss." in the heading is a legal formalism frequently found in affidavits. It stands for "silicet," which roughly means "to wit" or "let it be known," and simply indicates that the affiant publicly asserts the facts in the affidavit.

It is entirely proper to submit affidavits in support of a motion, to establish the facts necessary for the court to rule on the motion. See Fed. R. Civ. P. 43(c). In the case of Jones's motion to dismiss for lack of personal jurisdiction, for example, the earlier pleadings do not indicate whether Jones has sufficient contacts with Massachusetts to support jurisdiction over him for this claim. Jones's affidavit provides the court with admissible evidence (since it is sworn personal testimony of the affiant), which supports the position taken in his motion.

If the other parties have countervailing evidence, they may submit their own affidavits or other materials in opposition to the motion. The court may decide the motion on the basis of the facts presented or, if issues of credibility are involved or further evidence needed, may take testimony from the witnesses in a full evidentiary hearing on the motion.

4. You may have been puzzled as to why Jones's lawyers have included a paragraph in the affidavit stating that several potential witnesses no longer work for Ronan and do not live within 100 miles of Boston. These facts are relevant to the motion to transfer: If these witnesses still worked for Ronan they would presumably be subject to his control and therefore would appear to testify at a trial in Massachusetts. If they no longer work for Ronan, however, and are outside the subpoena power of the Massachusetts federal court, they will probably not be available to testify at a trial in Boston. See Fed. R. Civ. P. 45(b)(2) (authorizing service of subpoenas within the judicial district where suit is pending or within 100 miles of the place of trial). The New Hampshire federal court, however, could subpoena witnesses from any place within New Hampshire, thus supporting the argument for transfer.

5. It is entirely proper to file combined motions for more than one form of action by the court. Jones's lawyers could, for example, decide to file a combined "Motion to Dismiss for Lack of Personal Jurisdiction, or in the Alternative to Transfer Venue under 28 U.S.C. §1404(a)." Torres drafted the two separately because the tactical decision whether to file them together or separately had not yet been made.

6. Torres's suggestion that Philbrook contact Ronan's counsel is interesting. It would certainly lend credence to the motion if the original defendants also sought transfer. Although Jones and Ronan are adversaries on the merits, their interests may coincide on this issue or others in the suit. As Chapter 30 indicates (supra p. 624), it is appropriate to contact Ronan's counsel to discuss a possible joint motion or any other such issues that arise in the course of the litigation.

Further, the point that Torres makes about the potential difference in interests between Ronan and his attorneys is a delicate and interesting one. If the case is transferred, Ronan's insurance company may retain local counsel in New Hampshire to handle it, and the Boston firm may lose the case. However, Ronan's counsel is there to represent his clients' interests, not his own, and should join in the motion to transfer if Ronan prefers to litigate in New Hampshire, or if other tactical considerations point to New Hampshire as the preferable forum.

7. This book-writing business is frustrating. I started out to create a fairly straightforward case for illustration purposes, but like all lawsuits, *Schulansky v. Ronan* refuses to be simple. The motion to transfer presents a good example. There is some authority for the proposition that the third-party defendant has no standing to object to venue or, apparently, to move to transfer. Instead, the court should consider any inconvenience to the third-party defendant in deciding whether to allow him to be impleaded in the first place. See *Gundle Lining Constr. Co. v. Adams County Asphalt*, 85 F.3d 201, 209-210 (5th Cir. 1996); see also *Pelinski v. Goodyear Tire & Rubber Co.*, 499 F. Supp. 1092, 1095 (N.D. Ill. 1980) ("some question" whether a third-party defendant can seek transfer under §1404(a)); but see *Krupp Intern., Inc. v. Yarn Industries, Inc.*, 615 F. Supp. 1103, 1107 (D. Del. 1985) (third-party defendant has standing to seek transfer).

To be truthful, your humble author never knew this arcane bit of procedural lore until his research assistant stumbled on the point in researching the standards for transfer. It is hardly surprising that Jones's attorneys have not yet discovered it. They well may when they reach the stage of briefing the transfer issue. Or they may not. If they don't, the issue may be raised by one of the other parties or the judge. Or it may not; perhaps no one will think of it. If the court decides that Jones lacks standing to seek a transfer (or that transfer is not warranted, since the plaintiff and defendants are happy with the forum), he could still dismiss the third-party claim in his discretion under Rule 14(a). Or, Jones can try to convince Ronan to sponsor the motion, since Ronan clearly has standing to seek a transfer.

8. An important limitation on transfer is the requirement that the suit "might have been brought" in the transferee district. 28 U.S.C. §1404(a). In *Hoffman v. Blaski*, 363 U.S. 335, 342-343 (1960), the Supreme Court held that this phrase limits transfer to districts in which venue is proper and service could have been made on the defendant. This requirement is obviously met here, since venue in the initial action would be proper under 28 U.S.C. §1391(a)(1) or (a)(2) and all defendants would be subject to personal jurisdiction in New Hampshire. In paragraph eight of his motion, Torres represents that this requirement for transfer is satisfied.

9. It is fortunate that Philbrook, a New Hampshire practitioner,[2] re-
   membered to have Torres check the local rules for the District of
   Massachusetts. Most federal districts have their own rules, in addition
   to the Federal Rules of Civil Procedure, and they frequently cover
   important aspects of local practice. In this case, Rule 7.1(B)(1) of the
   Local Rules for the District of Massachusetts specifically requires that
   supporting affidavits and memoranda be filed with the motion, or
   else only with leave of court. One effect of this requirement is to
   discourage "shotgun" motions raising a long laundry list of possible
   objections. Since counsel must brief all the issues at the outset, they
   are much more likely to separate the wheat from the chaff in raising
   preliminary objections. If there is no viable argument for an objection, that will become clear to counsel when he tries to support the
   argument in a brief. Thus, the need to brief the question right off will
   often lead counsel to drop the objection instead.

   Rule 7.1(D) further requires that a request for a hearing be
   included in the motion if the moving party wants one and that the
   party seeking a hearing indicate in the motion the amount of time
   needed for oral argument, as Torres has done at the end of each
   motion.

   Rule 7.1(B)(2) of the local district court Rules imposes another
   requirement that may trap the unwary litigant. Under that Rule, a
   party who *opposes* a motion must file an opposition to the motion
   within fourteen days. There is nothing in the Federal Rules of Civil
   Procedure that requires that an opposition be filed. It is thus essential for counsel to be familiar with the local rules as well as the
   Federal Rules themselves, which apply generally to *all* federal district
   courts.

10. Note that the draft motion to dismiss for lack of personal juris-
    diction says nothing about Rule 4(k)(1)(B) or the line of cases
    Torres unearthed in his research. It simply asserts the position that
    there is no jurisdiction because Jones lacks minimum contacts with
    Massachusetts. However, because the local rule requires a sup-
    porting memorandum of law, Jones would have to set out his
    argument as to why such contacts are necessary. Thus, he would
    have to cite the few cases in support of his argument, and this

---

2. Philbrook will not automatically have the right to appear on behalf of Jones in the
Massachusetts Federal District Court, unless he is a member of the Massachusetts bar.
However, Rule 83.5.3 of the Massachusetts District Court Local Rules authorizes the district
court to allow an attorney admitted to practice in another state to appear in particular cases.

would doubtless trigger a response from Ronan with a wealth of contrary authority. Torres is probably right to suggest that, given the strength of the opposing case law and the expense of the motion, it is better to let this one go. While the lawyer's job is to raise arguments that benefit his clients, that does not require him to abandon good judgment in tilting at litigation windmills. Such unrestrained aggressiveness will simply raise the cost of litigation and provoke similar unproductive conduct from the opposition.

# Index

# Index